Energy efficiency in buildings

CIBSE Guide F

CIBSE

© Second edition January 2004; reprinted with corrections July 2006; The Chartered Institution of Building Services Engineers London

Registered charity number 278104

ISBN 1 903287 34 0

Typeset by CIBSE Publications Department

Printed in Great Britain by Page Bros. (Norwich) Ltd., Norwich, Norfolk, NR6 6SA.

Note from the publisher

This publication is primarily intended to provide guidance to those responsible for the design, installation, commissioning, operation and maintenance of building services. It is not intended to be exhaustive or definitive and it will be necessary for users of the guidance given to exercise their own professional judgement when deciding whether to abide by or depart from it.

Foreword to the second edition

Guide F has been a leading source of guidance on energy efficiency in buildings over the last five years. This revised edition of the Guide has been brought up-to-date in the light of current domestic legislation, specifically Part L of the Building Regulations. CIBSE Applications Manual AM 5: *Energy audits and surveys* has been incorporated within this volume for completeness. This edition of Guide F covers both the energy requirements committed by the design and the energy costs in use, as design and management cannot be separated. It has become larger as some new sections have been added, such as the checklist *Why buildings fail on energy*, and there are useful practical enhancements including a *Design checklist*, *How to carry out an energy survey* and Part C: *Benchmarks*.

The Guide seeks to inform a very diverse audience and aims to be pertinent to many groups involved in buildings besides building services engineers, including building developers/financiers, specifiers, architects, surveyors, letting agents, energy managers and consultants and building owners/operators.

Guide F deals with the building as a whole. The technical content is guidance from an energy perspective and extra information is available elsewhere in the CIBSE Guides and other sources listed in the bibliographies at the end of each section. The Guide also complements energy efficiency publications provided under the Carbon Trust's Action Energy programme (formerly the Energy Efficiency Best Practice programme). The CIBSE has had a long and productive relationship with the Best Practice Programme and I am pleased that this relationship continues under the Action Energy banner.

The importance and relevance of Guide F has been given added emphasis because of the EU Energy Performance of Buildings Directive which came into force on 4 January 2003. This Directive will give public profile to the energy efficiency performance of buildings across the UK. It will raise awareness of how energy efficient different buildings really are. Prospective owners and occupiers will, for the first time, be able to compare one building with another and see what could be done to bring energy efficiency performance up to the standards of the best. The Directive should help stimulate substantial increases in investments in energy efficiency measures in all buildings both commercial and domestic.

The environmental prize for the application of the good design and management principles set out in this Guide is huge. It is estimated that around 22% of the present energy consumed in buildings can be saved by 2010. This challenge is reflected in the CIBSE Energy Policy Statement included in Appendix A1.

I should like to thank the members of the Guide F Revision Steering Committee, see below, who put in many hours of work doing research, reading drafts and providing comments and suggestions.

Thanks also the committee secretary Alan Watson and technical editor/revision author Phil Jones for their significant personal contributions.

Barry Hutt
Chairman, Guide F Revision Steering Committee

Guide F Revision Steering Committee

Barry Hutt (Chairman)
John Field (Target Energy Services)
Debbie Hobbs (Faber Maunsell)
Tony Johnson (BRE)
John Palmer (Faber Maunsell)
Alan Watson (Secretary)

Revision author and technical editor (second edition)

Phil Jones (Building Energy Solutions)

Copy editors

Ken Butcher
Justin Rowe

CIBSE Publishing Manager

Jacqueline Balian

Acknowledgements (second edition)

Gina Barney (Gina Barney Associates)
Tony Johnson (BRE Ltd. Energy Division)

The Institution gratefully acknowledges the work of the authors and contributors to the first edition of Guide F, published in 1998, which forms the basis of this second edition.

Extracts from Crown copyright publications are reproduced by permission under licence number C02W0002935.

Foreword to the first edition

This is the first time that the CIBSE has endeavoured to bring together in one volume a range of information related entirely to energy efficiency in buildings. Energy plays a part in all aspects of building services and this is reflected in most of the Institution's publications.

It is perhaps surprising that, until now, there has been no CIBSE Guide which deals exclusively with the many facets of energy efficiency in buildings. This publication seeks to fill that gap and at the same time confirm the Institution's dedication to energy conservation and the preservation of the environment.

This volume in the series of CIBSE Guides is essentially a reference book, which also identifies other documents dealing with the various topics in more detail. It is not intended that it should be read from beginning to end in one go, but rather that the reader can consult a section that is of particular interest in respect of the project in hand.

Those involved in the production of this Guide have recognised that the content cannot cover every aspect of what is, after all, a very extensive and sometimes controversial subject. There will, however, be opportunities in the future to up-date the content in order to deal with further subjects and areas of concern, as well as covering new developments.

The Institution offers its grateful thanks to all those who have contributed to this volume and, in particular, to the Department of the Environment, Transport and the Regions and BRECSU/BRE, without whose collaboration and perseverance this Guide would not have seen the light of day.

D D Lawrence
Chairman, CIBSE Energy Publications Joint Steering Committee, March 1998

Acknowledgements (first edition)

The Chartered Institution of Building Services Engineers gratefully acknowledges the support and funding provided for the development of this CIBSE Guide by the Department of the Environment, Transport and the Regions. This support was provided as part of the Department's Energy Efficiency Best Practice programme managed on behalf of the Department by the Building Research Energy Conservation Support Unit (BRECSU) at the Building Research Establishment (BRE). The BRECSU project managers were Colin Lillicrap, Chris Hall and Tony Johnson and many other BRE staff contributed to the guide.

Contents

Part B: Operating and upgrading the building

Why buildings fail on energy

Principles of energy efficiency

An energy efficient building provides the required internal environment and services with minimum energy use in a cost effective and environmentally sensitive manner.

The following principles have been developed from the CIBSE policy statement on energy, see Appendix A1.1, and provide a framework for engineers to put the policy into practice. Where possible, building services engineers should make every effort to follow the principles shown below.

Principle	Measures for implementation of principle	Relevant section(s) of Guide F		
		Part A: Designing the building	Part B: Operating and upgrading the building	Part C: Benchmarks
Integrated building design	Design the most energy efficient buildings and services possible. Provide holistic designs which are responsive to the external climate whilst still meeting the needs of the occupants.	2 to 13	—	20
The energy efficient brief	Ensure the client's brief includes energy efficient criteria and targets for all buildings, new or refurbished. Review the project in relation to these targets and criteria as the design progresses.	2	—	20
Benchmarking	Compare designs and in-use performance of buildings with appropriate benchmarks to ensure that best practice energy efficiency is being achieved.	2 to 13	19	20
The integrated design team	Work with other members of the design team in order to optimise building energy performance.	2	—	—
Reduce demand	Keep energy demand to a minimum through careful design of built form and services using renewable energy sources, ambient energy and passive solutions. Make every effort to avoid the need for air conditioning.	2 to 13	—	—
Design for operation	Design for commissionability, maintainability and manageability bykeeping solutions simple and eliminating potential failure pathways.	2 to 13	—	—
Optimise plant	Select the most efficient plant, using certified or otherwise independently verified product performance data, and ensure that plant and equipment are not oversized.	7 to 12	18	—
Use effective controls	Introduce energy efficient controls which operate systems efficiently, safely and economically, whilst still allowing individual occupants to alter their own comfort levels, but avoiding systems defaulting to 'on'.	6 to 11	18	—
Ensure complete handover	Ensure that building services are properly commissioned and handed over to managers, operators and occupants.	14	—	—
Improve operation	Encourage energy efficient operation of buildings through management, policy, maintenance, monitoring and control.	—	15 to 19	20
Understanding the building	Provide managers, engineers, operators and occupants with suitable documentation to ensure they understand the design intention and how the buildings are meant to function.	14	15	—
Monitoring and feedback	Develop a strong element of feedback to improve understanding from previous good and bad experience related to these principles. Introduce appropriate metering to improve information and to detect faults rapidly.	13, 14	19	20
Build-in energy efficiency	Always consider introducing energy efficient technologies throughout the design and upgrade processes but avoid unnecessary complications. Seek opportunities for improving existing buildings during operation, maintenance, alteration and refurbishment.	3 to 12	15–19	—
Environmental impact	Minimise adverse effects on the external environment. Minimise emissions and select environmentally friendly materials and fuels, utilising renewable sources as much as possible..	3 to 12	15–19	—

1 Introduction

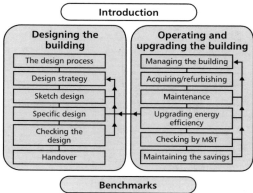

1.0 Objectives and scope

This Guide shows how to improve energy performance, reduce running costs and minimise the environmental impact of buildings by:

— designing energy efficient new buildings and refurbishment of existing buildings

— managing and operating buildings in an energy efficient way

— upgrading buildings to improve ongoing energy efficiency

— demonstrating the value of energy efficiency to clients, developers and tenants

— enabling engineers to overcome barriers to energy efficiency in discussions with clients and other members of the design and construction team.

An energy efficient building provides the required internal environment and services with minimum energy use in a cost effective and environmentally sensitive manner. There is, therefore, no conflict between energy efficiency and comfort. Hence, energy efficiency can be combined with other aspects of sound engineering practice, as set out in the other CIBSE Guides.

This document is primarily targeted at building services engineers and takes an holistic approach to designing and operating buildings. The early sections will also be useful to other members of the design team including architects and surveyors. The latter sections should also be useful to other building professionals such as energy managers, facilities managers, developers, clients, property agents and occupiers. Sections of particular relevance to each reader are shown in 1.2.

This document covers opportunities for achieving energy efficiency and complements existing guidance by CIBSE and others. It refers readers to more detailed guidance including the Carbon Trust's Action Energy programme. It does not cover process energy or detailed design methods. Although it concentrates on non-domestic buildings, much of the information is also relevant to the domestic sector.

The document promotes an holistic approach to design by recognising that there is a strong interaction between the building envelope, heating and cooling systems, lighting, etc. The overall design intent should always be considered before implementing individual measures.

1.1 Energy efficiency drivers

Buildings consume nearly half the energy used in the UK. All building professionals have a responsibility to reduce this through good practice. Tangible benefits from energy efficiency ranging from the individual to the national level are:

— improved design and operation of buildings

— better working environments

— life-cycle cost savings

— environmental: mainly through reduced emissions of carbon dioxide (CO_2) and reduced consumption of finite fossil fuels. Energy efficiency is a key performance measurement in most environmental management systems (EMS)

— added market value of buildings, when energy efficiency is perceived as a significant benefit by developers and letting agents

1.1.1 National energy use

The energy bill for most existing commercial and public buildings could be reduced by at least 20% using measures regarded as cost effective by most common investment criteria.

New buildings and major refurbishment represent even greater potential. New low-energy buildings consume 50% less energy than similar existing buildings and 20% less than typical new buildings.

In 2000 the total energy consumption of the UK was 6695 PJ* (1.93×10^9 MW·h) of which 3080 PJ was used in buildings[1]. The total cost of energy in buildings was

---

* 1 petajoule = 1×10^{15} joules

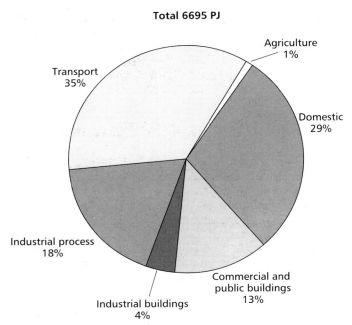

Total 6695 PJ

Figure 1.1 Total UK delivered energy consumption by sector in 2000

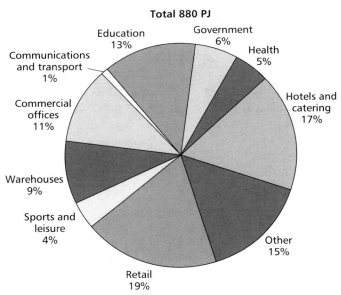

Total 880 PJ

Figure 1.3 UK delivered energy consumption by end use in 2000

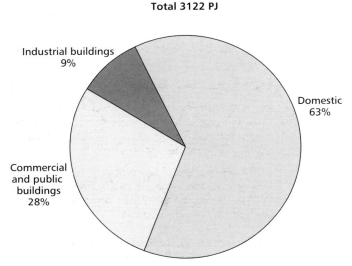

Total 3122 PJ

Figure 1.2 Total UK delivered energy consumption by buildings in 2000

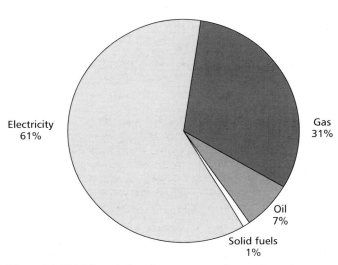

Total 81.1 Mt CO$_2$/year

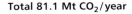

Figure 1.4 UK CO$_2$ emissions from energy use in non-domestic buildings by fuel in 2000[1]

around £21.3 billion per annum. Figures 1.1 to 1.3 illustrate national energy use by sector, building type, and fuel used in non-domestic buildings.

Typical energy breakdowns for various types of building are shown in section 20 and in the Action Energy's Energy Consumption Guides[2]. Electricity consumption is rising in many existing buildings, often due to increased amounts of office equipment, and sometimes air conditioning to remove internal heat gains emanating from this office equipment. Although small, it is hoped that the current trend in new-build toward more passive solutions, improved design integration and more efficient engineering systems may mitigate this rising trend.

1.1.2   Environmental issues

Burning fossil fuels contributes to atmospheric pollution, resulting in a wide range of damage both to the environment and public health, see CIBSE policy statement on global warming, Appendix A1.4. Increased atmospheric concentration of CO$_2$ caused by burning fossil fuels is

increasing global temperature[3,4]. Improving energy efficiency will help reduce global warming. Burning fossil fuels also results in emissions of SO$_x$ and NO$_x$, both of which contribute to acid rain.

The efficiency of electricity production in most thermal power stations is typically between 30% and 50%. The consumption of electricity can therefore lead to two to three times the CO$_2$ emissions per delivered unit of energy than the consumption of fossil fuels.

Under the Kyoto protocol, the UK government is committed to reducing the emission of CO$_2$ to 12.5% below 1990 levels by the year 2010, and have set a more stringent internal target to reduce it by 20% by 2010. UK CO$_2$ emissions from energy use in non-domestic buildings are shown by fuel type in Figure 1.4 and by end use in Figure 1.5. These could be reduced by roughly 20% through the introduction of cost-effective energy efficiency measures. The government has therefore published a strategy to achieve these reductions[5] covering a wide range of

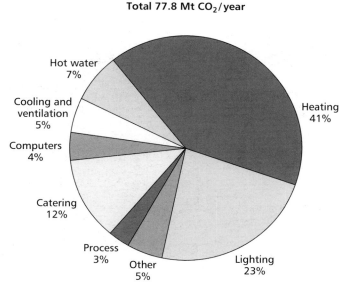

Total 77.8 Mt CO$_2$/year

- Heating 41%
- Lighting 23%
- Catering 12%
- Hot water 7%
- Cooling and ventilation 5%
- Other 5%
- Computers 4%
- Process 3%

Figure 1.5 UK CO$_2$ emissions from energy use in non-domestic buildings by end use in 2000

policies, some of which have a direct impact on the buildings industry:

— *Taxation*: the Climate Change Levy was introduced in 2001 and effects almost all non domestic buildings. The levy is an additional cost on top of the previous price of energy and is currently set at 0.43 p/kW·h for electricity, 0.15 p/kW·h for natural gas and 0.07 p/kW·h for LPG. There are exemptions for renewable forms of energy and for 'good quality' CHP installations, as defined under the government's CHP Quality Assurance Scheme[6]. It is a fiscally neutral tax as most is returned in the form of reduced National Insurance contributions from employers. A proportion is used to support the Action Energy programme, additional research and development and financial support for energy efficient technologies (see below).

— *Financial support*: enhanced capital allowances (ECAs) provide a tax incentive to encourage the purchase of energy efficient technologies as defined on the energy efficiency technology list (www.eca.gov.uk). This covers a wide range of technologies including 'good quality' CHP, boilers, lighting, variable speed drives, refrigeration, pipework insulation and wide range of controls.

— *Regulation*: Part L of the Building Regulations★[7] imposes new and upgraded requirements aimed at improving the energy efficiency of domestic and non domestic buildings, see section 1.1.3.

A recent development has been the publication of an energy 'white paper', *Our energy future — creating a low carbon economy*[8]. This sets out a new objective of reducing carbon emissions by 60% by 2050. It also makes a commitment that a further update to Building Regulations Part L will be introduced by 2005, which will include implementation of the European Directive on the Energy Performance of Buildings[9], see section 1.1.3.

Where possible, building professionals should use more sustainable materials when designing and upgrading buildings. In particular, the embodied energy used in

manufacturing and delivering construction materials, including that related to local sourcing and recycling of building services components, should always be considered at the design stage. Wider environmental issues related to buildings and building services are covered in BSRIA's *Environmental Code of Practice*[10].

1.1.3   Legislation and codes of practice

There is an increasing level of legislation addressing energy and environmental issues.

The Building Regulations★[11] for England and Wales impose new and upgraded requirements aimed at improving the energy efficiency of domestic and non domestic buildings. Building Regulations Approved Document L (2002)[7], and its equivalents for Scotland[12] and Northern Ireland[13], offer various means for meeting these requirements. These include:

- — limiting the heat loss and gains through the fabric of new and refurbished buildings

- — providing space heating and hot water systems which are energy efficient

- — providing lighting systems with appropriate lamps and sufficient controls so that energy can be used efficiently

- — limiting exposure to solar overheating

- — making provisions where air conditioning and mechanical ventilation systems are installed, so that no more energy needs to be used than is reasonable in the circumstances

- — providing sufficient information so that the building can be operated and maintained in such a manner as to use no more energy than is reasonable in the circumstances.

The Regulations have also been extended to include significant changes to controlled services and fittings in existing buildings, e.g. boiler replacement situations.

The wide ranging nature of the 2002 requirements will have a significant effect on energy efficiency of all new buildings and on the existing UK building stock.

The European Directive on the Energy Performance of Buildings[9] will be highly influential in the future. This Directive requires (by January 2006) member states to implement:

- — a common methodology for calculating the energy performance of buildings

- — minimum standards on energy performance of new and some existing buildings

- — certification schemes when buildings are constructed sold or rented out, with public display of energy performance certificates in public service buildings and buildings frequented by the public

- — specific inspection and assessment of boilers and air conditioning systems.

A CIBSE Briefing summarises the requirements of this directive[14].

★ Requirements may differ in Scotland[12] and Northern Ireland[13]

Statutory Instrument 1980 No. 1013: *Control of Fuel and Electricity*[15] specifies a maximum heating level of 19 °C in all non-domestic buildings. However, this law has not been rigorously enforced because, in some circumstances, it reduces the comfort of occupants.

Although not statutory, BS 8207: *Code of practice for energy efficiency in buildings*[16] makes recommendations for achieving energy efficient performance in buildings. It considers both design and operation and provides a framework which can be applied to new designs or to refurbishment. It also highlights the timing of critical design decisions in relation to the RIBA *Plan of Work*[17].

BS EN ISO 14001: *Environmental management systems*[18] encourages energy efficiency, as it requires monitoring of any significant environmental impact and a commitment to its reduction. Energy is normally the most significant factor in EMSs in buildings.

The Building Research Establishment Environmental Assessment Method (BREEAM)[19] is a non-statutory means of judging buildings against environmental targets and standards.

1.1.4   The role of building professionals

Rethinking Construction[20] ('The Egan Report') said that the construction industry must change significantly in order to meet the needs of clients and government. Amongst other things, the report urged:

—   a quality driven agenda with integrated teams and processes

—   integration of design and production

—   a culture of performance measurement and continuous improvement in seven areas: cost, time, predictability, defects, accidents, productivity and profitability.

The issues raised have a significant impact on energy efficiency and, if implemented, should help to improve buildings in this respect. Conversely, focussing on improving energy efficiency in buildings necessitates and often results in many 'Egan' outcomes. e.g. greater integration of teams and processes, integration of design and production and a culture of performance measurement. Energy efficiency plays a central role in achieving better buildings, leading to improved occupant satisfaction and productivity.

For these reasons, all building professionals should make energy efficiency a key part of their professional activities. They should always encourage clients, owners and operators to include energy efficiency in the brief at all stages in a building's life whether designing, operating or upgrading. Clients and financiers should be made aware of the investment case for energy efficiency. Building professionals should help clients to develop a brief which sets out both user and client requirements and constraints, balancing these against capital costs, running costs, whole life costs and environmental objectives.

Integrating energy into a clear brief is particularly necessary in projects carried out under 'Public Private Partnerships' (PPPs) where additional competition for investment can sometimes lead to a lowering of standards.

Building professionals will benefit by:

—   providing an added-value service to their clients by improving their buildings

—   reducing plant capital cost, particularly where mechanical cooling has been avoided or minimised

—   enhancing the standing of all building professionals by improving occupants' use and perception of buildings

—   increasing building marketability by promoting buildings as assets in which to invest

—   obtaining repeat work through satisfied customers.

The overall goal is 'better buildings' and this can often be achieved by focussing on energy efficiency. Recent work[21,22] has indicated that buildings that are designed and managed in an energy efficient way can be more comfortable and their staff more productive, making investment in good energy efficient design and management even more cost effective to a client organisation.

1.2   How to use this Guide

1.2.1   Structure

This Guide starts by setting out an overall framework for energy efficiency within which the building professional has the freedom to design, operate or upgrade a building. The 'principles of energy efficiency' stated at the front of this Guide are broadly based on the CIBSE policy statement on energy, see Appendix A1.1, and aim to help professionals put the policy into practice.

The main body of this Guide is divided into three parts as shown in Figure 1.6.

—   Part A: *Designing the building*: consists of sections 2 to 14 and deals with new buildings and major refurbishment.

—   Part B: *Operating and upgrading the building*: consists of sections 15 to 19 and covers the management and maintenance of buildings, highlighting measures that can be retrofitted in existing buildings. The reader is referred back to Part A where there is a large element of design.

—   Part C: *Benchmarks*: consists of section 20 and provides 'typical' and 'good practice' energy benchmarks for a wide range of buildings, components and end-uses.

A diagram at the top of the first page of each section indicates the relationship of that section to the rest of the Guide.

The first section in each part provides a strategic overview of the process being covered. The last two sections in each part help check that the main options have been considered and that the final outcome meets expectations. The sections of this Guide particularly relevant to readers

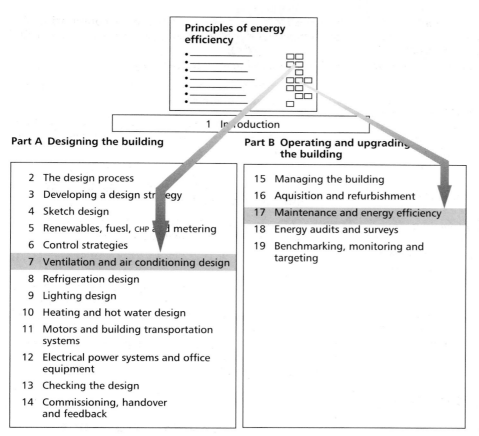

Figure 1.6 Structure of the Guide

from various professions are shown in Table 1.1. Appendix A1 consists of relevant CIBSE Policy Statements and Appendix A2 gives some standard conversion factors and properties of fuels. Appendix A3 considers the role of energy consultants and provides model briefs for commissionins energy audits and surveys. Useful websites are listed in Appendix A4.

1.2.2   Investing in energy efficiency

Some organisations are now investing in energy efficiency to directly improve their overall environmental performance. This is usually in response to an overall environmental policy laid down by senior management or as a result of government initiatives in the public sector. The benefits of measuring and reporting environmental performance against targets can also significantly enhance corporate image which may influence future investors.

Although environmental reasons are strong, in practice cost savings usually drive energy efficiency. This Guide therefore concentrates on cost effective measures. Savings

Table 1.1 Sections relevant to readers from various professions

Reader	Part	Section
Building services designers	Designing the building	1–14
Building owners/operators	Operating and upgrading the building	15–20
Energy managers/consultants	Operating and upgrading the building	15, 18–20
Architects/surveyors	Designing the building	1–14
Developers/financiers	Designing the building	1–6, 15

in operating costs will flow directly into the building user's profit. Well-managed organisations tend to re-invest some of the savings in further energy-efficiency measures, setting up a snowball effect. Additional investment may also be justified for environmental reasons e.g. emissions trading.

Energy efficiency measures should generally be considered in their order of economic payback, complexity and ease of application. Measures fall into three broad types:

— no-cost/low-cost requiring no investment appraisal

— medium cost requiring only a simple payback calculation

— high capital cost measures requiring detailed design and a full investment appraisal.

Investment in energy efficiency should be treated on the same basis as any other financial decision, and should have no more onerous conditions placed upon it than any other investment. A variety of financial appraisal methods can be used to assess the viability of energy saving measures (see 18.8). Assessments should always take into account the wider benefits such as improvements in comfort and the environment. This can be achieved using a life-cycle approach.

Energy efficient buildings need cost no more to build than conventional buildings. The integration of the fabric and services design can present opportunities to reduce capital cost. For example, the cost of external shading can be offset by minimising or avoiding air conditioning plant.

References

1   *Digest of UK energy statistics* (London: The Stationery Office) (published annually)

2   (Various titles) Energy Efficiency Booklets (Action Energy) (1994) (www.actionenergy.org.uk)

3   *Climate Change 2001* (Geneva: Intergovernmental Panel on Climate Change) (July 2001) (www.ipcc.ch)

4   *Energy — the changing climate* Twenty Second Report of the Royal Commission on Environmental Pollution (London: Royal Commission on Environmental Pollution) (June 2000) (www.rcep.org.uk)

5   *Climate Change — The UK programme* (London: The Stationery Office) (2000)

6   *Quality Assurance for Combined Heat and Power* (London: Department for Environment, Food and Rural Affairs) (2001) (www.chpqa.com)

7   The Building Regulations 2000 Statutory Instrument 2000 No. 2531 and the Building (Amendment) Regulations 2001 Statutory Instrument 2001 No. 3335 (London: The Stationery Office) (2000/2001)

8   *Our energy future — creating a low carbon economy* CM5761 (London: The Stationery Office) (2003)

9   Directive 2002/91/EC of the European Parliament and of the Council of 16 December 2002 on the energy performance of buildings *Official J. of the European Communities* 4.1.2003 L1/60 (Brussels: Commission of the European Communities) (2001)

10   *Environmental code of practice for buildings and their services* BSRIA COP 6/99 (Bracknell: Building Services Research and Information Association) (1991)

11   *Conservation of fuel and power* The Building Regulations 2000 Approved Document L1/L2 (London: The Stationery Office) (2001)

12   *Technical standards for compliance with the Building Standards (Scotland) Regulations 1990 (as amended)* (London: The Stationery Office) (2001)

13   *Conservation of fuel and power* Building Regulations (Northern Ireland) 1994 Technical Booklet F (London: The Stationery Office) (1999)

14   *The Energy Performance of Buildings Directive* CIBSE Briefing 6 (London: Chartered Institution of Building Services Engineers) (2003)

15   Control of Fuel and Electricity. The Fuel and Electricity (Heating) (Control) (Amendment) Order 1984 Statutory Instrument 1980 No. 1013 (London: The Stationery Office)

16   BS 8207: 1985: *Code of practice for energy efficiency in buildings* (London: British Standard Institution) (1985)

17   *Plan of work for design team operation* RIBA Handbook (London: Royal Institute of British Architects) (1973)

18   BS EN ISO 14001: 1996: *Environmental management systems. Specification with guidance for use* (London: British Standards Institution) (1996)

19   R Baldwin, A Yates, N Howard and S Rao *BREEAM 98 For Offices* (London: Construction Research Communications) (1998)

20   *Rethinking construction — the report of the Construction Task Force to the Deputy Prime Minister, on the scope for improving the quality and efficiency of UK construction* ('The Egan Report') (London: Department of the Environment, Transport and the Regions) (now DEFRA) (July 1998)

21   Bordass W T, Bromley A K R and Leaman A J *Comfort, control and energy efficiency in offices* BRE Information Paper IP3/95 (Garston: Building Research Establishment) (1995)

22   Special Issue on Post Occupancy Evaluation *Building Research and Information* **29** (2) (March/April 2001)

Bibliography

Pout C et al. *Non-domestic energy fact file* (London: Construction Research Communications) (1999)*Energy efficiency in buildings* House of Commons Environment Committee Fourth report Session 1992–93 (London: The Stationery Office) (1993)

Wyatt T *Adapt or die: the major challenges ahead for the building services industry* CIBSE Presidential Address 2003 (London: Chartered Institution of Building Services Engineers) (2003)

Environmental issues in construction RP 445 (London: Construction Industry Research and Information Association) (1992)

Energy on the boardroom agenda — Making a corporate commitment (Action Energy) (1992) (www.actionenergy.org.uk)

Organisational aspects of energy management General Information Report GIR 12 (Action Energy) (1993) (www.actionenergy.org.uk)

Reviewing energy management General Information Report GIR 13 (Action Energy) (1993) (www.actionenergy.org.uk)

Part A: Designing the building

Energy design checklist

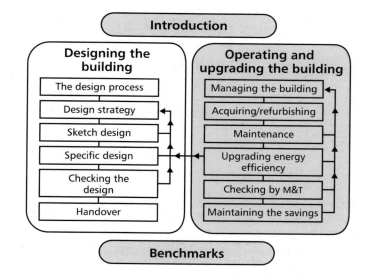

Energy design checklist

HAS THE BRIEF BEEN MET?
- [ ] Have clients requirements and investment criteria been satisfied?
- [ ] Have original power density targets (W/m^2) been met?
- [ ] Have original energy ($kW{\cdot}h/m^2$ per year) or CO_2/m^2 per year targets been met?
- [ ] Have original environmental targets been met? e.g. BREEAM
- [ ] Have life cycle cost targets been achieved?

DESIGN INTEGRATION
- [ ] Will the fabric and services work well together?
- [ ] Will individual services operate without conflict?
- [ ] Has every effort been made to minimise requirements for services?
- [ ] Has every effort been made to include renewables?
- [ ] Can thermal storage, heat recovery, free cooling be used to minimise services further?
- [ ] Has natural ventilation been optimised to minimise services?
- [ ] Has daylight been optimised to minimise services?

BUILDING FABRIC
- [ ] Is this the optimum site layout to improve orientation, shading and footprint?
- [ ] Is this the best building orientation?
- [ ] Is this the optimum shape?
- [ ] Is this the most appropriate thermal response? e.g. heavyweight or lightweight
- [ ] Is this the optimum level of insulation?
- [ ] Is this the optimum percentage fenestration?
- [ ] Are the windows the most appropriate design for this situation?
- [ ] Has every effort been made to minimise/utilise solar gains? e.g. shading
- [ ] Will design detailing help minimise unwanted air infiltration?

VENTILATION
- [ ] Has every effort been made to use a natural ventilation strategy?
- [ ] If natural ventilation is not possible, can a mixed-mode approach be used?
- [ ] If mixed-mode is not possible then has every effort been made to use efficient air conditioning?
- [ ] Has every effort been made to avoid humidification and/or de-humidification?
- [ ] Has night cooling been considered?
- [ ] Where mechanical plant is essential, is it the most efficient possible?
- [ ] Is ductwork designed to give low pressure drops?
- [ ] Does the ventilation design have effective controls including VSDs, good zoning and local user controls?

COOLING/INTERNAL GAINS
- [ ] Has every effort been made to reduce cooling loads and minimise internal gains?
- [ ] Where mechanical plant is essential, is it the most efficient possible?
- [ ] Can supply temperatures be raised?
- [ ] Have free cooling, thermal storage and heat recovery been considered?
- [ ] Can the evaporating temperature be increased and/or the condensing temperature be reduced to increase COP?
- [ ] Does the cooling system have effective controls including VSDs, good zoning and local user controls?

LIGHTING
- [ ] Has every effort been made to bring in additional daylight?
- [ ] Will the daylight be utilised in conjunction with responsive controls?
- [ ] Have daylight controls been zoned in relation to occupants needs?
- [ ] Has every effort been made to avoid over lighting compared to recommended illuminance levels?
- [ ] Can lighting be provided by more localised systems e.g. task lighting?
- [ ] Are the light sources (lamps, luminaires and control gear) the most efficient possible?
- [ ] Are lighting controls effective in controlling consumption related to occupancy and daylight with good local user controls?

HEATING AND HOT WATER
- [ ] Has every effort been made to reduce heating loads, heat losses and hot water demands?
- [ ] Is heating and hot water plant the most efficient possible? (e.g. condensing boiler)
- [ ] Are heating and hot water plant separate and has a decentralised approach been considered?
- [ ] Has CHP been considered?
- [ ] Does the heating system have effective controls including VSDs, good zoning and local user controls?

MOTORS
- [ ] Have high efficiency motors been specified throughout the design?
- [ ] Have VSDs been specified where appropriate?

BEMS/CONTROLS
- [ ] Has a suitable balance been found between central and local control?
- [ ] Are controls reasonably simple for both management and occupants?
- [ ] Will management have suitable overall controls that encourage good operation? e.g. BEMS
- [ ] Does the BEMS provide central control, monitoring and alarms with a good user interface?
- [ ] Do occupants have good local controls with simple interfaces?
- [ ] Will controls cause conflicts between systems?
- [ ] Is the building zoned appropriately using controls?
- [ ] Has variable flow control using VSDs been included?

OVERALL BUILDING
- [ ] Is the design simple, avoiding over-complexity?
- [ ] Is the building easy to commission?
- [ ] Is the building easy to manage and operate?
- [ ] Is the building easy to maintain?
- [ ] Is the building flexible enough to meet the needs of future changes in work practices?

ENERGY REGULATIONS
- [ ] Has Part L of the building Regulations been satisfied?
- [ ] Has every effort been made to go well beyond the minimum standards in Part L?

METERING AND DOCUMENTATION
- [ ] Has a building log book been prepared showing design estimates of future consumption?
- [ ] Has a metering strategy been developed and included in the log-book?
- [ ] Are all sub-meters shown on the design drawings?
- [ ] Have detailed O&M manuals been prepared including details of design, commissioning, equipment etc?

2 The design process

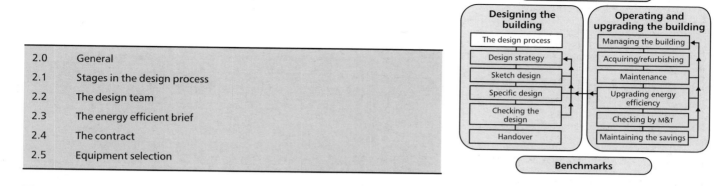

This section shows how and when energy efficiency can be included in the design process, in line with the principles given at the front of this Guide. Designers should seek a balance between overall cost and good design practice, while meeting the occupier's business needs. Energy efficiency plays a central part in any good design and is exceptional in being cost-effective over the life cycle of the building.

2.0   General

The process of energy efficient design should always include:

—   identifying user requirements

—   designing to meet these requirements with minimal energy use

—   establishing an integrated design team with a brief and contract that promotes energy efficiency

—   setting energy targets at an early stage, for each fuel and individual end-uses, and designing within them

—   designing for manageability, maintainability, operability and flexibility

—   checking that the final design meets the targets and that the selected equipment conforms with product performance benchmarks.

Success depends on understanding the interactions between people, building fabric and services, as shown in Figure 2.1[1]. This integrated design approach requires the successful collaboration of client, project manager, architect, engineer and quantity surveyor at the early conceptual stage of the project[2–4].

The most significant influence in energy efficiency is often the way the building is used by the management and occupants. Hence, the principles of energy efficiency at the front of this guide place great emphasis on management issues. Activity, hours of occupancy, control settings etc. all vary enormously and represent the greatest unknown at the design stage. Designers need to take account of this variability and promote better building management through improved design. A good management regime, which is responsive to the needs of the occupants and fully in control of the building, can have a major effect on energy consumption.

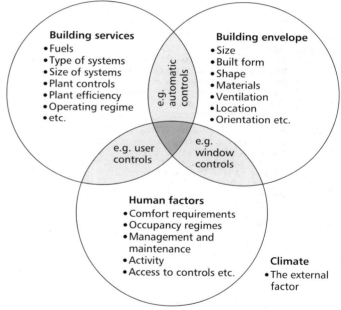

Figure 2.1 Key factors that influence energy consumption

The integration of building envelope, services and 'human factors' should be covered in the brief and is a key part of the sketch design stage. The early design concept needs to be tested against the client's criteria, which normally include cost, quality of the internal environment and compliance with energy and environmental targets, e.g. by using BREEAM[5]. If it does not meet the criteria, the design team should review the design concept or the client's requirements. This iterative process is essential in reaching an effective energy efficient design.

Generally, owner-occupiers will be more interested in low running costs than will speculative developers. However, developers should recognise that buildings that are energy efficient and therefore have low running costs can attract a premium in the market place and are increasingly likely to do so in the future.

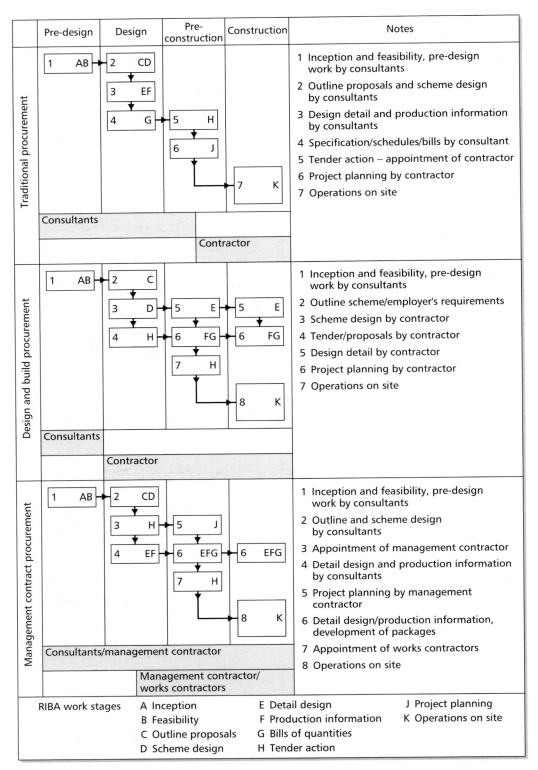

Figure 2.2 Common methods of procurement

	Pre-design	Design	Pre-construction	Construction	Notes
Traditional procurement	1 AB →	2 CD / 3 EF / 4 G →	5 H / 6 J	7 K	1 Inception and feasibility, pre-design work by consultants 2 Outline proposals and scheme design by consultants 3 Design detail and production information by consultants 4 Specification/schedules/bills by consultant 5 Tender action – appointment of contractor 6 Project planning by contractor 7 Operations on site

Consultants

Contractor

	Pre-design	Design	Pre-construction	Construction	Notes
Design and build procurement	1 AB →	2 C / 3 D / 4 H →	5 E / 6 FG / 7 H →	5 E / 6 FG / 8 K	1 Inception and feasibility, pre-design work by consultants 2 Outline scheme/employer's requirements 3 Scheme design by contractor 4 Tender/proposals by contractor 5 Design detail by contractor 6 Project planning by contractor 7 Operations on site

Consultants

Contractor

	Pre-design	Design	Pre-construction	Construction	Notes
Management contract procurement	1 AB →	2 CD / 3 H / 4 EF →	5 J / 6 EFG / 7 H →	6 EFG / 8 K	1 Inception and feasibility, pre-design work by consultants 2 Outline and scheme design by consultants 3 Appointment of management contractor 4 Detail design and production information by consultants 5 Project planning by management contractor 6 Detail design/production information, development of packages 7 Appointment of works contractors 8 Operations on site

Consultants/management contractor

Management contractor/works contractors

RIBA work stages	A Inception	E Detail design	J Project planning
	B Feasibility	F Production information	K Operations on site
	C Outline proposals	G Bills of quantities	
	D Scheme design	H Tender action	

2.1 Stages in the design process

Standard plans of work[6] usually need to be modified to meet the requirements of the building users and the contract being undertaken. In particular, provision should be made to review energy issues throughout the plan to ensure that the energy concepts are not gradually diluted or dropped. The plan should also formalise the responsibility for energy and ensure that energy issues are well communicated during the design process[7,8]. A speculative development that will be fitted out by the occupant will need a different approach to energy efficiency than a

bespoke building for an owner-occupier. Examples of these different approaches are shown in Figure 2.2.

The plan of work should identify specific points at which the design team will report on how the design meets the client's brief. Table 2.1 illustrates this in relation to RIBA Plan of Work stages.

There will be a significant level of overlap between the individual activities taking place throughout the design process. This is illustrated in Figure 2.3, taken from BS 8207[9] which highlights the timing of critical design decisions that influence the energy performance. BS 8207 also makes recommendations for achieving energy

Table 2.1 Reporting on energy efficient design

Work stages	Details to be reported by the design team	Energy efficiency considerations
(A) Inception	Prepare general outline of requirements	Establishment of energy and environmental objectives, criteria and targets
	Plan future action	Establish an appropriate team
(B) Feasibility	Appraisal and recommendations of how project will proceed	Ensure good communication within the design team with a good plan of work
	Show it is feasible, functionally, technically and financially	Develop a clear design strategy that integrates fabric, services and human factors
(C) Outline proposals	The brief as far as has been developed	Site considerations
	Explanation of major design decisions and definition of user requirements	Building form and arrangement on site
	Firm estimate with outline cost plan	Outline servicing and energy strategy, e.g. naturally ventilated, mechanically ventilated, air-conditioned, daylighting etc.
		Selection of fuel/energy types
(D) Scheme design	Statement of the fully developed brief	Design of fenestration taking into account the ramifications on heating, cooling fans and pumps, and lighting energy
	Explanation of scheme outline specification	Selection of building thermal characteristics; levels of insulation and thermal response
	Cost plan	Decisions on main plant arrangements and control strategies, and main vertical and horizontal routes for services
	Future timetable	Decisions made on lighting and daylighting systems, and their control
(E/F) Detail design/production information	Preparation of the production drawings, specifications, schedules etc.	Detailed plant/system design. Select equipment using certified product performance data to comply with performance benchmarks
		Detailed design of system controls
		Provisions for monitoring system condition and energy use
		Commissioning requirements and acceptance procedures
		Building/system management requirements and documentation

efficient performance in buildings and hence provides a framework that can be applied to new designs or refurbishment. It should be noted that the environmental objectives of reducing carbon dioxide emissions and environmental pollution are particularly important for design decisions 1, 4, 6, 10 and 16 in Figure 2.3.

2.2 The design team

The multi-disciplinary design team should be appointed at inception, prior to the conceptual stage of the design, and comprise typically an architect, building services engineer, quantity surveyor, structural engineer and client representatives. Each member should consider the energy implications of each design decision; the design team should also obtain feedback from the client during the design process.

The design team should:

— make the client aware of the implications that decisions have on life cycle costs

— provide an energy efficient design that takes account of energy management, maintenance needs and occupant comfort/control

— provide projections of energy performance and running costs

— propose further options for energy efficiency, highlighting the potential benefits

— produce good documentation which makes the design intent clear.

Ideally, all team members should be involved for the entire duration of the project[2]. The client's requirements must be clearly identified and any changes addressed by the team as the project develops, any implications being reviewed with the client, as necessary.

2.3 The energy efficient brief

The energy efficient brief should be no more complex than is appropriate for the type and size of building[2,10]. It should incorporate:

— the client's intentions, requirements and investment criteria

— energy targets for each fuel and individual end-uses e.g. based on benchmarks from section 20

— environmental targets e.g. BREEAM credits

— life cycle costs

— the intentions to include energy efficient equipment, based on certified performance information where available (see www.ukepic.com)

— a requirement to undertake integrated design.

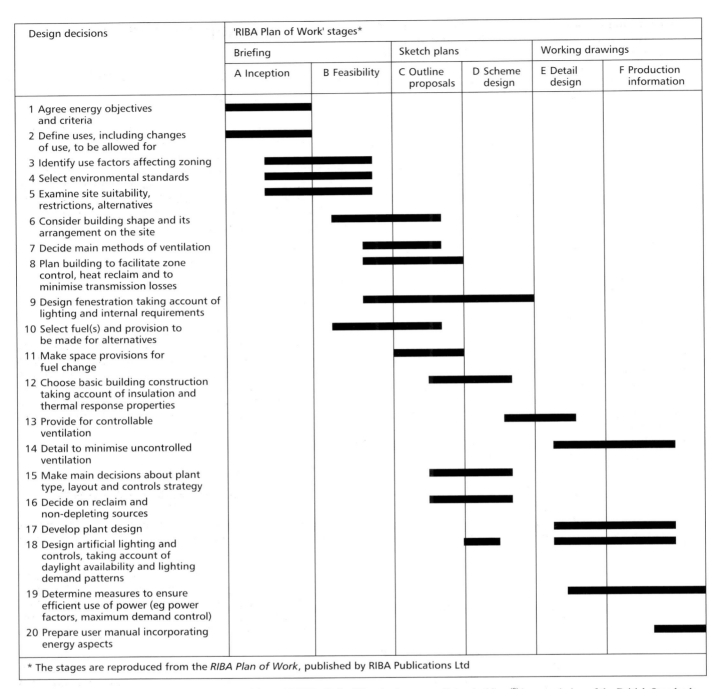

Design decisions	'RIBA Plan of Work' stages*					
	Briefing		Sketch plans		Working drawings	
	A Inception	B Feasibility	C Outline proposals	D Scheme design	E Detail design	F Production information
1 Agree energy objectives and criteria	▬					
2 Define uses, including changes of use, to be allowed for	▬					
3 Identify use factors affecting zoning		▬				
4 Select environmental standards		▬				
5 Examine site suitability, restrictions, alternatives		▬				
6 Consider building shape and its arrangement on the site		▬				
7 Decide main methods of ventilation		▬				
8 Plan building to facilitate zone control, heat reclaim and to minimise transmission losses		▬				
9 Design fenestration taking account of lighting and internal requirements			▬			
10 Select fuel(s) and provision to be made for alternatives		▬				
11 Make space provisions for fuel change			▬			
12 Choose basic building construction taking account of insulation and thermal response properties				▬		
13 Provide for controllable ventilation					▬	
14 Detail to minimise uncontrolled ventilation					▬	
15 Make main decisions about plant type, layout and controls strategy				▬		
16 Decide on reclaim and non-depleting sources				▬		
17 Develop plant design					▬	
18 Design artificial lighting and controls, taking account of daylight availability and lighting demand patterns				▬		
19 Determine measures to ensure efficient use of power (eg power factors, maximum demand control)					▬	
20 Prepare user manual incorporating energy aspects						▬

* The stages are reproduced from the *RIBA Plan of Work*, published by RIBA Publications Ltd

Figure 2.3 Timing of design decisions (reproduced from BS 8207: *Code of Practice for energy efficient buildings*[9] by permission of the British Standards Institution and the Royal Institute of British Architects. This extract from BS 8207: 1995 is reproduced with the permission of BSI under licence no. PD\1998 0963. Complete editions of the standard can be obtained by post from BSI Customer Services, 389 Chiswick High Road, London W4 4AL.)

Where possible, a range of options should be considered before deciding on the overall design concept. GPG287: *The design team's guide to environmentally smart buildings*[11] is particularly helpful in considering the available options. It is possible to meet a particular brief through a number of design solutions, and it is important at the briefing stage to establish the aims and objectives of the design to ensure that they are reflected in these solutions.

The energy implications of the internal environment and loads specified in the brief should be explained to the client by the building services engineer. Unrealistic criteria can result in plant being oversized with energy and cost penalties. For example, excessive lighting levels will increase both capital and running costs. Equally, specifying very narrow bands of temperature or humidity is likely to increase energy consumption. This is particularly true if air conditioning is required as this can increase building energy consumption by up to 50%[12]. Humidification and dehumidification should only be specified where absolutely essential.

Internal and external design conditions should be selected in accordance with CIBSE Guide A: *Environmental design*[13]. However, designers should agree an acceptable range for the internal environmental standards, as these can have a significant effect on plant sizing and energy consumption. For example, maximum summer indoor temperatures might be selected that typically are not exceeded for 97.5% of the time. Flexible options should also be considered. e.g. to allow bands of temperature, humidity or ventilation to float across seasons.

Higher air change rates usually mean increased energy consumption, particularly with mechanical ventilation, although heat recovery and 'free cooling' may redress the balance. Areas where smoking is allowed require around four times the ventilation rate per person, so restricting these areas reduces energy consumption and improves the quality of the internal environment.

The level of occupant control can have a very significant impact on the way systems are used and hence on future energy consumption. Occupants' response to their environment is influenced by:

— the quality of the environment.

— the perceived level of individual control.

— the quality of the management of services and response to complaints.

— the desire to be close to a window.

Results from building user surveys[14] show a 'virtuous circle' of characteristics, with responsive and effective management of buildings leading to staff satisfaction, better energy efficiency and improved productivity. Where occupants' tolerance of the internal environment is low, the building is unlikely to function efficiently. This is more likely to be the case in air conditioned buildings as they tend to exclude the external environment.

In essence, this means that buildings that make good use of natural light and ventilation, in which occupants have the opportunity to make local adjustments, often provide more acceptable environments and hence greater energy efficiency.

2.4   The design contract

The building design contract should promote energy efficiency by ensuring that all building professionals work together creatively to achieve an integrated and energy efficient design. Energy efficient buildings often require greater professional skill and design input. The team must, therefore, have enough time at an early stage to formulate an integrated sketch design.

To realise energy efficient designs, each stage of a contract needs to be carefully assessed to ensure that the design intent is followed through appropriate procurement and careful commissioning to actual performance, and the predicted returns realised. Although this can sometimes result in increased design fees at an early stage, these can be compensated by lower fees later in the contract. It also ensures that the client's brief is fully addressed.

Fee structures based entirely on the capital cost of the building services may not encourage energy efficiency, which often requires more design input and a lower plant capital cost. Lump sum fees based on the estimated time spent are therefore becoming more common, allowing greater scope for energy efficient design.

2.5   Equipment selection

2.5.1   Importance of product certification

Product performance may not necessarily be as manufacturers claim in their literature. This could result in systems being unable to cope with demands, and/or operating less efficiently than design. There are industry-run certification schemes that aim to guarantee that products achieve their claimed performance. Selecting products whose performance is certified or otherwise independently verified means that:

(a)   safety factors may often be reduced leading to smaller plant and lower running costs, and

(b)   system performance and efficiency levels are more likely to be achieved.

The Eurovent Certification Company Ltd (www.eurovent-certification.org) operates a scheme that certifies many important HVACR components including packaged chillers and fan coil units. The Association of European Refrigeration Compressor and Controls Manufacturers (ASERCOM) (www.asercom.org) certifies refrigeration compressors. Other schemes exist for particular types of plant/equipment.

2.5.2   Product performance benchmarks and databases

There are several sources of product performance information and databases which can aid product screening and/or selection:

— The European Committee of Air Handling and Refrigerating Equipment Manufacturers (EUROVENT) operates on-line HVACR product databases (www.eurovent-certification.org) but these do not enable comparison of products from competing suppliers.

— The UK Environmental Products Information Consortium (UKEPIC) (www.ukepic.com) is a government-sponsored initiative that publishes searchable product performance databases, indicative performance targets and other procurement guidance.

Other sources of data and benchmarks exist.

References

1   Jones P G, Cheshire D and Lillicrap C Energy efficient buildings: what is integrated design? *CIBSE Nat. Conf., Harrogate, 4–5 October 1997* (London: Chartered Institution of Building Services Engineers) (1997)

2   *Briefing the design team for energy efficiency in new buildings Good Practice Guide* GPG 74 (Action Energy) (1994) (www.action energy.org.uk)

3   *Environmental code of practice for buildings and their services* BSRIA COP 6/99 (Bracknell: Building Services Research and Information Association) (1999)

4   *The benefits of including energy efficiency early in the design stage —
        Anglia Polytechnic University* Good Practice Case Study GPCS
        334 (Action Energy) (1997) (www.actionenergy.org.uk)

5   Baldwin R, Yates A, Howard N and Rao S *BREEAM 98 For
        Offices* (London: Construction Research Communications)
        (1998)

6   Phillips R *The Architect's Plan of Work* (London: RIBA
        Publications) (2000)

7   Parsloe C J *The allocation of design responsibilities for building
        engineering services — a code of conduct to avoid conflict* BSRIA
        TN 8/94 (Bracknell: Building Services Research and
        Information Association) (1994)

8   Wild L J *Design information flow* BSRIA TN 17/92 (Bracknell:
        Building Services Research and Information Association)
        (1992)

9   BS 8207: 1985: *Code of Practice for energy efficient buildings*
        (London: British Standards Institution) (1985)

10   *A performance specification for the energy efficient office of the future*
        General Information Report GIR 30 (Action Energy) (1995)
        (www.actionenergy.org.uk)

11   *The design team's guide to environmentally smart buildings* Good
        Practice Guide GPG287 (Action Energy) (2000)
        (www.actionenergy.org.uk)

12   *Energy use in offices* Energy Consumption Guide ECON 19
        (Action Energy) (2000) (www.actionenergy.org.uk)

13   *Environmental design* CIBSE Guide A (London: Chartered
        Institution of Building Services Engineers) (1999)

14   Bordass W T, Bromley A K R and Leaman A J *Comfort, control
        and energy efficiency in offices* BSRIA IP3/95 (London:
        Construction Research Communications) (1995)

Bibliography

Environmental criteria for design Section 1 in CIBSE Guide A:
Environmental design (London: Chartered Institution of Building Services
Engineers) (2000)

Best practice in the specification for offices (Reading: British Council for
Offices)(2000)

Guide to ownership, operation and maintenance of building services (London:
Chartered Institution of Building Services Engineers) (2000)

Hancock C, Oreszczyn T and Iwaszkiewicz C Energy conscious design;
the role of design advice *Proc. CIBSE Nat. Conf., Brighton, 2–4 October
1994* (London: Chartered Institution of Building Services Engineers)
(1994)

Al-khafaji M Effective energy management : the designer's role *Proc.
CIBSE Nat. Conf., Brighton, 2–4 October 1994* (London: Chartered
Institution of Building Services Engineers) (1994)

Halliday S and Smerdon T Feedback as part of the building design
process *Proc. CIBSE Nat. Conf., Eastbourne, 1–3 October 1995* (London:
Chartered Institution of Building Services Engineers) (1995)

*The benefits of including energy efficiency early in the design stage — Anglia
Polytechnic* University Good Practice Case Studies GPCS 334 (Action
Energy) (1997) (www.actionenergy.org.uk)

Energy efficiency in offices — A guide for the design team Good Practice
Guide GPG 34 (Action Energy) (1993) www.actionenergy.org.uk

De Saules T *Handover information for building services* BSRIA TN15/95
(London: Building Services Research and Information Association)
(1995)

Blyth A and Worthington J *Managing the brief for better design* (London:
Spon) (2001)

The Elizabeth Fry Building, University of East Anglia New Practice Report
NPR 106 (Action Energy) (1998) (www.actionenergy.org.uk)

3   Developing a design strategy

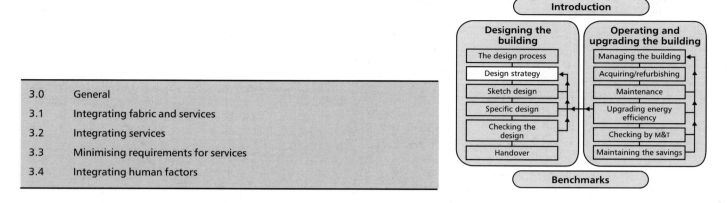

3.0   General

3.1   Integrating fabric and services

3.2   Integrating services

3.3   Minimising requirements for services

3.4   Integrating human factors

A coherent sketch design is at the heart of an energy efficient building[1-4]. This section outlines how to develop an integrated design strategy in line with the principles at the front of this Guide. Section 4 contains more detail on site considerations, built form, ventilation, daylighting and fuel selection.

3.0   General

Building design is an iterative process, often requiring design teams to re-think fundamental aspects of the design. Figure 3.1 indicates how an energy efficient design can be achieved through an integrated approach.

An overall design philosophy should be established to underpin the whole design process. Some key issues that have a strong influence on the energy efficient design philosophy are shown in Table 3.1.

3.1   Integrating fabric and services

The first step in developing an integrated design is to establish the function of the building envelope as the primary climatic modifier, supported by the services to trim conditions. Good fabric design can minimise the need for services. Where appropriate, designs should avoid simply excluding the environment, but should respond to factors like weather and occupancy and make good use of natural light, ventilation, solar gains and shading, when they are beneficial.

For example, decisions taken on the provision of daylight will directly influence the window design, the amount of glazing and the type of glass. They will also affect the building's susceptibility to solar gain and influence:

—   the need for solar control and/or air conditioning

—   the size, capacity and space required to accommodate central plant

—   the air and water distribution systems.

Several iterations may be needed to reach an effective design as it is tested against the performance criteria of:

—   cost

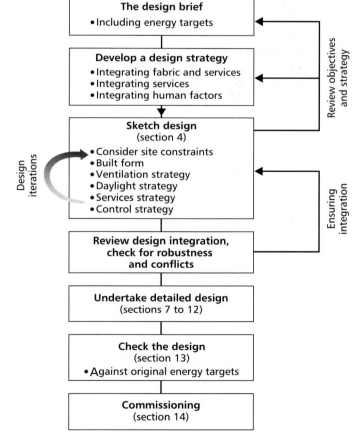

Figure 3.1 Integrated design

—   quality of the internal environment

—   space requirements

—   energy use

—   robustness

—   ease of operation.

Table 3.1 Issues that influence the energy efficient design philosophy

Building envelope	Building services	Human factors
Climate excluding or climate responsive?	Heavily serviced, mixed mode or passive solutions?	Balance between central automation and local occupant controls?
Use building fabric for thermal storage?	Use natural daylight and/or ventilation?	Responsive to occupancy/activity or fixed systems?
Thermally heavyweight or lightweight?	Complex or simple systems/controls?	Do occupants require 'loose' or 'tight' comfort bands?
Deep or shallow plan?	Use flexible comfort criteria?	Easy or difficult to manage?
Highly glazed or little glazing?	Use heat recovery and free cooling?	Easy or difficult to maintain?
Openable or fixed windows?	Use combined heat and power?	Allow for future flexibility?

Select issues on the x and y axes to see how they may interact

Sevices issues	Deep plan/ shallow plan	Orientation	Percentage glazing	Lightwells and atria	Airtightness	Thermal response
Cooling	Deep plan may need greater cooling and mechanical ventilation	Consider locating cooled zones on north façade to reduce potential cooling loads	Minimise solar gains	Minimise solar gains	Take care that facilities for summer cooling are airtight in winter	Store heat in thermal mass and effect on response times
Heating	Deeper plan reduces heat loss area	Position less heated buffer zones on north façade to reduce heat loss	Solar gains contribute to heating	Minimise heat loss via atria i.e. avoiding heating	Minimise air infiltration to reduce heat loss	Store heat in thermal mass and effect on response times
Electric lighting and daylight	Use shallow plan for maximum daylight penetration or lightwells/atria	Calculate sun angles and use north light or shading to limit solar gains	Increased glazing will increase daylight but may also increase solar gains and need for shading	Use atria to increase natural daylight		
Natural ventilation	Use shallow plan to allow natural ventilation	Draw air from north façade to give cooler air	Ventilation depends on number of openable windows	Use atria to encourage natural air circulation	Seal building envelope and allow only controlled ventilation	Utilise effect of thermal mass on response of building to external conditions
Mechanical ventilation and air conditioning	Consider shallow plan with mixed-mode to allow natural ventilation at certain times	Orientated to avoid solar gains	Reduce percentage glazing to minimise effect of solar gains on air conditioning	Consider atria with mixed mode to allow natural ventilation and daylight at certain times	Ensure building envelope is sealed	Utilise effect of thermal mass on response time of air conditioning

Fabric issues

Figure 3.2 Interaction between fabric and services

Avoiding dependence on mechanical plant, e.g. air conditioning, can reduce capital and running costs. Where air conditioning is unavoidable, the principles of integrated design can still help to reduce the size and complexity of the system, and hence its capital and running costs.

Figure 3.2 indicates some of the issues that need to be considered when integrating fabric and services. For example, a low percentage glazed area may result in higher lighting loads than expected. However, a large glazed area may not be helpful if the blinds have to be used to limit glare.

3.2   Integrating services

The next step is to ensure that the services operate in harmony without detrimental interaction or conflict. For example, the levels, control and efficiency of lighting have a significant effect on the need for cooling. It may also be appropriate to reconsider the building form so that more use can be made of daylight if this minimises energy demands for lighting and cooling.

Many energy problems can be traced to a conflict between building services. An energy efficient design strategy should avoid such conflicts. Some of the key interactions are shown in Figure 3.3.

	Cooling	Heating	Electric lighting	Daylight/ glazing	Natural ventilatiion
Heating	Avoid simultaneous heating and cooling	Select issues on the X and Y axes to see how they may interact			
Electric lighting	Reduce incidental gains from lights to minimise cooling	Include contribution of lighting towards heating			
Daylight/ glazing	Minimise solar gains to reduce cooling loads	Minimise heat loss and maximise useful heat gain through glazing	Use suitable switching and daylight linking controls to minimise use of electric lighting		
Natural ventilation	Consider mixed-mode to use natural ventilation and avoid mechanical cooling where possible	Account for effect of open windows		Balance solar gains from glazing with increased natural ventilation. Avoid conflicts between window opening and blinds	
Mechanical ventilation and air conditioning	Use free cooling and 'coolth' recovery	Use heat recovery	Reduce electric lighting to reduce loads on air conditioning	Solar gains from glazing may increase loads on air conditioning, Heat loss may require simultaneous perimeter heating	Use natural ventilation instead of air conditioning where possible, or consider mixed-mode

Figure 3.3 Interaction between building services

Simultaneous heating and cooling can be a major problem. Although this can be minimised by good controls, sometimes the problem originates from the basic design. For example, perimeter heating with core air conditioning may result in wasted energy if controls are adjusted by the occupants to compensate for local discomfort.

Zoning services is an important factor in achieving an energy efficient integrated design. Services should be matched to the actual requirements of each area. Areas with different requirements should not be heated, cooled, or lit to the same standards. Zones should be established in relation to the building, its occupancy and use, and the means of supplying the services. Generally, it helps to establish the same zones for each service to minimise conflict. For example, where a heating zone overlaps a cooling zone there is potential for simultaneous heating and cooling.

Excessive casual gains from lighting due to poor control can lead to significant cooling loads. This is particularly true in summer, when daylight levels may be sufficient for lights to be turned off. Good lighting control, including suitable manual override, can help to avoid this problem.

Mechanical cooling systems often operate when the external air could be used for cooling. Air conditioning systems may operate solely to negate the heat added to the air by the fans. The change to 'free' cooling and/or natural ventilation during winter can save significant energy, when humidification is not required.

Heat recovery provides a means of integrating services. For example, integrating lighting and air conditioning systems by extracting air through luminaires enables a proportion of the energy consumed by the lamps to be recovered to supplement heating in winter. The summer cooling load is also reduced by preventing a proportion of the lighting heat load from entering the room. The light output of fluorescent lamps also increases due to the lower operating temperature, although over-cooling must be avoided.

Many conflicts between services are control issues (see section 6). However, the underlying reasons for conflict should be identified and eliminated to prevent carrying a flawed design forward. It is not good policy to hope that the control system will resolve these conflicts.

3.3 Minimising requirements for services

Over-specification of services should be avoided in order to minimise capital and running costs[5]. Continually reviewing the need for services, the true demands likely to be made on them, and avoiding unnecessary complexity will improve energy efficiency and will often result in a better building.

Building services engineers have a responsibility to challenge the assumptions underpinning the design in order to avoid over provision of services. An over-serviced building does not necessarily mean a 'high quality' building[6–8]. For example:

— Are the design margins excessive? (See section 4.)

— Are the design parameters unnecessarily restrictive? (For example, attempting to control relative humidity to 50% ±5% all year round in an office.)

— Is the plant over sophisticated, necessitating more complex controls and increasing the likelihood that systems will be difficult to understand and control?

— Have natural sources such as daylight and cooler outdoor air been used to the full?

— Is the overall design intrinsically energy efficient, or is it likely to result in high running costs?

At an early stage, it should be possible to modify the design to reduce the capacity, size and complexity of the services. This can reduce the capital cost of the services without having to remove features from the design. For example, reducing the need for air conditioning by adopting a mixed mode approach could prevent the loss of a well-specified BMS through budget cuts, thus retaining good control.

In general, a 'simple' approach is the best way of promoting good installation, operation and maintenance[6–8]. Simple services promote a good understanding of how the building and plant are intended to work. This generally improves building management and hence energy efficiency.

3.3.1 Optimising internal heat gains

Internal gains arising from occupants, equipment, lighting and solar radiation, etc. will normally offset a significant part of the fabric and ventilation heat losses. This can reduce heating plant capacity and running costs provided that the controls can respond to changes in internal gains, preventing overheating.

In summer, these heat gains can increase the need for mechanical cooling. To allow passive control of summertime temperatures, the level of heat gains within the space should be kept to a minimum[9–11].

To minimise energy consumption, it is important to establish a balance between the benefits of the gains in winter and the disadvantages in summer[12,13]. Office case studies[6] suggest that too many buildings use over elaborate methods to remove or avoid heat that could have been designed out. Common problems included:

— excessive window area with inappropriate or non-functioning solar control systems: reasonable window sizes (say 30% of main facade area) with simple, useable blinds and control devices are often preferable (see section 4).

— inefficient lighting: some 'passive' offices had installed lighting loads of 25 W·m^{-2}, while good practice is 10–12 W·m^{-2} to achieve 400 lux (see section 9).

— poor lighting control: often caused by a lack of appreciation of the associated human factors, e.g. occupants objecting to frequent automatic switching.

— unnecessary internal heat gains: gains can be either from inefficient office equipment; excessive operation or poor location.

— over-design: can occur through over estimation of heat gains, particularly office equipment (see section 12). Recently there has been a trend to more realistic equipment gain levels (typically 10–15 W·m^{-2} in many offices)[5] and to treat higher gains as special cases.

3.3.2 Optimising natural ventilation

Establishing a ventilation strategy can help to minimise the need for services[9] (see section 4). Natural ventilation can be optimised by the following measures:

— Question the need for full air conditioning: a passive or mixed mode approach may reduce capital cost.

— Further reduce the need for mechanical ventilation in mixed mode designs: e.g. improved zoning can lead to the separation of areas of high heat gain and result in smaller plant.

— Enhance window design to prevent poor usability: too often there are not enough types of opening, insufficient user choice, and operational difficulties because window control gear is unsuitable or out of reach

— Use stack-assisted ventilation: this is often achieved via roof lights in atria, to help ventilate deep plan buildings. Air outlets should be at least 3 m above the windows of the uppermost floor to prevent upper floors becoming much warmer than lower floors. In addition, people sitting near ventilation stacks or atria are not always as tolerant of high summertime temperatures as those sitting near external windows.

— Consider storing heat in the fabric during the day and removing it at night: case studies[6] have indicated that windows for night ventilation need to be more useable, weather-tight and secure. Fan-powered systems often consume too much additional electricity and yet provide inefficient cooling[14].

3.3.3 Optimising daylighting

Daylighting should be an integral part of an overall lighting strategy (see section 4). Natural lighting may be optimised by:

— ensuring that electric lights remain off when there is sufficient daylight

— ensuring that daylight does not produce glare as this can lead to a blinds-down/lights-on situation, particularly where there are display screens

— ensuring that daylight is useable through good distribution using splayed reveals, light shelves, prisms etc.

— avoiding dark internal surfaces which absorb useful daylight

— introducing light into deep plan rooms by means of light wells or atria in order to minimise the use of electric lights

— ensuring that lighting controls take account of daylight availability, workstation layout and user needs; careful integration of manual and automatic control often provides the most effective solution.

It is essential to achieve a balance between useful daylight and unwanted solar gains. Increased daylight may result in less use of electric lighting and hence reduced cooling loads. However, increased solar gains during the summer could outweigh the benefits.

3.3.4 Thermal storage

Using the building itself as a passive thermal store can sometimes improve energy efficiency. In particular, night cooling of the building fabric is possible by passing cool night air across internal surfaces or through ventilation ducts in the structure (see section 4). It may be possible at the sketch design stage to further optimise the thermal response of the building to allow better use of the fabric as a storage medium. This requires a balance between:

— thermal capacity

— thermal response

— insulation levels

— complexity of controls.

All these should be matched to the occupancy patterns and method of heating and cooling being employed.

Active thermal storage devices like water tanks and ice storage have often been used effectively to smooth out peak demands, reducing the peak capacity of plant[15]. This can also help to keep plant operating at improved load factors and better efficiencies. Thermal storage can result in reductions in plant capital costs due to lower capacities, although the costs of the storage and the more complex controls can sometimes outweigh the savings. Reduced efficiency can arise from losses where there are less favourable operating regimes. For example, in the case of ice storage where chiller CoPs tend to be reduced and pumping increased.

3.3.5 Heat recovery

Heat recovery systems can form a fully integrated part of a design, resulting in lower running costs and possibly reduced plant capacities. These systems most commonly recover heat from ventilation systems, using devices such as heat wheels or run-around coils to recover energy from exhaust air, then use it to pre-heat or pre-cool supply air. There must be sufficient energy being rejected at times when it can be used to justify the added complications and running costs of installing heat recovery devices (see 4.2.5.5 and 7.3.5).

3.3.6 'Free' cooling

Generally, 'free' cooling uses the cooling capacity of ambient air to directly cool the space. External air at say 10 °C can be used to meet a cooling load and hence reduce the energy consumed by mechanical refrigeration plant (see 7.3.4).

Because the maximum cooling requirement usually coincides with maximum outside temperature, free cooling is unlikely to reduce the peak cooling load or size of chiller. However, it can reduce the running hours of the chiller and associated equipment, particularly when internal gains occur all year. These savings usually occur at lower cooling demand and hence at lower chiller efficiencies. Enthalpy controls are generally used in air recirculation systems to automatically increase the amount of fresh air when the ambient conditions can provide a useful cooling and/or dehumidification effect.

Free cooling can also be achieved using a mixed mode (changeover) approach (see 4.2.5.3). Fan energy consumption can be reduced by shutting-off the air conditioning system in winter, provided that adequate ventilation is maintained by natural means. Free cooling can also be obtained direct from cooling towers (see section 8).

3.3.7 Minimising distribution losses

Minimising the distribution lengths of ducts and pipework by siting pumps and fans as near to the loads as possible reduces transport losses. Distribution lengths are influenced by:

— the shape of the building

— the number and location of plant rooms

— the provision of space for distribution (riser shafts and ceiling voids).

This emphasises the need for an integrated design to ensure that plant room requirements are properly considered at the earliest design stage. It may be possible to reduce transport losses by decentralising plant, although this should be balanced against possible reduced plant efficiencies and increased maintenance costs. Usually, it is more energy efficient to transport hot water to a heater battery than warm air to a terminal unit.

Significant energy savings can also be achieved by reducing unnecessary pressure drop in the system by the careful sizing, routing and detailing of ductwork and pipework. In particular, pinch points or index runs require much higher pressure drops than much of the rest of the system.

3.4 Integrating human factors

Although human factors often have a bigger influence on energy consumption than the services and fabric design, the way people use buildings is little understood. Ensuring that management and occupants' requirements are met is a central part of energy efficient design. In particular, management needs full control of the whole building whilst occupants need to feel in-control of their own local surroundings. Controls are the main interface between the occupants and the building services; these are discussed further in section 6. However, it is common to find automatic controls that deprive and infuriate rather than empower the user e.g. closing blinds when they wanted the sun and switching lights on unnecessarily. Difficulties in getting automatic controls to work as intended as a result of poor design, installation, commissioning and usability also lead ultimately to poor energy consumption.

Buildings and services that are responsive to the needs of the occupant are generally more successful in achieving comfort, acceptability and energy efficiency[16]. However, comfort levels do not always need to be within a tight specification to achieve an acceptable environment. Psychologically, peoples perception of comfort is often based on whether they feel in control of their surroundings, with easily adjustable parameters that effect their own local environment. Given an openable window or a responsive thermostat, occupants can 'feel' comfortable even though conditions are outside what might be considered normal comfort limits. For instance, the tight comfort conditions expected in air conditioned offices are somewhat contradictory to those expected in the home.

It is the responsibility of the services designer (not the controls contractor) to ensure that the control 'user interfaces' are designed to encourage good use of systems by the occupants. Equally important is to ensure that simple user guidance is produced to explain the systems and the controls interfaces in order to promote good use of systems.

A building will only provide comfortable conditions and low running costs for the user if it can be readily managed and easily maintained, and if it responds speedily to the changing needs of occupants[17]. These attributes must be planned for at the design stage since rectifying problems near completion, or when the building is occupied, seldom works and is always more expensive.

3.4.1   Manageability

Many buildings do not realise their full potential for energy efficiency, often due to over complex design,

effectively making them difficult to manage and sometimes unmanageable[17]. Buildings can be more or less technologically complex, and have higher or lower management input. Four main types can be identified, as shown in Figure 3.4[18,19]. Newer buildings tend to be more complex in order to service an increasing range of activities, facilities and user needs. Avoiding unnecessary complexity and agreeing management requirements can improve energy efficiency but demands a strategic approach at an early stage. The energy efficient management of buildings is covered in more detail in section 15.

Potential conflicts need to be kept to a minimum and interactions between systems anticipated, rather than left to chance. Systems should default to off or standby, not allowed to by-pass or be left on continuously. They should also operate robustly, rapidly and predictably, giving intelligible responses, especially during intense use. Good ergonomic design, rapid feedback and clear diagnostics are essential features in the design, not optional extras.

It is important to take account of the different points of view of designers, managers, users and corporate decision-makers. This approach helps to reduce misunderstandings between members of the design team, between the design team and client and within the client group. Effective strategy combines vision, clarity, attention to detail and requires regular review.

3.4.2   Commissionability and maintainability

Ease of commissioning and maintenance will influence future energy efficiency and should be addressed at the design stage. The CIBSE's *Guide to ownership, operation and maintenance of building services*[20] provides a key source on commissioning and maintenance including a design guide to maintainable buildings. CIBSE Commissioning Code M: *Commissioning management*[21] also discusses commissionability. The requirements of space, position, access, repair and replacement of services should be

Technological complexity

	More	Less
More (Building management input)	**Type A** Effective but often costly	**Type D** Can be thoughtful and imaginative but rarely 'user friendly'
Less (Building management input)	**Type C** Risky with performance penalties	**Type B** Effective but often small scale

Type A
A complex building with well-resourced management. This suits organisations where the extra management is regarded as an investment in staff comfort and productivity, thus improving the business and enhancing the corporate image.

Type B
A simply serviced building that needs only low management input and will suit most occupiers, if the design team can achieve it.

Type C
Clients often feel that new buildings should be able to 'look after themselves' but, in practice, complex buildings with inadequate fine-tuning of innovative systems and insufficient management input are likely to operate very inefficiently.

Type D
Rarely found in practice, this category is exemplified by buildings occupied and managed by the designers themselves, where high levels of commitment and enthusiasm can make simple, but not necessarily 'user friendly', systems perform well.

Figure 3.4 Complexity and management options for buildings (reproduced from Building Services Journal[19], by permission of Builder Services Publications Ltd.)

considered so that equipment can be commissioned, monitored and maintained. Designers should include adequate access and monitoring facilities. It should be easy to change features such as set-points, control authority, filter elements, and to check boiler/chiller efficiencies, and also for alarms and faults to be registered quickly and easily. Where commissioning and maintenance are difficult, they seldom get done and energy efficiency suffers.

The specification should also make clear the need for, and extent of, properly planned operating and maintenance procedures so that the design targets for the minimum use of energy are achieved. Energy efficiency will only be achieved in practice if the building is operated as the designer intended. Commissioning buildings is covered in section 14 while maintaining buildings for energy efficiency is covered in section 17 and in various BSRIA publications[22,23].

3.4.3 Flexibility

Inflexible designs can become prematurely redundant, whereas designing for flexibility can influence future energy efficiency. Flexibility is often best achieved by considering future adaptation of the building and its services and planning contingency strategies, rather than trying to create all-purpose spaces and systems. For example, one might allow space in plant rooms for upgrades, space for cooling coils in the air handling units and provision for additional cooling capacity in spaces where occupancy and equipment densities may increase. CIBSE TM 27[24] and BSRIA TN 12/96[25] provide further guidance on flexible building services.

References

1   *A performance specification for the energy efficient office of the future* General Information Report GIR 30 (Action Energy) (1995) (www.actionenergy.org.uk)

2   *Avoiding or minimising the use of air-conditioning — A research report from the EnREI Programme* General Information Report GIR 31 (Action Energy) (1995) (www.actionenergy.org.uk)

3   Baker N V *Energy and environment in non-domestic buildings — A technical design guide* (Cambridge: Cambridge Architectural Research/Building Research Energy Conservation Support Unit) (1994)

4   *Daylighting in buildings* Thermie Maxibrochure (Action Energy) (1994) (www.actionenergy.org.uk)

5   *Best practice in the specification for offices* (Reading: British Council for Offices)(2000)

6   Bordass W T and Leaman A J Future buildings and their services — Strategic considerations for designers and their clients *Proc. CIBSE Nat. Conf., Eastbourne, 1–3 October 1995* (London: Chartered Institution of Building Services Engineers) (1995)

7   Bordass W T, Bromley A K R and Leaman A J *Comfort, control and energy efficiency in offices* BRE Information Paper IP3/95 (London: Construction Research Communications) (1995)

8   Special Issue on Post Occupancy Evaluation *Building Research and Information* **29** (2) (March/April 2001)

9   *Natural ventilation in non-domestic buildings* CIBSE Applications Manual AM10 (London: Chartered Institution of Building Services Engineers) (1997)

10   *Code for lighting* (London: Chartered Institution of Building Services Engineers) (2002)

11   *Internal heat gains* Section 6 in CIBSE Guide A: *Environmental design* (London: Chartered Institution of Building Services Engineers) (1999)

12   *Energy demands and targets for heated and ventilated buildings* CIBSE Building Energy Code 1 (London: Chartered Institution of Building Services Engineers) (1999)

13   Baker N V and Steemers K *The LT Method 2.0. An energy design tool for non-domestic buildings* (Cambridge Architectural Research/Building Research Energy Conservation Support Unit)(1994)

14   Barnard N *Dynamic energy storage in the building fabric* BSRIA TN 9/94 (Bracknell: Building Services Research and Information Association) (1994)

15   *Ice storage systems* CIBSE TM18 (London: Chartered Institution of Building Services Engineers) (1994)

16   Bordass W T *Factors for success* (London: Workplace Comfort Forum) (1998)

17   Bordass W T and Leaman A Design for manageability *Proc. Conf. Buildings in The Age Of Paradox, Institue of Architectural Studies, University of York, 1995* (York: University of York) (1995)

18   *The design team's guide to environmentally smart buildings* Good Practice Guide GPG287 (Action Energy) (2000) (www.action energy.org.uk)

19   Probe 19: Designer feedback *Building. Serv. J.* **21** (4) 35–38 April 1999

20   *Guide to ownership, operation and maintenance of building services* (London: Chartered Institution of Building Services Engineers) (2000)

21   *Commissioning management* CIBSE Commissioning Code M (London: Chartered Institution of Building Services Engineers) (2003)

22   *Building services maintenance* BSRIA Reading Guide RG6/95 (Bracknell: Building Services Research and Information Association) (1995)

23   Parsloe C *Design for maintainability* BSRIA AG 11/92 (Bracknell: Building Services Research and Information Association) (1993)

24   *Flexible building services for office-based environments* CIBSE TM27 (London: Chartered Institution of Building Services Engineers) (2000)

25   Johansson M *Contingency planning* BSRIA TN 12/96 (Bracknell: Building Services Research and Information Association) (1996)

Bibliography

Fundamentals ASHRAE Handbook (Atlanta, GA: American Society of Heating, Refrigeration and Air Conditioning Engineers) (2001)

HVAC Applications ASHRAE Handbook (Atlanta, GA: American Society of Heating, Refrigeration and Air Conditioning Engineers) (2003)

Daylight and window design CIBSE Lighting Guide LG10 (London: Chartered Institution of Building Services Engineers) (1999)

BS 8206: *Lighting for buildings*: Part 2: *Code of practice for daylighting* (London: British Standards Institution) (1985)

BS 8207: *Energy efficiency in buildings* (London: British Standards Institution) (1985)

Halliday S and Smerdon T   Feedback as part of the building design process *Proc. CIBSE Nat. Conf., Eastbourne, 1–3 October 1995* (London: Chartered Institution of Building Services Engineers) (1995)

Brown A and Steemers K Integrating shading and daylighting for energy efficiency and comfort *Proc. CIBSE Nat. Conf., Eastbourne, 1–3 October 1995* (London: Chartered Institution of Building Services Engineers) (1995)

Energy efficiency in offices — A technical guide for owners and single tenants Energy Conservation Guide ECON 19 (Action Energy) (1997) (www.actionenergy.org.uk)

Jaunzens D and Bordass W T Building design for mixed mode systems *Proc. CIBSE Nat. Conf., Eastbourne, 1–3 October 1995* (London: Chartered Institution of Building Services Engineers) (1995)

Air-to-air heat recovery CIBSE Research Report RR2 (London: Chartered Institution of Building Services Engineers) (1995)

Thermal storage — the environmental benefits CIBSE Research Report RR6 (London: Chartered Institution of Building Services Engineers) (1998)

Engineering design calculations and the use of margins CIBSE Research Report RR4 (London: Chartered Institution of Building Services Engineers) (1998)

Daylighting in atrium buildings BRE Information Paper IP3/98 (London: Construction Research Communications) (1998)

The Elizabeth Fry Building, University of East Anglia New Practice Report NPR 106 (Action Energy) (1998) (www.actionenergy.org.uk)

The Ionica Building, Cambridge — Feedback for designers and clients Good Practice Case Study GPCS 115, (Action Energy) (2000) (www.actionenergy.org.uk)

The Inland Revenue Headquarters — Feedback for designers and clients Good Practice Case Study GPCS 114 (Action Energy) (2000) (www.actionenergy.org.uk)

4   Sketch design

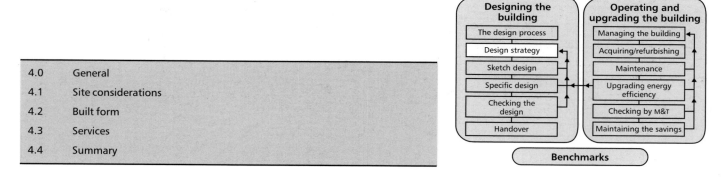

This section highlights some of the issues to be considered in developing an energy efficient sketch design and complements the strategic guidance given in section 3. The principles at the front of this Guide provide a framework for energy efficient design.

4.0   General

The sketch design stage should resolve any issues concerning the interrelationship between architecture and building services whilst confirming their respective contributions to the energy efficiency of the building. Decisions which affect the holistic concept need to be taken during this stage, so that the members of the design team can proceed with detailed design work (covered in the following sections) fully aware of the relationship between the components and the whole.

Site layout, the potential size of the building and the fuels available present both opportunities and constraints. The site conditions influence the built form and can be used to advantage to promote passive ventilation and daylight strategies[1-6]. The sketch design process is shown in Figure 4.1.

4.1   Site considerations

Some of the key site issues that effect energy efficiency are shown in Figure 4.2.

4.1.1   Local weather and microclimate

An effective design will take advantage of any local variations in climate, for instance by using local wind conditions to drive natural ventilation. Geography, topography, landscape, shelter, shading and surrounding buildings can all influence the development of built form and services, sometimes in different ways on different facades. These effects can be further enhanced by building arrangement and added landscape features[7].

The level of external pollution and noise, particularly in urban areas, may influence the choice of ventilation system and could exclude natural ventilation as an option. In these cases, careful design can provide acceptable

solutions, e.g. by placing areas requiring low noise levels furthest away from noise and pollution sources.

4.1.2   Site layout and shape

The nature of the site will have a strong effect on built form and orientation, as well as a knock-on effect on services design. Planning requirements, local and national bye-laws and fire protection requirements may further restrict the building shape and orientation, affecting its services and energy performance. The position of approach roads and the requirements for vehicle parking could also influence the energy efficiency of the design. Often, such features can be used to advantage, e.g. by using a parking structure to form a noise barrier.

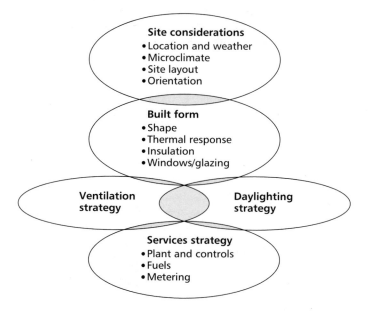

Figure 4.1 Sketch design

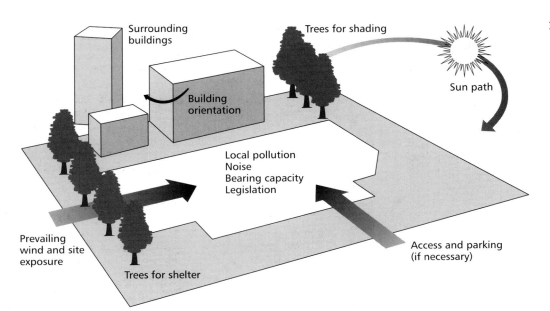

Figure 4.2 Site considerations

4.1.3   Building orientation

Choosing the optimum orientation to maximise daylight and to minimise summer heat gain and winter heat loss can have a significant impact on energy efficiency, particularly if it avoids or minimises air conditioning. For example, north-facing windows suffer very little solar gain and benefits are often gained by having the major building axis pointing east/west. East or west-facing glazing is harder to shade from direct sunlight, as the sun angles are low at some times of year. South facades receive both direct and diffuse radiation and are relatively easy to control.

4.2   Built form

The building envelope should be considered as a climate modifier rather than solely a means of excluding external climatic conditions. The envelope generally has four main functions:

—   In cold weather, to reduce heat loss through the fabric, to maximise the benefits of solar and internal heat gains, and reduce losses associated with uncontrolled air infiltration.

—   In warm weather, to minimise solar heat gain and avoid overheating, also to use window shading and thermal mass to attenuate heat gain.

—   To allow optimum levels of natural ventilation.

—   To allow optimum levels of daylighting.

Relatively simple adjustments to built form at the sketch design stage can have a substantial effect upon future energy performance. If left until later stages, more complex and costly solutions may be necessary to make similar energy savings. Energy efficiency can be influenced through built form via:

—   shape

—   thermal response

—   insulation

—   windows and glazing

—   ventilation strategy

—   daylighting strategy.

These inter-related items, discussed below, need to be fully integrated during the sketch design process.

4.2.1   Shape

4.2.1.1   Building form

Compact building forms have a relatively small exposed surface area for a given floor area, thus reducing the influence of the external environment. A compact design may also benefit by requiring less space for the distribution of horizontal and vertical services, particularly for air ductwork. However, if commercial pressures and/or a compact design lead to a deep plan, i.e. over 15 m in depth, there may be a greater complexity of servicing. The core of the building may then require continuous electric lighting[8] and internal activities may prompt mechanical ventilation or air conditioning[9]. The energy efficiency benefits from natural ventilation and daylight penetration are most easily obtained up to 6 metres inwards from the windows. Taller constructions can increase energy consumption due to greater exposure and the need for lifts. Figure 4.3 shows examples of how building shape may effect energy efficiency.

4.2.1.2   Atria

Atria are rarely incorporated in designs for the main purpose of energy saving. The most likely motivation is architectural or the desire to make effective use of the site but their impact on the building services design can be significant. Energy efficient atria work best as a buffer between the inner and outer environments and should be carefully integrated into the sketch design and related to the heating, ventilation and daylighting strategies. Various forms of atria are shown in Figure 4.4. Building Regulations Approved Document L★[10] sets out requirements aimed at avoiding energy inefficient atria and conservatories.

★ Requirements may differ in Scotland[11] and Northern Ireland[12]

Tall, slender
- Additional exposure
- Requires lifts
- Higher heat loss

Shallow plan
- Higher heat loss
- Increased daylight
- Natural ventilation

Deep plan
- Lower heat loss
- Less daylight
- Greater use of artificial lighting
- More likely to need air conditioning

Deep plan with atrium or courtyard
(effectively shallow plan)
- Lower heat loss
- Increased daylight penetration
- Potential natural ventilation strategy

Figure 4.3 Examples of built form and its effect on energy

To ensure that an atrium does not increase overall energy consumption, the following points are suggested:

— Daylighting levels should be maximised by using reflective finishes and clear glazing to reduce the need for daytime electric lighting. The electric lighting must then be controlled to gain the benefits.

— The atrium should be used as a heat recovery/buffer space, e.g. pre-heating incoming fresh air or passing exhaust air through the atrium on its way out of the building.

— Shading and high rates of ventilation should be provided in summer to prevent overheating.

The advantages and disadvantages of atria are shown in Table 4.1. Atrium design is also covered by IP3/98: *Daylight in atrium buildings*[13]. The LT Method[14] provides a detailed design methodology and atrium ventilation is discussed in CIBSE Applications Manual AM10[15].

The daylight performance of an atrium is complex and depends on:

— its orientation and geometry

— the character of its wall and floor surfaces

— the nature of its roof and glazing.

In addition, the proportions of the atrium determine the amount of direct daylight reaching the floor; wide, shallow, square atria perform better in this respect than do deep, narrow, rectangular ones.

The design of atrium walls significantly affects the distribution of light once it has entered the atrium. Dark finishes reduce internal reflectance and, the deeper the

Table 4.1 Possible advantages and disadvantages of atria

Advantages	Disadvantages
Conversion of open courts to daylit and protected spaces	Added fire and smoke risks
Reduced conduction losses	Need to make provision for ventilating spaces which may otherwise be open to ambient air, e.g. light well construction
Possible use of the atrium as a sink for warm extract air	Cost of glazing; total building costs can be less, depending on the form of the atrium
Enhanced use of daylighting in the building core	Risk of overheating
Possible use of the atrium as a thermal flue to promote air flow through the rest of the building	Delicate plants may require precise lighting and temperatures, increasing energy consumption
Ability to pre-heat ventilation air	Loss of daylighting compared with courtyards

atrium, the more important this becomes. Windows in the atrium wall also reduce internally reflected daylight. Spaces facing into the atrium should have requirements corresponding with those of the atrium — rooms at the upper levels tend to receive plenty of light but need protection from glare while those at the base need to maximise the amount of light they receive. Other design strategies include making rooms near the base shallower, increasing their floor to ceiling heights, or successively stepping back the upper floors so that all rooms have some view of the sky.

Putting a glass roof over an open courtyard reduces daylight levels in the courtyard by at least 20%. The structure of an atrium roof, therefore, should minimise obstructions to the glazing area, and its connections to the building should ensure that light is allowed to wash the atrium walls.

Poorly designed atria can present problems with glare and excessive solar gains, leading to occupant dissatisfaction and sometimes higher energy consumption. Careful design of shape, orientation, room reflectance and shading can avoid these problems.

4.2.2　　Thermal response

The dynamic thermal response of a building can be used to reduce energy consumption[16]. This response is a measure of the ability of the building to exchange heat with the environment when subjected to cyclic variations. It depends on the admittance of the contents and components of the structure and their surface areas. This ability smoothes out transient temperature variations and is especially important in reducing maximum summer time temperatures[2,5], thus avoiding or minimising the use of air conditioning. Increasing admittance also smoothes out transient heating/cooling loads and results in longer heat-up and cool-down periods. The thermal response can be different depending upon where the mass is placed e.g. floors, facades, internal walls, contents, etc. To make effective use of this mass it is necessary to ensure a good heat transfer to and from the structure, for example by using embedded coils or ducts[1]. Further guidance on

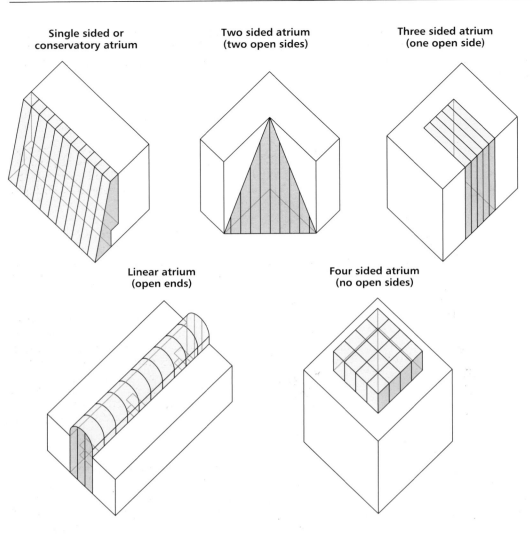

Single sided or conservatory atrium

Two sided atrium (two open sides)

Three sided atrium (one open side)

Linear atrium (open ends)

Four sided atrium (no open sides)

Figure 4.4 Generic forms of atrium buildings (reproduced from *Atrium Buildings* by Richard Saxon by permission of the author)

exploiting thermal inertia is shown in CIBSE AM13: *Mixed mode ventilation*[17].

A well managed heavyweight building with high admittance can cope with a wide variation in gains and can often provide a robust solution if effective natural or mechanical night ventilation or cooling of the structure can be ensured (see 4.2.5.2). However, a high thermal mass does not guarantee a comfortable environment and night ventilation is critical to avoiding summer overheating. If the building could be subject to high heat gains, it may benefit from a high thermal response to slow down temperature swings, reducing cooling energy. If an intermittent heating regime predominates, a less thermally massive building would have shorter preheat periods and use less heating energy, provided that any tendency to overheat is well controlled.

If night ventilation cannot be assured a lower thermal mass may be more appropriate, although mass can still be useful in restricting peak temperatures and air conditioning loads. Attempts should then be made to minimise solar and internal gains, and maximise useful daytime ventilation.

Where a heavyweight structure and significant night ventilation are considered necessary, the operation of windows should be explained to the management and other building occupants, and possibly automated. Effective automatic control would need to be integrated with the rest of the control system (see section 6) and provide management feedback.

Intuitive manual control by the occupants depends on the feedback they get. In a low thermal response building, internal and external heat gains would prompt window opening for cooling, although the temperature swings could be so large that cooling would not be achieved without excessive air movement. On the other hand, in a thermally massive building, the structure would absorb heat and delay the time when conditions would become uncomfortable. However, the structure's ability to absorb heat gains depends on it being cooled down at some time before the gains occur. Occupants will be unable to anticipate this, and so will need to be educated on how to undertake manual night cooling. Once they have learned this technique, feedback (in the form of discomfort) will prompt corrective action on days when overheating is likely.

Internal partitions and furniture increase the thermal response of the building. Cellular buildings often have a high thermal mass, regardless of the admittance of the materials used, as the extra surface area increases the thermal response. This can balance the effect of a lack of cross-ventilation, but effective night ventilation still needs to be assured. However, a full fit-out by interior designers can reduce the thermal response by covering exposed slabs and walls, changing their admittance. Thus the occupants of the building also need education so that they are aware of this when they brief initial and future fit-out contractors.

Heavyweight buildings may have areas that perform as lightweight buildings; for example, a large glazed entrance hall. Such areas may receive excessive solar gain and also be subject to higher heat losses than the remainder of the building, so they will need to be zoned separately using appropriate fast response zone controls.

4.2.3　　Insulation

Reducing the thermal transmittance of the building envelope by adding insulation can help reduce heating demand and result in lower heating energy consumption[18]. Building Regulations Approved Document L*[10] calls for measures to ensure the continuity of insulation in both domestic and non-domestic buildings. The requirements can be met by either:

— avoiding excessive thermal bridging using approved design details, or

— conducting infra-red thermography inspections[19,20] to identify gaps in insulation that need to be blocked.

Insulation is much cheaper to include at initial construction stage than later in the building's life. Greater insulation in a building can simplify and reduce the capacity of its heating system. The resultant capital cost saving should be balanced against the additional insulation cost.

The location of insulation has a strong effect on the admittance and thus the thermal response. In intermittently heated buildings, it is sometimes preferable to place the insulation close to the interior surface of the wall. This will modify the thermal response of the room by reducing the ability of the masonry to absorb or emit heat and thus allow the heating system to track rapid changes in heating requirement. This may be desirable with intermittent heating, but may lead to rapid overheating if heat gains change rapidly. Insulation located on the external surface tends to de-couple the mass of the structure from the influence of the external environment and hence enables it to stabilise the internal environment.

In buildings with high internal heat gains[9], the effect of insulation on total energy use requires careful assessment. Removal of heat gains will become more reliant on ventilation if the building fabric cannot readily dissipate internal heat gains. This will require more careful design and will increase the need for, or capacity of, mechanical cooling systems.

Design issues include:

— *Internal insulation*: the structure is cold leading to greater likelihood of interstitial condensation or frost damage. Condensation can be avoided with extra ventilation and/or extra heating to raise surface temperatures, but this has an energy cost.

— *Interstitial insulation*: there is the possibility of thermal bridging at openings or junctions with internal walls and floors, with the risk of condensation or excess heat loss.

— *Composite structure*: fixing details are critical to avoid thermal bridging, particularly where masonry penetrates insulated components for structural reasons.

— *External insulation*: the structure remains warm, with less risk of surface condensation. The full benefit of the thermal capacity of the structure is obtained.

4.2.4　　Windows and glazing

The amount and type of glazing, along with the shape, location and functionality of the windows, are key factors in the effective control of heat losses and gains to the building with consequent effects on ventilation, daylight and control strategies, see 4.2.5 and 4.2.6.

Building Regulations Approved Document L*[10] sets out requirements for avoiding solar overheating which include maximum allowable areas of glazing as one means of achieving compliance. These are shown in section 4.2.6.4.

Strategic decisions at concept design require early collaboration between architects and building services engineers to review the factors that influence the glazing design. In particular, the percentage of glass, the likely user reaction, the provision of daylighting and the implications for the design and control of heating, lighting and cooling systems. CIBSE Lighting Guide LG10[8] provides information on window design and daylight design.

4.2.4.1　　Windows and window systems

Modern integrated window systems can offer good control of openable areas of glazing, built-in noise reduction and solar protection measures. These should be investigated as part of the strategic design intention of obviating the need for air conditioning. Types of opening windows are described in CIBSE Application Manual AM10[15] and window control systems are considered in AM13[17].

In terms of energy performance, windows have the advantages and disadvantages shown in Table 4.2.

The design of window/glazing systems must achieve a balance between:

— providing daylight (controls which integrate electric lighting with daylight and occupancy are essential to minimise energy consumption)[21]

— effective use/control of heat gains and losses

— providing natural ventilation (the usability of the window mechanisms and furniture are crucial to this)

— providing external views, controlling glare and privacy

— allowing some degree of occupant control over local environment.

Many types of window design are available, the relative ventilation characteristics varying significantly. There are a number of criteria to consider:

— *Ventilation capacity*: i.e. how much air can flow through a given window area of different designs. This will depend on the ratio of the effective open area to the facade area taken by the window unit.

---

* Requirements may differ in Scotland[11] and Northern Ireland[12]

Table 4.2 Advantages and disadvantage of windows in terms of energy performance

Advantages	Disadvantages
Provide daylight, avoiding the use of electric lighting at certain times	Possible source of glare requiring screening and additional use of electric lighting
Openable windows can provide natural ventilation, avoiding the need for mechanical ventilation in some cases	Source of uncontrolled air infiltration/drafts causing additional heating demand, e.g. badly fitting frames
Removal of internal heat gains	Allows high heat loss through conduction, increasing heating demands
Transmission of beneficial spring, autumn and winter solar gain which can reduce heating demand	May cause overheating due to solar gains possibly creating a need for mechanical cooling
Openable windows permit occupant control of local environment which can reduce heating and cooling demands	Control of natural ventilation is influenced by noise and pollution with no possibility of heat recovery

It will, in turn, depend on how the window opens (side, top/bottom, or centre pivot, sliding etc.) and the distribution of the open area in the vertical plane. In some cases, it may be possible to induce local stack ventilation via say low to high level windows.

— *Controllability*: i.e. how the air flow capacity changes with opening. Good control at small openings is particularly important for winter comfort.

— *Impact on comfort*: i.e. what effect will the position of the room air inlet have on such factors as draughts?

— *Integration with solar control strategies*: particularly the use of blinds: the physical movement of the window may be restricted by an independent blind. The blind elements can provide an obstruction to the free area of the opening or the effectiveness of the blind may alter with window position.

The relative benefits of different types of window design are as follows:

— *Horizontal pivot windows*: produce very effective ventilation because large open areas are created at a separation equivalent to the window height. Air will tend to enter at the lower level and exit via the top of the window. They are easily adjustable to provide control of the ventilation rate.

— *Vertical pivot windows*: less efficient ventilators than horizontal pivot windows because the open area is uniformly distributed through the height of the window rather than concentrated at the extremes; but they can work well in combinations.

— *Top/bottom hung windows*: even less effective as ventilators than pivot windows as all the opening area is concentrated at one end, the top or bottom of the window.

— *Sliding windows*: similar characteristics to the corresponding horizontal or vertical pivot windows. A good seal is important in reducing draughts and energy loss when closed.

— *Tilting top vents*: provide smaller opening areas than the other systems as they occupy only a relatively small proportion of the window height. However, they can provide good draught-free ventilation, especially in cross-ventilation mode.

Useful rules of thumb for opening window design are:

— high level for cross ventilation

— low level for local ventilation

— trickle ventilation for winter time

— large openings for still summer days.

Windows are the most obvious controllable opening for natural ventilation, especially in summer. Building Regulations Approved Document F[22] recommends an openable area of at least 1/20th of the floor area for rapid ventilation. Windows should:

— ventilate effectively (see Figure 4.5) but not cause draughts

— provide sufficient glare-free daylight and adequate view out of the building

— keep out excessive solar gain but allow a contribution during any heating period

— provide good insulation and avoid condensation

— allow occupants to adjust finely the openable area

— be simple to operate and make secure.

There can be a conflict between security and good ventilation, compromising energy performance, particularly for night ventilation. This can be alleviated by careful selection of window opening or, by separating the ventilation element from the window.

Selection of window areas must accommodate the factors which influence the health and well being of the occupant. Occupants generally prefer to work adjacent to a window for the external view and natural lighting on the working plane. Any restriction of glazed areas to less than 30% of the external wall area must, therefore, be considered with care. However, case studies[23] suggest buildings with greater glazed areas may often operate with blinds down and the lights on because of the effects of glare. A balance must be drawn between these needs.

4.2.4.1   Glazing

The energy efficiency of glazing depends on the following:

— *Single, double or multiple glazing*: the more layers, the less light transmittance but the better the thermal performance.

— *Window frame construction and detailing*: the area of the frame, its material and whether a thermal break is included, have a substantial effect on the composite thermal transmittance of the complete window system[8,16].

— *Type of coating*: modern coatings can have a greater effect on the energy consumption than the type of glass. Thin plastic films are used in some multi-layered windows to reduce weight and provide anti-reflective qualities. However, to significantly reduce heat transfer through multi-layered

Deeper windows can ventilate better.... .... but avoid draughts at working level Consider controllable opening lights

Figure 4.5 Effect of window shape on ventilation performance[33] (reproduced from BRE Information Paper 399 by permission of the Building Research Establishment)

windows they must control radiation heat transfer. Ideal glazing is transparent to short-wave radiation and reflective to long-wave radiation, allowing daylight and useful solar gains to enter while resisting radiative heat loss. 'Reflective glass' and solar control film reduce solar transmission, but at the expense of daylight and useful solar gain in winter. They can also create problems by reflecting sun onto other buildings or on to the northern facades of the same building.

— *Type of glass*: some tinted glass reduces solar heat gain but also cuts down daylight transmission and distorts the colour of the landscape. Heat absorbing glass does not reduce daylight transmission to quite the same degree and it only reduces heat gain by 10% since a large percentage of the heat absorbed by the glass is re-radiated into the interior.

— *Insulating layer in sealed glazing*: heavy gases such as argon have lower thermal conductivity than air. Vacuum and translucent insulating fills are also becoming available.

It is always more cost effective to include energy efficient glazing at the initial construction stage rather than retrofitting. Selective low-emissivity double glazing, with a heat loss equivalent to that of triple glazing, has a light transmission factor of approximately 80% and can provide a robust solution.

4.2.5   Ventilation strategies

Establishing a clear ventilation strategy is key to reaching an integrated energy efficient design. The strategy should provide:

— control over unwanted ventilation

— the correct quantity of fresh air for health and odour/moisture control, and for the rejection of excessive heat gains, if needed

— a driving force to move air into and around the building

— a means of controlling the air movement to and from the right place and at the right time, preferably involving the occupants so that it can match their needs.

Figure 4.6[15] provides a flow chart to assist in the design process, indicating a strong dependence on the depth of the building (see 3.3). A move towards air conditioning or mechanical ventilation is likely to increase consumption

significantly and, although this may be unavoidable in some circumstances, it can be mitigated by energy-efficient fabric, systems, controls and the effective operation of the building.

4.2.5.1   Control of unwanted ventilation

Building Regulations Approved Document L★[10] calls for measures to minimise air leakage in both domestic and non-domestic buildings. The requirements can be met by either:

— conducting air leakage test according to CIBSE TM23[24] and hence showing that air leakage does not exceed 10 $(m^3 \cdot h^{-1})/m^2$ at 50 Pa, or

— for buildings less than 1000 m^2 gross floor area, installing air barriers by using appropriate design details and construction techniques

The building fabric should be as airtight as possible to take advantage of a well-designed ventilation strategy. 'Build tight, ventilate right' is true for both mechanical and naturally ventilated buildings[25]. Background ventilation can be provided by trickle ventilators.

The reduction of infiltration relies on good building details[26] and on the quality of the building construction. The architect and builder must collaborate in implementing this part of the strategy because the performance of ventilation systems, and particularly the achievement of energy efficiency and comfort conditions, is dependent on the amount of infiltration occurring through the building envelope. Leaky buildings will interfere with the performance and energy efficiency of mechanical systems and will greatly reduce the net efficiency of heat recovery devices.

Typical infiltration openings include:

— the openable perimeter of windows and doors

— the window/door frame to wall interface

— wall to wall, wall to ceiling and wall to floor junctions

— porous and semi-porous building materials

— perimeter leaks around penetrations such as service ducts

— open flues

— open doorways.

★ Requirements may differ in Scotland[11] and Northern Ireland[12]

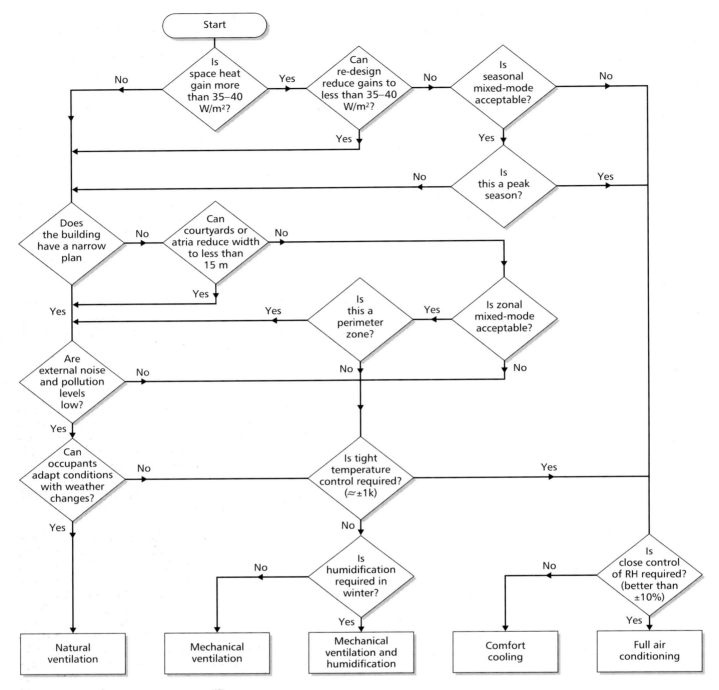

Figure 4.6 Selecting a ventilation strategy[15]

Good attention to sealing is needed to minimise leakage routes. The leakage performance of openable windows and doors, and the performance of weather-stripping components for windows and doors, is covered by BS 6375[27] and BS 7386[28]. However, the greatest leakage has often occurred at the perimeter of the window assembly, particularly in buildings that are ostensibly sealed.

Particular attention should be paid to detailing at the junctions of building elements, e.g. the junction of curtain walling panels with mullions, window frames with openings in the external wall, junctions at eaves and in prefabricated structures. At these junctions, components built to factory tolerances often meet elements that are subject to site accuracy. The use of sealants and gaskets may be a solution, provided that suitable materials and procedures are specified.

4.2.5.2   Natural ventilation

Naturally ventilated buildings generate the driving force for air movement by relying on a range of techniques which maximise the potential of the stack effect, using air passages at differing heights and wind effects, often by ventilating from at least two facades. Guidance and case studies on natural ventilation are provided in CIBSE AM10[15] and BSRIA TN11/95[29]. CIBSE Guide A, section 4: *Air infiltration and natural ventilation*[30] and BS 5925[31] give simple equations to estimate ventilation flows. Figure 4.7 shows various natural ventilation strategies[32].

The design of a naturally ventilated building should reflect the different requirements for winter and summer occupancy. In winter, excess ventilation should be minimised with background ventilation controlled by trickle ventilators or low level mechanical ventilation to meet occupants' needs for health and comfort. In summer, ventilation rates may need to exceed what is required for moisture and odour removal to satisfy occupants' needs to avoid overheating. As part of this process, the careful distribution of fresh air within the space is important to achieve the objectives without causing draughts.

Ventilation controls should be ergonomically efficient and respond rapidly; their use should also be explained to the occupants. Where ventilation controls do not work properly (e.g. inaccessible window catches or insufficient fine control), occupants will often undermine the original strategy by taking alternative steps, e.g. introducing desk fans or making requests for air conditioning.

Background (trickle) ventilation

Trickle ventilators are designed to provide the required minimum fresh air rate, particularly in winter, but without the increase in heating energy loss caused by opening windows. Building Regulations Approved Document L*[10] recommends a provision of 400 mm^2 per m^2 of floor area, with a minimum provision in each room of 4000 mm^2. These should be placed at a high level (typically 1.75 m above floor level) to avoid draught problems (see Figure 4.7).

The advantages and disadvantages of trickle ventilation are shown in Table 4.3.

Single-sided ventilation

This occurs when large, natural ventilation openings (such as windows and doors) are situated on only one external wall. Exchange of air takes place by wind turbulence, by outward openings interacting with the local external air streams and by stack effects driven by temperature difference. The rules of thumb shown in Figure 4.7 apply for moderate to high heat gains.

Single sided ventilation should only be used when the building form or location limits ventilation to one facade. Until recently, the practical limits of single sided natural ventilation have been considered to be 6 m. However, research[32] concludes that, for low-heat gain, single-sided ventilation may be effective over a depth of up to 10 m, and may even be incorporated into open plan offices. Care should be exercised to minimise draughts for occupants at the perimeter when fresh air is required deep into the space. Also, people remote from the window can exercise less control and are therefore less tolerant of adverse conditions.

Cross ventilation

Cross ventilation occurs when inflow and outflow openings in external walls have a clear internal flow path between them (see Figure 4.7). Flow characteristics are determined by the combined effect of wind and temperature difference. Cross ventilation depends on the co-operation of occupants on opposite sides of the building to open windows appropriately, but can also be affected by internal partitions.

* Requirements may differ in Scotland[11] and Northern Ireland[12]

Table 4.3 advantages and disadvantages of trickle ventilation

Advantages	Disadvantages
Low cost	Variable rates of air change
Little maintenance needed	Little or no control of air flow pattern
Provides a safe level of background ventilation	No possibility of heat recovery
	Poor control can result in unnecessary heat loss

Stack induced ventilation

Ducts, shafts, solar chimneys etc. can be used to create a column of air at higher temperature thus generating pressure differences that give rise to the stack effect (see Figure 4.7). Passive stack effects can also be promoted through an atrium that will additionally act as a buffer to reduce fabric heat losses.

Stack ventilation can be controlled by automatic vents at the top of the stack, operated by temperature sensors in the space. Advantages and disadvantage of passive stack ventilation are shown in Table 4.4.

Night cooling

Increased ventilation at night can help remove heat that is stored in the building structure during the daytime to avoid high summer temperatures. A range of passive and active night cooling strategies can be used to achieve this objective, the simplest generally relies on good window design to allow ventilation at night (see Figure 4.7). Further guidance on night cooling can be found in CIBSE AM13[17], GIL 85[33] and BRE IP4/98[34].

Solutions include using the thermal capacity of the building (see 4.2.2) by passing air through the building structure, e.g. hollow core slabs[33]. In this way, the building envelope can be used to dissipate at night, heat that has been absorbed during the day. Thus, the fabric provides a reservoir for incidental heat gains. These can be used for space heating in cold weather, or dissipated to ambient air using a night purge in warm weather. However, it is important to take account of the fan energy used to move the air through the structure. Low energy mechanical ventilation systems operating at around 1 kW/(m^3·s^{-1}) should always be the design target. It is also essential that the controls ensure that the summer night purge is undertaken during the coolest part of the night.

Night ventilation in well insulated buildings with high thermal response factors can reduce the maximum

Table 4.4 Advantages and disadvantages of passive stack ventilation

Advantages	Disadvantages
Possible to achieve a consistent flow pattern that can remove pollutants at source	Only limited control of the air flow rate is possible; unless the building is very well sealed (i.e. airtight), the combination of passive stack ventilation and infiltration may lead to excessive air flow rates, particularly during the heating season
No electrical power needed	Poor installation (such as bends in ductwork or excessive duct lengths) can result in low air flow rates

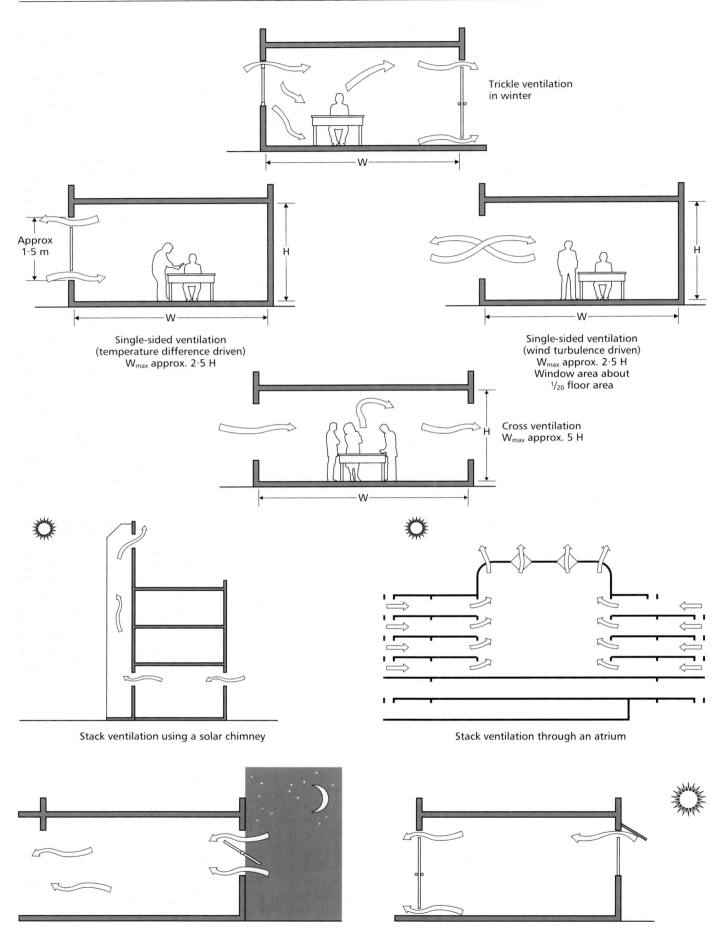

Trickle ventilation
in winter

Approx
1·5 m

Single-sided ventilation
(temperature difference driven)
W_{max} approx. 2·5 H

Single-sided ventilation
(wind turbulence driven)
W_{max} approx. 2·5 H
Window area about
$^1/_{20}$ floor area

Cross ventilation
W_{max} approx. 5 H

Stack ventilation using a solar chimney

Stack ventilation through an atrium

Night ventilation to restrict temperature rise next day

Figure 4.7 Ventilation strategies[32] (reproduced from BRE Digest 399 by permission of the BRE Ltd.)

daytime temperatures by 2–3 °C, provided the thermal mass is exposed and a good control strategy deployed, see BSRIA Technical Notes TN 11/95[29] and TN 5/96[35].

4.2.5.3   Mixed mode ventilation

If a complete mechanical or natural ventilation strategy is not feasible, a mixed mode approach may be considered rather than full air conditioning[17,36–38]. Mixed mode alternatives can stretch the performance of natural ventilation by using mechanical systems only when and where necessary. Mixed mode designs can be seen as a logical extension to shell-and-core, as mechanical cooling only needs to be added where the occupant confirms it is required. Over-design can be avoided, capital expenditure reduced and adaptation to meet changes in use can be allowed.

Mixed mode design strategies

There are three distinct approaches; contingency, complementary and zoned. Each of these can be developed in a wide variety of ways:

— *Contingency designs*: make provision for future addition or removal of mechanical systems. For example, a naturally ventilated building may be planned to allow mechanical ventilation and/or air conditioning to be added easily (locally or generally). Equally, an air conditioned building may be planned so that natural ventilation, or a combination of natural and mechanical systems, could easily be used if the air conditioning was no longer needed. This approach is particularly useful where occupancy/activity may change. Although there is a premium due to the space set aside, this is less than the capital cost of installing air conditioning.

— *Complementary designs*: have natural and mechanical systems present together. This may seem like a 'belt and braces' solution (and sometimes it is) but appropriate combinations can achieve an effective result at less cost than full air conditioning.

— *Zoned designs*: have different systems, or combinations of systems, in parts of the building which differ in their requirements for ventilation and cooling, owing to either their occupancy and usage or to their planning and location. Zoning is particularly efficient where problems can be grouped, for example, where a building is poorly located for passive cooling but has high occupancy and high equipment gains co-existing with relatively high solar gains. In this case, local air conditioning can do several jobs. However, studies suggest that the cooled areas may acquire higher status and 'concurrent' or 'changeover' approaches may then be preferable.

Mixed mode operating strategies

It is important that natural and mechanical systems work together without clashing. In principle, there are three ways of achieving this:

— *Concurrent operation*: where the natural and mechanical systems operate together, for example in a building with openable windows and background mechanical ventilation. With some care, this can be an effective and energy efficient solution. For example, a building designed for high thermal stability, background ventilation (typically in the range 1–3 air changes per hour), with efficient fans, heat recovery and night cooling, may be able to maintain a steady temperature economically. The mechanical ventilation may also be used to extract hot or polluted air at source. Even if the mechanical system seldom makes it necessary to open the windows, the ability to do so increases tolerance and choice for occupants, provides additional ventilation if required and can permit the mechanical systems to be more modestly sized.

— *Changeover operation*: where the natural and mechanical systems can operate together in a variety of different ways that may alter with the seasons, the weather, occupancy levels or even the time of day. The intention is to maximise the use of natural ventilation but to introduce the necessary mechanical systems as and when required. A simple example would be a building that is naturally ventilated during the day but, if it becomes too hot by the evening, can use a mechanical system to pass night air to extract heat and pre-cool the structure. Another is where room cooling units, such as fan coils or chilled panels, have interlocks that only permit them to operate when the window is shut.

— *Alternate operation*: like changeover operation but with a much longer time scale. The building, or zone, operates in one mode for a long period, typically years, but certainly months. For example, part of a building may be air conditioned with the windows locked shut to suit one type of occupancy or use. However, if the occupancy and use were to change, natural ventilation or some hybrid could be used instead. Another example is where a cooling system is activated only in very hot weather, when the occupants would be alerted and asked not to open the windows while the cooling was running.

A flowchart to help select mixed mode strategies is shown in Figure 4.8.

4.2.5.4   Mechanical ventilation and air conditioning

Introducing mechanical ventilation and/or air conditioning into a design can increase electrical energy consumption by up to 50%. There are instances where some form of forced ventilation system is unavoidable e.g. deep plan buildings, high internal gains, exacting environmental conditions etc. Even then, designers should seek to make effective use of ambient conditions with a view to minimising demand. Good zoning and controls are a key factors in making any mechanical ventilation strategy energy efficient, see sections 6 and 7, although controlling humidity will always increase energy consumption. Variable flow systems are preferable for energy efficiency, see section 11. Also control strategies that use free cooling at times when ambient conditions are suitable.

Building Regulations Approved Document L2*[10] sets out requirements aimed at minimising the energy consumed in air conditioning and/or mechanical ventilation systems (AC/MV). This is a recognition that AC/MV should be minimised or even avoided where possible in order to improve energy efficiency. Basic requirements are that buildings with AC/MV should be designed and constructed such that:

— the form and fabric of the building do not result in a requirement for excessive installed capacity of AC/MV equipment. In particular, the suitable specification of glazing ratios and solar shading are an important way to limit cooling requirements

— components such as fans, pumps and refrigeration equipment are reasonably efficient and appropriately sized to have no more capacity for demand than is necessary for the task

— suitable facilities are provided to manage, control and monitor the operation of the equipment and the systems.

One way of achieving compliance in offices is to show that the 'Carbon Performance Rating' (CPR) in kgC·m^{-2} per year falls within certain limits. The CPR is a rating based

* Requirements may differ in Scotland[11] and Northern Ireland[12]

on standardised occupancy patterns that relates system performance to a benchmark based on Energy Consumption Guide ECG 19[39]. A calculation method, and targets, are set out for a variety of scenarios such as new-build, replacement etc.

A second way of achieving compliance in offices is to meet 'whole-office' CPR targets set out in Approved Document L2. Other buildings can comply by meeting specific fan power targets of 2.0 W/(litre·s^{-1}) in new buildings and 3.0 W/(litre·s^{-1}) in refurbishments. Hospitals and schools can comply by following National Health Service (NHS) and Department for Education and Employment (DfEE) guidelines respectively.

4.2.5.5   Heat recovery

Heat recovery systems use heat energy that would otherwise be rejected to waste, resulting in lower running costs and possibly reduced plant capacities. These systems are most commonly applied in ventilation systems, using devices such as heat wheels, plate heat exchangers or run-around coils to recover energy from exhaust air, then use it to pre-heat or pre-cool supply air[40]. Also consider preheating incoming air through atria, conservatories, roof spaces etc. or using waste heat from air-cooled condensers, e.g. industrial refrigeration and computer rooms.

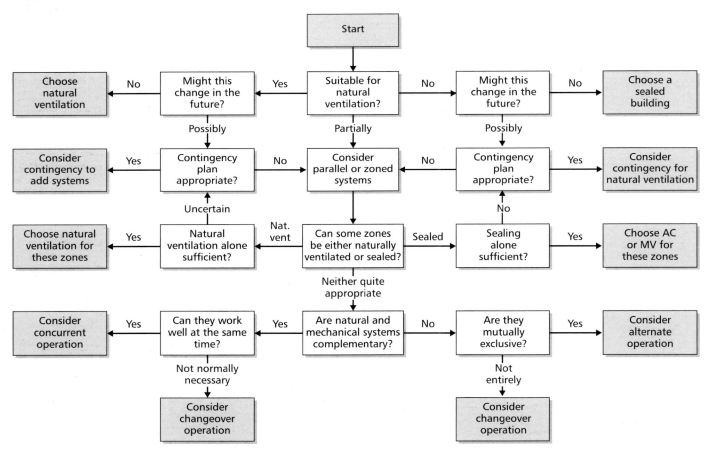

The above flowchart defines three operating strategies for mixed mode systems:
— *concurrent*: designed to allow the windows to be opened if required while the mechanical systems are running
— *changeover*: designed for either the mechanical or the natural systems to be operating, according to the circumstances at the time
— *alternate*: where a long-term management choice is made to operate the building in one particular mode; e.g. windows locked during 24-hour occupancy

Figure 4.8 Selecting mixed mode strategies[36] (reproduced from General Information Report 56) (Crown copyright)

Heat recovery devices can sometimes be difficult to justify on a purely economic basis. There must be sufficient energy being rejected at times when it can be used to justify the added complications and running costs of installing heat recovery devices. Check that any additional electrical energy input required, e.g. fan power to overcome resistance of heat exchangers or coils, does not negate the energy saved, bearing in mind that it uses electricity rather than the fossil fuel energy. Note that extra fan power is needed whenever the system is in operation, although the degree of heat recovery varies throughout the year. Include the additional fan or pump running costs when calculating the viability of the scheme. Use effectiveness as a measure of the heat recovered, as shown in Figure 4.9.

Run-around coils

These comprise finned-tube copper coils located in supply and exhaust air streams connected by pipe work through which water or antifreeze solution is pumped. The advantages and disadvantages are summarised in Table 4.5. Typical thermal effectiveness is 45–65% depending on the number and spacing of coil rows and the temperatures prevailing. The additional air resistance and pumping energy should be taken into account, as should temperature conditions across the whole season when assessing viability.

Thermal wheels

These cylindrical drum heat exchangers rotate slowly between supply and exhaust air streams, absorbing heat from the warmer air and transferring it to the cooler air. Typical effectiveness is 60–85% depending on the media construction in the thermal wheel. A sensible heat exchanger may recover up to about 65% sensible heat, whilst the hygroscopic exchanger can recover around 80%

total heat (i.e. sensible plus latent heat). The advantages and disadvantages are summarised in Table 4.6.

Plate heat exchangers

Cross-flow plate heat exchangers are inexpensive, have low hydraulic resistance and require no motive power. Effectiveness can be in the range 30–70%, depending on the spacing of the plates, but is typically less than 50%. The advantages and disadvantages are summarised in Table 4.7. Placing the fan on the downstream side of the device on the supply side and the upstream side on the exhaust side maximises the ability to pick up the fan energy.

Heat pipes

These devices make use of a closed fluid cycle within a sealed tube to give a reversible heat recovery system. Supply and exhaust air ductwork must be adjacent in order to install the heat pipes.

Heat pumps

These should be used only where it is necessary to take advantage of small temperature differences between supply and exhaust air or where it is appropriate to convert rejected latent heat into sensible heat e.g. swimming pool ventilation. Energy is required to drive the compressor, although high CoPs are possible (see 7.3.3 and 10.1.5).

Table 4.5 Advantages and disadvantages of run-around coils

Advantages	Disadvantages
Supply and exhaust air flows are separated, thus avoiding any possibility of cross contamination	Direct transfer of latent heat is not generally possible
Can be used where the supply and exhaust ducts are not in close proximity	Overall heat recovery effectiveness is not likely to be greater than 65%
Seasonally reversible, providing preheating in winter and pre-cooling in summer	Frost protection should be provided
Multiple supply and exhaust systems can be incorporated in a single loop where appropriate	Easy to fit with minimum disturbance
Use conventional finned tube technology	

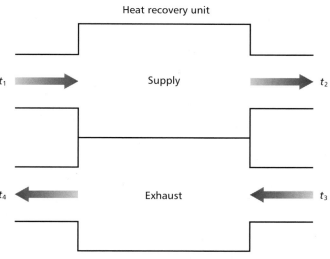

t_1 = supply air temperature (dry-bulb) into unit (°C)
t_2 = supply air temperature (dry-bulb) out of unit (°C)
t_3 = exhaust air temperature (dry-bulb) into unit (°C)
t_4 = exhaust air temperature (dry-bulb) out of unit (°C)
W_s = supply flow rate
W_e = exhaust flow rate
W_{min} = minimum value of W_s or W_e

$$\text{Sensible effectiveness} = \frac{W_s (t_1 - t_2)}{W_{min} (t_1 - t_3)} = \frac{W_e (t_4 - t_3)}{W_{min} (t_1 - t_3)}$$

Figure 4.9 Heat recovery effectiveness

Table 4.6 Advantages and disadvantages of thermal wheels

Advantages	Disadvantages
Can be controlled by varying the rotational speed	Possibility of cross contamination from exhaust to supply (can be minimised using a purge section)
Possible to recover both latent and sensible heat using hygroscopic materials	Difficult to clean
Highest heat recovery effectiveness of all devices; efficiency may be as high as 65% in sensible heat reclaim and 80% in enthalpy terms for the hygroscopic type	Supply and extract ducts must be adjacent

Table 4.7 Advantages and disadvantages of plate heat exchangers

Advantages	Disadvantages
Simple static devices; easy to commission and maintain	No modulation, so rate of heat recovery cannot be controlled unless a by-pass duct is provided (i.e. overheating could occur when heating requirements are small); over-recovery of heat also possible if there is a building cooling requirement (i.e. could result in heat being dumped into a cooled space, thereby increasing the cooling load)
Minimal risk of cross contamination unless mechanical damage occurs	Supply and exhaust ducts must be adjacent, and ductwork needs to be arranged to allow heat transfer through the plates
May be constructed so as to be easily removed for cleaning	

Air re-circulation

This is essentially a form of heat recovery, and in common use. The effectiveness is equal to the re-circulation percentage, e.g. 10% fresh air gives a 90% heat recovery effectiveness.

4.2.6   Daylighting strategies

The daylight strategy will have a significant influence on built form and, hence, the overall design concept. Strategies can vary significantly from, say, a building incorporating an atrium and light wells, with daylight for a large percentage of the year, to deep plan buildings that can only provide daylight around the perimeter of each floor. These different approaches hinge on the nature of the site (including the surrounding building etc.) and using the available daylight to its full extent, together with any necessary shading to avoid overheating and glare. CIBSE Lighting Guide LG10: *Daylight and window design*[8] provides simplified design guidance.

4.2.6.1   Using daylight

Good lighting design maximises the use of natural daylight to provide illumination, minimising installed lighting loads and lighting consumption and, thereby, reducing internal heat gains[41]. Daylight strategy, therefore, has a strong effect on the requirement for mechanical ventilation and air conditioning. The additional capital cost of improving daylighting should be offset against the running cost savings in lighting, and the capital and running costs of mechanical ventilation or air conditioning to remove the heat it produces. The LT method provides a 'ready-reckoner' for optimising daylight penetration[14].

The amount and distribution of daylight depends on the size and position of the windows, the window construction, the external and internal obstructions and the type of glazing material. To maximise the use of daylight, high room surface reflectances should be used to promote good distribution[8,41,42]. Effective control of the electric lighting is the key to realising the potential energy saving from daylight. The electric lighting control system should reduce light output when daylighting levels are adequate and when the space is unoccupied[21,43,44], see 9.5.

Figure 4.10 shows a range of daylighting solutions that can be employed to fully utilise and control the use of natural light[6,42,45].

4.2.6.2   Daylighting levels

The level and availability of daylight varies with time, season and weather conditions[46]. In temperate climates, where an overcast or diffuse sky predominates, it is quantified in terms of 'daylight factor' which is a measure of the amount of daylight reaching the working surface in the room[8]. The amount of daylight illuminance for particular tasks will be the same as for electric lighting[42].

The average daylight factor indicates the appearance of the interior in daylight. For example, a room with an average daylight factor of not less than 5% will appear 'light' and many tasks will not require electric lighting during daytime. However, a room with an average daylight factor of 2% or less will require electric lighting for most of the day[42,47]. A regular schedule for cleaning windows and internal room surfaces is necessary to ensure that daylighting levels are maintained, thus avoiding energy waste.

The variation of daylight throughout the day, and the year, affects the length of time it can be used to offset the use of electric lighting energy. These can be established using calculation procedures shown in CIBSE Lighting Guide LG10[8]. CIBSE Guide J: *Weather, solar and illuminance data*[46] also provides values of probable sky illuminance hours for Kew. To prevent summer overheating, it is generally preferable to keep out the high sun of summer by good fabric, shading and window design[8,42,46].

4.2.6.3   Zoning electric lighting in relation to daylight

To maximise daylighting, the electric lighting installation should be zoned to take account of occupancy patterns and daylight distribution. Zones should start at the perimeter and work towards the central area. They should be parallel to windows and depending on the glazing ratio of the building facade, solar shading etc., the daylit zone may vary in depth to over 6 m. The number of zones and complexity of the lighting system should be balanced against the value of the likely electricity saving. Intranet or hand held remote controls should be investigated to reduce wiring costs. The control or switching system also needs to be fully integrated with these zones in order to achieve potential savings, see 9.5.

4.2.6.4   Avoiding solar overheating

Building Regulations Approved Document L2★[10] sets out requirements aimed at avoiding solar overheating. Buildings should be constructed such that:

—   those occupied spaces that rely on natural ventilation should not overheat when subject to a moderate level of internal heat gain, and

---

★ Requirements may differ in Scotland[11] and Northern Ireland[12]

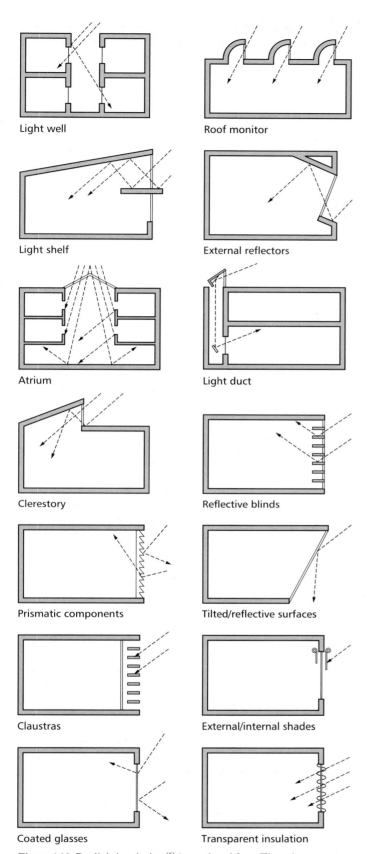

Light well

Roof monitor

Light shelf

External reflectors

Atrium

Light duct

Clerestory

Reflective blinds

Prismatic components

Tilted/reflective surfaces

Claustras

External/internal shades

Coated glasses

Transparent insulation

Figure 4.10 Daylighting devices[6] (reproduced from Thermie Maxibrochure *Daylighting in buildings*)

— those spaces that incorporate mechanical ventilation or cooling do not require excessive cooling plant capacity to maintain the desired space conditions.

Some of the ways of meeting the requirements would be through:

— the appropriate specification of glazing, and

— the incorporation of passive measures such as shading (detailed guidance being given in BRE Report BR364)[48], and

— the use of exposed thermal capacity combined with night ventilation.

A way of achieving compliance for spaces with glazing facing only one orientation would be to limit the area of glazed opening as a percentage of the internal area of the element under construction to the values given in Table 4.8.

4.2.6.5 Shading

Daylight can be controlled either actively, e.g. with external adjustable manual or automatic blinds, or passively using architectural features such as orientation and overhangs to reduce solar gains when the building may be susceptible to overheating[48]. Figure 4.11 shows a range of external shading devices.

The appropriate type, size and positioning of any shading device will depend on climate, building use and the source of the light to be excluded (high or low angle direct sunlight, diffuse sky light or perhaps reflected light from paving on the street outside). Deciduous trees or vines can be used to screen the solar heat and glare in summer and filter light in winter, and planting can sometimes solve the problem of reflected light from neighbouring structures, water or ground finishes. Designers should balance the benefits of having moveable external blinds against the relative robustness of fixed external shading. i.e. movable blinds will have higher capital and maintenance costs but should provide better shading.

Interior shades protect occupants against the immediate effects of direct sunlight and against glare. But when infra-red radiation penetrates the glazing most of it is trapped in the room and must be dissipated by ventilation or mechanical cooling. Mid-pane blinds are often a useful compromise and tend to require less maintenance and cleaning.

Horizontal shading elements are effective in reducing peak summer solar gain where high solar attitudes are experienced, primarily on southerly facades. Vertical elements are effective for restricting solar gain to facades subject to lower solar attitudes, i.e. east and west.

Fixed external shading devices include permanent facade features such as overhangs and window reveals. Unlike external blinds, the shading effect cannot be adjusted and the obstruction to daylight is permanent.

Table 4.8 Maximum allowable area of glazing

Orientation of opening	Maximum allowable area of opening (%)
N	50
NE/NW/S	40
E/SE/W/SW	32
Horizontal	12

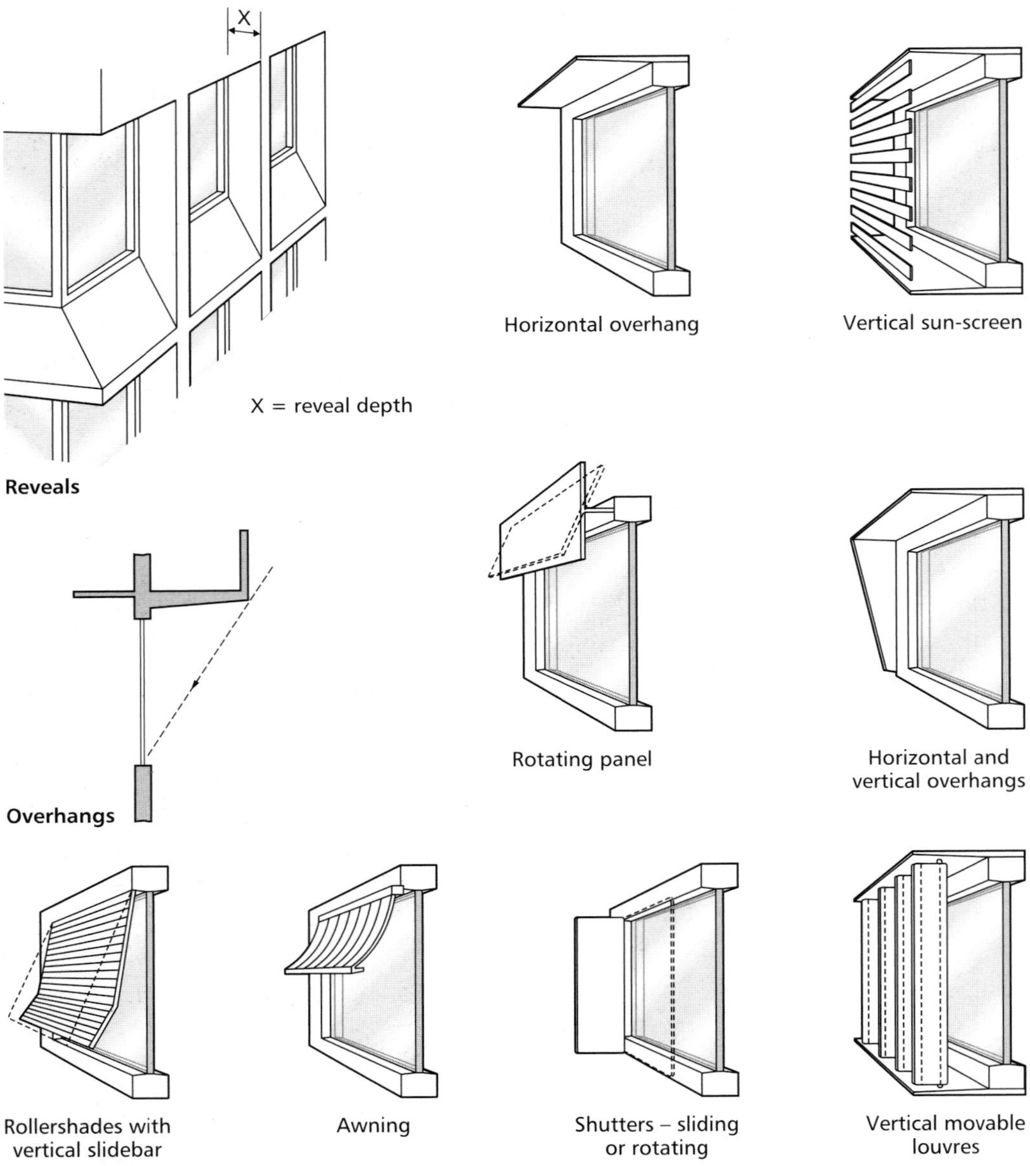

Figure 4.11 External shading devices

Horizontal overhang

Vertical sun-screen

X = reveal depth

Reveals

Overhangs

Rotating panel

Horizontal and vertical overhangs

Rollershades with vertical slidebar

Awning

Shutters – sliding or rotating

Vertical movable louvres

Reveals can be used to set back the window/glazing systems from the building envelope's opaque fabric to provide both vertical and horizontal shading effects, for east/west facades and south facades respectively. Overhangs can also be used to shade and are most effective on apertures that have a southerly orientation. Horizontal overhangs are not as effective on east or west facing walls, where reveals are more suitable.

Where large overhangs are used, the daylight factor is reduced and the result may be a greater use of electric lighting; this may offset the energy savings made on the HVAC systems. In air conditioned buildings, the investment in fixed external shading devices will also reduce central plant size and capital costs.

Automatically controlled shading devices can provide improvements by shading when there is excessive solar gain, and retracting to utilise daylight and winter solar gain. Control is a critical element and, in particular, the integration with electric lighting control is essential. Systems that default to a condition of 'blinds down' and 'lights on' must be avoided. However, a 'seamless' variation between daylight and electric lighting can be difficult to achieve. Large step changes prompted by

automatic controls should be avoided as this can prove irritating to occupants[21,43]. Individual control, rather than fully automatic modulation, is generally preferred by occupants. Automatic external shading devices need to be provided with overrides to permit manual adjustment by the occupants, and automatic retraction to prevent wind damage. BRE IP 11/02[49] describes the shading systems commonly used in retrofit situations and gives guidance on their selection and design. BRE IP 12/02[50] provides guidance on whether to use automatic or manual controls and describes practical control strategies.

4.3   Services

4.3.1   Concepts for services

Selecting the most appropriate and energy efficient systems is fundamental to the overall sketch design. Good selection of zones and effective means of control is also vital to energy efficiency. At times when passive natural ventilation and daylight can not alone meet the needs of occupants, the building services should meet the remaining demands as simply and effectively as practicable, in harmony with the occupants and the building as a whole.

Further details on the selection and design of particular systems is provided in sections 7 to 12.

4.4 Summary

The sketch design can be regarded as complete only when:

— the overall strategy is clearly stated and understood by all those involved

— the inter-relationships between the architectural and services aspects of the design have been resolved

— the contributions to energy efficiency made by each aspect of the design have been established

— decisions which affect the holistic concept of the design have been made, e.g. whether mechanical ventilation or cooling is needed, whether the building form will encourage the use of daylight and how the lighting will be controlled

— all members of the design team appreciate the impact that their components have on the whole.

References

1 *A performance specification for the energy efficient office of the future* GIR 30 (Action Energy) (1995) (www.actionenergy.org.uk)

2 *Avoiding or minimising the use of air-conditioning — A research report from the EnREI Programme* GIR 31 (Action Energy) (1995) www.actionenergy.org.uk

3 *The design team's guide to environmentally smart buildings* GPG287 (Action Energy) (2000) www.actionenergy.org.uk

4 *Best practice in the specification for offices* (Reading: British Council for Offices) (2000)

5 Baker N V *Energy and environment in non-domestic buildings: a technical design guide* (Cambridge: Cambridge Architectural Research/Building Research Energy Conservation Support Unit)(1994)

6 *Daylighting in buildings* Thermie Maxibrochure (Action Energy) (1994) www.actionenergy.org.uk

7 *Climate and site development* Digest 350 (London: Construction Research Communications) (1990)

8 *Daylight and window design* CIBSE Lighting Guide LG10 (London: Chartered Institution of Building Services Engineers) (1999)

9 *Environmental design* CIBSE Guide A (London: Chartered Institution of Building Services Engineers) (1999)

10 *Conservation of fuel and power* The Building Regulations 2000 Approved Document L1/L2 (London: The Stationery Office) (2001)

11 *Technical standards for compliance with the Building Standards (Scotland) Regulations 1990 (as amended)* (London: The Stationery Office) (2001)

Key points to consider during design

- Select the most efficient source, e.g. boiler, chiller, lamp etc. Where available, base selection on certified product performance data

- Use renewables where possible and/or the most environmentally friendly fuel, see 4.3.2.

- Ensure that plant is not oversized and output can be matched to demand e.g. using a modular approach.

- A 'keep it simple' approach is often best to ensure that design intentions can be achieved and energy consumption kept under control.

- Do not simply employ 'add-on' energy saving features; ensure they are part of an integrated strategy.

- Always consider part load conditions and efficiencies, and provide modulating systems where appropriate.

- Zone the building carefully to meet the needs of occupants. Select appropriate controls for each zone to allow, for example, the building manager to isolate unoccupied areas. These should ensure services only operate when, where, and to the level required.

- Select effective controls for the central plant to minimise plant running hours and cycling. Controls should be designed to give priority to natural resources, e.g. daylight, before electric lighting.

- Ensure that large central systems do not operate to meet small loads, e.g. if summer hot water demand is low; install separate heating and hot water systems rather than a combined central system.

- Consider a mixed mode approach to avoid having one large system operating all year round. Demands can be met using different design strategies (contingency, complementary, or zoned) and/or different operating strategies (concurrent, changeover or alternate) (see 4.2.5.3).

- Special needs, e.g. additional lighting, should be met locally and not used for the entire area.

- The temperatures of the heating and cooling media supplied to heat exchangers should be kept at the minimum and maximum values, respectively, that are able to achieve the necessary performance.

- Provide some element of user control with well designed interfaces and, thereby, promote comfort and energy efficiency. Controls should be sufficiently flexible to satisfy different occupancy levels and activities, e.g. the necessary switching to allow a half level of lighting for cleaners or security staff outside normal working hours.

- Systems should revert to safe and energy-efficient 'off' or 'standby' levels after use rather than automatically left on.

- Controls should be appropriate to the user, e.g. building management systems (BMS) can be very effective in large buildings or estates with resident engineers, whereas less complex controls may be more appropriate in smaller buildings.

- It is essential that feedback mechanisms are put in place to monitor the status and operation of the building. These mechanisms should ensure that building managers know if energy consumption is greater than expected.

12   *Conservation of fuel and power* The Building Regulations (Northern Ireland) 1994 Technical Booklet F (London: The Stationery Office) (1999)

13   Littlefair P J and Aizlewood M E *Daylight in atrium buildings* BRE Information Paper IP3/98 (Construction Research Communications) (1998)

14   Baker N V and Steemers K *The LT Method 2.0. An energy design tool for non-domestic buildings* (Cambridge: Cambridge Architectural Research) (1994)

15   *Natural ventilation in non-domestic buildings* CIBSE Applications Manual AM10 (London: Chartered Institution of Building Services Engineers) (1997)

16   *Thermal properties of building structures* Section 3 in CIBSE Guide A: *Environmental design* (London: Chartered Institution of Building Services Engineers) (1999)

17   *Mixed mode ventilation* CIBSE Applications Manual AM13 (London: Chartered Institution of Building Services Engineers) (2000)

18   *Thermal insulation: avoiding risks* BRE Report BR262 (London: Construction Research Communications) (2001)

19   *A practical guide to infra-red thermography for building surveys* BRE Report BR176 (London: Construction Research Communications) (1991)

20   Pearson C and Barnard N *Guidance and standard specification for thermal imaging of non-electrical installations* BSRIA FMS 6/00 (Bracknell: Building Services Research and Information Association) (2000)

21   *Electric lighting controls — A guide for designers, installers and users* GPG 160 (Action Energy) (1997) (www.actionenergy.org.uk)

22   *Ventilation* The Building Regulations 1991 Approved Document F (London: The Stationery Office) (1994)

23   Bordass W T, Bromley A K R and Leaman A J *Comfort, control and energy efficiency in offices* BRE Information Paper IP3/95 (London: Construction Research Communications) (1995)

24   *Testing buildings for air leakage* CIBSE TM23 (London: Chartered Institution of Building Services Engineers) (2000)

25   Potter N *Air tightness specifications* BSRIA S10/98 (Bracknell: Building Services Research and Information Association) (1998)

26   Perera E S, Turner C H C and Scivyer C R *Minimising air infiltration in office buildings* BRE Report BR265 (London: Construction Research Communications) (1994)

27   BS 6375: 1989: *Performance of windows*: Part 1: 1989: *Classification for weathertightness (including guidance on selection and specification)*; Part 2: 1987: *Specification for operation and strength characteristics* (London: British Standards Institution) (dates as indicated)

28   BS 7386: 1997: *Specification for draughtstrips for the draught control of existing doors and windows in housing (including test methods)* (London: British Standards Institution) (1997)

29   Martin A J *Control of natural ventilation* TN 11/95 (Bracknell: Building Services Research and Information Association) (1995)

30   *Air infiltration and natural ventilation* Section 4 in CIBSE Guide A: *Environmental design* (London: Chartered Institution of Building Services Engineers (1999)

31   BS 5925: 1991 (1995): *Code of practice for ventilation principles and designing for natural ventilation* (London: British Standards Institution) (1995)

32   *Natural ventilation in non-domestic buildings* BRE Digest 399 (London: Construction Research Communications) (1994)

33   *New ways of cooling – information for building designers* GIL 85 (Action Energy) (www.actionenergy.org.uk)

34   Kolokotroni M *Night ventilation for cooling office buildings* BRE Information Paper IP4/98 (London: Construction Research Communications) (1998)

35   Martin A *Night cooling control strategies* BSRIA TN 5/96 (Bracknell: Building Services Research and Information Association) (1996)

36   *Mixed-mode buildings and systems* GIR 56 (Action Energy) (1999) (www.actionenergy.org.uk)

37   Jaunzens D and Bordass W T Building design for mixed mode systems *Proc. CIBSE Nat. Conf., Eastbourne, 1–3 October 1995* (London: Chartered Institution of Building Services Engineers) (1995)

38   Bordass W T, Entwisle M J and Willis S Naturally ventilated and mixed mode office buildings — Opportunities and pitfalls *Proc. CIBSE Nat. Conf., Brighton, 2–4 October 1994* (London: Chartered Institution of Building Services Engineers) (1994)

39   *Energy use in offices* Energy Consumption Guide ECG 19 (Action Energy) (2000) (www.actionenergy.org.uk)

40   *Air-to-air heat recovery* CIBSE Research Report RR2 (London: Chartered Institution of Building Services Engineers) (1995)

41   Bell J and Burt W *Designing buildings for daylight* BRE Report BR288 (London: Construction Research Communications) (1995)

42   *Code for lighting* (London: Chartered Institution of Building Services Engineers) (2002)

43   *People and lighting controls* BRE Information Paper IP6/96 (London: Construction Research Communications) (1996)

44   *Photoelectric control of lighting: design, set-up and installation issues* BRE Information Paper IP 2/99 (London: Construction Research Communications) (1999)

45   Littlefair P J *Designing with innovative daylighting* BRE Report BR305 (London: Construction Research Communications) (1996).

46   *Weather, solar and illuminance data* CIBSE Guide J (London: Chartered Institution of Building Services Engineers) (2001).

47   Gould J R, Lewis J O and Steemers T C *Energy in architecture: The European passive solar handbook* EUR 13445 (London: Batsford) (1992)

48   *Solar shading of buildings* BRE Report BR364, (London: Construction Research Communications) (1999)

49   *Retrofitting solar shading* BRE Information Paper IP 11/02 (London: Construction Research Communications) (2002)

50   *Control of solar shading* BRE Information Paper IP 12/02 (London: Construction Research Communications) (2002)

Bibliography

General

Special Issue on Post Occupancy Evaluation *Building Res. and Information* **29** (2) (March – April 2001)

Fundamentals ASHRAE Handbook (Atlanta, GA: American Society of Heating, Refrigeration and Air Conditioning Engineers) (2001)

HVAC Applications ASHRAE Handbook (Atlanta, GA: American Society of Heating, Refrigeration and Air Conditioning Engineers) (2003)

Energy standard for buildings except low rise residential buildings ASHRAE/IESNA Standard 90.1-1999 (Atlanta, GA: American Society of Heating, Refrigeration and Air Conditioning Engineers) (1999)

ASHRAE/IESNA Standard 90.1: User's manual (Atlanta, GA: American Society of Heating, Refrigeration and Air Conditioning Engineers) (2000)

Environmental code of practice for buildings and their services —Case studies BSRIA CS4/96 (Bracknell: Building Services Research and Information Association) (1996)

Building services and environmental issues: bibliography BSRIA LB 74/92 (Bracknell: Building Services Research and Information Association) (1992)

Selecting windows by performance BRE Digest 377 (London: Construction Research Communications)

Energy efficiency in dwellings BRE Digest 355 (London: Construction Research Communications)

Comparative life cycle assessment of modern commercial buildings BRE SC98 (London: Construction Research Communications) (1997)

Thermal response of buildings Section 5 in CIBSE Guide A: *Environmental design* (London: Chartered Institution of Building Services Engineers) (1999)

Braham D, Barnard N and Jaunzens D *Thermal mass in office buildings* BRE Digest 454 (London: Construction Research Communications) (2001)

Barnard N *Fabric energy storage of night cooling* Proc. CIBSE Nat. Conf., Brighton, 2–4 October 1994 (London: Chartered Institution of Building Services Engineers) (1994)

Mills F A *Atrium building performance* Proc. CIBSE Nat. Conf., Eastbourne, 1–3 October 1995 (London: Chartered Institution of Building Services Engineers) (1995)

Archard and Gicquel *European passive solar handbook — Basic principles and concepts for passive solar architecture* CEC DG XII for Science Research and Development (Brussels: Commission of European Communities) (1986)

Passive solar design — Netley Abbey Infant School General Information Leaflet GIL 12 (Action Energy) (1996) (www.actionenergy.org.uk)

Passive solar design — Looe Junior and Infant School General Information Leaflet GIL 33 (Action Energy) (1996) (www.actionenergy.org.uk)

The benefits of including energy efficiency early in the design stage -- Anglia Polytechnic University Good Practice Case Studies GPCS 334 (Action Energy) (1997) (www.actionenergy.org.uk)

Energy efficiency in offices. A guide for the design team Good Practice Guide GPG 34 (Action Energy) (1993) (www.actionenergy.org.uk)

Designing energy efficient multi-residential buildings Good Practice Guide GPG 192 (Action Energy) (1997) (www.actionenergy.org.uk)

Irving S J *Air-to-air heat recovery* Proc. CIBSE Nat. Conf., Brighton, 2–4 October 1994 (London: Chartered Institution of Building Services Engineers) www.actionenergy.org.uk (1994)

HVAC thermal storage BSRIA AG 11/2000 (Bracknell: Building Services Research and Information Association) (2000)

Ventilation

White M *Trickle ventilators in offices* BRE Information Paper IP12/98 (London: Construction Research Communications) (1998)

Jackson A J *Air conditioning and energy efficiency* Proc. CIBSE Nat. Conf., Eastbourne, 1–3 October 1995 (London: Chartered Institution of Building Services Engineers) (1995)

Liddament M W *A guide to energy efficient ventilation* (Coventry: Air Infiltration and Ventilation Centre) (1996)

Leaman A, Cohen R R and Jackman P J *Ventilation of office buildings: Deciding the appropriate system* Proc. CIBSE Nat. Conf., Brighton, 2–4 October 1994 (London: Chartered Institution of Building Services Engineers) (1994)

De Saulles T *Free cooling systems — design and applications guide* BSRIA RR16/96 (Bracknell: Building Services Research and Information Association) (1996)

Daylighting

Thompson M W and Mucibabic A *Model studies of daylight factor: light shelves, curved ceilings and external obstruction* Proc. CIBSE Nat. Conf., Eastbourne, 1–3 October 1995 (London: Chartered Institution of Building Services Engineers) (1995)

Loe D *Interior lighting quality and the potential for energy saving* Proc. CIBSE Nat. Conf., Eastbourne, 1–3 October 1995 (London: Chartered Institution of Building Services Engineers) (1995)

Lynes J A and Littlefair P J *Lighting energy savings from daylight estimation at the sketch design stage* Lighting Res. Technol **22** (3) (1990)

Littlefair P J *Innovative daylighting: review of systems and evaluation methods* Lighting Res. Technol **22** (1) 1990

Baker N, Franchotti A and Steemers K *Daylighting in architecture -- a European reference book* (London: James and James) (1993)

Littlefair P J *Site planning for daylight and sunlight* BRE Report BR209 (London: Construction Research Communications) (1991)

Lighting for people, energy efficiency and architecture — an overview of lighting requirements and design Good Practice Guide GPG272 (Action Energy) (2000) (www.actionenergy.org.uk)

HVAC strategies for well-insulated airtight buildings CIBSE TM29 (London: Chartered Institution of Building Services Engineers) (2001)

Desktop guide to daylighting — for architects (Action Energy) (1998) (www.actionenergy.org.uk)

5 Renewables, fuels, CHP and metering

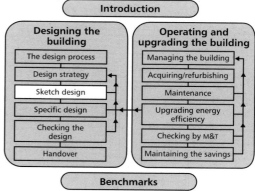

5.0 General

5.1 Renewables

5.2 Fuels

5.3 Distributed energy sources and CHP

5.4 Metering

This section discusses fuel selection including the possibility of including renewables and other means of generating energy (e.g. CHP) in the design. It also highlights the need for appropriate metering and sub-metering to ensure that future building performance can be monitored in line with the principles at the front of this Guide.

5.0 General

An essential part of integrated design is to ensure that the energy supply and monitoring strategy is as coherent and environmentally sustainable as possible. The following issues should be considered in the order shown:

(a) Where possible, include renewable sources of energy as an integral part of the building design

(b) Where fuels are necessary, to select those least harmful to the environment

(c) Where possible include on-site generation using CHP or fuel cells

(d) Include metering and sub-metering to ensure that future building performance can be continually monitored by the building operator

Designers should include a clear summary of this overall energy supply strategy in the building log book alongside a metering strategy, as required for England and Wales by Building Regulations Approved Document L2[1]*.

5.1 Renewables

5.1.1 Renewable energy opportunities

Renewable energy describes energy flows that occur naturally and repeatedly in the environment, e.g. from the sun, wind and the oceans, and from plants and the fall of water. It also includes energy available from wastes and the emerging clean technologies e.g. fuel cells (see section 5.3.2). There are a wide range of renewable energy sources/technologies, varying in technical and commercial viability. These include:

— wind power

— hydroelectric power

— wave and tidal power

— photovoltaics

— active solar heating

— passive solar design

— municipal and general wastes

— landfill gas

— geothermal energy

— agricultural and forestry wastes

— energy crops.

Renewable energy produces few, if any, harmful emissions. Exploiting renewables also reduces the rate at which other energy resources are consumed. Renewables therefore promise to play an increasingly significant role in the future.

Renewable energy technologies in the UK are now establishing themselves as viable, credible contributors to energy supplies. An assessment of renewable energy opportunities in the UK in the early 1990s[4] indicated limited opportunities for exploiting geothermal power but considerable resources for wind, wave and tidal power. In 2000, the UK produced 2.8%[5] of its electricity from renewable sources, of which just under half was by large-scale hydroelectricity. The remainder came largely from combustion of bio-fuels, led by landfill gas and refuse combustion. Wind power was the largest contributor, other than large-scale hydro and bio-fuels, but amounted to only 0.26% of total electricity produced. Although the contribution from renewables is still relatively small, renewable generating capacity doubled between 1996 and 2000.

The Government has set a target that 5% of UK electricity needs should be met from renewables by the end of 2003 and 10% by 2010, as long as the cost to consumers is acceptable. This has led to the introduction of a new Renewables Obligation (RO), to succeed the Non-Fossil Fuel Obligation (NFFO), which includes exemption of

---

* Requirements may differ for Scotland[2] and Northern Ireland[3]

renewable electricity and heat from the Climate Change Levy and an expanded support programme for renewable energy. The new RO requires power suppliers to derive a specified proportion of the electricity they supply from renewables, with the cost to consumers limited by a price cap. In the short term much of the expansion in renewables is expected to come from wind and land-fill gas.

The use of naturally renewable energy resources is becoming more common in buildings. Waste incineration, bio-fuels, wind, bio-gas and hydroelectric schemes should all be considered at the design stage, depending upon local conditions and availability. Active and passive solar energy systems are becoming more common in buildings although the economics still require careful assessment. Photovoltaic cells to produce electricity are becoming cheaper and are beginning to have applications in buildings, particularly when integrated into the building fabric. Simple solar systems for heating domestic hot water have been used extensively in hot climates although they have not generally provided a good return on investment in the UK. The calorific value of some renewable sources are shown in Appendix A2.

The main constraints on the use of renewables are the costs of the energy they produce and the local environmental impact. Currently, the cost of energy from renewables is generally higher than that produced by conventional energy sources. However, as renewables become more established and the benefits of mass production take effect, the gap will reduce. Indeed, in the case of wind power and some other technologies, this is already happening.

There are a number of key issues not specific to any individual renewable energy technology that affect both the uptake of renewables and the development of the industry. These cross-technology issues include:

— planning

— financing

— development of the UK electricity market.

No renewables scheme can proceed without planning permission. A range of guidance aimed at the planning community is available (e.g. ODPM Planning Policy Guidance 22: *Renewable energy*[6]) to ensure that planning authorities make informed decisions when faced with applications for renewables projects. The government has recently introduced a regional strategic approach to planning with regional targets for renewable energy. Local authorities also play a key role in stimulating renewable energy under their Local Agenda 21 UK[7] and post-Kyoto activities.

Obtaining finance can represent a major barrier to the progress of a renewables project. In 1990, very few renewables projects existed (beyond large-scale hydro-electricity) and the technologies were largely untried in a commercial sense. Now, through the mechanism of the NFFO, hundreds of schemes are generating power. The Department of Trade and Industry's New and Renewable Energy Programme in the financial sector has encouraged investors into a new market and allayed financiers' concerns about what they originally perceived as a risky industry.

The integration of renewables into, and their acceptance by, the electricity supply industry will play a key role in ensuring that they make an increasingly significant contribution to UK energy supplies. The market for 'green' electricity is growing, with an expanding number of electricity companies now offering 'green' tariffs. The industry is also addressing barriers that might prevent significant increases in renewables-based generating capacity by working with the renewables and wider small generator community to define and implement the New Electricity Trading Arrangements (NETA). The OFGEM/DTI Embedded Generation Working Group is also building an industry consensus on the way forward to achieve Government targets for embedded renewables and CHP generation.

5.1.2   Wind power

As the UK is the windiest country in Europe, wind power is one of the UK's most promising renewable energy technologies and already provides electricity for nearly a quarter of million homes. Wind turbines are a technically proven technology that use aerodynamic forces ('lift' and 'drag') to produce mechanical power that can then be converted to electricity. There are already nearly 1000 wind turbines in operation around the UK.

The costs of installing wind energy plant are very site-specific, usually related to the terrain and distances from grid lines and access roads. Current capital costs are around £500–750 per kW of installed capacity. Typically, around two thirds of the cost are the wind turbines themselves, about a quarter are for roads, foundations and electricity cables, and the rest are for installation, planning and legal costs etc. Operation and maintenance costs are on average about 0.5 p/kW·h.

Wind turbines are being developed over a range of power outputs from kilowatt to multi-megawatt units and are available commercially up to 2 MW. Small wind generators rated at a few watts are also available for battery charging, meeting small on-site power needs etc. Large-scale generation of electricity requires a number of large machines to be grouped together, in wind farms, for economy and ease of operation. The machines are usually spaced 5 to 10 rotor diameters apart to ensure they do not interfere with each other's performance. As a result, a wind farm of about 20 machines usually extends over an area of 3–4 km^2, although the actual machines occupy only about 1% of this area and, if sited on agricultural land, the remaining land can be farmed as usual. The reliability of wind turbines has increased steadily during the past decade and modern turbines now operate with a typical machine availability of 95–98%. Offshore wind farms use similar technology, but the harsher climate, relative inaccessibility and additional cost of foundations reduce the viability, particularly for machines less than one megawatt.

Global indications show that wind energy costs are likely to fall further, because of economies of scale in manufacture and technical improvements leading to lower capital equipment costs. It is expected that by 2010 wind energy might be supplying 6% of UK electricity. However, there is still considerable debate about the acceptability of wind farms in the UK landscape. Visual impact is a significant planning issue. For good wind speeds, needed to give more economic generation of electricity, wind power projects need to be sited on high, exposed land. A wind turbine typically has a tower height of 40–50 m and a rotor diameter of 80–100 m. There is a delicate balance to be struck between the change in the landscape and wind power's environmental benefits. Careful design, siting and operation ensure that wind turbine noise is no longer a nuisance although it may be an issue when used near buildings. Aerodynamic noise from the blades needs to be assessed but mechanical noise from the rotating machinery can normally be minimised using well-proven engineering practices.

5.1.3 Wave power

Ocean waves are caused by winds as they blow across the surface of the sea and the energy contained in the waves can be harnessed and used to produce electricity. Due to the direction of the prevailing winds and the size of the Atlantic ocean, the UK has one of the largest wave energy resources in the world. However, the lack of commercial schemes means that the cost and performance of wave power devices are difficult to estimate. UK wave energy resources are either shoreline or offshore.

Shoreline wave devices are mainly oscillating water columns (OWC). These consists of a partially submerged, hollow structure that is open to the sea below the water line. This encloses a column of air on top of a column of water. Waves cause the water column to rise and fall, which alternately compresses and depressurises the air column. This trapped air is allowed to flow to and from the atmosphere via a Wells turbine, which has the ability to rotate in the same direction regardless of the direction of the airflow. The rotation of the turbine is used to generate electricity.

Offshore wave devices exploit the more powerful wave regimes available in deep water. Several different types of offshore device have been developed, but none has yet been deployed commercially.

Following the decommissioning of a prototype shoreline 75 kW OWC on the Hebridean island of Islay, there has been no UK installed wave power capacity. Recently, three projects have gone ahead. One of these is the 'land-installed marine-powered energy transformer' (LIMPET) which is a 500 kW shoreline OWC on Islay, which was commissioned in 2000. There is currently a further 350 kW of wave energy devices installed worldwide, mainly OWCs. Installed capacity in the UK is expected to grow with demonstration schemes such as the LIMPET and world capacity is expected to increase to nearly 6 MW.

5.1.4 Hydroelectric power

Hydroelectric power accounts for around 2% of the UK's total installed electricity generating capacity. Hydroelectricity is produced when a flow of water, either from a reservoir or a river, is channelled through a turbine connected to an electricity generator. The amount of power produced depends on the rate of flow and the volume of water available. Hydroelectric schemes are generally divided into two broad categories: 'large-scale' (i.e. more than 5 MW) and 'small-scale' (less than 5 MW). Systems of a few tens of kilowatts are often referred to as

'micro-hydro' and these are not usually connected to the electricity grid but could provide significant opportunities in or around buildings.

The cost of generation by existing large-scale schemes is estimated to be 1–2.5 p/kW·h. For small-scale schemes, the initial costs are lowest for sites with high hydraulic heads. These costs increase as the hydraulic head decreases, while scheme viability decreases as generating capacity decreases. However, the initial costs are very dependent on the details of a particular scheme e.g. land prices. If existing engineering structures are used, capital costs can be considerably reduced. The principles of operating small-scale and large-scale hydro schemes are essentially the same. They require:

— a suitable rainfall catchment area.

— a hydraulic 'head' (i.e. vertical distance from the reservoir or river to the turbine)

— a water intake placed above a weir or behind a dam

— a pipeline or channel to transport the water from the reservoir or river to the turbine

— a flow control system

— a turbine, a generator, associated buildings and grid connection

— an outflow, where the water returns to the main water course.

Hydroelectric schemes do not produce any atmospheric emissions once commissioned. The turbines and generators create some noise but this is confined to plant rooms. The noise level from a hydroelectric plant depends on the operating conditions, in particular the installed capacity, hydraulic head and volumetric flow of water.

Small-scale hydroelectric devices have environmental impacts that require careful consideration. Visual impact of the water intake, dam or weir, and the turbine buildings may be an issue and the ecological impact of diverting water flow and the need to maintain sufficient flow through normal river channels needs careful thought. Small-scale schemes with suitable insulation in the turbine house do not create significant noise but the possibility of damage to fish and other organisms passing through hydro turbines must be avoided.

It should be noted that small-scale schemes which do not involve collecting water behind dams or in reservoirs have considerably less impact on the environment. Some small-scale hydroelectric power schemes can be successfully developed with minimal environmental impact using existing infrastructure such as water-supply reservoirs and flood control weirs.

5.1.5 Energy from waste

Household, commercial and industrial wastes can represent an asset in energy terms. Many UK projects use waste to produce electricity, heat or both. Waste generally has a calorific value about two thirds that of coal and produces around 50% more ash. The costs of producing energy from waste depend very much on the scale of the operation. Developments in environmental legislation and trends in disposal practice also significantly influence costs. Energy can be obtained from waste in a number of ways:

— *incineration*: combustion of raw waste

— *refuse-derived fuel* (RDF): combustion after processing to remove undesirable components or material that can be recycled

— *anaerobic digestion* (AD): biological process under controlled conditions in digester systems (also see section 5.1.8)

— *landfill gas collection and utilisation*: biological processes that occur spontaneously when the waste is land-filled (see section 5.1.6)

— *gasification of waste*: by heating in a low-oxygen atmosphere to produce a combustible gas

— *pyrolysis of waste*: by heating in an oxygen-free atmosphere to produce a liquid oil.

Incineration of raw waste is widely practised in many parts of the world. The heat produced during incineration can be used for electricity production, or for CHP, with the heat often used in district heating schemes. Energy from waste plant that dispose of municipal waste typically handle 12–80 tonnes of waste per hour (90 000–600 000 tonnes per year) and produce 6–40 MW of electricity. Incineration can also be used to dispose of other types of waste, e.g. chicken litter (several such plants are in operation in the UK), straw (the first UK plant is now operating near Ely) etc. In the UK at present, around 2.5 million tonnes of waste a year is being used to fuel 180 MW of power generation, enough for a quarter of a million homes.

Refuse-derived fuel (RDF) has been under development for some years and involves processing waste to remove undesirable components or material that can be recycled before combustion. Approaches range from schemes where waste is pulverised and used with little additional treatment (coarse RDF), through to schemes where waste is extensively processed to allow recovery of recycled material and production of a refined, dried and densified fuel product (densified RDF). Historically developments in the UK largely focused on the production of densified RDF aimed at the industrial boiler market. These developments were largely unsuccessful. However, a recently built plant in Dundee is using coarse RDF in a fluidised bed combustion plant.

Anaerobic digestion (AD) involves treating organic waste using bacteria in an oxygen-free environment and is a biological process under controlled conditions in a digester. As well as consuming the waste, the bacteria give off a methane-rich bio-gas that can be used as a fuel. AD has a long and successful pedigree in the sewage treatment industry where sewage gas is produced from digestion of sewage sludge. Some of the gas produced is used to maintain the optimum temperature for the digestion process. Attention is now focusing on treating animal slurries in a growing range of applications as AD can provide a viable means of disposing of highly polluting wastes, e.g. cattle slurry. The digestate produced as a by-product can also have value as a fertiliser. AD could be used to process the organic fraction of household and commercial waste, either as part of source separation schemes or to complement centralised plant set up for recycling or to produce RDF.

All waste disposal options have some impact on the environment. However, the energy recovery option can offer environmental benefits, in addition to the usual advantages of renewable energy. For example, incineration plant enables the expansion of recycling, e.g. through metals recovery, and thus reduces the volume of unrecycled waste. Incineration schemes also enable landfills to be more easily managed as landfilling incineration residues rather than untreated mixed waste reduces the potential for emissions from landfill sites to air, ground and water.

Concerns about emissions from incineration, particularly heavy metals and dioxins, have produced strict emissions regulations in the UK. This has led to the evolution of incinerators and of gas-cleaning systems that can meet these standards. Nonetheless, incineration projects often still face opposition at the planning stage because of fears about their emissions. In general, these emissions are small and easily monitored.

5.1.6   Landfill gas

Landfilling is the main disposal method for the UK's waste, with up to 90% of all domestic waste taking this route. It is estimated that there are over 10 000 landfill sites in the UK. Landfill gas is formed when the waste deposited in landfills breaks down as a result of the action of microbes. It consists of a mixture of carbon dioxide and methane, with a large number of trace components. The methane content of the gas (typically around 40–60% by volume) makes it a potential fuel. The calorific value of landfill gas is 15–25 $MJ \cdot m^{-3}$, depending on its methane content. Landfill gas is mostly used without processing, other than the removal of moisture and dust. It is suitable for heat generation when it can be produced close to a heat load, which favoured its early exploitation for brick kilns adjacent to clay pits used for land fill. In other cases, it is used to generate electricity from gas turbines or reciprocating engines.

Of all the renewable energy technologies (except large-scale hydro power), landfill gas projects have been closest to full commercialisation and have produced power closest to the UK electricity pool price. Some projects even operate outside the protected NFFO marketplace. Future costs of landfill gas schemes are expected to decrease further because of increased sales volumes and increased competition between suppliers of generator sets. It is also likely that gas collection costs will have to be borne as part of a landfill site's environmental control system and will no longer be costed into the overall landfill gas utilisation scheme.

Landfill gas is collected through a series of wells drilled into the waste. A wide variety of designs of wells and collection systems are available. The choice will depend to some extent on site-specific factors, such as type and depth of waste. Gas collection for energy production can often complement environmental protection measures in force at landfill sites. There is a potential risk to the local and global environment from the escape of landfill gas, and its control is often required to comply with environmental legislation. A well-designed landfill site and gas collection system can ensure integration of effective environmental protection and energy recovery.

Gas turbines, dual-fuel (compression ignition) engines and spark ignition engines are all used to combust landfill gas and convert it into energy. Fuel conversion efficiency can range from 26% (typically for gas turbines) to 42% (for dual-fuel engines) although efficiency can be increased significantly by using CHP. In the UK, there are currently around 150 sites generating electricity for the grid. The UK landfill gas resource is estimated to be equivalent to around 6.75 TW·h* per year (around 2% of current UK electricity demand). This equates to around 850 MW of installed capacity.

In general, emissions from landfill gas combustion will include (at different concentrations) all the pollutants produced by flaring off landfill gas at sites that do not have gas utilisation equipment, but at different concentrations. These emissions include particulates, traces of heavy metals and organic compounds such as dioxins. Emissions of some pollutants (e.g. carbon monoxide) are less than those from flaring, because of the more controlled combustion conditions employed in energy recovery schemes. Using landfill gas for energy generation provides an additional incentive to maximise gas collection at a site and so reduces uncontrolled methane emissions. While some noise is generated by the gas utilisation equipment, appropriate siting and design can keep noise levels within acceptable limits.

5.1.7 Energy crops

Energy crops are plants grown specifically for use as a fuel. Energy crops are important as a renewable energy technology because they can be grown to meet the needs of the market. This sets them apart from other renewable resources that must be harnessed where they occur. In common with other biomass options, energy crops provide energy on demand and are not as subject to variations due to external influences such as the weather. In these respects they resemble the fossil fuels on which the current energy infrastructure is based.

The most advanced energy crop for northern European conditions is coppiced willow, grown on a rotation of 2 to 4 years. This is commonly referred to as short rotation coppice (SRC). The crop is established by planting 10–15 000 cuttings per hectare. After 1 year these are cut back close to the ground ('coppiced'), which causes them to form multiple shoots . The crop is then allowed to grow for 2 to 4 years, after which time the fuel is harvested by cutting the stems close to the soil level. This cycle of harvest and re-growth can be repeated many times. The shoots can be harvested as chips, short billets or as whole stems of 25–50 mm diameter and 3–4 metres length.

Of the grasses, those of tropical origin use sunlight more efficiently and produce higher yields than native plants. However, they are less well adapted to the climate in the north of the UK. *Miscanthus* has been the most extensively studied. It is similar to coppice in that it is perennial and harvested in the winter, but on a 1 year cycle. Similar machinery could be used for harvesting, and the chipped product requires the same infrastructure for storage and transport. The fuel has a similar calorific value to wood and could possibly be used in power plants designed for wood or agricultural residues. The harvested fuel is

relatively dry and the yield potential is significantly higher than that for willow.

It is also feasible to convert some crops into liquid fuels. These are normally crops with a high protein and carbohydrate content compared with food crops. For example, the oil from crops such as rape can be converted to a diesel substitute, known as bio-diesel. Crops producing carbohydrates such as cereals or sugar beet can be fermented to give alcohol that can be used as a petrol extender. Alcohol can also be used as a petrol replacement, although this will necessitate extensive engine modifications. However, the capital and operating costs of producing liquid fuels from carbohydrates and oilseeds are unlikely to reduce significantly in the future.

5.1.8 Agricultural and forestry residues

Agricultural and forestry wastes fall into two main groups: dry combustible wastes (e.g. forestry residues, straw, and chicken litter) and wet wastes (e.g. green agricultural crop wastes, such as root vegetable tops, and farm slurries). The first group can be converted to electricity and/or heat by combustion. The second group is best used to produce methane-rich biogas through the process of anaerobic digestion (also see section 5.1.5).

Typical costs for a power plant based on conventional boiler technology for clean forestry residues will be around £1600 per kW installed for a 5 MW installation. Poultry litter plants tend to be more expensive due to the nature of the fuel. Capital costs for AD plant vary from £3000 to £7000 per kW, depending on size.

Straw is available from cereal and other crops such as oilseeds. It is produced seasonally and is localised, with highest production centred in East Anglia. As straw is a low-density material, transport and storage can be a significant part of the fuel cost. This has led to the adoption of large high-density Hesston bales. Straw is a relatively low heating value fuel, with an energy content of around 18 GJ·(dry tonne)$^{-1}$. An increasing number of UK farms have straw-fired boilers to help meet their on-site heat requirements. Currently, these offset the use of the equivalent of 72 thousand tonnes of oil a year.

Forestry residue wood for fuel, in commercial quantities, can be produced as a by-product of forestry/tree management. The residual material from these operations (e.g. branches, treetops) is a clean fuel that can be converted to useful energy. Wood has a relatively low calorific value of around 19 GJ·(dry tonne)$^{-1}$ and, when harvested, has a moisture content around 55% by weight. In the UK, contracts to generate electricity from forestry residues have been allocated under the NFFO. Outside of the NFFO, electricity generation from wood fuel is restricted in the UK to locations where sawmill or paper-making residues are co-fired with fossil fuels in existing plant. Domestic wood use is also significant in the UK, offsetting the use of the equivalent of 200 thousand tonnes of oil a year. This includes the use of logs in open fires, Aga-type cookers/boilers and other wood-burning stoves.

Poultry litter is the bedding material from broiler houses. It usually comprises material such as wood shavings, shredded paper or straw, mixed with droppings. As received, the material has a calorific value slightly lower

---

* 1 terawatt = 1 × 10^{12} watts

than wood at 9–15 GJ/tonne. It has a high variable moisture content of between 20% and 50% depending on husbandry practices.

Wet agricultural wastes or farm slurries are derived from three major sources: cattle, pigs and poultry. (*Note*: this is different to poultry bedding material.) When not correctly managed, these slurries can present serious environmental problems, e.g. by polluting watercourses and producing odours. Farm slurries can be turned into fuel through AD. Typically, 40–60% of the organic matter present is converted to biogas; the remainder consists of a stabilised residue with some value as a soil conditioner. The technology is now well developed and a range of digesters are commercially available. Six projects have received NFFO contracts to generate electricity from farm slurries using AD.

Green agricultural residues mainly arise from the processing of root vegetables and sugar beet. Most are produced seasonally and can present the farmer with a disposal problem. Currently, they are either ploughed-in green, allowed to rot prior to ploughing-in, or left to decompose. A further option is to use the wastes as animal feed. The use of these wastes as a fuel has not been seriously considered. However, they can be co-digested with slurry to produce methane. The addition of green wastes will increase both the amount of methane produced and the fibre content, and therefore the value, of the final compost.

There are few environmental concerns regarding the use of forestry residues as fuel. Forestry machinery can compact the soil and after a site has been cleared there is more water run-off, which could lead to soil erosion. However, these are manageable by using good forestry practice. There are no significant environmental issues related to using straw as a fuel. There are no emissions requirements for AD plant, but there are requirements regarding the handling of the potentially explosive methane produced by the process. For chicken litter, gaseous emissions from the combustion process can be reduced by state-of-the-art clean-up technology to meet statutory requirements. Ash produced as a combustion by-product can be recovered from the furnace ('bottom ash') and from the exhaust flue (via a baghouse filter). It can then be used as an environmentally friendly fertiliser. Transporting fuel to a power plant could increase traffic locally and will need to be taken into account in planning. All power plant will need to meet emissions regulations appropriate to their size and location.

5.1.9   Active solar heating (solar water heating panels)

Active solar heating systems convert solar radiation into heat which can be used directly, stored for use in the future, or converted to electricity. They are widely used around the world to provide domestic hot water, particularly where sunshine is plentiful and fuel is relatively expensive. Due to the climate, active solar heating in the UK is best suited to low temperature heating applications, which do not require direct sunlight, the great majority of installed systems being in dwellings.

The most common approach is the provision of heat for domestic hot water. These consist of solar collectors, a preheat tank (optional), a pump, a control unit, connecting pipes, the normal hot water tank, and a conventional heat source. The collectors are usually mounted on the roof and provide heat to a fluid circulated between the collectors and a water tank. In most domestic hot water (HWS) systems, only the collectors are visible, similar in appearance to dark roof lights. A rule of thumb is that a house requires 2–4 m² of panel area, which will yield around a 1000 kW·h per year of heat and meet around half of annual hot water requirements. BS 5918[8] gives a method for sizing solar hot water systems for individual houses, taking account of climate, panel orientation and collector performance. CIBSE Guide B1[9] and GIR 58[10] also provide further details.

The efficiency of solar collector panels depends on a number of factors[11], including the type of collector, the spectral response of the absorbing surface, the extent to which the panel is insulated and the temperature difference between the panel and the ambient air. Different sorts of collectors, which concentrate direct sunlight, can be used to produce electricity although climatic conditions appear to make this thermal solar power technology impractical in the UK.

The current commercial price of a typical hot water system for a house varies greatly from £2000 to £6000. It is possible to buy systems that can be installed as a 'DIY' kit, which can be considerably cheaper. The installation of systems in new-build properties, with no value added tax (VAT) payable and more straightforward installation, is also significantly cheaper than retrofit applications. There are some indications that the cost of systems is falling, increasing the economic attractiveness of systems and the range of viable applications. Typically, solar collectors cost £300 to £750 per m² to install (depending on the technology) and would produce approximately 300 kW·h·m⁻² of hot water in the UK. Evacuated tube systems are about 30% more efficient but are at the expensive end of the market. A collector area of 4–5 m² can save approximately 1 tonne of CO_2 emissions per year.

Active solar heating systems can be used for water heating in non-domestic applications, e.g. for caravan sites, holiday camps, office buildings, hotels and guest houses, and schools. They can also be used to provide space heating in houses. However, this is not common because large areas of collectors (typically 20–40 m²) are required to supply heat in winter, when it is most needed.

The other major use for active solar technology in the UK is for swimming pool heating. A collector area equivalent to more than half the pool area is usually required. The pool water can be passed directly through the collectors, often using the filter pump, though for larger pools a more complex system is required.

Active solar heating offers the advantages common to all renewable technologies, e.g. in terms of displacing fossil-fuelled power production. The only visible part of the system is the collector array and the extent of visual impact would therefore be determined by the size of the array in any given instance. The environmental impact of collector manufacture is limited to that associated with the normal production of the component materials, e.g. steel, copper, glass and insulation.

5.1.10   Photovoltaics

Solar radiation can be converted directly into electricity using photovoltaic (PV) cells. The technology was first utilised for powering satellites, but is now increasingly being used to meet electricity requirements around the world. PV materials are usually solid-state semiconductors which generate electricity when exposed to light. The PV material and its electrical contacts are usually referred to as a cell. There are three common types of PV cell and they have different efficiencies, costs and appearances. Interconnected cells encapsulated into a sealed unit producing a useful voltage and current are called a PV module.

Building-integrated photovoltaics (BIPV) is achieved by using PVs to replace conventional roofing or cladding materials such as tiles or natural stone. CIBSE TM 25: *Understanding building-integrated photovoltaics*[12] provides detailed design guidance. BIPV systems have been identified as the most attractive means of exploiting PV technology in the UK. This is because they reduce CO_2 emissions, have no additional requirement for land and most importantly the cost of the PV system can be offset against the cost of the building element it replaces. PV is a mature technology, and some systems have already been in use for 15 years. In the UK, it is estimated that installed PV rose from 172 kW in 1992 to about 400 kW in 1996, and is now about 1 MW. One reason for this expansion is the technology's potential, via stand-alone systems, to provide power to locations not served by the electricity grid. However this installation rate is likely to be eclipsed by installation of grid-connected systems which attract a substantial government subsidy. This subsidy is potentially as much as £150m. over ten years, and is intended to encourage a British PV industry, leading to a dramatic fall in prices.

The main components of a PV system are an array of PV modules containing photovoltaic cells which generate DC power and a power conditioning unit which converts the DC power to AC with associated control and protection equipment. The electrical efficiency of most modules is less than 15% and can be as low as 5%. The energy output is mainly dependent on the amount of solar radiation available which ranges from 1000 $kW \cdot h \cdot m^{-2}$ in southern England to 800 $kW \cdot h \cdot m^{-2}$ in northern Scotland. Shading (from other buildings etc.), temperature and soiling can also have a significant effect on the system output. 1 m^2 of monocrystaline array will produce roughly 150 $kW \cdot h$ per year (assuming reasonable tilt, orientation and system efficiency). A roof mounted system will produce approximately 700 $kW \cdot h$/yr for each kW installed.

Typically, PV currently costs £280 to £780 per m^2 installed and would produce approximately 70–150 $kW \cdot h \cdot m^{-2}$ of renewable energy each year in the UK (depending on the technology). A PV installation is unlikely to pay for itself in energy savings alone over its useful life. However, BIPV can be used to replace building cladding or be used as roofing material, in a variety of colours. A 1 kW panel can save 0.5 to 1 tonne of CO_2 emissions per year.

BIPV systems are still expensive although costs have been reducing. Installed costs range from £500 per m^2 for roof tile systems to over £900 per m^2 for the most expensive facades. Smaller systems are relatively more expensive. For a building-integrated PV system, costs will depend on system size and module detail, but typically installed costs are likely to be in the range of £5 to £10 per W.

The operation and maintenance costs of a PV system appear to be low, but actual maintenance costs for mains-connected PV systems are still a relatively unknown quantity. For example, it is unclear whether the inverter will need to be replaced during the lifetime of the PV system. Routine maintenance may include the cleaning of the PV modules, although if this is part of routine building maintenance the cost may not be directly attributable to the PV. It is expected that further development of PV material, manufacturing improvements and higher-volume production will bring costs of PV modules down over the next 25–30 years. Improvements in costs are also expected for inverters and wiring.

PV is emission-free, systems require no fuel or cooling water, and therefore raise no issues of supply or use of these resources. Silent operation and suitability for integration into buildings make PV particularly appropriate for the urban environment. However, the manufacture of PV materials involves the use of a number of hazardous materials.

5.1.11   Passive solar design

Passive solar design (PSD) uses the fabric and orientation of a building to capture the sun's energy. It thus reduces the need for artificial heating, cooling and lighting.

PSD is not new. Modifying the design of buildings to encourage natural ventilation or to let in more daylight has been common practice since the beginnings of architecture. Usually, modifications were made for aesthetic or health reasons. People prefer daylight and appreciate the other benefits of windows, e.g. providing a view and natural ventilation. It is only recently that the potential energy benefits of the wider use of PSD have been appreciated. PSD measures need to be considered in combination with the energy efficiency of the building as a whole; an integrated approach is required to achieve an optimal result. This approach to building design is covered in detail in sections 2 to 4.

The basic principles behind PSD are as follows:

— *Heating*: orientating buildings, laying out rooms and distributing glazing in a way that allows the interior to be heated by solar radiation, while at the same time minimising heat losses from shaded facades and maintaining thermal comfort of the building's occupants.

— *Lighting*: arranging glazing to increase the amount of daylight available, so reducing the need for artificial lighting, while maintaining visual comfort.

— *Ventilation and cooling*: allowing solar-heated air to assist natural convection e.g. using the stack effect, so minimising the need for mechanical ventilation and utilising cool night time air to minimise the use of mechanical cooling systems.

PSD is a proven design approach that can be cost-effective in terms of reduced energy costs for buildings. If incorporated at the design stage, the space-heating requirement of individual houses can be reduced by around 1000 kW·h per year. In the UK, significant progress has been made in the non-domestic buildings sector although uptake in the house building sector has been slower due to misconceptions that passive solar houses are more expensive and too futuristic for most buyers' tastes.

Providing adequate attention is paid to good design to avoid problems such as glare and overheating (which could result in additional energy use through increased need for artificial lighting and air conditioning), PSD saves energy. PSD causes no emissions to the environment, apart from those associated with the normal production of building materials and components. There is also increasing evidence that high levels of natural lighting and natural ventilation can significantly improve the working environment inside buildings.

5.1.12 Geothermal heating

There is a large amount of heat just below the Earth's surface and this geothermal energy can be extracted for use in generating electricity or in heating systems. There are two methods of extracting the heat:

— *Aquifers*: geothermal aquifers extract heat from the Earth's crust through deep, naturally occurring, ground waters in porous rocks at depth. A borehole is drilled to access the hot water or steam which is then passed through a heat exchanger located on the surface. If the temperature is about 150 °C then it can be used to generate electricity, otherwise it is more suited as a source of warm water. Use of thermal aquifers is well established in certain geologically favoured countries. A borehole in Southampton has resulted in a district heating scheme in the city centre. However, in the UK there are very few sources above 60 °C, making it one of the lowest potential renewables.

— *Hot dry rocks*: much of the heat in the Earth's surface is stored in relatively impermeable rocks such as granite. Attempts to extract the heat have been based on drilling two holes from the surface. Water is then pumped down one of the boreholes, circulated through the naturally occurring fissures,

and returned to the surface via the second borehole. In the UK it would be necessary to drill to depths of 7 km to reach the temperatures required for electricity production. The engineering of the underground heat exchanger has turned out to be formidable technical problem which has never been satisfactory solved and, as a result, there are no commercial schemes in existence in the world.

5.1.13 Ground and water cooling

There are a range of opportunities for using the natural energy storage of the earth, the sea, rivers and lakes for cooling buildings, see CIBSE Guide B2[13] and GIL 85[14]. Opportunities include:

— *Ground coupling using air*: by passing air through underground pipes at depths of 2–5 m to take advantage of the 12 °C, or lower, soil temperatures. The cooled air from the underground pipes can be used directly to provide cooling although close temperature/humidity control is difficult. During the heating season ground temperatures can be above ambient and these systems can then be used for pre-heating ventilation air.

— *Ground water cooling (aquifers)*: consist of two wells drilled into the ground. Water is pumped from one well to the other via a heat exchanger to provide cooling. Ground water has greater thermal capacity than air, allowing more energy to be stored. It is also possible to reverse the flow during winter to take advantage of the heat collected during summer.

— *Ground coupled heat pumps*: using the thermal mass of the ground as a heat sink to improve the COP of a reversible heat pump, see 10.1.5.

— *Surface water cooling (sea/river/lake)*: by pumping water from these sources and extracting cooling via a heat exchanger it is possible to directly cool the space/supply air or to pre-cool the chilled water circuit. Great depth is required to reach cold water and fouling/corrosion problems must be avoided. Alternatively, the surface water could be used as a heat sink/source for a heat pump.

Table 5.1 Factors to consider when choosing fuels

Factor	Coal	Waste-derived fuel	Natural gas	Fuel oil	Electricity	Multi-fuel	Waste heat
Local availability							
Security of supply	—	3	—	—	—	3	5
Fuel cost	3	3	3	3	5 5	3 3	3 3
Flexibility/ controllability	5	5	3	3	3	5	5
Capital cost of plant	5	5	—	—	3	5 5	—
Space and civil works required	5	5	3	—	3	5	—
Complexity of ancillary plant	5	5	—	—	—	5	5
Attendance and maintenance	5	5	3	—	3 3	5	5
Chimney requirements	—	—	3	—	3 3	5	—
Noise	5	5	—	—	—	5	—
Environmental emissions	5	—	—	—	5	—	3

Key: 5 unfavourable; 3 favourable (double ticks/crosses emphasise favourability/unfavourability)

5.2 Fuels

5.2.1 Fuel selection

Where it is not possible to use renewable sources of energy, an essential part of minimising emissions from buildings is to use the most environmentally friendly fuel possible. Fuel selection is a strategic decision that can drive the choice and design of building services and hence future energy efficiency. The decision is often dominated by practical issues, such as the availability of fuels on site, access for delivery, as well as the space and cost of fuel storage. Fuel costs are a significant driving force but environmental emissions should be regarded as a key issue.

Typical fuel specifications and combustion details are shown in CIBSE Guide C5: *Fuels and combustion*[15] and CIBSE Guide B1[9]. Conversion factors are provided in Appendix A2. Table 5.1 summarises the factors to consider when choosing different fuels.

5.2.1.1 Fuel prices

The price of fuel remains a very important factor affecting fuel choice and a strong determinant of life-cycle cost. Current energy prices and recent price trends may be obtained from the Department of Trade and Industry[16]. Even though prices fluctuate, electricity has a much higher price (p/kW·h) than gas, oil and coal. Electricity should therefore be reserved for purposes in which its special advantages are needed. This normally precludes its use as a principal source of space heating, although it can be economical for localised and occasional use, particularly as radiant 'spot' heating.

5.2.1.2 Environmental emissions of fuels

The use of energy affects the environment both at the point of use and indirectly, through the upstream activities associated with production, conversion and delivery. It can have detrimental impacts locally on air quality and acid deposition and, on a global scale, on stratospheric ozone depletion and greenhouse gas concentration in the atmosphere, which is widely recognised as a cause of climate change.

Burning fossil fuels results in emissions to the environment and contributes to the threat of climate change, primarily through carbon dioxide emissions. Table 5.2 shows a comparison of the different fuels and their relative CO_2 emissions. Electricity production causes emissions at the power station whereas on-site use of gas etc. results in local emissions. Use of electricity generally results in about twice the emissions (per kW·h consumed) than most other fuels. However, the factor is generally falling as power stations become more efficient and use fuels with lower CO_2 emissions. By comparison, renewable sources of energy produce little or no greenhouse and acid gas emissions. Table 5.3 shows an example of how to calculate the CO_2 emissions from a building using these CO_2 equivalents.

The *Digest of UK Energy Statistics*[5] shows that the generation mix for electricity in the UK has changed radically since 1992, when gas-fired power stations began to come on stream displacing coal-fired plant. In 1991, 65% of all fuel used for generating electricity was coal and less than 1% gas. In 2000, these proportions had changed to 33% and 35% respectively. Taking account of the higher efficiency of gas generation, the proportion of electricity supplied from gas generation is even higher, at 39% (c.f. 31% from coal generation). Nuclear power accounted for 21% of electricity supplied in 2000, a proportion that has not changed substantially over recent years. Hydro-electricity contributed only 1.3%, although pumped-storage hydroelectric stations perform an important role in balancing system loads. The shift towards gas generation has several important implications. Gas produces negligible emissions of sulphur dioxide to the atmosphere, and reduced concentrations of other atmospheric pollutants. The amount of carbon dioxide released per unit of heat energy obtained from gas is also lower than that for coal and the current generation of gas-fired power stations using combined cycle technology are more efficient than coal-fired stations. The overall effect is that the electricity generated by gas is responsible for the emission of under half of the carbon dioxide per unit than electricity generated by coal.

5.2.1.3 Other factors affecting fuel choice

Availability of a mains supply of natural gas is a key factor in the choice of fuel, given its advantages of clean combustion and low price. In remote areas, the absence of mains gas normally leaves a choice between oil, LPG and solid fuel, all of which require significant space for storage and access for delivery. Solid fuel is often the lowest in price but has greater maintenance costs than oil or LPG.

Table 5.2 CO_2 equivalents of electricity and fuels (1998 data)[17]

Energy source	CO_2 emission / kg·(kW·h)$^{-1}$
Electricity (grid):	0.43*†
Coal (typical)	0.29
Coke	0.42
Coke oven gas	0.24
Smokeless fuel	0.39
Natural gas	0.19
Petroleum (average)	0.27
Heavy fuel oil	0.26
Diesel	2.98 kg/litre
Petrol	2.54 kg/litre
Propane	1.75 kg/litre

* per kW·h delivered
† 1998 figure; this has been adopted as the official standard for carbon dioxide reporting until further notice

Table 5.3 Example of calculation of building CO_2 emissions

Fuel	Consumption	Delivered energy / kW·h	CO_2 ratio	CO_2 emission / kg
Oil	27 000 litres	286 200	0.27	77 274
Gas	—	140 000	0.19	26 600
Electricity		35 000	0.43	15 050
				Total: 118 924

LPG may be cleanest and most convenient but is generally significantly more expensive than heating oil. Renewables now present a significant option for fuel supply in more remote buildings where electricity and/or gas supply would be costly or impractical.

5.2.2 Electricity

Electricity is generally a premium fuel but relatively expensive (currently 2.5 to 7 p/kW·h). Although it is usually easy and cheap to install electricity supplies, and it is clean at the point of use, some forms of generation cause high CO_2 emissions, see 5.2.1. High voltage transformer losses can be around 1% of energy consumed on larger installations and therefore transformer efficiency should be considered at the design stage.

Electricity is the most versatile form in which energy is delivered and may serve almost any end-use of energy, including those for which fuels are consumed directly. However, the high quality and versatility of electricity must be seen in the context of its high cost, which reflects the high primary energy input to electricity generation.

Lower power factors lead to higher electricity costs, greater energy consumption and larger switchgear and cables. It is desirable to keep power factors above about 0.9 and this should be addressed when selecting equipment, particularly lighting, electronics and motors. Where necessary, power factor correction equipment should be installed. For example, improving the power factor of a 100 kW demand from 0.75 to 0.93, the current would be reduced from 186 A to 150 A. Typically, a payback period of less than two years could be expected depending upon the supply contract and usage.

5.2.3 Gaseous fuels

The key properties of the main gaseous fuels are shown in Table 5.4.

5.2.3.1 Natural gas

Natural gas is a convenient, cheap and clean fuel, but it is not available on all sites and connection costs can be significant. Where gas is supplied at high pressure, temperature and pressure adjustments usually need to be made to establish the actual volume used. Care should also be taken to ensure that the true calorific value is used in any energy calculation.

5.2.3.2 Liquid petroleum gas (LPG)

Liquid petroleum gas (LPG) is a clean fuel (normally propane or butane) but comparatively expensive. It is usually delivered by tanker (requiring access) and stored as a liquid under pressure. Consumption is normally measured using a standard gas meter.

5.2.4 Liquid fuels

Fuel oil is supplied in a range of densities and calorific values from kerosene to heavy fuel oil. Heavier fuel oils are generally cheaper but have lower calorific values and require heating to ensure that they have the correct viscosity at the burner. They also produce more harmful emissions when burnt. Monitoring fuel deliveries does not provide an accurate reflection of consumption and integrating meters should be installed for monitoring and targeting purposes, see section 5.3.

BS 2869[18] contains specifications for various classes of liquid fuels designated by the letters A to G. The fuels commonly used for heating are Class C2 (kerosene or burning oil), Class D (gas oil), Class E (light fuel oil), Class F (medium fuel oil) and Class G (heavy fuel oil). The key properties of these fuels are shown in Table 5.5. More detailed information can be found in CIBSE Guide C[15].

Fuel oils Class E to H require heating to provide the recommended storage temperatures, which are shown in

Table 5.4 Properties of commercial gas supplies at standard temperature and pressure

Gas	Property			
	Density relative to air	Gross calorific value / MJ·m^{-3}	Supply/working pressure / Pa	Stoichiometric air-to-gas volume ratio
Natural gas	0.60	38.7	1750 to 2750	9.73
Commercial propane	1.45 to 1.55	93	3700	24
Commercial butane	1.9 to 2.10	122	2800	30

Table 5.5 Key properties of typical petroleum fuels

Fuel	Property				
	Density at 15 °C / kg·m^{-3}	Kinematic viscosity at 40 °C / mm^2·s^{-1}	Kinematic viscosity at 100 °C / mm^2·s^{-1}	Gross calorific value / MJ·kg^{-1}	Net calorific value / MJ·kg^{-1}
Class C2	803	1.0 to 2.0	—	46.4	43.6
Class D	850	1.5 to 5.5	—	45.5	42.7
Class E	940	—	≤ 8.2	42.5	40.1
Class F	970	—	≤ 20.0	41.8	39.5
Class G	980	—	≤ 40.0	42.7	40.3

Table 5.6 Storage temperatures for fuel oils

Class	Minimum storage temperature / °C	
	Storage	Outflow
E	10	10
F	25	30
G	40	50
H	45	55

Table 5.6. Heating may be provided by steam or hot water coils, or by electric immersion heaters. It is usual to maintain tanks at the temperatures given in column 2 of Table 5.6 and raise the temperature further by a separate outflow heater to the level shown in column 3. Class C and D fuels do not generally require heating, but some Class D fuels may require heat to ensure an adequate flow of oil.

5.2.5 Solid fuels

Solid fuels are normally inexpensive although they require more handling, boiler management and storage space. They also have significant environmental impact, see 5.2.1. Coal is classified according to its chemical composition and graded according to size. CIBSE Guide C[15] gives the properties of numerous varieties of coal, including moisture, ash and sulphur content. Gross calorific value ranges from 24 to 34 MJ·kg^{-1}. These fuels are normally delivered by weight and come in various sizes and calorific values. Unless there is a recording meter on the grate or screw feed to the boiler, accurate measurement of consumption can be difficult. A crude arrangement using storage bays can be employed to estimate usage.

5.3 Distributed energy sources and CHP

5.3.1 Combined heat and power (CHP)

For many buildings, combined heat and power (CHP) offers a highly economic method of providing heat and power which is less environmentally harmful than conventional methods. Where applicable, CHP is the single most effective means of reducing building-related CO_2 emissions and running costs. Building designers, specifiers and operators should always consider the option of CHP as an alternative means of supplying energy.

A full option appraisal[19,20] should always be carried out when replacing major plant or designing new systems. If CHP begins to look like a viable option then a full feasibility study will need to be carried out. For more detailed information, see CIBSE AM12[21].

The use of CHP has proved highly cost-effective in a wide range of buildings[22,23]. There are now over 1000 installations providing more than 300 MW electrical power (MWe) in buildings. Small scale CHP is used as the prime source of heat and power in many hospitals, hotels, leisure centres, universities, residential building and defence establishments. Large-scale CHP installations[24] are being used with community heating schemes[25] and on some multi-building sites such as major hospitals, airports and universities.

The UK government has set a target to encourage the installation of at least 10 000 MWe of CHP by 2010 which amounts to more than 20% of the Kyoto carbon target. Roughly 1000 MWe of this is expected to be in buildings and community heating. 'The CHP Club' (www.chpclub.com) has been established under the Carbon Trust's Action Energy programme to support existing and potential CHP users by providing a forum for sharing knowledge and experience of CHP. Government initiatives also include exemption from Climate Change Levy for 'good quality' CHP, which can often turn a 5 year payback into 4 years and tax incentives called Enhanced Capital Allowances (ECAs) (www.eca.gov.uk) are also available to encourage the purchase of 'good quality' CHP. The CHP Quality Assurance Scheme[26] (CHPQA) sets out what is meant by 'good quality' CHP.

Building Regulations Approved Document L2★[1] suggests minimum efficiencies (based on maximum carbon intensities) for heating systems at full load and 30% load, based on the overall output of the system, as a means of compliance with the Building Regulations 2000[27]. Where CHP is included then special adjustments can be made to take into account the benefit of the on-site electricity generation in reducing emissions from power stations. Including CHP is therefore a simple way of meeting these regulations, particularly the requirement at 30% load. These regulations apply when replacing boilers or a heating system as well as in new and refurbished buildings.

5.3.1.1 Types of CHP

Most small scale CHP installations in buildings are packaged units, based on reciprocating engines, with an electrical output not exceeding 1 MWe and usually less than 500 kWe. Small scale units are most commonly retrofitted to existing installations although CHP can prove to be even more beneficial in new buildings. Small gas turbines and 'micro-turbines' are now available for these applications (see later). Larger multi-building installations (e.g. hospitals, universities) commonly use gas turbines or diesel engines, fuelled by either gas or oil. Gas turbines are favoured particularly when high grade heat is required for steam raising or if a high ratio of electricity to heat is required through operation in combined cycle mode.

CHP installations can run on natural gas, bio-gas or diesel (gas oil). They have a similar reliability to conventional boilers and availability factors of over 95% are common. The energy balance of a typical CHP unit is shown in Figure 5.1.

The high efficiencies achieved are much greater than conventional power stations, thus reducing the amount of primary energy required to satisfy a given heat and electrical load. Site energy cost can be reduced significantly using CHP. The primary energy consumed on a site

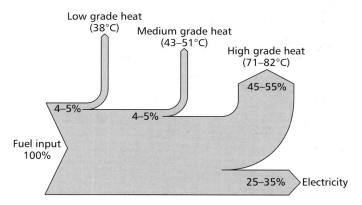

Figure 5.1 Energy balance of a typical reciprocating CHP unit[22]

★ Requirements may differ for Scotland[2] and Northern Ireland[3]

will increase due to CHP but overall energy consumption and CO_2 emissions will decrease[24].

Simple paybacks of 4 to 5 years can be achieved if the CHP unit operates for about 4500 hours per year or about 12–14 hours per day. Such paybacks can only be achieved where there is a significant demand for heating and hot water, e.g. in hospitals, hotels or swimming pools. However, CHP can be used to provide the heat source for absorption chillers to supply cooling and standby generation capacity (see 5.3.1.4).

CHP plant should always operate as the lead boiler to maximise savings. The electricity generated is best utilised on site, although it is also possible to export electricity back to the electricity companies. This is often uneconomic since the 'sell back' tariffs are usually at low rates.

CHP cannot be considered in isolation and requires good integration with other energy systems on site. It is unlikely that all the power and heat requirements will be supplied by the CHP plant. Additional heat and/or power will usually be required from conventional sources.

5.3.1.2   Connection to heating plant

Although CHP plant often replaces significant boiler capacity, boilers are retained to meet peak heat demands. Most small-scale units provide low temperature hot water (LTHW), i.e. 80–90 °C, and can therefore be directly connected to standard building heating systems.

A CHP unit can be connected into an existing heating system in two ways, see Figure 5.2.

— in series as a by-pass in a suitable return to the boilers (generally used in new installations)

— in parallel with the boilers (usually for retrofit installations).

Connection in series is most frequently used when retrofitting CHP to an existing heating system, as it creates the minimum interference with existing flow and control arrangements. Connection in parallel is more common in completely new installations, especially where the CHP unit is likely to supply a significant proportion of the total heat load.

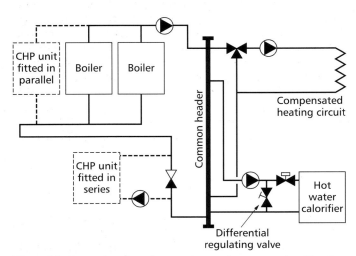

Figure 5.2 Alternative ways of connecting CHP into conventional heating plant[22]

Whichever connection method is used, it is vital that the control system ensures that the CHP unit runs as the lead boiler, thus maximising its operating hours. Careful consideration must be given to the integration of the CHP plant into the heating circuit to ensure correct balancing of flows through the various items of plant. Due to the number of heat exchangers, CHP plant has a significantly higher water flow resistance than conventional boiler plant. General Information Report GIR 82[23] illustrates these requirements in some detail.

5.3.1.3   Connection to electrical services

In building applications, the CHP generator is most commonly connected to the low voltage distribution network. The grid can then either meet the peak demand or supply the whole demand if the CHP is not operating. In order to operate the CHP unit in parallel with the grid, technical approval must be obtained from the electricity supplier. It will be necessary to ensure that the CHP unit can be isolated from the grid in the event of a failure of either the CHP unit or the grid. The existing electrical services may require some modification in order to achieve this when installing CHP.

5.3.1.4   CHP units as standby generators

Where standby generators are required, there is an opportunity to use a CHP unit to provide all or part of the standby capacity. By using CHP, the reliability of the standby facility is sometimes improved over conventional generators as the engine is operated more frequently and for longer periods. Furthermore, the capital saved by reducing conventional standby capacity can be offset against the cost of the CHP.

However, if CHP is to provide all the standby capacity, it may be necessary to install more than one CHP unit to ensure that the facility is available even when maintenance is being carried out. Heat dump radiators may be required so that the CHP can still provide standby power when there is a low heat demand. It is also important to take into account the special control requirements necessary for any standby generators, see CIBSE AM8[28].

5.3.1.5   Plant sizing and economic appraisal

Good Practice Guides GPG 176[22] and 227[29] provide a methodology and examples for assessing the financial benefits of introducing a CHP scheme. Simple payback may be acceptable at a very early stage of the investigation, but a more rigorous approach using discounted cash flow and life cycle costing is required for the detailed appraisal. The economics of CHP vary significantly with changes in fuel prices and a sensitivity analysis should be carried out to assess the risks of future changes in fuel prices.

The capital investment in CHP plant may be substantial, so it is essential to achieve maximum returns. Idle plant accrues no benefits, so it is important that the CHP plant operates for as many hours as possible. This means matching CHP capacity to base heat and power loads. CHP in buildings is usually sized on heat demand, as this is generally the limiting factor, although the most cost-effective solution often involves sizing slightly above the base heat load with some modulating capability and/or heat dumping. Any feasibility study should optimise the plant size by assessing the economics of a range of CHP sizes. Overall efficiency does fall when modulating or dumping heat whereas maintenance costs remain the same. A careful balance must therefore be achieved between the drop in efficiency and the increased savings.

Economic viability is heavily dependent on the demand for heat and the price of electricity and gas. Detailed energy demand profiles for both heat and electricity are fundamental to accurately sizing CHP and hence its ultimate viability[23]. A computer program for sizing CHP and optimising the capacity of CHP units is available free of charge under the government's Action Energy programme[30]. When sizing the CHP plant, it is important that all other no-cost and low-cost energy efficiency measures have been carried out first, in order to reach 'true' energy demands.

Figure 5.3 shows an example load duration curve of a system with two engines, one of 180 kW (thermal) running for about 6500 hours per annum and a second of 200 kW running for about 5000 hours. The remaining thermal load should be met by the conventional boiler plant. Designers can use this technique to optimise the number and size of CHP units alongside the top-up boilers required.

5.3.1.6 Financing options

Whilst the capital and installation costs of CHP plant are significantly higher than conventional boiler plant, CHP can yield very considerable savings in running costs. Any economic appraisal should only consider the marginal capital cost of CHP plant over and above any avoided costs of boiler or standby generation plant. A range of alternative financial arrangements exist, see GPG 176[22], including:

— *Capital purchase*: in this case the host organisation bears all the capital cost, and realises all the subsequent savings.

— *Equipment supplier finance* (ESF): where the CHP supplier offers an arrangement whereby they supply and maintain the equipment free of charge in exchange for a proportion of the savings achieved. This is typically for the site that does not

have funds available and is looking for a straight-forward 'one-stop' approach to CHP.

— *Energy services companies* (ESCO): formerly known as contract energy management (CEM) companies, whereby an organisation contracts out its energy services. Contracts can be based on a fixed fee, an agreed unit price for energy (energy supply) or a shared savings approach.

5.3.1.7 Maintenance

CHP requires more maintenance than conventional boiler plant. This represents a significant running cost which must be taken into account in the feasibility study. Good maintenance underpins economic outcome, maximising availability and minimising downtime. Percentage availability and reliability are key factors that represent the success of the maintenance regime. Maintenance is nearly always contracted out to a specialist company, usually the CHP supplier itself. Contracts are usually based on performance, typically guaranteeing an availability well above 90%, see GPG 226[32]. Typical maintenance costs are as shown in Table 5.7. Example maintenance schedules are shown in GPG 227[29] and CIBSE AM12[21].

Table 5.7 Typical CHP maintenance costs

Maintenance option	Cost for stated CHP output / (p/kW·h)	
	50–150 kWe	200–800 kWe
Service only (with remote monitoring including consumables)	0.6–0.7	0.3–0.5
Comprehensive service (with remote monitoring; for a minimum period of five years)	1.1–1.3	0.6–0.9
Comprehensive service (with remote monitoring and performance guarantees normally for a minimum period of five years)	1.3–1.5	0.9–1.3

5.3.1.8 New CHP technologies

Absorption cooling and CHP

Absorption chillers are driven by a supply of heat and linking them with CHP provides a base demand for heat in situations where cooling is required. This combination provides heating, cooling and electricity, and opens up building sectors like air conditioned offices, call centres and internet hotels as potential CHP installations. Absorption units have no CFCs or HCFCs but have a much poorer coefficient of performance than electrically driven chillers, which has a significant effect on the overall economics. The high capital cost and complexity of the plant are also key factors that will influence selection. GPG 256[33] provides detailed guidance on linking CHP and absorption cooling.

Air CHP

These units are based on a CHP unit inside a purpose-built air handler with heat exchangers to give up the recovered heat to the air. Often around 1 MWe output, this type of plant has proved economic in large factory-like spaces such as warehouses and large postal sorting offices.

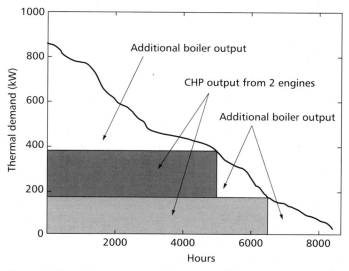

Figure 5.3 Load duration curves and CHP sizing[31] (reproduced from Good Practice Guide GPG 1; Crown copyright)

Micro-turbines

Small gas turbines (down to 500 kWe) have been commonly available for a number of years but the introduction of packaged micro-turbines, with outputs as low as 30 kWe, presents a new option to designers. These units have comparable capital costs to those of reciprocating CHP with lower maintenance costs as there are less moving parts. However, micro-turbines with optional recuperators to pre-heat inlet air have slightly lower efficiency (i.e. 70–75% overall, 25% power, 45–50% MTHW/LTHW). Without a recuperator, efficiencies are generally too low to be classed as good quality CHP. Integrated packages are also available with mini-turbines and absorption cooling, see above.

Micro-CHP

'Micro-CHP' is now available providing outputs of around 5 kW (electricity) and 10–15 kW (heat) and even smaller units (1 kWe) are being offered. These devices are principally aimed at the domestic market

5.3.1.8   CHP: summary

The following summarises the key features of CHP:

— CHP provides on-site electricity generation with heat recovery.

— CHP is typically over 80% efficient.

— The most appropriate applications are those with a year-round heat demand.

— In general, CHP will be economic if it runs for more than 4500 hours per year.

— An independent feasibility study is essential, based on reliable demand profiles.

— CHP should always be the lead 'boiler'.

— The economics of CHP improve if standby generation or boiler replacement is considered.

— Sizing CHP somewhat above the base heat load usually provides the best economics.

— Oversizing CHP leads to excessive heat dumping which undermines the economics.

5.3.2   Fuel cells

Fuel cells are devices that convert the 'free' energy of a chemical reaction, typically between hydrogen and oxygen (generally from air), directly into low-voltage DC electricity and into heat. Fuel cells have the potential to revolutionise the way power is generated. For building applications, fuel cell systems offer modularity, high efficiency across a wide range of loads, minimal environmental impact and opportunities for use as CHP systems[34]. Stationary fuel cells are ideal for power generation, either connected to the electricity grid to provide supplemental power and backup for critical areas, or installed as a grid-independent generator for on-site services. Since fuel cells are silent in operation they reduce noise pollution as well as air pollution. The waste heat from a fuel cell can be used to provide hot water or space heating. They are highly efficient and low maintenance. In the stationary power sector, if fuel cell manufacturing costs are reduced to the level expected through volume production, electricity generating costs would be as low as 3–4 p/kW·h (with no utilisation of heat).

A fuel cell consists of two electrodes sandwiched around an electrolyte. Oxygen (or air) passes over one electrode (the cathode) and hydrogen over the other (the anode), generating electricity, water and heat. Encouraged by a catalyst, the hydrogen atom splits into a proton and an electron, which take different paths to the cathode. The proton passes through the electrolyte. The electrons create a separate current that can be utilized before they return to the cathode, to be reunited with the hydrogen and oxygen in a molecule of water. It will produce energy in the form of electricity and heat as long as fuel is supplied.

Typically, individual fuel cells generate power outputs of a few tens or hundreds of watts. Cells are therefore combined into assemblies known as stacks to provide a larger voltage and current. Fuel cells running on hydrogen derived from a renewable source will emit nothing except water vapour.

A fuel cell system which includes a 'fuel reformer' can utilise the hydrogen from any hydrocarbon fuel, e.g. natural gas, methanol or gasoline. Since the fuel cell relies on chemistry and not combustion, emissions from this type of system would still be much smaller than emissions from the cleanest fuel combustion processes.

A number of types of fuel cell are currently the focus of development work:

— *Solid oxide fuel cells* (SOFCs): significant progress has been made in recent years and SOFCs remain one of the most promising fuel cell systems for stationary power and CHP applications. However, work remains to develop fully engineered systems.

— *Solid polymer fuel cells* (SPFCs): SPFCs are very promising for automotive and stationary applications and there is a massive global effort underway to develop commercial systems. SPFCs are now being demonstrated in a range of commercial applications including buses, cars, CHP and distributed power.

— *Phosphoric acid fuel cells* (PAFCs): PAFCs are more developed than the SOFCs and SPFCs and almost 400 pre-commercial systems have been sold worldwide (total capacity ~44 MW). Demonstrated in the bus sector, it has been pursued as a candidate for CHP and distributed power applications. Increasingly, it is being marketed as a technology for uninterruptible power supplies (UPS) and premium power applications.

— *Alkaline fuel cells* (AFCs): A relatively simple device, the AFC is still the preferred system for applications in space and remains a candidate for mobile applications, particularly in captive fleet vehicles.

— *Molten carbonate fuel cells* (MCFCs): The MCFC is a candidate for stationary power and CHP applications that has been demonstrated at 2 MW scale.

Installed fuel cell capacity is still very small because truly commercially competitive products are not yet available. However, in the future there is likely to be an increasing demand for the high efficiencies and low (even zero) emissions offered by fuel cells. Initial assessments for SPFCs and SOFCs has shown that early markets are now opening up, although widespread uptake is unlikely before 2010. More than 200 stationary fuel cell systems have been installed all over the world in hospitals, nursing homes, hotels, office buildings, schools, power plants, and an airport terminal, providing primary power or backup. In large-scale building systems, fuel cells can reduce facility energy service costs by 20% to 40% over conventional energy service. Many of the prototypes being tested and demonstrated for residential use extract hydrogen from propane or natural gas and are particularly useful for areas that are inaccessible by power lines.

Fuel cells are more efficient than conventional engine-based plant because the lack of a combustion stage means their efficiencies are not limited to those achievable by heat engines. This higher efficiency means reduced energy use and less emission of CO_2.

5.4 Metering

It is essential that feedback mechanisms are put in place to monitor the status and operation of the building. These mechanisms should ensure that building managers can determine whether energy consumption is greater than expected. A key part of this is to include metering and sub-metering in the design to ensure that future building performance can be continually monitored by the building operator. A good maxim is 'if you can't measure it, you can't manage it'.

Good metering is fundamental to the monitoring and targeting process that is, in turn, an essential part of energy management.

Improved sub-metering and benchmarking of end-uses will help operators to understand and manage their buildings better, resulting in greater energy savings. Sub-metering is particularly important where there are large process loads which may mask the true performance of the building, e.g. a computer suite or kitchen. It will also enable fair billing for energy use where a building may be subdivided for occupation by more than one organisation, or where one occupant has a variety of cost centres. It is generally cheaper to install sub-meters as part of the design than to retrofit at a later stage.

A meter that identifies pumps being left on 24 hours a day, seven days a week, may save 60% of the energy passing through it, whereas a meter measuring well-controlled services, or a meter which is not read (or not acted upon) may save nothing. Generally, actions taken as a result of installing and monitoring meters can often save 5–10% of the energy being metered and sometimes much greater than this.

Building Regulations Approved Document L2*[1] includes recommendations for sub-metering in non-domestic buildings. To enable owners/occupiers to measure their actual energy consumption, they should be provided with sufficient energy meters and sub-meters. They should also be given sufficient instructions, including an overall

metering strategy, that show how to attribute energy consumptions to end uses and how meter readings can be used to compare operating performance with published benchmarks. Reasonable provision would be to enable at least 90% of the estimated annual energy consumption of each fuel to be accounted for. Reasonable provision of meters would be to install incoming meters in every building greater than 500 m² gross floor area (including separate buildings on multi-building sites).

Reasonable provision of sub-metering would be to provide additional meters such that the following consumptions can be directly measured or reliably estimated:

— electricity, natural gas, oil and LPG provided to each separately tenanted area that is greater than 500 m²

— energy consumed by plant items with input powers greater or equal to that shown in Table 5.8.

— any heating or cooling supplied to separately tenanted spaces.

— any process load that is to be discounted from the building's energy consumption when comparing measured consumption against published benchmarks.

The Building Regulations seek to ensure that building designers include appropriate metering at the design stage and hence provide building operators with a clear procedure to establish where the majority of energy is being consumed. GIL 65[35] helps designers meet the metering requirements of the Building Regulations in new buildings and major refurbishments. It provides a flexible and practical method to reach a metering schedule and metering strategy, both of which should be included in the building log book and the necessary meters included on the design drawings.

Ideally, enough direct metering would be installed to measure all significant building services and energy end-uses in new buildings. However, this is not always practical or economic. Electricity has a high unit cost but metering is cheap, reliable and accurate, relative to other fuels. Energy used in main plant, e.g. gas or oil, is often easy to meter. However, metering of services such as heat, chilled water and air conditioning can require more complex metering arrangements. Hours-run meters are very cheap and easy to install and can help to deduce the breakdown of energy used on significant items of equipment. Metering costs need to be optimised but accuracy should be the determining factor in deciding whether or not to meter directly. It is almost always cost-effective to purchase meters that allow connection to a building

Table 5.8 Size of plant for which separate metering would be reasonable

Plant item	Rated input power / kW
Boiler installations comprising one or more boilers or CHP plant feeding a common distribution circuit	50
Chiller installations comprising one or more chiller units feeding a common distribution circuit	20
Electric humidifiers	10
Motor control centres providing power to fans and pumps	10
Final electrical distribution boards	5

* Requirements may differ for Scotland[2] and Northern Ireland[3]

Table 5.9 Key considerations when selecting meters[34]

Service	Type of meter	Approximate installed cost	Typical accuracy	Key issues
Electricity	Single phase Three phase	£100–200 £500 upwards	±1%	Single or three phase? Will current transformers be needed?
Gas	Diaphragm Turbine	£300–700 £700–1300	±2%	Pressure drop? Will pressure and temperature compensation be needed? (May cost an extra £1000.)
Oil	—	£350–2800	±1%	Strainer needed to avoid blockages?
Water	—	£250–700	±1%	
Heat	Electromagnetic Turbine	£450–1200 £400–900	±(3 to 5)%	Electromagnetic meters are more accurate. Dirty systems can be a problem

management system (BMS) or automatic metering system (AMS). Table 5.9 shows some of the key considerations when selecting meters.

Meters should always be sized to match the actual throughput. Accuracy falls away when very small throughputs are measured and therefore meters must be not be oversized. Smaller meters will cost less and may perform adequately. Check at commissioning that the sum of all the sub-meters is reasonably close to the main meter reading. This may not summate exactly due to differences in accuracy, compensation etc. but significant differences should be investigated.

5.4.1 Practical considerations

5.4.1.1 Electricity meters

Check that any current transformers are matched to the meters, and the correct meter factors are used. Also check that these current transformers are installed the correct way round, otherwise the load on one phase can negate that of the others.

5.4.1.2 Oil, water and heat meters

Install in straight pipework to ensure accurate operation. This is specified by the manufacturer as a number of pipe diameters of straight pipe before and after the meter. Specify this on the design drawings and check at the commissioning stage. Install in clean systems, avoiding heating/cooling systems that carry significant amounts of sludge and particulates. Dirty systems reduce accuracy, reliability and can ultimately lead to blockage. Some meters e.g. oil, may need to have a strainer installed to prevent blockage.

5.4.1.3 Gas meters

To ensure accuracy, adjust readings to compensate for pressure and temperature of the supply, particularly where large volumes are being measured. The lack of temperature/pressure compensation can sometimes explain differences between the sum of sub-meters and the main incoming meter.

5.4.2 Methods of metering

Directly metering all the energy consumption is the best approach. However, Building Regulations Approved Document L2[1] allows various metering methods to be used, providing flexibility where direct metering is impractical or uneconomic. These methods are:

— *Direct metering*: it is always preferable to directly meter as this provides high accuracy and increased reliability in the overall energy audit.

— *Estimation from hours-run* (constant loads only, e.g. fans): install an hours-run meter to measure the operating hours at a constant known load and use the following formula:

$$kW \cdot h/year = kW \times hours~run \times load~factor$$

— *Estimation based on an indirect meter*: use readings from an indirect meter to estimate end use energy consumption (e.g. measure cold feed water consumption and temperature difference to estimate hot water consumption).

— *Estimation by difference*: readings from two direct meters can often be used to estimate a third end use by difference. e.g. measuring total gas consumption and catering gas consumption, the difference being an estimate of the heating/hot water consumption.

— *Estimation of small power usage*: using methods outlined in the section 12.2 it is possible to achieve reasonable estimates of small power loads (e.g. office equipment etc.) without installing extensive metering.

A hierarchy of these metering methods is shown in Figure 5.4 indicating the balance between cost, accuracy, reliability and ease of design/installation. GPG 231[36] provides further information on metering and introducing information systems for energy management.

5.4.3 Building management and automatic meter reading systems

Due to the number of meters and their location it may be impractical to carry out manual meter reading with any regularity. Meter reading may then become too onerous

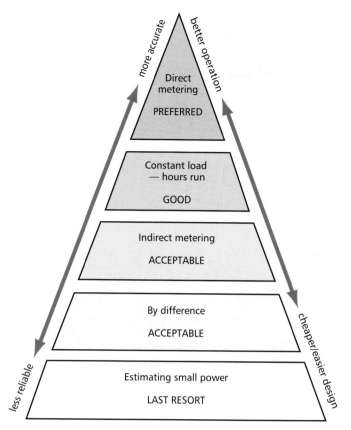

Figure 5.4 Hierarchy of metering methods[34]

for building operators and might not allow them to pick up dynamic wastage that occurs at specific times of the day.

These problems can be overcome by introducing an automatic means of reading meters and analysing the results, such as a building management system (BMS) or a dedicated automatic meter reading system (AMR). BMS/AMR systems are ideal in larger buildings, for building operators with a large stock of buildings or on multi-building sites. They also promote the introduction of energy cost centres to improve energy management and cost reduction. Automatic systems should reduce manpower required for monitoring and may provide results more rapidly. An AMR provides automatic meter reading and automatic real-time analysis. The automatic presentation of consumption data as simple profiles and reports can be the most practical way to get users to recognise problems and take action. This allows consumption to be audited against targets or consumption profiles with exception reporting to highlight waste. The whole process can be automated, providing the busy manager with reports only when something needs rectifying.

Automatic metering can be achieved using a BMS and standard monitoring and targeting (M&T) software but a dedicated AMR system may provide a more tailored solution in many instances. Metering, communication technology and analysis software have become less expensive whilst becoming increasingly reliable.

Demand patterns are readily available from BMS and AMRs and from most energy suppliers. These can be very useful for investigating faults or atypical consumption. Clear analysis is essential as the downfall of monitoring systems is often due to excessive print-outs and incomprehensible

analysis. Consumption profiles give an immediate indication of where and when the problem has occurred e.g. high base/overnight load, out of hours consumption (start-up and shut-down) which would otherwise not be seen.

References

1   *Conservation of fuel and power* The Building Regulations 2000 Approved Document L1/L2 (London: The Stationery Office) (2001)

2   *Technical standards for compliance with the Building Standards (Scotland) Regulations 1990 (as amended)* (London: The Stationery Office) (2001)

3   *Conservation of fuel and power* The Building Regulations (Northern Ireland) 1994 Technical Booklet F (London: The Stationery Office) (1999)

4   *An assessment of renewable energy for the UK* (London: Her Majesty's Stationery Office) (1994)

5   *Digest of UK Energy Statistics* (London: The Stationery Office) (published annually)

6   *Renewable energy* ODPM Planning Policy Guidance 22 (London: Office of the Deputy Prime Minister) (www.odpm.gov.uk)

7   *Local Agenda 21 UK* (London: Improvement and Development Agency) (www.scream.co.uk)

8   BS 5918: 1989: *Code of practice for solar heating systems for domestic hot water* (London: British Standards Institution) (1989)

9   *Heating* CIBSE Guide B1 (London: Chartered Institution of Building Services Engineers) (2002)

10   *Solar air collectors for buildings — domestic and non-domestic* General Information Report GIR 58 (Action Energy) (2000) (www.actionenergy.org.uk)

11   Hunn B D, Carlilse N A, Franta G and Kolar W *Engineering principles and concepts for active solar systems* NREL Report SP271-2829 (Golden, CO: National Renewable Energy Laboratory) (1987) (www.nrel.gov)

12   *Understanding building integrated photovoltaics* CIBSE TM 25 (London: Chartered Institution of Building Services Engineers) (2000)

13   *Ventilation and air conditioning* CIBSE Guide B2 (London: Chartered Institution of Building Services Engineers) (2001)

14   *New ways of cooling — information for building designers* General Information Leaflet GIL 85 (Action Energy) (2001) (www.actionenergy.org.uk)

15   *Fuels and combustion* Section 5 in CIBSE Guide C: *Reference data* (London: Chartered Institution of Building Services Engineers) (2001)

16   *Quarterly energy prices* (London: Department of Trade and Industry) (published quarterly)

17   *Undertaking an industrial energy survey* Good Practice Guide GPG 316 (Action Energy) (2002) (www.actionenergy.org.uk)

18   BS 2869: 1998: *Specification for fuel oils for agricultural, domestic and industrial engines and boilers* (London: British Standards Institution) (1998)

19   *Heating system option appraisal — a managers guide* Good Practice Guide GPG 182 (Action Energy) (1996) (www.actionenergy.org.uk)

20   *Heating system option appraisal — an engineers guide for existing buildings* Good Practice Guide GPG 187 (Action Energy) (1996) (www.actionenergy.org.uk)

21   *Small scale CHP in buildings* CIBSE Applications Manual AM12 (London: Chartered Institution of Building Services Engineers) (1999)

22   *Combined heat and power for buildings* Good Practice Guide GPG 176 (Action Energy) (2004) (www.actionenergy.org.uk)

23   *Managers guide to packaged CHP* GIR 82 (The CHP Club) (www.chpclub.com)

24   *Manager's guide to cusom-built CHP systems* General Information Report GIR 83 (The CHP Club) (www.chpclub.com)

25   *Guide to community heating and CHP* Good Practice Guide GPG 234 (Action Energy) (2002) (www.actionenergy.org.uk)

26   *CHPQA — A quality assurance for combined heat and power* CHP Standard (Action Energy) (2000) (www.actionenergy.org.uk)

27   The Building Regulations 2000 Statutory Instrument 2000 No. 2531 and the Building (Amendment) Regulations 2001 Statutory Instrument 2001 No. 3335 (London: Stationery Office) (2000/2001)

28   *Private and standby generation* CIBSE Applications Manual AM8 (London: Chartered Institution of Building Services Engineers) (1992)

29   *How to appraise CHP* Good Practice Guide GPG 227 (Action Energy) (1997) (www.actionenergy.org.uk)

30   *CHP sizer software package* Version 2.0 (Action Energy) (2004) (www.actionenergy.org.uk)

31   *Guidance notes for the implementation of small scale combined heat and power* GPG 1 (Action Energy) (www.actionenergy.org.uk)

32   *The operation and maintenance of small scale CHP* Good Practice Guide GPG 226 (Action Energy) (1998) (www.actionenergy.org.uk)

33   *An introduction to absorption cooling* Good Practice Guide GPG 256 (Action Energy) (1999) (www.actionenergy.org.uk)

34   Ellis F W *Fuel cells for building applications* (Atlanta, GA: American Society of Heating, Refrigeration and Air Conditioning Engineers) (2002)

35   *Metering energy use in new non-domestic buildings — A guide to help designers meet Part L2 of the Building Regulations* General Information Leaflet GIL 65 (Action Energy 0800 585794) www.actionenergy.org.uk (2002)

35   *Introducing information systems for energy management* Good Practice Guide GPG 231 (Action Energy) (1998) (www.actionenergy.org.uk)

Bibliography

Fundamentals ASHRAE Handbook (Atlanta, GA: American Society of Heating, Refrigeration and Air Conditioning Engineers) (2001)

Environmental code of practice for buildings and their services BSRIA Case Studies CS4/96 (Bracknell: Building Services Research and Information Association) (1996)

Comparative life cycle assessment of modern commercial buildings SC98 (London: Construction Research Communications) (1997)

Fordham M *Photovoltaics in buildings — a design guide* ETSU Report No. S/P2/00282/REP (London: The Stationery Office) (1999)

Sick F and Erge T (eds) *Photovoltaics in buildings* (London: James and James) (1996)

Photovoltaics in Buildings — Testing, commissioning and monitoring guide ETSU Report No. S/P2/00290/REP (London: The Stationery Office) (1998)

Photovoltaics in Buildings — a survey of design tools ETSU Report No. S/P2/00289/REP (London: The Stationery Office) (1997)

Selling CHP electricity to tenants — opportunities for social housing landlords New Practice Report NPR 113 (Action Energy) (1999) (www.actionenergy.org.uk)

Community heating, a guide for housing professionals Good Practice Guide GPG 240 (Action Energy) (1999) (www.actionenergy.org.uk)

Simple measurements for energy and water efficiency in buildings Fuel Efficiency Booklet 21 (Action Energy) (2001) (www.actionenergy.org.uk)

The design team's guide to environmentally smart buildings Good Practice Guide GPG 287 (Action Energy) (2000) (www.actionenergy.org.uk)

Best practice in the specification for offices (Reading: British Council for Offices) (2000)

6 Control strategies

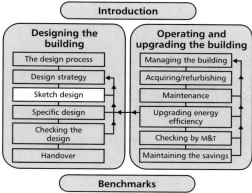

This section sets out some of the key issues to be considered in developing energy efficient control strategies for building services, in line with the principles at the front of this Guide. Guidance on designing specific controls is given in sections 6 to 10. Upgrading controls is covered in section 19 and maintenance of controls in section 17. Further guidance on controls can be found in the CIBSE Guide H: *Building control systems*[1], CIBSE Guide B2: *Ventilation and air conditioning*[2], Fuel Efficiency Booklet FEB 10[3], BSRIA *Standard specification for BEMS*[4], BSRIA *Library of system control strategies*[5] and BRECSU General Information Reports GIR 40[6] and GIR 41[7].

6.0 General

Good control is essential to maintain the desired levels of service, comfort and safety in an energy efficient manner. Even well designed systems can perform badly if the controls are inadequate or incorrectly installed. Conversely, the inherent problems of a poorly designed system are unlikely to be corrected by adding controls, whatever their complexity. Good controls can:

— improve the comfort of occupants

— prevent systems from being on when not needed

— switch systems on just early enough to achieve comfort by occupancy time, and off early enough to minimise consumption

— ensure that services are provided at the right level, e.g. at an appropriate temperature

— minimise maintenance requirements by preventing over-use of services

— reduce energy consumption, running costs and minimise emissions to the atmosphere.

In order to reach an energy efficient building design it is essential to form a clear and integrated control strategy. Controls provide the main interface between the occupant and the building services and it is therefore essential to include user controls within the strategy. Whatever strategy is devised, the following are some basic guidelines for controls:

— User interactive controls should be territorial, i.e. their operation should influence the space occupied by one person (if possible), and they should be near the area that they control.

— They should be intuitive, i.e. as obvious as reaching for a light switch; there should be a clear indication that control action has been initiated.

— User interactive controls should be located in obvious places, not where they will be difficult to reach or obscured by furnishings.

— Systems should be robust and capable of being easily re-configured, e.g. when office layouts change.

— Automatic systems should have simple overrides that revert to 'off' after a set time period and management should always be aware when these overrides are being used.

— Management should be provided with a clear understanding of the system controls and their correct settings in the building log book[8]. In particular, how the systems interact, and how to avoid possible conflicts. e.g. simultaneous heating and cooling.

— Occupants should be provided with a simple explanation of how to use the controls relevant to them. e.g. how to use their local thermostats and TRVs.

— Where possible, the default state should be the low-energy state, and systems should switched off automatically when there is no further need for them.

— All services should be controllable. For example, unsuitable hydraulic arrangements can lead to systems that are uncontrollable no matter how sophisticated the control system. Hydraulic interaction between systems is a major cause of control stability problems and often occurs between primary and secondary circuits (see 10.3).

— Systems should be sized correctly. Controls can become unstable (e.g. causing hunting) if primary plant is oversized, leading to energy waste and, often, poor reliability. Conversely, generously sized distribution systems can significantly reduce transport losses and aid control stability, particularly with variable flow systems, as there is less variation in differential pressure throughout the system.

— Sensors should be located where they will feed back a true value of the variable being monitored.

— Where possible, controls should monitor themselves for efficient operation in accordance with the design intentions, and alert management if they detect problems, e.g. simultaneous cooling and heat recovery in an air handling plant.

6.1 Developing a strategy

Establishing a practical control strategy that is appropriate to the structure, occupancy, activity and services is an essential step in achieving energy efficiency and ensuring that the building and its services work in harmony. The design team needs to establish this in outline at an early stage. It is essential that they ultimately pass this strategic overview to the building contractor and the operator to ensure that the design concept can be put into practice correctly. This strategic overview of controls should be set out in the building log book[8] to ensure that anybody working on the building throughout its life has a good understanding of the design intent. When systems are altered/upgraded then the building log book should be modified to keep the control strategy up to date.

Occupants should enjoy reasonable comfort under automatic control, but should also be able to alleviate discomfort manually when necessary. Designers need to seek a balance between central control and local occupant control. Occupants should have good 'perceived' control, which does not necessarily require a plethora of building services control devices[9]. It is a choice between a closely-specified environment with relatively low perceived control and a less-exactly controlled one which offers more adaptive opportunity. Staff satisfaction and comfort can also be linked to better health and productivity, so that in well designed and well managed buildings, 'virtuous circles' begin to emerge, where comfort, control, productivity and energy efficiency all go together[10].

Studies[10] show that improved controls usually lead to energy savings. However, a successful control strategy addresses issues well beyond simple energy savings. The more complex the building, the more difficult it can be to manage, and the greater the requirement for a clear control strategy to provide an achievable balance between energy and comfort.

Unfortunately, if the complex technical systems designed to increase comfort or reduce energy consumption are too complicated, they can actually bring about a situation where the management loses control of the building. Consequently, comfort levels can reduce or energy consumption can increase and the building is in a vicious circle. It is, therefore, better to introduce a few well-chosen techniques into the design correctly, rather than to smother a building with energy-saving features which require complex and elaborate controls.

In general, the better the controls interface between occupants and the building services the better will be the energy efficiency. Control systems should have good interfaces for both management and staff, particularly in more highly serviced buildings and where responsibilities are divided between landlord, tenant and contractors. Controls should be simple, intuitive, territorial and located in obvious places to encourage good building management and energy efficiency.

Energy efficient buildings are not automatically comfortable. In buildings where comfort and energy efficiency go together successfully, the unifying reason appears to be good management, not just of energy, but also of the entire process of procuring, designing, building, occupying, operating and maintaining the buildings.

Designers should seek to make their intended operating strategies obvious, convenient, and effective. It is especially important not to ignore the original control strategy when spaces are being fitted out and refurbished. For example, access to perimeter controls for windows, blinds or HVAC systems is often blocked by furniture[10].

6.1.1 Avoiding conflicting controls

It is essential that interaction between individual systems and their controls is considered at the design stage to ensure that the whole building is controllable, maintainable, and can be commissioned successfully. Unwanted interaction between systems, e.g. cooling and heating, can cause major energy wastage and result in failure to obtain desired comfort conditions. Factors to consider include:

— *Maximise control stability*: control of the system should not cause any effect which upsets the stability or operation of the system's component parts, e.g. compensated circuit valve position should not effect flow through boilers.

— *Minimise zone interaction*: systems must be designed such that the effect of control on one zone does not affect another zone.

— *Minimise system interaction*: systems must be designed such that control of one system does not have an adverse effect on other systems.

— *Keep it simple*: wherever possible, designers should aim for simple and understandable control strategies, capable of producing the conditions required. However, elements of these strategies (such as optimum start) will inherently be sophisticated.

— *Simple user interfaces*: regardless of the underlying complexity of control, local and central user interfaces should be as intuitive and easy to understand as possible. Don't assume that users will understand the overall control strategy.

— *Use appropriate accuracy*: it could be uneconomic to provide controls that operate with a degree of accuracy to which a plant or building is unable to respond, or to select equipment that is capable of producing more precise control than the application requires.

— *Use appropriate response times*: controls should be appropriate to the thermal response of the building and its services, e.g. lightweight buildings need services and controls that can respond rapidly to changes externally and internally, as there is no capacity to store heat or 'coolth' within the building fabric. The services in heavyweight buildings can be very difficult to control and will need controls to be set up with an inherent lag to avoid excessive cycling, and possibly an element of predictive control to anticipate conditions and avoid overshoot.

— *Variable speed drives*: can provide significant savings, even for constant loads in some circumstances.

6.1.2 Zoning the building and services

Services are often required at different times and levels (e.g. temperatures) in different areas of a building. A successful control system will provide a good match between these requirements on a zone by zone basis. A zone is defined as a part of the building whose services are capable of independent control, either in time or in level of service (e.g. temperature), or in both. On multi-building sites, each individual building supplied by a central service should also be regarded as a separate zone within the overall system.

All but the smallest of buildings will require some form of zoning. The choice of zones plays an important part in designing the overall control strategy. The building use, layout and services will influence the choice of controls. Questions to be addressed are:

— Does the layout of the building lend itself to particular zones, e.g. floor-by-floor?

— Is there scope for more zones?

— Is more than one building involved? Can they be treated separately?

— Is more than one tenant involved? Should each tenant's space be one zone?

— Do the services have some obvious circuits, e.g. secondary heating circuits?

— Is it possible to integrate the building layout zones with the services zones?

— Are there different activities, occupancy patterns, temperature and lighting requirements?

— Does the building need to be zoned due to the orientation and solar gain on certain facades?

Good zone control can provide greater comfort and save energy. Objective zoning of services can add to the controllability of systems where load profiles vary between areas of the building. Zones should also be chosen to meet the needs of occupants. It is particularly important to avoid large systems defaulting to 'on' when there is little or no local demand to be met.

Multiple zone control is most advantageous:

— in larger buildings

— in poorly insulated buildings (or parts of buildings)

— where a section of the building is not often used

— where the rooms have different uses and requirements

— where different systems are used

— depending on orientation, buildings that are subject to wide variations in sunlight throughout the day.

Buildings that receive solar gain on one side in the morning and the opposite side in the afternoon should have the heating for each facade zoned separately. Lighting controls should be zoned parallel to windows in order to compensate for additional daylighting. Where small areas, such as cellular offices are intermittently occupied, occupancy sensing control in individual rooms would provide more economical operation.

Multi-zone air conditioning systems, with a common cooling coil and zone re-heater batteries, should avoid over-cooling the primary air. Where possible, zones should have a similar load profile to prevent wasteful common cooling and zone reheat. Separate air handling units, or zone cooling coils, are desirable for areas with a higher cooling load profiles.

There is normally little benefit in zoning tempered air systems unless occupancy varies considerably between zones. Hydraulic systems serving fan coils and induction units may benefit from zoning where load profiles or usage hours vary significantly between zones.

VAV systems will benefit from zoning where load profiles vary significantly[11]. However, this should not compromise duct sizes or flow measurement. Preference should be given to reducing duct losses, ensuring good time and temperature control of the VAV units and good control of the supply and extract fans.

Where perimeter heating is used in conjunction with internal zones which are predominantly in need of cooling, consideration should be given to linking the controls in adjacent internal and perimeter areas to minimise simultaneous heating and cooling.

6.1.3 Accuracy of control

Excessively tight specification of acceptable temperatures and humidities can waste energy and may not be essential to achieve comfort conditions. It is normally acceptable to allow space conditions to float, commonly by 2–3 °C, although a greater variation is often acceptable, particularly where space temperatures are reset with respect to external conditions. Allowing seasonal variations, e.g. higher summer temperatures, can also provide acceptable conditions and energy savings.

Far greater variations in humidity are acceptable, as very few buildings require control to +5% relative humidity, and occupants will normally tolerate a range of say 30–70%. In the UK, it is usual to maintain minimum humidity levels during cold spells in winter when the moisture content of the outside air is very low.

For systems with both heating and cooling, a dead-band should be incorporated where no control action takes place. The width of the dead-band between heating and cooling is a balance between an acceptable variation in space temperature and minimising energy consumption.

6.1.4 Variable flow control

Variable flow control of air and water based services can give very considerable savings in fan and pump energy, and variable flow control can be used on most distribution systems. For example, controlling heating pump speed to respond to variations in load caused by two-port valves and TRVs is highly cost effective. Equally, VAV systems have potentially significant air distribution savings over other central plant systems, provided that pressures are well controlled and air handling plant and drives are intrinsically efficient.

Variable speed drives also allow rapid matching of pump and fan duties during commissioning and will provide significant savings compared with manual system regulation. Typical energy savings are 20% at 10% regulation and 40% at 20% regulation dependent upon characteristics. Manual system regulation increases system resistance and is inherently inefficient.

6.2 Strategic control functions

Figure 6.1 identifies the four main areas in which control systems should aim to perform if they are to combine manual and automatic functions[10]. Control functions are classified as manual or automatic (vertical axis) and as reactive or forward-looking (horizontal axis). Effective control strategies should aim for good performance in all quadrants.

Historically, there has been a tendency to expect that automatic systems alone will cope and, in particular, feedback controls (top left quadrant). Forward-looking items need a good understanding by users of the functions and purposes of systems and good feedback on achieved performance.

Even among automatic controls, anticipatory control (top right) has been the poor relation, and is often limited to time control. Effective anticipation is becoming increas-ingly important in strategies proposed for energy efficient buildings, but it has often proved difficult to get right, as it needs careful attention.

Appropriate manual intervention (i.e. the bottom half of Figure 6.1) can be effective in avoiding waste, discomfort or dissatisfaction. Occupants who can influence conditions appear to be more tolerant of environments which, in sealed air conditioned buildings, would be unacceptable.

In order to improve both comfort and energy efficiency, the aim should be to:

— provide comfort with automatically controlled systems that keep people comfortable, without waste, for a high proportion of the time (top left of Figure 6.1)

— provide facilities that permit the occupants to alter conditions quickly and easily (bottom left of Figure 6.1), particularly where the comfort band adopted is wide.

More sophisticated systems involving anticipation should have:

— simple, accessible facilities for occupants to adjust controls in advance (bottom right of Figure 6.1) and for managers to re-program automatic controls intended to anticipate changing conditions (top right of Figure 6.1)

— effective information feedback to management on the performance of these systems, particularly where they operate unseen or outside normal occupancy hours, e.g. the controls of mechanical night ventilation/cooling systems need to alert management if the supply air temperature rises significantly above the outside temperature due to plant or control faults (e.g. damper seizure or unwanted heater battery operation).

The control system objectives should be clearly defined at an early stage alongside the response times for events. In particular, controls should ensure that systems are switched off when there is no demand.

The choice of controls has a direct effect on the operation and energy consumption of a building. CIBSE Guide H: *Building control systems*[1] and the BSRIA *Library of system control strategies*[5] provide extensive guidance on the selection of controls.

6.3 Building management systems

Building management systems (BMS) can significantly improve the overall management and performance of buildings, promoting an holistic approach to controls and providing operational feedback. Energy savings of 10–20% can be achieved by installing a BMS compared with independent controllers for each system. However, BMSs cannot compensate for badly designed systems, poor management or incorrect maintenance, although user experiences show that even the earliest systems were normally of significant benefit. A BMS also needs to be well

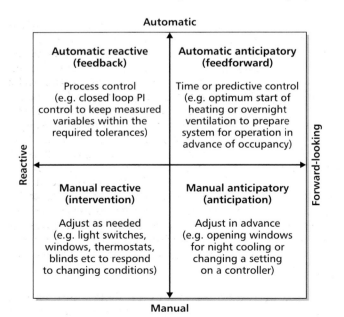

Figure 6.1 Strategic features of controls (reproduced from BRE Information Paper IP3/95[10], by permission of BRE)

specified[12] and engineered, with good documentation and user interfaces if it is to be used effectively[13].

Recent work[14,15] shows that BMS are not being used to their full potential. While BMS are most successful in their role as plant control systems, the strategic functions including energy metering, monitoring and targeting, are under utilised. The work also shows that a strong working relationship with the BMS vendor underpins successful operation and that a close involvement of the user in the specification process is a key factor in this.

The monitoring facilities of a BMS allow plant status, environmental conditions and energy to be monitored, providing the building operator with a real-time understanding of how the building is operating. This can often lead to the identification of problems that may have gone unnoticed, e.g. high energy usage. Energy meters connected to a BMS, providing real-time energy consumption patterns and ultimately a historical record of the buildings energy performance, can be logged and analysed in a number of ways both numerically and graphically. BMSs can, therefore, improve management information by trend logging performance, benefiting forward planning/costing. This can also encourage greater awareness of energy efficiency among staff.

Alarms can also be monitored providing instantaneous indications and records that plant has shut down, maintenance is required, or environmental conditions are outside limits.

Most modern microprocessor-based control systems have communication facilities that permit the addition of a BMS central facility at relatively low cost. Additional monitoring is often desirable, as are additional points for individual control of pumps and fans, etc. However, these may add to overall cost compared with more basic control strategies. BMS that integrate security, access control and lighting control are now available. These can, where appropriate, reduce the total cost of incorporating a range of services and, hence, help to justify the additional cost.

As with controls, staff must be trained in the use of BMSs and over-sophistication should be avoided.

The following issues need to be considered when a BMS is to be included in a design:

— The BMS supplier should be given a clear brief and a full functional specification[12], together with input/output schedules, monitoring requirements and schematic drawings[4]. Many functions can be incorporated at little or no cost when specified initially, but can be expensive to incorporate at a later stage.

— A formal handover demonstration procedure should be agreed. The greater the understanding, the greater the likely energy savings.

— A significant level of support should be provided by the BMS supplier during commissioning[16] and to prove systems software[17].

— The scope for system expansion at each outstation should be considered. Often the addition of a single point may require a complete outstation if all points on the original are occupied.

— The provision for future retraining in the event of staff changes. To minimise day-to-day reliance on suppliers for simple maintenance measures, suitable user documentation should be made available for system fault finding and maintenance.

— The ability of the system to integrate with other hardware and software should be considered when selecting a BMS. In particular, the integration of a BMS with an energy monitoring and targeting software package can benefit energy management.

— A graphical user interface, provided it is clear, informative and usable can promote better understanding and use of a BMS and, hence, energy savings. Colour dynamic displays can provide useful aids to fault diagnosis, as well as a visual indication of plant status and relationships between points.

— The financial justification for a BMS should ideally include a full life-cycle costing calculation based on discounted cash flow. Estimates of potential savings should, where possible, account for contributions from improved maintenance and increased reliability, in addition to reduced energy consumption.

— The ability to interrogate local outstations should be carefully considered when selecting a BMS. Some systems provide a communication interface to allow local override control and local checking of functional integrity following maintenance action.

6.4 Occupant controls

User interactive control systems and achieving 'perceived control' are important for the long-term success of a building[9] and these issues require careful consideration at an early stage in the design. Occupants often feel more comfortable when there is a general perception of being in control. This can be as important as having objectively good comfort conditions.

People like control and rapid response, particularly when they experience a 'crisis of discomfort'[18]. Current trends, however, can tend to take control away from occupants. These trends include open-plan spaces with interlocked furniture which does not allow the working position to be moved (to avoid local glare or draughts), and choosing automated systems with poor, or no manual over-rides. This can create a dependency culture in which management has to solve problems which individuals might have been able to deal with themselves. Without good, attentive and responsive management, this culture can start to spread in any building in which the occupants are unable to make their own adjustments, not just in relation to air conditioning[19]. However, an effective response does not always require good and well placed individual controls. A skilled and committed building manager with a well-configured BMS can give similar results in response to a telephone request.

Air conditioned buildings are usually better at providing controlled comfort conditions for most occupants for most of the time. However, they are difficult to adapt to people who may wish to alter conditions. Naturally ventilated buildings are usually better equipped for alleviating discomfort quickly when it does occur, albeit sometimes only marginally. For example, local control of TRVs can provide good comfort conditions in an energy efficient manner, with occupant interaction via the TRV settings.

Local control problems are generally more prevalent in open-plan areas than in cellular offices where a small number of people can make choices relatively easily. For example, case studies show how lighting in open-plan offices is often left on, whereas lighting in cellular offices is switched off (and then remains off) more frequently.

More sophisticated control systems offer many occupant interaction options. These include local user reset of temperature, user hand-held remote control, telephone-based systems, intranet/internet based systems, systems linked with security and occupancy control, all of which can help save energy if applied correctly. However, lack of clarity and over-complexity can often negate the potential savings and care must be taken to ensure that these facilities are intuitive and easy to use.

Where buildings are randomly occupied, such as village halls, a simple push button that runs the heating for a predetermined period (via a timer) is desirable with suitable frost and low temperature protection facilities. Anything more complicated can lead to unnecessary operation.

Where buildings have regular occupancy plus intermittent evening use, such as schools, simple user interfaces should also be provided for use out of normal hours. This will often require interfacing with an optimiser; some manufacturers provide pre-configured override options. User interfaces to change occupancy periods or check temperatures should be as easy to use as possible with each function clearly identified. Poor user interfaces can lead to poor control and in some cases to controls being disabled causing energy waste.

References

1   *Building control systems* CIBSE Guide H (London: Chartered Institution of Building Services Engineers) (2000)

2   *Ventilation and air conditioning* CIBSE Guide B2 (London: Chartered Institution of Building Services Engineers) (2001)

3   *Controls and energy savings* Fuel Efficiency Booklet FEB 10 (Action Energy) (1993) (www.actionenergy.org.uk)

4   Pennycook K *Standard specification for BEMS* BSRIA AG 9/2001 (Bracknell: Building Services Research and Information Association) (2001)

5   Martin A J and Banyard C P *Library of system control strategies* BSRIA Applications Guide AG 7/98 (Building Services Research and Information Association) (1998)

6   *Heating systems and their control* General Information Report GIR 40 (Action Energy) (1996) (www.actionenergy.org.uk)

7   *Variable flow control* General Information Report GIR 41 (Action Energy) (1996) (www.actionenergy.org.uk)

8   *Building log book toolkit* CIBSE TM 31 (London: Chartered Institution of Building Services Engineers) (2003)

9   Bordass W T *Factors for success* (London: Workplace Comfort Forum) (1998)

10   Bordass W T, Bromley A K R and Leaman A J *Comfort, control and energy efficiency in offices* BRE Information Paper IP3/95 (London: Construction Research Communications) (1995)

11   *Selecting air conditioning systems — a guide for building clients and their advisers* Good Practice Guide GPG 71 (Action Energy) (1993) (www.actionenergy.org.uk)

12   Pennycook K and Hamilton G *Specifying building management systems* BSRIA TN 6/98 (Bracknell: Building Services Research and Information Association) (1998)

13   Pennycook K *The effective BMS* BSRIA AG10/2001 (Bracknell: Building Services Research and Information Association) (2001)

14   Lowry G Factors affecting the success of building management system installations *Building Serv. Eng. Res. Techol.* **23** (1) (2002)

15   Levermore G J *Building energy management systems* (2nd. edn.) (London: Taylor & Francis) (2000)

16   Pike P and Pennycook K *Commissioning of BEMS — a code of practice* BSRIA AH 2/92 (Bracknell: Building Services Research and Information Association) (1992)

17   Pike P G *BEMS performance testing* BSRIA AG 2/94 (Bracknell: Building Services Research and Information Association) (1994)

18   Haigh D *User response in environmental control* in Hawkes D and Owers J (eds.) *The Architecture of Energy* (London: Construction Press/Longman) (1981)

19   Bordass W, Bunn R, Cohen R and Standeven M PROBE: Some lessons learned from the first eight buildings *Proc. CIBSE Nat. Conf., Alexandra Palace, 5–7 October 1997* vol. 1 7–16 (London: Chartered Institution of Building Services Engineers) (1997)

Bibliography

Fundamentals ASHRAE Handbook (Atlanta, GA: American Society of Heating, Refrigeration and Air Conditioning Engineers) (2001)

HVAC Systems and Equipment ASHRAE Handbook (Atlanta, GA: American Society of Heating, Refrigeration and Air Conditioning Engineers) (2000)

Fletcher J *Building control and indoor environmental quality* BSRIA TN9/98 (Bracknell: Building Services Research and Information Association) (1998)

Barnard N and Starr A *BEMS as condition based maintenance tools* BSRIA TN(S) 4/95 (Bracknell: Building Services Research and Information Association) (1995)

Intelligent buildings BSRIA Library Bulletin LB 51/89 (Bracknell: Building Services Research and Information Association) (1989)

Martin A *Night cooling control strategies* BSRIA TN 5/96 (Bracknell: Building Services Research and Information Association) (1996)

Brown R *Radiant heating* BSRIA AG 3/96 (Bracknell: Building Services Research and Information Association) (1996)

7   Ventilation and air conditioning design

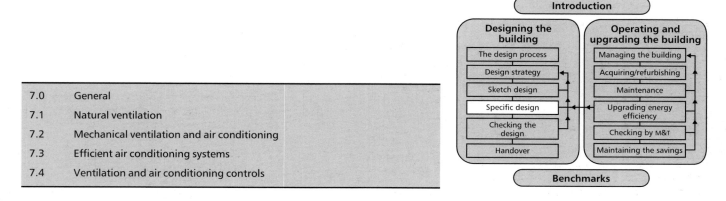

7.0	General
7.1	Natural ventilation
7.2	Mechanical ventilation and air conditioning
7.3	Efficient air conditioning systems
7.4	Ventilation and air conditioning controls

This section sets out some of the key issues for designing energy efficient ventilation and air conditioning systems, in line with the principles at the beginning of this Guide. Ventilation strategies are covered in section 4 and energy issues related to the maintenance of ventilation systems are covered in section 17. Further information on ventilation is provided in CIBSE Applications Manual AM10[1], CIBSE Guide B2[2], Good Practice Guides GPG 257[3], GPG 287[4] and GPG 291[5], CIBSE Guide A[6], ASHRAE Handbook: *HVAC Applications*[7], General Information Report GIR 31[8], BRE Digest 399[9] and BCO *Best practice in the specification for offices*[10].

7.0   General

The form of the building will influence the ventilation strategy as discussed in sections 3 and 4. Ventilation is often responsible for the largest energy loss from buildings and has grown in relative importance as improved levels of insulation have reduced conduction losses. Designers should:

— minimise uncontrolled air infiltration by designing a tight envelope: 'build tight—ventilate right'. Recommended air leakage standards are shown in CIBSE TM23[11]

— minimise demand by avoiding over-design which leads to high air change rates

— use 'passive' before 'active' solutions by giving preference to natural ventilation[1,8,9]

— choose efficient primary plant where mechanical ventilation is essential[3]

— consider energy recovery between air streams

— distribute air effectively by avoiding excessive duct lengths, system resistance and duct heat loss[3]

— use effective controls through good zoning, effective time control, and variable flow control where possible.

An energy efficient design aims to provide thermal comfort and acceptable indoor air quality with the minimum use of energy. Mechanical ventilation is a primary energy intensive process, and air conditioning is even more so. Therefore, an energy efficient building should provide the desired internal conditions by relying on natural means where possible. If factors such as excessive heat gains, noise, pollution etc. prevent this then designers should consider the next best energy efficient means of providing ventilation, following the ventilation design hierarchy shown in Figure 7.1. This approach is supported by figures in section 3 of the BCO's *Best practice in the specification for offices*[10].

A ventilation system (whether natural, mechanical, or a combination of the two) should be able to satisfy health, comfort and cooling needs, with a good degree of local control. Defining the optimum ventilation rate is crucial to energy efficiency. Too little fresh air will result in the internal air quality becoming unsatisfactory; too much causes excessive energy consumption. The minimum required is 5 litre·s^{-1} per person (or 0.5 litre·s^{-1} per m^2) while the recommended rate is generally 8 litre·s^{-1} per person (or 0.8 litre·s^{-1} per m^2)[2]. Cigarette smoking can double or quadruple this requirement. A good strategy should be, therefore, to avoid smoking in buildings, or to provide separately ventilated rooms for smokers.

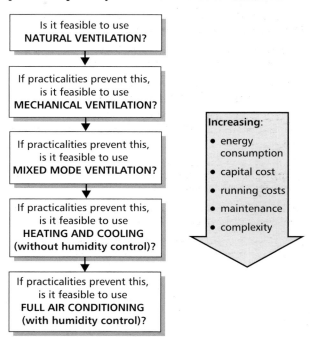

Figure 7.1 Ventilation design hierarchy

Building Regulations Approved Document L2★[12] sets out a number of recommendations related to ventilation including:

— building air leakage standards to minimise unwanted ventilation, see 4.2.5.1

— avoiding solar overheating, see 4.2.6.4

— minimising the energy consumed in air conditioned and/or mechanically ventilated (AC/MV) systems, see 4.2.5.4. This includes the carbon performance rating (CPR) for offices which sets out requirements for new and refurbished buildings as well as existing buildings where an AC/MV systems is to be significantly altered or replaced.

These requirement are summarised in the relevant parts of section 4, as they influence very early design decisions.

7.1   Natural ventilation

Designs which rely on natural ventilation can provide the following advantages[1,2]:

— lower running costs through lower energy consumption[8]

— decreased capital cost

— decreased maintenance costs[15]

— reduced transport energy associated with fans

— fewer possible problems of plant noise.

It is desirable, therefore, to begin by examining the provision of fresh air requirements by natural means (see section 4).

Heat gains are a critical factor in the success of natural ventilation strategies, as shown in Table 7.1[1].

Design tools, such as the LT method[16] can help establish a balance between internal/solar heat gains, the need for

* Requirements may differ in Scotland[13] and Northern Ireland[14]

heating and cooling, daylight and fresh air by optimising glazing, built form etc.

Any external environmental conditions which may limit or preclude the use of natural ventilation, e.g. high levels of noise or pollutants, should be identified at an early stage and minimised where possible, see CIBSE TM21[17]. When it is necessary to keep windows shut to exclude noise, fumes, smoke and dirt, it may force a move to a mechanical ventilation system with the consequence of higher energy consumption. Pollution levels that may require a mechanical ventilation system to be selected are shown in CIBSE AM10[1].

Even if some of these limitations are encountered, it may still be possible to design the building to take advantage of natural ventilation. This may require a reassessment of the ventilation strategy and sketch design (see section 4), or may suggest a mixed-mode approach could be appropriate, see 4.2[18].

7.2   Mechanical ventilation and air conditioning

Installing mechanical ventilation and/or air conditioning will significantly increase capital costs, running costs, environmental emissions and maintenance costs. Mechanical ventilation rates should be kept to a minimum commensurate with acceptable levels of indoor air quality. Therefore, the size of fan, fan power usage (specific fan power) and ventilation heating/cooling loads should be kept to a minimum, see 7.3.6.1. Designers are also advised to consider the possibility of meeting comfort requirements using mechanical ventilation alone without mechanical cooling.

Fan capacities larger than those shown in Table 7.2 suggest over-sizing of plant[19].

Specific fan power should be 2 $W/(litre \cdot s^{-1})$ or less to achieve good practice in offices[20]; very energy efficient systems can sometimes achieve 1 $W/(litre \cdot s^{-1})$ although

Table 7.1 The relationship between design features and heat gains

Design features	Total heat gains† / W·m⁻² floor area)			
	10	20	30	40‡
	Minimum room height / m			
	2.5	2.7	2.9	3.1
Controllable window opening (down to 10 mm)	Essential	Essential	Essential	Essential
Trickle vents for winter	Essential	Essential	Essential	Essential
Control of indoor air quality (may be manual)	May be required	May be required	Essential	Essential
Design for daylight to reduce gains	May be required	Essential	Essential	Essential
Daylight control of electric lighting	May be required	May be required	Essential	Essential
100% shading from direct sun	May be required	Essential	Essential	Essential
Cooling by daytime ventilation only	Essential	Essential	Problem	Problem
Cooling by day and night ventilation	Not necessary	May be required	Essential	Essential
Exposed thermal mass	Not necessary	Not necessary	Essential	Essential

† i.e. people + lights + office equipment + solar gain

‡ The guidance in this table is indicative of scale only and will vary depending on the characteristics of a particular building. In particular, heat gains greater than 40 W·m⁻² can be catered for by careful design of building form but will require very detailed analysis

Table 7.2 Basic fan capacity benchmarks

Building	Fan capacity / (litre·s⁻¹)·m⁻³ of ventilated space)
Offices	1.4
Retail stores, halls and theatres	2.1
Restaurants	3.5

this can be difficult. Above 4.0 W/(litre·s⁻¹) could be regarded as a poor level of efficiency[3].

Mechanical ventilation systems resolve a number of problems associated with natural systems. They require much smaller openings, they can be easier to control and they also provide sound absorption and security. However, they consume electricity and heat the air. In theory, fans can operate at better than 80% efficiency but, in practice, less efficient units tend to be specified to save money or provide a design safety margin. The loss of efficiency is dissipated as heat. Systems can have fan gains of up to 2 °C, which can make the difference between a comfortable building and one that is too warm.

If a building is sealed and mechanically ventilated, occupants may react to the loss of individual control by demanding a high degree of environmental stability that might not be possible without mechanical cooling. Full mechanical ventilation also tends to require significantly higher air change rates than where natural ventilation is also available, increasing HVAC capital and running costs. In order to minimise these costs, designers should consider the possibility of a mixed-mode approach before opting for a fully air conditioned building.

7.2.1 Mixed-mode buildings

Mixed-mode designs (see 4.2) can involve a variety of ventilation and cooling systems, possibly supplying different areas or at different times. It is essentially the provision of the least amount of mechanical air movement and cooling that can still achieve the conditions required. For example, it may be advantageous to turn off the air conditioning system for parts of the season, and rely on ventilation and cooling by opening windows. This so-called 'mixed-mode' approach requires the design rigours of both natural and mechanical ventilation.

7.2.2 Efficient ventilation

Fresh air rate is only one parameter in the design of a successful ventilation system, the second being ventilation efficiency. This relates to the way in which fresh air is distributed within the occupied space, and its consequent ability to remove pollutants. The various ventilation techniques are summarised in CIBSE AM10[1] and CIBSE Guide B2[2].

It is generally desirable and energy efficient to adopt a balanced ventilation system, comprising independently ducted supply and extract. The advantages and disadvantages of balanced ventilation are shown in Table 7.3.

Care must be taken in selecting the ratio between the supply and exhaust airflow volumes. For spaces where

Table 7.3 Advantages and disadvantages of balanced ventilation

Advantages	Disadvantages
Contaminants removed at source.	Building must be effectively sealed to prevent air ingress by infiltration.
Incoming air can be conditioned and cleaned.	Expensive, requiring two complete duct work systems.
Potential for heat recovery from exhaust air	Regular cleaning and maintenance is necessary.
Weather independent, provided structure is moderately airtight	Electrical energy consumed in fans

there are no noxious fumes and where moisture ingress is unlikely to be a problem it is generally recommended that the extract be slightly (10–20%) less than the supply. Conversely, where fumes or moisture problems exist, the supply flow rate should be 90–95% of the extract rate to encourage fumes to pass through the plant.

Energy efficiency will be improved by the following measures where appropriate:

— Provide heat recovery via thermal wheels, run around coils, etc. on full fresh air air handling units, including tempered air systems. Supply and extract systems must be designed such that heat recovery can be easily facilitated. Ensure that the energy flow can not be reversed when external conditions change e.g. provide a by-pass for summer operation.

— Provide effective control of dampers for minimum fresh air and free cooling on recirculation systems.

— Ensure that fresh air and exhaust dampers are closed when the building is not occupied.

— Ensure that only the minimum fresh air required is treated, preferably automatically by varying the minimum fresh air content during occupied periods with respect to air quality.

— Provide effectively-controlled free cooling wherever possible

— Minimise duct lengths and bends and providing adequately sized ducts[21] (case studies[22] have shown that with careful design fan energy can be halved compared with the norm)

— Correctly select and size the most efficient fans.

— Ensure that the control strategy considers all full and part load conditions, and is fully described and correctly configured.

7.2.3 Need for air conditioning

Introducing full air conditioning into a design can often add around 50% to the eventual running costs of the building and should therefore be avoided where possible.

Although full air conditioning involves humidity control, in the UK the term is commonly used for the provision of mechanical cooling to the conditioned space. In the UK, there is a limited set of circumstances in which a building will require air conditioning. However, it can be necessary in certain circumstances due to pollution, external noise and high heat gains.

When designing mixed-mode or mechanically ventilated buildings, a balance should be sought between moving small amounts of cool air rather than large amounts of tempered or ambient air.

Figure 7.2 provides useful guidance in assessing the need for full air conditioning, comfort cooling or mechanical ventilation[23].

7.2.3.1   Avoiding mechanical cooling

Avoiding the need for mechanical cooling is a function of integrated service and fabric design as discussed in section 4[8]. There are several steps to be taken to minimise the energy need for air conditioning:

—   Minimise the heat gains to the space by careful design of the building envelope.

—   Minimise internal heat gains from lighting, office equipment etc.

—   Wherever possible, meet the cooling requirements with free or passive cooling sources (see below).

—   Ensure the systems and controls are able to match the cooling requirements efficiently.

—   When mechanical cooling is required, limit where it is employed and ensure that the cooling plant operates as efficiently as possible.

In general, the liberation of more than about 40 W·m^{-2} from lighting and other sources may be regarded as excessive and will constitute grounds for reassessing the design to minimise these heat gains.

The main problem in avoiding mechanical cooling is that the period when heat gains are greatest usually coincides with periods when outside air temperatures are at a maximum, thus reducing the cooling potential. It is necessary, therefore, to consider ways in which stored 'coldness' can be exploited.

Using night air to cool the building fabric can avoid the need for mechanical cooling. The building fabric can be used as a thermal store acting as a heat sink during the occupied hours by absorbing the incidental gains.

The thermal mass of the building then needs to be directly available for heat exchange. Exposed concrete ceilings are widely used and can achieve an additional 2–3 °C reduction of the daytime internal temperature. The reduced surface temperature of the exposed concrete also influences the radiant thermal environment and enhances the effect (see 4.2.5).

7.2.3.2   Need for humidity control

Full air conditioning with humidity control is even more energy intensive than systems providing heating and cooling only. It is essential, therefore, to question the requirements, tolerances and need for humidity control[1,2,8]. For most human comfort applications, relative humidity can drift between 30% and 70%[6].

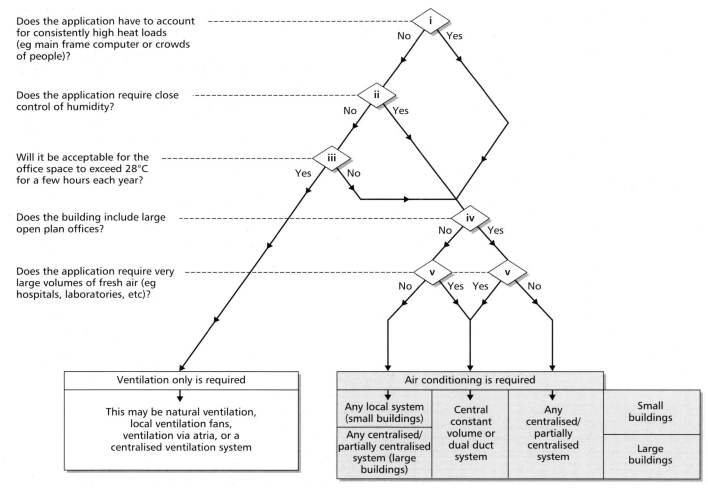

Figure 7.2 Assessing the need for air conditioning (adapted from Good Practice Guide 71[23]) (Crown copyright)

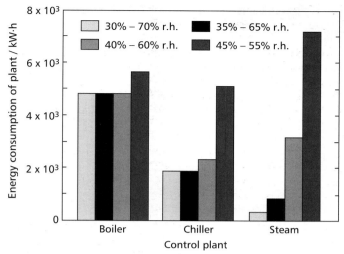

Figure 7.3 Effect of humidity control on energy use

Where humidity needs to be controlled within much tighter bands, both capital and running costs will be increased. In general, the closer the design humidity tolerances, the greater the energy consumption (see Figure 7.3).

The BCO's *Best practice in the specification for offices*[10] suggests that humidification is rarely needed for general office use and that humidity control should not be installed within the base office scheme unless a particularly high rate of fresh air is required. In which case it should be controlled to give a minimum of 35–40%.

Close control of humidity is sometimes required for specialist applications such as the protection of exhibits in a museum. Designers should carefully evaluate whether both humidification and de-humidification are required to maintain conditions within acceptable limits[24].

De-humidification is generally only required in summer. The most common method of removing moisture is by cooling the air to its dew-point using a chilled water cooling coil so that moisture condenses out. This commonly occurs when air is being cooled for comfort conditioning. For close control of relative humidity the air may be cooled further to the required moisture content, then re-heated to bring it back to the required temperature. Cooling then re-heating makes de-humidification an energy intensive process that should be avoided where possible, unless heat rejected from the cooling process can be used for re-heat[2].

Desiccants offer an alternative method to de-humidify air. Exposure of the air to chemicals such as calcium chloride or silica gel will remove moisture. In order for the desiccant to be re-used, it has to be regenerated by heating to drive off the moisture. Often much more air is dehumidified and reheated than is necessary, avoidable by using a by-pass plant. The cost of the regeneration plant and the cost of providing heat for the regeneration process have so far limited the take-up of this technology. However, it may become more attractive if a local source of waste heat exists for regeneration. It is also particularly appropriate if there is a need for de-humidification without the need for significant sensible cooling, e.g. clean rooms.

Humidification is mainly required in winter and can be achieved using a range of equipment including steam injection, water spray and ultra sound humidifiers. Spray humidifiers are now less common due to health concerns. The characteristics of different types of humidification equipment are discussed in CIBSE Guide B2[2] and in BSRIA AG10/94.1[25].

Steam injection systems, whether direct from a steam distribution system or from local electrode boilers, give rise to very significant energy consumption. Where steam is available on site, it is sensible to make use of it and directly inject steam to humidify. However, this will add significantly to the winter demand on the boiler plant. More commonly, local electrode humidification units are used to inject steam into the air stream. These units generally have independent controls and can often result in excessive electricity consumption if not maintained.

Humidification can be a significant energy user in air conditioned offices. Typical and good practice performance indicators are shown in Table 7.4[20]. The 'energy use indicator' (EUI) is the product of[26]:

(a)   the installed capacity in W·m⁻² of treated floor area. This typically varies between about 15 and 25 but should be kept to a minimum once the need for humidification has been established

(b)   the annual running hours

(c)   the average percentage utilisation of the plant expressed as a decimal fraction.

The result is then divided by 1000 to obtain the EUI in (kW·h)·m⁻² per year.

Energy use can be minimised by close control of the hours of operation and ensuring that the humidity set point is kept as low as possible.

Ultrasonic humidification systems are now becoming more common, using up to 90% less energy than electrode systems and, hence, provide a cost-effective alternative. Lower electrical consumption results in reduced electrical wiring costs, although a water purification plant is required to operate the system. Ultrasonic humidifiers require little energy themselves, although the air temperature will decrease due to the evaporative cooling effect. Re-heating is then necessary to bring the air up to the required supply temperature.

Table 7.4 Humidification benchmarks for air conditioned offices

Parameter	Benchmark for stated office type			
	Air conditioned standard office (Type 3)		Air conditioned prestige office (Type 4)	
	Good practice	Typical	Good practice	Typical
Installed capacity (W·m⁻²)	15	20	20	25
Running hours (h/yr)	2750	3500	3000	3700
Utilisation (%)	20	25	20	25
Energy use indicator (EUI) ((kW·h)·m⁻²)/yr	8	18	12	23

Note: factors for converting treated floor area to nett and gross are given in Table 20.1

7.3 Efficient air conditioning systems

There is a wide range of air conditioning plant, including some that offer greater scope for energy efficiency. For a more detailed description of the systems, see CIBSE Guide B2[2] and BSRIA TN15/92[27]. Good Practice Guide GPG 71[23] gives a useful summary of the relative advantages and disadvantages of the various systems. Figure 7.4[23] and Table 7.5[23] list the systems and indicate the capital and running costs of some of options, based on gross floor area and 1992 prices.

GPG 257[3] provides a useful comparison of capital and running costs for high, medium and low velocity systems.

This shows that running costs are reduced for low velocity systems and that some components become more expensive, others become cheaper. Systems velocity is therefore a key factor in the design of an energy efficient system.

7.3.1 Central all-air systems

7.3.1.1 Constant volume

In centralised constant volume single zone systems the heating and cooling loads of the conditioned space are met by changing the temperature of the supply air. Comfort requirements determine the supply temperature, which results in large air volumes and large ductwork consuming

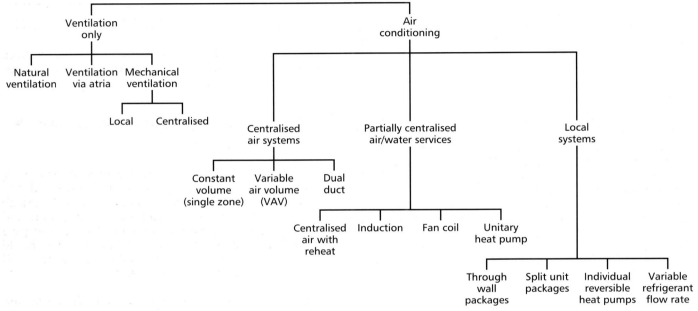

Figure 7.4 Types of air conditioning system[23] (reproduced from Good Practice Guide GPG 71[26]; Crown copyright)

Table 7.5 Air conditioning system costs in offices

System type	Costs			CO_2 emission / (kg·m⁻²) p.a.
	Capital / (£·m⁻²)	Energy / (£·m⁻²) p.a.	Maintenance requirement	
Centralised 'all-air' systems:				
— ventilation and heating (no air conditioning)	100	1.9	Medium	30
— constant volume (single zone)	160	3.0	Medium	50
— variable air volume (VAV)	180	2.4*	Medium to high	40†
— dual duct	210	3.4	Medium	55
Partially centralised air/water systems:				
— centralised air with reheat	200	3.1	Medium to high	50
— induction units	160	3.2	High	50
— fan coil units	170	3.2	Medium to high	50
— unitary heat pump	130	3.2	Medium to high	55
Local systems:				
— heat and local ventilation (no air conditioning)	90	1.1	Low	17
— 'through-the-wall' packages	70‡	3.5	Low	75
— split unit packages	85‡	3.5	Medium to high	75
— individual reversible heat pumps	110	3.0	Medium to high	55
— variable refrigeration flow rate	130	2.8	Medium to high	50

† System fitted with variable speed fan
‡ Excludes separate provision of heating

Note: figures are indicative only and based on gross floor area and 1992 costs; capital costs exclude related building work and cost of BMS

considerable transport energy, even when only small amounts of cooling are required.

These systems should only be used for single zones with common heating/cooling load characteristics such as large rooms, lecture theatres etc. where they can provide a well controlled and efficient system. Single zone systems must not be used for multiple zones with different heating/cooling loads because control of conditions will be very poor and operation very inefficient. However, correctly applied single zone systems are one of the few types of air conditioning system where simultaneous heating and cooling of the same air is not necessary except during de-humidification.

Centralised constant volume multiple zone systems are also available. However, multiple zone systems with local re-heats are more common (due to plant and duct space requirements) and characteristics are similar (see 7.3.2.1). Mixing losses on all but the lead zone make this system relatively inefficient.

7.3.1.2 Dual duct

Dual duct systems have high transport energy, heating and cooling loads. The heated and cooled air are required to be circulated separately and the two air streams then combined to produce an intermediate comfort temperature, thereby wasting heating and cooling energy. Such systems should not be used except where reclaimed energy can be applied. Where they are used, it is important that they have controls to automatically reset temperatures at the central air handling unit to provide minimum heating and cooling to satisfy the hottest/coolest zone. Dual duct VAV systems are available and offer significantly improved energy efficiency.

7.3.1.3 Variable air volume

In general, energy efficiency is improved by moving to variable air volume (VAV) systems to minimise transport energy. However, VAV systems should be matched to suitable applications. They are primarily suited to applications with a year round cooling load such as deep plan office buildings and can also have other limitations to their application such as ceiling height due to box throw etc. The VAV boxes for each zone should be individually controlled, making it necessary for appropriate locations for temperature sensors to be available. VAV systems can provide flexibility for future fit out and partition changes, provided the locations of supply and extract grilles and sensors are carefully considered.

VAV systems reduce the airflow rate in relation to the demand, rather than change the supply air temperature. The air handling unit (AHU) supplies cooled air (normally at 10–18 °C but this can be at 6 °C from ice storage) to VAV boxes which vary the volume with respect to space temperature. The supply fan is normally controlled with respect to static pressure and it responds to demand by varying volume. The location of the static pressure sensor is critical in achieving energy savings[28]. The extract fan volume is controlled with respect to the supply fan volume. The AHU fans achieve variable volume by variable speed drive (VSD), variable pitch or the less efficient inlet guide vane control. VAV boxes with reheat and fan assisted boxes are available but care must be taken to ensure that

Table 7.6 Advantages and disadvantages of variable air volume systems

Advantages	Disadvantages
Often the most efficient form of air-conditioning	Complex in comparison with other types of air conditioning system
Highly flexible for initial/future fit-out requirements	Integration of controls from concept stage essential
Opportunity to reduce AHU and duct size compared to multizone system if diversity allowed on cooling load	Special diffusers may be required for good room air distribution at low loads
VAV systems, using DDC controls with communications, will generally require less maintenance in occupied areas than multizone systems with reheat coils	VAV systems with conventional controls, or additional VAV box coils/fans, could require more maintenance than multizone systems
	Additional sound attenuation may be required for maximum velocity

these are only used where necessary to avoid wasting energy. The advantages and disadvantages of VAV systems are shown in Table 7.6.

7.3.2 Partially centralised air/water systems

Systems in which the air does not transport all the cooling and heating may offer energy savings due to reduced flow rates from the plant room to the spaces served. To satisfy zones that have variable requirements, both heating and cooling pumped water circuits are needed i.e. four pipe circuits. Three pipe systems with a common return should be avoided at all costs as cooling and heating energy will be wasted when the return water is mixed.

Tempered fresh air systems limit the humidification and de-humidification capacity. However, this is normally adequate for most applications and discourages attempts at unnecessary close control of humidity, which is very wasteful of energy.

Savings due to reduced air flows must be balanced against the restricted free cooling from fresh air, the additional energy used due to higher pressures and local fan energy, and the energy required for heating and chilled water distribution pumps.

The AHU should be sized for minimum fresh air duty only, to reduce transport energy. The minimum fresh air volume can be controlled with respect to air quality via VSDs to minimise the amount of heating and cooling of fresh air. Turndown may be limited, dependent upon application. Varying fresh air volume is unlikely to be satisfactory with induction systems due to the minimum pressure required at the induction terminal units. Heat recovery via thermal wheels or run around coils should be considered at the AHU.

Where the building is likely to require cooling in one area and heating in another, or where common cooling coils are used with multiple re-heater batteries, heat recovery from the chillers to supply the terminal unit heating coils, or re-heat batteries, should be considered. This will require a low temperature (warm water) heating circuit. Top-up heat can be provided by condensing boilers, which will always operate in the condensing mode.

All partially centralised systems should have local controls with communication to provide demand-based control of main plant.

7.3.2.1   Centralised air with reheat

These systems (commonly known as multi-zone) require the full volume of air necessary for heating and cooling loads to be transported to and from the AHU. The AHU should incorporate a controlled re-circulation system via dampers (or other means of heat recovery) and free cooling (enthalpy) control to minimise energy use.

Most systems incorporate a common cooling coil, which must be controlled with respect to the zone requiring the greatest amount of cooling. Additional re-heating for the other zones is therefore required, necessitating simultaneous heating and cooling of the same air. This increases energy consumption compared with correctly applied multiple single zone systems.

Systems with minimum air treatment at the AHU and local heating and cooling coils are likely to be far more efficient than systems with a common cooling coil at the AHU, although capital costs will be increased.

Dew-point systems provide saturated air at the cooling coil at all times to provide very stable humidity conditions when air is reheated to the desired space temperature. However, these systems are only necessary for special applications, such as laboratories, and should normally be avoided since they can be very inefficient. Systems with the cooling coil controlled in relation to the zone requiring greatest cooling are much more efficient and should normally be used.

7.3.2.2   Induction

In order to produce the air jet velocity needed to induce room air through the casing and over water coils, induction systems need to operate at higher pressures than those of low velocity systems. Also, having high pressure sufficient to drive room circulation in the furthest zone means that the extra pressure needs to be removed from other branches in an induction system. Typically, this is achieved by careful sizing of the ductwork, together with dampers for the final trimming. Restrictions such as jet nozzles and dampers for flow regulation inherently absorb fan power and thus it is important to consider how much energy is used compared with other means of creating room air circulation.

Two coil induction units should be used where both heating and cooling are required at the terminal. Systems with one coil terminal units require much higher air volumes from the AHU to provide the heating, increasing transport energy. Even where the common heating coil is effectively controlled, simultaneous heating and cooling is inevitable. This can be reduced by effective zoning of the AHUs serving areas with different load profiles such as facades with different orientations. Single-coil systems should have the supply temperature reset in a similar manner to multi-zone systems; they also require a sophisticated control system. Where this is not possible, such as in existing systems, the supply temperature should be scheduled in relation to ambient temperature.

Simultaneous heating and cooling is a common energy problem found in induction systems and often results in a poor user control with associated comfort problems. This can be avoided by good zone selection and control.

7.3.2.3   Fan coils

Fan coils place the motive power for distributing heat and cooling within or close to the zone being served. This means that fan power is not used to move this air down ducts from the central plant. However, additional power is required at fan coil units to circulate the room air. The cross-flow and tangential fans used in fan coil units typically have an efficiency of around 40% — around half that of the most efficient AHU fans.

The energy consumption of these alternative approaches should be assessed. Fan units with free cooling are suitable for some applications (on outside walls of low-rise buildings) and can provide additional economy of operation.

Simultaneous heating and cooling is a common energy problem that can be found in fan coil systems and often results in a poor user control with associated comfort problems. In particular, where there is perimeter heating fighting fan coils providing cooling. This can be avoided by good zone selection and control with interlocks to prevent conflicts with perimeter heating.

7.3.2.4   Chilled beams and ceilings

Conventional cooling methods such as fan coils and VAV systems provide cooling almost entirely by convective heat transfer. Chilled beams/ceilings can provide up to 60% of the cooling by radiation and therefore cool the objects within the space as well as the space itself.

Operating at a higher chilled water temperature than conventional systems offers improved energy efficiency and the possibility of using passive cooling instead of mechanical cooling[29]. Chilled beams/ceilings are often used with upward or positive displacement distribution systems which are inherently more efficient than conventional air conditioning. This system also requires less fan power due to the lower air flow requirements. The BCO's *Best practice in the specification for offices*[10] indicates annual CO_2 emissions of 60–90 kg·m^{-2} for displacement ventilation systems as opposed to 80–140 kg·m^{-2} for conventional air conditioning. The temperature control provided by any separate fresh air system is critical as simultaneous heating and cooling may occur and reduce the overall efficiency of operation.

7.3.2.5   Displacement ventilation

Displacement ventilation provides buoyancy-driven flow rather than less energy efficient conventional forced methods. 'Fresh' air is introduced gently at a low level and at a temperature just slightly below the room ambient, with a view to providing a local cooled environment around the people and heat sources, eliminating the need to temper the entire space, e.g. a theatre. Any local heat sources in the lower part of the room create convection currents that also contribute to the general upward movement. The warmed air and contaminants collect below the ceiling and are then exhausted at high level. The temperature of the stratified air near the ceiling can be allowed to rise above comfort conditions allowing greater temperature differential between supply and extract, increasing cooling capacity (typically 40 $W \cdot m^{-2}$). The higher supply temperature also achieves energy savings by improving the COP of central cooling plant.

Displacement systems operate with lower volume airflow (typically 4 ACH) than traditional methods, thus saving energy. However, supply air has to be warmer than for mixing ventilation, thereby increasing heating requirements, although cooling may be more important in these situations. There may also be more opportunity to utilise free cooling. Further information about displacement ventilation can be found in section 4.2.5 of CIBSE Guide B2[2], General Information Leaflet GIL 85[29] and BSRIA TN 2/96[30].

7.3.2.6 Unitary heat pumps

For buildings where there is a significant spatial variation in load, especially if there is a need for simultaneous heating and cooling in different zones, the use of localised reversible heat pumps connected to a circulating water system can be advantageous. This provides the opportunity to transfer energy around the building, i.e. by carrying heat from a cooled zone into a zone requiring heat. This effectively recovers heat or coldness from different parts of the building. Controls should be linked where more than one unit is used in a common zone, to avoid individual heat pumps simultaneously heating and cooling the same space.

A boiler and cooling tower are normally connected to the water system to top up or reject heat as necessary. This system also has reduced transport losses by circulating low temperature water as the heat source/sink. Also, because there are several items of plant around the building, areas with several heat pumps will not lose the service completely during individual unit breakdowns. Conversely, maintenance is costly and can cause considerable disturbance in occupied areas.

The efficiency of the local heat pumps is reduced compared with other types of air conditioning due to the common circuit being used as both a heating and cooling source. This reduction in efficiency can be minimised by scheduling the circuit temperature in relation to outside temperature so that it increases when cold and vice versa.

Typically, the cooling COP for smaller individual units is 2.4 to 2.6[31], although it is important to consider the energy consumption by the other components in the system, such as the boiler, cooling tower and pumps for the low temperature water circuit. A tempered fresh air system will also be needed for minimum fresh air requirements.

7.3.3 Local air conditioning

Local air conditioning systems include through-the-wall packaged units and split systems to provide comfort cooling, or heating and cooling, but not humidity control. Ventilation air needs to be handled separately, and thus there is little scope for controlled free cooling. Whilst it is not common to base a major new design on individual local air conditioning units, they are commonly used to introduce air conditioning in major refurbishment of naturally ventilated buildings.

Individual local units have lower COPs than centralised plant and often lack a coherent control strategy. However, they provide scope for energy savings through:

—   avoiding multiple heat exchange (into/out of chilled water and condenser water) and fouling at each water heat transfer surface

—   avoiding pumping large volumes of chilled and condenser water

—   simpler heat rejection equipment (i.e. direct air cooled condensers instead of cooling towers with their energy consumption and water treatment consequences)

—   plant operating only in those areas that need cooling at a given time.

Although more localised plant may increase maintenance costs, this approach may provide greater standby in areas served by a number of local units.

Where it has been decided that air conditioning is unnecessary in the building as a whole, it may be appropriate to use highly localised units to cool hot spots in a mixed-mode approach, thus avoiding larger cooling systems. A similar approach may be appropriate where cooling requirements are more stringent in one small area than in the building as a whole.

7.3.3.1 'Through-the-wall' packages

These units are difficult to integrate into a coherent system, but may be applicable where a single room within a building needs to be cooled, either to different temperatures, or at different times, from the remainder which has a co-ordinated system. Cooling COP lies in the range 1.5 to 2.3. Heating is sometimes provided by electric resistance heaters, which should be appraised carefully in life cycle cost terms. Care should be taken to ensure that they do not operate in conflict with any separate space heating system, or with other similar units in the same zone, and that they are time controlled to function only when required. Where possible, free cooling by directing fresh air through the unit without mechanical cooling should be adopted.

7.3.3.2 Individual reversible heat pumps

Packaged heat pumps have much the same limitations as through-the-wall packages except that heating can be provided more efficiently by reversing refrigerant flow through the indoor and outdoor coils. This saves energy in comparison with electric resistance heating, but care needs to be taken to compare the total running cost of heat from this source with other alternatives such as a separate central heating system.

7.3.3.3 Split unit packages

Split units have a separate outdoor unit to house the compressor and condenser thus avoiding noise problems in the space being served. Some units offer variable speed compressors that enable cooling to be modulated, and thus the energy use can be matched more closely to cooling requirements. Split systems provide cooling COPs of 2.5 to 3.0 whereas through the wall units only give 1.5 to 2.3. Otherwise, they should only be used in the same context as individual packaged units, with extra care taken to avoid the prospect of leaks from the connecting refrigerant lines. Most typically used in refurbishments, they often lack a coherent control strategy when multiple units supply the same space leading to simultaneous heating and cooling.

7.3.3.4   Variable refrigerant flow rate

Variable refrigerant flow rate (VRF) multi-split systems are generally regarded as local systems but are increasingly used as distributed cooling systems. More than one indoor unit can be connected to the same outdoor unit. However, it is important to comply with the manufacturer's recommendations on horizontal pipe runs, number of bends and vertical lift, in order to minimise energy losses[31].

In each circulation loop, the refrigerant flow rate can be varied to match the heat transport requirements, thus making energy savings. Some suppliers offer heat recovery between zones on the same circulation loop, and it is in this mode that the system operates at its peak COP of 3.1[32]. In heating only, or cooling only, modes the best system COPs lie in the range 2.3 to 2.5.

In some installations, several outdoor units for individual refrigerant loops have been located in a bank adjacent to each other, but not connected, which can give the false impression of a co-ordinated system. Care should be taken to ensure a coherent control strategy with this approach. In particular, controls for multiple units serving the same space should be linked to avoid simultaneous heating and cooling. Dead-bands between heating and cooling set points should be adequate to avoid individual units cycling between heating and cooling modes.

7.3.4   'Free' cooling

Before considering a system that depends on mechanical cooling, every opportunity should be taken to use 'free' cooling, of which fresh air is the most obvious source. In systems where sufficient air quantities can be delivered to the space, it can be used to reduce demands on mechanical cooling when ambient temperatures are sufficiently low. All-air recirculation systems are ideal applications where savings can be achieved. However, care must be taken to consider the resulting relative humidity, as the energy used for humidification, particularly electric, can offset the refrigeration savings. Additional energy used for air transportation should also be compared with the mechanical cooling savings. Effective controls for free cooling, linked with system demand and fresh air high limit override or enthalpy control, are essential for efficient operation (see 7.4.4).

7.3.5   Heat recovery

Integrating heat recovery systems into the design of air conditioning and ventilation systems is essential for energy efficiency. Including heat recovery as an integral part of an overall design will always be more cost effective than retrofitting at a later stage. In some cases, this can reduce the capacity of primary plant required and may also reduce the overall capital cost of the building services.

There must be sufficient energy being rejected to justify the added complications and running costs of installing heat recovery devices (see 4.2.5.5). With some equipment, the likelihood of cross-contamination between air streams is a key consideration. The extra power consumption of pumps or fans to overcome additional air resistance should always be taken into account. This is particularly important where system operating hours are much greater than heat recovery hours.

Effective controls for heat recovery, linked with system demand and fresh air high limit override or enthalpy control, are essential for efficient operation. In particular, situations where energy flow is reversed, rejecting rather than recovering energy, should be avoided e.g. where temperature differences between air streams have reversed due to weather conditions.

Heat recovery systems are most applicable and cost effective in ventilation systems that reject large amounts of heat, e.g. where high moisture content air is exhausted from swimming pools, or where there is no possibility of re-circulating air (e.g. in full fresh air hospital theatre systems). In both these cases, cross-contamination must be avoided.

A further method of recovering heat is to extract air through luminaires to recover a proportion of the energy consumed by the lamps. The heat in this air may be reclaimed and re-used where needed. This system also reduces the cooling load in the room by preventing a large part of the lighting heat load entering the room and the system can also increase the light output of fluorescent lamps.

7.3.6   Minimising transport losses

Keeping air transport losses to a minimum is an essential part of an energy efficient design. Good Practice Guide GPG 33[33] shows that for typical air conditioned offices, energy used by fans is comparable to that used by the refrigeration plant itself. Many of the 'passive' technologies, which offer reductions in refrigeration load, can cause an increase in fan power requirements. A balance needs to be struck between this additional fan power and reduced refrigeration loads.

The four main ways of reducing fan energy consumption are:

— optimising the fan characteristic

— efficient system regulation (see 11.4)

— reducing air transport losses

— switching off the system when not required.

7.3.6.1   Fan power

The selection of a fan type is primarily determined by the application and, where a choice is available, the most efficient should be chosen. In general, centrifugal fans are more efficient, controllable and quieter. Aerofoil-bladed centrifugal fans can be up to 30% more efficient than a forward curved centrifugal fan for a typical application. The additional capital cost is normally recovered within two years. See section 5.11 Guide B2[2] and Good Practice Guide GPG 257[3] for guidance on fan selection.

All mechanical ventilation fans should be sized as close to the actual demand as possible in order to keep capital and running costs to a minimum. Motors should not be significantly oversized as efficiency and power factor will reduce.

Fan characteristics should be matched to the chosen method of volume control[27]. This can be achieved through various means, such as variable speed motors and, now less commonly, variable pitch fans to optimise fan performance at part load. Variable speed drives are covered in 10.4 and Good Practice Guide GPG 2[34]. Inlet guide vanes, disc throttles and dampers are not generally recommended for energy efficiency due to the 'throttling' effect.

Air handling is one of the largest energy users in air conditioned offices. Typical and good practice performance indicators are shown in Table 7.7[20]. The energy use indicator (EUI) is the product of:

(a)   the amount of air handled in litre·s^{-1} per m^2 of treated floor area. This typically varies between about 1 and 8

(b)   the average efficiency with which it is handled, called specific fan power, in (W/(litre·s^{-1}))

(c)   the annual running hours.

The result is divided by 1000 to obtain the EUI in (kW·h)·m^{-2} per year.

Specific fan power should be kept to a minimum and energy efficient systems should achieve around 2 to 3 W/(litre·s^{-1}). Many ventilation systems can operate with reduced volumes for much of the year, allowing significant energy savings if the fans have variable speed controls. While fans usually have to operate for normal occupancy periods, building operators should ensure that fans do not run too liberally. Common reasons for extended operation are that parts of the building continue in use into the evening, or that the building takes a long time to heat up or cool down prior to occupation at the start of the day.

Table 7.7 Air handling benchmarks for air conditioned offices

Parameter	Benchmark for stated office type			
	Air conditioned standard office (Type 3)		Air conditioned prestige office (Type 4)	
	Good practice	Typical	Good practice	Typical
Air handled ((litre·s^{-1})·m^{-2})	4	4	4	4
Specific fan power (W/(litre·s^{-1}))	2	3	2	3
Running hours (h/yr)	2750	3500	3000	3700
Energy use indicator (EUI) ((kW·h·m^{-2})/yr)	22	42	24	44

Note: factors for converting treated floor area to nett and gross are given in Table 20.2

This extended running can be alleviated by careful zoning so that the only fans to function are those which serve the parts of the building in use, and by selecting heating/cooling systems which can pre-condition all or part of the building without operating all the fans.

7.3.6.2   Air transport losses

Transport energy losses can also be minimised by reducing resistance to air movement through good ductwork design. This is constrained by increased capital costs and by the space requirements for the larger ductwork, but careful consideration at the design stage can reduce energy consumption significantly. The following guidelines should be followed:

—   Ductwork should be designed to achieve minimum pressure loss. This requires low velocities, the use of low-loss fittings (swept bends rather than elbows etc.) and to undertake pressure loss design to minimise damper requirements.

—   Central plant filters provide a significant resistance to airflow. A careful balance must be struck between filtration efficiency and pressure drop which both vary with time for a given installation.

—   The length of ducts should be minimised by carefully siting the plant room and air-handling units. Excessive ductwork increases pressure drop, and increases fan duty and consumption.

Guidance on ductwork design can be found in CIBSE Guide B3[21]. Further guidance on minimising ductwork pressure drop is given in Guide B2[2] (section 4.4.3) and Good Practice Guide GPG 257[3]. This also provides a comparison of the effect of pressure drop through various system components, highlighting the trade-off between capital and running costs. The figures show how running costs are reduced using low velocity systems and how some components become more expensive (notably ductwork) while others become cheaper (notably fans).

7.4   Ventilation and air conditioning controls

Air systems generally provide a more rapid response than wet systems, so good control is essential for comfort conditions and energy efficient operation. DDC or BMS controls are generally recommended as they provide more accurate control of temperature and volumes (see section 6). The control of ventilation and air conditioning is covered in CIBSE Guides B2[2] and H[35], and Good Practice Guide GIR 41[28]. Table 7.8 provides guidance on the selection of controls for mechanical ventilation systems.

7.4.1   Plant start/stop

Air systems should generally be started and stopped in accordance with the guidance given in 5.5. Due to the faster response of air systems, optimum start control has a lesser effect but should still be used. Optimum stop is not normally used with ventilation systems due to the need to maintain minimum fresh air rates. Night purge systems pre-cool the building structure overnight to limit the

Table 7.8 Selection of controls for mechanical ventilation systems

Plant	Control function
Ventilation systems start/stop up to 30 kW heating	Time switch; resolution better than 15 minutes, spring reserve/battery back up
Ventilation systems start/stop 30–100 kW heating	Optimum start/stop recommended
Ventilation systems start/stop over 100 kW heating	Optimum start/stop required by current Building Regulations
Fresh air and exhaust dampers; tempered air systems	Open/closed linked with time control of plant
Fresh air, re-circulation and exhaust dampers; central air handling units; minimum fresh air	Full re-circulation when unoccupied; minimum fresh air position when occupied; minimum fresh air preferably controlled with respect to air quality
Fresh air, re-circulation and exhaust dampers; central air handling units; free cooling	Free cooling override of minimum fresh air from heating/cooling sequence; fresh air temperature high-limit or preferably enthalpy control
Tempered air systems	Heating/cooling sequence for constant supply temperature; possible reset supply condition according to ambient temperature or summated demand if appropriate
Single zone air handling units	Heating/cooling sequence from space or return air temperature; possible minimum supply air temperature to prevent dumping of cold air; systems for large spaces (lecture theatres, etc.) reset supply air temperature from return air
Multi-zone air handling units; common cooling coil	Re-heater batteries controlled with respect to space or return air temperature. Common cooling coil controlled from zone requiring most cooling; do not control cooling coil at constant off coil temperature, except in rare case of dew-point system
VAV air handling units: temperature	Heating/cooling sequence for constant supply temperature; possible reset supply temperature according to ambient temperature or summated demand if appropriate
VAV air handling units; supply fan	Speed or pitch control with respect to duct pressure 2/3 of the way along supply duct
VAV air handling units; supply fan, alternative methods	Speed or pitch control with respect to point near supply fan with reset from summated system demand, plus low limits; demand based control strategies based on VAV box positions can be used but can be unduly influenced by poorly sized boxes
VAV air handling units; extract fan	Control with respect to supply/extract differential volume
VAV boxes	Control velocity between minimum and maximum with respect to space temperature
Dual duct air handling units	Control hot and cold decks for a constant temperature. Possible reset according to outside temperature or summated demand
Dual duct mixing boxes	Mix hot and cold duct supplies according to space temperature
VAV dual duct	Fans as for VAV; temperature as for dual duct
Fan coil units	Return air (or space) temperature control of heating & cooling in sequence
Induction units	Heating and cooling control in sequence from space or return air temperature; segregation of heating and cooling hydraulic distribution essential for efficient operation
Intermittently occupied areas	Occupancy sensing controls with appropriate default values dependent upon system response
Humidification	Control from space or return relative humidity, supply modulating high limit
De-humidification	Over-ride temperature control of cooling coil to cool air below dew-point; re-heat via re-heater batteries as per normal temperature control; supply temperature low limit may be required

daytime peak cooling requirement and require operation at night.

Heater and cooler batteries, humidifiers, etc. should always be interlocked with the fan to ensure they are only able to operate when required. Terminal units such as fan coil units, fan assisted VAV boxes, etc. should all have effective time control. Demand based control systems to operate central plant only when required should be considered to minimise energy consumption.

7.4.2   Set points, dead-bands and summated signals

Temperature and humidity set points must be selected for the minimum energy consumption consistent with comfort conditions. Adequate dead-bands between heating and cooling are essential to minimise energy consumption and avoid simultaneous heating and cooling.

Where DDC is used with P+I control, the results of the heating and cooling calculations should be summated and a common signal produced to avoid simultaneous heating and cooling due to the integral action. The signal should then split into heating, free cooling (where appropriate) and mechanical cooling.

7.4.3   Sensor location

Sensors must be located in representative positions for the services being controlled. Where multiple terminal units are used in air conditioning systems, such as VAV systems, one sensor per terminal unit is normally required.

7.4.4   Free cooling control

Free cooling can significantly reduce the running costs of air conditioning systems. Central air handling units should have the supply, re-circulation and extract dampers controlled in parallel to provide fresh air as the first stage of cooling. When the system calls for cooling and outdoor enthalpy is below the setting on the enthalpy controller, the fresh air dampers modulate open. If the outdoor air enthalpy is above the enthalpy set point then the fresh air dampers remain closed. If the outside air can not satisfy cooling requirements of the conditioned space then mechanical cooling will be brought on in stages. Free cooling control is improved by enthalpy control which compares fresh air and return air enthalpy, controlling the fresh air to meet demand. Enthalpy control is essential where controlled humidification and/or de-humidification are provided by the AHU.

Free cooling is available with some packaged air conditioning units and should be used wherever possible. Free cooling is also available via cooling towers providing cooled water without chillers operating (see 8.1.3). Complex control strategies and additional filtration are necessary for effective operation, although significant savings are claimed.

7.4.5   Humidity control

Most comfort cooling applications do not require close control of relative humidity in the occupied space and do not require controlled de-humidification, see section 7.2.3.2.

Humidification may be required with air conditioning systems to provide a minimum relative humidity in winter. A relative humidity limit in the supply air is required to prevent saturation in the distribution ductwork.

Energy efficient humidifiers should be used, preferably with modulating control rather than control in stages or simple on/off control.

Where both humidification and de-humidification is essential, a wide dead-band between humidification and de-humidification set points is recommended to minimise energy consumption.

Humidistats or humidity sensors can suffer from drift causing inaccurate relative humidities and possibly higher energy consumption. Specifying a high quality sensor and regular calibration can help avoid this.

7.4.6   Multi-zone systems

Multi-zone systems with a common cooler battery must have the cooler battery effectively controlled with respect to the space requiring the greatest amount of cooling, as poor control can lead to excessive energy use. These systems must not be controlled at a constant supply temperature, except in the rare case of a dew-point system.

7.4.7 CO_2 demand-controlled ventilation

Where spaces have a large and unpredictable occupancy, there is potential to save energy by matching air supply to ventilation demand. This is most commonly achieved by sensing CO_2 and can provide significant energy savings for both full fresh air and re-circulation systems. CO_2 control is more expensive than conventional forms of control but can be set up more easily. However, it often has a rapid payback.

In recirculation systems, the minimum fresh air quantity is normally controlled via the supply, re-circulation and extract dampers in relation to air quality. This is particularly effective for VAV systems where fixed minimum damper positions would provide varying fresh air content.

The air volume can be controlled on full fresh air systems in relation to CO_2 via variable speed drives or variable pitch axial fans. However, minimum ventilation rates may be required to provide adequate heating and cooling, air distribution, etc. Significant energy savings can still result even where turndowns in volume are limited (see GIR 41[28]).

BSRIA TN 12/94[36] suggests that significant energy savings may accrue from the use of CO_2 control. However, each application has to be judged on the ventilation requirements based on predicted occupancy profiles for the particular building and TN12/94 contains the means of assessing the viability of given schemes. In general, the energy benefits of a CO_2 controlled ventilation system manifest themselves in buildings with spaces subject to variable occupancy.

7.4.8   VAV control

The control of VAV systems is far more complex than other air conditioning systems. VAV systems should normally only be used where the load is predominantly cooling throughout the year, such as a deep plan office building. Good space and duct sensor locations are essential for energy efficient operation[29].

Proportional space temperature control is preferable for stability, ease of commissioning and efficient operation. A dead-band between heating and cooling is necessary where reheat occurs.

Most modern VAV systems use velocity reset VAV boxes. Primary air volume is reset between minimum and maximum settings in relation to space temperature. These are pressure dependent and the system is substantially self-balancing. Reheat is normally at minimum volume to prevent energy wastage. Fan-assisted VAV boxes generally have greater energy consumption, additional maintenance and higher capital costs.

Supply fans are normally controlled in relation to static pressure, two thirds of the way along the supply duct. Care must be taken to ensure the static pressure setting is not higher than necessary as this will waste energy and possibly cause increased noise at the terminal units at low loads. Extract fans are normally controlled in relation to differential volume. Difficulties can arise due to velocity sensor locations from which the volumes are calculated. A wide range of VAV controls is discussed in detail in CIBSE Guide H[35] and Good Practice Guide GIR 41[28].

References

1   *Natural ventilation in non-domestic buildings* CIBSE Applications Manual AM10 (London: Chartered Institution of Building Services Engineers) (1997)

2   *Ventilation and air conditioning* CIBSE Guide B2 (London: Chartered Institution of Building Services Engineers) (2001)

3   *Energy efficient mechanical ventilation systems* Good Practice Guide GPG 257 (Action Energy) (1999) (www.action energy.org.uk)

4   *The design team's guide to environmentally smart buildings* Good Practice Guide GPG287 (Action Energy) (2000) (www.action energy.org.uk)

5   *A designers guide to the options for ventilation and cooling* Good Practice Guide GPG 291 (Action Energy) (2001) (www.action energy.org.uk)

6   *Environmental design* CIBSE Guide A (London: Chartered Institution of Building Services Engineers) (1999)

7   *HVAC Applications* ASHRAE Handbook (Atlanta, GA: American Society of Heating, Refrigeration and Air Conditioning Engineers) (2003)

8   *Avoiding or minimising the use of air-conditioning — A research report from the EnREI Programme* General Information Report GIR 31 (Action Energy) (1995) www.actionenergy.org.uk

9   *Natural ventilation in non-domestic buildings* BRE Digest 399 (London: Construction Research Communications) (1994)

10   *Best practice in the specification for offices* (Reading: British Council for Offices) (2000)

11   *Testing buildings for air leakage* CIBSE TM23 (London: Chartered Institution of Building Services Engineers) (2000)

12   *Conservation of fuel and power* The Building Regulations 2000 Approved Document L2 (London: The Stationery Office) (2001)

13   *Technical standards for compliance with the Building Standards (Scotland) Regulations 1990 (as amended)* (London: The Stationery Office) (2001)

14   *Conservation of fuel and power* The Building Regulations (Northern Ireland) 1994 Technical Booklet F (London: The Stationery Office) (1999)

15   *Office service charges analysis* (7th edn.) (London: Jones, Lang and Wootton) (1992)

16   Baker N V and Steemers K *The LT Method 2.0. An energy design tool for non-domestic buildings* (Cambridge: Cambridge Architectural Research)(1994)

17   *Minimising pollution at air intakes* CIBSE TM21 (London: Chartered Institution of Building Services Engineers) (1999)

18   *Mixed mode buildings* CIBSE Applications Manual AM13 (London: Chartered Institution of Building Services Engineers) (2000)

19   Brittain J R J *Oversized air handling plant* BSRIA GN 11/97 (Bracknell: Building Services Research and Information Association) (1997)

20   *Energy efficiency in offices* Energy Consumption Guide ECG 19 (Action Energy) (2000) (www.actionenergy.org.uk)

21   *Ductwork* CIBSE Guide B3 (London: Chartered Institution of Building Services Engineers) (2002)

22   *Energy efficiency in offices — 1 Bridewell Street* Good Practice Case Study GPCS 21 (Action Energy) (1991) (www.actionen-ergy.org.uk)

23   *Selecting air conditioning systems. A guide for building clients and their advisers* Good Practice Guide GPG 71 (Action Energy) (1993) (www.actionenergy.org.uk)

24   Cassar M *Environment management: Guidelines for museums and galleries* (London: Museums and Galleries Commission) (1994)

25   *Efficient humidification in buildings* BSRIA AG10/94.1 (Bracknell: Building Services Research and Information Association) (1995)

26   Bordass W (private communication)

27   *Refrigeration and the environment — typical applications for air conditioning* BSRIA TN 15/92 (Bracknell: Building Services Research and Information Association) (1992)

28   *Variable flow control* General Information Report GIR 41 (Action Energy) (1996) (www.actionenergy.org.uk)

29   *New ways of cooling — information for building designers* General Information Leaflet GIL 85 (Action Energy) (2001) (www.actionenergy.org.uk)

30   Alamdari F and Eagles N *Displacement ventilation and chilled ceilings* BSRIA TN2/96 (Bracknell: Building Services Research and Information Association) (1996)

31   Jones W P *Air conditioning applications and design* (2nd edn.) (London: Edward Arnold) (1997)

32   King G R and Smith M H *VRF based air conditioning systems — performance, installation and operation notes* BSRIA TN 10/97 (Bracknell: Building Services Research and Information Association) (1997)

33   *Energy efficiency in offices. Understanding energy use in your office* Good Practice Guide GPG 33 (Action Energy) (1992) (www.actionenergy.org.uk)

34   *Energy savings with electric motors and drives* Good Practice Guide GPG 2 (Action Energy) (1998) (www.action energy.org.uk)

35   *Building control systems* CIBSE Guide H (London: Chartered Institution of Building Services Engineers) (2000)

36   Potter I N and Booth W B *CO_2 controlled mechanical ventilation systems* BSRIA TN 12/94.1 (Bracknell: Building Services Research and Information Association) (1994)

Bibliography

HVAC systems and equipment ASHRAE Handbook (Atlanta, GA: American Society of Heating, Refrigeration and Air Conditioning Engineers) (2000)

Martin A J *Control of natural ventilation* BSRIA TN11/95 (Bracknell: Building Services Research and Information Association) (1995)

Martin A J *Night cooling strategies* BSRIA RR5/96 (Bracknell: Building Services Research and Information Association) (1996)

Energy demands and targets for heated and ventilated buildings CIBSE Building Energy Code 1 (London: Chartered Institution of Building Services Engineers) (1999)

Energy demands for air conditioned buildings CIBSE Building Energy Code 2 (London: Chartered Institution of Building Services Engineers) (1999)

Martin P L and Oughton D L *Faber and Kell's Heating and air-conditioning of buildings* (London: Butterworth Heinemann) (1995)

Steer J W and Doig R The specification of efficient ventilation systems in the decommissioning of redundant plant at Sellafield *Proc. CIBSE Nat. Conf., Eastbourne 1–3 October 1995* (vol. 2) 26–35 (London Chartered Institution of Building Services Engineers) (1995)

Green R H, Taylor M S and Fletcher P G The performance of a prototype, commercial building, balanced ventilation, heat pump *Proc. CIBSE Nat. Conf., Eastbourne 1–3 October 1995* (vol. 2) 36–43 (London: Chartered Institution of Building Services Engineers) (1995)

Riffat S B, Shao L and Shehata Mop fan for removal of air-borne pollutants *Proc. CIBSE Nat. Conf., Eastbourne 1–3 October 1995* (vol. 2)

44–51 (London: Chartered Institution of Building Services Engineers) (1995)

Leaman A J, Cohen R R and Jackman P J Ventilation of office buildings: deciding the appropriate system *Proc. CIBSE Nat. Conf., Brighton 2–3 October 1994* (vol. 2) 90–101 (London: Chartered Institution of Building Services Engineers) (1994)

Channer G R A mixed mode ventilation system for an office tower which addresses the problems of infiltration, internal comfort and energy consumption *Proc. CIBSE Nat. Conf., Brighton 2–3 October 1994* (vol. 2) 109–120 (London: Chartered Institution of Building Services Engineers) (1994)

Butler D J G Chilled ceilings and beams — BRE research *Proc. CIBSE Nat. Conf., Alexandra Palace 5–7 October 1997* (vol. 1) 53–60 (London: Chartered Institution of Building Services Engineers) (1997)

Edwards M, Linden P and Walker RR Theory and practice — natural ventilation modelling *Proc. CIBSE Nat. Conf., Brighton 2–3 October 1994* (vol. 2) 102–108 (London: Chartered Institution of Building Service Engineers) (1994)

W P Jones *Air conditioning engineering* (5th edn) (London: Edward Arnold) (2001)

Trott A R and Welch T C *Refrigeration and air conditioning* (London: Butterworth Heinemann) (1999)

Chilled ceilings and beams CIBSE Research Report RR5 (London: Chartered Institution of Building Services Engineers) (1998)

Air-to-air heat recovery CIBSE Research Report RR2 (London: Chartered Institution of Building Services Engineers) (1995)

Fletcher J *Pre-cooling in mechanically cooled buildings* BSRIA TN16/95 (Bracknell: Building Services Research and Information Association) (1995)

De Saulles T *Free cooling systems — design and application guide* BSRIA RR16/96 (Bracknell: Building Services Research and Information Association) (1996)

Jackman P J *Air distribution in naturally ventilated offices* BSRIA TN 4/99 (Bracknell: Building Services Research and Information Association) (1999)

Guide to air distribution technology for the internal environment (Heating, Ventilating and Air Conditioning Manufacturers Association) (2000)

A guide to energy efficient ventilation (Coventry: Air Infiltration and Ventilation Centre) (1996)

A practical guide to air leakage testing HVCA DW143 (London: Heating and Ventilating Contractors Association) (2000)

Kendrick C and Martin A *Refurbishment of air conditioned buildings for natural ventilation* BSRIA TN 8/98 (Bracknell: Building Services Research and Information Association) (1998)

REHVA guide to displacement ventilation in non-industrial premises (Brussels: Federation of European Heating and Ventilating Associations (REHVA)) (2002)

Ventilation and cooling option appraisal — a clients guide Good Practice Guide GPG 290 (Action Energy) (2001) (www.actionenergy.org.uk)

HVAC strategies for well-insulated airtight buildings CIBSE TM29 (London: Chartered Institution of Building Services Engineers) (2001)

Air handling units HEVAC Guide To Good Practice (Marlow: HEVAC Association)

Fan application guide (Marlow: Fan Manufacturers Association/HEVAC Association)

Fan and ductwork installation guide (Marlow: Fan Manufacturers Association/HEVAC Association)

Butler D Pushing the limits of displacement ventilation for cooling *Proc. CIBSE Nat. Conf., London 2002* (vol. 1) 53–60 (2002)

8 Refrigeration design

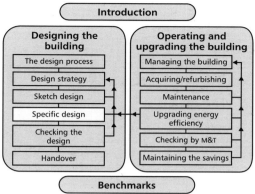

This section sets out key issues to be considered when designing energy efficient refrigeration systems and should be read in conjunction with section 6, which covers mechanical ventilation and air conditioning. There is considerable potential at sketch design stage to minimise or even avoid the need for mechanical cooling and this is addressed in section 4. Energy issues related to the maintenance of refrigeration systems are covered in section 17. For further detail on refrigeration, refer to the CIBSE Guide B4[1], Fuel Efficiency Booklet FEB 11[2], BSRIA TN15/92[3], Good Practice Guides GPG 280[4] and 283[5], and ASHRAE Handbook: *Refrigeration*[6].

8.0   General

Most refrigeration plant is electrically driven and can add significantly to energy costs and CO_2 emissions. Moreover, the need for cooling is increasing, due to the greater use of information technology and increasing comfort expectations.

Building Regulations Approved Document L2[7]* sets out a number of issues related to refrigeration plant, in particular minimising the energy consumed in air conditioning and/or mechanically ventilated (AC/MV) systems, see 4.2.5.4. This includes the 'carbon performance rating' (CPR) for offices which sets out requirements for new and refurbished buildings as well as existing buildings where an AC/MV system is to be significantly altered or replaced. The CPR for air conditioned offices is based on the total installed capacity ($kW·m^{-2}$) of refrigeration plant and a series of factors representing plant management and control.

These requirement are summarised in the relevant parts of section 4 as they influence very early design decisions.

8.1   Minimising cooling requirements

Minimising the need for cooling can reduce energy costs and, in some cases, the capital cost of plant. The need for cooling can be minimised by:

— reducing cooling loads

— raising cooling supply temperatures

— using 'free' cooling.

* Requirements may differ in Scotland[8] and Northern Ireland[9]

8.1.1   Reducing cooling loads

Cooling loads can be reduced in many ways, as discussed in section 4, for example by:

— selecting office equipment with lower power use

— improved management (e.g. turning off lights and personal computers when not in use)

— optimising set points (e.g. space temperature, air supply temperature, recirculation rate and humidity)

— improved, but not necessarily closer, control of temperatures, flows and humidities.

8.1.2   Raising supply temperatures

Raising the temperature at which cooling is delivered allows higher evaporating temperatures which increases refrigeration efficiency and, therefore, reduces energy consumption. It may also increase the cooling capacity of a given size of refrigeration plant. For example, the energy cost of delivering water at 6 °C is some 10% more than at 10 °C. Furthermore, the capital cost of the central plant is likely to be lower, although this may be offset by higher costs of fan coil units, distribution systems, terminal units and other emitters. Temperatures at which cooling is delivered can be raised by:

— installing larger, more efficient heat exchangers for cooling air, but with increased capital cost

— increasing chilled water or supply air volume flow rates, and increasing pipe and duct sizes to maintain the same pump or fan power

— increasing chilled water flows through heat exchangers and increasing pipe sizes to avoid increasing pumping energy e.g. using chilled ceilings

— separating cooling duties that require low temperatures (e.g. de-humidification or areas where cooling loads are exceptionally high) from more general cooling duties that can be achieved with higher temperatures

— raising set points at times of lower cooling demand (e.g. compensating chilled water temperatures).

8.1.3 'Free' cooling

'Free' cooling using ambient air to cool a secondary fluid, usually water or glycol, can also be used to cool air in the building. The secondary fluid can be cooled via cooling towers, air-cooled heat exchangers (dry air-cooling coils) or evaporative heat exchangers. Some options are shown in Figure 8.1[10]. Free cooling systems such as these can be particularly effective in situations where the cooling demands are high and unrelated to ambient temperature, for example in computer suites and telephone exchanges.

The direct system or 'strainer cycle' circulates water directly through a cooling tower without running the chiller. The potential for this 'free' cooling is demonstrated by the fact that, in London, the ambient wet bulb temperature is below 8 °C for more than 40% of the year. A diverter valve causes cooled water to circulate directly from the cooling tower to the cooling coils in the chilled water system. A strainer is provided in the circuit so that the cooling tower water can be kept sufficiently clean to prevent blockage of the small waterways in the cooling

coils. The pressure drop across the strainer will increase the pumping pressures, and this has to be balanced against the free cooling provided. The potential for contamination and fouling of the chilled water circuit can also be a significant problem.

To avoid some of the drawbacks, indirect systems are available, incorporating a plate heat exchanger with a closed-circuit cooling tower[11]. However, use of this system reduces the amount of potential free cooling due to the temperature difference across the heat exchanger.

8.2 Designing energy efficient systems

Refrigeration (including heat rejection) can be a significant energy user in air conditioned offices although it is seldom as much as that used in the pumps and fans that distribute the cooling. New more energy efficient ways of cooling are discussed in GIL 85[12]. Typical and good practice performance indicators for conventional systems are shown in Table 8.1[13]. The energy use indicator (EUI) is the product of:

(a) the installed capacity in $W \cdot m^{-2}$ of treated floor area; the installed capacity typically varies between about 90 and 135 $W \cdot m^{-2}$ but should be kept to a minimum once the need for refrigeration has been established; BSRIA *Rules of thumb*[14] indicates 125 $W \cdot m^{-2}$

Table 8.1 Refrigeration (including heat rejection) benchmarks for offices[13]

Parameter	Benchmark for stated office type					
	Naturally ventilated open plan office (Type 2)		Air conditioned standard office (Type 3)		Air conditioned prestige office (Type 4)	
	Good practice	Typical	Good practice	Typical	Good practice	Typical
Installed capacity ($W \cdot m^{-2}$)	5	8	90	125	100	135
Average COP	2.0	2.0	3.0	2.5	3.0	2.5
Running hours (h/yr)	1500	2000	1500	2500	2500	3000
Utilisation (%)	30	30	30	25	25	25
Energy use indicator (EUI) (($kW \cdot h) \cdot m^{-2})/yr$	1.1	2.4	14	31	21	41

Note: factors for converting treated floor area to nett and gross are given in Table 20.2

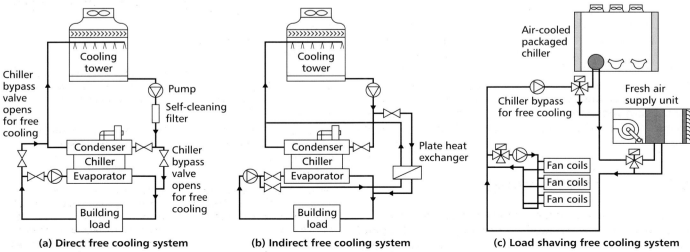

(a) **Direct free cooling system**   (b) **Indirect free cooling system**   (c) **Load shaving free cooling system**

Figure 8.1 Options for free cooling[10] (reproduced from *Premises and Facilities Management* by permission of the publisher)

(b)　　　the reciprocal of the average COP of the plant

(c)　　　the annual running hours

(d)　　　the average percentage utilisation of the plant expressed as a decimal fraction.

The result is divided by 1000 to obtain the EUI in $(kW \cdot h) \cdot m^{-2}$ per year.

Cooling plant and the associated pumps need to be carefully controlled to run only when there is a genuine demand. Small 24-hour loads should be independently cooled.

Oversizing refrigeration plant increases capital and running costs unnecessarily. Chiller capacities greater than those shown in Table 8.2 suggest oversizing[15].

Table 8.2 Basic chiller plant capacity benchmarks

Building type	Chiller capacity (cooling load) / $W \cdot m^{-2}$
Offices, health-care, retail stores	140
Restaurants	220
Computer suites	400

Note: Indicated capacities on equipment nameplates may not be applicable; actual cooling loads may be significantly lower than those shown in table

The lower the chilled water (evaporator) temperature, the more energy used and the greater danger of freeze-up. Therefore, arrangements that segregate chillers used for low temperature circuits will improve energy efficiency. Direct expansion (DX) cooling can more easily provide lower air temperatures, and it can be worthwhile installing separate DX systems for specific dehumidification duties.

Where possible, include interlocks to hold off chillers and pumps when external air temperature drops below a preset level, say 12 °C.

Designs should deal with common problems to maintain efficiency[5]. For example, in large chiller plant, an automatic air purging system will prevent the build-up of air and other non-condensable gases in the condenser, and effective oil separation and recovery systems will prevent evaporator fouling, both helping to maintain good heat transfer.

Instrumentation should be incorporated for monitoring the performance[16] of large chiller plant. As a recommended minimum, power use, condensing and evaporating temperatures, chilled fluid and ambient temperatures should be measured. Leakage of refrigerant and oil usage should also be monitored. Refrigerant leakage can cause a significant increase in energy consumption and should, therefore, be minimised through adherence to good practice[17].

8.3.1　　Thermal storage

Thermal storage techniques can smooth out the peaks and troughs in cooling demand, improving the loading and efficiency of chillers[18]. The economics are highly dependent on the electricity tariff. Opportunities include:

—　　chilled water storage during periods of low demand

—　　ice storage, where ice is formed on plates or tubes and subsequently defrosted to provide chilled water

—　　other phase change and eutectic materials that freeze at certain temperatures depending on the particular substance (they can be frozen during periods of low load e.g. night-time, and then defrosted at peak periods)

—　　use of the building's thermal inertia (see section 4).

The main advantages/disadvantages of thermal storage systems are shown in Table 8.3.

The chiller and thermal store can be used for partial or full storage. Partial storage provides load levelling, with the chiller still operating during the day to meet the peak cooling load. Full storage eliminates the daytime operation of the chiller altogether, thus reducing electrical energy costs, but increasing the store size. These various operational modes are discussed in CIBSE TM18[18] and Guide H[19].

Short term thermal storage, where cooling is smoothed out over say half an hour to a couple of hours, provides a number of benefits:

—　　it allows plant to be operated more efficiently by not exactly matching demand (e.g. compressors may be operated at full load and then switched off, rather than to running continuously at part load)

—　　it allows high electricity charges to be avoided (e.g. maximum demand)

—　　it may allow plant sizes and capital costs to be reduced.

Longer term thermal storage, over several hours, can take advantage of off-peak electricity prices. However, refrigeration efficiency can be reduced because the production of ice and the over cooling of a building require cooling to be delivered at lower temperatures.

Table 8.3 Advantages and disadvantages of thermal storage systems

Advantages	Disadvantages
Smaller chiller required, running for longer hours at or near its design duty, thus maximising its COP and therefore improving overall system efficiency	Mixing losses in the storage vessel
Reduced operating cost e.g. ability to operate for longer periods on low cost tariffs and reduced maximum demand charges	Increased conduction losses from the system because of the lower temperatures and the larger surface area
Steadier load operation increases reliability and reduces maintenance costs (i.e. reduced plant cycling)	Increased plant room space required to allow for the storage vessel
Operation at lower condensing temperatures because of reduced night time temperatures, thus enhancing COP	Ice systems operate at lower evaporating temperatures to enable ice production, thus reducing COP (new phase-change materials that 'freeze' at higher temperatures may overcome this disadvantage)

In ice storage systems, ice storage tanks use the latent heat of fusion of ice to store energy at 0 °C and are particularly economic where there is a large differential between peak and off-peak electricity costs[12]. Energy consumption is often greater than conventional systems in producing ice rather than cooling water directly but costs can be reduced by shifting the load to night time. Ice storage cycles are usually daily, although weekly and seasonal cycles are also used. Refrigeration plant capacity can be reduced but the overall plant will require more space and more complex controls than conventional plant. Ice thermal storage systems use the low temperature store to cool air to lower levels (say 5 °C) which can result in reduced primary air volumes and subsequently reduced fan power in normally sized ducts.

8.2.2   Heat recovery

Efficient heat recovery from refrigeration systems in buildings is often difficult to achieve. Heat is available from the de-superheating, condensing and sub-cooling of the high pressure refrigerant, and this heat can be used to supplement space and domestic hot water heating.

Heat recovery is cost-effective where there is a simultaneous demand for heating and cooling and it is feasible to use heat recovered from cooling one area to heat another. Some systems are particularly suited to such situations, e.g. unitary heat pumps (see 7.3.2.5).

Heat recovered from the condenser can be used in those parts of the building that require it. This may often be the case in a deep plan building where the core is in continuous cooling mode, but in winter and mid season the perimeter may require heating. The main drawback is that only low grade heat is available. Heat recovery is usually achieved through a double bundle condenser, which consists of an oversized shell containing two separate tube bundles — one taking water to the open cooling tower, the second to the heating circuit. The energy benefit of this approach has to be offset against the increased pumping costs associated with the recovery system. The likely difference in fuel cost between the electricity for pumping and the fossil fuel for the boiler plant should also be taken into account.

Where air cooled condensers are adjacent to a heating requirement, such as in a warehouse, it may be possible to duct the warm air from the system condensers into the areas requiring heat. The heat generated in plant rooms can also be used for similar purposes, but care must be taken not to raise the plant operating temperatures excessively by doing so as this would reduce CoP and increase the plant energy consumption.

De-superheating using a separate heat exchanger can be cost-effective if a suitable heat sink can be found for the recovered heat. There can also be a saving in condenser size and cost, which can help to offset the cost of the heat recovery system.

8.3   Refrigeration efficiency

Many factors can affect the energy efficiency of a refrigeration system. Knowledge of these is essential if an energy efficient design is to be achieved. Temperature 'lift', the difference between the evaporating and condensing temperature, is probably the single most important factor for a system designer. Each 1 °C reduction in lift gives a 2–4% decrease in energy consumption, and increases capacity[4].

8.3.1   Refrigeration cycle efficiency

The higher the coefficient of performance (CoP), the better the efficiency[4]. A plant operating with a CoP of 4 will use 25% less power to achieve the same cooling than one operating with a CoP of 3.

CoP depends on condensing and evaporating temperatures, although it is also influenced by compressor efficiency and the choice of refrigerant.

The lower the condensing temperature and pressure, the higher the CoP (see Figure 8.2[20]). A drop in condensing temperature of 1 °C reduces energy use by around 3%.

Lower condensing temperatures can be achieved when:

—   ambient temperatures are lower

—   larger and more efficient condensers are installed

—   condenser performance is maintained.

The higher the evaporating temperature, the higher will be the CoP, see Figure 8.3. A rise in the evaporating temperature of 1 °C will reduce energy use by approximately 3%.

The evaporating temperature is affected by the performance of the evaporator and the expansion valve. Higher evaporating temperatures can be achieved by:

—   raising the temperature of the fluid being chilled

—   installing larger, more efficient evaporators

—   maintaining evaporator and expansion valve performance.

The choice of refrigerant can also affect CoP, but energy efficiency is likely to be secondary to safety and environmental considerations. Designers should note that the phased withdrawal of many common refrigerants under the 1990 Montreal Protocol may influence their choice of refrigerant[21-25].

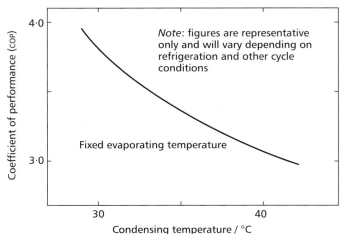

Figure 8.2 Effect of condensing temperature on system performance (reproduced from GPG 42[20]; Crown copyright)

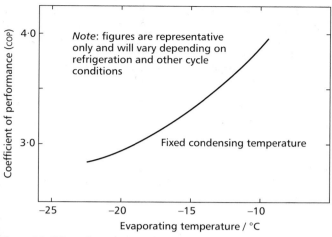

Figure 8.3 Effect of evaporating temperature on system performance (reproduced from GPG 42[20]; Crown copyright)

8.3.2 System and seasonal performance

Improving the performance of the refrigeration cycle alone will not ensure an efficient design. Energy is also used by the auxiliary equipment, including the condenser, evaporator pumps and fans. The coefficient of system performance (CoSP) is generally a more useful measure of energy efficiency than CoP, and can be defined as:

$$\text{CoSP} = \frac{\text{Cooling achieved by refrigeration system}}{\text{Power used by all compressors and auxiliary plant}}$$

Furthermore, it is not sufficient to consider CoP and CoSP at the plant design conditions alone. CoSP should be calculated for all likely conditions, and a seasonal CoSP (a weighted average CoSP for a year) should be estimated. It is important to recognise that most refrigeration systems will operate at part load for most of the year.

8.4 Primary plant

Where the need for mechanical cooling has been clearly established, designers should select the most energy efficient cooling plant. The plant options, normally vapour compression or absorption chillers, will have a major influence on overall system efficiency.

The CoP of vapour compression machines can approach 4.0 and that of absorption chillers up to about 1.0, in terms of delivered energy. When primary energy is considered, the CoPs of the different types of plant are much closer, because the vapour compression cycle uses electricity and the absorption process uses heat. It is, therefore, particularly important to consider primary energy and cost when comparing these chillers.

8.4.1 Selecting efficient components

Selection of efficient plant is based on selecting efficient components — condensers, evaporators, expansion valves, compressors, pumps and fans.

8.4.1.1 Evaporators and expansion valves

Evaporators can be 'flooded' or 'direct expansion' types. In general, they should be as large and efficient as is cost-effective to achieve the highest possible evaporating temperature. Raising the evaporating temperature increases the CoP and therefore reduces energy costs. A circuit diagram of a single stage vapour compressor and the associated pressure enthalpy diagram are combined in Figure 8.4.

In Figure 8.4, the expansion valve (4–1) controls the flow of liquid refrigerant to the evaporator (1–2), and can have a significant impact on performance. It controls the flow of refrigerant to maintain a level of superheat (1a–2) at the evaporator outlet (2), sufficient to ensure that all the liquid has been boiled before it enters the compressor.

Figure 8.4 Single stage vapour compressor circuit and pressure–enthalpy diagram (adapted from Fuel Efficiency Booklet FEB 11[2])

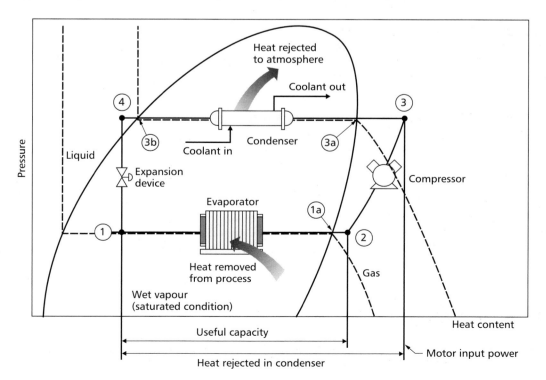

It is important to ensure that these valves are correctly commissioned. They are very often found operating with unnecessarily high superheats, which means that the evaporator is starved of liquid and its performance is impaired.

Thermostatic expansion valves generally operate within a limited range of pressure drop. For this reason, it is sometimes necessary to install head pressure control to prevent condensing pressures (and corresponding temperatures) falling too low in mild and cold weather. Since this is inefficient, it is vital to ensure that the head pressure set point is set as low as possible.

Compressor refrigeration duty and system energy efficiency can be increased by using electronic expansion valves. These provide a robust and more efficient alternative to the thermostatic expansion valve, the valve opening being controlled electronically. The valve can control superheat far more effectively. Also, it does not have the restricted pressure operating range of the thermostatic valve.

8.4.1.2   Compressors

There are a variety of compressors, including reciprocating, screw, scroll and centrifugal, each with different efficiency characteristics[4]. In selecting compressors, it is important to select machines that will be reliable and easy to maintain, and have a high efficiency under all likely conditions.

The energy efficiency of a compressor can vary between 40 and 85%. Furthermore, manufacturers' data sometimes quote the shaft power into the compressor, while others quote motor input power. For a motor/drive efficiency of 90%, this results in a significant apparent difference in quoted efficiency.

An efficient design will usually consist of multiple compressors in order to meet all demands effectively, avoiding inefficient part load operation. Overall efficiency can often be improved by selecting more compressors of a smaller size and with different capacities.

An efficient control system, combined with the use of effective buffering (thermal storage), will also help avoid poor part-load operation as discussed in 8.2 and Good Practice Guide GPG 280[4]. Hot gas by-pass and suction gas throttling should be avoided as a means of control on all but the smallest plant where very close control of temperature is required.

8.4.1.3   Condensers and heat rejection plant

Heat rejection plant is required to cool the condenser; the efficiency of this process will affect the system COP. Overall seasonal efficiencies are therefore influenced by energy efficient design of heat rejection systems. BSRIA TA 1/93[26] compares the operating costs of the different systems.

The two basic types of condenser are:

—   *direct*: air-cooled or evaporative

—   *indirect*: condenser heat is rejected via a water system by using cooling towers or dry air coolers.

Evaporative condensers are the basis for the most efficient refrigeration systems since the condensing temperature can closely approach the ambient wet bulb temperature. A cooling tower system achieves a similar performance, although the condensing temperature may be somewhat higher because of the additional heat transfer stage.

Direct air-cooled condensers are less efficient, producing condensing temperatures several degrees above ambient dry bulb temperature. Water-cooled condensers in conjunction with dry air coolers are the most inefficient option, producing even higher condensing temperatures, often with associated high water pumping and fan costs.

Water treatment is also a key issue for cooling towers and evaporative condensers. Effective treatment is essential to avoid legionella, corrosion and fouling[26]. Poor water treatment can greatly increase energy and water costs. Legionella can be controlled if the tower is designed and operated in accordance with CIBSE TM13[27].

The larger the condensing system, the better the plant performance, but with correspondingly higher capital costs.

Air-cooled condensers

Air-cooled condensers are the simplest form of condenser heat rejection plant, in which air is blown over finned tubes containing the condensing refrigerant. They are generally found on stand-alone plant such as packaged air conditioners, split systems or some packaged air handling plant. They lose efficiency by having to operate at a relatively high condensing temperature, since they do not have the benefit of evaporative water cooling outside the coil. However, they gain by not having pumping and other auxiliary energy consuming plant associated with condenser water systems.

Evaporative condensers

An evaporative condenser is an extension of an air-cooled condenser. As well as air being blown over the tubes, the tubes themselves are continuously wetted by a recirculating water system. They are able to achieve a similar performance to water-cooled condensers and open circuit cooling towers, but eliminate the condenser water pumps. The other potential benefit of using evaporative condensers is that they can make use of the thermo-syphon effect to provide free cooling during periods of low demand and low ambient temperature.

The thermo-syphon effect involves the natural circulation of refrigerant without being pumped by the compressor. Thermo-syphoning which requires specially designed chillers can only take place during cold or cool weather when the condensing temperature is lower than the evaporating temperature.

Wet cooling towers

There are two types of wet cooling tower:

—   *Open circuit*: water from the condenser is pumped to the cooling tower and is cooled by the evaporation of some of the condenser water. This requires all the water passing through the condenser circuit to be treated and results in increased water consumption due to drift losses.

— *Closed circuit*: condenser water is circulated in a closed loop and a separate water circuit is pumped through the cooling tower, cooling the condenser water by transferring heat through a heat exchanger. This minimises water treatment costs but it also reduces energy efficiency due to the temperature difference across the heat exchanger, although this effect can be minimised by specifying a high-efficiency heat exchanger.

Wet cooling towers minimise condensing temperatures and thus enhance chiller COP since they reduce the water temperature to near the ambient wet bulb temperature. However, the auxiliary power to drive a wet cooling tower is greater than other types of heat rejection system.

Dry coolers

Dry coolers reject heat from the condenser water without making use of evaporative cooling. Since there are two heat exchangers between the refrigerant and the final point of heat rejection, such systems are the least energy efficient.

8.4.2 Vapour compression chillers

Most chillers are based on the vapour compression cycle, using either a positive displacement or centrifugal machine. Whilst machines designed for use with the new zero ozone depleting potential refrigerants can be as efficient as the older technologies, refurbishment of existing machines can result in significant reductions in both refrigeration capacity and efficiency[21–25].

Designers have some flexibility in the selection of temperatures over which the system operates (see Figure 8.5). For example, the condensing temperature will be lower for an evaporative condenser than for an air-cooled condenser.

At part load, the temperature differences in the evaporator and condenser are reduced, and so the evaporating temperature rises and the condensing temperature falls. Part-load COP is, therefore, a balance between increased efficiency due to smaller temperature lift and decreased efficiency due to increased losses[28,29]. Figure 8.6 shows how the balance works for compressor COP alone. However, Figure 8.7 shows the effect of part load operation on system performance, which includes the power taken by the pumps etc. The reduction in compressor COP is particularly significant with screw and centrifugal compressors at low loads.

For much of the time, a chiller installation will operate at part-load, so it is important to maintain energy efficient performance. For example, the design duty may require an evaporator temperature of 4 °C and a condenser temperature of 40 °C, corresponding to an outside design temperature of 28 °C. For much of the year, the outside temperature will be lower, so the condensing temperature will also be significantly reduced unless restricted by head pressure control (see 8.4.1.1).

The COP at design full load should not be less than those shown in Tables 8.4 and 8.5.

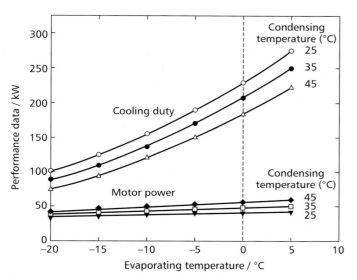

Figure 8.5 Typical compressor performance data (reproduced from Fuel Efficiency Booklet FEB 11[2]; Crown copyright)

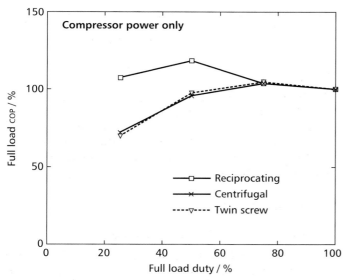

Figure 8.6 Part load compressor performance (reproduced from Fuel Efficiency Booklet FEB 11[2]; Crown copyright)

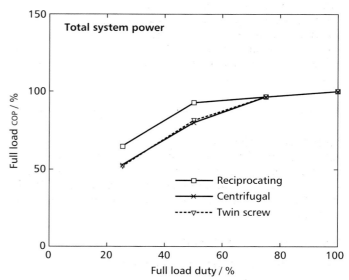

Figure 8.7 Part load system performance (reproduced from Fuel Efficiency Booklet FEB 11[2]; Crown copyright)

Table 8.4 Coefficients of performance of reciprocating water chillers

Cooling capacity / kW	Overall COP for stated type of chiller	
	Air cooled	Water cooled
<120	2.6	3.2
>120	2.8	3.4

Table 8.5 Coefficients of performance, water chillers with centrifugal compressors

Cooling capacity / kW	Overall COP for stated type of chiller	
	Air cooled	Water cooled
< 800	2.2	3.8
> 800	2.3	4.0

8.4.2.1   Reciprocating compressors

Reciprocating compressors are common and often cheaper than other compressor types. However, they have many moving parts and can be more expensive to maintain.

Capacity control to enhance part-load performance can be achieved by cylinder unloading or variable speed control. Cylinder unloading enables output to be reduced in fixed steps, according to the number of cylinders in the machine. For a typical reciprocating compressor, the absorbed power at 25% part load may be about 40% of the full load power.

Variable speed drive gives more flexible control with greater energy savings, although the minimum capacity is much higher because of the need to maintain cylinder lubrication. Compressors are available with improved efficiencies through reduced clearance volumes, better flow through valves and reduced heat transfer. Savings can be up to 20%, although compressor costs are higher.

8.4.2.2   Rotary compressors

In general, rotary compressors are less efficient when operating away from their ideal pressure ratio, but they do not have the valve losses found with reciprocating compressors. They are also more suited to variable speed operation and can sometimes offer a more significant operating range than reciprocating compressors due to effective oil cooling.

Screw compressors are expensive and tend to be used in the middle range of compressor sizes, say 150–1500 kW of cooling. The machines are compact and, because of their limited number of moving parts, require less maintenance.

Capacity control can be achieved by use of a slide valve to give continuously variable loading down to about 10% of full load. At 25% of full load, the absorbed power will be about 50% of the full load power. Lift valve unloading can be used, but it only provides unloading in discrete steps (usually 25, 50 and 75%). This ability to provide a high turn-down ratio makes them more attractive than reciprocating compressors for larger installations.

Scroll compressors are used in smaller units such as unitary heat pumps and these tend to be up to 10% more efficient than the equivalent sized reciprocating machine.

Centrifugal compressors tend to be used towards the top end of the range (i.e. above 500 kW of cooling). They generally have good efficiency at the design condition. Capacity control is usually by inlet guide vanes, but this is very inefficient at reduced loads.

8.4.3   Absorption chillers

The COP of absorption chillers tends to be much less than that of vapour compression machines, particularly at part load[28-31]. However, absorption cooling is worth considering if:

—   there is CHP but cannot use all the available heat, or if you are considering a new CHP plant

—   waste heat is available

—   a low cost source of heat is available (e.g. landfill gas)

—   the site has an electrical load limit that will be expensive to upgrade

—   the site is particularly sensitive to noise or vibration

—   HCFCs need to be avoided

—   the site needs more cooling, but has an electrical load limitation that is expensive to overcome, and you have an adequate supply of heat.

Table 8.6 shows the range of absorption chillers currently available. Quoted COPs are based on manufacturers' data and are ideal rather than achievable. Their attraction is that they can be operated using waste heat. Where this is readily available, the economics can be very attractive. When combined with CHP, it provides the opportunity to extend the period of the year over which there is a demand for heat, further enhancing the viability of the CHP scheme (see section 10).

A low coefficient of performance results in a high rate of heat rejection. When comparing water cooled vapour

Table 8.6 Coefficients of performance, heat operated water chillers

Chiller type	Characteristics			COP*
	Heat source	Refrigerant	Condenser	
Single effect	Direct fired natural gas	NH_3	Air-cooled	0.5
	Hot water (80–130 °C)	H_2O	Water-cooled	0.7
	Steam (0.2–1 bar)	H_2O	Water-cooled	0.7
Double effect	Direct fired natural gas	H_2O	Water-cooled	1
	Steam (3–9 bar)	H_2O	Water-cooled	1.2
	Exhaust gases (280–800 °C)	H_2O	Water-cooled	1.1

* ideal rather than achievable

compression chillers with absorption chillers it is important to take account of the additional capital and running cost of the heat rejection equipment plus the associated pumps. Good Practice Guide GPG 256[32] shows examples of sizing absorption chillers, separately or when using it with CHP.

8.4.4 Heat pumps

Where there is both a heating and cooling requirement, packaged heat pumps can provide an efficient option[33–35] (see 10.1.5 and 7.3.3).

8.4.5 Desiccant cooling

Desiccant dehumidification offers an alternative to using mechanical regeneration to dehumidify[12], see section 7.2.3. It is particularly applicable in full fresh air systems, or where low humidity is required and can utilise waste heat to regenerate (drive the moisture from) the desiccant.

8.4.6 Evaporative cooling

Water evaporated in non-saturated air will produce a drop in dry bulb temperature and an associated rise in moisture content. This evaporative cooling can provide an energy efficient alternative to mechanical cooling. It can be applied in three ways[12]:

— *direct evaporation*: where evaporation takes place in the supply air stream

— *indirect evaporation*: where the exhaust stream is cooled using evaporation and then used to cool the supply via a heat exchanger

— *direct/indirect combination*: the two methods used in series to increase the cooling delivered.

Larger plant is required than conventional systems and there are legionella concerns although the risk is limited by the lower water temperatures involved.

8.5 Distribution systems

Conventional chilled water systems are covered in CIBSE Guide B4[1]. Most chilled water systems are constant volume, using the same amount of energy for pumping throughout the year, regardless of load. Variable flow systems use modulating two port valves which close on reduced load, thus reducing the total flow of the system. Variable speed pumps respond to the reduced demand and decrease the flow of the pumps to match the load of the system. Considerable energy savings can be achieved with the use of variable flow systems. Coil bypass pipework and regulating valves can be eliminated, thus reducing capital costs and commissioning[36–38].

Where there is likely to be a large disparity in load between one zone and another, for instance the north and south facades of a building, separately pumped circuits should be considered. Separate zone circuits can add considerably to the controllability of systems and consequently to the economy of operation, although capital cost may be increased.

Pumps are often selected with a safety margin of around 10% surplus pressure (head) at design flow rates and/or 15% additional flow at design pressure head. The pump with the next highest performance curve is then selected, thereby increasing the oversizing margin. Pumps should be sized close to the actual demand in order to keep power factor, capital and runnig costs to a minimum[15]. Energy efficiency can be improved by selecting more efficient electric motors (see section 11) and/or introducing variable chilled water flow[39] as shown in Figure 8.8.

---

* Requirements may differ in Scotland[8] and Northern Ireland[9]

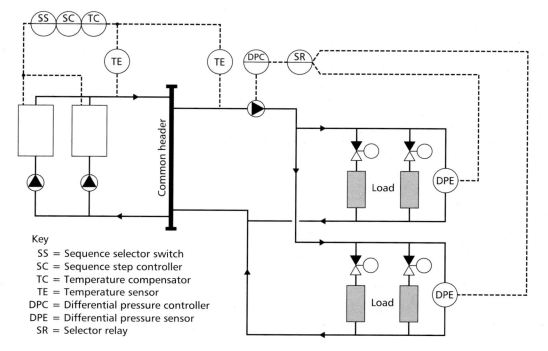

Figure 8.8 Connecting chillers in parallel with variable flow

Key
SS = Sequence selector switch
SC = Sequence step controller
TC = Temperature compensator
TE = Temperature sensor
DPC = Differential pressure controller
DPE = Differential pressure sensor
SR = Selector relay

Building Regulations Approved Document L2★[7] suggests that all pipework, ductwork and vessels for space cooling, including chilled water and refrigerant pipework, should be insulated to the standards in BS 5442[40].

8.6   Controls

Good controls can avoid high refrigeration operating costs. Key requirements are as follows:

— Chillers and chilled water systems should only operate when there is a real cooling demand.

— Maximise full load operation of compressors.

— Keep condensing temperatures low and avoid head pressure control.

— Maintain higher evaporating temperatures.

— Avoid rapid cycling of unloading mechanisms.

— Ensure that auxiliaries can be controlled effectively at low loads.

CIBSE Guide H[19] provides further detail on controls for refrigeration, heat rejection and cooling distribution systems.

8.6.1   Individual compressor capacity control

A variety of systems are used to provide compressor capacity control[41]. Nearly all capacity control methods reduce the overall system COP to a greater or lesser extent. Control methods include:

— *On/off operation*: simple and reliable, but frequent on/off cycling of the compressor is potentially harmful and should be avoided.

— *Cylinder unloading of multi-cylinder reciprocating compressors*: the power requirement reduces as the capacity decreases, although not in exactly the same proportion since frictional and other parasitic losses still exist within an unloaded cylinder.

— *Variable speed drives*: can be employed to provide efficient capacity control of reciprocating, vane, screw and scroll compressors. Oil pump performance and avoiding speeds that create critical resonant frequencies should be carefully considered[37].

— *Slide valves*: used to provide capacity control of screw compressors. The slide valve provides smooth step-less regulation down to 10% of design capacity, although screw compressors consume a significant proportion of full load power when operating at part-load.

— *Variable inlet guide vanes on centrifugal compressors* (to be avoided): capacity reduction is achieved by changing the direction of flow, prior to the refrigerant vapour entering the impeller. This is an extremely inefficient way of providing capacity control, since it reduces the isentropic efficiency of the compressor, and hence system COP.

The following control methods should be avoided:

— *Suction throttle devices*: particularly wasteful as they lower the compressor inlet pressure. This is equivalent to operating with evaporator temperatures lower than design, with all the inherent efficiency penalties.

— *Hot gas by-pass*: circulates high pressure hot gas from the compressor discharge, through an expansion valve to the low pressure side of the system. This is very inefficient since no useful cooling is undertaken by the by-pass gas and there is no attendant reduction in compressor power input. Also, hot gas by-pass can result in excessive superheating of the suction vapour, which can lead to overheating of the compressor.

— *Head pressure control*: condensing temperatures should ideally be allowed to float downwards in cool ambient conditions, which means lower temperature lift for much of the year.

8.6.2   Multiple chiller sequence control

It is not uncommon to find large refrigeration systems operating inefficiently while meeting small cooling loads. This often involves multiple compressors all operating at part load and the associated auxiliaries (fans, pumps etc.) operating at full load. Effective sequence control can achieve significant savings in multiple chiller installations by minimising excessive part load operation of compressors and ensuring that associated auxiliary equipment is automatically switched off when not required.

Operating two chillers at three-quarters load can be more efficient than running one at full load and one at half load. The load efficiency characteristics of the chiller should be used to determine the most efficient combination of chillers and chiller stages, for a typical range of loads.

Reciprocating compressors generally demonstrate better part load performance than do screw or centrifugal compressors and should be used, wherever practicable, to provide modulation. Screw and centrifugal compressors are ideally suited to providing the base load of refrigeration, preferably with systems that have reasonably constant evaporating and condensing temperatures.

Sequence control can be used to allow the chiller to operate under its own capacity controls. This is normally less efficient than full capacity control via a common control signal from the sequence control system. Individual capacity control of multiple chillers must only be considered where the total load can be determined at all times, such as from the return temperature on constant flow systems. Sequence control from the flow temperature, where each chiller operates under its own capacity controls, invariably results in ineffective control, poor operation and reliability.

Good control of multiple chiller installations requires:

— effective hydraulic arrangements

— adequate system water volume capacity (often requiring a buffer vessel)

— high standards of commissioning and maintenance.

Reference should be made to General Information Report GIR 41[39] and CIBSE Guide H[19] for details of variable flow control systems.

8.6.2.1   Evaporators connected in parallel

Poor hydraulic arrangements can result in reduced efficiencies. Evaporators connected in parallel should be individually pumped to avoid the chilled water being diluted with that flowing through off-line chillers. Evaporators should also normally be constant flow and separated from the effects of any flow variation in the secondary circuits. Individual chiller primary pumps should be sized for the full duty flow of the chiller, and non-return valves incorporated on each evaporator to prevent reverse flows through off-line chillers.

Secondary circuits should preferably be variable flow to minimise pumping energy and reduce the possibility of freeze-up due to higher differential temperatures. A buffer vessel should be used to separate primary and secondary circuits and add to system capacity (see Figure 8.8). To prevent flow reversal in the buffer vessel and re-circulation of secondary return into secondary flow, primary circuit flow should normally be greater than secondary flow at all loads.

Constant-flow secondary circuits can be used where there is less danger of freeze-up, but with a greater seasonal pumping energy cost. Where constant-flow secondary circuits are used, sequence control can be with respect to return water temperature in a proportional manner.

An alternative to temperature control is to enable chillers, with individual capacity control, with respect to secondary circuit flowrate. Total heat load of the secondary circuit can be used, but slight inaccuracies in temperature sensing can give significant errors due to the low differential temperature. Therefore, accurate flow metering via magnetic flow meters or vortex meters, etc. should provide an adequate indication of total load based on design differential temperature and should also ensure flow is not reversed in the buffer vessel.

8.6.2.2   Evaporators connected in series

Chillers connected in series can be used where evaporator pressure drop is relatively low and does not cause excessive pumping losses. This will normally limit the number of chillers to two, although three have been used in some instances. By-pass pipes and manual isolation valves may be provided for maintenance purposes.

Secondary circuits should preferably be variable flow to minimise pumping energy and reduce the possibility of freeze-up due to higher differential temperatures. Series connected evaporators should normally be constant flow and separated from the effects of flow variation in the secondary circuits via a buffer vessel (see Figure 8.9). Sequence control should be proportional to primary circuit return water temperature.

Where constant flow chilled water systems are used, a simple hydraulic layout results, as shown in Figure 8.10. However, seasonal pumping energy costs will be higher.

8.6.3   Condenser control

The control of condensers is an important issue. Condensing systems should ideally be operated to reject heat at the lowest possible condensing temperatures. However, there can be a minimum condensing temperature, corresponding to a particular refrigerant pressure, below which plant will not operate. Head pressure controls are implemented in these cases to prevent the condensing pressure falling below the minimum value in cool weather (see 8.4.1.1). The most common and effective technique is to cycle condenser/cooling tower fans on and off. Alternatives include the use of variable speed fans and the less efficient use of dampers to restrict airflow. In some cases, water flow can be restricted, using a valve or variable speed pump, or the cooling tower can be bypassed (which is wasteful). The efficient control of fans and pumps is discussed in section 10.

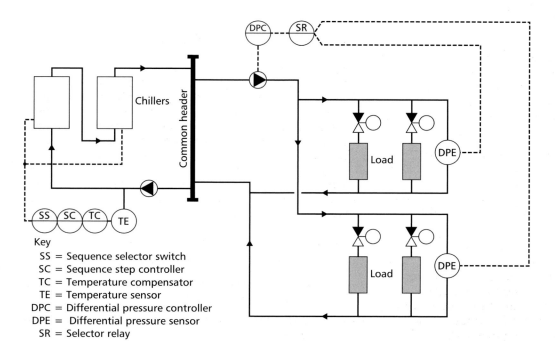

Figure 8.9 Chillers connected in series with variable flow

Key

SS = Sequence selector switch
SC = Sequence step controller
TC = Temperature compensator
TE = Temperature sensor
DPC = Differential pressure controller
DPE = Differential pressure sensor
SR = Selector relay

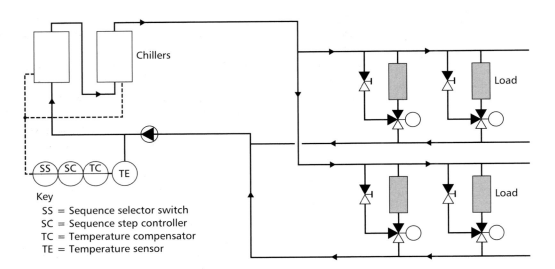

Figure 8.10 Chillers connected in series with constant flow

Key

SS = Sequence selector switch
SC = Sequence step controller
TC = Temperature compensator
TE = Temperature sensor

8.6.4   Cooling tower control

Cooling towers are normally controlled by modulation of the water flow over the tower, and up to one third of the cooling can be provided without the fan operating. Beyond this point the fan is switched on and off to provide control of the water temperature. More sophisticated systems have two-speed fan motors on centrifugal fans which give better control and reduce energy consumption. Variable speed fans give much better control than two speed fans and are much more energy efficient than inlet dampers.

8.6.5   Distribution system control

There is a range of standard controls that can be included in the design of a typical chilled water system. At the very least, simple time control should be provided, but an optimum start/stop control will provide greater savings. Weather compensation (to vary chilled water temperature in relation to outside conditions) can also be beneficial, producing savings from increased operating temperatures and improvements in CoP. System temperatures can also be set back during periods of low load, similar to the use of reset control on weather compensators in heating systems.

Pumping power can be significant in chilled water systems, although it can be reduced by introducing variable speed pumps[36–38] (see 8.5).

References

1   *Refrigeration and heat rejection* CIBSE Guide B4 (London: Chartered Institution of Building Services Engineers) (2003)

2   *The economic use of refrigeration plant* Fuel Efficiency Booklet FEB 11 (Action Energy) (1993) (www.actionenergy.org.uk)

3   *Refrigeration and the environment — typical applications for air conditioning* BSRIA TN 15/92 (Bracknell: Building Services Research and Information Association) (1992)

4   *Energy efficient refrigeration technology — the fundamentals* Good Practice Guide GPG 280 (Action Energy) (2000) (www.action energy.org.uk)

5   *Designing energy efficient refrigeration plant* Good Practice Guide GPG 283 (Action Energy) (2000) (www.actionenergy.org.uk)

6   *Refrigeration* ASHRAE Handbook (Atlanta, GA: American Society of Heating, Refrigeration and Air Conditioning Engineers) (2002)

7   *Conservation of fuel and power* The Building Regulations 2000 Approved Document L2 (London: The Stationery Office) (2001)

8   *Technical standards for compliance with the Building Standards (Scotland) Regulations 1990 (as amended)* (London: Stationery Office) (2001)

9   *Conservation of Fuel and Power* The Building Regulations (Northern Ireland) 1994 Technical Booklet F (London: Stationery Office) (1998)

10   Retrofitting for free cooling *Premises and Facilities Management* (June 1997)

11   De Saulles T *Free cooling systems — design and applications guide* BSRIA RR 16/96 (Bracknell: Building Services Research and Information Association) (1996)

12   *New ways of cooling — information for building designers* General Information Leaflet GIL 85 (Action Energy) (2001) (www.actionenergy.org.uk)

13   Bordass W (private communication)

14   Boushear M *Rules of thumb* BSRIA TN 15/00 (Bracknell: Building Services Research and Information Association) (2000)

15   Brittain J R J *Oversized cooling and pumping plant* BSRIA GN 13/97 (Bracknell: Building Services Research and Information Association) (1997)

16   Calder K *Practical chiller system monitoring* BSRIA TN 7/94 (Bracknell: Building Services Research and Information Association) (1994)

17   *Cutting the cost of refrigerant leakage — an introductory guide for users of small to medium sized refrigeration systems* Good Practice Guide GPG 178 (Action Energy) (1997) (www.action energy.org.uk)

18   *Ice storage systems* CIBSE TM18 (London: Chartered Institution of Building Services Engineers) (1994)

19   *Building control systems* CIBSE Guide H (London: Chartered Institution of Building Services Engineers) (2000)

20   *Industrial refrigeration plant — energy efficient operation and maintenance* GPG 42 (Action Energy) (1992) (www.action energy.org.uk)

21   *CFCs, HCFCs and halons: Professional and practical guidance on substances which deplete the ozone layer* CIBSE GN1 (London: Chartered Institution of Building Services Engineers) (2000)

22   *CFCs in buildings* BRE Digest 358 (London: Construction Research Communications)

23   *Minimising refrigerant emissions from air conditioning systems in buildings* BRE Information Paper IP1/94 (London: Construction Research Communications) (1994)

24   *Phase-out of CFCs and HCFCs: options for owners and operators of air conditioning systems* BRE Information Paper IP14/95 (London: Construction Research Communications) (1995)

25   *The safety and environmental requirements of new refrigerants* BRE Information Paper IP16/95 (London: Construction Research Communications) (1995)

26   *Heat rejection systems — some methods and their operating costs* BSRIA TA 1/93 (Bracknell: Building Services Research and Information Association) (1993)

27   *Minimising the risk of Legionnaires' disease* CIBSE TM13 (London: Chartered Institution of Building Services Engineers) (2002)

28   Smith J and Webb B A fair COP *Building Services J.* 15 (9) 26–27 (September 1993)

29   Smith J and Webb B A comparison of the CO_2 emission rates from gas fired and electrically driven chillers *Proc. CIBSE Nat. Conf., Eastbourne, 1–3 October 1995* (London: Chartered Institution of Building Services Engineers) (1995)

30   Tozer R M and James R W *Chiller operating comparison, absorption and centrifugal* Research Memorandum 140 (London: South Bank University School of Engineering) (1993)

31   Tozer R M and James R W Theory and application of absorption refrigeration systems *Proc. Inst. Refrigeration* 92 12–29 (1996)

32   *An introduction to absorption cooling* Good Practice Guide GPG 256 (Action Energy) (1999) (www.actionenergy.org.uk)

33   *Heat pumps in the UK* Genral Information Report GIR 72 (Action Energy) (2000) (www.actionenergy.org.uk)

34   *Selection and application of heat pumps* CIBSE TM11 (London: Chartered Institution of Building Services Engineers) (1985)

35   *Design guidance for heat pump systems* CIBSE TM15 (London: Chartered Institution of Building Services Engineers) (1988)

36   Parsloe C J *Variable speed pumping in heating and cooling circuits* BSRIA AG 14/99 (Bracknell: Building Services Research and Information Association) (1999)

37   *Variable speed drives for chillers* CADDET Results 344 (Didcot: AEA Technology) (2000) (www.caddet-ee.org)

38   *Variable speed drives on cooling water pumps at Manchester Airport* Good Practice Case Study GPCS 89 (Action Energy) (1992) (www.actionenergy.org.uk)

39   *Variable flow control* General Information Report GIR 41 (Action Energy) (1996) (www.actionenergy.org.uk)

40   BS 5442: 2001: *Methods for specifying thermal insulation materials on pipes, ductwork and equipment in the range –40 °C to +700 °C* (London: British Standards Institution) (2001)

41   Calder K Optimising the control of chillers *Building Services J.* 17 (5) 23–29(May 1995)

Bibliography

Ventilation and air conditioning CIBSE Guide B2 (London: Chartered Institution of Building Services Engineers) (2001)

HVAC systems and equipment ASHRAE Handbook (Atlanta, GA: American Society of Heating, Refrigeration and Air Conditioning Engineers) (2000)

HVAC Applications ASHRAE Handbook (Atlanta, GA: American Society of Heating, Refrigeration and Air Conditioning Engineers) (2003)

Refrigeration systems CIBSE Commissioning Code R (London: Chartered Institution of Buildings Services Engineers) (2002)

Refrigeration efficiency investment — putting together a persuasive case Good Practice Guide GPG 236 (Action Energy) (2000) (www.actionenergy.org.uk)

Purchasing efficient refrigeration — the value for money option Good Practice Guide GPG 278 (Action Energy) (2000) (www.actionenergy.org.uk)

Running refrigeration plant efficiently — a cost-saving guide for owners Good Practice Guide GPG 279 (Action Energy) (2000) (www.actionenergy.org.uk)

Saving money with refrigerated appliances — a guide for smaller retailers, pubs, clubs, hotels and restaurants Good Practice Guide GPG 277 (Action Energy) (2000) (www.actionenergy.org.uk)

Installation and commissioning for efficient refrigeration plant — a guide for technicians and contractors Good Practice Guide GPG 281 (Action Energy) (2000) (www.actionenergy.org.uk)

Service and maintenance for efficient refrigeration plant — a guide for technicians and contractors Good Practice Guide GPG 282 (Action Energy) (2000) (www.actionenergy.org.uk)

Smith J Refrigeration system design for part-load *Building Services J.* 17 (6) 47–49 (June 1995)

Dossat R J andHoran T J *Principles of refrigeration* (London: Prentice Hall) (2001)

Oughton D L and Hodkinson S *Faber and Kell's Heating and air-conditioning of buildings* (London: Butterworth Heinemann) (2001)

Thermal storage: environmental benefits CIBSE Research Report RR6 (London: Chartered Institution of Building Services Engineers) (1998)

Roper M A *Energy efficient chiller control* BSRIA TN 16/00 (Bracknell: Building Services Research and Information Association) (2000)

King G R and Smith M H *VRF-based air conditioning systems — performance, installation and operation notes* BSRIA TN 10/97 (Bracknell: Building Services Research and Information Association) (1997)

Arnold D Chilled beams in naturally ventilated buildings *Proc. CIBSE Nat. Conf., Harrogate, September 1996* (vol. 1) 333–338 (London: Chartered Institution of Building Services Engineers) (1996)

Butler D J G Chilled ceilings — free cooling opportunities *Proc. CIBSE Nat. Conf., Bournemouth, October 1998* 273–279 (London: Chartered Institution of Building Services Engineers) (1998)

Jones W P *Air conditioning engineering* (London: Architectural Press) (2000)

Bardard N and Jaunzens D (eds.) *Low energy cooling technologies selection and early design guidance* IEA Energy Conservation in Buildings and Community Systems Programme EP56 (London: Construction Research Communications) (2001)

Fletcher J *Pre-cooling in mechanically cooled buildings* BSRIA TN 16/95 (Bracknell: Building Services Research and Information Association) (1995)

Efficient air conditioning — the role of refrigeration *Proc. Ann. Conf. Inst. Refrigeration, November 2001* (Carshalton: Institute of Refrigeration) (2001)

Teekaram A J H and Brown R *Retrofitting of heating and cooling systems* BSRIA TN 15/99 (Bracknell: Building Services Research and Information Association) (1999)

Chan K T and Yu F W Part load efficiency of air cooled multiple-chiller plants *Building Services Eng. Res. Technol.* 23 (1) 31–41 (London: Chartered Institution of Building Services Engineers) (2002)

9 Lighting design

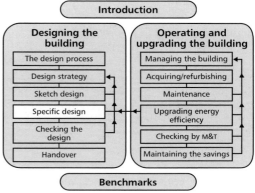

This section sets out some of the main issues in designing energy efficient lighting systems in line with the principles at the front of this Guide. Energy issues related to lighting maintenance are considered in 9.1.2 and section 17. For further detail on lighting issues, reference should be made to the CIBSE *Code for lighting*[1], CIBSE Lighting Guides LG3[2], LG7[3] and LG10[4], and Fuel efficiency Booklet FEB 12[5].

9.0 General

Energy efficient lighting should:

— maximise natural daylight

— avoid unnecessarily high illuminance

— incorporate the most efficient luminaires, control gear and lamps

— include effective lighting controls.

Lighting is often the single largest electrical consumption and cost in non air conditioned buildings. For example, lighting can account for over 40% of electricity costs in naturally ventilated offices. Good lighting design can reduce these running costs and can also reduce internal heat gains, thus reducing the need for air conditioning. Attention to fabric detail at the sketch design stage to ensure the integration of daylighting is particularly important in achieving this (see section 4 and 9.5).

9.1 Design objectives

Good lighting design is covered in detail in the *Code for lighting*[1] and Lighting Guide LG10[4]. Designers should specify the adopted design criteria in order that clients may fully understand what they are likely to get from the system.

The energy efficiency actions to consider in achieving the design objectives are:

— Identify the visual tasks and locations where they will be performed and consider the type of lit environment that is required for the space (see 9.1.5).

— Select the design maintained illuminance, colour rendering index and unified glare rating required for the tasks, or interior, in accordance with the *Code for lighting*[1], noting any special requirements (see 9.1.1).

— Consider the amount of daylight that may be used to minimise running costs (see section 4 and LG10[4]).

— Consider the most energy effective maintenance programme for adoption throughout the life of the installation (see 9.1.2).

— Select the preferred type of lighting system, i.e. general, localised or local (see 9.1.3 and Figure 9.1).

— Select the most appropriate controls to ensure that lighting is reduced or switched off when not required (see 9.5 and Table 9.11).

— Select the most efficient lamp, ballast and luminaire that also meet the optical, control and design requirements (see 9.2, 9.3, 9.4, and Figures 9.2 and 9.3).

— Calculate the installed power density and check that it comes within the recommended range (see 9.6, Table 9.1 and 9.1.4).

9.1.1 Illuminance and power density

The *Code for lighting*[1] provides an extensive list of illuminances (lighting levels), consistent with BS EN 12461-1[6], for various areas and tasks. Using the *Code*, it is the responsibility of designers to determine the appropriate task illuminance for each project.

Design of the visual environment is more than simply illuminating the task. Room surface reflectance and the illuminance received on the walls and ceiling affect the efficiency of an installation, as well as the visual comfort and satisfaction of occupants (see 9.1.3). In general, the lighter and more reflective the finishes, the less light is required to achieve a given illuminance. The *Code for lighting*[1] provides further guidance on reflectance.

9.1.1.1 Design maintained illuminance

The *Code for lighting*[1] gives recommendations in terms of maintained illuminance. This is defined as 'the value below which the average illuminance on the specified area should not fall. It is the average illuminance at the time maintenance should be carried out.

Table 9.1 provides some examples of standard maintained illuminance for various 'typical' tasks or interiors, a more detailed list is provided in the *Code for lighting*[1]. Identifying the task correctly is a key part of the design process and will help minimise installed load and running costs.

Maintained illuminance takes into account luminaire, lamp and room surface depreciation due to soiling, as well as the loss of lamp light output over the lamp's life. The maintenance factor (the ratio of initial illuminance to the maintained illuminance) will be affected by:

— *the choice of lamp*: the lumen depreciation and mortality rate will determine the economic lamp life (see Table 9.3)

— *the choice of luminaire*: the accumulation of dirt and dust will be dependent on the environment, the cleaning cycle and the design of the luminaire

— *the room surfaces*: the frequency of cleaning will affect the reflected component of light.

Regular planned maintenance of a lighting installation can reduce the installed lighting load due to the higher maintenance factor for the design illuminance calculation. Avoid specifying long periods between maintenance since it can result in excessive depreciation which, in turn, can lead to higher connected loads and higher initial illuminance than can be justified.

9.1.1.2 Power density

Once the design solution has been established, it should be checked against installed power density targets for maintained illuminance. This is to ensure that the maintenance regime has not resulted in over-design by keeping the installation within the target ranges.

Table 9.1[1] also provides targets of power density, averaged over the space, for general lighting for a range of applications with particular task illuminance values. The values of average installed power density are based on current good practice using efficient lamps and luminaires in good quality installations. However, improvements on these values could be possible. The targets are for an average sized space (room index of 2.5), with high room surface reflectances (ceiling reflectance of 0.7, wall reflectance of 0.5 and floor reflectance of 0.2) and a high degree of installation maintenance. The values are in average $W \cdot m^2$ for the space and at particular task illuminance levels.

Recent benchmarks for office lighting[7,8] indicate that a lighting load of less than $12\ W \cdot m^2$ of treated floor area can be regarded as good practice, based on a level of 350–400 lux at an efficiency of $3\ W \cdot m^2$ per 100 lux. For 500 lux, or an uplighting installation of 300–350 lux, $15\ W \cdot m^2$ of treated floor area may be required.

9.1.2 Types of lighting system

There are three types of electric lighting system as shown in Figure 9.1, and these are distinguished by the balance between task and building, or ambient, illuminance.

Local or localised task lighting schemes normally consume less energy than general lighting systems, but care must be taken to co-ordinate the lighting layout with

Table 9.1 Lighting energy targets[1]

Application	Lamp type	CIE general colour rendering index (Ra)	Task illuminance / lux	Average installed power density / $W \cdot m^2$
Commercial and other similar applications, e.g. offices, shops and schools†	Fluorescent (triphosphor)	80–90	300 500 750	7 11 17
	Compact fluorescent	80–90	300 500 750	8 14 21
	Metal halide	60–90	300 500 750	11 18 27
Industrial and manufacturing applications	Fluorescent (triphosphor)	80–90	300 500 750 1000	6 10 14 19
	Metal halide	60–90	300 500 750 1000	7 12 17 23
	High pressure sodium	40–80	300 500 750 1000	6 11 16 21

† Values do not include energy for display lighting

Figure 9.1 Basic types of lighting system[1]

A general lighting system employs a regular array of luminaires to provide a uniform illuminance across the working plane.

A localised lighting system uses luminaires located adjacent to the work stations to provide the required task illuminance. The necessary ambient illuminance in the surrounding areas is provided by additional luminaires if required.

A local lighting system employs a general lighting scheme to provide the ambient illuminance for the main area with additional luminaires, located at the workstations, to provide the necessary task illuminance.

task positions and orientation. On the other hand, control systems that integrate daylight with ceiling mounted general lighting (see 9.5) can achieve lower energy consumption.

With both local and localised systems, the average illuminance over non-task and circulation areas should not be less than one third of the illuminance over the task areas.

The problem of variation of illuminance over the working plane is covered by two measures:

— *Uniformity*: the ratio of the minimum illuminance to the average illuminance over the specified task areas (i.e. the task and the immediate surround) for a local or localised lighting system or the core area[1] of the working plane for a general lighting installation. This should not be less than 0.8.

— *Diversity*: the ratio of the minimum to the maximum illuminance over the core area of the working plane of a room when task lighting is used. This should not be less than 0.2. In this case, of course, a uniformity of 0.8 must be achieved over the specified task areas.

9.1.3 Visual comfort and satisfaction

If visual performance is impaired by poor lighting, poor controls or glare[9], the system is not effective. In these circumstances, low energy consumption is being achieved at the cost of reduced staff productivity. The lighting designer should, therefore, find a balance between energy efficiency and a sufficient quantity and quality of illumination to perform the visual task efficiently without experiencing discomfort or disability glare. Discomfort glare is avoided by meeting the recommended limiting unified glare rating for the interior[1]. Disability glare is most commonly caused by the veiling reflections of windows and luminaires on visual display screens.

The Health and Safety (Display Screen Equipment) Regulations[10] require that any possible disturbing glare on display screens should be prevented by co-ordinating the work space location and the electric lighting design. While calling for lighting of workspaces to be naturally lit where reasonably practicable, windows should be fitted with adjustable coverings to attenuate the daylight that falls on the workstation. The Regulations also require a minimum illuminance of 200 lux in any continuously occupied workspace. The Health and Safety Executive's *Display screen equipment work — Guidance on regulations*[10] and CIBSE LG3[2] (with its 2001 addendum) provide further guidance on compliance with the Regulations.

Good visual satisfaction can be achieved by ensuring the observed brightness patterns are not too bland and don't have excessive contrasts, whether the interior is lit by daylight or electric lighting. Following the recommended values of illuminance ratios, surface reflectance, limiting glare index, etc. should help meet these aims. Giving users some control of their luminous environment can also contribute to their satisfaction.

Lamps with a colour-rendering index lower than 80 should not be used in interiors where people work or stay for longer periods. Exceptions may apply for some places and/or activities (e.g. high-bay lighting), but suitable measures shall be taken to ensure lighting with higher colour rendering at fixed continually occupied work places and where safety colours have to be recognised.

9.2 Selecting luminaires

A luminaire comprises a housing, a reflector, a lamp and shielding (either louvres, or a lens or diffusing material) and, for discharge lamps, some form of control gear. The photometric efficiency is measured in terms of its light output ratio. This is the ratio of the total light output of the luminaire to that of the lamp(s) under reference conditions. The higher the light output ratio, for a given light distribution, the more efficient the luminaire. The distribution and other characteristics of over 70 generic types of luminaire are described in the *Code for lighting*[1].

Designers must select equipment by comparing manufacturers' published photometric data. If it is found that recommended power density targets are not met, it is probable that an inefficient luminaire has been selected.

The maintenance characteristic of a luminaire is an important consideration in arriving at the maintenance factor in the design calculation. This means that well sealed or ventilated self-cleaning designs will contribute more to lower installed loads than other luminaires with poorer maintenance characteristics.

9.3 Selecting light sources

Lamp and circuit selection is a crucial part of energy efficient design[11–16]. Information on lamp efficacies,

lumen output and wattage range is given in Figures 9.2[1] and 9.3[1], while Table 9.2[12] provides a summary of applications, advantages and disadvantages of the main lamp types. Lamp manufacturers should be consulted for information on specific lamps.

The factors involved in lamp selection are:

— luminous efficacy (lumen output/watts input)

— rating (consumption watts)

— mortality (rated life of the lamp)

— lumen maintenance (lumen depreciation over life)

— operating position (in some cases this may affect efficacy)

— size (physical properties can affect optical efficiency of light control)

— control gear type and controllability (switching or dimming)

— colour appearance (appearance of the source in terms of 'warm' or 'cool')

— colour rendering

— starting, run-up and re-start times

— minimum starting temperatures.

Within the overall design requirement, lamps with the highest efficacy, and circuits with the lowest losses, should be selected to minimise installed load and running costs.

Figures 9.3 and 9.4[1] show the relationship between initial lamp luminous efficacy (excluding gear losses) and the lamp-lumen 'package' for each lamp type. For clarity, fluorescent lamps are shown separately in Figure 9.4. The most commonly used lumen package range is from 2000 to

Table 9.2 Energy efficient light sources[12]

Type of source	Application	Advantages	Disadvantages
Tungsten and tungsten halogen	Display lighting only as they do not meet the requirements of Building Regulations Part L2[13]	Cheap to buy; dimmable; instant light; excellent colour rendering	Inefficient; short life; no longer meets requirements of Building Regulations Part L2[13]
Linear fluorescent	Can be used in ceiling mounted, surface or suspended luminaires, as part of a direct, localised or task-ambient installation	Cheap to buy; dimmable with special ballasts; instant light; energy efficient; long life (12 000–15 000 hours); good colour rendering for triphosphor types	Linear luminaires or concealed lighting must be used
Compact fluorescent	Can be used in ceiling mounted, surface or suspended luminaires, as part of a direct, localised or task-ambient installation; larger lamp wattages can be used as uplighters	Cheap to buy; instant light; energy efficient; long life (10 000 hours); good colour rendering; small sizes available	Dimming can be difficult although some dimming ballasts are now available
High pressure discharge:			
— metal halide	Wide range of applications, often used in an uplighter as part of a task-ambient installation. They are point sources that are very bright when viewed directly	'White' light source; energy efficient; good colour rendering; small size; relatively long life	Expensive; requires warm-up period after switch on; restrike period up to 15 mins after switch off; not dimmable; many types do not meet Ra 80 requirement; older types not colour stable
— mercury vapour	As for metal halide	Relatively cheap; long life	Poor colour rendering; average efficiency; warm-up and restrike period required
— sodium	As for metal halide	High efficiency; long life (except 'white' SON)	Poor colour rendering except 'white' SON and SON deluxe which are average; warm-up and restrike period (around 30 seconds) required

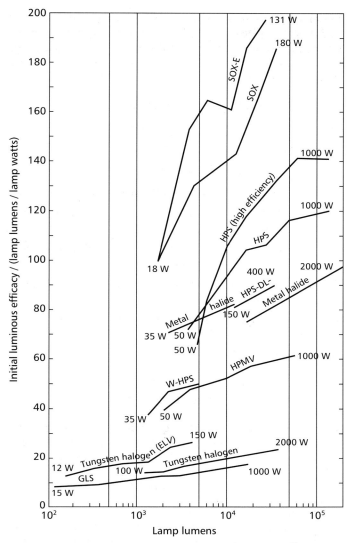

Figure 9.2 Initial luminous efficacies of various types of lamp[1]

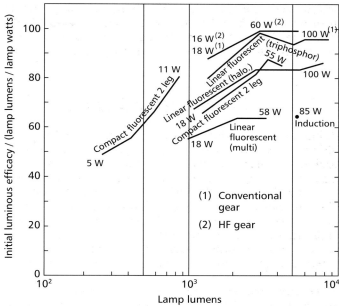

Figure 9.3 Initial luminous efficacies of fluorescent lamps[1]

10 000 lm. Lamps below 2000 lm tend to be used for domestic, display and local lighting applications. Lamps above 10 000 lm tend to be used for heavy industrial and exterior lighting.

Where controllability is important, lamps that can be switched on and off or dimmed easily should be chosen[12]. Fluorescent lamps are the most energy efficient available that meet these criteria. It is now possible to dim some high pressure discharge lamps, although not completely to zero. However, sodium and mercury discharge lamps have longer run-up and re-strike times and are generally less appropriate for use with automatic controls, other than simple time controls for the beginning and end of the working day.

9.3.1   Building Regulations and minimum efficacy of lamps

Building Regulations Approved Documents L1/L2[17]★ state that lighting systems should be reasonably efficient and make effective use of daylight where appropriate.

Requirements include★:

—   minimum efficacies of lamps (see below)

★ Requirements may differ in Scotland[18] and Northern Ireland[19]

—   minimum efficiencies of lamp/luminaire/control gear combinations

—   maximum power consumption of high efficiency control gear (see 9.4)

—   minimum levels of control (see 9.5)

—   meeting the above new-build requirements when replacing lighting systems serving more than 100 m² in existing buildings.

For offices, industrial and storage buildings, Approved Document L2[17] suggests that one way of meeting the requirements of the Regulations is to ensure that the initial efficacy averaged over the whole building is not less than 40 lumens per circuit watt (calculated according to a procedure given in the Approved Document). However, this should be regarded as a minimum requirement. The *Code for lighting*[1] recommends that an average initial circuit lamp luminous efficacy of at least 65 lm·W⁻¹ should be achieved. The BCO's *Best practice in the specification for offices*[8] recommends that commercial office installations should be at least 75 lm·W⁻¹.

For electric lighting systems serving other building types the requirements can be met if the installed lighting capacity is at least 50 lumens per circuit watt. A way of achieving this would be to provide at least 95% of the installed lighting capacity using lamps with circuit efficacies no worse than those in Table 9.3.

For display lighting the requirements can be met if the installed lighting capacity is at least 15 lumens per circuit watt. An alternative would be to provide at least 95% of the installed display lighting capacity comprises lighting fittings with circuit efficacies no worse than those in Table 9.4

9.3.2   Tungsten filament and tungsten halogen lamps

Where it is essential to use tungsten lamps for reasons of colour rendering or light control, e.g. lighting for display and special effects, low voltage tungsten halogen sources

Table 9.3 Light sources meeting the criteria for general lighting given in Building Regulations Approved Document L2[17] (reproduced from Building Regulations Approved Document L2; Crown copyright)

Light source	Types and ratings
High pressure sodium	All types and ratings
Metal halide	All types and ratings
Induction lighting	All types and ratings
Tubular fluorescent	26 mm diameter (T8) lamps; 16mm diameter (T5) lamps rated above 11W, provided with high efficiency control gear; 38 mm diameter (T12) linear fluorescent lamps 2400 mm in length
Compact fluorescent	All ratings above 11 W
Other	Any type and rating with an efficacy greater than 50 lumens per circuit watt

Table 9.4 Light sources meeting the criteria for display lighting as given in Building Regulations Approved Document L2[17] (reproduced from Building Regulations Approved Document L2; Crown copyright)

Light source	Types and ratings
High pressure sodium	All types and ratings
Metal halide	All types and ratings
Tungsten halogen	All types and ratings
Compact and tubular fluorescent	All types and ratings
Other	Any type and rating with an efficacy greater than 15 lumens per circuit watt

should be used in preference to the equivalent mains voltage general lighting service (GLS) or PAR reflector lamps since the former have the highest efficacy and longest life for lamps of this type. The advantages and disadvantages of the two types of tungsten lamp are shown in Tables 9.5 and 9.6. Where possible, GLS and tungsten-halogen lamps should be replaced with compact fluorescent lamps[20] (see also 9.3.4).

9.3.3   Tubular fluorescent lamps

Fluorescent lamps have high efficacy, long life, good controllability and relatively low cost. The older argon-filled 38 mm diameter lamps are largely superseded and should only be used for replacements in starter-less circuits. The modern range of krypton-filled, 26 mm diameter, triphosphor lamps are the preferred choice for switch-start circuits, suitable electronic start circuits, and electronic high frequency ballasts.

Because of their characteristics, fluorescent lamps are used for the majority of commercial lighting applications. Where appropriate, heat recovery should be considered by extracting air through the luminaires. This can improve the light output by maintaining the lamp at its optimum operating temperature (see section 8). The advantages and disadvantages of tubular fluorescent lamps are shown in Table 9.7.

9.3.4   Compact fluorescent lamps

Compact fluorescent lamps (CFLs) are available in various configurations, some types having integral control gear, others with a separate ballast.

Table 9.5 Advantages and disadvantages of tungsten filament (GLS) lamps

Advantages	Disadvantages
Low purchase price	Low efficacy, i.e. 8 to 15 lm·W⁻¹
Excellent colour rendering	Short life, usually 1000 hours
Immediate full light when switched on	High running costs
No ballast required	
Ease of dimming	
Sparkle lighting effects can be created	
Operates in any plane (universal operating position)	

Table 9.6 Advantages and disadvantages of tungsten halogen lamps

Advantages	Disadvantages
Life of 2000 to 5000 hours depending on type	Lower efficacy than low and high pressure discharge lamps
Excellent colour rendering	Transformer required for low voltage lamps
Brighter, whiter light	Operating positions of double ended types is limited to horizontal
No ballast required	Requires careful handling
Sparkle lighting effects can be created	
Can be dimmed	
Immediate full light output when switched on	

CFLs provide the equivalent light output of GLS filament lamps for about 20–25% of the power. So that the lamp size and weight (of those with integral gear) can be kept to a minimum, some of these lamps operate at a low power factor. However, a wide range of luminaires designed specifically for compact fluorescent lamps is available and the extra available space usually allows the incorporation of power factor correction in these luminaires.

Before retrofitting CFLs in existing GLS luminaires[20], it is necessary to ensure that the light distribution and light output ratio is not adversely affected and that the operating position and temperature of the lamp do not significantly reduce its efficacy.

CFLs were originally developed as energy efficient replacements for filament lamps with ratings up to about 20 W. However, the same lamp technology has been applied to higher wattages giving light outputs equivalent to some linear fluorescent lamps. There are several formats including the short twin-leg and '2D' variations. The shorter twin-leg construction means that these can be housed in more compact luminaires for general and localised lighting. The advantages and disadvantages of compact fluorescent lamps are shown in Table 9.8.

9.3.5   Mercury and sodium discharge lamps

High pressure sodium (SON) and metal halide (MBI) lamps offer greater efficacies than high pressure mercury lamps

Table 9.7 Advantages and disadvantages of tubular fluorescent lamps

Advantages	Disadvantages
Low running cost	Excessive switching shortens life
High efficacy	Requires ballast
Up to 8% energy saving when replacing equivalent 38 mm lamps on switch-start circuits	Can be dimmed but requires special ballast and dimmer
Long life in normal use	Limited operation at low ambient temperatures
Minimal reduction of light output through life	
Prompt start and restart with quick run-up to full light output	
Very good to excellent colour rendering	
Universal operating position	

Table 9.8 Advantages and disadvantages of compact fluorescent lamps (CFLs)

Advantages	Disadvantages
Low running cost	Excessive switching shortens life
Replacement for tungsten lamps	Ballast required (but built-in on some lamps)
Five times the efficacy of equivalent tungsten lamps	Not suitable for use on standard domestic dimmers
Average life of 8000 to 10 000 hours	Limited operation at low ambient temperatures
Very good colour rendering	
Prompt start and restart, and quick run up to full light output	
Four pin lamps can be dimmed with suitable ballast and dimmer	
Universal operating position but light output may be reduced with some types for certain positions	

(MBF). The colour rendering properties of the SON range, particularly the SON-DL lamp has increased the range of applications from industrial use to some commercial applications. The efficacy of the MBI lamp is generally lower than the SON lamp but comparable to that of the SON-DL lamp.

The increasing popularity of free-standing and wall-mounted uplighters means that these high pressure lamps are now being used in office installations, although it is advisable to check the colour rendering characteristics before fitting an entire installation. Metal halide and high pressure sodium lamps operated on standard control gear have significant run-up and re-strike times, limiting their use with lighting control systems.

The advantages and disadvantages of SON lamps are shown in Table 9.9.

9.4 Control gear (ballasts)

All discharge lamps require a ballast to start and control the lamp and, possibly, power factor correction. Matching the control gear to the lamp achieves the optimum lamp performance and circuit efficacy. Until recently, ballasts consisted of a wire-wound choke with losses representing 10–20% of the total load. Low-loss wire wound ballasts are now available which are specifically designed to be more energy efficient.

High-frequency (around 30 kHz) electronic ballasts are available for a wide range of fluorescent and compact lamps[21]. These can reduce losses by more than 50% and, as the efficacy of a fluorescent tube increases at high frequency, this provides further energy savings. Additional advantages are virtually instantaneous starting, the possibility of dimming, flicker-free lighting, softer starting conditions that increase lamp life and a power factor of 0.95. It should be noted that there have been cases of interference between some older types of high frequency ballast (operating at frequencies lower than 33 kHz) and infra-red computer mouses. This should not occur with later (33 kHz) ballasts.

Electronic ballasts for lower ratings of metal halide (MBI) lamps are being introduced. These provide faster warm-up

Table 9.9 Advantages and disadvantages of SON lamps

Advantages	Disadvantages
Low running cost	High purchase cost
High efficacy	Moderate colour rendering limits use for general interior lighting
Very long life	Requires ballast
Universal operating position	Requires 1.5 to 6 minutes to reach full output
	Delayed restart when hot on most lamps

Table 9.10 Maximum power consumption of high efficiency control gear as defined in Building Regulations Approved Document L2 (reproduced from Building Regulations Approved Document L2[17]; Crown copyright)

Nominal lamp rating / W	Control gear power consumption / W
Less than or equal to 15	6
Greater than 15, not more than 50	8
Greater than 50, not more than 70	9
Greater than 70, not more than 100	12
Greater than 100	15

periods, instant re-strike, improved circuit efficacy and extended lamp life, but are more expensive than wire wound ballasts.

Ballasts for fluorescent and compact fluorescent lamps are now covered by an efficiency labelling scheme.

Building Regulations Approved Document L2★[17] defines high efficiency control gear as low loss or high frequency control gear that has a power consumption (including the starter component) not exceeding Table 9.10

9.5 Lighting controls

Effective control of electric lighting is the key to realising the potential energy saving from daylight. The control system for the electric lighting should reduce light output when daylighting levels are adequate, and when the space is unoccupied. The integration of daylight and electric

Table 9.11 Recommended types of lighting control[25]

| Type of space | Recommended options for stated lighting type and occupancy | | | |
| | Daylit | | Non-daylit | |
	High occupancy	Low occupancy	High occupancy	Low occupancy
Owned: e.g. small rooms for one or two people such as cellular offices	Manual by door Flexible manual Timed 'off', manual 'on' Photoelectric dimming†	Manual by door Flexible manual Timed 'off', manual 'on'	Manual by door Flexible manual†	Manual by door Flexible manual† Presence detection†
Shared: e.g. multi occupied areas such as open plan offices and workshops	Flexible manual Timed 'off', manual 'on' Photoelectric dimming	Flexible manual Timed 'off', manual 'on' Photoelectric dimming† Presence detection†	Flexible manual† Time switching†	Flexible manual Presence detection†
Temporarily owned: e.g. meeting rooms and hotel bedrooms, where people expect to operate the lighting controls when present	Local manual Flexible manual† Presence detection† Timed 'off', manual 'on'† Photoelectric dimming†	Local manual Presence detection Flexible manual† Timed 'off', manual 'on'† Key control†	Local manual Presence detection†	Local manual Presence detection Flexible manual† Timed 'off', manual 'on'† Key control†
Occasionally visited: e.g. storerooms, book stacks in libraries, aisles of warehouse and toilets	Not applicable	Presence detection Full occupancy linking† Local manual† Timed 'off', manual 'on'† Key control†	Not applicable	Presence detection Full occupancy linking† Local manual† Timed 'off', manual 'on'† Key control†
Unowned: e.g. circulation areas where people expect their way to be lit, but often do not expect to operate lighting controls	Photoelectric dimming Photoelectric switching†	Full occupancy linking Presence detection† Timed 'off', manual 'on'† Photoelectric dimming† Photoelectric switching†	Time switching† Presence detection†	Full occupancy linking Presence detection† Timed 'off', manual 'on'†
Managed: e.g. atria, concourse, entrance halls, restaurants, libraries and shops, where someone is in charge of the lighting, but usually too busy to control it; individual users do not expect to control the lighting	Photoelectric dimming Time switching Centralised manual Photoelectric switching† Programmed scene setting†	Photoelectric dimming Time switching Centralised manual Photoelectric switching† Programmed scene setting† Full occupancy linking†	Centralised manual Time switching Programmed scene setting†	Centralised manual Time switching Programmed scene setting† Full occupancy linking†

† Assess suitability for particular installation

lighting requires planning, the correct choice of light source and the correct controls to facilitate it. Daylight in a building will not in itself lead to energy efficiency. Even a well daylit building may have high energy use if the lighting is left on because controls are inappropriate. Case studies have shown that in a conventionally daylit building the choice of controls can make up to 30–40% difference in lighting use.

Lighting controls should ensure that light is provided in the right amount, in the right place for the required time[22–24]. Table 9.11[25] provides guidance on the selection and application of lighting controls. Further details on implementing lighting controls can be found in CIBSE LG10[4] and CIBSE Guide H[25], which also discusses human interaction with automatic lighting control.

There are many factors influencing the specification of lighting controls, including:

— occupancy pattern

— available daylight

— type of lighting (i.e. can it be dimmed?)

— the desired level of control sophistication

— capital costs and the potential for saving.

Even with efficient lamps and luminaires, the energy used for lighting can be wasted in various ways[23]. For example, users cannot be relied upon to turn lighting off when they leave an area, or when daylighting has increased. Exhortation can be helpful in the short term, but the ideal solution is to provide manual 'on' switching and some form of automatic 'off' switching. Energy is also wasted where a large area of lighting is controlled by a small numbers of switches, or where the switches are not located in convenient positions. Clear labelling of manual switches will also help avoid energy being wasted.

The choice of the number of control zones is a balance between cost and energy saving. The more zones of electric lighting, the better the match between lighting and demand. Zones should start at the perimeter and work away from the windows, corresponding to the reduction in daylight factor (see section 4). It is generally cost-effective to have zones from 1.5–3.0 m deep since this coincides with the minimum module for one person.

The five basic methods of lighting control that can be used separately or in combination are:

— localised manual switching

— time control

— reset control (timed off, manual on)

— occupancy control (presence detection)

— photoelectric switching and dimming.

9.5.1 Lighting control and Building Regulations

With respect to lighting controls, Building Regulations Approved Document L2★[17] makes the following observation:

> 'Where it is practicable, the aim of lighting controls should be to encourage the maximum use of daylight and to avoid unnecessary lighting during times when spaces are unoccupied. However, the operation of automatically switched lighting systems should not endanger the passage of building occupants. Guidance on the appropriate use of lighting controls is given in BRE Information Paper IP 2/99'[22].

The Approved Document suggests ways of meeting this requirement as follows.

9.5.1.1 Offices and storage buildings

A way of meeting this requirement in offices and storage buildings would be the provision of local switches in easily accessible positions within each working area or at boundaries between working areas and general circulation routes. The distance from any switch to the furthest luminaire it controls should generally not be more than eight metres or three times the height above floor level of the light fitting if this is greater, as shown in Figure 9.4. Local switching can be supplemented by other controls such as time switching and photo-electric switches where appropriate. Local switches could include:

(a)   switches that are operated by the deliberate action of the occupants either manually or by remote control. Manual switches include rocker switches, push buttons and pull-cords. Remote control switches include infra-red transmitter, sonic or ultra-sonic transmitters and telephone handset controls.

(b)   automatic switching systems, including controls which switch the lighting off when they sense the presence of occupants.

9.5.1.2 Buildings other than offices and storage buildings

For buildings other than offices and storage buildings, a way of meeting the requirement would be to provide one or more of the following control systems to maximise the beneficial use of daylight as appropriate:

(a)   local switching (as described above)

* Requirements may differ in Scotland[16] and Northern Ireland[17]

(b)   time switching, for example in major operational areas which have clear timetables of occupation.

(c)   photoelectric switching

9.5.1.3 Display lighting

A way of meeting the requirement would be to connect display lighting in dedicated circuits that can be switched off when people will not be inspecting exhibits or merchandise.

9.5.2 Localised manual controls

Switching arrangements should permit individual rows of luminaires parallel to window walls to be controlled separately. Switches should be well labelled and as near as possible to the luminaires that they control. One simple method that has been used effectively is a pull-cord switch adjacent to each luminaire.

Localised switching is important where the electric lighting only needs to be on in part of a large space, either because the other parts are unoccupied or because daylight is adequate. Controls that allow for these variations can produce significant energy savings compared with single switch lighting. In general, the area controlled by a particular switch should have a similar daylight level in all parts, related to the occupancy pattern. For example, in an office where individual occupants may be absent, it should cover the space of a single occupant or small working group; in a factory, it could be related to a particular production line or process.

Arrangements must be made to ensure that no one has to enter an unlit space, or be in a space where all lighting is out of their control.

9.5.3 Time controls

If the occupation of a building, or particular zones, ceases at a fixed time each working day, it may be worth installing a time-switch for the lighting, although arrangements will need to be made for security lighting. Individuals working late should be able to override the controls in their zone (see 9.5.4), and an extension timer should be used to avoid lights being left on. The building cleaning routine may also need special arrangements. Sequential control of lighting may be appropriate when a cleaning gang moves from floor to floor. Again, arrangements must be made to ensure that no one has to enter an

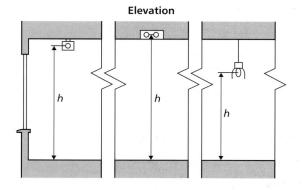

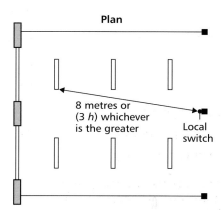

Figure 9.4 Location of local switch controls as recommended by Building Regulations Approved Document L2[17]

unlit space, or be in a space where all lighting is out of their control.

The introduction of time controls and/or photoelectric controls is particularly important in external lighting to minimise energy consumption. Simple time switches are highly cost-effective but only allow fixed 'on' and 'off' times. Photoelectric controls can ensure that external lighting is only on when it is dark.

9.5.4   Reset controls (timed 'off', manual 'on')

Time control systems that automatically switch the whole lighting installation off at predetermined times are available. Occupants are provided with local switches, often pull-cords, to restore the electric light if still required. Reset control is particularly applicable in open plan spaces where energy savings of 20–30% are possible. Maximum savings can be achieved through the careful selection of switching times. Post-cleaning, lunchtime and soon after the working day has ended are particularly advantageous times. Signals are transmitted to luminaires through mains wiring or through a dedicated low voltage wiring bus connected to receivers in each luminaire. The use of remote switching (e.g. by infra-red transmitters) to fulfil the localised override facility is also possible.

9.5.5   Occupancy controls (presence detection)

Occupancy detectors use infra-red, acoustic, ultrasonic or microwave sensors, to detect either movement or noise in the space. These usually switch the lighting on when occupancy is detected and off when they have failed to detect occupancy for a pre-set time. A time delay built into the system can help avoid excessive switching which reduces lamp life. In some cases, occupancy controls can allow manual switches to be dispensed with, thus reducing capital costs.

Lighting linked to occupancy can show considerable savings in energy usage particularly in intermittently occupied spaces. For example, lighting in warehouse aisles can be switched in response to a detector which senses the approach of a fork-lift truck. This form of control can be applied to a wide range of lamp types as long as the run-up and re-strike characteristics are taken into account. However, it is essential to ensure that the use of presence detection does not leave escape/exit routes dark when some spaces are unoccupied.

9.5.6   Photoelectric switching and dimming controls

Photoelectric daylight linking can take two forms, either simple on/off switching, or dimming. Tables 9.12 and 9.13 summarise the advantages and disadvantages of switched and dimming controls.

An externally mounted photocell provides very coarse control and should be applied only to the rows of luminaires closest to the windows. Photocells mounted inside the space measure the actual daylight penetration by monitoring the illumination under the first (and possibly the second) row of luminaires from the window walls. In both cases, it is important to incorporate time delays into the control system to avoid repeated rapid switching caused, for example, by fast moving clouds.

Photoelectric switching can cause sudden and noticeable changes in lighting level and can lead to occupant complaints. It is, therefore, suited to well-daylit areas and those areas where the switching frequency will be low. In order to reduce this effect, the illuminance at which the switching occurs should not be too low. Switch-off should occur when the total illuminance is around 3 to 4 times the required task illuminance and switch-on when the daylight illuminance is around 2 to 3 times the required task illuminance.

To achieve energy savings from daylighting, it is essential to integrate the control of daylight with the control of electric lighting. For example, an automatic, external, blind control system should be linked to an internal dimming lighting control system. In addition, consideration should be given to occupant override of either the blind or electric lighting control, using 'user-friendly' controls[22].

Tungsten lamps and most standard tubular and compact fluorescent lamps above 13 W, with suitable control gear, can be dimmed. Unlike photoelectric switching, photoelectric dimming control is relatively unobtrusive. The control system ensures that the sum of daylight and electric lighting always reaches the design level by sensing the total light in the controlled area and adjusting the output of the electric light to top-up the daylight as necessary. The energy saving potential of dimming control is greater than that of photoelectric switching. The mode of control is also more likely to be acceptable to the occupants, although initial cost is greater.

Table 9.12 Advantages and disadvantages of switch control

Advantages	Disadvantages
Cheap	Changes in illuminance noticeable
	Frequent switching of light source will, in the main, shorten lamp life
	Energy savings limited
	High pressure discharge sources require warm-up period, restrike period 15 mins

Table 9.13 Advantages and disadvantages of dimming control

Advantages	Disadvantages
Suitable high frequency ballasts can be used	More expensive than switch control
Digital ballasts produce smooth dimming	High pressure sources can be dimmed but only with special equipment
Task illuminance can be set and maintained	
Energy savings can be maximised	
Circuits have soft start, increasing lamp life	
Can be less obtrusive to occupants	

Photoelectrically-controlled dimming, particularly with high frequency fluorescent electronic ballasts, can also be used to maintain the design illuminance at a constant level throughout the life of the installation. When the lamps are new and the installation is clean, the luminaires are operated at low power and this is increased automatically as lamp lumen and luminaire depreciation occurs. This can be a very effective means of saving energy as it applies to all luminaires, whereas daylight linking only achieves energy savings for the luminaires close to the windows.

Discharge lamps are less easily dimmable, requiring special equipment to achieve this effect. The reductions in power and light output do not have a linear relationship and lamp colour may change.

9.5.7   Lighting management systems

Lighting management systems (LMS) can integrate the control strategies mentioned above and provide many of the advantages of building management systems (BMS) (see section 6) by including centralised control, monitoring and alarms. LMS can control individual luminaires, groups of luminaires or lighting zones. Space layout alterations can be made and the lighting adjusted through a central interface to suit the new layout, avoiding the need for the expensive relocation of luminaires and alterations to switching arrangements. Modern LMS also provide monitoring capabilities so that lamp performance and hours run can be logged allowing better maintenance regimes to be undertaken. User interfaces can include intranet/internet, telephone and hand held remote controls. It is possible to interface a BMS and an LMS in order to provide certain control commands from the BMS to the lighting although most BMS can carry out the function of the LMS directly.

9.5.8   Selection of controls

The cost of a control system installation should be compared with the cost of a traditional hard-wired installation, and the difference related to the projected energy savings. Any control system must ensure that acceptable lighting conditions are always provided with safety, visual effectiveness and comfort taking priority over energy saving.

Automatic controls need to be selected carefully since perceived changes in lighting levels can prove distracting and an irritation to occupants. Control systems that are obtrusive are counter-productive and may even be sabotaged by the staff. Problems of this kind can often be minimised by making staff aware of the purpose behind the control system, how it works and how they can interact with it (see section 6).

Experience in use can improve the operation of lighting control systems by gradually fine tuning settings to meet the needs of the occupants. Only the occupants can determine the absolute level at which switching should occur to suit their needs. This requires a responsive management approach to the control system.

Lighting needs to be carefully controlled to ensure that it is only on when there is a genuine need. Automatic control generally works best to switch lights off or reduce their brightness when daylight is sufficient or when people are absent. Provide occupants with the maximum amount of manual control appropriate, only automatically switching on where this is necessary for safety.

9.6   Energy consumption

Lighting is often the single largest end-use of electricity in buildings, accounting for over 40% of electricity costs in naturally ventilated offices. Typical and good practice performance indicators for offices are shown in Table 9.14[7]. The energy use indicator (EUI) is the product of:

(a)   the installed capacity in $W \cdot m^{-2}$ of treated floor area

(b)   the annual running hours

(c)   the average percentage utilisation of the plant, expressed as a decimal fraction.

The result is divided by 1000 to obtain the EUI in $(kW \cdot h) \cdot m^{-2}$ per year.

The installed power density ($W \cdot m^{-2}$) can be estimated by adding up all the lamp wattages in an area, adding control gear losses (typically 10–20%, but 5% for high frequency ballasts) then dividing by the floor area. The good practice benchmark of 12 $W \cdot m^{-2}$, also recommended by the BCO's *Best practice in the specification for offices*[8], is based on 350–450 lux at a luminous efficacy of 3 $W \cdot m^{-2}$ per 100 lux. This is achievable with good luminaires and high

Table 9.14 Overall lighting benchmarks for offices[7]

Parameter	Benchmark for stated office type							
	Naturally ventilated cellular office (Type 1)		Naturally ventilated open plan office (Type 2)		Air conditioned standard office (Type 3)		Air conditioned prestige office (Type 4)	
	Good practice	Typical	Good practice	Typical	Good practice	Typical	Good practice	Typical
Installed capacity ($W \cdot m^{-2}$)	12	15	12	18	12	20	12	20
Running hours (h/yr)	2500	2500	3000	3000	3200	3200	3500	3500
Utilisation (%)	45	60	60	70	70	85	70	85
Energy use indicator (EUI) (($kW \cdot h) \cdot m^{-2}$)/yr)	14	23	22	38	27	54	29	60

Note: factors for converting treated floor area to nett and gross are given in Table 20.2

frequency lighting with a small allowance for decorative lighting. For 500 lux or an uplighting installation of 300–350 lux, an installed capacity of 15 W·m^{-2} may be required.

References

1   *Code for lighting* (CD-ROM) (London: Chartered Institution of Building Services Engineers/Society for Light and Lighting) (2002)

2   *The visual environment for display screen use* CIBSE Lighting Guide LG3 (with addendum) (London: Chartered Institution of Building Services Engineers) (1996/2001)

3   *Lighting for offices* CIBSE Lighting Guide LG7 (London: Chartered Institution of Building Services Engineers) (1993)

4   *Daylighting and window design* CIBSE LG10 (London: Chartered Institution of Building Services Engineers) (1999)

5   *Energy management and good lighting practice* Fuel Efficiency Booklet No. 12 (Action Energy) (1994) (www.actionenergy.org.uk)

6   BS EN 12464-1: *Light and lighting. Lighting of work places. Indoor work places* (London: British Standards Institution) (2002)

7   *Energy efficiency in offices* Energy Consumption Guide ECG 19 (Action Energy) (2000) (www.actionenergy.org.uk)

8   *Best practice in the specification for offices* (Reading: British Council for Offices) (2000)

9   *Daylighting requirements for display screen equipment* BRE Information Paper IP14/93 (London: Construction Research Communications) (1993)

10   *Display screen equipment work — Guidance on regulations* HSC Legislation Series L26 (London: HSE Books) (1992)

11   *Energy efficient lighting — a guide for installers* Good Practice Guide GPG 199 (Action Energy) (1996) (www.actionenergy.org.uk)

12   *Lamp guide* (London: Lighting Industry Federation) (2001) (incorporated in CIBSE *Code for lighting*[1])

13   *Energy efficiency in hotels. A guide to cost-effective lighting* Good Practice Guide GPG 189 (Action Energy) (1996) (www.actionenergy.org.uk)

14   *Energy efficiency in lighting for industrial buildings* GPG 158 (Action Energy) (1995) (www.actionenergy.org.uk)

15   *Energy efficient lighting in the retail sector* Good Practice Guide GPG 210 (Action Energy) (1997) (www.actionenergy.org.uk)

16   *Energy efficient lighting — a guide for installers* Good Practice Guide GPG 199 (Action Energy) (1997) (www.actionenergy.org.uk)

17   *Conservation of fuel and power in buildings other than dwellings* The Building Regulations 2000 Approved Document L2 (London: The Stationery Office) (2001)

18   *Technical standards for compliance with the Building Standards (Scotland) Regulations 1990 (as amended)* (London: The Stationery Office) (2001)

19   *Conservation of fuel and power* The Building Regulations (Northern Ireland) 1994 Technical Booklet F (London: The Stationery Office) (1999)

20   *Converting to compact fluorescent lighting — a refurbishment guide* Good Practice Guide GPG 159 (Action Energy) (1995) (www.actionenergy.org.uk)

21   *High frequency luminaires: Specification, construction, installation* Technical Statement No. 21 (London: Lighting Industry Federation) (1997)

22   *Photoelectric control of lighting — design, set-up and installation issues* BRE Information Paper IP 2/99 (London: Construction Research Communications) (1999)

23   Slater A I, Bordass W T and Heasman T A *People and lighting controls* BRE Information Paper IP6/96 (London: Construction Research Communications) (1996)

24   *Electric lighting controls — a guide for designers, installers and users* Good Practice Guide GPG 160 (Action Energy) (1997) (www.actionenergy.org.uk)

26   *Building control systems* CIBSE Guide H (London: Chartered Institution of Building Services Engineers) (2000)

Bibliography

Lighting for people, energy efficiency and architecture — an overview of lighting requirements and design Good Practice Guide GPG 272 (Action Energy) (2000) (www.actionenergy.org.uk)

Baker N V and Steemers K *The LT Method 2.0. An energy design tool for non-domestic buildings* (Cambridge: Cambridge Architectural Research) (1994)

Baker N V *Energy and environment in non-domestic buildings. A technical design guide* (Cambridge: Cambridge Architectural Research) (1995)

Slater A I Occupant use of lighting controls: a review of current practice, problems and how to avoid them *Proc. CIBSE Nat. Conf., Eastbourne, 1–3 October 1995* (1) 204–209 (London: Chartered Institution of Building Services Engineers) (1995)

Rohde M F Concerted light — day and artificial light as interaction with architecture *Proc. CIBSE Nat. Conf., Eastbourne, 1–3 October 1995* (1) 210–218 (London: Chartered Institution of Building Services Engineers) (1995)

Environmental comfort and productivity BSRIA LB 79/94 (Bracknell: Building Services Research and Information Association) (1994)

Office lighting for good visual task conditions BRE Digest 256 (London: Construction Research Communications)

Desktop guide to daylighting — for architects (Action Energy) (1998) (www.actionenergy.org.uk)

Lighting controls — are they working? *Light & Lighting* (7) 14–15 (April 1999)

10 Heating and hot water design

10.0 General

10.1 Primary plant

10.2 Distribution systems

10.3 Controls

10.4 Energy consumption

10.5 Domestic heating

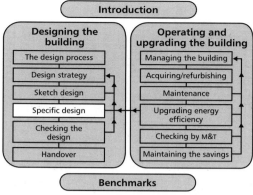

This section sets out key issues in designing energy efficient heating and hot water systems, in line with the principles at the front of this Guide. In most buildings, heating and hot water account for the largest annual consumption of delivered energy and hence CO_2 emissions from heating systems are often high. For each unit of delivered energy, the most common fuels used for heating, such as gas and oil, produce lower emissions to the atmosphere than electricity. Attention to fabric detail at the sketch design stage to minimise the requirement for space heating is particularly important in reducing energy consumption (see section 4). Efforts should also be made to minimise hot water demand by incorporating low-flow alternatives such as showers and spray taps.

Energy issues related to heating maintenance are covered in section 17. For further detail on heating issues see CIBSE Guide B1[1], Fuel Efficiency Booklets FEB 3[2], 7[3], 14[4], 15[5], and 17[6], General Information Reports GIR 40[7], 41[8] and Good Practice Guide GPG 132[9]. Domestic heating is covered in the *Domestic heating design guide*[10] and Good Practice Guides GPG 284[11] and GPG 302[12].

10.0 General

Energy efficient heating should:

— incorporate the most efficient primary plant to generate heat/hot water

— ensure that heat/hot water is distributed effectively and efficiently

— include effective controls on primary plant and distribution systems to ensure that heat/hot water is only provided when and where it is needed and at the correct temperature

— be responsive to changes in climate, solar gains, occupancy, activity, and internal gains.

10.1 Primary plant

The mix of primary plant can have a major influence on overall system efficiency, e.g. CHP with condensing boilers. In particular designers should:

— select fuels and tariffs that promote efficiency and minimise running costs

— segregate hot water services generation wherever possible

— consider de-centralised heating and hot water services generation plant on large sites to reduce standing losses and improve load matching

— locate plant to minimise distribution system and losses

— insulate pipework, valves etc. effectively

— provide appropriate margins but avoid oversizing

— ensure that the base load is provided by the most efficient plant.

10.1.1 Building Regulations requirements

As a means of demonstrating compliance with the Building Regulations[13], Building Regulations Approved Document L2*[14] states that heating plant serving hot water and steam heating systems, electric heating and heat pumps at full and part load should have carbon intensities not less than those shown in Table 10.1.

Table 10.1 Maximum allowable carbon intensities of heating systems

Fuel	Maximum allowable carbon intensities of heating systems for stated heat output / $(kgC \cdot (kW \cdot h)^{-1})$	
	At max. heat output	At 30% of max. heat output
Natural gas	0.068	0.065
Other fuels	0.091	0.088

Where there are multiple pieces of heat generating equipment, the carbon intensity of the heating plant is the rating weighted average of the individual elements calculated using the following equation:

* Requirements may differ in Scotland[15] and Northern Ireland[16]

$$\varepsilon_c = \frac{1}{\sum R} \sum \left(\frac{R \, C_f}{\eta_t} \right) \qquad (10.1)$$

where ε_c is the carbon intensity of the heating system (kgC·(kW·h)$^{-1}$ of useful heat), R is the rated output of an individual element of heat raising plant (kW), η_t is the gross thermal efficiency of that element of heat raising plant (kW·h of heat per kW·h of delivered fuel) and C_f is the carbon emissions factor of the fuel supplying that element of heat raising plant (kgC emitted per kW·h of delivered fuel consumed), see Table 10.2.

Table 10.2 Carbon emissions factors

Delivered fuel	Carbon emissions factor / kgC·(kW·h)$^{-1}$
Natural gas	0.053
LPG	0.068
Biogas	0
Oil	0.074
Coal	0.086
Biomass	0
Electricity	0.113
Waste heat	0

This requires a typical 100 kW gas boiler, or multiple boiler installation, to be at least 79.9% efficient at full load and 81.5% at 30% of full load. Some atmospheric boilers are unlikely to meet the requirement at 30% load and a simple solution might be to introduce some condensing boilers into the installation to increase the part-load efficiency.

10.1.2   Boilers

10.1.2.1   Boiler efficiency

By definition, the outside design condition is only exceeded on a certain percentage of days so that heating plant will operate for much of the time at less than full load. Designers should therefore consider boiler efficiency across the whole range of likely loads, not just at the design condition.

Table 10.3 Typical seasonal efficiencies

System	Seasonal efficiency / %
Condensing boilers:	
— underfloor or warm water system	90 or greater
— standard size radiators, variable temperature circuit (weather compensation)	87
— standard fixed temperature emitters (83 °C flow, 72 °C return)	85
Non-condensing boilers:	
— modern high efficiency non-condensing boilers	82
— good modern boiler design closely matched to demand	80
— typical good existing boiler	70
— typical existing oversized boiler (atmospheric cast-iron sectional)	45–70

Quoted instantaneous boiler efficiencies are not generally representative of practical situations in buildings. Seasonal (or annual) efficiencies, as shown in Table 10.3, provide a measure of true operation, averaged over a season or a year, based on the total useful heat output versus the total energy input over the period in question. This takes into account the low efficiency of some boilers at part load (see Figure 10.1). In practice, seasonal efficiency is not easy to measure but can be estimated.

High efficiency boilers

High efficiency boilers are now the minimum standard for new and replacement installations after 1997[17] having some or all of the following characteristics:

— low water content and/or low thermal mass

— improved heat exchangers and insulation

— a packaged modular arrangement (sometimes slightly more expensive than the more basic atmospheric boilers)

— greater efficiency; e.g. 10% improvement in efficiency in comparison with a good existing boiler across the range of loads

— higher part-load efficiencies, which make boilers of this type particularly suitable for applications with a wide range of loads.

Condensing boilers

Condensing boilers are generally gas fired, although oil fired versions are available. Condensing boilers:

— use an additional heat exchanger to extract extra heat by condensing water vapour from the products of combustion

— operate at a minimum efficiency of around 85%, even when not condensing

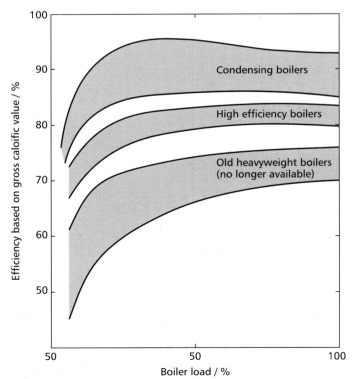

Figure 10.1 Typical seasonal LTHW boiler efficiencies at part load

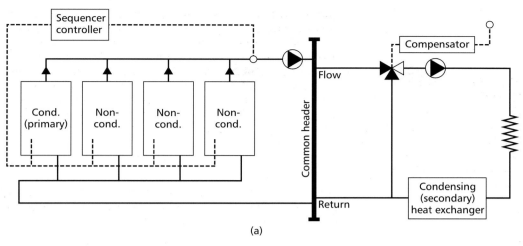

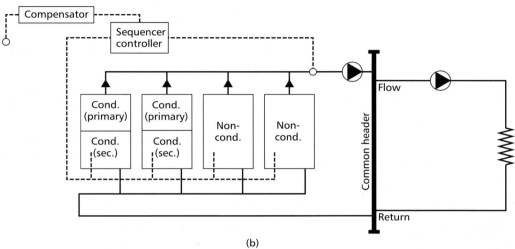

Figure 10.2 (a) Single condensing boiler with weather compensation using a three-port valve; (b) two condensing boilers with direct weather compensation on the primary circuit

— can achieve efficiencies in the range 85–95% and efficiency can sometimes be higher at part-load than at full load (see Figure 10.1)

— are more expensive than basic atmospheric boilers, typically 20–50% although some are now the same cost as high efficiency modular boilers

— are most commonly installed in combination with non-condensing boilers to keep capital costs to a minimum. The optimum economic combination is often 50–75% condensing boilers; low temperature systems should be 100% condensing

— should normally be the first choice, at least for 'lead' gas boilers; controls should ensure that the condensing boiler operates as the lead boiler

— provide energy savings of 10–20% with paybacks of 2–5 years[18].

Lower return water temperatures lead to more condensation, resulting in higher efficiencies. There are a number of hydraulic arrangements and controls that can promote these lower temperatures[7], weather compensation being the most common and conventional method, as shown in Figure 10.2.

The operation of a condensing boiler with weather compensation is shown in Figure 10.3[19]. The boiler moves into the condensing mode (and higher efficiencies) in the milder parts of the season when return water temperatures are lower, giving seasonal efficiencies of around 87–88%.

10.1.2.2 Plant sizing

Careful consideration should be given to the size and number of boilers to be installed as oversizing heating plant will generally reduce seasonal efficiency and increase capital cost unnecessarily.

Boiler plant is sized for mid-winter requirements, giving it considerable over capacity for the rest of the year. Heating plant is often oversized due to excessive design margins and this exacerbates the part-load efficiency problem.

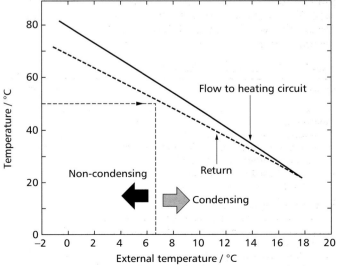

Figure 10.3 Weather compensation and condensing boilers (reproduced from Good Practice Guide GPG 16[18]; Crown copyright)

Heating design loads for the purpose of sizing HVAC systems should be determined in accordance with the procedures detailed in the CIBSE Guide A[20].

BSRIA Guidance Note 12/97[21] covers the oversizing of heating plant and indicates that heating plant capacities larger than those shown in Table 10.4 are likely to be oversized.

Table 10.4 Boiler plant oversizing limits

Building type	Boiler plant yardstick (heating load) / W·m^{-2}
Offices and industrial	90
Retail, health care and education	110

10.1.2.3   Centralised versus decentralised systems

The argument for the selection of centralised or de-centralised services is complex (see Tables 10.5 and 10.6). For example, if a building is multi-tenanted with diverse periods of occupancy, the use of de-centralised services could match the type of operation better than a centralised arrangement. However, for a building having a large energy demand with a high load factor, the use of centralised plant working at high efficiencies and possibly using dual fuel facilities, may provide a better solution.

Table 10.5 Advantages and disadvantages of centralised heating

Advantages	Disadvantages
Capital cost per unit output falls with increased capacity of central plant	Capital cost of distribution systems is high
Convenient for some institutions	Space requirements of central plant and distribution systems are significant, particularly ductwork
Central plant tends to be better engineered, operating at higher efficiencies, (where load factors are high) and more durable	As the load factor falls the total system efficiency falls as distribution losses become more significant
Some systems will naturally require central plant, e.g. heavy oil and coal burning plant	
Flexibility in the choice of fuel	
Better utilisation of CHP etc.	

Table 10.6 Advantages and disadvantages of de-centralised heating

Advantages	Disadvantages
Low overall capital cost, savings made on minimising the use of air and water distribution systems	Equipment tends to be less robust with shorter operational life
Zoning of the systems can be matched more easily to occupancy patterns	Flueing arrangements can be more difficult
Maintenance less specialised	Fuel needs to be supplied throughout the site
Can be readily altered and extended	May require more control systems
Energy performance in buildings with diverse patterns of use is usually better	
Plant failure only affects the area served	

The argument for de-centralised heating often hinges on the price and availability of fuels, the space available for plant and distribution pipework, flueing arrangements and the losses in a centralised system and the size of the loads involved.

10.1.3   Hot water plant

Hot water plant should always be sized correctly thus minimising capital and running costs[1]. CIBSE Guide G[22] provides sizing methods for hot water plant.

Reducing temperatures saves energy and the risk of scalding, but should not be achieved at the expense of safety. To avoid multiplication of *legionella*[23], hot water should be stored at 60 °C and distributed such that a temperature of 50 °C is achieved within one minute at outlets.

Primary and secondary distribution losses should always be minimised as part of an energy efficient design. Hot water circulation loops should be compact and well insulated, while dead legs should be kept to a minimum size and length. The length of pipe between an outlet and a storage vessel, or a secondary flow and return system, should not exceed the lengths given in Table 10.7.

Table 10.7 Maximum lengths of pipe to outlet

Nominal bore of pipe / mm	Maximum length / m
Up to 20	12
21 to 25	7
Over 25	3

Hot water systems should be equipped with effective, automatic temperature controls (see 10.3.8).

The four main types of hot water system are:

— central calorifiers, supplied by the main heating boilers

— central self-contained gas or electric

— local storage, gas or electric

— local point of use, usually electric.

10.1.3.1   Central calorifier systems

Where hot water loads are high and distribution systems compact, a well controlled central boiler/calorifier plant can operate reasonably economically. However, where hot water loads are not substantial, particularly in summer, separate heating and hot water systems will be more energy efficient.

Combination boilers can also provide an energy efficient approach to both heating and hot water in small (domestic sized) centralised systems. Hot water is heated almost instantaneously on demand, although interaction between the heating and hot water may occur where winter demand is high.

10.1.3.2   Central self-contained systems

Self-contained central hot water systems are normally much more efficient than systems combined with the main heating. This is because standing losses are lower and the poor part-load efficiencies characteristic of boilers sized for the full heating duty are avoided during summer operation. Relatively high efficiency storage water heaters are commonly used and condensing versions offer a further high efficiency option.

Electric immersion heating is generally only economic where there is adequate capacity for off-peak storage. Suitable tariffs must be available, and the system well controlled to minimise daytime top ups. This method can be used during summer, with heat generation via the main boilers in winter. Although highly efficient in terms of delivered energy, with comparable running costs to storage water heaters, the primary energy consumption and CO_2 emissions are relatively high.

10.1.3.3   Local storage systems

Small de-centralised gas fired storage water heaters close to the point of use can significantly improve efficiency since standing and distribution losses are greatly reduced, particularly for larger buildings. Problems associated with minimising the risk of *legionella* are also normally reduced with localised systems. Capital and maintenance costs can be higher, but this is normally more than offset by the increased efficiency and other advantages. This option can also be useful for catering and sports facilities with high peak demand.

Local electric storage systems are usually designed to take advantage of off-peak electricity tariffs, and can be located close to the point of demand. The disadvantages are as described for central electric storage systems in 10.1.2.2.

10.1.3.4   Point of use water heaters

Monitored projects suggest that local instantaneous point of use water heating is extremely economical where hot water demand is low, e.g. for offices without catering facilities. Capital cost and delivered energy consumption is generally low. Water softening may be desirable to prevent units scaling up, therefore avoiding premature failure.

10.1.4   Combined heat and power

Combined heat and power (CHP) has a wide range of applications in buildings and commonly provides the single biggest CO_2 reduction that can be achieved in a building where CHP is appropriate. It can be connected in series (usually in retrofit installations) or parallel (usually in new installations) with boiler plant and should always operate as the lead boiler to maximise savings. CHP should always be considered when evaluating, new designs, refurbishment schemes or boiler replacement. See Section 5.2 for further details.

10.1.5   Multiple boiler arrangements

Multiple boiler arrangements match the demand for heat more closely and hence improve energy efficiency. These may comprise an integrated package of modules or independent boilers, including CHP. As the load increases, individual modules are progressively switched on. Since each boiler performs close to its individual design duty, efficiency is maintained. The overall plant can therefore provide an improved part load efficiency characteristic, as shown in Figure 10.4. (Note that Figure 10.4 is based on older, less efficient boilers but the principle still applies.) Careful sequence control is fundamental to this approach (see 10.3).

Within practical limits, and where the dilution effect of parallel connected boilers is not significant, the greater the number of stages of sequence control, the better the efficiency. It is normally preferable to use a greater number of smaller boilers to provide more stages of control, than create more stages by switching combinations of different sized boilers. Different sized boilers are often used where one acts as the summer boiler for hot water services. However, complete segregation of hot water services is normally more efficient. Different sized boilers also require more complex sequence control systems when being controlled from return water temperature as they could have different response times. Whilst these problems can be overcome by careful engineering and commissioning, boiler sequence control systems are normally best kept to simple principles for long term efficient operation. Identical boilers also reduce potential maintenance and spares problems.

In some instances, particularly for low temperature systems, it can be economic to specify all the boilers in a multiple arrangement as condensing. However, in most instances it is more economic to specify the lead boiler(s) as condensing, with high efficiency boiler(s) to top-up. This minimises capital cost while still keeping overall plant efficiency high[18].

Figure 10.5 provides a means of estimating the overall seasonal efficiency when combining condensing and high efficiency boiler plant. Moving from left to right increases the proportion that is condensing and hence there is a rise in overall efficiency. Whilst there is only a relatively small drop in overall efficiency in moving from 100% to two thirds condensing, this will reduce significantly the capital cost of the plant. It is common to find that 50–75% condensing often provides the shortest payback periods.

Condensing and high efficiency boilers can also be combined with CHP plant, as shown in Figure 10.6. The most efficient plant should take the base load, i.e. the CHP plant first and the condensing boilers second. In the past, CHP plant was specifically sized to meet only the base load. However, the most cost-effective solution often involves

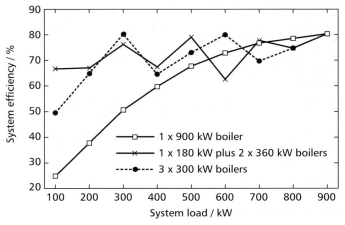

Figure 10.4 Effect of multiple boilers on overall efficiency

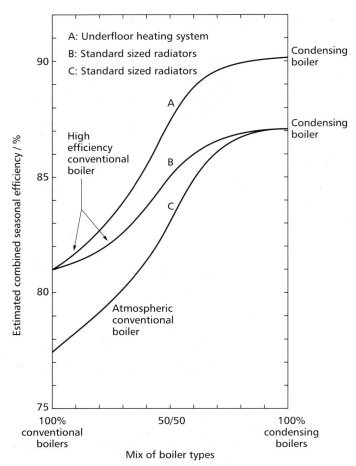

Figure 10.5 Seasonal efficiency of mixed boiler systems

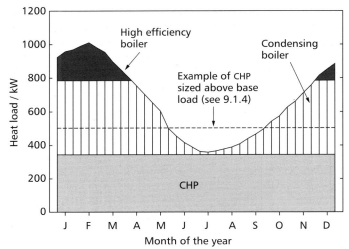

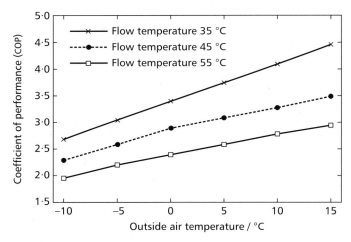

Figure 10.6 Combining CHP and boiler plant (adapted from Good Practice Guide GPG 176[23])

Figure 10.7 Effect of temperature range on heat pump performance

sizing CHP at a greater capacity than the base load with some CHP modulating capacity and/or heat dumping capacity to cope with periods of low heat demand (summer) (see the dotted line in Figure 10.6). A full option appraisal should consider all the available possibilities and gradually focus on the most efficient, economic and practical combination, as shown in Good Practice Guide GPG 187[25]. See Section 5.2 for further details on CHP.

10.1.6   Heat pumps

Heat pumps can produce high coefficients of performance (COP) when operating at low temperature differentials, as shown in Figure 10.7. Heat pumps have found wide use in applications where low grade heat is available, e.g. where low grade process heating is being dumped, or for ventilation extract heat recovery such as in swimming pools and supermarkets.

Heat pumps are available in a number of different forms and exploit different sources of low grade heat. Air source heat pumps may be used to extract heat either from outside air or from ventilation exhaust air. When outside air is used as a heat source, the COP tends to decline as the air temperature drops. Problems with the heat exchanger icing can be experienced where outside air humidity is high, which is frequently the case in the UK. This requires periodic defrosting, often achieved by temporarily reversing the heat pump, reducing the COP. Air-to-air heat pumps supplying heating only, using outside air as a

source in a typical UK climate, can therefore have relatively low COP.

When used to provide heating only, the COP of heat pumps does not usually compensate for the increased financial and environmental cost of using electricity. Where the need for cooling has been established, e.g. in retail outlets, reversible heat pumps can be an effective way of providing both cooling and heating. Small split-unit heat pumps are common in small shops and office and these require good interlinked controls to ensure that units providing heating do not fight nearby units supplying cooling. The coefficients of performance for heat pumps in the heating cycle should not generally be less than shown in Table 10.8.

Table 10.8 Minimum coefficients of performance for heat pumps in heating cycle

Heating capacity / kW	COP
Up to 20	2.2
21 to 60	2.4
61 to 120	2.5
Over 120	2.6

Ground or water source heat pumps extract heat from the ground, bodies of water at ambient temperature, or from the outflow of waste heat. These heat sources have greater specific heat than air and, provided it has sufficient mass, vary much less with outside temperature. Small ground source heat pumps can therefore have a seasonal COP of around 2.8 in a typical UK climate[26].

The CoPs given above are for electrically driven vapour compression cycle heat pumps. Absorption cycle heat pumps have a much lower CoP but have the advantage that they can be powered directly by gas. When used for heating, the CoP obtainable in practice (of around 1.4) still offers a considerable advantage over a boiler.

10.1.7 Electric heating

Panel radiators, natural draught and fanned electric convectors are available with outputs up to 5 kW. Electric heating systems:

— are generally inexpensive to install

— can reduce space requirements

— require little or no maintenance

— provide very quick response to controls

— are highly efficient but can have high CO_2 emissions

— are suitable for intermittently heated areas

— have high running costs.

Owing to the high unit cost of electricity, high levels of insulation and good central/local control are essential for the efficient use of electric heating. Simple, effective systems can give heating energy consumption in the range 40–60 $(kW \cdot h) \cdot m^{-2}$ per year[27].

Electric storage heaters can take advantage of low electricity costs at night. They also have a low capital cost, are easy to install and maintenance free. However, their main disadvantages are the limited charging capacity and the difficulty of controlling output often leading to expensive daytime re-charging. This lack of control can give rise to comfort problems and higher than necessary energy consumption. Use of 'CELECT'-type integrated system controls for electric storage and panel heaters can address these problems. Electronic sensors fitted in the main rooms are linked to a central controller which optimises the charging of all storage heaters individually. It also provides separate time and temperature control in all system zones.

10.2 Distribution systems

The characteristics of distribution circuits for space heating systems can have a significant effect on thermal performance and energy consumption. The main sources of inefficiency are:

— incorrectly sized distribution systems resulting in high pump and fan energy consumption; the position of plant rooms, and the consequent length of pipework will influence both the capital and running cost of the distribution system

— unwanted heat losses from the pipework or ductwork; Building Regulations Approved Document L*[14] recommends that, for compliance with the Building Regulations, all pipework, ductwork and vessels for space heating and hot

* Requirements may differ in Scotland[14] and Northern Ireland[15]

Table 10.9 Typical distribution system utilisation efficiencies

Type of distribution system	Utilisation efficiency η_s
Intermittent:	
— automatic centrally-fired radiator or convector systems	0.97
— automatic centrally-fired warm air ventilation systems	0.93
— fan assisted electric off-peak heaters	0.90
— direct electric (non-storage) floor and ceiling systems	0.95
— district heating/warm air systems	0.90
Continuous:	
— automatic centrally fired radiator or convector systems	1.00
— automatic centrally fired warm air ventilation systems	1.00
— electric storage radiator systems	0.75
— direct electric floor and ceiling systems	0.95
— district heating/radiator systems	1.00
Water heating:	
— gas circulator/storage cylinder	0.80
— gas or oil fired boiler/storage cylinder	0.80
— off-peak electric storage with cylinder and immersion heater	0.80
— local instantaneous electric water heaters	1.00
— instantaneous gas heaters	0.95
— district heating with local calorifiers	0.80
— district heating with central calorifier and distribution	0.75

water supply should be insulated to the standards in BS 5422[28]

— wasteful operation at part loads.

Table 10.9 shows typical utilisation efficiencies of various systems. Multiplying these by the seasonal boiler efficiency provides an overall system efficiency.

As heating demands reduce due to improved standards of insulation and air tightness, the relative importance of distribution losses increases. More detailed information on the sizing of emitters and the design of individual heating systems is provided in CIBSE Guide B1[1].

Different types of emitter have different output characteristics in terms of the split between convective and radiant heat. Where there is a high ventilation rate, the use of a radiant heating system results in lower energy consumption. Fully radiant systems heat occupants directly without heating the air to full comfort temperatures.

Where convection is the predominant form of heat in tall spaces, care must be taken to avoid vertical temperature stratification. Increased temperatures at high level also increase heat losses through the roof in atria or warehouse/factory buildings.

10.2.1 Wet systems

10.2.1.1 Radiators

Radiators have a convective component of between 50% and 70% and provide a positive room air temperature gradient. They are cheap and easily controlled with a reasonably quick response.

10.2.1.2 Natural convectors

Natural convectors have a radiant/convective split of 20:80 and tend to produce a more pronounced vertical temperature gradient that can result in inefficient energy use.

They are best used in well insulated rooms with low air change rates.

10.2.1.3 Fan convectors

Fan convectors, like natural convectors, are suitable for well insulated rooms with low air change rates. Fan convectors:

— provide good temperature control and the possibility of using a fan-only operating mode in summer

— respond rapidly to control

— can have a variable speed and, hence, a variable output

— require compensated circuits with a high minimum flow temperature and should be separated from circuits serving other types of emitter

— require additional wiring for fan interlock with time control.

The minimum flow temperature for circuits serving fan convectors should not be below 50–55 °C to prevent cold draughts. Disadvantages include higher capital costs, higher maintenance requirements, the need to have an electrical supply to every unit and an increased electrical requirement due to the fans.

10.2.1.4 Underfloor heating

Underfloor heating usually consists of a low temperature warm water distribution system set into the floor slab giving a slow response that is more suited to areas of continuous occupation. However, the system does have some built-in self-regulation; as the room warms up, the temperature difference between the floor and the room air decreases, reducing the heat output. Generally, operating at 45–35 °C, these systems provide an ideal opportunity to use condensing boilers as seasonal efficiencies of over 90% can be achieved due to the low return water temperature. Heat pumps are equally advantageous in underfloor systems. The selection of heating zones and their control will have a considerable impact on comfort and energy. There is a high thermal inertia with underfloor heating and less opportunity to respond to local heat gains.

10.2.1.5 Radiant panels

Radiant panels can be supplied with medium or high temperature hot water, or steam, and can have a radiant component of up to 65%. They are suitable for use in large spaces with high air change rates such as factories or warehouses[29].

10.2.2 Warm air systems

The three main types of warm air systems are direct gas fired units; indirect gas or oil-fired units and indirect units fitted with water or steam coils. Operation can be with either air recirculation to maintain space temperature, or with a full fresh air supply to provide the minimum fresh air requirement. Direct gas fired unit heaters have additional fresh air requirements for combustion. See CIBSE Guide B1[1] and Good Practice Guide GPG 303[29] for further details.

Warm air systems:

— have a quick response to control but can promote stratification

— often require significant lengths of ductwork and, therefore, fan power can add to overall energy consumption

— are generally more difficult to control in zones, requiring air dampers and room thermostats.

Direct gas fired unit heaters should preferably have modulating burners controlled in relation to the discharge temperature and room temperature. Also available are gas-fired condensing unit heaters that operate in the condensing mode constantly.

10.2.3 Radiant systems

These are typically used in large volume buildings that have high air change rates, such as factories, warehouses and garages. Radiant systems:

— are more efficient because they only heat the occupants and building fabric and do not generally raise the temperature of the internal air to full comfort levels

— generally provide a rapid response, requiring less heat up time at the beginning of the day.

Significant energy savings compared with convective systems are therefore possible. Types of radiant heater include gas fired tube heaters, plaque heaters and electric quartz-halogen units. See CIBSE Guide B1[1], Good Practice Guide GPG 303[29] and BSRIA AG 3/96[30] for further details.

The radiant effect is only maintained when heater surfaces are above a certain temperature, hence two stage switching which operates above and below the critical temperature gives closer control than simple on/off switching.

Temperature control is required for each heater and time control for the overall system. Black-bulb radiant heat sensors should be used to achieve good temperature control of radiant heating systems. The sensors must be located in positions that are representative of the radiant effect of the panels being controlled.

The height of radiant heaters is particularly important as overheating can occur if they are positioned too low. Locating them too high can result in comfort problems and increased energy consumption due to the heaters often being left on continuously.

Where areas have different temperature requirements, they should be zoned accordingly. This necessitates the use of a sensor and controller plus a time switch for each zone. In general, the more zones the better the control, although large zones are acceptable in areas requiring low heat levels.

Electric quartz heaters use a quartz lamp to provide a high intensity radiant effect. Due to their high capital and running cost they are mainly used for spot heating in intermittently occupied areas. They have very rapid response times and can therefore be used in conjunction with occupancy sensors or local run-back timers to control heat output.

10.3 Controls

Good control of primary heating/hot water plant and distribution systems is a vital part in achieving low energy consumption. The key requirement is to provide heat/hot water only when and where it is needed, and at the right temperature, whilst minimising boiler cycling.

Section 5 covers overall control strategies and more detailed guidance is available in CIBSE Guide H[31] and Good Practice Guide GPG 132[9]. General Information Report GIR 40[7] also provides a series of application sheets explaining the operation of controls for particular systems. Domestic heating controls are covered in section 10.4.1 and Good Practice Guide GPG 302[12].

Good Practice Guide GPG 132[9] sets out minimum and good levels of control for wet central heating systems in small commercial and multi residential buildings, which are summarised in Figure 10.8. Building Regulations Approved Document L2★[14] states that, for buildings with heating systems having a maximum output not exceeding 100 kW, following these recommendations is one way of meeting the requirements of the Building Regulations.

10.3.1 Circuit design

The successful operation of controls depends heavily on good circuit design. A constant, or near constant, water flow is normally required for modern boilers. A variable flow is created by the action of automatic back-end valves and individually pumped boilers. Therefore, for most applications, systems should be designed with:

— a single primary pump driving a constant flow primary circuit to ensure that the sequence control sensor can then detect a temperature that is representative of the load on the system

---

★ Requirements may differ in Scotland[15] and Northern Ireland[16]

MINIMUM < 50 kW

TIME	TIMESWITCH if intermittent occupancy	Controlling a single zone
TEMPERATURE	WEATHER COMPENSATOR (if constant occupancy consider night set back)	Controlling a single zone
	AND	
	ZONE CONTROL OF SPACE TEMPERATURE (e.g. motorised valves and thermostats or TRVs)	Controlling multi-zones
BOILER	BOILER INTERLOCK to link the system controls with the boilers to ensure that they do not operate when there is no demand for heat	

MINIMUM > 50 kW

TIME	OPTIMUM START if intermittent occupancy	Controlling a single zone
	AND	
	ZONES TIMED FOR OCCUPANCY (e.g. motorised valves and timeswitches)	Controlling multi-zones
TEMPERATURE	WEATHER COMPENSATOR (if constant occupancy consider night set back)	Controlling a single zone
	AND	
	ZONE CONTROL OF SPACE TEMPERATURE (e.g. motorised valves and thermostats or TRVs)	Controlling multi-zones
BOILER	BOILER INTERLOCK to link the system controls with the boilers to ensure that the boiler output matches demand, e.g. using wiring, software and/or an integrated controller	

GOOD < 50 kW

TIME	OPTIMUM START if intermittent occupancy	Controlling a single zone
	AND	
	ZONES TIMED FOR OCCUPANCY (e.g. motorised valves and timeswitches)	Controlling multi-zones
TEMPERATURE	WEATHER COMPENSATOR (if constant occupancy consider night set back)	Controlling a single zone
	AND	
	ZONE CONTROL OF SPACE TEMPERATURE (e.g. motorised valves and thermostats or TRVs)	Controlling multi-zones
BOILER	BOILER INTERLOCK to link the system controls with the boilers to ensure that they do not operate when there is no demand for heat	BOILER ENERGY CONTROL to link the system controls with the boilers to ensure that they do not operate when there is no demand for heat

GOOD > 50 kW

TIME	ZONE OPTIMUM START where appropriate, e.g. separate intermittent occupancy buildings	Controlling a single zone
	AND	
	ZONES TIMED FOR OCCUPANCY (e.g. motorised valves and timeswitches)	Controlling multi-zones
TEMPERATURE	ZONE WEATHER COMPENSATORS e.g. separate buildings (if constant occupancy consider night set back)	Controlling a single zone
	AND	
	ZONE CONTROL OF SPACE TEMPERATURE (e.g. motorised valves and thermostats or TRVs)	Controlling multi-zones
BOILER	BOILER INTERLOCK to link the system controls with the boilers to ensure that the boiler output matches demand, e.g. using wiring, software and/or an integrated controller	
	AND	
	MINIMISE STANDING LOSSES in heavyweight boilers	

Figure 10.8 'Minimum' and 'Good' levels of control for wet central heating systems in small commercial and multi residential buildings (reproduced from Good Practice Guide GPG 132[9]; Crown copyright)

separately pumped secondary circuits which are 'decoupled' from the primary circuit by a common header or buffer vessel (see Figures 10.9 and 10.10) avoiding any interaction between circuits that could destabilise the controls.

Small, single boiler applications are often provided with a single pumped circuit. This can cause problems due to reduced flow through the boiler. A differential pressure by-pass can be provided to maintain a minimum boiler flow[8]. A more satisfactory arrangement is shown in Figure 10.9. In this arrangement the primary and secondary circuits are separately pumped but, since the boiler is directly compensated, no compensated valve is necessary.

10.3.2   Boiler controls

Effective control of boilers is a significant factor in achieving good energy efficiency. Inadequate or incorrect application of boiler control can add 15–30% to fuel consumption. The following points should be noted:

— the control of multiple boilers is often poor

— the reduced standing losses and improved part load efficiency of modern well insulated, low water content boilers normally allows very simple hydraulic arrangements to be used for multiple boilers

— simple layouts do not require the use of individual boiler pumps, or automatic isolation valves, which are the cause of many problems associated with the control of multiple boilers

— boiler controls must be considered at an early stage in the design; adding controls after plant layouts are designed can often result in uncontrollable systems.

10.3.2.1   Avoiding boiler dry cycling

Preventing excessive boiler cycling saves energy. Small (domestic) boilers should have boiler inhibit so that their operation is interlocked with the main heating and hot water thermostats[8]. Interlocking in this way ensures that the boiler and pump only operate when there is a real demand for heat.

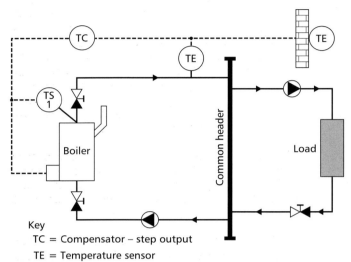

Key
TC = Compensator – step output
TE = Temperature sensor
TS1 = Burner control and high limit thermostat

Figure 10.9 Directly compensated single boiler system plant (reproduced from General Information Report GIR 40[7]; Crown copyright)

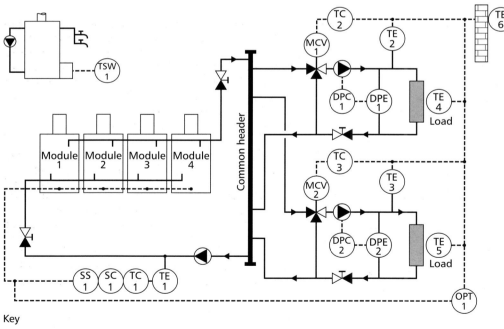

Figure 10.10 Pumped primary circuits with multiple secondary circuits plant (reproduced from General Information Report GIR 40[7]; Crown copyright)

Key

TE1	= boiler return water temperature sensor	TC2	= zone 1 compensator
TE2	= zone 1 compensated flow temperature sensor	TC3	= zone 2 compensator
TE3	= zone 2 compensated flow temperature sensor	SC1	= boiler sequence control step controller
TE4	= zone 1 space temperature sensor	SS1	= boiler sequence selector switch
TE5	= zone 2 space temperature sensor	MCV1	= zone 1 compensator valve
TE6	= outside temperature sensor	MCV2	= zone 2 compensator valve
TSW1	= HWS timeswitch	DPE1	= zone 1 differential pressure sensor
OPT1	= heating optimiser	DPE2	= zone 2 differential pressure sensor
TC1	= boiler sequence proportional temperature controller	DPC1	= zone 1 differential pressure controller
		DPC2	= zone 2 differential pressure controller

Boiler anti-cycling controls

Stand-alone boiler anti-cycling controls that delay boiler firing to reduce unnecessary cycling by increasing the 'off' time of the boiler are available. These devices provide little or no improvement to boiler efficiency compared with good, standard controls[8,10].

Demand-based boiler control and system inhibit

Standing losses and excessive part load operation can be reduced where boilers and associated primary pumps are only enabled when there is a demand. This can significantly reduce energy consumption where boilers and systems have high standing losses. However, response times must be adequate to meet demand, particularly where the boilers serve hot water services systems. For modern high efficiency, low standing-loss, boilers the benefit is reduced but still worthwhile.

Sophisticated strategies can be developed with advanced control systems and some lower cost systems (such as boiler energy managers) are now available with demand-based control of central plant dependent upon zonal demand. Boiler energy managers often combine optimisers and compensators alongside system inhibition and daytime optimisation. These can be very successful for small buildings but can cause problems in larger buildings due to response times. Demand-based control strategies should be used for larger buildings.

10.3.2.2   Boiler sequence control

Controlling multiple boilers in sequence:

—   matches the number of boilers firing to suit the load

—   minimises the number of boilers firing, thus, maximising overall efficiency

—   avoids short cycling of burner operation and, therefore, enhances energy efficient and stable operation

—   is normally carried out with respect to boiler circuit return temperature, although flow temperature can be used.

Sequence control will not operate correctly where the flow varies as a result of individual boiler pumps or automatic isolation valves. Systems must have:

—   a single primary pump, see above

—   a common header or buffer vessel to 'decouple' primary and secondary circuits, see above

—   a margin between the boiler thermostats and the sequence control setting to prevent interaction; this is normally 8 °C to allow for boiler thermostat switching differential and dilution effect of flow through off-line boilers.

Individual boiler thermostats must be set in accordance with HSE Guidance Note PM5[32]. Therefore, systems must have an adequate head of water or be pressurised to permit boiler thermostat settings higher than 82 °C[33].

Where boilers have individual pumps, or automatic isolation valves are used, the primary circuit flow will vary. The flow/return temperature is therefore not representative of the load on the system and boiler sequence control will not operate correctly.

Where boilers do not have separate primary and secondary heating circuits (e.g. domestic), TRVs will reduce the flow through the boilers and hence boiler control is lost at low load. To give near constant flow through the boiler(s), a differential pressure regulating valve should be installed in a by-pass. At periods of low heat load, this will circulate the flow back to the boiler, maintaining the required flowrate through the boiler. TRVs in this situation will slightly reduce the savings possible with a condensing boiler but they should still be used as they provide important zone control. These problems can be avoided by using a more energy efficient system, in which the primary boiler circuit is separately pumped and connected to the secondary circuit via a common header. A variable flow compensated secondary circuit can also be used with variable speed drives for energy efficient operation.

Sequence control related to outside air temperature can provide reasonably stable sequencing of boiler plant. However, it is a totally open loop control and does not respond to actual system load. It should only be used, therefore, where other methods are not possible.

Sequence selection can be manual or automatic, based on time or usage with more sophisticated control systems. Condensing boilers should always operate first; and modular boilers with a common combustion chamber normally require a fixed sequence of operation.

10.3.2.3   Burner controls

Single-stage, two-stage and modulating burners are available. Two-stage high/low burners provide more stages and therefore improved part load efficiency compared with single-stage burners. Where high/low boilers are more efficient at low fire (e.g. with a flue damper) then the sequence should gradually bring them all on at low fire before bringing any on at high fire. The sequence is therefore 'low–low–low' then 'high–high–high'.

Modulating burners provide the most efficient part load operation as air/fuel ratios can be maintained across the output range, ensuring high combustion efficiency. LTHW boilers with modulating burners are now becoming more widely available, providing a means of matching the load more accurately across the full output range. In larger boilers this offers the opportunity for oxygen trim control to further optimise the air/fuel ratio. Oxygen trim control can provide savings from 2% for a well maintained boiler, up to 5% for older boilers with hysteresis in linkages, etc.

10.3.2.4   Directly compensated boilers

Direct compensation of non-condensing boilers is normally of little benefit with modern high efficiency boilers due to their low standing losses and the need for separately pumped secondary circuits (see 10.3).

However, directly compensating the primary circuit is an ideal way of achieving low return water temperatures and therefore high efficiencies with condensing boilers (see

10.3.1 and Figure 10.9). Where heating and hot water are being supplied from a common plant then compensation must be overridden when hot water is required, possibly resulting in overheating of the space. Use a separate hot water supply where possible.

10.3.2.5   Reducing boiler standing losses

Significant energy savings can be achieved by minimising the standing losses in older, heavyweight poorly insulated boilers. Modern boiler standing losses are typically 0.75% of rated output for recent designs (but can be as low as 0.2% for high efficiency and condensing boilers). Older boiler designs with higher water content can have standing losses up to 7% of rated output. Whilst these older boilers may need back-end shut-off valves to minimise standing losses, modern boilers will not. The Boiler (Efficiency) Regulations[17] stipulate minimum efficiency levels for new boilers at full and part load efficiency from January 1998. Manufacturers have therefore improved their plant to meet these standards, resulting in low standing losses. Building Regulations Approved Document L*[14] suggests even higher standards at 30% load, which will force standing losses even lower. Losses on modern plant are therefore too small to justify installing shut-off valves.

Automatic boiler isolation valves can be used in multiple boiler installations to isolate the flow through off-line boilers and reduce losses from individual boilers. However, this adds to the complexity of multiple boiler systems and often leads to control problems. Using boilers with low standing losses alleviates the need to isolate flows through off-line boilers. Isolation of flow through off-line boilers is rarely effective and the additional cost of automatic isolation valves is wasted, particularly when they leak between ports or are set to part-open.

When boiler output is not required, boilers and primary circuits should be inhibited to minimise boiler and pipework standing losses, as well as pump energy. Inhibition should occur when compensator valves are on full re-circulation and time delays are required to prevent rapid cycling. The complete heating system should shut down when outside temperatures are high.

It is difficult to achieve satisfactory standing losses with large high water content boilers. Effective automatic isolation is normally complex and losses from associated distribution systems are often high. Distributed systems with smaller boilers located nearer the loads reduce distribution losses and, with well designed control and monitoring systems such as a BMS, can often be operated more efficiently.

Boilers with forced, or induced, draught fans should have the fans interlocked with burner operation to minimise standing losses. Large boilers should have air inlet or flue dampers interlocked with burner operation to prevent standing losses from natural draughts.

10.3.3   Time controls

Time controls should be provided to automatically control the number and duration of operating periods, with

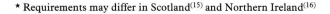

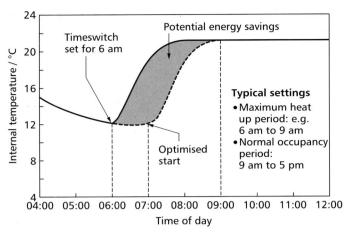

Figure 10.11 Example of the operation of optimum start control plant (reproduced from Good Practice Guide GPG 132[9]; Crown copyright)

provision for day omissions. Programmers with separate weekday/weekend settings are now cheap and easy to install. Programmable room thermostats can be a cheap and flexible means of providing both time and temperature zone controls.

10.3.3.1   Fixed time controls

A time switch provides a simple, robust and easily understood means of saving energy and should have a resolution of 15 minutes or less for effective operation.

'Run-back' timers giving a fixed additional period of operation are useful where occupancy is particularly unpredictable or where extensions to the normal heating period are needed. They are particularly useful in offices and shops where evening work is sometimes carried out, and in function rooms where occupancy is unpredictable.

10.3.3.2   Optimum start/stop control

Optimum start controls are weather-dependent time switches that vary the start-up time in the morning to achieve the building temperature by the required time of occupation. Heat-up times are reduced during milder weather, thus saving 5–10% of heating energy[10]. Figure 10.11 shows the operation of optimum start controls and the potential energy savings compared with a time switch. Optimum start controls can be relatively simple using a single internal sensor and a linear delay of start-up. However, sophisticated self-learning units with an external sensor are available. These can also provide optimum stop facilities to turn the boiler off early at the end of the day in milder weather.

The greatest energy savings from optimum start control are likely to be gained in buildings of lightweight construction and with heating systems of low thermal capacity. Heavyweight buildings are less influenced by external fluctuations and are likely to require smaller variations in required start-up times. Similarly, heating systems with a slow response require a longer preheat time and are, therefore, likely to realise reduced savings with optimum start control.

The thermal inertia of the building and its heating system should be considered when determining heating plant termination times. Boiler operation can be terminated early and the thermal mass of the plant relied upon if some degradation of inside temperature is acceptable towards the end of the occupied period.

10.3.4 Temperature controls

Good control of space temperature is required for energy efficient operation. Control of space temperature can often be achieved at low cost using TRVs. Reducing the room temperature by 1 °C can reduce the fuel use by around 10%.

Distribution systems should be weather compensated unless constant temperature is absolutely necessary (e.g. air heater batteries or domestic hot water). This reduces system losses and provides basic space temperature control, although it will not react to internal gains etc. Multiple compensated circuits are ideal for zoning a building to allow for different occupancy patterns. etc. Where different emitters are used, or parts of the building are better insulated, the compensator schedule can be set to reflect the differing zonal temperature requirements.

10.3.4.1 Weather compensation

The flow temperature of compensated circuits reduces as ambient temperature increases (see Figure 10.3). This provides basic control of space temperature and reduces distribution system losses. The compensator slope is normally linear, often with a maximum and minimum flow temperature. In milder weather, the system operates at lower temperatures thus saving energy. Compensators with non-linear slopes are also available to match heat output more closely to ambient temperature.

The most common version requires a three-port motorised valve to control water temperature, although direct boiler compensation is also possible. Weather compensation can provide low return water temperatures in milder weather causing condensing boilers to operate at higher efficiencies.

The controls should be installed so that the weather compensator is overridden during the heat up period. Many units provide a high temperature limit, which shuts off the heating entirely above a set external temperature (ambient temperature shutdown). Other units provide room reset control, whereby a room sensor signals the compensator to lower (reset) the temperature when the required space temperature is reached. Compensated circuits with space temperature reset provide more effective control than temperature averaging systems for control of a large number of emitters.

Space temperature reset of compensators is often desirable to take into account local heat gains. The maximum number of reset sensors should be limited to four, with a reset of 3 °C flow temperature to 1 °C space temperature. This is to prevent an undue influence from space temperature which may be unrepresentative of the total area served.

Proper siting of the external sensor is crucial, since it must reflect the ambient weather condition. Placing it near the building exhaust or on a wall exposed directly to solar radiation can lead to incorrect operation.

Deep plan buildings often require heating at their perimeter during the winter and mid-seasons, while the core may not require any heating at all. Where a compensated wet heating system is being used around the perimeter of a building in conjunction with an air conditioning system, care must be taken to ensure that there is no interaction between systems. Where the compensated circuit has a relatively small duty, primarily to prevent cold down draughts etc., space temperature control of the heating may not be required. Where the perimeter heating has a higher duty, space temperature control can be difficult due to differing reaction times for the two systems, and space temperature controls sensors need careful siting to prevent interaction between the two systems. In some circumstances, it may be possible to link the space temperature and air conditioning controls.

10.3.4.2 Night set-back

These controls reduce or set back the temperature during a given time period and are often part of the weather compensator controls. This is particularly useful at night in continuously occupied buildings, e.g. in elderly persons' homes. Night set-back provides an alternative to simply switching the heating off at night, allowing a minimum temperature to be maintained during the night and thus providing energy savings compared with continuous operation. However, generally it is more economical to switch the heating off at night with a low limit to bring it back on.

10.3.5 Zone controls

Heating is often required at different times, temperatures and areas of a building. A successful control system will satisfy these different requirements on a zone by zone basis. A zone may be regarded as a part of the building the heating system of which is capable of independent control, in terms of time, temperature, or both.

Building Regulations Approved Document L★[14] recommends that space temperature control, by means of thermostats, TRVs etc., should be provided for each part of the system designed to be separately controlled. Individual emitters should have separate control wherever possible for energy efficient operation. However, emitters should not have local control where sensors are located for space temperature reset of compensators.

Zone control can be implemented by:

— thermostatic radiator valves (TRVs)

— motorised valves and room thermostats.

10.3.5.1 Thermostatic radiator valves

Thermostatic radiator valves (TRVs) provide a low cost method of local temperature control on individual emitters, particularly where there are high incidental gains. TRVs are normally two-port and should be used in association with variable speed pumps to provide good control (see 10.3.7). Correct direction of flow through the TRV is essential, this may require the TRV to be fitted to the radiator return connection, rather than the flow.

★ Requirements may differ in Scotland[15] and Northern Ireland[16]

Lockable tamper-proof heads are also recommended. These can either be completely locked on one setting, or provide a minimum level of control for the adjacent occupants.

10.3.5.2   Motorised valves and room thermostats

Motorised valves and room thermostats can be used to provide temperature and/or time control of a zone. This method is probably best used in areas with a small group of emitters, say totalling over 5 kW. Sensing locations are better than TRVs and a wider range of emitters can be controlled. Reset of space temperature for unoccupied periods can also be more easily achieved.

Further energy savings can be achieved by installing time control in zones using two-port motorised valves, room thermostat and time control independent from the main heating time control. Programmable room thermostats are a convenient way of achieving this as they combine the roles of time switch and electronic room thermostat, e.g. by varying the room temperature at different times of the day in an elderly persons' day centre.

Larger zones should also be weather compensated, particularly where a boiler supplies a number of buildings or to allow for solar gains on different facades. Multiple secondary circuits should normally be connected in parallel across a common header so that each one has the full heat source available to it (see Figure 10.10). This system is relatively simple and allows good control to be achieved. More sophisticated space temperature control systems are also available including occupancy sensing[3].

10.3.6   Temperature sensor location

Correct installation of sensors is crucial to the efficient and effective operation of control systems. Poor siting can result in excessive energy consumption.

Room thermostats and sensors must be positioned:

—   around 1.5 m (approx. 5 feet) above floor level

—   out of direct sunlight

—   away from draughts

—   away from sources of heat

—   not in a partitioned office, if it also serves others.

Internal sensors for optimum start control should always be located in the coldest part of the building to signal how much heat is still stored in the building.

External sensors also need careful siting:

—   on a north or north west wall, out of the sun

—   in a position which is representative of the zone being controlled

—   away from heat sources such as openable windows, extract ducts and chimney stacks.

10.3.7   Variable flow control

Most heating systems are constant volume and use the same amount of energy for pumping power throughout the year regardless of the load on the system. Heating systems normally only require maximum flow during the boost period, which is a small percentage of total heating time. Variable speed pumps can respond to the reduced demand and decrease the flow of the pumps so that they match the load on the system[9,31].

Considerable pumping energy savings and improved space temperature control can be achieved by controlling the speed of distribution system pumps to respond to system demand (see section 11). Pumps are now available with in-built variable speed drives, which provide rapid payback of the additional capital cost.

Typically between 25 and 50% of annual pumping energy consumption can be saved by using variable flow heating systems. This is commonly achieved using two port control valves and a differential pressure controller on a by-pass. The pump speed is then controlled using a variable speed drive to maintain a constant differential pressure. Capital costs and commissioning is also reduced as coil by-pass pipework and regulating valves can be eliminated[9,31].

10.3.8   Hot water controls

Hot water generators and calorifiers should have time and temperature control as recommended in Building Regulations Approved Document L★[14]. The controls should be capable of holding the water temperature to within ±3 °C of the set-point temperature. The controls should also include a time switch to turn off the heating source and any circulating pumps (both primary and secondary) during periods when hot water will not be needed[7].

Segregation of hot water generation from heating systems is recommended (see 10.1.2). Where possible, hot water should be generated locally to minimise distribution losses. To avoid *legionella*[22], hot water should be stored at 60 °C and distributed such that a temperature of 50 °C is achieved within one minute at outlets.

10.4   Energy consumption

In most buildings, heating and hot water accounts for the largest annual consumption of delivered energy. Around 40–50% of CO_2 emissions in naturally ventilated offices are from heating systems. For each unit of delivered energy, the most common fuels used for heating, such as gas and oil, produce lower emissions to the atmosphere than electricity.

Upper limits for fossil fuel consumption in new buildings are provided in section 13 and typical/best practice targets for existing buildings are shown in section 19. These provide an indication of fuel consumed collectively in space heating, domestic hot water and catering. All-electric buildings where heating, hot water and catering

---

★ Requirements may differ in Scotland[14] and Northern Ireland[15]

are supplied by electricity will have quite different consumptions and CO_2 emissions to those using fossil fuel. They should be compared to the relevant all-electric whole building benchmarks.

10.4.1 Space heating energy consumption

Typical and good practice performance indicators for space heating in offices are shown in Table 10.10[34]. The energy use indicator (EUI) is the product of:

(a) the installed capacity in $W \cdot m^{-2}$ of treated floor area

(b) the annual running hours

(c) the average percentage utilisation of the plant, including allowances for boiler efficiency, expressed as a decimal fraction.

The result is divided by 1000 to obtain the EUI in $(kW \cdot h) \cdot m^{-2}$ per year.

For new offices, good practice EUIs should be seen as the upper limit and no office, of any age, should have an EUI greater than that given for a 'typical' office. Space heating EUIs for some other buildings are given in section 20. Where buildings provide 24-hour occupation, or have significant special end-uses like swimming pools, the EUIs will be significantly higher than those given in Table 10.10. Buildings with electric space heating should be compared using CO_2.

10.4.1 Domestic hot water energy consumption

Typical and good practice performance indicators for domestic hot water in offices are shown in Table 10.11[35,36]. These figures are based on systems which are both matched to hot water need and sensibly controlled.

Domestic hot water EUIs for some other buildings are given in section 20. Where buildings provide 24-hour occupation including bathing/showers or have significant special end uses like showers in sports halls, then EUIs will be significantly higher than those in given in Table 10.11.

Central systems combining heating and hot water can be very inefficient when meeting small hot water loads in summer. Where options of electric water heating and

fossil fuel fired water heating are being compared then CO_2 should be used as the basis[35,36].

10.5 Domestic heating

Heating and hot water systems for individual dwellings are covered by CIBSE/HVCA *Domestic heating design guide*[10] and Good Practice Guide GPG 284[11]. Building Regulations Approved Document L1★[14] states that the requirements of the Building Regulations with regard to boiler efficiency will be met if the boiler has a 'SEDBUK' (i.e. 'seasonal efficiency of domestic boilers in the UK', as defined under the Government's 'Standard Assessment Procedure for the Energy Rating of Dwellings' (SAP), not less than those given in Table 10.12. SEDBUK values for particular boilers may be obtained from the SEDBUK website (www.sedbuk.com).

The provision of controls is crucial in achieving satisfactory in-use efficiencies. Controls for a range of domestic heating systems are covered in Good Practice Guide GPG 302[12] which also provides the basis for meeting the Building Regulations. This indicates running cost savings of 4–17% by improving controls. Minimum and best practice levels of control for regular boilers in wet central heating systems are shown in Table 10.13. Further improvements include zone control using motorised valves, weather compensation and optimum start control.

★ Requirements may differ in Scotland[15] and Northern Ireland[16]

Table 10.11 Domestic hot water benchmarks for offices[34,35]

Function	Energy source	Consumption per m² of treated floor area / $(kW \cdot h) \cdot m^{-2}$	
		Good practice	Typical
Hand washing	Local electric	4	7
Hand washing	Central gas boiler	7	10
Hand washing and catering kitchen	Central gas boiler	12	20

Note: factors for converting treated floor area to nett and gross are shown in Table 20.2

Table 10.12 Minimum boiler SEDBUK as stated in Building regulations Approved Document L1

Central heating system fuel	SEDBUK / %
Mains natural gas	78
LPG	80
Oil	85

Table 10.10 Space heating benchmarks for offices[33]

Parameter	Benchmark for stated office type							
	Naturally ventilated cellular office (Type 1)		Naturally ventilated open plan office (Type 2)		Air conditioned standard office (Type 3)		Air conditioned prestige office (Type 4)	
	Good practice	Typical	Good practice	Typical	Good practice	Typical	Good practice	Typical
Installed capacity ($W \cdot m^{-2}$)	80	125	80	125	90	140	90	140
Running hours (h/yr)	2000	2500	2000	2500	2500	3000	3000	3700
Utilisation (%)	45	45	45	45	40	40	35	35
Energy use indicator (EUI) $((kW \cdot h) \cdot m^{-2})/yr$	72	141	72	141	90	168	95	181

Note: factors for converting treated floor area to nett and gross are given in Table 20.2

Table 10.13 Levels of control in wet central heating systems with regular boilers

Best practice	Minimum
Programmable room thermostat with additional hot water timing capability	Room thermostat
	Full programmer
Cylinder thermostat	Cylinder thermostat
TRVs on all radiators except in rooms with a room thermostat	TRVs on all radiators except in rooms with a room thermostat
Automatic bypass valve	Automatic bypass valve

References

1   *Heating* CIBSE Guide B1 (London: Chartered Institution of Building Services Engineers) (2002)

2   *Economic use of fired space heaters for industry and commerce* Fuel Efficiency Booklet FEB 3 (Action Energy) (1993) (www.actionenergy.org.uk)

3   *Degree days* Fuel Efficiency Booklet FEB 7 (Action Energy) (1993) (www.actionenergy.org.uk)

4   *Economic use of oil-fired boiler plant* Fuel Efficiency Booklet FEB 14 (Action Energy) (1993) (www.actionenergy.org.uk)

5   *Economic use of gas-fired boiler plant* Fuel Efficiency Booklet FEB 15 (Action Energy) (1993) (www.actionenergy.org.uk)

6   *Economic use of coal-fired boiler plant* Fuel Efficiency Booklet FEB 17 (Action Energy) (1993) (www.actionenergy.org.uk)

7   *Heating systems and their control* General Information Report GIR 40 (Action Energy) (1996) (www.actionenergy.org.uk)

8   *Variable flow control* General Information Report GIR 41 (Action Energy) (1996) (www.actionenergy.org.uk)

9   *Heating controls for wet central heating systems in small, commercial and multi-residential buildings* Good Practice Guide GPG 132 (Action Energy) (2000) (www.actionenergy.org.uk)

10   *Domestic heating design guide* (London: Heating and Ventilation Contractors Association) (2000)

11   *Domestic central heating and hot water systems with gas and oil fired boilers* Good Practice Guide GPG 284 (Action Energy) (2000) (www.actionenergy.org.uk)

12   *Controls for domestic central heating and hot water — a guidance for specifiers and installers* Good Practice Guide GPG 302 (Action Energy) (2001) (www.actionenergy.org.uk)

13   The Building Regulations 2000 Statutory Instrument 2000 No. 2531 and the Building (Amendment) Regulations 2001 Statutory Instrument 2001 No. 3335 (London: Stationery Office) (2000/2001)

14   *Conservation of fuel and power* The Building Regulations 2000 Approved Document L2 (London: The Stationery Office) (2001)

15   *Technical standards for compliance with the Building Standards (Scotland) Regulations 1990 (as amended)* (London: The Stationery Office) (2001)

16   *Conservation of fuel and power* The Building Regulations (Northern Ireland) 1994 Technical Booklet F (London: The Stationery Office) (1999)

17   The Boiler (Efficiency) Regulations 1993 Statutory Instrument 1993 No. 3083 (London: The Stationery Office) (1993)

18   *Condensing boilers. Part 1 — an introduction to more efficient boiler houses in the 90s* BSRIA TA 1/90 (Bracknell: Building Services Research and Information Association) (1990)

19   *Guide for installers of condensing boilers in commercial buildings* Good Practice Guide GPG 16 (Action Energy) (1990) (www.actionenergy.org.uk)

20   *Environmental design* CIBSE Guide A (London: Chartered Institution of Building Services Engineers) (1999)

21   *Oversized heating plant* Guidance Note GN 12/97 (Bracknell: Building Services Research and Information Association) (1997)

22   *Public health engineering* CIBSE Guide G (London: Chartered Institution of Building Services Engineers) (1999)

23   *Minimising the risk of Legionnaires' disease* CIBSE Technical Memoranda TM13 (London: Chartered Institution of Building Services Engineers) (2002)

24   *Small scale combined heat and power for buildings* GPG 176 (Action Energy) (2004) (www.actionenergy.org.uk)

25   Heating system option appraisal — an engineer's guide for existing buildings Good Practice Guide GPG 187 (Action Energy) (1996) (www.actionenergy.org.uk)

26   *Ground source heat pumps — a technology review* BSRIA TN18/99 (Bracknell: Building Services Research and Information Association) (1999)

27   *Energy efficiency in offices. BRE Low Energy Office* Good Practice Case Study GPCS 62 (Action Energy) (1993) (www.actionenergy.org.uk)

28   BS 5422: 2001: *Methods for specifying thermal insulating materials on pipes, ductwork and equipment (in the temperature range $-40\,^{\circ}C$ to $+700\,^{\circ}C$)* (London: British Standards Institution) (2001)

29   *The designer's guide to energy-efficient buildings for industry* Good Practice Guide 303 (Action Energy) (2000) (www.actionenergy.org.uk)

30   Brown R *Radiant heating* BSRIA AG 3/96 (Bracknell: Building Services Research and Information Association) (1996)

31   *Building control systems* CIBSE Guide H (London: Chartered Institution of Building Services Engineers) (2000)

32   *Automatically controlled steam and hot water boilers* Guidance Note PM5 (London: Health And Safety Executive) (2000)

33   *Energy efficient multiple boiler systems* (Poole: Hamworthy Heating Ltd) (1998)

34   Bordass W (private communication)

35   *Energy use in offices* Energy Consumption Guide ECG 19 (Action Energy) (2000) (www.actionenergy.org.uk)

36   *Energy Assessment and Reporting Methodology — Office assessment method* CIBSE TM22 (London: Chartered Institution of Building Services Engineers) (2004)

37   *Energy consumption in hospitals* Energy Consumption Guide ECG 72 (Action Energy) (2000) (www.actionenergy.org.uk)

Bibliography

Energy efficiency in schools: potential benefits of boiler replacement Good Practice Case Study GPCS 73 (Action Energy) (1996) (www.actionenergy.org.uk)

Commissioning of water systems in building BSRIA AG 2/89.3 (Bracknell: Building Services Research and Information Association) (1998)

Day A R *A better way of sizing central boiler plant* Proc. CIBSE Nat. Conf., Regent's College, 18 October 2001 (London: Chartered Institution of Building Services Engineers) (2001)

All-electric office of simple design with low electricity consumption General Information Leaflet GIL 10 (Action Energy) (1999) (www.actionenergy.org.uk)

Teekaram A J H and Brown R *Retrofitting of heating and cooling systems* BSRIA 15/99 (Bracknell: Building Services Research and Information Association) (1999)

Central heating system specifications (CHeSS) General Information Leaflet GIL 59 (Action Energy) (2000) (www.actionenergy.org.uk)

11 Motors and building transportation systems

11.0	General
11.1	Minimising the motor load
11.2	Motor sizing and selection
11.3	Motor drives
11.4	Controlling the motor load
11.5	Building transportation systems

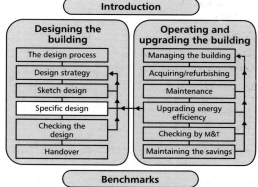

This section sets out key issues in designing systems to minimise the energy consumption of motors and drives, in line with the principles at the front of this Guide. It covers minimising the motor load, sizing and selecting motors, motor drives and controlling the motor load, including that of variable speed drives (VSDs). The operation and maintenance of motors and drives is covered in section 17 and upgrading motor driven systems to improve energy efficiency is covered in section 18. Further details on the energy efficient use of motors and drives can be found in Good Practice Guide GPG 2[1], Fuel Efficiency Booklet FEB 9[2], CIBSE Guide H[3] and General Information Report GIR 41[4]. Internal heat gains from electric motors are shown in CIBSE Guide A[5].

11.0 General

The motor load should always be minimised by good system design prior to motor selection. Effective system regulation and control are also essential for efficient operation.

Electric motors and drives can account for a significant part of the energy demand in buildings. A modestly sized 11 kW induction motor costing £300 to buy can build up a running cost of over £8000 in an intermittently occupied building over ten years, and up to £30 000 with continuous operation.

The following are key issues for electric motors and drives:

— Systems should be carefully designed to minimise pressure loss and hence reduce energy consumption.

— High-efficiency motors should always be considered as they often have no additional capital cost and they offer efficiency and economic benefits in virtually all situations.

— Motors should be sized correctly to avoid the greater losses when part loaded.

— Use direct drives rather than belt drives where practical.

— Where belt drives are used, consider modern flat, synchronous, or ribbed belt drives rather than traditional V-belts, to reduce drive losses.

— Efficient system regulation by matching fan and pump characteristics to the system (normally via speed change) can provide significant energy savings compared with increased system resistance. Typically, 20% energy saving for a 10% flow regulation and 40% saving for a 20% regulation can be expected.

— Variable flow control can provide significant opportunities for energy saving. Building services are sized for peak loads and spend most of their time operating well below full output. Typically, only 20% of full volume energy is required to move air and water at 50% of maximum volume.

— The use of VSDs should always be considered for efficient system regulation and variable flow control.

11.1 Minimising the motor load

Considerable energy savings can be achieved by good system design to minimise the motor load. Accurate calculations of system resistance are essential for effective fan and pump selection. Due to fundamental relationships, a small increase in duct and pipe size can significantly reduce system losses and thus a greater reduction in the power required. Guidance on pipe and duct sizing is given in CIBSE Guides B1[6], B3[7] and C[8].

11.1.1 Ventilation systems

Energy can be wasted by:
— poor fan efficiency
— unnecessary bends
— reduced duct size
— excessive duct length
— poor inlet and outlet conditions
— accumulation of dirt.

Select an efficient fan, keeping the specific fan power to a minimum. Energy efficient systems should achieve 2–3 W/(litre·s^{-1}). Poor fan performance, and hence inefficient operation, can also be caused by poor inlet and outlet conditions, often referred to as 'installation effects'. Measures to reduce installation effects at the fan inlet and outlet include the following:

Fan inlet:

— Ensure that air enters axial fans without spin by improved inlet design or a splitter.

— Include turning vanes where there is a duct bend close to fan inlet.

— Include a transition piece where the duct size reduces.

— Ensure flexible connections are correctly fitted without offset or slack.

— Where fans are installed in plenum chambers, ensure the fan inlet is a minimum of one diameter from plenum wall with no obstructions.

Fan outlet:

— Ensure a minimum of two diameters straight duct.

— Where bends are close to the outlet, ensure that they radius bends with splitters are used.

— Preferably, axial and propeller fans should be fitted with guide vanes to provide energy recovery. Where guide vanes are not fitted, air swirl will significantly increase system resistance. This can be corrected by a carefully designed cross-piece.

Ventilation energy consumption is shown in Section 7.3.6. Additional guidance on efficient fan and ventilation system design can be found in various HEVAC Association publications[9–11].

11.1.2   Pumps and hydraulic systems

Energy can be wasted by:

— poor pump efficiency

— unnecessary bends

— reduced pipe size

— excessive pipe lengths.

Select an efficient pump and ensure it is operated close to its rated design flow and head. On large sites, decentralised generation of heating and hot water will reduce pumping power requirements as well as thermal losses.

Typical and good practice performance indicators for pumps in offices are shown in Table 11.1[12]. The energy use indicator (EUI) is the product of:

(a)   the installed capacity in W·m^{-2} of treated floor area

(b)   the annual running hours.

The result is divided by 1000 to obtain the EUI in (kW·h)·m^{-2} per year.

For new offices, good practice EUIs should be seen as an upper limit and no office, of any age, should have an EUI greater than that given for a 'typical' office. Pump EUIs for some other buildings are given in section 20. Where buildings provide 24-hour occupation or have significant special end-uses like swimming pools then EUIs will be significantly higher than those in Table 11.1.

11.2   Motor sizing and selection

There is scope for saving capital and running costs through better sizing of electric motors. Motors are often rated well above the power levels at which they operate. For example, the basic duty may require a delivered power of 7.5 kW. Designers may specify a 10% margin and the project engineer responsible for the system may apply a further 10% contingency, resulting in a power requirement of 9.1 kW. As 9.1 kW is not a standard rating, an 11 kW motor is selected. The installed motor, therefore, always operates at two thirds or less of its rated output.

By far the most common type of motor in HVAC applications is the three-phase squirrel cage induction

Table 11.1 Energy consumption benchmarks heating and cooling pumps in offices[12]

Parameter	Benchmark for stated office type							
	Naturally ventilated cellular office (Type 1)		Naturally ventilated open plan office (Type 2)		Air conditioned standard office (Type 3)		Air conditioned prestige office (Type 4)	
	Good practice	Typical	Good practice	Typical	Good practice	Typical	Good practice	Typical
(a) Heating pump								
Installed capacity (W·m^{-2})	0.8	1.875	1.2	2.5	1.35	2.8	1.35	2.8
Running hours (h/yr)	2000	2500	2000	2500	2500	3000	3000	3700
Energy use indicator (EUI) ((kW·h)·m^{-2})/yr	1.6	4.9	2.4	6.3	3.4	8.4	4.1	10.4
(b) Cooling pump								
Installed capacity (W·m^{-2})	—	—	—	—	1.8	3.1	2.0	3.4
Running hours (h/yr)	—	—	—	—	1500	2500	2500	3000
Energy use indicator (EUI) ((kW·h)·m^{-2})/yr	—	—	—	—	2.7	7.8	5.0	10.2

Note: factors for converting treated floor area to nett and gross are given in Table 20.2

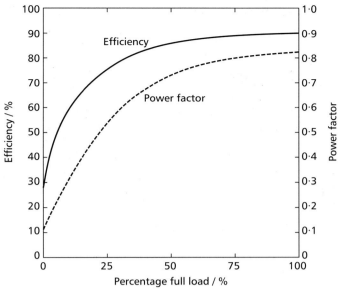

Figure 11.1 Standard induction motor efficiency and power factor (adapted from Fuel Efficiency Booklet FEB 9[2]; Crown copyright)

motor. Modern motors are designed for maximum efficiency at 75% full load, although between 50 and 100% load there is minimal variation in efficiency. Significant reductions in efficiency occur at 25% or less of full load, and it is at this level that serious consideration should be given to fitting a reduced-rating 'higher-efficiency' motor with a lower capital cost.

Figure 11.1 shows how the efficiency of standard motors falls rapidly at low load. At low loading, power factor falls off even more rapidly than efficiency. Smaller motors also reduce the cost of associated cabling and switchgear.

Therefore, over-sizing of motors increases:

— the capital cost of the motor

— the capital cost of associated switch gear and wiring

— the capital cost of power factor correction equipment

— the running cost due to lower efficiencies.

Typical efficiencies of electric motors are shown in Table 11.2

11.2.1   High efficiency motors

High efficiency motors (HEMs) are designed to minimise the inherent losses and save, on average, 3% of energy consumption compared with standard motors. Percentage savings will be larger on smaller motors but less on bigger

Table 11.2 Average efficiencies of electric motors[5]

Motor output rating / kW	Average motor efficiency / %			
	DC motors	AC motors		
		Single phase	Two phase	Three phase
0.75	76	65	73	74
3.75	83	78	84	85
7.5	86	81	87	88
15	88	83	88	90
38	90	85	91	91
56	92	86	92	92

motors, although the actual cost savings will be larger for bigger motors. Many manufacturers now offer 'energy efficient' or 'high efficiency' motors as their standard product for no extra capital cost. Purchasing policies should reflect the wide availability of HEMs[13]. The improvement in efficiency is greatest at part load, as shown in Figure 11.2. Good Practice Guide GPG 2[1] shows examples of how to calculate energy savings from installing HEMs.

11.2.2   Rewinding motors

The cost of rewinding a motor can be high compared with the cost of a new motor and, unless the motor is rewound to high standards, the efficiency can be reduced by between 0.5 and 2%. Therefore, the decision to rewind or to replace with a new high efficiency motor should be based on life cycle costs. In practice, it is rarely economic to repair standard induction motors of less than 7.5 kW and some motor users would choose a much higher cut-off point. Good Practice Guide GPG 2[1] and Association of Electrical and Mechanical Trades' *The repair of induction motors*[14] provide further guidance on when to repair and when to replace motors.

11.3   Motor drives

Efficiency losses will occur in the motor drive and these vary with the type of equipment being used. Typical efficiencies of motor drives are shown in Table 11.3

11.3.1   Direct drives

Directly driven fans and pumps avoid the need for belt drives and therefore eliminate belt drive losses and maintenance. Belt drives have traditionally been used to enable the matching of fan and pump speeds to duty. However, this can normally be achieved more easily and efficiently using VSDs, see 11.4.1.

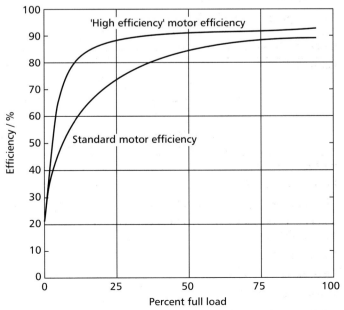

Figure 11.2 Comparison of efficiencies of standard and high efficiency motors (reproduced from Fuel Efficiency Booklet FEB 9[2]; Crown copyright)

Table 11.3 Average drive efficiencies[5]

Drive	Drive efficiency / %
Plain bearings	95–98
Roller bearings	98
Ball bearings	99
V-belts	96–98
Spur gears	93
Bevel gears	92

11.3.2   Belt drives

There are now a number of alternatives to the traditional V-belt which offer better efficiency and lower maintenance costs:

— Modern synchronous, flat and ribbed belts are typically 5–6% more efficient than V-belts.

— Wedge and ribbed wedge belts are normally around 2% more efficient than V-belts.

— The efficiency of wedge and V-belts deteriorates by around 4% over the life of the belt when well maintained and a further 5–10% if poorly maintained.

— Over-sizing or under-sizing of V- and wedge belts produces additional losses.

— Multiple belt drives should be avoided where possible since equal tension on each belt is rarely maintained, causing inefficiency.

— Where used, always replace belts on multiple drives with complete sets of matched belts.

— Ensure pulleys are not misaligned.

— Ensure belts are checked and properly tensioned at the recommended intervals.

— Consider changing the drive type when pulleys require replacement.

11.3.3   Motor location

Where possible, motors in ventilation systems should be located out of the air stream to avoid additional unwanted heat input, although this is reduced with HEMs.

11.4   Controlling the motor load

Further information on motor control and variable speed controls can e found in CIBSE Guide H[3] and General Information Report GIR 41[4].

11.4.1   Variable speed drives

Variable speed drives (VSDs) can be used for both efficient system regulation and variable flow control.

VSDs vary motor speed through output waveforms at reduced frequencies. VSDs for fans and pumps are normally pulse width modulation inverters with variable torque characteristics. Modern VSDs are very efficient and reliable with sophisticated features for setting speeds, acceleration rates etc. Little, if any, allowance has to be made for de-rating motors when used with modern VSDs. VSDs also normally provide a high power factor at all loads.

Electronic variable voltage VSDs provide a far less efficient drive system than pulse width modulation inverters but are acceptable for very small (fractional kW) motors. They should be avoided on larger drives because special motors with extra cooling are required. The additional cooling requirement is an indication of an inefficient drive system.

As a rule of thumb, the capital cost of VSDs is roughly £115/kW motor rating, excluding installation costs. Costs are normally higher per kW for small drives, although real costs are continuing to fall. There is an increasing number of pump and fan manufacturers who supply in-built VSDs that provide significant cost savings compared to separate VSDs. Reference should be made to General Information Report GIR 41[4] and Good Practice Guide GPG 2[1] for further information on VSDs for building services applications.

11.4.2   Efficient system regulation

Fans and pumps are normally at least 15–20% over-sized due to safety factors and available pressure/flow characteristics making it necessary for them to be regulated to provide design flow rates. Fan and pump pressure/flow characteristics must be matched as closely as possible to the system characteristics to provide the design flow rate. Increasing system resistance to reduce flow rates is inherently inefficient as fan or pump absorbed power is in proportion to the pressure generated. Energy is often wasted due to insufficient care being taken with system regulation.

11.4.2.1   Traditional regulation

Traditional regulation methods match the fan or pump to the system as closely as possible, then using system regulation through increasing system resistance until the flow is reduced to the design figure. The amount of system regulation should be minimised as far as possible due to its inherent inefficiency.

At the first stage the fan or pump is matched to the system as follows:

— For belt drives, a change of pulleys normally allows the pump or fan speed to be reduced and the duty to be matched to within 5–10% (belt drives have additional losses, see 11.3.2).

— Smaller impellers can be used with pumps, although this will cause a slight reduction in pump efficiency.

— Multiple speed motors have coarse adjustment of speed and will rarely permit an accurate matching of fan/pump characteristics.

— Axial fans often permit accurate matching of characteristics by blade pitch adjustment.

Lack of time, or readily available components, should not be used as an excuse for inadequately matching the fan or pump to the system.

At the second stage, the system is regulated as follows:

— System resistance is increased, by regulating valves or dampers, until the flow rate is reduced to the design flow rate.

11.4.2.2 Regulation using VSDs

VSDs can be used to match fans or pumps to the system, their additional cost often being justified purely for regulation. Regulation using VSDs offers the following advantages:

— Very rapid results are possible compared with traditional first stage regulation methods.

— There is no need for a second stage.

— Accurate setting of speeds and flow provides minimum energy consumption.

— Ease of resetting to match flow to actual loads is possible where system flow requirements are changed.

— Additional flexibility allows variable flow control, maximum demand control, etc.

— There are cost savings for regulating valves or dampers.

— 20 to 40% savings are possible with 10 to 20% regulation.

— They normally (but not always) operate nearer the point of maximum efficiency, compared with conventional flow regulation.

In the unlikely event of an exact match of pump/fan to system, there would be an energy penalty of up to 10% with a typical VSD. However, for most applications, VSD regulation will often dramatically reduce energy consumption and the savings can justify the cost of the VSD on grounds of regulation alone.

Examples in General Information Report GIR 41[4] indicate the following key points:

— Nearly 20% of the energy is saved by using a VSD for 10% flow regulation.

— For general guidance, unless the pump or fan curves are exceptionally flat, it is safe to assume around 20% saving for 10% flow regulation and 40% for 20% flow regulation using a VSD compared with a regulating valve.

— In many instances, these savings make the use of VSDs viable purely for regulation.

— Similar savings can be achieved through speed matching by pulley changes where belt drives are used (although the belts will consume additional energy), or impeller changes, etc. However, in practice, time and the availability of components often preclude optimising the fan or pump characteristic.

For further information on regulation using VSDs, reference should be made to General Information Report GIR 41[4], CIBSE Guide H[3] and Good Practice Guide GPG 2[1].

11.4.3 Variable flow control

Building services are generally sized for peak loads and spend most of their operating life at part load. Power absorbed by fans and pumps is proportional to the speed (volume) cubed and, typically, less than 20% of full volume input energy is required at 50% flow. The significant potential energy savings of variable flow control are illustrated in Figure 11.3.

Figure 11.3 illustrates the savings for a heating pump in a typical office on an average heating system day. It shows that:

— full flow is only required during boost

— the average flow rate is 53%

— the average energy saving is 66.9%.

Effective variable flow control requires a well designed system, with controllability considered from very early stages. Methods of controlling variable flows in building services are discussed in some detail in General

Hour	1	2	3	4	5	6	7	8	9	10	Average
Flow rate / %	100	90	70	55	40	30	30	32	38	45	53·0
Energy consumption / %	110·0	82·9	42·3	23·6	13·4	9·7	9·7	10·3	12·5	16·1	33·1
Energy saving / %	−10·0	17·1	57·7	76·4	86·6	90·3	90·3	89·7	87·5	83·9	66·9

Figure 11.3 Heating pump energy savings (reproduced from General Information Report GIR 41[4]; Crown copyright)

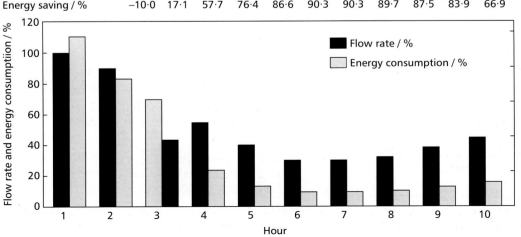

Information Report GIR 41[4]. Types of fans are summarised in CIBSE Guide B2[15].

11.4.3.1 Mechanical variable flow control methods

Variable pitch axial fans provide a very efficient method of variable flow control and ,unlike variable speed fans, can maintain high static pressures at low volumes. However, care must be taken with the selection of variable pitch axial fans to avoid stall problems. Complex hub mechanisms and actuation systems can also cause problems.

Other methods of mechanical variable flow control are very inefficient compared with VSDs and variable pitch axial fans. However, dampers used in association with VSDs and variable pitch axial fans, such as VAV terminal units, provide an efficient system.

Where mechanical variable flow methods result in variable motor loads the power factor will also vary, making automatic power factor correction desirable.

Reference should be made to General Information Report GIR 41[4] for further information on mechanical variable flow control methods.

11.4.3.2 Ventilation and air conditioning systems

Variable air volume (VAV) systems are suitable for buildings where there is predominantly a cooling load throughout the year, such as deep plan office buildings, where they can be an energy efficient form of air conditioning. VAV systems are complex compared with other forms of air conditioning and considerable care has to be taken in system design and control. In particular, sensor locations must be carefully considered.

There are a number of opportunities for variable flow control with other ventilation and air conditioning systems, such as air quality control and heating/cooling demand control. These systems normally have limited flow reduction due to factors such as cold air dumping. However, due to the 'cube law' relationship between flow and absorbed power, significant energy savings are also possible.

Fans for dry air coolers and air-cooled condensers are normally controlled in stages by multiple fans and/or multiple speed motors. The control and energy efficiency of cooling towers is normally improved by variable speed control of the fans (via VSDs) rather than on/off control or staged control by multiple speed motors.

Reference should be made to General Information Report GIR 41[4] for further information on variable flow control of ventilation and air conditioning systems.

11.4.3.3 Variable flow heating and chilled water systems

Variable flow can be applied to most heating and chilled water distribution systems with significant pumping energy savings. Care must be taken in system design to ensure design water flow rates through boilers and chillers are maintained. This can best be achieved using a constant flow primary pump with secondary circuits served via a buffer vessel (or common header), as shown in Figure 11.4.

Capital cost savings can be made by using two-port valves instead of three-port valves for applications such as air conditioning. By-pass pipework and regulating valves are also eliminated. Many heating systems use two-port TRVs for emitter control so that there will be no system capital cost savings, although effective variable flow control will permit TRVs to operate effectively and provide further energy savings.

The design of variable speed circuits needs to allow two-port control valves to close without causing unwanted flow or pressure variations in other parts of the circuit. The most common method of controlling pump speed is to maintain a constant pressure differential between two points in the index circuit. CIBSE Guide H[3] recommends about two thirds the way between the pump and the index circuit. BSRIA AG 14/99[16] describes procedures for the design of systems with variable speed pumping.

Pumps are now available with in-built VSDs and differential pressure control. These include control strategies that reduce pump differential pressure at low loads, allowing differential pressure control similar to that

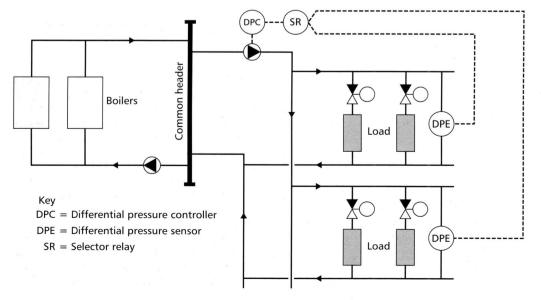

Figure 11.4 Variable flow heating or chilled water system (reproduced from General Information Report GIR 41[4]; Crown copyright)

Key
DPC = Differential pressure controller
DPE = Differential pressure sensor
 SR = Selector relay

above. These pumps significantly reduce the cost of variable flow heating and chilled water systems.

Reference should be made to General Information Report GIR 41[4] for further information on variable flow heating and chilled water systems.

11.4.4 Additional control methods

11.4.4.1 Demand based control

Energy consumption is minimised where plant only runs when required. Demand based control will only run central plant when there is a demand from the zones served. Pump, fan, boiler and chiller energy, plus distribution system thermal losses, can all be reduced.

Care must be taken to ensure that response times are adequate if central plant and distribution systems are allowed to start and stop according to zone demand. Logical strategies (often incorporating time delays and minimum operating times) must be developed to permit safe and reliable operation in all circumstances. Additional control functions such as optimum stop/start, which then demand central plant operation, will be required at each zone.

Demand based control strategies are available with a number of modern control systems and these can provide additional economy of operation at minimal, or zero, cost. However, where fixed strategies are built into controllers, care must be taken to ensure that they are suitable for the application.

11.4.4.2 Duty cycling

Duty cycling switches off plant for a percentage of the normal operating time and is normally on a fixed cyclical basis, such as 15 minutes in an hour. This can disturb building occupants and cause problems such as additional belt wear due to more frequent starting.

Duty cycling is an indication of over-sized systems and should not be necessary for well designed and controlled plant. Where services are over-sized it is normally much better to reduce fan or pump output by efficient system regulation, such as by using a VSD. This will give far greater gains than duty cycling due to the cube relationship between flow and absorbed power.

Duty cycling can make savings, but should normally be regarded as a stop-gap measure prior to the implementation of more satisfactory and energy efficient methods.

11.4.4.3 Maximum demand control

Reducing the maximum electrical demand of a building can reduce supply costs with many tariffs. Maximum demand control limits the maximum load and hence eliminates charges imposed for exceeding the agreed supply limit. Effective control can offer the opportunity for lower limits with the consequent reduction in supply costs.

The use of maximum demand control has often been limited because building users are reluctant to allow any item of plant to be switched off. Where VSDs are used, maximum demand control can be used effectively as the cube law relationship between flow and absorbed power permits significant power reductions for a small reduction in flow.

Plant with a high energy consumption such as chillers can also have the number of stages limited at times of maximum demand, rather than be turned off. Care must be taken to ensure that safe and reliable operating strategies are devised.

11.4.4.4 Motor energy optimisers

Motor energy optimisers, also known as 'motor controllers' or 'power factor controllers' are connected between the motor and the mains supply. At low load they can reduce the iron losses by chopping the waveform which reduces the average voltage and current. This technique can give reasonable energy savings in some applications with long running hours, mainly at very low load. Table 11.4 shows when this approach might be applicable. See Good Practice Guide GPG 2[1] for more details.

Table 11.4 Potential energy savings from energy optimising[1]

Motor load	Effect on energy consumption
Less than $1/3$ load	Useful energy savings possible
Between $1/3$ and $2/3$ load	Little effect
Greater than $2/3$ load	Energy consumption may increase

Small motor energy optimisers have commonly been introduced on domestic freezers and 'fridge–freezers'. A study[1] indicated that most appliances showed savings of 0% to 15%. Average energy savings found were:

— large chest freezers: 6%

— ice cream cabinets: 3.8%

— drinks cabinets: 2.9%

— dairy cabinets: 2% increase.

11.5 Building transportation systems

This section sets out some important issues in designing energy efficient transportation systems for buildings, in line with the principles at the front of this Guide. Lifts and escalators can consume 5–15% of total energy costs in some buildings, depending on the layout and use of the building. Where possible, designers should aim to minimise transportation requirements through good building layout during the sketch design stage (see section 4 and CIBSE Guide D[17] section 2: *Interior circulation*).

The number and type of lifts installed in a building is determined by the traffic requirements of the building occupants (see Guide D section 3: *Traffic planning and selection of equipment and performance*). Energy cannot sensibly be saved by reducing the number of lifts installed.

Lifts are designed to be counterbalanced when 50% loaded (see Guide D section 7.6), when the least demand is made on the drive motor. Thus, the most energy efficient loading for an electric traction lift is when the car is 50% full of passengers.

During the peak periods of morning ('uppeak'), evening ('downpeak') and midday traffic, the lifts will generally be loaded close to 100% capacity and nothing can be done to reduce energy useage. During off-peak periods of inter-floor activity during the working day, lifts tend to be occupied by one or two passengers only. During these periods energy can be saved, without significantly lengthening the passenger waiting times, by the traffic control system by introducing a minimum passenger waiting time. This can increase the number of passengers present in the lift at any one time and thereby increase the loading towards its optimum value of 50%. The same strategy can be applied to the 'out of hours' service, during which there is little activity. This is equivalent to 'machine shut down' employed on the older Ward-Leonard systems, but implemented by a computer program.

Increased energy efficiency can often involve higher initial capital cost, this may be recovered through energy savings and, therefore, each application warrants a full cost analysis. Detailed design of transportation systems are covered CIBSE Guide D[17] and BS 5655: Part 6[18].

Guide D section 13 provides more comprehensive information on lift and escalator energy consumption. In particular, it provides an assessment of three different methods of estimating lift consumption and a further method for escalators. Guide D indicates that as a general rule of thumb, and taking the two-speed AC system as a benchmark of 100%, the AC variable voltage system draws 70% of the energy and the variable voltage variable frequency (VVVF) system draws 50%. Hydraulic lifts are the least efficient. The other interesting point is that energy consumption rises dramatically with the increase in rated speed in all but the VVVF system. The VVVF and AC variable voltage systems are forms of variable speed drive commonly used in the lift industry.

A software model has been developed to predict more accurately the energy consumption of lifts[19].

11.5.1 Lifts

The following issues should be taken into account when designing energy efficient vertical transportation systems:

— Aim to group lifts together in order to group their controls as this may help minimise the number of journeys and, hence, reduce energy consumption.

— Locate lifts as appropriate and locate stairs before lifts. If passengers pass a well signposted staircase on the way to the lift, the demand for the lift may be less[20,21].

— Select the lift control strategy to minimise the number of journeys as this may reduce energy consumption[20,21].

— Select lift speeds that are appropriate to the task, e.g. slower speeds for goods lifts.

— Select an energy efficient drive for the lift and consider regeneration systems where the electricity can be used on-sit[17].

— Consider recovering heat from lift motor rooms if the lifts are used intensely. Typically, a 20 kW lift motor can produce 7 kW of heat in the machine room, see Table 11.5.

Energy consumption of lifts is affected by:

— rated speed

— rated capacity

— travel distance

— duty cycle (i.e. starts per hour, average run distance, load variation, direction when loaded, idle time etc.)

— drive system

— method of drive and speed control

— system losses (e.g. machinery inefficiencies, controller power consumption)

— traffic control system.

Lift motors do not work continuously, nor at constant load. To take proper account of these factors requires specialist knowledge applied to specific applications and appropriate methods are given in CIBSE Guide D[17]. Measured average power consumption of passenger lift motors is shown in Table 11.6[5].

11.5.2 Escalators and conveyors

Escalators, conveyors and travelling walk-ways operate constantly and require constant speed, but widely varying torque. Their motors run at the same speed whether they are fully or partially loaded. Factors affecting escalator energy consumption are:

Table 11.5 Waste heat generated in machine rooms[17]

Capacity of lift / person	Geared electric traction			Gearless electric traction			Oil hydraulic		
	Motor size / kW	Lift speed / m·s⁻¹	Heat output / kW	Motor size / kW	Lift speed / m·s⁻¹	Heat output / kW	Motor size / kW	Lift speed / m·s⁻¹	Heat output / kW
8	8.7	1.6	4.9	—	—	—	20	0.63	4
10	10.5	1.6	5.2	—	—	—	20	0.63	4
13	14	1.6	5.8	21	2.5	5.7	20	0.4	4
16	20	1.6	6.9	21	2.5	6.5	20	0.3	4.4
21	24.5	1.6	7.7	34	2.5	7.9	24	0.3	4.9

Note: Based on serving 7 floors at 240 starts per hour (electric traction) and 5 floors at 45 starts per hour (hydraulic)

Table 11.6 Measured average power consumption of passenger lift motors[5]

Drive type	Speed / m·s⁻¹	Number of passengers									
		8		10		13		16		21	
		Motor rating / kW	Average power / kW	Motor rating / kW	Average power / kW	Motor rating / kW	Average power / kW	Motor rating / kW	Average power / kW	Motor rating / kW	Average power / kW
Geared variable voltage	1.0	10	2.4	10	2.4	2.4	10	12	2.9	15	3.6
	1.6	15	3.6	15	3.6	15	3.6	17.6	4.2	22	5.3
Geared variable frequency	1.0	5.5	1.0	7.5	1.3	9.5	1.6	11	1.8	15	2.4
	1.6	9.5	1.6	11	1.8	13	2.2	18.5	3.0	22	3.6
Gearless static direct drive	2.5	—	—	—	—	—	3.8	—	4.2	—	5.2
	4.0	—	—	—	—	—	6.7	—	7.6	—	8.6

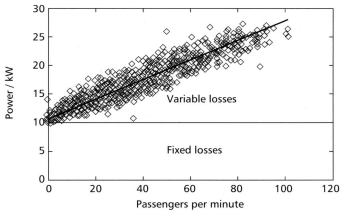

Figure 11.5 Fixed and variable losses for an up-escalator[14]

— rise

— mechanical design

— number of passengers

— walking factor[14].

Consumption can be broken down into fixed and variable losses, as indicated in Figure 11.5. Variable losses for a down-escalator will have a negative gradient. Variable losses account for only 20% of consumption in general.

The motors driving these loads often use a power factor controller. Variable speed drives that reduce speed when traffic is light can also provide control for these loads, but at a higher cost. Other options include 'delta' to 'star' switching of motors and systems that switch off when traffic is zero. High efficiency motors and 'soft start' are now in common use on passenger conveyors, escalators and baggage handling systems.

A method for estimating the energy consumption of escalators is given in CIBSE Guide D[17]. Examples of the energy consumption for escalators calculated using this method are shown in Table 11.7.

Table 11.7 Examples of energy consumption for escalators

Rise / m	Hours run / h	Passengers per hour	Daily energy consumption / kW·h	
			Up	Down
3	8	1000	30.0	27.6
		5000	34.9	22.7
	10	1000	37.2	34.8
		5000	42.1	29.9
	12	1000	44.4	42.0
		5000	49.3	37.1
6	8	1000	43.2	40.8
		5000	48.1	35.9
	10	1000	53.7	51.3
		5000	58.6	46.4
	12	1000	64.2	62.8
		5000	69.1	56.9

References

1   *Energy savings with electric motors and drives* Good Practice Guide GPG 2 (Action Energy) (2000) (www.actionenergy.org.uk)

2   *Economic use of electricity in industry* Fuel Efficiency Booklet FEB 9 (Action Energy) (1993) (www.actionenergy.org.uk)

3   *Building control systems* CIBSE Guide H (London: Chartered Institution of Building Services Engineers) (2000)

4   *Variable flow control* General Information Report GIR 41 (Action Energy) (1996) (www.actionenergy.org.uk)

5   *Environmental design* CIBSE Guide A (London: Chartered Institution of Building Services Engineers) (1999)

6   *Heating* CIBSE Guide B1 (London: Chartered Institution of Building Services Engineers) (2002)

7   *Ductwork* CIBSE Guide B3 (London: Chartered Institution of Building Services Engineers) (2002)

8   *Reference data* CIBSE Guide C (London: Chartered Institution of Building Services Engineers) (2001)

9   *Guide to good practice — air handling units* (Marlow: HEVAC Association) (1991)

10 *Fan application guide* (Marlow: HEVAC Association)

11 *Fan and ductwork installation guide* (Marlow: HEVAC Association)

12 Bordass W T (private communication)

13 *Purchasing policy for higher efficiency motors* Good Practice Case Study GPCS 222 (Action Energy) (1994) (www.actionenergy.org.uk)

14 *The repair of induction motors* (Nottingham: Association of Electrical and mechanical Trades)

15 *Ventilation and air conditioning* CIBSE Guide B2 (London: Chartered Institution of Building Services Engineers) (2001)

16 *Variable speed pumping in heating and cooling circuits* BSRIA AG 14/99 (Bracknell: Building Services Research and Information Association) (1999)

17 *Transportation systems in buildings* CIBSE Guide D (London: Chartered Institution of Building Services Engineers) (2000)

18   BS 56555: Part 6: *Code of practice for the installation of new lifts* (London: British Standards Institution) (2002)

19   al-Sharif L and Peters R Lift energy consumption: modelling and simulation *Proc. CIBSE Lifts Group Annual Seminar, London, 12 November 2003* (London: Chartered Institution of Building Services Engineers) (2003)

20   Barney G C *Elevator traffic handbook — Theory and practice* (Basingstoke: Spon Press) (2002)

21   Barney G C Vertical transportation *Proc. CIBSE Nat. Conf., London, 18 June 2002* (London: Chartered Institution of Building Services Engineers) (2002)

Bibliography

Variable speed drive on a boiler fan Good Practice Case Study GPCS 35 (Action Energy) (www.actionenergy.org.uk)

Two-speed motors on ventilation fans Good Practice Case Study GPCS 219 (Action Energy) (1994) (www.actionenergy.org.uk)

Variable speed drives on secondary refrigeration pumps Good Practice Case Study GPCS 124 (Action Energy) (1992) (www.actionenergy.org.uk)

Variable speed drives on cooling water pumps Good Practice Case Study GPCS 89 (Action Energy) (1992) (www.actionenergy.org.uk)

Variable speed drives on water pumps Good Practice Case Study GPCS 88 (Action Energy) (www.actionenergy.org.uk) (1991)

High efficiency motors on fans and pumps Good Practice Case Study GPCS 162 (Action Energy) (1993) (www.actionenergy.org.uk)

Higher efficiency motors on HEVAC plant Good Practice Case Study GPCS 266 (Action Energy) (1997) (www.actionenergy.org.uk)

Variable speed drive on a cooling tower induced draught fan Good Practice Case Study GPCS 270 (Action Energy) (1995) (www.action energy.org.uk)

Higher efficiency induction motors Future Practice Profile FPP 50 (Action Energy) (1996) (www.actionenergy.org.uk)

Permanent star running of a lightly loaded motor Good Practice Case Study GPCS 267 (Action Energy) (1996) (www.actionenergy.org.uk)

Lifts BSRIA Library Bulletin LB 2/96 (Bracknell: Building Services Research and Information Association) (1996)

Barney G C and Dos Santos S M *Elevator traffic analysis design and control* (London: Peter Peregrinus) (1995)

Guidelines on energy efficiency of lift and escalator installations (Hong Kong: Government of the Hong Kong/Electrical and Mechanical Services Department) (2000)

12 Electrical power systems and office equipment

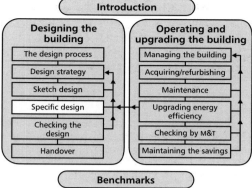

12.0	General
12.1	Large power users
12.2	Office equipment
12.3	Energy consumption
12.4	Heat gains and air conditioning

This section sets out some of the key issues in the energy efficient design of electrical power systems and office equipment in buildings, in line with the principles at the front of this Guide. It discusses installed power loads and the impact that office equipment, particularly information technology (IT), has on the ultimate design and energy consumption of the building services. Purchasing policies for office equipment are discussed in section 15 and upgrading systems for energy efficiency in section 18. CIBSE Guide A[(1)] covers internal heat gains from computers and office equipment and discusses future trends that might impact on heat gains and power consumption.

12.0 General

Both large and small electrical power loads form a significant part of the total energy use in buildings. Currently, office equipment accounts for more than 20% of the energy used in a typical office[(2)]. With equipment levels doubling every few years, this is likely to become increasingly important. However, power use is often over estimated at the design stage, and this has led to oversized or unnecessary air conditioning and consequent energy wastage.

12.1 Large power users

In larger offices, particularly high-tech situations, a significant amount of energy is consumed by power systems supplying IT equipment e.g. uninterruptible power systems (UPS). Careful design and selection of this equipment can result in very large energy savings in the longer term as many of these systems operate continuously.

12.1.1 Transformers

Most large buildings and multi-building sites are supplied at high voltage, usually 3.3 kV or 11 kV and have transformers to bring this down to 415 V. All transformers have losses, typically 1% of the throughput although this will vary with the load. Whilst this is a small percentage, it is a proportion of the electrical load of the whole building and can therefore amount to a significant energy loss. Select the most efficient transformer possible and ensure that it is not oversized as efficiency reduces at low loadings.

12.1.2 Uninterruptible power supplies

Uninterruptible power supplies (UPSs) provide 'clean' power to critical IT equipment and act as a back-up in case of mains failure. They include batteries and are generally rated by the energy (in kVA) they can provide during a power outage.

'Off-line' UPSs monitor the line constantly whilst passing incoming mains power (sometimes with a little conditioning) through to the output sockets while the supply is good. If there is a power failure then it switches on its inverter and supplies output power until the mains voltage has been restored. These systems are normally smaller supplies but are more efficient because the inverter is not running continuously.

'On-line' UPSs convert all the incoming power to direct current, which both tops up the batteries and feeds the inverter. The inverter is constantly producing fresh alternating current to supply the load and is consequently less efficient, although more secure, than an off-line system. When the mains fails, the batteries hold up the incoming DC supply to the inverter, so the load continues to be supplied.

UPSs have fixed losses which become a bigger proportion of output as the load falls, reducing efficiency. Select the most efficient UPS possible and ensure that it is not oversized as efficiency reduces significantly at low loadings.

12.1.3 Main frame computer and server rooms

The amount of equipment, and hence the energy consumption, in computer suites and server rooms can vary widely. However, energy consumption in main frame computer suites can be so significant that it can skew a building energy performance assessment, often turning 'typical' practice into 'poor'. Where possible, it should be removed from the assessment to give a more honest picture of performance, as described in CIBSE TM22[3]. These installations should be independently sub-metered to allow building operators to separately account for the consumption. Energy Consumption Guide ECG 19[2] provides best practice energy use indicators for computer suites of 87 kW·h/m² treated area in prestige offices and 14 kW·h/m² in standard offices. BSRIA *Rules of thumb*[4] indicates installed power loads of 200–400 W·m⁻² (based on nett area) for small computer rooms.

Computer room air conditioning is often wasteful. Typically, it uses as much as the computer equipment although in best practice installations this can be reduced to about two thirds of that used by the computers and less if humidity control is not required. Select efficient air conditioning, avoiding humidity control unless absolutely necessary, ensure that plant is sized correctly and provide controls that help prevent over-cooling.

12.2   Office equipment

12.2.1   Installed power loads

Many client organisations refer to power demands in terms of W·m⁻² of floor area. These figures are very useful in assessing installed loads, calculating heat gains and power consumption. However, care needs to be taken as W·m⁻² is heavily influenced by occupancy density, occupancy patterns, type of activity etc. It is also important to establish the floor area definition being used, as nett, gross and treated floor areas are measured in different ways. See Energy Consumption Guide ECG 19[2] for floor areas definitions.

The actual energy used by office and other equipment is often far less than design calculations predict[5–7]. A report[8] based on measurements in six buildings indicates that allowances of 15 W·m⁻² are more than adequate for all but the most intensive users. Recent figures indicate that less than 10 W·m⁻² of treated floor area in a naturally ventilated office and less than 15 W·m⁻² in a prestige air conditioned office can be regarded as good practice. The BCO's *Best practice in the specification for offices*[9] also state that power consumption in new offices rarely exceeds 15 W·m⁻² when diversified and measured over an area of 1000 m². Typically, desktop and associated IT equipment such as computers, printers and fax machines average

about 160 W per work location. Typical average operational power demands are shown in Figure 12.1. Most equipment is found in the areas of heaviest shading. The power consumed by most items of office equipment is often considerably less than that stated on equipment nameplates, as shown in Figure 12.2.

Average power consumption can vary between similar items of equipment, even from the same manufacturer[7]. It is advisable, therefore, to obtain energy consumption data on specific equipment. However, not all manufacturers provide representative data. Some may only provide maximum power demand values rather than representative average loads.

Most modern office equipment has a standby or 'sleep' mode whereby power consumption is considerably less than that for normal operation. These standby levels should be taken into account in determining true installed power loads. Typical levels of stand-by power consumption are shown in Table 12.1.

12.2.2   Diversity of use

Diversity of use is an important variable in predicting installed electrical loads and energy consumption. The actual use of equipment depends heavily upon the individual's job function and routines. The degree to which computers are used by staff in various branches of commerce is shown in Figure 12.3.

The average operating time for a computer and, hence, the average power demand, can be assessed using Figure 12.3. This is based on the percentage operating time for intermittent users and allowing for the time that staff are absent from the office.

The number of computers in operation within each user group will also vary from hour to hour and day to day. For example, if 100 computers are in operation for an average of 20% of the time, it is probable that up to 30% of them could be in use simultaneously. To determine the likely maximum power demand, a usage diversity factor has to be applied to the average percentages to determine the likely maximum number of computers in use at any one time. Usage diversity factors for groups of computers are shown in Figure 12.4 and the typical daily use of office equipment in Table 12.2.

Sites with high power demands per unit floor area (W·m⁻²) tend to be relatively densely populated e.g. 8 m² per person, therefore the power demand per person may be

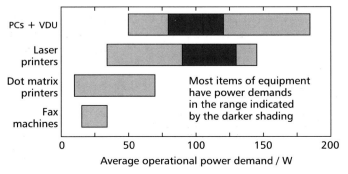

Figure 12.1 Average operational power demand for ranges of office equipment (reproduced from Good Practice Guide GPG 118[6]; Crown copyright)

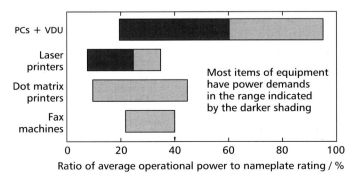

Figure 12.2 Ratio of average operational power demand to nameplate ratings (reproduced from Good Practice Guide GPG 118[6]; Crown copyright)

Table 12.1 Typical levels of energy used by office equipment[6]

Item	Peak rating / W	Average power consumption / W	Stand-by energy consumption obtainable / W	Typical recovery time
PC and monitor	300	120–175	30–100	Almost immediate
Personal computer	100	40	20–30	Almost immediate
Laptop computer (PIII 600 MHz)	100	20	5–10	Almost immediate
Monitors	200	80	10–15	Almost immediate
Printer:				
— laser	1000	90–130	20–30	30 seconds
— ink jet	800	40–80	20–30	30 seconds
Modern printer/scanner/copier	50	20	8–10	30 seconds
Photocopiers	1600	120–1000	30–250	30 seconds
Fax machines	130	30–40	10	Almost immediate
Vending machines	3000	350–700	300	Can be almost immediate

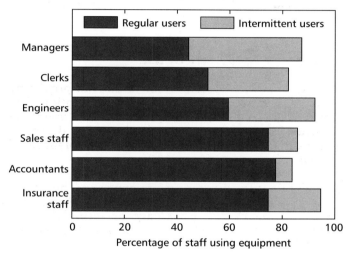

Figure 12.3 Percentage of staff using PCs (reproduced from Good Practice Guide GPG 118[6]; Crown copyright)

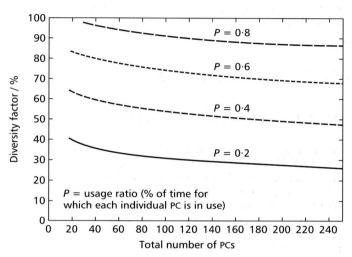

Figure 12.4 Usage diversity factors for groups of PCs (reproduced from BSRIA TN 8/92[7] by permission of the Building Services Research and Information Association)

more representative. Surveys indicate that for most general purpose office buildings, the power demand of general IT equipment is within the range 5–30 W·m⁻² or 100–200 W per person[5]. Lower values are possible where organisations operate successful energy efficiency policies. However, for intensive users, the load can increase to as much as 50 W·m⁻².

In modular offices, there is less opportunity to apply a diversity factor since the distribution of heat gains is more concentrated. The heat gain allowance for an individual room may be much higher than the average load for the floor area as a whole.

The average power demand of variable load machines, such as vending machines and photocopiers, is closely related to the amount of work done by them. Most

Table 12.2 Typical daily use of office equipment

Equipment	Time per day that equipment is in use
Personal computers	4 hours
Printers	1–2 hours
Photocopiers	1–2 hours
Fax machines	20–30 minutes
Vending machines	8–10 hours

vending machines only have a small standing load with only nominal local heat gains. Figure 12.5 shows typical average power demands relative to the number of hot drinks supplied per 8 hour working day.

The power demand of photocopiers while printing is approximately 80% of the nameplate rating, and while idling is approximately 20%. Typically, photocopiers are in use for around 10% of the time in general offices and 40% in typing pools. However, large print runs can lead to an increase in the time spent printing up to as much as 80% in print rooms. Based on this assumption, Figure 12.6 indicates average power demand values.

Machines such as laser printers, photocopiers and fax machines are usually shared between a number of users. Table 12.3 indicates the minimum likely staff numbers per machine for larger offices.

Table 12.3 Minimum likely staff numbers per machine[7]

Machine	Persons per machine
PCs	1
Laser printers	3
Photocopiers	20
Fax machines	20

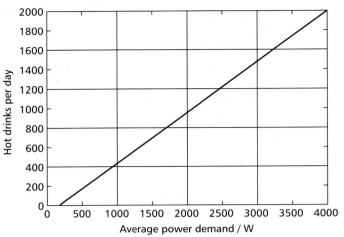

Figure 12.5 Average power demands for vending machines (reproduced from BSRIA TN 8/92[7] by permission of the Building Services Research and Information Association)

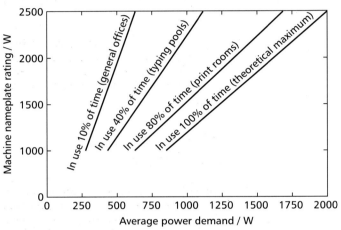

Figure 12.6 Average power demands for photocopiers (reproduced from BSRIA TN 8/92[7] by permission of the Building Services Research and Information Association)

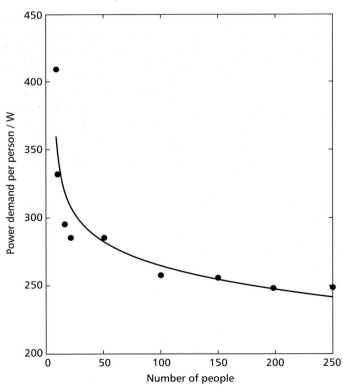

Figure 12.7 Worst case power demands per person for self-contained offices (reproduced from Energy Consumption Guide ECG 35[5]; Crown copyright)

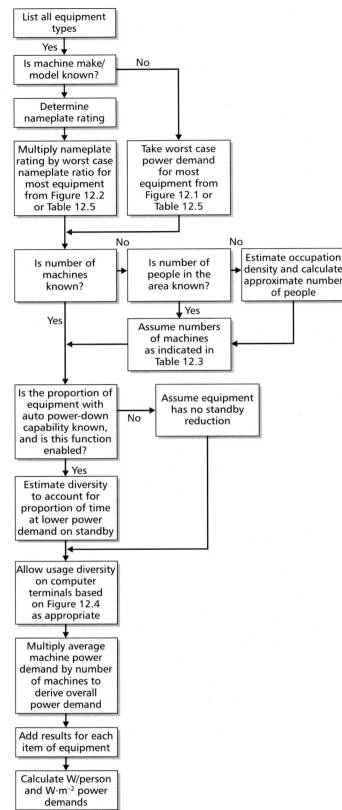

Figure 12.8 Decision guide for estimation of likely power demands (adapted from Energy Consumption Guide ECG 35[5] and BSRIA TN8/92[7])

If the highest consumption machines are chosen from Figure 12.1 and the worst case numbers are assumed from Table 12.3, then for self-contained offices of around 50 persons the load could in theory reach 300 W/person.

Localised 'hot spots', where the heat gain is much higher than the average power demand across the floor, should be identified and taken into account in the design. For example, offices with less than 10 staff will still require access to photocopiers, printers and fax machines, as well as individual computer terminals. Locating all these facilities in the same area could result in a power demand between 30 and 40 W·m⁻². Where cooling is necessary in these hot-spots, it may be supplied more efficiently by dedicated plant.

Figure 12.7 indicates worst case power demands per person for offices of different staff numbers. The values are based on the worst case individual machine loads and worst case numbers of persons sharing. The steps indicated in Figure 12.8 will assist in estimating the office power demands.

Designers will need to acquire information about the future office functions and the numbers and types of equipment. If the office is a speculative new development, designers may have little information on which to base estimates. In these situations, a design estimate for equipment power demands and numbers of machines can be made based on Figure 12.1 and Table 12.3, with further additions to allow for 'hot spot' areas and future trends.

12.3 Energy consumption

Personal computers (PCs) and associated monitors typically account for two-thirds of energy used by office equipment. Often left on all day, they are used for only a few hours. A typical PC (including monitor) left on for 24 hours each day can use 1000 kW·h of energy per year. Turning it off at night, holidays and weekends can reduce energy costs by 75%. Half to two thirds of the energy is consumed by the monitor. Screen savers primarily prolong screen life, but can reduce consumption by 10–20% as an interim measure. Automatic stand-by and switch-off modes should be implemented wherever possible to reduce energy consumption and therefore heat gains by a further 60% or more.

The annual energy consumption for laser printers can be reduced from 1000 kW·h per year for 24-hour operation to just 250 kW·h per year if their operation is restricted to 8 hours per day, 5 days per week and turned off at night.

Half of the annual 2000 kW·h energy consumption for a typical photocopier can be the result of having to ensure

that the unit is ready when required. Therefore, good stand-by modes are essential.

In naturally ventilated offices, office equipment is the second largest end use of energy after lighting. Typical and good practice performance indicators for offices are shown in Table 12.4[2,10]. The energy use indicator (EUI) is the product of:

(a)   the installed capacity (load density) in W·m⁻² of floor area with IT

(b)   the annual running hours

(c)   the IT area as a percentage of overall treated floor area, expressed as a decimal fraction.

The result is divided by 1000 to obtain the EUI in (kW·h)·m⁻² per year.

These benchmarks do not include dealing rooms or computer rooms.

Overall office equipment consumption will probably continue to rise, the dominant factor being the ever increasing use of IT equipment. However, advances in technology will probably result in a gradual reduction in equipment loads.

12.4 Heat gains and air conditioning

In air conditioned offices, it can take 50% more energy to remove the heat that the equipment generates than that used to run the equipment itself. Therefore, it is important to obtain an accurate estimate of the heat gains from office equipment and not rely on the nameplate ratings given by manufacturers.

Over sized cooling plant and air conditioning affects the selected air handling plant and ductwork sizes, as well as chillers and chilled water pipework. Apart from the initial cost penalty, over estimating will reduce the operating efficiency of cooling installations and can affect comfort levels[8]. Chillers will operate for large proportions of the time under part load conditions with, consequently, lower energy efficiency. Although this effect will be less marked with modular chillers and good capacity control, fans and pumps will still be over sized. Internal heat gains from a wide range of equipment are given in CIBSE Guide A[1] and Figure 12.1.

Table 12.4 Office equipment benchmarks for offices[2,10]

Parameter	Benchmark for stated office type							
	Naturally ventilated cellular office (Type 1)		Naturally ventilated open plan office (Type 2)		Air conditioned standard office (Type 3)		Air conditioned prestige office (Type 4)	
	Good practice	Typical	Good practice	Typical	Good practice	Typical	Good practice	Typical
Installed capacity for floor area with IT (W·m⁻²)	10	12	12	14	14	16	15	18
Running hours (h/yr)	2000	2500	2500	3000	2750	3250	3000	3500
IT area as % of treated floor area (%)	60	60	65	65	60	60	50	50
Office equipment (EUI) ((kW·h)·m⁻²/yr)	12	18	20	27	23	31	23	32

Note: factors for converting treated floor area to nett and gross are given in Table 20.2

Table 12.5 shows the worst case power demands for office equipment in normal use based on a sample of machines tested[7]. It should be noted that the power demand values in the table are not usually the same as the manufacturers nameplate ratings. Typical variations, identified as the 'nameplate ratio', are also shown in Table 12.5.

In new-build or refurbishment, consideration should be given to clustering shared equipment to avoid full air conditioning, or to minimise its effect on the overall air conditioning system. Localised air conditioning can be sized to meet the specific loads within a zone and appropriate zone controls can be installed.

Catering equipment, such as hot water boilers, kettles, refrigerators and particularly vending machines, can also contribute significantly to the heat gains. Table 12.6 indicates sensible and latent heat emissions from miscellaneous electrical cooking appliances under normal use. The values shown in the table incorporate diversities of up to 50% to allow for intermittent use and the effects of thermostatic controls. More detailed figures are provided in CIBSE Guide A[1].

Table 12.5 Average heat emissions from equipment (1992 data)[7]

Item	Worst case power demand / W	Worst case nameplate ratio / %
Personal computers with VDU	187 (116)	70 (46)
Mini/mainframe computer workstations	160	60
Laser printers	150 (98)	20 (15)
Dot matrix printers:		
— nameplate rating 100–120 W	54	45
— nameplate rating 120–220 W	67	31
Plotters:		
— monochrome A4–A0 electrostatic	300	60
— colour A4–A0 electrostatic	850	75
— colour A4 thermal	400	51
— colour A0 thermal	750	56
Pen plotter	200	43
Fax machine	38	25
Electronic typewriters	38	40
Modems	20	—
Punching machines	110	44
Microfiche viewers	150	50
Overhead projector	300	99
Slide projector	350	100

Notes:
(1) Values in brackets represent typical averages for these machines
(2) Nameplate ratio = (actual power demand × 100) / nameplate rating

Table 12.6 Sensible and latent heat emissions from equipment

Item	Nameplate rating / W	In average use		
		Sensible heat gain / W	Latent heat gain / W	Total heat gain / W
Kettle	1850–2200	430–500	270–315	700–815
Hot water urn	3500	800	500	1300
Hot water urn	5000	1000	700	1700
Gas hot plate	3000–5000	1300–2300	900–1600	2200–3900
Electric hot plate	1200–1800	1200–1800	—	1200–1800
Grill (300 mm × 300 mm)	3000	600	1200	1800
Microwave	600–1400	600–1400	—	600–1400
Toaster:				
— two slice	2200	1500	400	1900
— four slice	3000	1800	800	2600
Dishwasher	7600	1120	2460	3580
Refrigerator	125	50	—	50
Freezer	810	320	—	320

References

1   *Environmental design* CIBSE Guide A (London: Chartered Institution of Building Services Engineers) (1999)

2   *Energy efficiency in offices* Energy Consumption Guide ECG 19 (Action Energy) (2000) (www.actionenergy.org.uk)

3   *Energy assessment and reporting methodology: Office assessment method* CIBSE TM22 (London: Chartered Institution of Building Services Engineers) (1999)

4   *Rules of thumb — Guidelines for assessing building services* BSRIA TN 15/2001 (Bracknell: Building Services Research and Information Association) (2001)

5   *Energy efficiency in offices — small power loads* Energy Consumption Guide ECG 35 (Action Energy) (1993) (www.actionenergy.org.uk)

6   *Managing energy use: Minimising running costs of office equipment and related air-conditioning* Good Practice Guide GPG 118 (Action Energy) (1996) (www.actionenergy.org.uk)

7   Hejab M and Parsloe C *Small power loads* TN 8/92 (Bracknell: Building Services Research and Information Association) (1992)

8   LoPinto, Fairfield and Eaves *An assessment of small power loads for commercial buildings* (London: Stanhope Properties PLC) (April 1993)

9   *Best practice in the specification for offices* (Reading: British Council for Offices) (2000)

10   Bordass W T (private communication)

13 Checking the design

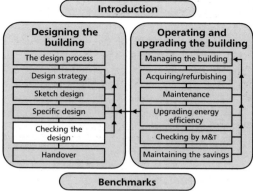

This section sets out how and when the design should be checked for energy efficiency, in line with the principles at the front of this Guide. The design team must spend time, at each stage in the process, checking that energy efficiency objectives and briefing requirements have not been compromised. A comprehensive set of benchmarks for various building types is presented in section 20.

13.0   General

The early checks on the overall conceptual design philosophy are covered in section 2. However, both qualitative and quantitative checks should be carried out at various stages throughout the design process to ensure that it meets the energy targets set at the briefing stage. Time for ongoing checks must be included in the plan of work and the design reviewed if it does not meet the targets. There is a range of indicators that contribute to understanding the performance of a building, see section 19, Figure 19.9[1,2].

Checks against benchmarks should be carried out at a number of levels across all the main energy end-uses, including:

—   overall building CO_2 emissions

—   overall energy consumption ($kW·h·m^{-2}$) of each fuel

—   installed power loads ($W·m^{-2}$) of each major service, e.g. lighting, pumps, fans etc.

—   end-use energy consumption ($kW·h·m^{-2}$) of each major service

—   efficiency indicators, such as specific fan power and lighting ($W·m^{-2}$ per 100 lux).

In the early stages of design these checks can be quick comparisons between rough estimates and simple rules of thumb. The checks should become increasingly detailed as the design progresses. They might involve manual methods for estimating energy consumption through to sophisticated computer simulation techniques for option appraisal. In all cases, the assumptions, accuracy and reliability of the data should always be presented alongside any estimated consumption[1,2].

The targets set at the briefing stage should be simple to interpret and apply. This is often best achieved using installed power densities in $W·m^{-2}$. Targets should also allow an element of design flexibility. For example, it may be appropriate to allow one target to drift in favour of another if that allows a more integrated energy efficient design overall. In general, 'total' delivered energy should not be used when rating overall building energy efficiency. Electricity and fossil fuel should always be considered separately, and converted to CO_2 or primary energy if one single indicator is required[1–4].

The principal 'integration' of the building and its services takes place in the very early stages of design. The team needs to confirm that its original design intent and energy philosophy still underpins the developing design and that energy efficiency features have not been discarded. Specifically, this should include a check on the likely interactions between the building services, and on the controls necessary to optimise energy consumption (see section 3.2).

In cases where a building is composed of several parts having significantly different environmental conditions or patterns of occupancy, separate targets should be established for comparison with the corresponding design calculations. Targets are usually based on installed capacity ($W·m^{-2}$) or energy use ($kW·h·m^{-2}$) per unit floor area. Care should be taken to use the correct measurement of floor area when comparing buildings[1–4]. Definitions are as follows:

—   *gross area*: total building area measured inside external walls

—   *treated area*: gross area less plant rooms and other areas not directly heated or cooled (e.g. stores)

—   *net area*: gross area less common areas and ancillary spaces (the letting agent's 'lettable' floor area).

Factors for converting office treated floor area to nett and gross are shown in Table 20.2. In general, treated area is to be preferred, although many of the available benchmarks are based on gross floor area.

13.1 Checking installed power loads

Rules of thumb for installed power loads that are based on gross floor area are shown in Table 13.1[5]. In the absence of confirmed data, these figures can be used as rough indicators, but are likely to be considerably higher than those for modern, low energy designs. Although these are not strict limits, they can be used to highlight significant over-design which could lead to high energy consumption. Best practice figures for building services in offices are shown in sections 6 to 11, and section 20 provides a wide range of overall, end-use and component benchmarks. It is anticipated that these figures will gradually be reduced over time due to improvements in design and the data available. GIR 31[6] provides some specific installed load data for seven low energy offices. Educational buildings should meet DfEE guidelines[7] and hospitals should meet NHS Estates guidance[8].

13.2 Checking against energy targets

13.2.1 Estimating energy consumption

Energy consumption may be estimated using installed loads, estimated hours run and simple diversity factors, as shown in CIBSE TM22[2]. The tree diagram shown in Figure 13.1 provides the basis for this approach and can be modified for use in other buildings. Initial estimates can be useful in providing an early order of magnitude indica-

tion of the likelihood that targets will, or will not be met. As the design progresses and the available data is firmed up, more accurate estimates can be established to compare against briefing targets.

Other tools are available to support this process including:

— Calculations based on CIBSE Guide A: *Environmental design*[9].

— CIBSE Building Energy Codes 1[10] and 2[11] provide a monthly average method to give preliminary assessments at an early design stage. A primary objective of the code is to compare early design options so that a suitable energy efficient scheme can be selected for development. However, the Codes are intended for comparing design options, not for forecasting the future energy consumption of a building.

— The ASHRAE 'Bin Method'[12].

— The 'LT method'[13] can be used to review optimum building shapes and glazing specifications to maximise passive potential and assess the need for cooling etc. This is an example of a refined manual technique for predicting annual energy consumption and optimising solar gains, daylighting etc. The technique is based on the results of detailed simulations of a large number of design options which are presented on a set of charts. The applicability of the LT method depends upon the match between the user's intention and the simplifying assumptions, e.g. fixed values for such things as opaque fabric U-values, room height, ventilation rate, internal gains, occupancy pattern, etc. An element of good design is assumed in that

Table 13.1 Thermal and electrical installed loads[5]

Load	Type of building (or load)	Load / $W \cdot m^{-2}$
Heating load	General buildings	90
	Offices	70
	Industrial	80
	Educational	100
	Retail	110
	Residential	60
Total cooling load	General office	125
	Interior zones (more than 7 m from windows)	75
	Perimeter zones (up to 6 m):	
	— 65% glazing	180
	— 60% glazing	120
	Typical buildings:	
	— retail	140
	— banks	160
	— restaurants	220
	— hotels	150–300
	— computer suites	400 (approx.)
Solar heat gains	Windows with internal blinds:	
	— south facing (June–Sept.)	250 ($W \cdot m^{-2}$ of glass)
	— east-west facing (June–Sept.)	150 ($W \cdot m^{-2}$ of glass)
Other heat gains (offices)	Metabolic	10
	Lighting	12
	Office machinery	15–25
Electrical services load	Lighting	10–12 (2.5 $W \cdot m^{-2}$/100 lux)
	Small power	15–45
	Air conditioning	60
	Passenger lifts	10
	Small computer rooms	200–400 (net area)
	Bespoke call centre	500–1000 (net area)

automatic lighting and blind controls are incorporated. Potential users may find these restrictions too severe.

— The 'carbon performance rating' (CPR)[14] as used in Building Regulations Approved Document L2*[15]. In the elemental method, this provides upper limits on the design of air conditioning and mechanical ventilation systems. In the whole building method this is extended to include space heating and lighting in offices.

— The 'carbon emissions calculation method' (CECM)[18] in Building Regulations Approved Document L2*[15] which allows flexibility between design elements in order to reach an integrated energy efficient building.

13.2.1.1 Dynamic building simulation

Dynamic models can provide hour-by-hour simulations based on average climatic data for predicting energy consumption and, in particular, for investigating the consequences of design modifications. Software can simulate the characteristics of one or more factors such as heat, light, mass (air and moisture) and can be used to assess alternative design options to help develop the design throughout the project. More detail is available in CIBSE AM11: *Building energy and environmental modelling*[19]. In general, simulation can be expensive and is heavily dependent on the assumptions and/or data fed into the model. Current simulation software is good at comparing design features/modifications but poor at predicting absolute energy consumption. Dynamic models are often required to estimate energy use of new designs. However, they rarely take account of realistic plant operation or parasitic losses and estimates can therefore be optimistic.

Important issues that must be addressed when using a dynamic model include the following[20]:

— suitability for the required purpose

— method of use

---

* Requirements may differ in Scotland[16] and Northern Ireland[17]

— data requirements

— data validation

— method of checking requirements

— training.

Suitability relates to the level of detail the model requires. For example, models that need a full geometrical description of the building may not be suitable for use at early stages in the design. The level of detail used to represent the plant and controls also varies.

13.2.2 Comparing against good practice benchmarks

Good practice benchmarks based on the energy performance of existing buildings are given in section 20. Roughly 25% of existing buildings have an energy consumption less than these benchmarks. New designs, with improved windows, controls, insulation etc. should have a target energy consumption very much less than these good practice benchmarks. In some instances it may be possible to set a design target of half these figures although the targets must be achievable within the constraints of budget, location, etc. It is anticipated that these benchmarks will change as data and design are improved. The 'good practice' benchmarks for existing buildings provide a useful upper limit for new design. GIR 31[6] presents a number of energy efficiency design case studies and these could also be used as targets. End-use/component benchmarks for various building types are presented in section 20. Where several design options that meet the targets are being considered, the cost-effectiveness of each approach should dictate the final choice.

Comparisons at a more detailed level based on end-uses are valuable in identifying where the design needs further attention. An example is shown in Figure 13.2[4].

Energy from renewable sources (e.g. photovoltaics) can be used to offset the demand for fossil fuels and electricity and hence improve on the target. On sites including CHP, a single overall CO_2 or primary energy benchmark and estimate should be developed, as indicated in section 13.3.

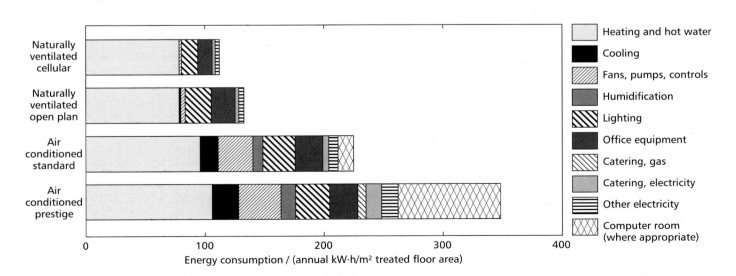

Figure 13.2 Good practice energy consumption benchmarks for particular services in offices (adapted from Energy Consumption Guide ECG 19[4])

13.3   Checking against environmental targets

The energy consumption benchmarks (kW·h·m^{-2}) given in section 20 can be converted into CO_2 emissions (kg·m^{-2}) by multiplying by the conversion factors shown in Table 13.2. The emissions can then be summed to provide a single target for a particular building against which estimates of future CO_2 emissions can be compared, as shown in CIBSE TM22[2]. Primary energy may also be used as a common basis to develop a single target/estimate.

The Building Research Establishment Environmental Assessment Method[21–25] (BREEAM) provides a methodology for assessing various environmental factors for new and existing buildings, and includes CO_2 emissions as an environmental indicator of energy use. The method has been developed for specific building sectors[21–25].

The environmental issues covered are grouped under three main headings:

— *Global issues*: covering global warming, acid rain and depletion of a limited natural resource.

— *Local issues*: e.g. water conservation, legionnaires' disease and transport.

— *Indoor issues*: including lighting and air quality.

The assessment of existing buildings is in two parts. The first relates to the building fabric and services, and the second to the operation and management of the building. Depending on the amount of credits obtained under each heading, a certificate is awarded expressed as a single rating of 'fair', 'good', 'very good' or 'excellent'.

Table 13.2 CO_2 equivalents of electricity and fuels (1998 data)[26]

Energy source	kgCO$_2$ / kW·h
Grid electricity (from 1998)*	0.43
Coal (typical)	0.29
Coke	0.42
Smokeless fuel	0.39
Natural gas	0.19
Petroleum (average)	0.27
Diesel	2.98 kg/litre
Petrol	2.54 kg/litre
Propane	1.75 kg/litre

* Electricity figures are per kW·h delivered; the figure of 0.43 has been adopted as the official standard for carbon dioxide reporting until further notice.

References

1 Field J, Soper J, Jones P G, Bordass W, Grigg P Energy performance of occupied non domestic buildings: Assessment by analysing end-use energy consumptions *Building Serv. Eng. Res. Technol* **18** (1) (1997)

2 *Energy Assessment and Reporting Methodology — Office Assessment Method* CIBSE TM22 (London: Chartered Institution of Building Services Engineers) (1999)

3 *Introduction to energy efficiency in buildings* Energy Efficiency Booklets EEB 1–13 (Action Energy) (1999) (www.action energy.org.uk)

4 *Energy efficiency in offices* Energy Consumption Guide ECG 19 (Action Energy) (2000) (www.actionenergy.org.uk)

5 *Rules of thumb — Guidelines for assessing building services* BSRIA TN 15/2001 (Bracknell: Building Services Research and Information Association) (2001)

6 *Avoiding or minimising the use of air-conditioning — a research report from the EnREI Programme* General Information Report GIR 31 (Action Energy) (1995) (www.actionenergy.org.uk)

7 *Guidelines for environmental design in schools* DfEE Building Bulletin 87 (London: Stationery Office) (2003)

8 *Achieving energy efficiency in new hospitals* NHS Estates (London: Stationery Office) (1999)

9 *Environmental Design* CIBSE Guide A (London: Chartered Institution of Building Services Engineers) (1999)

10 *Energy demands and targets for heated and ventilated buildings* CIBSE Building Energy Code 1 (London: Chartered Institution of Building Services Engineers) (1999)

11 *Energy demands for air conditioned buildings* CIBSE Building Energy Code 2 (London: Chartered Institution of Building Services Engineers) (1999)

12 *Fundamentals* ASHRAE Handbook (Atlanta, GA: American Society of Heating, Refrigeration and Air Conditioning Engineers) (1997)

13 Baker N V and Steemers K *The LT Method 2.0. An energy design tool for non-domestic buildings* (Cambridge Architectural Research) (1994)

14 *The Carbon performance rating for offices* BRE Digest 457 (London: Construction Research Communications) (2001)

15 *Conservation of fuel and power* The Building Regulations 2000 Approved Document L2 (London: The Stationery Office) (2001)

16 *Technical standards for compliance with the Building Standards (Scotland) Regulations 1990 (as amended)* (London: The Stationery Office) (2001)

17 *Conservation of fuel and power* The Building Regulations (Northern Ireland) 1994 Technical Booklet F (London: The Stationery Office) (1999)

18 *Guidance on the use of the carbon emissions calculation method* CIBSE TM32 (London: Chartered Institution of Building Services Engineers) (2003)

19 *Building energy and environmental modelling* CIBSE Applications Manual AM11 (London: Chartered Institution of Building Services Engineers) (1998)

20 *Computer modelling as a design tool for predicting building performance* Building Serv. Eng. Res. Technol **16** (4) B41–B54 (1995)

31 *BREEAM/New Offices Version 1/98 — An environmental assessment for new offices* (London: Construction Research Communications) (1998)

32 *BREEAM Version 2/91 — An environmental assessment for new superstores and supermarkets* BR207 (London: Construction Research Communications) (1991)

33 *Environmental standard: Homes for a greener world* BR 278 (London: Construction Research Communications) (1995)

34 *BREEAM/Existing offices Version 4/93 — An environmental assessment for existing office buildings* BRE240 (London: Construction Research Communications) (1993)

35 *BREEAM/New Industrial Units Version 5/93 — An environmental assessment for new industrial, warehousing and non-food retail units* BRE252 (London: Construction Research Communications) (1993)

36 *Undertaking an industrial energy survey* Good Practice Guide GPG 316 (Action Energy) (2002) (www.actionenergy.org.uk)

14   Commissioning, handover and feedback

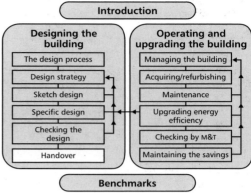

This section reviews the energy issues that arise when commissioning and handing over new or refurbished buildings, along with feedback mechanisms to improve future energy efficient designs (see the principles at the front of this Guide). It should be read in conjunction with sections 2 and 13. Further information on commissioning and handover can be found in the CIBSE Commissioning Codes[1–7] and in CIBSE's *Guide to ownership, operation and maintenance of building services*[8].

14.0   General

Good installation, commissioning, documentation and handover are essential in achieving energy efficiency. Lack of attention to these issues has resulted in poor building performance leading to greater requirements for pre- and post-occupancy performance checks and troubleshooting.

The period immediately after completing construction can be a make-or-break situation for future energy efficiency. It is during this period that the robustness of the design should be tested, the plant checked and set into operation. This time also allows steps to be taken to ensure that building managers understand how the building and its services are meant to work. Beyond this period, initial and ongoing post-occupancy evaluation provides an important tool to get the building operating correctly and to keep in this state.

Often, designers and contractors are under pressure to meet deadlines and clients are preoccupied with preparations for fitting-out and occupation. This situation can lead to inadequate checks and problem solving with poor handover procedures and, in consequence, high energy consumption in the future. In some cases, it can lead to a building being out of control for the remainder of its life. Careful preparation and management is essential to ensure that energy objectives are retained, since many energy problems can be traced back to poor commissioning and handover.

14.1   On-site checks

The following checks need special attention:

—   Check the integrity of the building envelope including the continuity of insulation and air/vapour barriers, as required by the building regulations (see section 4.2.5.1)

—   Check air tightness, especially in buildings assembled dry from components; checks of detailing and specification, as well as pressure tests may be necessary, as required by the building regulations (see section 4.2.5.1).

—   Check any ductwork for air tightness and proper insulation, since excessive leakage will make it difficult to balance the HVAC system, resulting in excessive energy consumption. Most importantly, the controls wiring/software should be checked carefully to ensure that systems can actually be commissioned and balanced correctly.

—   Check lighting equipment to ensure that fixtures are installed in the proper places. A lighting strategy that mixes high efficiency and regular fittings can be confusing to installers.

—   Check insulation of hot and chilled water pipework, valves and storage vessels to minimise losses.

14.2   The commissioning process

Successful commissioning of a system should ensure safe and reliable operation in accordance with manufacturers' instructions and design intentions. It should seek to identify and resolve operational faults while maximising plant efficiency and working life. Commissioning is the advancement of the system from static completion to working order so that it operates as intended and meets the building regulations and any health and safety requirements. The commissioning process acts as a checking procedure to ensure that:

—   the installed equipment is as designed

—   the building and its services operate correctly, safely and efficiently when set to work

—   equipment is tested and adjusted repetitively, balanced and fine tuned to achieve the specified performance whilst optimising flow rates, temperatures etc.

— automatic controls have been calibrated, set-up and tested

— any design faults or over specification are highlighted

— systems are clean

— the system settings and performance test results that have been recorded and accepted as satisfactory.

Building Regulations Approved Document L*[9] requires that a commissioning report be drawn up to indicate that inspection/commissioning has been completed to ensure that the work complies with Building Regulations. The report should include a commissioning plan to show that every system has been inspected/commissioned in an appropriate sequence. It should also include the results of the tests confirming performance is reasonable in accordance with the design.

It is the designers responsibility to ensure that systems are inherently commissionable. Where commissioning is difficult, it is seldom done correctly and future energy efficiency suffers, see section 3.4. Designers need to address the issue of 'commissionability' of building services early on, and the client should be encouraged to participate in this exercise. It is essential to allow adequate time and a suitable budget for commissioning by competent personnel. If this completion stage is squeezed, poor operation and high energy consumption are likely. CIBSE Commissioning Codes[1–7] and CIBSE *Guide to ownership, operation and maintenance of building services*[8] should be followed and BSRIA commissioning guidance consulted.

14.3   Handover

At handover, the client should be provided with:

— a building-log book for the building operator, as required by the Building Regulations*[9]

— full documentation on the commissioning of the building services, including a comparison with the original specifications to ensure compliance with the design intent and a check on the control of all systems under operating conditions

— operating and maintenance manuals for the building operator.

The design team should provide a brief overview of:

— the overall design and control strategy and the building services operation

— how to operate the plant efficiently in relation to seasonal changes, out of hours use, start-up and shut down

— the issues that management need to pass on to the building occupants, including the way to operate controls, window, shading etc.

A provision should be included in the contract for the contractor and designer to carry out familiarisation and training sessions for operators and managers. If the client

intends to outsource all or part of the maintenance work, this should be arranged well in advance of the training to ensure attendance by the maintenance contractor.

CIBSE *Guide to ownership, operation and maintenance of building services*[8] provides further information on handover.

14.4   Documenting the building

14.4.1   Building log books

Building Regulations Approved Document L*[9] includes requirements for 'building log books' in new and refurbished buildings. They are also required for existing buildings when 'controlled services', such as boilers, are upgraded or replaced. The building log book is intended to provide the building owner or occupier:

> "… with details of installed building services plant and controls, their method of operation and maintenance, and other details that collectively enable energy consumption to be monitored and controlled."

Approved Document L includes building log books because they are seen as an essential tool to promote energy efficient operation of buildings[12]. Building log books should improve understanding, management and operation resulting in sustainable buildings with lower running costs. Specifically, they provide a vehicle for continually recording and comparing building energy performance.

CIBSE TM31[13] explains the process of developing log books and provides a template to aid this, along with some example log books for different sizes and types of building. A small business template is also included for buildings or tenancies less than about 200 m². The log book should include a schedule of the building's energy supply meters and sub-meters, indicating for each meter, the fuel type, its location, identification and description, and instructions on their use. See section 5.4 and GIL 65[14]. The instructions should indicate how the energy performance of the building (or each separate tenancy in the building where appropriate) can be calculated from the individual metered energy readings to facilitate comparison with published benchmarks.

The log book should be an easily accessible focal point of current information for all those working in the building. It has four main functions:

— *Building summary*: it is a summary of all the key information about the building, including the original design, commissioning and handover details and information on its management and performance. One of the main things it will provide is a strategic understanding of how the building is meant to work, i.e. the design intent. As a summary, it should not duplicate the O&M manuals (or other existing documents) but should refer to the appropriate parts of them.

— *Key reference point*: it is the single document in which key building energy information is logged and kept. It could be regarded as the hub document linking other relevant documents. The log book should provide key references to the

---

* Requirements may differ in Scotland[10] and Northern Ireland[11]

detail held in O&M manuals, BEMS manuals and commissioning records. It should therefore be kept in a readily accessible (designated) location in the main building operations room and should not be removed without the approval of the facilities manager.

— *Source of information/training*: it provides a key source of information for anyone involved in the daily management or operation of the building and to anyone carrying out work on the building and its services. It will be relevant to new staff and external contractors and consultants and should play a role in training and induction.

— *Dynamic document*: it is a place to log changes to the building and its operation. It is also used to log building performance, maintenance and continual fine-tuning commissioning. It is essential that it is kept up to date. Alterations should only be made with the approval of the facilities manager and should be signed and dated by that person.

The closest analogy to the building log book is the simple 'owners handbook' that explains how a new car is meant to work. O&M manuals are usually too large and indigestible to help the building manager with the overall design and management philosophy. In order to run the building effectively and efficiently, the facilities manager needs to know how the designers intended the building, and its systems, to work, without having to understand all the detailed information contained in O&M manuals. The analogy to the O&M manual might be the detailed car workshop manual.

Good Practice Guide GPG 348: *Building log books — a user's guide*[15] helps facilities managers to get the most out of their log books when putting them into practice. This shows how to use a log book on a day-to-day basis and how to conduct an annual review as part of the organisation's quality assurance procedures. This review ensures that the log book is up to date and includes any alterations to the building and its services. In particular, it provides worked examples of how to log and compare energy performance.

14.4.2 Operating and maintenance manuals

Appropriate contractual provision must also be made for suitable operating and maintenance (O&M) manuals and drawings. O&M manuals should hold detailed information in support of summary information in the log book.

Information requirements should be carefully planned by the design team with a structured approach to handover. BSRIA Technical Note TN15/95[16] provides recommended contents for O&M manuals alongside legislation relevant to operating and maintaining building services. The Construction (Design and Management) Regulations 1994[17] require the inclusion of a health and safety file.

Typically, the operating element of O&M information is limited to plant room procedures. With the advent of low energy solutions, it is increasingly important that broader issues are included, in particular the overall design intent and how the building occupants are expected to control their environment.

Some contract allowances may cover the cost of providing only rudimentary O&M information. This may be sufficient for relatively small projects incorporating basic services but, for more complex installations, the building operator should be involved throughout the project to establish a maintenance brief and specific operating/maintenance procedures.

Responsibility should be allocated for producing the logbook, O&M manuals and record drawings. This could be a specialist author, which can be advantageous when producing comprehensive O&M information. Timescales need to be set for production and a system introduced to record and explain changes to the services that often occur during installation. Designers should also set up a procedure for checking the O&M manual at specific points during the project.

Detailed guidance on specifying and procuring O&M manuals is provided in BSRIA Application Guide AG1/87[18], which includes a model specification and details of contractual arrangements. Further information on O&M manuals is given in CIBSE *Guide to ownership, operation and maintenance of building services*[8].

14.5 Post-occupancy evaluation and feedback

Few buildings achieve maximum energy performance immediately. Complex buildings often require a 'troubleshooting' phase and clients should be made aware of this at an early stage. Troubleshooting represents an early part of the feedback process and may involve problems associated with unexpectedly high energy consumption.

It is now well recognised that most buildings require a period of 'sea-trials' to ensure that they operate correctly. In all but the most simple buildings, these sea-trials need to include post-occupancy evaluation, preferably involving the design team, to give useful feedback on the success of the building to all stakeholders. BSRIA AG 21/98[19] provides practical guidance on how to implement effective feedback systems.

The PROBE studies[20] revisited buildings, typically three years after they were first occupied, to assess how they were really working and what occupants and management thought of them. The results provide lessons to designers and clients throughout the whole industry. PROBE is one example of a range of post-occupancy evaluation activity including technical performance, energy and environmental performance, cost-effectiveness and client and occupant satisfaction.

Post-occupancy evaluation techniques[21] include questionnaires, focus groups, interviews, observational checks and physical measurements. These can be applied separately or together for many different purposes, for example to:

— review how a building is performing in relation to its design brief; repeat clients can also consider how successful the brief has been and areas which may need to be changed

— identify whether environmental systems and/or facilities provision are satisfactory from the staff's perspective, and where improvements should be directed

— evaluate the performance of facilities, energy, or environmental management

— demonstrate to project sponsors that money (including public funds) has been well spent

— help a project team to see how they have performed and to learn lessons for their next project

— evaluate the impact of a building on business performance.

The integration of natural ventilation and daylighting with the services creates a greater need for post-occupancy evaluation. Details may need fine-tuning; design intentions should be discussed with the occupants and management. Actual occupancy patterns may have changed since the system was designed resulting in a need for some re-thinking. Continuous feedback and fine-tuning is essential throughout the whole life of the building but particularly in the early years. All seasonal modes of operation will have occurred and all possible problems should therefore have been identified.

Later in the life of the building, the original design brief should become the benchmark for post-occupancy evaluation, which objectively explores whether or not the brief has been met. The information gained may then be fed into new building briefs, thereby closing the quality improvement loop. Guidelines are being developed[21] on the frequency and detail of post-occupancy evaluation using a checklist approach to ensure that all the key issues are addressed. Six critical areas have been identified:

— commissioning and fine-tuning of building services and controls

— initial technical information, support and training

— information and training for non-technical staff

— keeping information and support up to date

— client feedback and learning

— client/design team communication.

The cost of post-occupancy evaluation is normally recovered many times over as building performance is enhanced, problems and disputes avoided, and everyone learns about the building faster[20,21].

References

1 Air distribution systems CIBSE Commissioning Code A (London: Chartered Institution of Building Services Engineers) (1996)

2 Boiler plant CIBSE Commissioning Code B (London: Chartered Institution of Building Services Engineers) (2003)

3 Automatic controls CIBSE Commissioning Code C (London: Chartered Institution of Building Services Engineers) (2001)

4 Refrigeration systems CIBSE Commissioning Code R (London: Chartered Institution of Building Services Engineers) (2002)

5 Water distribution systems CIBSE Commissioning Code W (London: Chartered Institution of Building Services Engineers) (2003)

6 Lighting CIBSE Commissioning Code L (London: Chartered Institution of Building Services Engineers) (2003)

7 Commissioning management CIBSE Commissioning Code M (London: Chartered Institution of Building Services Engineers) (2003)

8 Guide to ownership, operation and maintenance of building services (London: Chartered Institution of Building Services Engineers) (2000)

9 Conservation of fuel and power The Building Regulations 2000 Approved Document L1/L2 (London: The Stationery Office) (2001)

10 Technical standards for compliance with the Building Standards (Scotland) Regulations 1990 (as amended) (London: The Stationery Office) (2001)

11 Conservation of fuel and power The Building Regulations (Northern Ireland) 1994 Technical Booklet F (London: The Stationery Office) (1999)

12 Jones P G and Davies H Bridging the great divide — building log books Proc. CIBSE/ASHRAE Conference, October 2003, Edinburgh (London: Chartered Institution of Building Services Engineers) (2003)

13 Building log books — a guide and templates for preparing building log books CIBSE TM 31 (London: Chartered Institution of Building Services Engineers) (2003)

14 Metering energy use in new non-domestic buildings GIL 65 (Action Energy) (2002) (www.actionenergy.org.uk)

15 Building log books — a user's guide Good Practice Guide GPG 348 (Action Energy) (2003) (www.actionenergy.org.uk)

16 De Saules T Handover information for building services TN 15/95 (Bracknell: Building Services Research and Information Association) (1995)

17 The Construction (Design and Management) Regulations 1994 (London: Stationery Office) (1994)

18 Armstrong J H Operating and maintenance manuals for building services installations BSRIA AG 1/87.1 (Bracknell: Building Services Research and Information Association) (1990)

19 Lawrence-Race G, Pearson C and De Saules T Feedback for better building services design BSRIA AG 21/98 (Bracknell: Building Services Research and Information Association) (1998)

20 Bordass W T et al. Special Issue on Post Occupancy Evaluation, Building Research and Information 29 (2) (March/April 2001)

21 Jaunzens D, Bordass W and Davies H More POE means better buildings Building Serv. J. 24 (2) 48 (February 2002)

Bibliography

Standard specification for the commissioning of mechanical engineering services installations for buildings (Horsham: Commissioning Specialists Association) (1999)

Fletcher J HVAC troubleshooting manual BSRIA AG 25/99 (Bracknell: Building Services Research and Information Association) (1999)

Parsloe C J Commissioning of water systems in buildings BSRIA AG 2/89.2 (Bracknell: Building Services Research and Information Association) (1998)

Part B: Operating and upgrading the building

Why buildings fail on energy

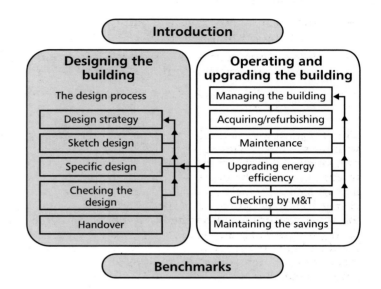

Why buildings fail on energy
"Too much optimism from designers, too much pessimism from operators"*

Failure situation	Energy consequences	Avoidance measures
FABRIC		
— excessive solar gain	Energy required to cool the space	Reduce fenestration, introduce external shading and/or automatic blinds.
— deep plan spaces	Core requires heavy servicing resulting in excessive energy use	Provide good well zoned user controls, reduce internal gains, attempt to bring in more daylight and natural ventilation.
VENTILATION		
— excessive uncontrolled air infiltration	High energy required to heat/cool unwanted air	Seal building fabric, particularly around windows and in service shafts.
— poor use of windows	Overheating leading to requirement for cooling	Improve window access and furniture, educate occupants on window use.
— air transportation problems	High energy required to transport air due to excessive air volumes	Consider reducing air volumes, reduce ductwork pressure loss, and/or inefficient fans and/or high pressure ductwork improve fan efficiency and introduce VSDs. Also consider a mixed-mode approach.
— central system operating at low loads for much of the year	Poor system efficiency leading to energy waste	Introduce VSDs, move to a mixed-mode approach where possible for some periods.
LIGHTING		
— over-lighting	High energy use due to excessive illuminance	Consider down-grading lighting, (photoelectric?) dimming controls and task lighting
— blinds down, lights on	Often due to problems with direct glare, leads to high lighting consumption	Introduce external shading and/or automatic blinds to alleviate glare. Improve internal blind controls and educate occupants.
— lights always on	High energy use	Improve light switch arrangements, consider automatic reset controls.
— lights on when sufficient daylight available	Losing potential energy savings	Introduce photoelectric controls and link to blinds.
HEATING/HOT WATER		
— poor heating distribution	Energy used in supplementary heating	Re-commission distribution system, consider VSD pumps.
— poor system controls	Boilers cycling excessively and/or low boiler efficiency, poor primary–secondary interaction with comfort and energy problems	Upgrade or re-commission BEMS/controls.
— poor user controls	Overheating; wasting energy, underheating leading to use of supplementary heating	Design-in simple user interfaces, re-train occupants (in simple terms) how to use the controls.
— simultaneous heating and cooling	Often poor controls leading to energy waste	Ensure integrated controls by upgrading or re-commission BEMS/controls.
— poor summer efficiencies	Large combined central plant supplying small hot water loads leading to poor efficiency	Split heating and hot water; consider localised hot water if demand is always small.
COOLING/INTERNAL GAINS		
— excessive internal gains	Energy wasted in cooling the space	Improve management/purchase of office equipment and lighting, improve lighting efficiency. Consider night cooling.
— central plant running at low loads	Poor plant efficiency and unstable control	Use free cooling, consider night cooling and VSDs, consider thermal storage.
— excessive use of split units (cooling and reversible heat pumps)	Often overcooling, or simultaneous heating and cooling, with no integration of controls leading to conflict between units; also poor user controls	Integrate controls of adjacent units into zones and improve user controls. Consider mixed-mode options.
— poor central system controls	Chillers cycling excessively and/or low chiller efficiency, poor primary–secondary interaction with comfort and energy problems	Upgrade or re-commission BEMS/controls.
MANAGEMENT		
— over complex buildings/building services/controls	Leads to poor understanding, mis-use and abuse	Keep designs simple, train management, develop a building log book
— poor understanding of building design	Operation often works against the original design intent	Re-train management, develop a building log book.
— poor understanding of building performance	Energy waste not being picked up	Introduce monitoring procedures with regular summary reporting.
— poor maintenance	Plant runs at low efficiency, poorly controlled and wasting energy	Improve maintenance policy, contracts, maintenance procedures and access to plant.
BEMS/CONTROLS		
— poor understanding of the BEMS capability and over-reliance on BEMS maintenance contractor	Energy wasted in poor control (and contractor does not have to live with the building)	Re-train operational staff; re-commission BEMS; introduce BEMS checking procedures.
— over-centralisation of controls through BEMS	Energy wasted and poor comfort due to lack of user controls	Provide more user controls with simple interfaces.
— poorly set-up BEMS	Energy wasted in poor control	Re-commission BEMS including a thorough check of settings against occupant requirements.
— lack of monitoring	Energy waste not being picked up	Introduce monitoring procedures using BEMS with regular summary reporting.
— 'tail wags dog' effect	Large central systems operating to supply a small local need	Supply small load separately or introduce good zone controls.
OCCUPANTS		
— poor understanding of systems	Energy lost in mis-use of systems	Re-train occupants on how the systems are meant to work (in simple terms)
— poor use of controls	Energy wasted in overheating, over lighting, over cooling etc.	Design-in simple user interfaces; re-train occupants on how the systems are meant to work (in simple terms).
— blocking services	Blocked vents, radiators, convectors, windows etc. leads to poor comfort and high energy use	Re-train occupants on consequences of blocking services.
OTHER		
— inflexible buildings	Systems become disrupted by changes to work space	Allow flexibility in design and consider systems carefully when introducing partitions etc.
— poor commissioning, handover and a lack of 'sea-trials'	Systems operate poorly from the start and never recover	Design systems for ease of commissioning; don't rush commissioning or handover; involve designers in 'sea-trials'.
— lack of continuous feedback	Energy waste not being picked up	Introduce M&T procedures with regular summary reporting to senior management.
— excessive base load and night/weekend consumption	Suggests a high energy waste, often when occupancy is low	Use night surveys to establish whether consumption is sensible and related to occupancy; use timeswitches to switch-off equipment not required.

* Bordass W T *et al.* Assessing performance in use — 2: Technical performance of the PROBE buildings *Building Res. Information* **29** (2) (2002)

15 Managing the building

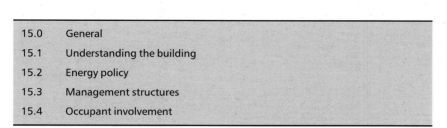

15.0 General
15.1 Understanding the building
15.2 Energy policy
15.3 Management structures
15.4 Occupant involvement

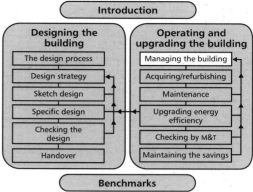

This section outlines the issues to be taken into account when operating, maintaining and managing existing buildings in an energy efficient manner, in line with the principles at the front of this Guide. It provides an overview of the main policy issues underpinning the energy efficient management[1-4] of existing buildings, and is primarily aimed at the facilities manager or building operator.

15.0 General

The energy used by a building is broadly determined by the building fabric, the building services and the management of the building. The influence of management on energy consumption is commonly underestimated[1]. Although improvements may be made to the fabric and services, the management of the building often has the biggest impact on the day-to-day energy consumption. It is common to find well-designed buildings operating badly due to poor management. Conversely, poorly designed buildings can be optimised to a great extent through good management practices[6].

Even where all the technical measures have been fully considered and implemented, there is often considerable scope for improving energy efficiency by adopting changes in the management, operation and maintenance of the building. The key to energy efficient management of existing buildings is to:

— gain a sound understanding of how the building is meant to work, at both strategic and detailed levels

— set out a clear energy management policy alongside a clear maintenance policy for the building and the building services, and implement these policies rigorously

— put into place organisational structures to ensure that responsibilities are clear, regular reporting/ feedback is taking place and the necessary resources are made available

— encourage occupants to use the building correctly and motivate them to reduce energy consumption

— set energy targets and continually monitor performance in order to keep consumption under control (see section 19).

The energy management matrix[3,4] shown in Figure 15.1 can be used to review the current state of energy management and to identify areas for improvement.

15.1 Understanding the building

The key to understanding an existing building is to:

— gain a strategic overview of the design intent

— ensure that the building is well documented

— identify the current status of the building

— identify and address problem areas.

Problems experienced in operating buildings are often due to misunderstandings about how the building design was originally intended to work. Designers' intentions are not always fully communicated to the building operator and, sometimes, designers have not necessarily appreciated the operational requirements. This often happens when the client is not the ultimate occupant of the building, or where there are changes of occupants or operational staff. Building log books can assist facilities managers in understanding the buildings for which they are responsible, see section 14.4.1.

15.1.1 Gaining an overview

The engineer managing specific items of plant often finds it difficult to form a strategic overview of the building and, in particular, an overview of the design intent. It is essential, therefore, to establish how the building is intended to be used and how this relates to the overall heating, lighting, ventilation and control strategies. This strategic understanding is important in providing a framework within which the building can be operated efficiently.

The key to gaining an overview of the building is to establish:

— occupancy levels, including cleaners, late working etc.

Level	Energy Policy	Organising	Motivation	Information Systems	Marketing	Investment
4	Energy policy, action plan and regular review have commitment of top management as part of an environmental strategy	Energy management fully integrated into management structure. Clear delegation of responsibility for energy consumption	Formal and informal channels of communication regularly exploited by energy manager and energy staff at all levels	Comprehensive system sets targets, monitors consumption, identifies faults, quantifies savings and provides budget tracking	Marketing the value of energy efficiency and the performance of energy management both within the organisation and outside it	Positive discrimination in favour of 'green' schemes with detailed investment appraisal of all new-build and refurbishment opportunities
3	Formal energy policy but no active commitment from top management	Energy manager accountable to energy committee representing all users, chaired by a member of the managing board	Energy committee used as main channel together with direct contact with major users	M&T reports for individual premises based on sub-metering, but savings not reported effectively to users	Programme of staff awareness and regular publicity campaigns	Same payback criteria employed as for all other investment
2	Unadopted energy policy set by energy manager or senior department manager	Energy manager in post, reporting to adhoc committee, but line management and authority are unclear	Contact with major users through adhoc committee chaired by senior departmental manager	Monitioring and targeting reports based on supply meter data. Energy unit has adhoc involvement in budget setting	Some adhoc staff awareness training	Investment using short-term payback criteria only
1	An unwritten set of guidelines	Energy management the part-time responsibility of someone with only limited authority or influence	Informal contacts between engineer and a few users	Cost reporting based on invoice data. Engineer compiles reports for internal use within technical department	Informal contacts used to promote energy efficiency	Only low cost measures taken
0	No explicit policy	No energy management or any formal delegation of responsibility for energy consumption	No contact with users	No information system. No accounting for energy consumption	No promotion of energy efficiency	No investment in increasing energy efficiency in premises

Figure 15.1 Energy management matrix[3,4]

— a breakdown of the building into areas with different uses

— the gross and treated floor areas and a breakdown of these in relation to use and tenancies

— the landlord/tenant agreement, e.g. which energy uses relate to the landlord and what is the consumption that is the responsibility of the tenant

— the key items of plant, what they supply and which areas they serve

— the means of heating/cooling, the areas served and how these systems are controlled

— how the building is ventilated (see section 7) and how ventilation is controlled

— the types of lighting, the areas they serve and how these should be controlled, particularly in relation to available daylight

— the means of managing, maintaining and monitoring the operation of the building.

The above can be gained using a combination of operation and maintenance (O&M) manuals, drawings, surveys and inspection but should be directly available from the building log book[7] where this is in place. The most important aspect is to establish the design intent, alongside what is actually happening in the building. Comparing the two can help to identify energy inefficiency.

15.1.2 Documentation

Good documentation is necessary to support the efficient operation of the building. Where available, the building log book should provide a useful overview of the building, particularly for external consultants and contractors. More often, documentation is in the form of very detailed O&M manuals, architectural and building services drawings, plant details, manufacturers' information and commissioning records, together with a detailed maintenance schedule. It can be very difficult to gain a good understanding of the overall building design from these detailed sources and a log book should be developed to provide this rapid access strategic overview. Log books[7] and O&M manuals are discussed in section 13.

Energy efficient buildings are inherently designed with less margin for error and less tolerance to very extreme circumstances. As a result they tend to be particularly sensitive to changes in use or layout. Therefore, the documentation should also provide a convenient means of logging changes that are made to the building. This also helps avoid changes that may contradict the original design intent since these can have major consequences for energy use and comfort.

A written explanation of the occupants' involvement in the operation of the building should be provided for distribution to staff. This should give guidance on practical matters such as energy efficient:

— use of office equipment

— use of windows for ventilation

— use of local heating controls

— use of lighting/shading to maximise the use of daylight.

A written explanation of the overall design intent may also be helpful, e.g. the ventilation strategy, as this could deter occupants from adopting bad practices such as placing books on top of fan convectors.

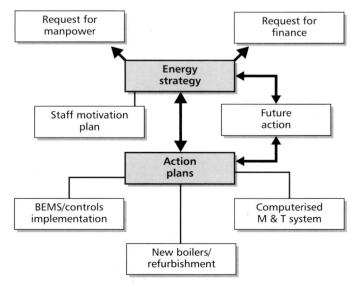

Figure 15.2 A framework for developing energy policy[11] (reproduced from *Educated Energy Management* by permission of the publisher)

15.1.3 Identifying the current status

Identifying the current status and operation of the building compared with the design intent will help building managers to understand the building better, particularly when they are new to a building. Initially, this can be achieved through overall performance indicators, such as £/m^2 for energy[8] and maintenance. The approach should gradually become more detailed, establishing performance indicators for specific services etc., as shown in Figure 19.9[9]. A qualitative measurement of the building can also be established by:

— developing a building log book[7] where this is not already in place (see section 14)

— floor area surveys

— energy audits and surveys (see section 18)

— an analysis of monitoring and targeting (M&T) data (see section 19)

— condition surveys of fabric and plant

— reviewing maintenance contracts and practices (see section 17)

— occupant surveys, to establish comfort and satisfaction levels

— monitoring plant operation and energy consumption

— post occupancy evaluation techniques (see section 14).

15.1.4 Identifying problem areas

Problems should be investigated promptly and the root causes sought. Many energy problems develop from poor interaction between fabric, services and occupants. Conflict can prevent the building operating in a coherent manner. For example, partitions may prevent natural cross ventilation and cause heating/lighting sensors to become separated from their respective zones. Section 18 provides guidance on identifying energy problems and Table 8.15 shows a list of possible energy saving measures that might be introduced.

Building services controls are often the key to solving energy and comfort problems. Poor controls can result in under or over provision and conflict between services, e.g. simultaneous heating and cooling. Improving the function, location and set points of controls can help to avoid such problems. Where installed, a BMS can be a particularly effective tool for rapidly identifying and solving problems. Section 5 gives further guidance on effective controls and BMS.

15.2 Energy policy

15.2.1 General

Adopting an appropriate and realistic energy policy delivers increased and sustainable performance improvements and provides a clear sense of direction. Any new policy should review current practices and provide a good starting point to an energy campaign[10].

Figure 15.2[11] shows a framework for developing an energy policy. The process will educate the decision-makers and secure financial approval for investment. For most organisations, a policy document will comprise a few pages. It should be reviewed annually. It is important that the energy manager gains the support and agreement of all his colleagues, particularly senior management, at each review.

An energy policy will:

— establish senior management commitment to energy efficiency

— improve the overall approach to energy management

— help to keep the main objectives in full view

— maximise the use of resources, both in time and money

— provide goals against which to monitor

— provide a clear direction for the energy team

— give senior management a way forward.

The long-term policy document is likely to cover five years, but would almost certainly be supported by other documents providing more detail on a shorter time scale. One such supporting document might be an annual action plan[2] showing specific energy saving projects with target dates and costs, together with the staff charged with the actions.

The energy policy should ideally be developed in conjunction with the maintenance policy (see section 17). It should also be integrated with any environmental policy, where this exists.

Energy management and policy should be reviewed regularly[1]. Using a management matrix[2–4,12–14] to help draw an 'organisational profile' of the current position will highlight strengths and weaknesses in policy, communication, investment, information, planning and audit. Senior management should also complete the matrix from their own perspective in order to secure their commitment and identify any differences between their view and that of the energy manager.

15.2.2   Energy policy checklist

The following checklist[11] provides a starting point for energy management. It is by no means exhaustive and needs to be tailored to suit the organisation. However, this skeleton checklist poses some of the key questions that need to be addressed in formulating a policy document.

(a)   *Overall objectives*:

— Energy saving or cost cutting?

— Attempt to save on all sites?

— Attempt to save on all fuels?

— Attempt to conserve water to indirectly save energy?

— Overall target saving?

— Over what time-period?

(b)   *Management reporting structures*:

— Who is responsible overall?

— Duties/responsibilities of the energy manager?

— Who is accountable in each cost centre?

— Who implements savings?

— Are management structure/lines of reporting in place?

— Who needs to meet and when?

(c)   *Manpower resources*:

— Total person–years invested?

— At what levels of seniority?

— Use of external consultants?

— Use of contract energy management?

— Who monitors consumption/cost?

— Who checks the bills?

(d)   *Financial resources*:

— Total funds to be invested?

— Separate energy budget?

— Capital versus maintenance?

— Mechanism for reinvesting savings?

— Use of contract energy management?

— Allow reinvestment of savings?

(e)   *Financial criteria*:

— Maximum acceptable payback period?

— Should NPV/DCF be used?

— Is life cycle costing appropriate?

(f)   *Monitoring*:

— What management information is required?

— Use of energy statistics to raise staff awareness?

— Is trend logging required? If so, which parameters?

— Use of performance indicators?

— Construct a league table of buildings to assess priorities?

— Is there a need for a bill checking mechanism?

— Is there a need for remote monitoring via a BMS?

(g)   *Targets*:

— Cost or consumption?

— Targeted percentage savings over one and five years?

— Targets for individual cost centres?

— Targets for individual fuels?

(h) *Motivation*:

— Publicity campaigns?

— Competitions?

— General staff training to raise awareness?

— Staff suggestion schemes?

— Incentive schemes?

(i) *Training*:

— Have staff training needs been investigated (initial and ongoing)?

— Has a list of planned course attendance been developed (technical and managerial)?

— Have building instructions been given to occupants?

(j) *Energy surveys*:

— Has a list of buildings targeted for surveys been developed?

— Means of funding surveys?

— Use in-house expertise or consultants?

— Choice of consultant?

15.3   Management structures

The location, role, responsibility and reporting lines of staff involved in energy management are important issues for the success of the programme. It is important that energy managers and building operators understand the framework within which they can affect energy use. This may vary significantly from one organisation to another. Although energy management is sometimes seen as a technical discipline, the bulk of the work requires general management skills.

15.3.1   Responsibility and reporting

Appointing an energy manager (i.e. allocating responsibility for energy conservation) is a key part of initiating an energy efficiency programme. Energy management needs to be an integral part of the general management structure with recognised reporting lines to senior management[3]. Someone needs to take overall responsibility for energy but all managers and staff have a role to play. In large buildings, and multi-building sites, it is often useful to nominate energy wardens for zones in order to act as the eyes and ears of the energy manager.

Larger organisations should consider setting up cost centres where line managers are responsible for their own energy costs. An energy committee with representatives from all departments may also be worthwhile.

Whatever structure is in place, it must be capable of implementing the energy policy[2,3]. This requires reporting on a regular basis; weekly, monthly, annually, to allow senior management to monitor energy costs (see section 19), identify savings made and make decisions on further investment. The energy manager will also need to identify opportunities for investment and prepare a financial case for consideration by senior management.

Where line managers are accountable for their own energy use, an effective method of feedback is necessary from the energy manager to occupants, as this can help to raise staff awareness and support for the campaign.

15.3.2   Roles and activities

All energy staff involved in the energy campaign should:

— improve staff awareness, motivation and commitment

— assist in collecting and analysing information

— take informed action and review the benefits that have accrued.

Senior management should:

— review energy policy

— agree and enforce targets

— agree resources and investment

— monitor progress of the energy efficiency programme

— provide recognition for success.

Without the commitment of senior management the programme is unlikely to succeed[2].

The energy manager should:

— develop the energy policy

— co-ordinate day-to-day energy management

— collate energy consumption and cost data and develop monitoring systems

— provide feedback and report on energy use

— identify and evaluate opportunities to improve energy efficiency

— prepare investment plans and implement agreed measures

— promote energy awareness and develop staff motivation

— gain the acceptance and support of staff at all levels

— educate staff in energy management techniques and efficient operating practices

— ensure adequate control and monitoring facilities are available

— review any historical energy data, allowing for changes in building use and, hence, examine the projected energy costs for a building.

The energy manager is the focal point of the energy efficiency programme and may often require specialist support to implement the programme[2].

General staff should:

— report energy waste

— suggest energy saving measures.

15.3.3   Obtaining resources

Energy managers may face difficulties in justifying why their organisation should invest in energy efficiency. Organisations often give priority to investment in their core activity and will usually demand faster rates of return on investment in energy savings.

In arguing for investment in energy savings it can be helpful for energy managers to suggest ways in which cost savings from energy management could be re-deployed within the organisation. These can be shown as:

— improving cost effectiveness and/or profits

— reducing operating costs

— increasing employee comfort and productivity

— enhancing the quality of service or customer care delivered

— protecting the environment and hence meeting environmental policy objectives.

15.3.3.1   Financial investment

Energy managers should have direct control of their own capital investment budget and the same criteria should apply for energy investment as in other areas of business planning. Planned capital investment can produce rapid revenue savings. If current accounting practices restrict funding, new procedures should be considered. For example by:

— re-investing some of the revenue savings in energy management

— allowing a share of the energy cost savings to be used for other purposes by those who achieve the savings

— treating some energy management costs as an overhead that contributes to staff comfort and productivity

— allowing use of revenue for capital expenditure when it can be recovered by revenue savings within the accounting period.

As a guideline, the level of investment that can be justified each year in energy management is of the order of 10% of the annual expenditure on energy[3]. This figure could be exceeded in the early stages of development, when there are more opportunities for investment. A lower figure may be considered adequate in a well-developed programme until new opportunities arise.

15.3.3.2   Manpower Investment

The specific number of staff required for energy management will depend on:

— the size of the energy bills

— the extent to which the programme of energy management has been implemented

— the required reduction in energy consumption

— the extent to which building/facilities management is outsourced.

The number of staff involved in energy management is likely to vary over time. However, it is suggested that there should be minimum of one full-time member of staff for every £1 million of energy expenditure up to £3 million per annum[3]. Beyond this, it is advisable to have one full-time member of staff for each additional £2 million up to £10 million and, above that, there should be one for every extra £4 million. If energy costs are less than £1 million p.a., organisations should consider appointing a part-time energy manager.

15.3.4   Sub contracting energy management

Senior management may take the view that as energy management is not a core activity, it should be sub-contracted, completely or in part. There are three main routes for sub-contracting:

— specialist energy consultants

— contract energy management (CEM) companies

— contract facilities management.

15.3.4.1   Specialist consultants

Should staff lack the technical knowledge or time to perform energy audits/surveys or other energy investigations, help or advice is available from specialist energy consultants[15,16] (see section 18).

15.3.4.2   Contract energy management (CEM)

Contract energy management companies offer a range of technical and financial services, some of which include the complete operation and maintenance of plant and building services. CEM companies can also provide investment in more efficient plant and will recover their investment from the saving achieved. Different types of contract are available but most incorporate improvements to energy efficiency.

Most large buildings are suitable for CEM. Small buildings with an energy bill less than say £50 000 p.a. would not normally be appropriate, except as part of a larger group. Using CEM, companies can transfer the investment risks to the contractor, who typically assumes responsibility for delivery of energy services and relevant maintenance. Figure 15.3 illustrates opportunities for introducing third-party services.

The suitability of CEM depends on:

— the availability of in-house technical expertise

— the availability of funding for energy saving projects

— the ability to find capital projects

— the suitability of the building

— the nature and status of occupancy

— the negotiation of an acceptable contract.

If CEM is selected as the preferred option, the client should identify and implement no-cost and low-cost measures before proceeding with the contract. Such measures can be

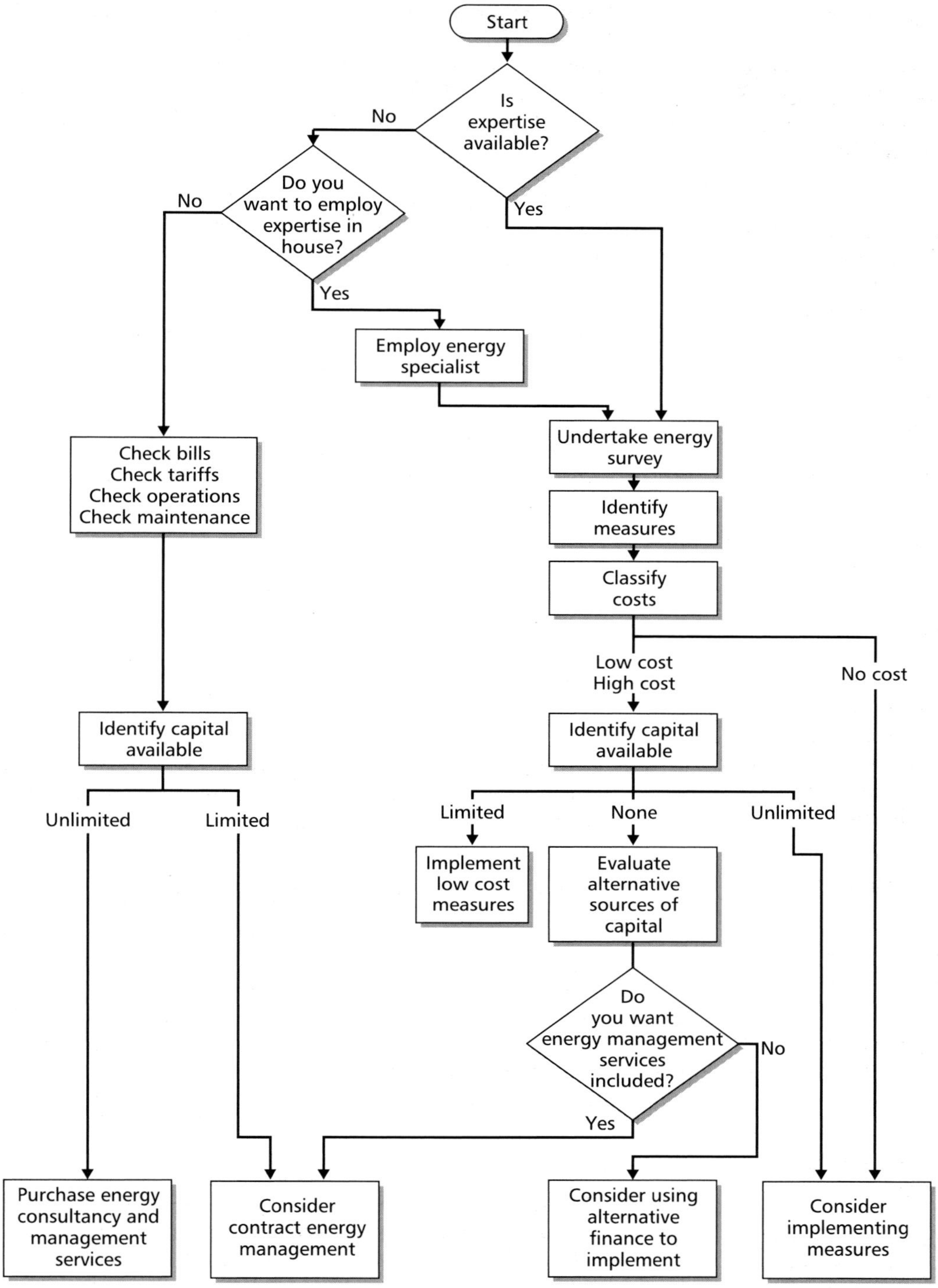

Figure 15.3 When to contract out energy management[18]

identified by the user and by the contractor carrying out an on-site energy survey (see section 18).

There are essentially three types of CEM contract. These are based on:

— variable heat charges (heat service)

— shared savings

— fixed fees.

Careful consideration is required in selecting the most suitable contract. Table 15.1 summarises the main advantages and disadvantages of the three types of contract.

15.3.4.3   Contract facilities management

Contracting out overall facilities management is now common. If facilities management is provided by an external contractor then effective liaison on energy matters should be incorporated within the contract. The contract should set out requirements for energy management, preferably in terms of a performance specification. Specifically, this should include a range of performance indicators for specific services as shown in Figure 19.9[9].

15.3.5   Purchasing policy

Purchasers of energy, sub-contracted services and equipment should be encouraged to consider energy efficiency as an important criterion.

Table 15.1 Advantages and disadvantages of CEM contracts

Contract type	Advantages	Disadvantages
Heat service	Simple payments based on energy use	No incentive for CEM company to reduce user's demand
	Full user control over amount of energy use	Cost savings strongly dependent on fuel prices
	User benefits directly from reduced consumption	Contracts of long duration
	Guaranteed supply	Usually limited to heat supply only
	Well established form of contract	
Shared savings	Performance basis encourages CEM company to achieve savings	Calculation of share of savings can be complicated
	Some savings guaranteed	Costs and savings not known in advance
	Incentive for user to increase savings	CEM companies may take unacceptable degree of control over energy supply
	Only savings achieved by CEM company's investment need to be shared	
	Flexible contracts allow higher rewards if user accepts more risk	
Fixed fee	Single, fixed payment	No incentive to user to reduce consumption
	No complicated calculation	Control may be surrendered to CEM company
	Cost known in advance	Not usually available as energy savings service on its own
	Single point of responsibility for all services included	
	Shorter contract lengths than other types	

15.3.5.1   Energy

The energy and purchasing managers should review periodically the arrangements for purchasing energy. There is a wide range of energy supply contracts available, with significant cost saving possible through judicious competitive tendering. Whilst this does not generally affect energy consumption, it can alter the energy supply tariff structures, and this can influence energy management procedures. A responsible energy strategy can often be combined with energy procurement services to give a valid environmental aspect to what otherwise might be purely a cost-saving exercise.

15.3.5.2   External contracts

Where general services, e.g. catering, cleaning and security, are to be sub-contracted, it is vital to include energy efficiency in the contract. Compulsory competitive tendering and selecting the lowest cost tender rarely results in an energy efficient solution, unless it is specifically requested in the brief. During the tendering procedure, it is advisable to check the contractor's ability to manage energy. This is particularly important when contracting:

—   cleaning staff (switching lighting on and off)

—   security staff (patrols can switch-off lighting and equipment)

—   catering staff (control of ovens, hot plates and use of hot water).

15.3.5.3   Office equipment

Managers should select the most efficient office equipment possible, with the energy consumption and energy saving features established before purchase (see section 12). Manufacturers should provide the average power consumed under typical conditions, the peak nameplate rating, provision to switch to standby 'sleep' modes and the corresponding consumption in these modes. It should be noted that average power consumption is not necessarily related to the nameplate rating. Modern PCs tend to have 'energy star' ratings and purchasing managers should acquire only equipment which satisfy these requirements. In particular, energy consumption should be carefully considered when purchasing network servers, main frame computers, telecoms equipment and any associated air conditioning that may be necessary.

Purchasing efficient equipment also applies to desk lamps and fans, vending equipment, photocopiers, fax machines and printers. This is particularly important when selecting catering equipment such as ovens and dishwashers.

15.3.5.4   High efficiency motors

Purchasing policies should specify that all new and replacement plant should have high efficiency motors as they now carry little or no additional capital cost. For new applications or spares, it is always cost-effective to buy high efficiency motors (see section 11). Motor rewinding and repair policies may also require review and amendment since it may be more economic to replace older motors by higher efficiency motors (see Table 18.15).

Improvement in efficiency using energy efficient motors range from 2 to 6%. Ideally, purchasing specifications should define precise performance requirements for each motor by application and size, including minimum acceptable efficiency. If this is impractical, the user should specify 'premium', rather than 'high' efficiency motors.

15.4   Occupant involvement

15.4.1   Motivation and training

The value of making energy a management issue and relying on people, rather than purely technical solutions, cannot be over emphasised. By raising awareness about the campaign, energy managers can enlist staff and management support to achieve success. For example, a good housekeeping campaign will recognise the importance of cleaning and security staff, particularly as they are often the first and last people in the building. Implementing a good housekeeping policy can also promote staff awareness of their responsibility to the environment as a whole[17,18]. Equipment will only be switched off if staff fully understand the benefits that can be realised e.g. less overheating of spaces, reduced emissions into the environment etc.

Whilst monetary saving is a driving factor for management it is seldom a motivator for staff in general. Therefore, it is the responsibility of the energy manager to find ways of convincing staff that energy efficiency is worthwhile. Possible motivators and de-motivators are shown in Table 15.2. The influence of these motivators on the staff will differ depending on their positions in the energy management structure. It is, of course, particularly important to communicate success at all levels in order to maintain the momentum of the campaign.

Technical and management training is essential for all those that have responsibility for energy management, particularly energy managers, wardens and those responsible for reading meters[19].

15.4.2   Occupant satisfaction

The comfort, health and safety of the occupants are primary aims of any building manager. However, well managed buildings can be both comfortable and energy efficient[20]. Occupant satisfaction is not only about providing the right temperature and light levels, but is also associated with peoples' ability to control their own surroundings. For example, delays in switching on the cooling system in response to warm weather may persuade occupants that their local environment is unsatisfactory.

The building manager will find that there are real energy saving benefits to be gained from securing the understanding and involvement of occupants. Staff should be:

Table 15.2 Examples of motivating and de-motivating factors

Motivators	Demotivators
Individual or group achievement	Unrealistic targets
Praise and recognition of success	Lack of support
Encouragement and support	Inadequate resources
Sense of individual control	Lack of recognition
Concern for environment	Failure to reward
Strong corporate image	Imposition of directives without explanation
Savings represent additional staff/equipment	Feeling of inability to influence or control

— advised how to use the building and control the local services

— informed and encouraged to improve energy efficiency

— kept informed about any problems together with the actions being taken.

Health and safety regulations based upon EU directives place significant responsibilities on building managers, clients and building professionals to maintain the indoor environment for buildings in which people work. These are:

— The Workplace (Health, Safety and Welfare) Regulations 1992[21]: affects ventilation, temperature and lighting standards.

— The Health and Safety (Display Screen Equipment) Regulations 1992[22]: affects the thermal and visual comfort of occupants using display monitors and requires the provision of adequate humidity in the space.

CIBSE guidance on complying with these regulations is available[23]. Whilst these regulations provide constraints for the building, the opportunity to install energy efficient services should not be missed where systems need to be replaced or upgraded in order to meet these regulations.

References

1   *A strategic approach to energy and environmental management* Good Practice Guide GPG 200 (Action Energy) (1996) (www.actionenergy.org.uk)

2   *Organising energy management — a corporate approach* Good Practice Guide GPG 119 (Action Energy) (1996) (www.action energy.org.uk)

3   *Organisational aspects of energy management* General Information Report GIR 12 (Action Energy) (1993) (www.action energy.org.uk)

4   *Energy management priorities — a self assessment tool* Good Practice Guide GPG 306 (Action Energy) (2001) (www.action energy.org.uk)

5   *Building log books — a user's guide* Good Practice Guide GPG 348 (Action Energy) (2003) (www.actionenergy.org.uk)

6   *Energy efficiency in the workplace — a guide for managers and staff* Good Practice Guide GPG 133 (Action Energy) (1994) (www.actionenergy.org.uk)

7   *Building log books — a guide and templates for preparing building log books* CIBSE TM 31 (London: Chartered Institution of Building Services Engineers) (2003)

8   *Introduction to energy efficiency in buildings* Energy Efficiency Booklets EEB 1–13 (Action Energy) (1999) (www.action energy.org.uk)

9   *Energy Assessment and Reporting Method* CIBSE TM22 (London: Chartered Institution of Building Services Engineers) (2004)

10   *Developing an effective energy policy* Good Practice Guide GPG 186 (Action Energy) (1996) (www.actionenergy.org.uk)

11   Somervell D and Talbot R *Educated energy management* (London: E and F N Spon) (1991)

12   *Is your energy under control? A practical guide to assessment and action* Good Practice Guide GPG 136 (Action Energy) (1994) (www.actionenergy.org.uk)

13   *Organisational aspects of energy management: a self-assessment manual for managers* Good Practice Guide GPG 167 (Action Energy) (1995) (www.actionenergy.org.uk)

14   *Putting energy into total quality. A guide for energy managers* Good Practice Guide GPG 169 (Action Energy) (1996) (www.action energy.org.uk)

15   *Choosing an energy efficiency consultant, what is energy consultancy and how can it benefit you* FL 89 (Action Energy) (2002) (www.actionenergy.org.uk)

16   *Energy audits for buildings* Fuel Efficiency Booklet FEB 1B (Action Energy) (1993) (www.actionenergy.org.uk)

17   *Managing and motivating staff to save energy* Good Practice Guide GPG 84 (Action Energy) (1993) (www.action energy.org.uk)

18   *Marketing energy efficiency — raising staff awareness* Good Practice Guide GPG 172 (Action Energy) (1997) (www.actionenergy.org.uk)

19   *Energy management training* Good Practice Guide GPG 85 (Action Energy) (1993) (www.actionenergy.org.uk)

20   Bordass W T, Bromley A K R and Leaman A J *Comfort, control and energy efficiency in offices* BRE Information Paper IP3/95 (London: Construction Research Communications) (1995)

21   The Workplace (Health, Safely and Welfare) Regulations 1992 (London: Stationery Office) (1992)

22   The Health and Safety (Display Screen Equipment) Regulations 1992 (London: Stationery Office) (1992)

23   *Health, Safety and welfare in the built environment* CIBSE TM 20 (London: Chartered Institution of Building Services Engineers) (1995)

Bibliography

Toolkit for building operation audits BSRIA Applications Guide AG 13/2000 (Bracknell: Building Services Research and Information Association) (2000)

Controlling energy use in buildings General Information Report GIR 47 (Action Energy) (1997) (www.actionenergy.org.uk)

Managing people, managing energy Good Practice Guide GPG 235 (Action Energy) (1998) (www.actionenergy.org.uk)

Maintaining the momentum, sustaining energy management Good Practice Guide GPG 251 (Action Energy) (1999) (www.actionenergy.org.uk)

Financial aspects of energy management in buildings — a summary Good Practice Guide GPG 75 (Action Energy) (1995) (www.action energy.org.uk)

Financial aspects of energy management in buildings Good Practice Guide GPG 165 (Action Energy) (1995) (www.actionenergy.org.uk)

Energy managers handbook (London: NIFES/Graham and Trotman) (1985)

Reviewing energy management General Information Report GIR 13 (Action Energy) (1993) (www.actionenergy.org.uk)

Parsloe C J *The allocation of design responsibilities for building engineering services — a code of conduct to avoid conflict* BSRIA TN 21/97 (Bracknell: Building Services Research and Information Association) (1997)

Gilham A and Shakespeare C Good management — managing energy efficiently — the role of the building services engineer in facilities management *Proc. CIBSE Nat. Conf., Eastbourne, 1–3 October 1995* (London: Chartered Institution of Building Services Engineers) (1995)

16   Acquisition and refurbishment

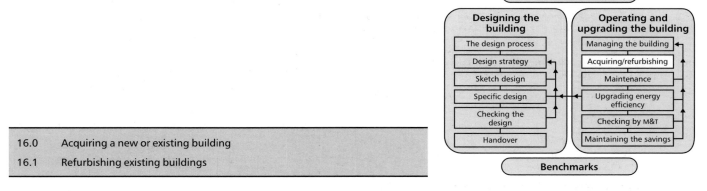

| 16.0 | Acquiring a new or existing building |
| 16.1 | Refurbishing existing buildings |

This section outlines the issues that need to be addressed when acquiring a new building or refurbishing an existing building (see the principles at the front of this Guide). These present major opportunities for improving energy efficiency[1,2].

16.0   Acquiring a new or existing building

Energy efficiency is seldom considered as part of the building procurement process even though purchase/rental could represent a long term commitment to high energy bills. Organisations should include energy efficiency targets in the brief for those entrusted with the task of searching for a suitable building. Considering running costs over the building's lifetime will highlight the long-term commitment being made.

In larger and more complex buildings, it may be appropriate to carry out a brief energy audit and assessment of the potential for savings. This may highlight wasteful features that are difficult to improve in the foreseeable future, and areas in which savings can readily be made. It can also be advantageous to re-commission the building services when taking responsibility for a building in order to ensure that the design intent is being met.

Older plant may be less efficient and hence may become increasingly costly to operate and maintain. The need to replace plant should be taken into account in the procurement process, alongside any improvement in efficiency, when upgrading to new plant.

16.1   Refurbishing existing buildings

Refurbishment provides excellent opportunities for improving energy efficiency[1,2], although it can sometimes increase energy consumption where services are enhanced, e.g. by the introduction of air conditioning. Major refurbishment will involve a significant amount of design and, therefore, reference should be made to sections 2 to 13. Minor refurbishment may present opportunities for introducing the specific energy saving measures discussed in section 19.

Action Energy Good Practice Guide GPG 35[3], which is supported by case studies[4,5], provides checklists that show what should be addressed in the refurbishment of offices, with appropriate benchmarks. A key decision is whether to provide air conditioning, 'design it out'[6], or adopt a mixed-mode approach (see section 4). BSRIA TN 8/98[7] and Action Energy New Practice Report NPCS 118[8] provide guidance and case studies on refurbishing air conditioned buildings to utilise natural ventilation.

Complete refurbishment of a building will normally require the whole design to meet the Building Regulations Approved Document L[9]*. The 2002 edition of Part L2 also covers less extensive work in existing buildings. Where windows, doors, heating, hot water, lighting, air conditioning or mechanical ventilation systems are replaced as part of a refurbishment then the new controlled service or fitting must meet Part L[9]* of the Building Regulations as if it were a new installation. The work must also be commissioned in line with the building regulations and the building log book[12] should be prepared/updated to include that work (see section 14). Also, the metering strategy should be prepared/revised to allow the energy consumption of the replacement services to be monitored (see section 5).

16.1.1   Complete refurbishment

This generally involves total replacement of plant and major changes to the building fabric, possibly only retaining the facade or structural frame. It nearly always involves radical strategic changes to the building services, which provides major energy saving opportunities, including:

—   introducing passive measures to reduce external heat gains while maximising daylight, e.g. replacing windows and introducing atria and rooflights

—   changes to the ventilation strategy to minimise the use of mechanical ventilation

* Requirements may differ in Scotland[10] and Northern Ireland[11]

— assessment of the need for air conditioning, leading to reduction and sometimes, complete avoidance [6–8]

— upgrading fabric thermal performance to reduce energy requirements for heating through improved insulation and better heating controls

— installing energy efficient plant, such as condensing boilers and CHP

— installing energy efficient lighting and lighting control systems

— improving building services monitoring and controls, possibly through the introduction of BMS.

Complete refurbishment should achieve standards comparable to energy efficient new buildings[13], as discussed in 12.2.

16.1.2   Major refurbishment

This usually involves replacement of major plant and can include some changes to the fabric, e.g. window replacement. It often allows significant changes to building services strategies. Energy saving opportunities include:

— adding atria and sun spaces to increase natural ventilation and daylight[1]

— increasing the use of passive measures or mixed mode strategies in air-conditioned buildings

— maximising use of free cooling

— removing (fully or partially) air conditioning through minor changes to fabric, lighting and controls, e.g. in shallow plan buildings on relatively quiet sites

— selecting efficient plant and flexible controls, including zone controls

— specifying an efficient and fully insulated hot water system, with consideration given to localised water heating where this will help to reduce standing losses.

Major refurbishment that involves upgrading the building envelope should enable energy use to be improved from 'typical' (medium consumption) to better than 'good practice' (i.e. low consumption)[14] as indicated in Table 20.1.

16.1.3   Minor refurbishment

This generally involves refitting the interior and making minor alterations to space layout and plant. Energy saving opportunities include:

— changing space layout to enhance daylight, ventilation and zone controls

— improving lighting and switching arrangements, including automatic controls

— improving window performance by adding blinds etc.

— using lighter coloured interior surfaces and furnishings to enhance the lighting efficiency

— improving perimeter services and window controls to avoid blockage by desks etc.

— introducing zoned areas for equipment etc. with high heat gains or special environmental requirements.

The aim in minor refurbishment should be to achieve 'good practice' (i.e. low consumption) as indicated in Table 20.1.

16.1.4   Passive refurbishment

Where possible, refurbishment should be based on passive solutions, e.g. daylighting and natural ventilation, to improve energy efficiency and reduce running costs. Passively refurbished buildings also offer potential environmental benefits[15,16] which can be used to promote the passive approach, including:

— more attractive, daylit interiors

— less dependence upon mechanical systems

— lower energy and maintenance costs

— good long term investment with less dependency on supplies of delivered energy

— less overheating, improved comfort, and possibly a healthier internal environment

— opportunities for better personal control of the local environment, particularly in cellular offices.

However, developers and investors are often worried about the marketability and financial returns from passive designs, especially for premium properties. Common concerns are:

— lower rental values; at present passive buildings enjoy no rental premium

— risks to thermal comfort, particularly if occupancy and equipment levels are high

— unfamiliar technologies may require changes of habits from management and occupants

— lack of flexibility in accommodating partitioning to suit occupiers' needs (partitions may block ventilation paths and interfere with control strategies).

Where these concerns are genuine, it helps to introduce contingency paths to allow extra services to be added easily, as necessary. For many building specifiers, wary of commitment to wholehearted passive redesign, this strategy offers a comforting 'halfway house' with an escape route[6–8,17], see section 4.2.5.3.

Wherever passive measures are introduced, it is important for those who operate and occupy the building to fully understand the design intent and operational strategies. This will ensure that the building functions correctly in the passive mode. Otherwise, operators may assume that the measures have failed and allow extra services to be installed. Once this has occurred, it is unlikely that the building will revert to its passive mode of operation.

References

1   Buckley M, Burton S and Bordass W *Passive refurbishment of offices, UK potential and practice* Lyons, November 1994

2   *Industrial building refurbishments: opportunities for energy efficiency* BRE Information Paper IP2/93 (London: Construction Research Communications) (1993)

3   *Energy efficiency in offices. Energy efficient options for refurbished offices — for the design team* Good Practice Guide GPG 35 (Action Energy) (1993) (www.actionenergy.org.uk)

4   *Naturally comfortable offices — a refurbishment project* Good Practice Case Study GPCS 308 (Action Energy) (1997) (www.actionenergy.org.uk)

5   *Energy efficiency in offices -- low cost major refurbishment. Policy Studies Institution, London* Good Practice Case Study GPCS 1 (Action Energy) (1989) (www.actionenergy.org.uk)

6   *Avoiding or minimising the use of air-conditioning —- a research report from the EnREI Programme* General Information Report GIR 31 (Action Energy) (1995) (www.actionenergy.org.uk)

7   Kendrick C, Martin A et al. *Refurbishment of air conditioned buildings for natural ventilation* BSRIA TN 8/98 (Bracknell: Building Services Research and Information Association) (1998)

8   *Comfort without air conditioning in refurbished offices* New Practice Report NPCS 118 (Action Energy) (2000) (www.action energy.org.uk)

9   *Conservation of fuel and power* The Building Regulations 2000 Approved Document L1/L2 (London: The Stationery Office) (2001)

10   *Technical standards for compliance with the Building Standards (Scotland) Regulations 1990 (as amended)* (London: The Stationery Office) (2001)

11   *Conservation of fuel and power* The Building Regulations (Northern Ireland) 1994 Technical Booklet F (London: The Stationery Office) (1999)

12   *Building log book toolkit* CIBSE TM 31 (London: Chartered Institution of Building Services Engineers) (2003)

13   *A performance specification for the energy efficient office of the future* General Information Report GIR 30 (Action Energy) (1996) (www.actionenergy.org.uk)

14   *Introduction to energy efficiency in buildings* Fuel Efficiency Booklets FEB 1–13 (Action Energy) (1994) (www.action energy.org.uk)

15   *Environmental code of practice for buildings and their services* BSRIA COP 6/99 (Bracknell: Building Services Research and Information Association) (1999)

16   *Environmental code of practice for buildings and their services — Case studies* BSRIA CS 16/99 (Bracknell: Building Services Research and Information Association) (1999)

17   *Mixed mode ventilation* CIBSE AM 13 (London: Chartered Institution of Building Services Engineers) (2000)

Bibliography

Martin A J and Gold C A *Refurbishment of concrete buildings — the decision to refurbish* BSRIA GN 7/99 (Bracknell: Building Services Research and Information Association) (1999)

Martin A J and Gold C A *Refurbishment of concrete buildings — structural and services options* BSRIA GN 8/99 (Bracknell: Building Services Research and Information Association) (1999)

Martin A J and Gold C A *Refurbishment of concrete buildings — designing now for future reuse* BSRIA GN 9/99 (Bracknell: Building Services Research and Information Association) (1999)

Flexible building services for office-based environments CIBSE TM 27 (London: Chartered Institution of Building Services Engineers) (2000)

Energy efficiency in refurbishment of industrial buildings. Parts warehouse Good Practice Case Study GPCS 175 (Action Energy) (1995) (www.actionenergy.org.uk)

Energy efficiency in refurbishment of industrial buildings. GEC Alsthom Large Machines Ltd., Rugby Good Practice Case Study GPCS 188 (Action Energy) (1995) (www.actionenergy.org.uk)

Booth W B and Williams R N Occupant satisfaction and environmental conditions following refurbishment of two air-conditioned office buildings to natural ventilation *Proc. CIBSE Nat. Conf., Harrogate, 29 September–1 October 1996* **1** 305–314 (London: Chartered Institution of Building Services Engineers) (1996)

Energy efficient refurbishment of retail buildings Good Practice Guide GPG 201 (Action Energy) (1997) (www.actionenergy.org.uk)

Energy efficient refurbishment of hotels and guesthouses — a guide for proprietors and managers Good Practice Guide GPG 205 (Action Energy) (1997) (www.actionenergy.org.uk)

Energy efficient refurbishment of hospitals Good Practice Guide GPG 206 (Action Energy) (1997) (www.actionenergy.org.uk)

Energy efficient refurbishment of schools Good Practice Guide GPG 233 (Action Energy) (1997) (www.actionenergy.org.uk)

Energy efficiency in offices — low cost major refurbishment Good Practice Case Study GPCS 1 (Action Energy) (1999) (www.actionenergy.org.uk)

17   Maintenance and energy efficiency

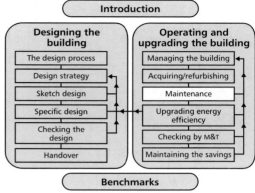

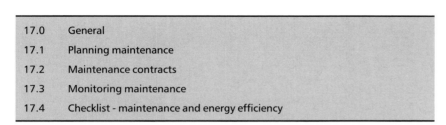

17.0   General

17.1   Planning maintenance

17.2   Maintenance contracts

17.3   Monitoring maintenance

17.4   Checklist - maintenance and energy efficiency

This section provides an overview of maintenance and its implications for energy management, in line with the principles at the front of this Guide. Table 17.4 provides a checklist of specific maintenance issues that influence energy efficiency. Detailed guidance on maintenance is available from CIBSE *Guide to ownership, operation and maintenance of building services*[1], HVCA[2], and other sources[3,4].

17.0   General

Effective maintenance contributes to the realisation of an energy efficient building by ensuring the efficient operation of systems and equipment; it also prolongs the useful life of the plant. Each building is unique and maintenance regimes should be tailored to the particular building.

A recent proposal for a European Directive on the Energy Performance of Buildings[5] is likely to have a significant impact on building services maintenance. It requires member states to implement regular inspection and assessment of boilers and air conditioning systems.

17.1   Planning maintenance

The overall approach should be set down in a clear concise policy for operation and maintenance.

17.1.1   Maintenance policy

The maintenance policy is the plan to provide and maintain the required environment for the occupants within the constraints of the owner's objectives and legal requirements.

Maintenance and energy policies should be co-ordinated with the support of top management (see section 15). Maintenance work can then include energy efficiency measures and checks, as appropriate.

Maintenance and energy management have the common objectives of:

— ensuring that a building and its services continue to function reliably, efficiently and effectively

— ensuring the health, safety and comfort of occupants

— protecting and enhancing the value of investment in a building and its equipment.

17.1.2   Types of maintenance

Maintenance tasks generally fall into two broad categories. These are:

— unplanned maintenance (reactive or breakdown)

— planned (preventative or condition-based) maintenance.

Maintenance duties might also include checks on plant operational efficiency and the installation of new services and equipment. Maintenance staff or contractors can maintain and improve energy efficiency by:

— servicing plant and equipment, e.g. boilers[6,7] to maintain optimum efficiency

— repairing faults that cause direct energy wastage

— identifying and implementing energy efficiency measures.

The recommendations in the checklist at the end of this section are maintenance tasks and can often be funded, sometimes at marginal cost, from maintenance or utilities budgets.

17.1.2.1   Unplanned maintenance

Although defects and emergencies are by their nature unplanned, they should not be identified and dealt with in the same way. Faults that result in loss of service tend to be reported promptly, whereas faults that result in energy wastage (but do not cause inconvenience) tend to be ignored. Building users should be encouraged to report all faults, whether or not they result in loss of service. This can help develop staff awareness and positive attitudes to energy efficiency. All reported defects should be assigned a priority and action taken accordingly.

Maintenance problems and energy losses that are not immediately evident can sometimes be detected by careful monitoring of energy use. Some can be identified directly by suitable BMS software. The use of energy monitoring and targeting systems in diagnosing faults is described in section 19.

Formal records should be kept of all repairs and breakdowns for management review. Regular reviews of the maintenance records can often highlight poor performance and energy problems. The timing and frequency of maintenance procedures is vital to the efficient running of equipment[10].

17.1.2.2   Planned maintenance

Planned preventative maintenance should reduce the risk of breakdown or loss of performance of an item of equipment. It may be carried out at set intervals ('time based') or when pre-determined conditions occur ('condition based'). Table 17.1 gives some examples of tasks falling into these categories which have energy implications.

The frequency of planned preventative maintenance should be reviewed where monitoring suggests that a change would be worthwhile. An assessment of the likely effect on energy costs should be included as part of any review. The condition based tasks are generally carried out in response to the results of routine checks, measured against target values[9]. Performance monitoring of this type can be assisted by the use of building management systems[10,11].

Table 17.1 Examples of planned maintenance tasks

Time based	Condition based
Annual service of boiler plant, clean adjust/replace items as necessary	Change air filters when pressure drop across filter exceeds given level
Daily/weekly/monthly checks for air, steam or water leaks	Clean gas side of boiler when flue gas temperature exceeds that in clean condition by, say 40 °C
Complete daily/weekly/monthly log sheets to monitor plant performance	Grease motor bearings when bearing temperatures or vibration exceeds a certain level
Carry out weekly/monthly test of boiler efficiency	

17.2   Maintenance contracts

It is common to rely on contractors for the maintenance of building services plant. External contractors require tight specifications with performance targets to maintain energy efficiency. The CIBSE's *Guide to ownership, operation and maintenance of building services*[1] and BSRIA AG 4/89.2[12] provide advice on all aspects that the client should consider when obtaining contract maintenance. They cover contract documents, conditions, specifications, tender procedures, and the monitoring and control of the ongoing contract. Maintenance contracts frequently lack a clear explanation of operational responsibilities and

standards. The result is that plant is often run liberally to avoid complaints, but energy efficiency suffers badly.

17.2.1   Performance specification

A brief from the client to the maintenance manager is required whether maintenance is carried out in-house or by external contractors. This should include budgets, levels of service, responsibilities, reporting procedures and policies such as energy, and health and safety. CIBSE's *Guide to ownership, operation and maintenance of building services*[1] provides a detailed checklist of issues that should be included.

Many contracts now include performance standards for particular items of equipment, e.g. a boiler must operate above a certain efficiency. This approach places a greater responsibility on the contractor to ensure that plant is maintained to a high level in order to achieve the required performance. This can be an effective way of building energy efficiency into the maintenance contract. However, requirements for efficient operation of the system as a whole are seldom included.

17.2.2   Use of maintenance contractors

Some of the advantages and disadvantages of using maintenance contractors are shown in Table 17.2.

An important issue in any maintenance contract is identifying those actions which should be undertaken by suitably qualified specialists as indicated in the manufacturer's documentation. The in-house capabilities can then be assessed to see if specialist contractors are required. Further guidance on the use of contractors is contained in the *Guide to ownership, operation and maintenance of building services*[1].

Table 17.2 Advantages and disadvantages of contract and direct labour

Contract	Direct labour
More competitive price	More difficult to assess costs
More flexible workforce with wide skills	Fixed workforce and fixed skills
May not be able to respond to all emergencies	Always available to respond to emergencies
Contract needs to be monitored	In-house supervision required
Specialist training and tools included	Need to provide specialist tools and training

17.3   Monitoring maintenance

While responsibility for maintenance should rest with those carrying it out, the client must institute some form of monitoring to ensure value for money and to identify any changes in the policy that need to be made. In particular, it is important to obtain feedback on whether the contractor is adhering to the maintenance policy and to determine the effectiveness of that policy in ensuring the energy efficiency of the plant.

17.3.1 Maintenance records

Maintenance records are a vital part of maintenance management and therefore have an important role in energy management. There are two broad categories of records:

— *Installation records*: include the building log book[13], operating and maintenance (O&M) manuals (see section 14), plant details, design performance data, maintenance instructions, commissioning data, record drawings and control set points. The building log book should include a metering strategy (see section 5) and design estimates of end use energy consumption to allow operators to compare the in-use performance of systems and the building as a whole. All documents should be updated when any modifications are made to the building.

— *Service records*: include log sheets, job records, work orders, inspection and test results and service performance data. Periodic checks on performance of plant and equipment in service can indicate when action should be taken before serious energy wastage occurs. Details should be kept of the time and nature of corrective action. Other adjustments of plant or control settings should also be recorded for future reference. In-use energy performance of the building and each main end use should be recorded in the log book[13] and compared against targets.

The schedule of installed assets, the planned maintenance programme and the service history are often combined in a computer based information system. This greatly simplifies the task of extracting and analysing information. Full details of test results or data logged during maintenance work (meter readings, flow and return temperatures, boiler flue-gas temperatures etc.) is more commonly kept in its original form on log sheets. Traditional log sheets can still be a useful source of information for energy management.

A BMS can help to collect this information and prepare inspection and maintenance routines for maintenance staff. A BMS can handle a greater volume of data in less time, and assists in monitoring complete systems, rather than individual assets, highlighting anomalies that would otherwise go unnoticed.

17.3.2 Checking maintenance standards

Building operators should monitor both technical and financial indicators to ensure that maintenance is effective.

Breakdown frequency provides a retrospective benchmark. A minimum period of data collection is necessary to provide a useful comparison. Judgements have to be made by the building owner over time, related to the expected life of the plant. Energy management through monitoring and targeting can also provide valuable information to assess the effectiveness of maintenance. Lack of maintenance or incorrect plant settings will increase energy consumption when compared with target figures.

As a rule of thumb, based on research by BSRIA[14] and data from Williams[15], the annual spend on building services maintenance should be about the same as that for energy. If the figures differ widely, something may be wrong, especially if the energy spend is high and the maintenance spend low.

Table 17.3 provides a guide to the costs of maintaining mechanical and electrical services for various types of buildings. Cost indices, such as those provided by Building Maintenance Information (a division of the Royal Institution of Chartered Surveyors' Business Services) can be used to obtain current values.

Table 17.3 Approximate costs for maintaining mechanical and electrical services

Building type	Cost / (£/m²)
Hospitals	12–14
Hotels	8–10
Offices, light industrial, university	6–9
Leisure	4–6
Major retail	3–5
Schools, residential homes	2–4

Note: based on BSRIA research (1991)

17.4 Checklist for maintenance and energy efficiency

Appendix 17.A1 provides a checklist of specific maintenance issues that influence energy efficiency. The appropriate checks should be included in a planned maintenance programme that promotes energy efficiency. Further checks are discussed in the CIBSE's *Guide to ownership, operation and maintenance of building services*[1].

Manufacturers' instructions should always be followed, particularly in relation to safety.

References

1   *Guide to ownership, operation and maintenance of building services* (London: Chartered Institution of Building Services Engineers) (2000)

2   *Professional maintenance management for HVAC businesses* (CD-ROM) (London: Heating and Ventilating Contractors' Association) (2001)

3   *Building services maintenance* BSRIA RG 6/95 (Bracknell: Building Services Research and Information Association) (1995)

4   *Planned maintenance for productivity and energy conservation* (London: Fairmount Press) (1989)

5   *Proposal for a Directive of the European Parliament and of the Council on the energy performance of buildings* COM(2001) 226 final 2001/0098 (COD) (Brussels: Commission of the European Communities) (2001)

6   *Maintaining the efficient operation of heating and hot water. A guide for managers* Good Practice Guide GPG 188 (Action Energy) (1996) (www.actionenergy.org.uk)

7   Armstrong J *The effect of maintenance on boiler efficiency* BSRIA TN 5/83 (Bracknell: Building Services Research and Information Association) (1983)

8   BS 5720: 1979: *Code of practice for mechanical ventilation and air conditioning in buildings* (London: British Standards Institution) (1979)

9   *Condition-based maintenance evaluation guide for building services* BSRIA AG 5/2001 (Bracknell: Building Services Research and Information Association) (2001)

10   Armstrong J *Planned maintenance and the use of computers* BSRIA TN 1/85.1 (Bracknell: Building Services Research and Information Association) (1991)

11   Barnard N and Starr A *BEMS as condition based maintenance tools* BSRIA TN 4/95 (Bracknell: Building Services Research and Information Association) (1995)

12   Smith M H *Maintenance contracts for building engineering services* BSRIA AG 4/89.2 (Bracknell: Building Services Research and Information Association) (1992)

13   *Building log books — a guide and templates for preparing building log books* CIBSE TM 31 (London: Chartered Institution of Building Services Engineers) (2003)

14   Smith M H *Maintenance and utility costs —- results of a survey* BSRIA TN 3/91 (Bracknell: Building Services Research and Information Association) (1991)

15   Williams B *The Economics of Environmental Services* **11** (11) 13–23 (1993)

16   *Commercial refrigeration plant: energy efficient operation and maintenance* Good Practice Guide GPG 36 (Harwell; ETSU) (1992) (www.actionenergy.org.uk)

17   *Industrial refrigeration plant: energy efficient operation and maintenance* Good Practice Guide GPG 42 (Harwell; ETSU) (1992) (www.actionenergy.org.uk)

18   *Code for lighting* (London: Chartered Institution of Building Services Engineers) (2002)

19   *Energy efficient lighting in buildings* Thermie Maxibrochure (Action Energy) (1993) (www.actionenergy.org.uk)

Bibliography

Everyone's guide to energy efficiency through effective maintenance FL 69B (Action Energy) (2001) (www.actionenergy.org.uk)

Cutting energy losses through effective maintenance — Totally productive operations Good Practice Guide GPG 217 9B (Action Energy) (1997) (www.actionenergy.org.uk)

Smith M and Tate A *Maintenance programme set-up* BSRIA AG 1/98 (Bracknell: Building Services Research and Information Association) (1998)

Nanayakkara R and Smith M *Operation and maintenance audits* BSRIA AG 24/97 (Bracknell: Building Services Research and Information Association) (1997)

Installation requirements and specifications for condition based maintenance BSRIA TN 8/00 (Bracknell: Building Services Research and Information Association) (2000)

Nanayakkara R *Condition survey of building services plant and installations* BSRIA AG 4/00 (Bracknell: Building Services Research and Information Association) (2000)

Parsloe C *Design for maintainability* BSRIA AG 11/92 (Bracknell: Building Services Research and Information Association) (1992)

Armstrong J *Fault finding procedures in the building services industry* BSRIA TN 12/86 (Bracknell: Building Services Research and Information Association) (1986)

Stonard P *Instruments for building services applications* BSRIA TN 14/86 (Bracknell: Building Services Research and Information Association) (1986)

Barnard N and Starr A *Vibration monitoring for building services* BSRIA TN 3/95 (Bracknell: Building Services Research and Information Association) (1995)

HVAC Applications ASHRAE Handbook (Atlanta, GA: American Society of Heating, Refrigeration and Air Conditioning Engineers) (1999)

Johansson M *Building services legislation* (5th edn.) BSRIA D 15/00 (Bracknell: Building Services Research and Information Association) (2000)

Infrared condition based maintenance for building services BSRIA TN 2/95 (Bracknell: Building Services Research and Information Association) (1995)

Energy efficiency in sports and recreation buildings — effective plant maintenance Good Practice Guide GPG 137 (Action Energy) (1999) (www.actionenergy.org.uk)

Appendix 17.A1: Checklist of energy related maintenance issues

Good housekeeping and maintenance

A 'switch it off' policy requires no capital expenditure but requires the co-operation of all staff, particularly maintenance staff who are responsible for a large part of good housekeeping. The following are typical good housekeeping measures:

☐ Adjust controls to match heating, cooling and lighting use to occupancy periods, and to ensure service levels meet the needs of occupants, i.e. avoid over-heating, over-cooling and excessive lighting levels.

☐ Establish responsibility for control setting, review and adjustment.

☐ Arrange partitioning and layout to make best use of natural lighting and building services.

☐ Concentrate out-of-hours occupancy in as few areas, or buildings, as possible and run plant in these areas only.

☐ Switch off non-essential office equipment when not in use.

☐ Close windows and doors when the building is unoccupied during the heating season.

☐ Ensure automatic door closers function properly.

☐ Discourage supplementary electrical space heating appliances except for out-of-hours use when, otherwise, central systems would have to be operated.

☐ Switch off miscellaneous extract fans when the building is unoccupied, unless continuing operation is essential.

☐ Use window shading devices during summer to minimise air conditioning loads. Close window shading devices during the heating season, and when dark outside to minimise radiation losses.

☐ Reduce heat generation from internal sources during the cooling season, i.e. lighting, machines, cooking equipment, etc.

☐ Ensure catering equipment is only on when necessary, particularly kitchen ovens, hot plates and dishwashers, but also local hot water urns, vending machines etc.

☐ Instigate a purchasing policy that considers energy consumption when buying new equipment.

☐ Ensure that security staff and cleaners practice a 'switch-it-off' policy

Building fabric

Maintenance of the building fabric is essential to avoid excessive air infiltration and to minimise heat losses. The following are examples of maintenance measures:

☐ Re-hang misaligned doors and windows.

☐ Replace weather stripping/sealant around windows and doors if damaged.

☐ Keep curtains and blinds clean and in good working condition.

☐ Ensure openable windows can be properly closed and latched, with a good seal.

☐ Replace broken or cracked glazing.

☐ Replace or upgrade damaged or missing insulation.

Controls

Regular checking/maintenance of controls to ensure correct setting and operation is fundamental to energy efficiency. Check to ensure that:

☐ controls are correctly commissioned and are set at the desired levels; also ensure that calibration of sensors and controls has not drifted

☐ the building environment is regarded as comfortable and that changes in building use have not occurred to warrant alterations in the controls

☐ zone controls meet the needs of the occupants and there are no occurrences of over-heating, over-cooling or annoyance due to automatic light switching

☐ plant operating times are optimised and time switches/optimisers operate in accordance with the intended settings, and provide appropriate flexibility in relation to occupancy patterns

☐ weather compensators and optimisers have been fine-tuned over a long period in order to find the best settings

☐ occupants understand the use of local controls, e.g. that room thermostats and trvs should be left alone once set, rather than used as on/off switches

☐ air conditioning terminal controls are linked to the central plant to give the lowest acceptable level for heating requirements, and the highest acceptable level for cooling

☐ central plant is modulating/sequencing to match the load while ensuring that controls are stable, i.e. not causing excessive cycling; unnecessary or standby plant should remain off, particularly during periods of low demand

☐ simultaneous heating and cooling does not occur except where maximum humidity control is essential

☐ a current record of the control settings is displayed near to the controls to assist in returning them to optimum settings if they have been tampered with.

Ventilation systems

Good maintenance of ventilation and air conditioning plant can have a significant effect on the overall success of the ventilation strategy, energy efficiency, comfort and indoor air quality. Cleanliness, balancing and control are particularly important. The following items should be checked:

☐ Correct operation of window ventilation fittings and furniture.

☐ Cleanliness of all equipment components, particularly, heat transfer surfaces, fan blades and interior fan casing.

☐ Motor drives: where necessary, replace worn bearings and ensure correct drive alignment. Correct tensioning of belts is critical.

☐ Operation of volume control devices, i.e. speed controls, vav boxes, dampers etc: ensure that damper blades and linkages for proper operation and tight shut-off for accurate control.

☐ Pressure drops: ensure that they are in accordance with manufacturers' data, e.g. heating and cooling coils, filters, casing interior, etc; clean outlet/inlet grilles regularly.

☐ Ductwork insulation: repair or replace where necessary.

☐ Absence of air 'short-circuiting'; absence of leaks in ducts as this increases heating/cooling load as well as fan consumption.

☐ Lubrication of fan/motor bearings.

☐ Regularly vent air from heat exchangers, particularly fan coil units, where they become noisy or output is reduced.

☐ Ensure correct operation of unitary air conditioning equipment, e.g. through-the-wall units and split systems; clean heat transfer surfaces and filters; ensure airflows are not obstructed and avoid unwanted air leakage around the outside of units.

Refrigeration systems

Refrigeration systems are often used intermittently to meet short periods of excessive heat gains. This places additional stress on components, requiring particular care in maintenance[17,18]. Checks should be made to ensure that:

☐ refrigerant is free of moisture by regularly inspecting moisture-liquid indicator; clean filters and/or re-charge refrigerant when necessary

☐ refrigerant charge is correct as low charge reduces heat transfer

☐ expansion valves are correctly set

☐ insulation on suction and liquid lines is in good order

☐ chilled water temperatures are increased when humidity or load conditions permit

- [ ] condenser water temperatures and/or flow rates are kept to a minimum

- [ ] compressor operating pressure and temperatures are correct, particularly suction pressure, discharge pressure and oil pressure; investigate any changes that occur

- [ ] compressor is not cycling excessively as this may indicate inefficient operation

- [ ] compressor noise level is not abnormal; excessive noise or vibration may indicate drive needs attention

- [ ] compressor joints and shaft seals are not leaking (open machines only)

- [ ] chiller performance is monitored regularly by recording water inlet and outlet temperatures and flow rate (or water-side pressure drop) to ensure cleanliness of water-side heat transfer surfaces; investigate any variations from the norm

- [ ] refrigerant pressures, air flow rates and temperatures are set correctly to keep air cooled condenser performance high

- [ ] heat rejection equipment (e.g. cooling towers) performance is monitored by recording ambient wet-bulb temperature, water inlet and outlet temperatures and flow rate

- [ ] cooling towers are kept clean to minimise air-side and water-side resistance including tower-fill or packing, nozzles (water distribution system, tower basin, water intake screens/strainers air intake screens etc.).

Lighting systems

Regular maintenance of lighting installations, including planned replacement of lamps, will sustain lighting levels and ensure continued efficiency. Cleaning lamps and luminaires, windows and internal walls is particularly important. Other checks should ensure that:

- [ ] efficient lamps and ballasts are used when replacement is carried out

- [ ] internal surfaces are decorated with light colours to obtain benefit from natural and electric lighting

- [ ] surfaces are kept clean

- [ ] the operation of controls is effective and they are suitable for space occupancy and use

- [ ] lights are switched off when not needed; research shows that leaving fluorescent lighting on unnecessarily for even a few minutes is not cost-effective; building managers should make occupants aware of this.

The reduction in light output due to luminaires and rooms becoming dirty can be very significant. In addition, the light output from most lamps decreases as they age. The illuminance from a lighting installation, therefore, decreases with time, and lack of maintenance will affect energy consumption and the productivity of occupants. The following measures should be taken:

- [ ] Clean uplighters more frequently as they are particularly prone to a rapid build-up of dust

- [ ] Use proper cleaning materials and techniques to reduce losses caused by chemical action or scratching of optics and electrostatic dust accumulation. Glass/acrylic diffusers generally have the longest useful life, whereas polystyrene tends to discolour with age and reduce the light output from a luminaire

- [ ] Plan group replacement of discharge lamps in all but the smallest installations. This is more sensible than only replacing individual lamps when they fail as it prevents efficiency and illuminance falling too low[19]. The effect of bulk lamp changing, luminaire cleaning, room surface cleaning and redecoration can be seen in Figure 17.A1[20].

Heating and hot water systems

Heating and hot water systems require regular maintenance in order to ensure efficient operation[7]. The following checks should be made:

- [ ] Check boiler operating pressures, temperatures, fuel consumption, and investigate any variations from the norm.

- [ ] Check flue gas analysis, adjust burners to achieve most efficient flue gas temperatures, CO_2, O_2 and excess air settings.

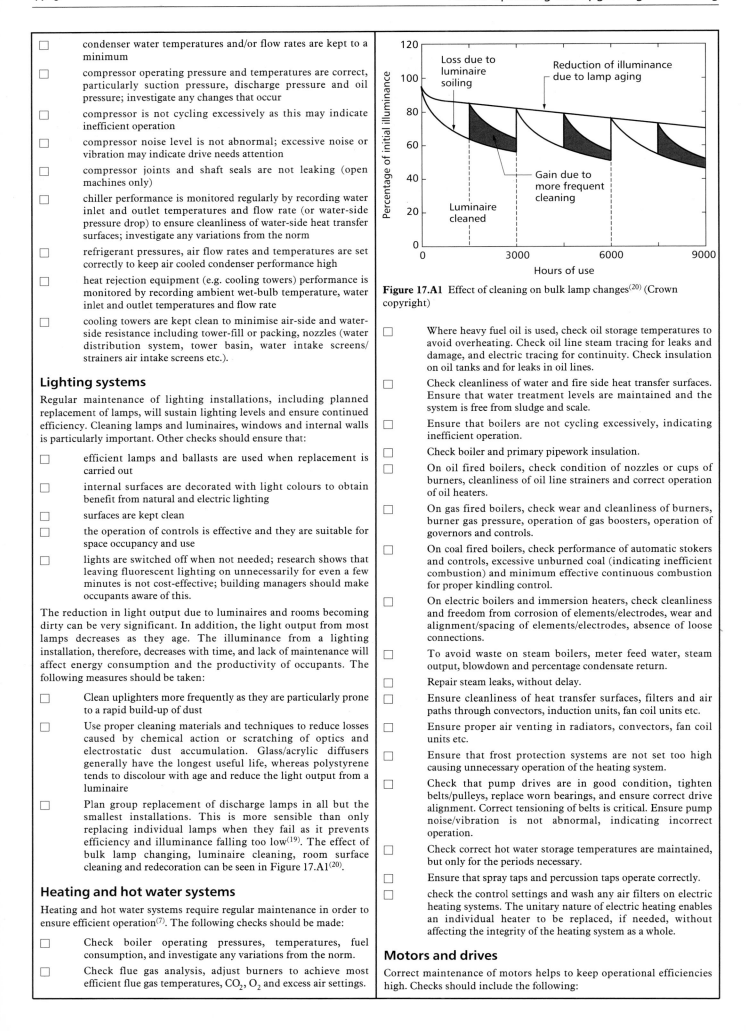

Figure 17.A1 Effect of cleaning on bulk lamp changes[20] (Crown copyright)

- [ ] Where heavy fuel oil is used, check oil storage temperatures to avoid overheating. Check oil line steam tracing for leaks and damage, and electric tracing for continuity. Check insulation on oil tanks and for leaks in oil lines.

- [ ] Check cleanliness of water and fire side heat transfer surfaces. Ensure that water treatment levels are maintained and the system is free from sludge and scale.

- [ ] Ensure that boilers are not cycling excessively, indicating inefficient operation.

- [ ] Check boiler and primary pipework insulation.

- [ ] On oil fired boilers, check condition of nozzles or cups of burners, cleanliness of oil line strainers and correct operation of oil heaters.

- [ ] On gas fired boilers, check wear and cleanliness of burners, burner gas pressure, operation of gas boosters, operation of governors and controls.

- [ ] On coal fired boilers, check performance of automatic stokers and controls, excessive unburned coal (indicating inefficient combustion) and minimum effective continuous combustion for proper kindling control.

- [ ] On electric boilers and immersion heaters, check cleanliness and freedom from corrosion of elements/electrodes, wear and alignment/spacing of elements/electrodes, absence of loose connections.

- [ ] To avoid waste on steam boilers, meter feed water, steam output, blowdown and percentage condensate return.

- [ ] Repair steam leaks, without delay.

- [ ] Ensure cleanliness of heat transfer surfaces, filters and air paths through convectors, induction units, fan coil units etc.

- [ ] Ensure proper air venting in radiators, convectors, fan coil units etc.

- [ ] Ensure that frost protection systems are not set too high causing unnecessary operation of the heating system.

- [ ] Check that pump drives are in good condition, tighten belts/pulleys, replace worn bearings, and ensure correct drive alignment. Correct tensioning of belts is critical. Ensure pump noise/vibration is not abnormal, indicating incorrect operation.

- [ ] Check correct hot water storage temperatures are maintained, but only for the periods necessary.

- [ ] Ensure that spray taps and percussion taps operate correctly.

- [ ] check the control settings and wash any air filters on electric heating systems. The unitary nature of electric heating enables an individual heater to be replaced, if needed, without affecting the integrity of the heating system as a whole.

Motors and drives

Correct maintenance of motors helps to keep operational efficiencies high. Checks should include the following:

☐ Lubricate motor bearings in accordance with manufacturers' instructions since inadequate lubrication results in excessive friction and torque, leading to overheating and power losses.

☐ Check motor shaft to load alignment to reduce running losses, bearing wear, noise and vibration; where necessary, tighten belts/pulleys.

☐ Clean motor fan inlets and frame surfaces so that generated heat can be removed effectively. An increase in the motor stator winding temperature of 1 °C can result in up to 0.5% increase in the $I^2 R$ losses, as well as shortening the life of the motor insulation. Ensure good ventilation to prevent over heating.

☐ Replace worn brushes, belts, sheaves, bearings and gears, as necessary.

☐ Check loading on large motors compared with rating and consider replacement.

☐ Check loads are balanced across the three phases as unbalanced supply voltage can lead to a significant increase in motor heat losses and reduced life.

☐ Check the power factor at varying loads is within acceptable limits; consider power factor correction where necessary.

☐ Check electrical connections and contacts for corrosion and arcing, and attend to loose connections or bad contacts. Thermography of drive systems offers an early warning of overheating and wasted energy, and can often help detect problems before there are signs of impending failure.

☐ Use motor circuit analysis (MCA) to measure the absolute and relative resistance, inductance, and capacitance of motor circuits and windings. MCA can also be used to predict circuit failure, enhancing a motor maintenance or replacement programme.

18 Energy audits and surveys

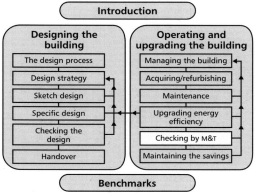

This section provides an overview of energy audits and surveys for retrofitting energy efficiency measures to upgrade existing buildings (see the principles at the front of this Guide). It is aimed predominantly at the energy manager/consultant. Table 18.15 provides a site survey checklist of specific energy saving measures that can be introduced. Where measures require significant amounts of design, reference should be made to the relevant section in Part A.

18.0 General

Energy audits and surveys are investigations of site energy use aimed at identifying measures for cost savings, energy savings and reductions in environmental emissions. They provide the information needed to make decisions on which are the most cost effective energy saving measures[1–6].

Energy audits and surveys are an essential part of the effective control of energy costs and should be undertaken regularly, typically every three to five years. All organisations, regardless of size, need to satisfy themselves that they are getting good value from their expenditure on energy. Audits and surveys, combined with routine monitoring, provide the vital information needed to ensure that energy is managed properly.

Nevertheless, financial rewards are normally the underlying reason for implementing energy efficiency measures. Every pound saved on energy costs could increase profits directly by the same amount. Even organisations operating efficiently can expect a survey to identify potential energy cost savings of up to 10%. Cost savings of over 60% have been achieved at sites where the potential had not previously been recognised. Such savings are usually obtained with payback periods of less than three years. A study of a sample of 4331 energy surveys showed that average savings of 21% of each site's energy bill were identified. The average payback period for recommendations was 1.5 years, providing an excellent opportunity for investment.

18.1 Retrofitting energy saving measures

The key to retrofitting cost-effective measures in existing buildings is to:

— identify high energy users using performance league tables etc.

— establish the potential for energy saving through measurement, audits, benchmarking etc.

— identify practicable measures to achieve these savings

— establish the financial case for introducing these measures

— select equipment on the basis of certified or otherwise independently verified product performance data

— establish any additional benefits e.g. environmental, comfort etc.

— obtain funding for the proposed measures based on the benefits

— implement the savings in a planned way with the least disruption to the building

— monitor the savings to confirm they have been achieved and to ensure they are maintained (see section 19).

Energy consumption of existing buildings can often be reduced by about 20% by introducing simple and cost-effective measures, usually with payback periods of less than 5 years. Any cost savings add directly to the profitability of organisations once the initial capital cost has been repaid. Identifying and implementing retrofit energy saving measures can, therefore, be highly cost-effective often with significant spin-off benefits including reduced environmental emissions, improved comfort and higher productivity.

Measures range from changes to working practices through low cost/no cost items to more significant alterations to the building and its services[2]. Many of these measures may require little or no design input and can be implemented by the building manager using contractors. Refurbishment is an ideal opportunity to improve energy efficiency, as discussed in section 15.

18.2 Developing an energy savings programme

Whilst it is possible to introduce ad-hoc measures, it is usually more beneficial to develop a prioritised programme to ensure best use of the funds available. A structured approach is also more likely to support the original design intent, while minimising disruption to the building.

18.2.1 Commitment and co-operation

An energy efficiency programme requires commitment from senior management. A senior member of staff must lead activities, and be responsible for ensuring the continued commitment and co-operation of management and staff (see section 15). The energy manager should initiate the following actions:

— Identify those measures and expected benefits that can produce energy savings with minimal expenditure.

— Produce a cost-benefit analysis for all measures that incur capital expenditure or changes in operational requirements.

— Obtain agreement on priorities, level of funding and economic criteria.

— Explain the impact of proposed energy efficiency measures on occupants and their work.

— In tenanted buildings, identify those aspects of the programme that are related to conditions in the lease and list the advantages to the owner and the tenants.

— Highlight the results achieved by others in the field of energy efficiency.

18.2.2 Planning

Since planning is essential, the first action should be to produce a fully costed plan of action, and obtain agreement to proceed with the programme, either as a whole or in stages.

All the original design information on the building and its services, plus the records, drawings, and maintenance and operating manuals, should be collected and reviewed in order to provide a good understanding of the original design intent (see section 15).

A simple audit of annual energy consumption based on invoices will establish if actual energy use is in line with expectations and targets (see section 19). It should then be possible to prepare an initial budget and action plan for discussion with maintenance and operations staff, for subsequent approval by owners and tenants. The action plan should include the following items:

— Preparation of a more detailed energy audit and building survey[1-6].

— Identification of measures where energy savings could be made.

— The effects of energy saving measures on the internal environment and activities within the building.

— Cost-benefit assessment of proposed measures.

— A list of priorities for the proposals.

— Involvement of maintenance staff and building occupants in additional activities.

— The implementation of the programme including time-scales and disruptions which could occur to normal operation.

— Identification of external sources of information which could be needed in assessing the returns achieved in the programme, e.g. meteorological data, case studies of energy usage in similar buildings.

— The planning of a monitoring and recording system to assess the effect of the programme.

Figure 18.1 shows the main stages in the retrofit process and indicates where professional assistance might be considered.

18.3 What are energy audits and surveys?

Audits, surveys and monitoring are all key elements of a good energy management policy. Figure 18.1 indicates their relative positions in a plan for reducing energy costs. Audits and surveys are defined below.

18.3.1 Energy audits

Similar to a financial audit, an energy audit is an attempt to allocate a value to each item of end-use energy consumption over a given period, and to balance these against overall energy use[1-6].

An energy audit, however imprecise, should be undertaken early in any energy efficiency programme to identify where energy is being used. It is then possible to direct energy efficiency action towards the highest consumers. Energy audits can bring to light and eliminate hitherto unknown mistakes (such as incorrect billing) and/or unnecessary uses of energy. Auditing should become progressively more accurate and can use all the analysis

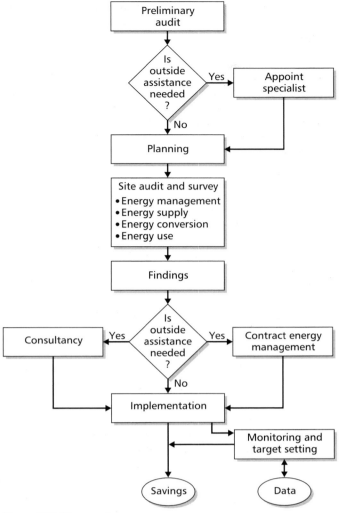

Figure 18.1 The retrofit process

techniques shown in section 19, including end-use bench-marking.

A simple preliminary audit can be performed with little specialist knowledge about energy. It will deal primarily with energy invoices, and therefore does not involve a detailed site investigation. An improved audit is often possible where site records of sub-meter readings are kept. Some engineering knowledge is useful for checking the reliability of site data. A full audit requires expertise to break down energy end-use on a service-by-service basis. The process normally involves measurement, analysis or direct assessment of energy consumption to indicate the proportions attributable to heating, lighting, air conditioning or other major uses. Such information can only be obtained by performing a site survey.

Where a whole stock of buildings is being considered, simple performance indicators (e.g. $kW \cdot h/m^2$ for fossil fuel and electricity) can be used to set up league tables of the highest consumers. Investigations should then target the worst buildings first, ultimately leading to detailed energy surveys where high consumption can not be easily explained and rectified (see section 19).

18.3.1   Energy surveys

An energy survey is an on-site technical investigation of the supply, use and management of energy to identify specific energy saving measures[1-6].

The survey should cover the main items affecting energy use, including the following:

— *building*: levels of insulation, ventilation, air infiltration etc.

— *pattern of use*: periods of occupancy, the types of control, the temperatures and humidities maintained, the use of electric lighting, the activities and processes being undertaken, including their operating temperatures, insulation etc.

— *energy supply*: examination of energy supply and distribution arrangements

— *main building services*: primary heating, cooling and air handling plant

— *electric lighting*: quality, illuminance, luminance efficiency, extent to which daylight could reduce energy use, flexibility of control etc.

— *transport of energy within the building*: fans and pumps, insulation of hot water and steam pipes and air ducts, evidence of leakage etc

— *plant room*: state and condition, insulation of boilers, chillers, tanks, pipe work, recovery of condensate, plant efficiency checks etc.

— *small power*: both on occupied floors and in common areas

— *energy management*: determining who is responsible for energy management in each department, how energy consumption is reviewed, recorded and analysed, monitoring and target setting, investment, planning and maintenance

— *building performance*: compared to standard benchmarks

— *identification of opportunities*: for energy and cost savings with recommendations for action.

A survey should be performed typically every 3–5 years, depending on the rate at which a site is changing, or following any major change in circumstances, including :

— change in building use or new tenants

— major refurbishment or development

— rationalisation leaving extensive unoccupied areas

— revised working practices or occupancy patterns

— substantial changes in fuel prices or availability

— significant upward movement in site energy consumption or costs.

It may sometimes be appropriate to perform a survey before major redevelopment to provide up-to-date information.

Measurements should be made systematically with correctly calibrated instruments. Guidance on instrumentation is given below. In the absence of instrumentation, it is possible to estimate energy use from nameplate and manufacturers' data, combined with an assumed proportion of full load operation. Such estimates are, however, second-best to actual measurement. Early in the energy efficiency programme, the larger energy-using systems should be instrumented, enabling actual energy consumption to be measured.

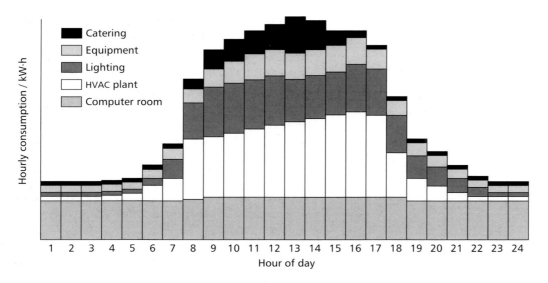

Figure 18.2 Identifying individual uses within the demand pattern (reproduced from Fuel Efficiency Booklet FEB 1[(1)]; Crown copyright)

Comprehensive surveys should aim to reach a detailed breakdown of end-uses and the constituent parts of typical load patterns. This allows the principal consumers to be identified and, in particular, the base load, as indicated in Figure 18.2. This is particularly helpful in indicating possible opportunities for reducing energy consumption as discussed in section 19.

Recent work[(1–7)] has emphasised the importance of accurate key data such as floor area, and the benefit of assessing the consumption of different energy sources separately, particularly electricity and fossil fuels. This work has provided a method for achieving a more accurate apportionment of end-uses by:

— using the most reliable data sources available

— reconciling the apportionment results with all useful metered data and avoiding ad hoc adjustments

— assessing the reliability of data and of the apportionment; if justified, seeking more data

— using specific techniques to obtain more details on uncertain loads.

These techniques underpin the benchmarking software in CIBSE TM22[(6)] and require little or no extra work but can provide more useful and reliable information in understanding the building's detailed performance. See section 19.6.

18.4   Planning a site survey

18.4.1   Level of detail required

The level and extent of an energy audit/survey should be determined by the likely potential for savings and the necessary investment in time and resources. In a small building with a relatively low energy bill, it may not be worth investing a great deal of time and effort in a survey. Large, complex buildings or sites will usually merit a detailed investigation of all areas of energy use.

A simple walkabout survey is often sufficient to identify some low-cost/no-cost measures and some areas requiring

further study. A detailed survey will be required to identify and assess more complex and costly measures.

Two basic levels of survey, concise and comprehensive, are shown in Appendix A3 in the form of standard specifications of what a survey should cover. These can be used to brief the survey team.

18.4.1.1   Comprehensive survey

A comprehensive survey is one that deals with specified areas or items in depth. It does not necessarily include every aspect of energy use but is annually expected to:

— determine the energy performance of buildings and major plant

— evaluate the principal energy flows

— identify precisely where savings can be made

— indicate the value of those savings

— provide costed recommendations or options as to how the savings can be achieved

— review procedures for energy management.

The report produced may, in addition to the recommendations and financial analyses, include:

— summaries of data collected

— details of rejected options

— outline or conceptual design work.

18.4.1.2   Concise survey

A concise survey also deals with specific areas or items, but not in depth. It will:

— assess the energy performance of buildings and major plant using little or no direct measurement

— determine the principal energy flows

— identify the main opportunities for savings

— indicate the scale of those savings

— provide outline recommendations and costs.

18.4.2   Using consultants

When an outside specialist is commissioned, a clear understanding must be established on both sides as to the objectives. With proper co-operation, the most effective use can be made of the combined skills and resources. A good brief is the key to the best use of consultants. Reference to the model briefs for comprehensive and concise surveys shown in Appendix A3 is strongly recommended, particularly where tenders for the work are to be invited.

18.4.3   Audit and survey costs

The cost of in-house work depends on internal accounting procedures. For outside assistance the cost will typically be a fixed sum or a function of a shared savings scheme. In assessing value for money for these services, similar criteria should be adopted to those applied to the rest of the organisation's business.

Whichever route is followed, the total audit and survey costs are not expected to exceed a small percentage of the annual cost of energy under investigation. A figure between 3% and 5% is not uncommon, perhaps falling towards 1% for energy-intensive sites with multi-million pound energy bills. More than 10% is unlikely to be justified even for small sites where the energy bill may be less than £10 000. Note that the percentage may remain at the higher level for an organisation with many small sites, even though the total energy bill may be several million pounds. The precise figure will depend largely on the depth of study undertaken. If audit and survey recommendations are implemented fully, the costs of these services are normally recovered from savings in the first year. The survey may also highlight measures requiring further study or design. These further study or design costs should also be identified at the time of implementation. Financial constraints and investment criteria for energy saving measures should be established at the outset.

18.4.4   Survey timing

Careful timing of a survey will produce the best results. Programming should seek to take advantage of seasonal factors and other planned activities.

—   Systems should generally be examined under operating conditions, i.e. heating in winter, cooling in summer, when performance can be measured.

—   The preliminary audit may well indicate which of the heating and cooling loads is likely to offer the greater potential for savings. A summer and/or winter survey can then be selected as required.

—   Examining plant after major maintenance is generally more appropriate than shortly before a shutdown. Ideally, examination both before and after will reveal the sensitivity of the equipment to maintenance.

—   Observation of equipment not in operation can still provide valuable information for a survey. For example, plant condition and control settings can be recorded.

—   Plan in conjunction with other proposed works, e.g. refurbishment or redevelopment.

—   Choose start and completion dates that are convenient to the pattern of normal business.

—   Select a period when key staff are available for consultation and not otherwise committed.

—   Aim to disrupt normal business as little as possible, but do not confine the survey to periods when normal operating patterns cannot be observed.

—   Plan around annual, weekend or overnight shutdown periods. These might be periods when no useful site work can be performed but might, conversely, allow access or observations not possible during normal operation. Base loads and standing losses might best be observed during 'quiet' periods

—   Assess the necessary duration of site investigation, particularly where measurements are required over some fixed period, e.g. load patterns or temperature profiles over one week.

The precise timing of the survey will be affected by the availability of resources. i.e. staff, funding and data. If existing records of consumption are limited, perhaps because site meter readings are not maintained, it may be preferable to defer the survey until more comprehensive records can be established. Once the programme has been finalised, time limits should be set and adhered to in order to maintain momentum.

18.4.5   Additional metering

It may be evident from the outset that additional meters installed at strategic points could provide much additional information. A period may be required before the survey to collect a useful number of readings from new meters or existing meters that have not previously been read.

Shortcomings in the metering arrangements can also become evident once the end users without sub-metering have been identified or where several are served by a single meter. The use of portable or temporary equipment for cross-checking old or disused meters should be considered.

Permanent metering should be considered where the cost of hiring, installing and removing temporary meters may be more than the purchase cost. The cost of sub-metering can usually be justified on major loads, particularly where little information on energy use is currently available (see section 5). The inconvenience of shutting down energy supplies for meter installation must also be considered. Shutdowns might only be possible during certain limited occasions if essential services cannot be interrupted.

18.4.6   Instruments and measurements

Good instrumentation and measurement is an essential part of site survey work. Measurements taken as part of energy surveys can indicate the potential for savings but it is also important to include metering in the implementation package in order to monitor the future savings achieved. BMS can provide a useful source of measurements although the accuracy of any information needs to be assessed carefully. More detailed information on consumption can be obtained through spot check measurements, demand profile recording and metering selected items of plant.

Table 18.1 Useful survey instruments

Instrument	Purpose/application
Electrical load profile recorder	Indicates pattern of overall building load or local use (e.g. 24-hour, 7-day); recordings can include (kV·A·h), voltage, current, power factor, dependent on type; useful for analysis, auditing and tariff review.
Clip-on power meter	Useful for auditing and checks on lighting circuits, motor consumption and small power usage. Preferably measuring watts directly.
Data logger (or chart recorder)	Inputs can include space temperature, duct air temperature, water temperature and relative humidity; pulsed outputs can also be used to provide gas/oil/water consumption, and indications of system and control performance
Boiler combustion test kit	Flue gas analysis; temperature, O_2, CO_2, CO, smoke number; spot check on boiler efficiency to highlight need for burner adjustment, boiler cleaning, etc.
Light meter	Spot checks on illuminance levels
Digital temperature indicator	Surface and immersion probes; spot checks on space/water/duct temperatures; surface temperatures for assessment of quality of pipework and vessel insulation
Sling hygrometer	Spot checks on wet and dry bulb space temperatures
Anemometer (or pitot tube and manometer)	Air flow rate to calculate supply/extract volumes, air change rates

Table 18.1[8] shows some common portable instruments found useful during surveys. All should have valid calibration certificates to ensure confidence in the results.

A concise survey may require minimal instrumentation. Comprehensive surveys are normally expected to include measurement of principal energy flows and performance assessment of major plant. Reliable measurements of building areas and volumes are also needed for detailed assessments.

18.4.7 Access to site

Restraints may be imposed on survey staff and working practices. The following issues should be raised before the survey begins:

— hazardous areas, e.g. high voltages, dangerous substances

— requirements for approved or authorised staff, e.g. qualified to work on high voltage equipment

— security clearance requirements

— medical health requirements

— need for protective clothing

— restrictions on use of survey instruments, e.g. intrinsically safe instruments operating on low voltage and containing no toxic materials

— safety procedures.

Department heads and security staff should be notified of the programme and asked to co-operate in the smooth running of the survey.

18.4.8 Integrating the measures

Energy surveys often identify stand-alone measures that will save energy on specific items. However, the wider effects of any measures should be considered carefully in relation to the whole building and the original design intent. Often, one set of problems can be exchanged for another. For example, turning off humidifiers on air

conditioning plant to reduce electricity consumption may lead to control problems and complaints of dryness.

It is essential that these measures are co-ordinated so that they form an integrated package, avoiding conflict between one measure and another. For example, the introduction of fast response lighting controls alongside the introduction of high pressure discharge lamps with long strike up times will result in significant problems. Equally, better building insulation without good heating controls may simply result in overheating.

Integration should also avoid double counting of savings. For example, if a boiler is upgraded and improved boiler controls are introduced then the savings from the controls should be based on the consumption expected after boiler replacement.

New measures should also be carefully integrated with the ability and resources of the existing management since additional burdens or complexity may prevent savings actually being achieved in practice.

18.5 How to carry out energy audits and surveys

Table 18.2 shows how to carry out an energy survey. This indicates that significant amounts of the work can be achieved off-site in preparation and analysis. It is also essential to take a structured approach based on clear principles. CIBSE TM22[6] is a tool that greatly assists this.

18.6 Preliminary audits: considerations

A preliminary audit seeks to establish the quantity and cost of each form of energy used in a building or site. If reliable data exist, a breakdown of energy use by area or by service may also be possible. Collated information should be used to prepare a plan for further action leading to a site survey. An audit period of one year is recommended, normally

Table 18.2 How to carry out an energy survey

Stage	Tasks
Identify objectives	Develop a good brief — see Appendix A3 for model briefs Determine scope e.g. whole site, building or particular fuel/system Determine the depth of the survey — how much detail is required? Establish start and finish dates Set out the reporting style — summary, concise or detailed
Preliminary data gathering (before site visit)	Gather what data possible before going to site Invoice consumption data (kW·h) for each incoming fuel are essential Floor areas and basic building layout plans are essential Occupancy patterns and typical building usage are essential An understanding of the basic heating, cooling, ventilation is valuable Any further monitored data, consumption profiles, system layout information are valuable
Preliminary analysis/audit (before site visit)	Familiarise yourself with building layout and systems Identify key areas to visit – plant rooms, BMS room, main meters etc. Complete CIBSE TM22[6] option A and hence: — calculate simple performance indicators in (kW·h)/m² per year for each incoming fuel — calculate a single overall performance indicator in (kg CO_2)/m² per year — compare actual performance with benchmarks to identify potential savings, see Appendix A3 — highlight the expected major end-uses to focus on-site activities
Initial site survey	Survey each main end-use system Gather sub-metering data and system information, e.g. W/m², hours run etc. for input to CIBSE TM22[6] option C Assess control and usage of each system as a control factor Review BMS operation and key settings with operator Take incoming and sub-meter readings over the survey period Gather sub-metering data, hours run etc. on any special end-uses for input to CIBSE TM22[6] option B Gather any other data, i.e. sub-meter readings, half hourly electronic data etc. Confirm floor area definitions and data plus any special end-use floor area data Throughout the survey, develop a list of possible energy saving measures that appear practical Discuss the use of the building and its systems with operational/maintenance staff Enquire about recent changes/problems and future plans for the building/systems
Analysis	Complete CIBSE TM22[6] option B accounting for special end-uses, weather and occupancy where appropriate Re-compare actual performance with benchmarks to identify potential savings, see Appendix A3 Complete CIBSE TM22[6] option C to assess detailed end-use breakdown Compare actual end-use performance with benchmarks Assess reasons and develop possible solutions for poorly performing systems Analyse any half hourly data/profiles and sub meter readings, see section 19.2 Apportion typical profiles to end-uses; build up base load and investigate shortfall Identify potential savings and areas for investigation from load profiles Continually update/improve list of possible energy saving measures that appear practical Estimate potential cost savings and implementation costs of each measure Calculate economic viability e.g. simple payback or whole life costs Identify data that is missing or poor accuracy that needs to be gathered/improved to support audit and savings
Final site survey	Gather any missing data and improve poor accuracy data Further investigate inefficient end-uses identified in analysis Firm-up all potential energy saving measures to ensure practicality Discuss measures with operational/maintenance staff to ensure feasibility Discuss implementation with potential equipment suppliers to confirm practicality/cost
Final analysis	Firm-up audit of energy in CIBSE TM22[6] Carry out a final check on actual performance versus benchmarks Firm-up likely cost savings and reductions in CO_2 emissions Firm-up implementation costs to get an indication of simple payback
Reporting	Write a brief overview of the building/system investigated Show the energy audit diagrammatically Show the actual performance versus benchmarks output from CIBSE TM22[6] Write a short section describing each energy saving measure showing brief calculations of economic return Indicate other spin-off benefits that may come from the measures e.g. improved comfort Develop a management summary List savings in order of priority — usually based on simple payback and ease of implementation Show the overall savings, implementation costs and payback

corresponding to the most recent financial year or other convenient period. The main steps can be summarised as:

(a)   collection of data

(b)   analysis of data

(c)   presentation of data

(d)   establishing priorities.

18.6.1   Data collection

Invoices are the principal source of data, supplemented where possible by site records.

18.6.1.1   Invoice data

Invoices are an essential source of information on energy input, costs and tariffs. Original invoices should always be obtained in preference to transcribed extracts as important data or errors can otherwise be missed. Actual meter readings and dates will assist with checking and interpretation.

— Collect copies of all monthly and quarterly invoices for energy used during the full audit year, not just those for which payment was made in this period.

— For fuels supplied in bulk (oil, solid fuel, liquefied petroleum gas, etc.) collect all invoices or delivery notes relevant to use during the audit period. Deliveries before the start of the period may have to be included but a delivery at the very end can usually be excluded.

— Check that all metering or supply points can be identified from invoices and that all supplies can be accounted for.

— Ensure that data for each type of energy refer, as closely as possible, to the same period.

— Note any estimated readings. Additional invoices with real readings should be collected for comparison if there are more than one or two estimates in the audit period.

— Approach suppliers for assistance if invoice information is inadequate or unavailable.

— Electricity and gas suppliers should also be able to supply half hourly data in electronic form allowing analysis of daily/weekly/monthly demand patterns

18.6.1.2   Site energy records

For large sites or buildings, site energy records may provide details of any sub-metered energy consumption, stock levels or use of bulk fuels. In small buildings they may be able to supplement incomplete or estimated invoice data.

— Collect any summaries of invoice data that have already been produced for the audit year and, to show overall trends, for the previous two years. Summaries may need validation before they can be used for analysis.

— Collect records of energy for the audit year. Monthly or weekly summaries are more useful than daily log books as anomalies may arise in the

shorter term and such detailed analysis is not expected for the audit.

— Confirm the arrangement of all sub-meters relative to their respective main meters, including any sub-meters for which records are not available but from which additional data could be obtained.

— Consider whether correction or multiplication factors should be applied and check the units of energy measurement. In particular note the addition of noughts following meter readings. The appropriate correction may be small enough in many cases to be unnecessary but this has to be established. Sub-meter readings in particular are likely to need correction, especially for pressures changes in gas or steam distribution. Further information on correction factors is given in Appendix A2.

— Where reliable sub-meter records are available, try to determine the consumption of users without sub-meters by difference. Care is needed as cumulative errors can often give inaccurate results.

18.6.2   Annual energy analysis

Analysis of consumption and cost from invoices assists the selection of priorities for survey. Data for individual sites should be analysed separately as follows :

— Identify each individual energy type to be analysed.

— Make special note of estimated readings, which can occur commonly for small electricity and gas supplies. Estimates are often based on the consumption for the corresponding period in the previous year and could well be inaccurate.

— Ensure that recorded annual totals apply to a full twelve-month period. An estimate in the middle of the audit year will not affect the recorded annual total. In the first or last period, an estimated or mistimed reading will need some interpretation. Interpolation can often be applied successfully to monthly readings, simply by assuming a uniform rate of consumption between the dates of two known readings. For quarterly readings, the results of this method are far less reliable and further analysis may be restricted.

— Convert the consumption of each energy type to a common unit (kW·h) using the standard conversion factors given in Appendix A2. The typical calorific values may be assumed if actual values are unavailable.

— Calculate the percentage breakdown of total energy consumption and cost by energy type and determine the average overall cost per kW·h of each energy type to indicate its relative significance.

— Prepare a table on the model of Table 18.3 showing the total annual consumption and cost of each fuel type for the audit year. It is useful, for reference, to include the respective proportions of total cost and energy and the overall unit costs for comparison.

— Prepare pie charts of the type shown in Figure 18.3 to illustrate the energy and cost contributions of each energy type

Table 18.3 Model table of annual energy input

Energy type	Purchased units	Consumption			Cost		
		/ kW·h	/ % of total	/ £	/ % of total	/ (p/kW·h)
Electricity	902 500 kW·h	0.90×10^6	15	37 400	57	4.16
Gas	5500 therms	0.16×10^6	3	1880	3	1.18
Oil (class G)	440 000 litres	5.13×10^6	83	26 200	40	0.51
Totals	—	6.19×10^6	100	65 480	100	1.06★ (av.)

★ Average cost (pence per kW·h) is defined as total cost divided by total energy purchased.

Table 18.4 Model table of changes in annual energy use and CO_2 emissions

Year	Electricity consumption / kW·h	Change / %	CO_2 emissions★ / tonnes	Gas consumption / kW·h	Change / %	CO_2 emissions★ / tonnes
1998	50 000	—	21 500	10 000	—	1900
1999	48 000	−4	20 640	9500	−5	1805
2000	49 000	+2	21 070	9500	0	1805
2001	47 000	−4	20 210	8200	−13	1558

★ Conversion factors (see Appendix A2, Table A2.7): electricity 0.43; gas 0.19

Note: no correction has been made for variable factors that might affect the comparison.

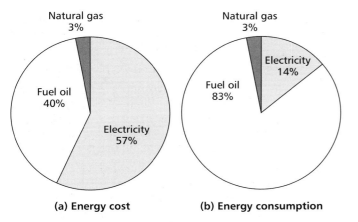

(a) Energy cost   (b) Energy consumption

Figure 18.3 Pie charts of annual energy cost and consumption

— Where the previous year's energy data are available, a comparison with the audit year should be made, as this may indicate any major overall trends as illustrated in Table 18.4.

18.7 Site surveys: considerations

18.7.1 Breaking down energy use

As part of a site survey it should be possible to produce a breakdown energy end-uses that corresponds reasonably well with the energy bought from the supplier. CIBSE TM22[6] (see section 19) provides a useful tool to help achieve this but where this is not available or applicable then:

(a) Prepare a table similar to Table 18.5, building on the preliminary audit, and insert all metered consumptions known from existing records. Keep each fuels separate as they have very different costs and environmental emissions. When assessing space heating and HWS this approach might sometimes be extended to show distribution or combustion losses separately if desired.

(b) Estimate the end-use consumptions using techniques shown in section 19 and/or CIBSE TM22[6]. In particular, use the tree-diagram approach to seek a reconciliation between end-use consumption and each incoming energy/fuel.

Two methods most applicable to fixed loads are:

— Multiply the design energy consumption of equipment of a known rating by its annual operating time, e.g. 12 kW × 8 hours per day × 5 days per week × 30 weeks per year = 14 400 kW·h per year. Ratings should be measured if possible as nominal ratings or design loads may not apply to the actual operating conditions.

— Multiply the actual energy consumption of the equipment measured over a limited period by its annual operating time. Electrical loads can often be assessed for this purpose from a simple measurement of current.

(c) Compare sub-metered totals with the end-uses and overall total quantities of fuel known to have been used.

(d) Once a reliable breakdown of end-uses has been reconciled with incoming metered use and any sub-metered use, then Table 18.5 can be redrawn as in the format shown in Table 18.6.

The estimated figures in the example are seen to agree closely with the purchased totals. If the calculated and purchased totals disagree then more reliable data should be sought in order to provide closer estimates of end-uses until a reliable balance (reconciliation) is achieved, see section 19.6.

Table 18.5 Model summary of metered energy use

Category of use	Energy source		
	Electricity	Gas	Oil
Space heating	U ⎫		
Hot water service	U ⎬	9000^M	2000^M
Air conditioning	U	—	—
Lighting	U	—	—
Process:			
— heating	—	500^U	—
— power	300^M	—	—
Unallocated	2300^D	0	0
Purchased totals:	2600^M	9500^M	2000^M

Note: M — metered figure; D — by difference (e.g. 9500 – 9000 = 500); U — unmetered

Table 18.6 Model table for allocation of purchased energy to end-uses

Category of use	Energy source		
	Electricity	Gas	Oil
Space heating	100^A	8000^A	2000^M
Hot water service	200^A	1000^A	—
Air conditioning	1200^A	—	—
Lighting	900^A	—	—
Process:			
— heating	—	500^D	—
— power	300^M	—	—
Calculated totals	2700	9500	2000
Purchased	2600^M	9500^M	2000^M
Unaccounted	(100)	0	0

Note: A — assessed; M — metered figure; D — by difference

18.7.2 Estimating the energy use of some principal services

18.7.2.1 Space heating

The energy used for space heating can be estimated using a variety of techniques some of which are described in CIBSE Guide A[9] and CIBSE Building Energy Code 1[10]. Estimates should take into account weather, building response and thermal properties, system characteristics and hours of use. In very simple terms, consumption might be expressed as:

$$F = 0.0036\, Q\, E \times (100 / \eta) \qquad (18.1)$$

where F is the annual fuel consumption (GJ), Q is the calculated building heat loss at design conditions (kW), E is the equivalent hours full load operation (hours per year) and η is the seasonal efficiency of the system (%).

Calculation of the building heat loss requires a knowledge of the thermal transmittance (U-value) of the building elements and the ventilation rate as a minimum. Reference should be made to CIBSE Guide A: *Environmental design*[9] for a formal derivation of the equivalent hours full load operation. Some typical ranges are given in Table 18.7.

Table 18.7 Typical ranges of equivalent hours full load operation

Building use	Hours
Offices, schools, lightweight buildings occupied 8 hour per day, 5 days per week	Under 1500
Public retail, catering; heavyweight buildings occupied 12 hours per day, 6 days per week	1500–2500
Hospitals, hotels, sheltered accommodation; continuously heated	2500–3500

Table 18.8, opposite, gives some typical examples of the seasonal efficiencies of different heating systems. A more rigorous treatment will also take account of solar and internal gains and the non-steady state conditions encountered in practice. Judgment must be applied in deciding the appropriate degree of accuracy in calculating space heating loads.

18.7.2.2 Hot water services

If the water consumption for hot water services is known, e.g. cold feed is metered, an estimate can be made of the energy consumption, see Table 18.9, opposite, for an example calculation.

Table 18.10, opposite, gives the typical seasonal efficiencies of various systems.

Where water usage is not known, the energy consumption may be estimated from the following equation:

$$Q_{hws} = 0.0864\, q_{hws}\, A_f\, N_w \times 10^{-3} \qquad (18.2)$$

where Q_{hws} is the energy consumed in providing hot water (GJ), q_{hws} is the mean power requirement from Table 18.11 (W·m^{-2}), A_f is the floor area under consideration (m^2) and N_w is the number of working days.

Table 18.9 Example calculation of the annual energy requirement to heat a known quantity of water from cold to full service temperature

Parameter	Value
Annual water consumption	120 000 litres
HWS temperature	60 °C
Cold make-up temperature	10 °C
Seasonal efficiency of system	60%
Specific heat content of water	4.2 × 10^{-6} GJ per litre
Annual energy required	= 120 000 × (60 – 10) × (4.2 × 10^{-6}) × (100/60) = 42 GJ

18.7.2.3 Lighting

The installed load (kW) can be multiplied by hours in use to give the energy consumption (kW·h). The load can be determined by counting the number of fittings and identifying their indicated rating. Allowance must be made for control gear losses, except for tungsten lighting, to give the total circuit load, see Table 9.14. Between 10 and 20 W·m^2 is typical for fluorescent lighting when the load is related to the floor area served. Less than 12 W·m^2 can be regarded as good practice, see Table 9.14.

Table 18.8 Seasonal efficiencies of heating systems

Type of system	Heat conversion efficiency / %	Utilisation efficiency / %	Seasonal efficiency of system / %
Intermittent:			
— automatic centrally-fired radiator or convector systems	65	97	63
— automatic centrally-fired warm air ventilation systems	65	93	60
— fan-assisted electric off-peak heaters	100	90	90
— direct electric (non-storage) floor and ceiling systems	100	95	95
— district heating/warm air systems*	75	90	67.5
Continuous:			
— automatic centrally-fired radiator or convector systems	70	100	70
— automatic centrally-fired warm air ventilation system	70	100	70
— electric storage radiator systems	100	75	75
— electric floor storage systems	100	70	70
— direct electric floor and ceiling systems	100	95	95
— district heating/radiator systems*	75	100	75

★ Allowance should be made separately for mains heat losses on a seasonal basis.

Notes:
1 Very high efficiency heat generators may raise the heat conversion efficiency.
2 Solid fuel appliances working in conjunction with intermittent systems may require allowance for rekindling.
3 Heavier liquid fuels will require preheating allowance.

Table 18.10 Seasonal efficiencies of water heating systems

Type of system	Heat conversion efficiency (%)	Utilisation efficiency (%)	Seasonal efficiency of system (%)
Gas circulator/storage cylinder*	65	80	52
Gas- and oil-fired boiler/storage cylinder*	70	80	56
Off-peak electric storage with cylinder and immersion heater	100	80	80
Instantaneous gas multi-point heater	65	95	62
District heating with local calofifiers*†	75	80	60
District heating with central calorifiers and distribution*†	75	75	56

* Dependent on the size of the heat generator, the summer conversion efficiency may deteriorate, thereby reducing the overall seasonal efficiency significantly.
† Allowance should be made separately for mains heat losses on a seasonal basis.

Notes:
(1) Very high efficiency heat generators may raise the heat conversion efficiency.
(2) Solid fuel appliances working in conjunction with intermittent systems may require allowance for rekindling.
(3) Heavier liquid fuels will require preheating allowance.

Table 18.11 Mean power requirements of hot water systems

Building type	q_{hws} / $W \cdot m^2$
Office:	
— 5-day	2.0
— 6-day	2.0
Shop:	
— 5-day	0.5
— 6-day	1.0
Factories:	
— 5-day, single shift	9.0
— 6-day, single shift	11.0
— 7-day, multiple shift	12.0
Warehouses	1.0
Residential	17.5
Hotels	8.0
Hospitals	29.0
Education	2.0

18.8   Assessing energy saving measures

18.8.1   Option appraisal

Before making a change to an existing system, it is important to consider all the available options, particularly where major investment is involved, e.g. new boilers or a BMS. A full optional appraisal will ensure that the most cost-effective and efficient plant is chosen[11,12]. Option appraisal can provide a number of benefits:

— correct sizing of plant to meet the real demands of the building, often leading to lower capital costs

— improved comfort levels through increased levels of control taking account of the needs of staff

— lower running costs through the installation of more efficient plant with better controls

— easier maintenance and improved reliability by using modern plant and careful choice of systems

— higher environmental standards by considering the environmental benefits of each option

— a formal justification for the recommendations made, including a well researched fall-back option in case the first recommendation is rejected by management

— an opportunity to investigate other forms of financing such as contract energy management.

Option appraisal compares possible solutions to a particular problem in order to arrive at the optimum solution to provide the required comfort conditions. The appraisal includes capital and operating costs, and environmental impact, as well as practical issues like flueing and plant location and the flexibility to cope with changes in building use and occupancy.

Option appraisal is a highly iterative process. Some options will be eliminated during the process due to the constraints on the project, such as economics or practical problems like the size of the plant room. Conversely, others may come to light during the analysis. It is important, therefore, to consider even what appear to be the most unlikely options. The appraisal should be treated as a flexible process of development; nothing should be fixed until final recommendations are made.

Strategic issues should be considered, including:

— What renewable energy sources are available?

— Should the plant be centralised or decentralised?

— Where will the plant be located?

— What fuels are available on site?

— Is in-house maintenance available or will it be contracted out?

— Are there complaints from staff about comfort levels?

— Will staff need to be trained or recruited to cope with increased plant complexity?

Future changes which may influence demand should also be considered, for example, use or occupancy patterns, alterations to the buildings including additions, refurbishments, demolitions etc.

Once ideas are seen as practical propositions, very simple comparisons of the rough payback and non-cost benefits of each option can be carried out. The worksheet shown in Table 18.12 illustrates a suitable format for estimating the paybacks and lists the information that will be required at this stage[11]. The aim is then to focus on the most feasible and economic options by gradually increasing the accuracy of costings and the engineering detail for those most favoured. The preferred options can be further refined by considering the practical problems e.g. flue heights, floor loadings etc.

18.8.2   Investment criteria

For low cost/low risk measures with quick returns, simple methods of appraisal are generally acceptable. Appraisals of large or long-term investments should take account of interest rates, inflation, project life and risk. Energy efficiency measures should be assessed on the same basis as other investments, taking into account the wider benefits that can accrue. Analysis of the sensitivity to changes in, for example, ambient temperature (as measured by degree-days), equipment performance or energy prices is also advisable.

The full implementation costs should always be considered including equipment, material and labour costs, consultants' fees, builders work and any disruption costs. In-house staff time, whether carrying out work directly or supervising the work of others should also be included.

Some of the methods used in investment appraisal are outlined below and are discussed in more detail in CIBSE Guide to Ownership, operation and maintenance of building services[13] and Action Energy Good Pracrtice Guides GPG 75[14] and GPG 165[15].

18.8.2.1   Simple payback

The crudest test of cost-effectiveness is simple payback period, which is the time taken for the initial capital expenditure to be equalled by the saving in energy cost.

This ignores interest rates and the benefit of continuing savings to the end of the life of the plant. A persistent and unthinking use of this method of testing cost-effectiveness may lead to under investment and a failure to seize good investment opportunities where payback periods are somewhat longer than anticipated.

The method is generally adopted for measures showing a return within five years, measures involving only minor investment, or for an initial assessment of measures that involve more substantial investment.

It should be made clear whether costs and savings are based on firm quotations or budget estimates. Where alternative measures are being compared, the marginal capital cost should be used to indicate the payback of one measure versus the other.

Table 18.12 Example format for an option appraisal worksheet

Option appraisal worksheet			
	Option 1	Option 2	Option 3
Plant output (kW)			
Hours run			
Seasonal efficiency			
Energy consumption (kW h)			
Fuel cost (pence/(kW h))			
Annual running cost			
Capital cost			
Payback period			
Environmental emissions			
Other benefits			

18.8.2.2   Discounted cash flow

Large projects and long term measures require the preparation of a cash flow statement to evaluate their true economic worth. Discounted cash flow (DCF) takes into account the timing of capital and revenue costs and savings. The decision on when to apply DCF methods should reflect normal business policy.

Such methods require the use of discount rates[13–15]. These discount rates differ widely between organisations but are usually between 5% and 20%. This is, in effect, saying that such a return on capital can be obtained by an alternative investment and an energy efficiency investment must yield a return no less than this. The results are often expressed as discounted payback or as the break-even period.

18.8.2.3   Net present value

Net present value (NPV) indicates the discounted cash flow over the life of the project[13–15].

The effects of taxation and capital allowances can be taken into account, as can changes in energy prices. The true worth of the proposed measure can then be seen as a sum of money in present day values.

18.8.2.4   Internal rate of return

Internal rate of return (IRR) provides an alternative approach to NPV, representing the rate of interest that money would have to earn elsewhere to be a better investment; the higher the IRR, the better the project.

IRR is defined as the discount rate at which the net present value of the project reduces to zero. There is no direct way of calculating IRR. The interest rate at which the NPV becomes zero is determined by successive approximations[13–15].

18.8.3   Life cycle costing

In addition to direct financial returns, there are nearly always wider benefits that should be taken into account, including:

—   improved manageability, for example through better control and monitoring

—   reduced maintenance and staff costs after replacing or upgrading plant

—   reduced harmful emissions to the atmosphere, e.g. less CO_2, NO_x etc; this is particularly important to organisations with environmental policies

—   improved management information and decision making

—   improved services, comfort and productivity.

The last point is often missed but is commonly one of the greatest benefits. Results from building surveys, have shown a combination of benefits comprising optimum levels of energy efficiency, people satisfied with their environment, and high productivity. This does not mean that installing measures will always directly improve productivity, but rather that well managed buildings tend to have satisfied occupants who pay attention to energy management.

Total life cycle costing involves evaluating all costs and benefits over the entire physical life of the asset, providing a more realistic basis for comparison. However, there is a risk of overestimating benefits and it should never be used as a means of enhancing the value of a project that has a poor payback.

18.9   Analysis and reporting

For action to be taken, recommendations for energy efficiency measures must reach the correct level of management, be presented in a form that assists, and offer a good case for investment. Energy survey reports should include:

—   a management summary suitable for non-technical managers

—   observations and data

—   an analysis of costs and non cost benefits

—   conclusions and interpretation of the findings

—   clear recommendations.

The energy account is often best presented in tabular form in a similar manner to a financial account. A graphical presentation can also be adopted, e.g. a pie-chart or Sankey diagram as shown in Figure 18.4. Where cost saving or environmental issues are a high management priority then the diagrams should be represented in (£) or (kg CO_2).

The audit and survey report should include future targets (see section 19), including emissions targets in (kg CO_2)·m^{-2} per annum.

Survey recommendations can range from simple non-technical measures to those needing major investment, and possibly more detailed investigation and/or design. A report can also include recommendations for savings solely in energy cost, e.g. tariff changes or control of electrical maximum demand. Such recommendations can often help the supplier reduce their primary energy consumption.

Measures can be summarised and ranked in as much detail as the data allows, as shown in the specimen summary illustrated in Table 18.13.

Measures are commonly grouped as follows:

—   *No-cost/low-cost measures*: Measures can normally be identified which require minimal investment and can often be implemented without further study. These include: general good housekeeping; 'switch-off' campaigns; avoiding wasteful practices adjustment of existing controls to match actual requirements of occupancy change of fuel purchasing tariffs, or correct selection of fuel where there is a dual-fuel facility rescheduling of activities; planning to take advantage of tariff structures; changing the use of building space small capital items such as installation of thermostats, time-switches and sections of pipework insulation or draught proofing.

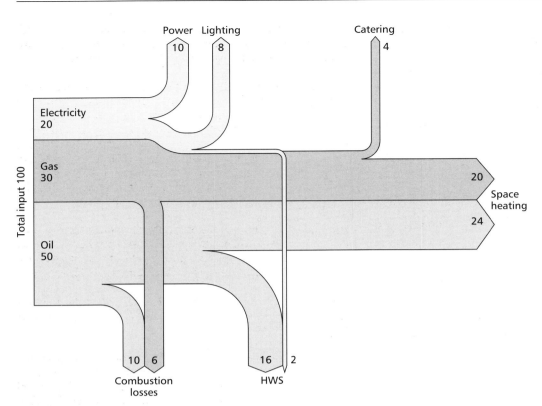

Figure 18.4 Sankey diagram showing where CO_2/costs/energy is going

Note: This diagram is probably best expressed in cost or CO_2 emissions to avoid adding electricity (kW·h) to fossil fuel (kW·h) as they have very different costs and CO_2 factors, see section 19.

— *Medium-cost measures*: These measures may still require little or no further design or study, but involve expenditure on works and will consequently take longer to implement. A convenient range of capital cost, e.g. £500 to 5000 per measure, can be defined to suit the requirements of any particular organisation. Common investment measures include: installation of new or replacement controls for heating, cooling or lighting, insulation or refurbishment of roofs, walls, windows and floors to reduce heat loss, prevent draughts or reduce solar gain. Some measures can have a low marginal cost when incorporated into major refurbishment work, e.g. flat roof insulation.

— *High-cost measures*: Measures in this category are expected to need further detailed study and design. Individual approval may have to be obtained at an executive level before implementation. Such measures could include: replacement or upgrading of plant and equipment, e.g. boilers, chillers, water heaters and luminaires, installation of a BMS, major

changes in the methods of generating heat or power, e.g. decentralisation of boiler plant or introduction of a CHP scheme.

The immediate end product of a survey is a report. Reporting procedures must therefore be considered at an early stage. Note that the effort involved in evaluating findings and preparing a final report is normally at least as great as that spent on site work.

A management summary is recommended for presentation to senior management. Interim reports can allow early implementation of simple measures during extended periods of site work. They can also help to ensure that effort continues to be applied most effectively. Circulation of a draft version of the final report is recommended, particularly in the case of a major report prepared by an outside organisation. Additional time must be allowed for discussion and amendments. The date specified for completing the final report may determine the whole programme. The final report should be presented to the

Table 18.13 Specimen summary of recommendations

Ref	Location	Description of recommendation	Fuel type	Net annual savings		Implementation costs (£)		Simple payback (years)
				(£)	(GJ)	Extra study and design if applicable	Total	
Totals (and overall payback period):								

level of management with authority to implement the capital schemes recommended.

Managing the implementation process is covered in section 18.10.

— Ensure the wider effects of any measures are considered carefully in relation to the whole building and the original design intent.

— Avoid exchanging one set of problems for another e.g. turning off humidifiers on plant to reduce electricity consumption may lead to air conditioning control problems and complaints.

— Ensure that the measures are co-ordinated to form an integrated package, avoiding conflict between one measure and another.

— Avoid double counting of savings e.g. savings from improved boiler should be based on the consumption expected after boiler replacement.

— Ensure that existing management can cope with additional burdens or complexity of any measures so that savings are actually achieved in practice.

18.10   Implementing savings

The principal object of the audit and survey stages is to identify worthwhile opportunities for saving energy. Production of a report must not be regarded as the end of a project but as a step leading to implementation. Every effort must be made to ensure that a project proceeds to implementation. The complete process involves final selection of the measures to be adopted, planning and carrying out the selected measures monitoring the results.

The final selection of measures is expected to be influenced strongly by the availability of funding and management time for implementation. Priorities are normally assigned on a financial basis although an increasing number of organisations use environmental emissions as a basis in the light of the recently formed emissions trading scheme. It is also preferable to establish a programme of measures within the capacity of management to implement and support. A highly cost-effective measure may not be so attractive if savings are dependent on a continued management and maintenance input.

A plan should be produced to implement the chosen options identifying: what action is necessary, e.g. design, tendering, installation, supervision, etc. who will carry out

the tasks who should be informed or may be affected, including external bodies where relevant when, and with what priority, each measure will be implemented

The plan developed will normally have to deal with measures in groups rather than individually. For the purposes of implementation the best groups are likely to be based on the type of work involved, e.g. mechanical, electrical or insulation works. This should assist tasks such as tendering or installation, particularly if work is to be let to an outside contractor. Priorities can still be assigned to individual items within a given group by taking account of their costs and benefits.

An implementation programme, as shown by the example in Table 18.14, can help to prioritise measures and to assist in managing individual projects. It should show the cost, responsibility and timing of each recommended measure.

Large scale energy saving projects need significant supervision to an extent that an independent project manager may be required.

One effective method is the rolling programme in which savings from the first energy saving measures are re-invested to produce further savings. Part of the initial investment can sometimes be raised by capitalising fuel cost savings from good housekeeping measures that need little or no capital expenditure.

Energy managers should publicise the programme and explain its importance and implications. Implementation should be planned so that measures are introduced with minimum disruption to normal activities but achieve savings at the earliest opportunity. Repetitive solutions may benefit from pilot projects to provide valuable experience and identify any pitfalls. Monitoring equipment should be installed as part of implementation in order to quantify the savings actually achieved. The implementation programme should be regularly reviewed, and all personnel should be kept informed of progress and the results achieved.

Tasks should be allocated with the authority and support of senior management. It is recommended that someone within an organisation, normally the site energy manager, be given the role of project manager with responsibility for co-ordinating the works. Liaison with in-house staff at a range of levels and with external organisations may be required. Large organisations may wish to consider setting up an energy working party. General good-housekeeping measures need the support and co-operation of all staff. Consultation with safety officers, staff representatives, etc.

Table 18.14 Example energy efficiency implementation programme

Proposed project	Location	Priority	Works order no.	Estimated cost	Estimated rate of return	Organisation actioned	Project manager	Date work ordered	Expected completion date	Comments

is often necessary where working conditions or practices will be affected. Some measures may also have to be explained to building occupants if they are to be introduced successfully e.g. automatic lighting controls.

18.11 Specific energy saving measures

Appendix 18.A1 provides a checklist of the main retrofit energy saving measures to consider when upgrading energy efficiency in existing buildings It should be read in conjunction with section 16 on maintenance issues.

Where windows, doors, heating, hot water, lighting, air conditioning or mechanical ventilation systems are replaced as part of a refurbishment then the new controlled service or fitting must meet the Building Regulations Approved Document L1/L2*[16] as if it were a new installation. The work must also be commissioned in line with the building regulations and the building log-book should be prepared/updated to include that work (see section 14). Also, the metering strategy should be prepared/revised to allow the energy consumption of the replacement services to be monitored (see section 5).

References

1   *Introduction to energy efficiency in buildings* Energy Efficiency Booklets FEB 1–13 (Action Energy) (1994) (www.action energy.org.uk)

2   *Energy audits for buildings* FEB 1B (Action Energy) (1993) (www.actionenergy.org.uk)

3   *Energy audits and surveys* BRE Information Paper IP12/92 (London: Construction Research Communications) (1992)

4   *Energy audit and survey guide: for building managers and engineers* Good Practice Guide GPG 28 (Action Energy) (1991) (www.actionenergy.org.uk)

5   *Energy audit and survey guide: for building financiers and senior managers* Good Practice Guide GPG 27 (Action Energy) (1991) (www.actionenergy.org.uk)

6   *Energy Assessment and Reporting Methodology — Office Assessment Method* CIBSE TM22 (London: Chartered Institution of Building Services Engineers) (1999)

7   Field J, Soper J, Jones P G, Bordass W and Grigg P Energy performance of occupied non domestic buildings: Assessment by analysing end-use energy consumptions *Building Services Eng. Res. Technol.* 18A (1) 39–46 (1997)

8   Stonard P *Instruments for building services applications* BSRIA TN 14/86 (Bracknell: Building Services Research and Information Association) (1986)

9   *Environmental design* CIBSE Guide A (London: Chartered Institution of Building Services Engineers) (1999)

10   *Energy demands and targets for heated and ventilated buildings* CIBSE Building Energy Code 1 (London: Chartered Institution of Building Services Engineers) (1999)

11   *Heating system option appraisal — an engineer's guide for existing buildings* Good Practice Guide GPG 187 (Action Energy) (1996) (www.actionenergy.org.uk)

12   *Heating system option appraisal — a manager's guide* Good Practice Guide GPG 182 (Action Energy) (1996) (www.action energy.org.uk)

13   *Guide to ownership, operation and maintenance of building services* (London: Chartered Institution of Building Services Engineers) (2000)

14   *Financial aspects of energy management in buildings — A summary* Good Practice Guide GPG 75 (Action Energy) (1995) (www.actionenergy.org.uk)

15   *Financial aspects of energy management in buildings* Good Practice Guide GPG 165 (Action Energy) (1991) (www.action energy.org.uk)

16   *Conservation of fuel and power* The Building Regulations 2000 Approved Document L1/L2 (London: The Stationery Office) (2001)

17   *Technical standards for compliance with the Building Standards (Scotland) Regulations 1990 (as amended)* (London: The Stationery Office) (2001)

18   *Conservation of fuel and power* The Building Regulations (Northern Ireland) 1994 Technical Booklet F (London: The Stationery Office) (1999)

19   *Economic thickness of insulation for existing industrial buildings* Fuel Efficiency Booklet FEB 16 (Action Energy) (1993) (www.actionenergy.org.uk)

20   Potter I N, Jones T J and Booth W B *Air leakage of office buildings* BSRIA TN 8/95 (Bracknell: Building Services Research and Information Association) (May 1995)

21   *Retail warehouses — the potential for increasing energy efficiency* BRE Information Paper IP 8/90 (London: Construction Research Communications) (1990)

22   *Condensation in roofs* BRE Digest 180 (London: Construction Research Communications)

23   *Building control systems* CIBSE Guide H (London: Chartered Institution of Building Services Engineers) (2000)

24   *Air-to-air heat recovery* CIBSE Research Report RR2 (London: Chartered Institution of Building Services Engineers) (1995)

25   *Oversized air handling plant* BSRIA GN 11/97 (Bracknell: Building Services Research and Information Association) (1997)

26   *The economic thickness of insulation for hot pipes* Fuel Efficiency Booklet FEB 8 (Action Energy) (1993) (www.action energy.org.uk)

27   BS 5422: 2001: *Methods for specifying thermal insulation materials on pipes, ductwork and equipment (in the temperature range −40 °C to +700 °C)* (London: British Standards Institution) (2001)

28   CFCs, HCFCs *and halons: Professional and practical guidance on substances which deplete the ozone layer* CIBSE GN1 (London: Chartered Institution of Building Services Engineers) (1993)

29   *Phase-out of* CFCs *and* HCFCs*: options for owners and operators of air conditioning systems* BRE Information Paper IP 14/95 (London: Construction Research Communications) (1995)

30   *Oversized cooling and pumping plant* BSRIA GN 13/97 (Bracknell: Building Services Research and Information Association) (1997)

31   *Code for lighting* (London: Chartered Institution of Building Services Engineers) (2002)

32   *Energy efficient lighting — a guide for installers* Good Practice Guide GPG 199 (Action Energy) (1996) (www.action energy.org.uk)

33   *Lamp guide* (London: Lighting Industry Federation) (1994)

34   *Lamp converting to compact fluorescent lighting — a refurbishment guide* Good Practice Guide GPG 159 (Action Energy) (1995) (www.actionenergy.org.uk)

---

* Requirements may differ in Scotland[17] and Northern Ireland[18]

35 *Electric lighting controls — a guide for designers, installers and users* Good Practice Guide GPG 160 (Action Energy) (1997) (www.actionenergy.org.uk)

36 *Oversized heating plant* BSRIA GN 12/97 (Bracknell: Building Services Research and Information Association) (1997)

37 *Public health engineering* CIBSE Guide G (London: Chartered Institution of Building Services Engineers) (1999)

38 *Reference data* CIBSE Guide C (London: Chartered Institution of Building Services Engineers) (2001)

39 *Variable speed drive on a boiler fan* Good Practice Case Study GPCS 35 (Action Energy) (1991) (www.actionenergy.org.uk)

40 *Steam* Fuel Efficiency Booklet FEB 2 (Action Energy) (1993) (www.actionenergy.org.uk)

41 *Combined heat and power in buildings* CIBSE AM12 (London: Chartered Institution of Building Services Engineers) (1998)

42 *Small scale combined heat and power for buildings* Good Practice Guide GPG 176 (Action Energy) (1996) (www.action energy.org.uk)

43 *Guidance notes for the implementation of small scale combined heat and power* Good Practice Guide GPG 1 (Action Energy) (1993) (www.actionenergy.org.uk)

44 *Energy efficiency in offices — a technical guide for owners and single tenants* Energy Consumption Guide ECG 19 (Action Energy) (1997) (www.actionenergy.org.uk)

45 *Purchasing policy for higher efficiency motors* Good Practice Case Study GPCS 222 (Action Energy) (1994) (www.action energy.org.uk)

46 *The repair of induction motors — best practices to maintain energy efficiency* AEMT Good Practice Guide (Nottingham: Association of Electrical and Mechanical Trades)

47 *Transportation systems in buildings* CIBSE Guide D (London: Chartered Institution of Building Services Engineers) (2000)

48 *Managing energy use. Minimising running costs of office equipment and related air-conditioning* Good Practice Guide GPG 118 (Action Energy) (1997) (www.actionenergy.org.uk)

49 *Energy efficiency in offices — small power loads* Energy Consumption Guide ECG 35 (Action Energy) (1993) (www.actionenergy.org.uk)

Bibliography

Bordass W T et al. Special Issue on Post Occupancy Evaluation, *Building Research and Information* 29 (2) (March – April 2001)

Energy management priorities — a self assessment tool Good Practice Guide GPG 306 (Action Energy) (2001) (www.actionenergy.org.uk)

Detecting energy waste — a guide for energy audits and surveys in the government estate Good Practice Guide GPG 311 (Action Energy) (2002) (www.actionenergy.org.uk)

Toolkit for building operation audits BSRIA AG 13/2000 (Bracknell: Building Services Research and Information Association) (2000)

Controlling energy use in buildings General Information Report GIR 47 (Action Energy) (1997) (www.actionenergy.org.uk)

Undertaking an industrial energy survey General Information Report GPG 316 (Action Energy) (2002) (www.actionenergy.org.uk)

Is your energy use under control? A practical guide to assessment and action General Information Report GPG 136 (Action Energy) (1994) (www.actionenergy.org.uk)

Choosing an energy efficiency consultant, what is energy consultancy and how can it benefit you FL89 (Action Energy) (2002) (www.actionenergy.org.uk)

Reviewing energy management General Information Report GIR 13 (Action Energy) (1993) (www.actionenergy.org.uk)

Energy efficiency in the workplace — A guide for managers and staff Good Practice Guide GPG 133 (Action Energy) (1994) (www.action energy.org.uk)

Educated energy management (London: E and F N Spon) (1991)

BS 7386: 1997: *Specification for draughtstrips for the draught control of existing doors and windows in housing (including test methods)* (London: British Standards Institution) (1997)

Farrar C H *Heat losses through ground floors* BRE Digest 145 (London: Construction Research Communications) (1972)

Choosing between cavity, internal and external wall insulation GG5 (London: Construction Research Communications)

Cavity insulation BRE Digest 236 (London: Construction Research Communications)

Industrial building refurbishments: opportunities for energy efficiency BRE Information Paper IP 2/93 (London: Construction Research Communications) (1993)

Thermal insulation: avoiding risks BRE Report BR262 (London: Construction Research Communications) (2001)

Pearson C and Barnard N *Guidance and standard specification for thermal imaging of non-electrical installations* BSRIA FMS 6/00 (Bracknell: Building Services Research and Information Association) (2000)

Pike P G *BEMS performance testing* BSRIA AG 2/94 (Bracknell: Building Services Research and Information Association) (1994)

Heat rejection systems — some methods and their operating costs BSRIA TA 1/93 (Bracknell: Building Services Research and Information Association) (1993)

Kew J *Heat pumps for building services* BSRIA TN 8/85 (Bracknell: Building Services Research and Information Association) (1985)

Armstrong J *Fault finding procedures in the building services industry* BSRIA TN 12/86 (Bracknell: Building Services Research and Information Association) (1986)

Lighting controls and daylight use BRE Digest 272 (London: Construction Research Communications)

Invest to save? Financial appraisal of energy efficiency measures across the government estate Good Practice Guide GPG 312 (Action Energy) (2002) (www.actionenergy.org.uk)

Maintaining the momentum, sustaining energy management Good Practice Guide GPG 251 (Action Energy) (1999) (www.actionenergy.org.uk)

Managing and motivating staff to save energy Good Practice Guide GPG 84 (Action Energy) (1993) (www.actionenergy.org.uk)

Marketing energy efficiency — raising staff awareness Good Practice Guide GPG 172 (Action Energy) (1999) (www.actionenergy.org.uk)

A strategic approach to energy and environmental management Good Practice Guide GPG 200 (Action Energy) (1996) (www.actionenergy.org.uk)

Organising energy management — a corporate approach Good Practice Guide GPG 119 (Action Energy) (1996) (www.actionenergy.org.uk)

Developing an effective energy policy Good Practice Guide GPG 186 (Action Energy) (1996) (www.actionenergy.org.uk)

Managing people, managing energy Good Practice Guide GPG 235 (Action Energy) (1998) (www.actionenergy.org.uk)

Energy Management Training Good Practice Guide GPG 85 (Action Energy) (1994) (www.actionenergy.org.uk)

Appendix 18.A1: Site survey checklist

Building fabric

As a retrofit measure, major energy saving building fabric measures are best applied when repairing or refurbishing the fabric. Major alterations are usually difficult to justify on energy saving grounds alone due to high capital costs and the resultant extended paybacks. Consequently, these projects often go ahead for other reasons, e.g. deterioration of existing fabric. When this is the case, it presents an opportunity to significantly improve the fabric energy efficiency in which case paybacks should be related to the marginal cost of including a superior specification. See section 4 and FEB 16[19].

Identifying problems

Problems can be identified by the following methods:

- *Thermography*: detects damaged or missing insulation and air leakage by identifying areas of fabric with high temperature in winter.
- *Building air pressure testing*: establishes the magnitude of infiltration leakage paths through the building fabric[20]; used in conjunction with smoke pencils or thermography, pressure testing can identify primary leakage paths.
- *Building simulation*: computer models are used to highlight major areas of heat loss and predict the effect of fabric changes on energy use.

Roofs

- Check the thickness of insulation above ceilings in pitched roof spaces. Areas may be found where insulation is missing or defective. Old, compact insulation may need to be upgraded.
- Installing a suspended ceiling beneath flat or pitched roofs could reduce the transmittance and the treated volume. Fitting a ceiling to a partitioned area to enclose a small treated volume within a much larger untreated building volume could be most cost-effective.

Note that additional ventilation, vapour barriers or other measures may be needed to prevent condensation in roof spaces. Insulation should not be allowed to obstruct ventilation, especially at the eaves of a roof. Services above an insulated ceiling may require protection against freezing.

Walls

- When considering cavity wall insulation, pay particular attention to the requirements for suitable materials and professional installation procedures.
- When considering internal dry lining or direct insulation of the outer faces of external walls or those between heated and unheated/cooled areas. Beware of the risk of condensation in the outer skin of an external wall with internal insulation.
- Identify problems of air infiltration through building openings, where services pass through walls or where dampers are left open unnecessarily.

Additional protection of services against condensation or frost damage may be needed.

Windows

- Examine the condition of windows for maintenance problems. Identify where work is needed to repair catches, replace broken panes, remove excess paint preventing closure, re-hang or replace distorted frames.
- Note the use of windows by occupants, who may need to be reminded of the good housekeeping value of keeping windows closed to minimise the space heating or air conditioning loads. Open windows during mild spells in the heating season can indicate that heating control is inadequate.

● indicates issue for consideration; ☐ indicates measure for action

Doors

- Examine the condition of doors for maintenance problems such as faulty catches or automatic closers, and misaligned or seriously distorted frames needing re-hanging or replacement.
- Consider providing personnel access doors to avoid frequent use of large vehicle access shutters or doors.

Floors

- Note problems of air infiltration under or through suspended or ventilated floors. Internal floor covering can be effective, provided the floor structure does not suffer adversely when ventilation is restricted.

Draught proofing

Draught proofing is often one of the most cost effective means of improving building fabric since uncontrolled air infiltration can be a cause of significant heat loss from buildings, particularly those that are well insulated.

External doors and entrances:

- ☐ Add draught lobbies to busy entrances, although capital cost may be high.
- ☐ Install weather stripping on doors or replace, if worn or broken.
- ☐ Use automatic door-closers on external doors, or entrances to unconditioned or unheated spaces.
- ☐ Provide signs and instructions for the operation of doors; and a reminder to keep closed.
- ☐ Consider using expandable entrance enclosures to connect to the back of delivery vehicles, or use automatic doors.
- ☐ Where there is regular traffic, consider using fast acting automatic doors, which give a pay back period of around two years[21].
- ☐ A simple and cheap option for factory doors is to use transparent plastic curtains which research indicates can reduce heat loss through factory doors by up to 50%[21].
- ☐ Consider making delivery entrances smaller.

Windows and skylights:

- ☐ Upgrade windows by repairing window furniture, seals, and 'ventilators'.
- ☐ Install weather stripping or replace if worn or broken; this gives a payback of under two years.
- ☐ Seal gaps between window frames and walls.
- ☐ Provide signs and instructions on how to use the windows, window furniture and ventilators, e.g. keep windows closed while the building is being heated or cooled.

Walls and roofs:

- ☐ Seal or draught proof at exterior joints, e.g. between walls and roof, and wall panels.
- ☐ Seal building openings at service penetrations, e.g. for piping and electrical conduits.
- ☐ Fit external covers or flaps to the outside air connections of window and wall fans, and unit air conditioners, thereby preventing infiltration when they are not in use.

Insulation

Upgrading insulation levels reduces heat loss and improves energy efficiency. FEB 16[19] contains methods of calculating the most economic thickness of insulation. Careful consideration should be given to avoiding any risk of interstitial condensation[22], particularly in the case of existing composite wall structures which already incorporate some insulation. Options are shown below.

Wall insulation

☐ Install external wall insulation: low risk of thermal bridges occurring, although the visual impact is significant. It is often expensive due to installation requirements e.g. scaffolding.

☐ Add internal wall insulation: no effect on the external appearance, but building use will be disrupted and there is a danger of thermal bridging at the junctions of building elements, e.g. where a floor slab penetrates an external wall.

☐ Install cavity wall insulation: often a more cost effective measure than internal or external insulation, with a payback of around 3–5 years; it also causes less disruption to building use. It is only possible where there is a suitable cavity, there is no danger of interstitial condensation and there is no risk of damp penetration due to driving rain.

Roof insulation

☐ Add insulation within the roof cavity (cold roof): can be very cost-effective often with paybacks under 3 years, although for flat roofs there is a danger of condensation.

☐ Apply insulation above the structure (warm roof): preferred option where there is no roof cavity. Careful detailing is necessary to avoid moisture penetration.

Floor insulation

☐ Add insulation to the exposed surfaces of floors, e.g. where the first floor overhangs the floor below, or is over unheated or unconditioned floors. Ground floor insulation is most appropriate when the floor is renewed.

Windows

☐ Specify double or triple glazing for replacement windows and consider low emissivity glass and multiple glass combinations (see section 4).

☐ Consider selective films/coatings on existing glazing: can help minimise solar gains (to avoid cooling loads) and reduce radiative heat loss, although they may have an adverse effect on daylighting levels.

☐ Replace existing clear glazing with special solar control glazing where solar gain is likely to cause overheating.

☐ Reduce the glazed area (if considered excessive) without compromising daylighting levels.

☐ Fit external or mid-pane shading devices to eliminate unwanted solar gains in the summer.

☐ Use internal shading to reduce glare, although this is unlikely to reduce solar gains significantly.

Controls

Upgrading controls is often the single biggest improvement that can be made to enhance the energy efficiency of existing buildings. Modern microprocessor controls are more accurate and more flexible, giving closer control and greater functionality and therefore better comfort conditions and lower running costs. Even well-designed building services will perform badly if controls are inadequate, incorrectly installed or misunderstood by the building operators. Many problems with building services can be traced back to poor control of the systems. Overall control strategies should always be considered when upgrading specific controls or diagnosing building services problems since they can sometimes be the root cause of symptoms that appear unrelated. Control strategies are covered in section 6 and maintenance issues are covered in section 17.

Diagnosing control faults

A number of studies have indicated common control problems that can reduce performance and increase energy consumption, with systems either defaulting to on when they could have been off, or operating inefficiently. The following can cause problems.

Excessive operation

Excessive operation occurs where whole-building systems are brought on to service small loads, for example:

● when the whole chilled water system is brought on to service a few small machine rooms

● when heating (or most wastefully air conditioning) is brought on early, or left on overnight, to avoid a few rooms otherwise being uncomfortable for out-of-hours use.

Demand-based control systems are the most energy efficient. However, where small areas are required frequently for out-of-hours use, plant dedicated to that area can be more economic to operate.

Unwanted operation

Unwanted operation is when systems run long hours, or constantly, due to:

● controls being over-ridden for a short-term purpose and not reset

● automatic controls (e.g. frost thermostats) bringing on systems unnecessarily due to poor settings or calibration, or incorrect interlocks

● time controls getting out of phase after a power failure.

'User-friendly' overrides are essential, normally providing a fixed period of operation.

Improving failure detection

Include a few diagnostic checks, either regular manual checks or within the BMS, that will identify major departures of important items of plant from the design intent and report exceptions. These checks need tailoring to the building in question, but will commonly include:

● monitoring daily hours run by major items of plant during periods when they should be off

● identifying simultaneous operation of potentially conflicting items of plant, e.g. chillers and heat recovery systems

● monitoring efficiencies of heat recovery devices and creating an alarm if the actual to anticipated efficiency in operation is less than, say, 65%

● raising an alarm if the supply air temperature for ventilation plant used for night cooling is more than say 3 K warmer than the outside air temperature.

Automatic controls should not be put forward as a solution to all the deficiencies of buildings or systems. Neither should they be seen as relieving staff of responsibility for controlling energy use. To be most effective, controls must be easy to understand and convenient to the user. Often a simple control system that is understood will be more effective than a complex system that is left to 'fend for itself', see CIBSE Guide H[23].

Time control

● Establish the precise pattern of occupancy in the areas served by a particular system; continuous, fixed daily or weekly pattern, highly variable, planned in advance, differences between areas on common system. Note any specific conditions to be maintained during or outside occupancy.

● Examine the controller in use for its suitability. A sufficient number and flexibility of on/off events must be available for different start/stop times or day omission. Complexity should not be such that use is discouraged or that mistakes in settings are common. Extension timers can be provided for occasional occupancy outside normal hours. Night set-back of space heating can be practised where fully intermittent operation is not acceptable.

● Ensure that controls are suitably located for the intended users. Local interval timers must be convenient for easy access; other controls may best be grouped in a central location to encourage full and proper use.

- Check the settings of the controller and observe the response of the system. Recordings of temperature over a day or a week can be used to identify where heating control settings should be changed.

- Identify where additional time controls are needed to meet the requirements of different areas on a common system.

Temperature control

- Establish the temperature requirements of each zone during and outside occupancy taking account of seasonal variations in comfort conditions. Review high/low limit and control settings.

- Consider whether the parameters measured provide satisfactory temperature control. Dry bulb/wet bulb/radiant temperature, solar/wind effects, water flow or storage temperature and duct air temperature are among the parameters that may need to be considered.

- Check that the location of sensors is representative of conditions. Space temperature sensors should be in a position not unduly influenced by direct heat gains or draughts but allowing free air circulation. 'Black-bulb' sensors for radiant heating should be located within line of sight of the heat source. Ensure that immersion, duct and surface sensors are fitted securely and identify where sensors and thermostats need additional protection to prevent tampering or accidental disturbance.

- Check that sensors have an appropriate range and resolution. Small errors can be significant, e.g. where the inside/outside temperature difference is small.

- Consider the suitability of the control type. Basic on/off control might be adequate. Some systems need a combination of proportional, integral and derivative control able to vary the rate of response to prevent overshoot and maintain stability.

- Check the settings and operation of the controls. Ensure that valves and dampers are free to operate. Compensating and reset controls may need to be checked over a range of ambient conditions. Recordings of temperature can assist in identifying where settings or controls need to be changed.

- Identify where additional controls are needed for central plant or complete zones. Heating circuit temperatures can be varied using a weather compensator to control boilers directly in response to outside temperature.

- Check the location and setting of the frost/low limit thermostat. For an internal location, a low-limit value of 10 ºC is normal. In a well insulated building the first stage of protection may only require pumps to be operated if circulation can prevent water circuits from freezing even without heat input.

Capacity control

- Ensure plant is operated in such a way as to minimise standing losses associated with less efficient part-load operation or excessive cycling. Output has to be controlled to match the load, whether steady or variable.

- Compare the plant capacity with the anticipated load range. A single plant item which is grossly oversized may be suitable for de-rating to prevent excessive cycling. Multiple plant with different ratings might permit a more appropriate combination of plant to be operated. Smoothing of peak loads may avoid the need to bring extra plant into operation.

- Examine the methods for controlling the number of plant items on-line.

- Consider the needs for standby plant. Complete isolation might be possible.

Building management systems

Introducing building management systems (BMS) as a retrofit measure can be a good way of upgrading the overall control strategy and improving both energy efficiency and comfort. A BMS can provide additional management benefits through improved monitoring of comfort conditions, plant operation and energy consumption (see section 6). Issues for introducing a BMS are as follows:

- Retrofitting a BMS can be expensive; payback periods are widely variable dependent upon how efficiently the plant has been operated but can be in excess of 5 years based on energy savings alone. The overall viability of BMS should take into account the additional benefits and wider management implications, such as gaining full control over large and complex buildings or large multi-building sites. Many buildings cannot be run effectively and efficiently without a BMS.

- The building user must be prepared to employ and train staff to operate the BMS and hence utilise all its facilities. If this aspect is neglected, poor performance and even complete failure of systems can result. Where site staff are not available to operate a BMS, off-site bureau services can be very cost-effective.

- A BMS is not a panacea for all ills and will not compensate for badly designed or badly maintained plant. However, a BMS can be used to identify poor design, operation and maintenance.

- Regularly review systems to ensure that they are being used effectively. Even a well installed and commissioned BMS can easily fall into misuse leading to a rise in energy consumption, if appropriate time is not spent in managing the system.

- Excessive alarms and monitoring can result in an information overload with so much information being generated by the BMS that little is actioned and the key information is hidden.

Time controls

- ☐ Ensure all plant turns off when there is no demand.

- ☐ Set time switches in relation to occupancy and use of the service. Where suitable, introduce time switches on energy using equipment, e.g. vending machines (some items may need power during standby periods).

- ☐ Upgrade major time controls to optimum start/stop controls and ensure that existing optimisers are actually minimising start up periods.

- ☐ Where override facilities are introduced to allow extensions to the occupancy period, these should always be self-resetting, e.g. a push button, to override the time controls for a preset fixed period of time. Incorporate an indication lamp to show that the system has been overridden, thereby indicating misuse.

Plant capacity controls

- ☐ Introduce sequence controls where appropriate e.g. modular boilers or chillers, and check that the sequence selection of boilers and chillers provides a minimum output matched to the load.

- ☐ Check that plant is not cycling excessively as this can reduce performance. Frequent cycling can normally be prevented using standard controls (see 10.3.2.1). Boiler-delay or anti-dry-cycling controls for heating systems should be avoided.

- ☐ Introduce variable speed drives where appropriate for central plant fans and pumps to minimise the power required during periods of low demand (see 11.2).

Temperature controls

- ☐ Check for overheating or over cooling and investigate the underlying reasons. Consider gradually lowering the flow temperature until overheating ceases.

- ☐ If the building overheats in some areas in order to maintain design conditions elsewhere, check the balance of the system and ensure that the circuit temperature is suitable for the emitter characteristic.

- ☐ Provide separately compensated zones where structure, orientation (solar gain), occupation, or emitters have different characteristics.

- [ ] Where small areas have different uses, consider time controlled local zone valves.
- [ ] Consider compensation of chilled water systems via reset of chillers.
- [ ] Consider separate provision of cooling (chilled water or DX) for de-humidification duties, rather than cooling all chilled water systems via reset central chillers.
- [ ] Check that local temperature controls are able to meet the needs of the staff and can respond to changes in occupancy etc.
- [ ] Consider varying set point temperatures depending upon external conditions. Use a fixed differential between inside and outside air temperature, e.g. a summer set point of say 3 K below external temperature.

Terminal unit controls

- [ ] Ensure settings are maintained at the lowest acceptable level for heating requirements, and the highest acceptable level for cooling requirements.
- [ ] Check the stability of terminal unit/controls: instability may be due to the proportional band being too narrow (adjust controls) or to incorrect selection of the unit and/or the controls (seek specialist advice).

Integrating the controls

(a)   Zoning arrangements

Services are often required at different times and levels (e.g. temperature or illuminance) in different areas of a building. Systems should be zoned according to occupancy, the layout of the services, building aspect and use so that each zone can be separately controlled. Options for zoning are as follows:

- [ ] Provide separately compensated zones where structure, orientation (solar gain), occupation or emitters have different characteristics.
- [ ] Consider time-controlled local zone valves where small areas have different uses.
- [ ] Zone light switches and automatic lighting controls, e.g. reset and/or photoelectric controls, in relation to daylighting and occupancy patterns.
- [ ] Consider decentralising primary cooling and heat generating plant to match the needs of each zone.

(b)   Simultaneous heating and cooling

- [ ] Set heating system and local controls correctly to avoid unauthorised local overrides by occupants, e.g. windows being opened to reduce the excess heating temperatures.
- [ ] Ensure that there is a dead band between heating and cooling.
- [ ] Ensure that, in addition to a dead band, P+I controllers have additional methods to prevent simultaneous heating and cooling, such as software or hardwired interlocks.
- [ ] Automatically reset the cold air supply temperature of reheat systems (other than VAV) to the highest to satisfy the zone requiring the coolest air. This minimises the effects of simultaneous heating and cooling in systems that supply more than one zone and use reheating for temperature control.
- [ ] Automatically reset the preheated air supply temperature in re-cool systems to the lowest to satisfy the zone requiring the warmest air. This minimises the effects of simultaneous heating and cooling in systems that supply more than one zone and use re-cooling for temperature control.
- [ ] Multi-zone dual duct systems will require the control described above for both the hot deck and the cold deck. Where simultaneous heating and cooling is unavoidable, either reclaimed heat or free cooling should be used wherever possible.
- [ ] Fully integrate the air conditioning with other systems within the building to minimise energy consumption. Attempts are sometimes made, on the grounds of energy efficiency, to shut down perimeter heating before the variable volume system is allowed to increase the cooling input. This may result in a better theoretical energy balance, but the occupants will often complain about cold down draughts from the windows. Setting the compensated circuit to the minimum temperature to avoid cold down draughts will be more satisfactory than turning the circuit off.

Ventilation and air conditioning

Ventilation is often responsible for the largest energy loss in well-insulated buildings. It therefore offers significant scope for retrofit energy saving measures. Further detail on ventilation issues is available in section 7. Where the measures alter the overall ventilation strategy or require a significant level of design, reference should be made to section 4.

- Establish the required conditions for the space(s) being served, including operational times, air change rates, dry-bulb temperature and relative humidity. It may be found that some conditioning processes are no longer necessary.
- Examine the installed plant to establish the type of system, the forms of energy used, the processes performed and the condition of the components.
- Estimate the heating/cooling loads, see CIBSE Guide A[9], taking account of incidental gains.
- In speculative developments in particular, compare the actual loads with those specified by the developer. Systems designed and commissioned for inappropriate loads may need fundamental reappraisal.
- With major systems, measure air volume flow rates, i.e. supply, extract, exhaust, recirculation and fresh air. Relate the measured values to building volume to determine air change rates and calculate the proportion of fresh air used. Compare with the actual requirements of occupancy.
- Measure building air conditions in terms of dry-bulb temperature and relative humidity and compare with requirements. Where anomalies are found, measure air conditions at terminal supplies and/or air extracts.
- For detailed surveys of major systems check air conditions at each stage of the air conditioning process, to ensure that excessive cooling or heating does not occur at any intermediate stage. Plotting the processes on a psychometric chart will assist in understanding them.
- Ensure that the volume of air handled is the minimum necessary to meet all occupancy and statutory requirements while maintaining effective operation of the system. Savings can be made in fan power and in heating/cooling a reduced volume. This might be achieved by introducing variable speed drives.
- Examine occupancy patterns and ensure that the system is switched off entirely whenever possible, e.g. overnight, at weekends or seasonally.
- Check the balance between supply and extract volumes. Pressurisation of a space results in a loss of treated air. A negative pressure can lead to infiltration of untreated air. Ensure that maximum permissible use is made of recirculated air or free cooling with external air as appropriate. Over-night/early-morning pre-cooling with untreated external air might be possible for further free cooling.
- Identify opportunities for recovering heat from exhaust air, particularly if recirculation is not possible. Ensure that heat recovery systems involving pumped circuits, heat wheels or other operating costs are only operated when economic.
- Review control arrangements and settings to ensure that controls allow maximum acceptable temperature with minimum cooling in summer and minimum acceptable temperature with minimum heating in winter. Check also that control interlocks are organised so that plant items do not run when there is no demand, i.e. not always to fixed schedules.
- Check that dehumidification is only operated when absolutely necessary in summer, since it involves cooling and subsequent reheating. This can be assisted by allowing relative humidity to rise to the maximum acceptable level; up to 70% should not cause discomfort in most environments.
- Ensure that heating/electricity loads are kept to a minimum by avoiding humidification whenever possible in winter.

- Ensure that terminals, grilles, diffusers and induction nozzles are clean and free from obstruction.
- Consider opportunities to reduce the temperature of perimeter heating circuits used to meet fabric heat loss and prevent cold downdraughts, and increase the temperature of chilled water circulation to terminal or induction units required to meet the cooling load.
- Ensure that separate heating/cooling units and humidifying/dehumidifying units or systems are not allowed to work in opposition in treated spaces.

Heat recovery systems

Use heating/cooling energy that would otherwise be rejected to waste.

- Consider air-to-air heat recovery devices which transfer sensible heat (or, depending on the device, total heat) from the exhaust air stream to the fresh air inlet. Several devices are available, the most common being run-around coils, plate heat exchangers and thermal wheels[24]. See section 4.2.5.5.
- Consider preheating incoming air through atria, conservatories, roof spaces etc. or using waste heat from air-cooled condensers, e.g. computer rooms.
- Check that any additional electrical energy input required, e.g. fan power to overcome resistance of heat exchangers or coils, does not negate the energy saved, bearing in mind that it uses electricity rather than the fossil fuel energy. Note that extra fan power is needed whenever the system is in operation, although the degree of heat recovery varies throughout the year. Include the additional fan or pump running costs when calculating the viability of the scheme.
- Consider air re-circulation, which is essentially a form of heat recovery. The effectiveness is equal to the re-circulation percentage, e.g. 10% fresh air gives a 90% heat recovery effectiveness.

Natural ventilation

The potential measures for natural ventilation are:

- [ ] Check that window ventilation systems are readily usable and operate correctly.
- [ ] Ensure natural ventilation is not obstructed by partitions.
- [ ] Ensure that heat and smoke relief vents are closed in winter.
- [ ] Ensure hot air is re-circulated from high level if stratification occurs during heating.
- [ ] Consider the introduction of cooling using external air at night.

Mixed-mode

Operation can be more energy efficient approach than full air conditioning. However, it needs to be introduced with care, and the overall ventilation strategy needs to be reassessed beforehand (see section 4).

- [ ] For changeover mixed mode, turn the air conditioning system off in the mid-season, opening windows for ventilation and cooling. Ensure that occupants understand when these various modes are in operation to avoid windows being opened when the air conditioning is on.
- [ ] Zoned mixed mode also provides a retrofit option for reducing mechanical ventilation by only serving the areas that actually require air conditioning.

Mechanical ventilation and air conditioning

The general aim should be to reduce the need for ventilation and cooling, commensurate with the required environmental conditions (see section 4). Where air conditioning is essential, ensure that it operates efficiently. Possible measures for mechanical ventilation and air conditioning are:

- [ ] Ensure plant is not oversized; BSRIA GN11/97[25] covers the monitoring, assessment and remedial action that should be taken where plant is likely to be oversized.
- [ ] Check that the minimum necessary air change rates are maintained.
- [ ] Consider switching off humidifiers when minimum humidity is not critical.
- [ ] Simultaneous heating and cooling should not occur except where close humidity control is essential.
- [ ] Check controls are set so that higher space temperature can be used in summer and lower space temperatures in winter.
- [ ] Ensure the cooling system is shut down in winter, when there are no cooling loads.
- [ ] Ensure heating is shut down whenever there are no heating loads, especially where internal heat gains are such that heating plant operation is unnecessary.
- [ ] Perimeter heating should be operated at the lowest temperature consistent with eliminating down draught.
- [ ] Fans, particularly those for toilet ventilation systems, should be switched off when the building is unoccupied. Where possible, they should operate in response to demand, e.g. controlled by presence detectors.
- [ ] Unless close control of humidity is required, allow the relative humidity to vary from 40% to 65%. Occasionally, over dry air can cause problems with static electricity and with respiration.
- [ ] Turn off reheat in all areas during the summer except where process or equipment requirements necessitate close humidity control.
- [ ] Readjust and rebalance systems to minimise over cooling and overheating which results from poor zoning, poor distribution, improper location of controls, or improper control.
- [ ] Review motor sizing and consider introducing variable speed drives to modulate fan speeds where loads vary significantly.
- [ ] Air curtains generally use more energy than they save and are not an efficient means of controlling heat loss through large openings.
- [ ] Ensure maximum use is made of re-circulated air and fresh air for 'free' cooling as appropriate. Introduce variable re-circulation where appropriate; using return air that retains an element of heating/cooling is the best form of energy recovery. Using automatic variable air dampers to control the amount of fresh air drawn into the system minimises the amount of air to be heated/cooled and consequently reduces energy consumed.
- [ ] Minimise air leakage from ductwork to prevent wasting fan power and the heating/cooling content of treated air; this also prevents unwanted heat gains/losses to other areas.
- [ ] Insulating ductwork is particularly important where treated air ducts pass externally or through unconditioned spaces[26,27]. FEB 8[26] provides a means of estimating the most economic thickness of insulation.

Constant volume systems

A reappraisal of existing ventilation requirements can result in reduced ventilation rates, and hence a downsizing of motors and fans. Reducing the air volume handled by the fan saves energy, taking care to ensure that poor air distribution or fan instability does not result. Limiting the temperature range of the supply air will also save energy. Re-commissioning of central-fan air volumes should be by changing pulleys to change the fan speed, rather than by closing dampers. Variable speed fan drives can often be used instead of overall system regulation dampers (see section 11).

Single zone systems

Single zone systems have a separate air handling plant for each zone and temperature control is achieved by means of a sensor situated within the controlled space.

- [ ] Reduce the air volume handled by the fan where appropriate.

☐ Switch off humidifiers when minimum humidity is not critical, or set humidity control to a maximum of 40%, as appropriate.

☐ Avoid simultaneous heating and cooling except where de-humidification is essential.

☐ Adjust or modify the control system so that higher space temperature can be used in summer and lower space temperatures in winter.

☐ Convert to variable air volume where practicable.

Multi-zone terminal re-heat systems

These systems use a single air handling plant to meet the requirements of several zones simultaneously. They provide air at a pre-determined temperature to air zones, where secondary terminal re-heaters raise the supply air temperature to suit space load requirements. Each zone therefore receives its own individually controlled air supply.

☐ Reduce the supply air volume where appropriate.

☐ Shut off reheat coils in summer, and raise the supply air temperature, as necessary.

☐ Install controls that ensure the control of common heating and cooling coils is based on the zone requiring the greatest load. This ensures that, while sufficient capacity is available for temperature control, excessive capacity is avoided.

☐ Convert to a variable air volume system where practicable, or heating and cooling coils for each zone.

Dual duct systems

Dual duct systems provide space temperature control by mixing the two air streams; one hot, one cold.

☐ Reduce air volume flow to all mixing boxes to the minimum acceptable level.

☐ Lower the hot deck temperature.

☐ Raise the cold deck temperature.

☐ Shut down the cooling system in winter when there are no cooling loads. Operate hot deck as a single duct system.

☐ Shut down heating system in summer when there are no heating loads. Operate cold deck as a single duct system.

☐ Convert to a VAV dual duct system; this should provide significant energy savings.

Induction systems

☐ Re-balance the system if the orifices have become enlarged due to cleaning.

☐ Reset the primary air heating and secondary chilled water temperatures according to load and season.

☐ Consider upgrading central plant and induction unit controls.

☐ Investigate the possibility of conversion of 2-pipe changeover and 3-pipe systems to 4-pipe operation to minimise change-over and mixing losses.

Room fan coil systems

☐ Reduce air volumes to the minimum acceptable level.

☐ Provide control interlocks between heating and cooling systems at each unit and within each zone to prevent simultaneous use.

☐ Convert zoned 2-pipe and 3-pipe systems to central 4-pipe systems to minimise change-over and mixing losses.

Variable air volume systems

☐ Use variable speed drives to control the air volume, rather than inlet guide vanes.

☐ Ensure that the static pressure sensor is located correctly so that the air volume reduces in relation to demand.

☐ Set terminal re-heat to operate only when the VAV terminal has turned down to the minimum amount for reasonable air distribution.

☐ Ensure that any perimeter heating is operated at the lowest temperature consistent with eliminating down draught.

☐ Automatically reset supply air temperature, where appropriate, to suit heating and cooling requirements.

Self-contained systems

These systems include unitary air conditioning, unitary heat-pumps and room-unit systems.

☐ Provide control interlocks between heating and cooling systems at each unit and within each zone to prevent simultaneous use.

☐ Replace old existing units with modern units or heat pumps with a higher efficiency rating.

☐ Improve local user controls to enable operation to match local requirements.

☐ Provide centralised automatic stop/start control (with manual over-ride) of multiple units.

☐ Ensure units operate only in occupied zones.

Industrial ventilation systems

☐ Introduce de-stratification fans where the upper part of the space is overheating.

☐ Use localised extraction for equipment emitting pollutants (e.g. welding, paint spraying etc.) in order to minimise ventilation losses.

☐ Improve hood design to reduce quantity of air handled and consider using unheated local outdoor make-up.

☐ Use 'ball-blankets' etc. on open tanks to limit evaporation and hence reduce ventilation rates.

Ventilation controls

Enthalpy control ('free' cooling)

Enthalpy control should be considered to reduce energy consumption. Enthalpy sensors detect the cooling capacity of the external air and then modulate the dampers to draw in more air than the basic fresh air requirement. This 'free' external cooling can significantly reduce the energy required for mechanical cooling (see sections 7.3.4 and 7.4.4).

Night cooling

Night cooling can be introduced as a retrofit measure to make use of the lower night-time air temperatures and the thermal capacity of the building. However, it is essential to ensure that the system is well controlled and fully integrated into the existing cooling and ventilation strategies. The cost of any energy used should be balanced against the cooling energy saved (see section 4.2.5).

Terminal and room controls

Good control of individual room and equipment controls is essential for the efficient use of energy. Options are as follows:

☐ Check the operation and settings of controls regularly, in order to maximise energy savings as well as comfort improvements.

☐ Upgrade to direct digital control (DDC) and electronic controls that can bring significant benefits; they are generally more accurate and responsive than older controls. An upgrade may be an opportunity to consider a more integrated control strategy, perhaps using a BMS.

Refrigeration

Where it is necessary in UK buildings, cooling is generally only required for parts of the year. However, plant is often found operating unnecessarily or inefficiently to supply small loads. There is significant energy saving potential in upgrading refrigeration systems and controls, or installing smaller plant to serve such loads.

Where measures alter the overall cooling strategy or require a significant level of design, reference should be made to section 8. Energy issues related to the maintenance of refrigeration systems are covered in section 17.

- Examine the demand for cooling and review the requirement for refrigeration. Cooling towers alone may sometimes cool water sufficiently to allow refrigeration plant to be by-passed other than on hot summer days. Uncooled ambient or recirculated air could be acceptable except when peak internal gains occur.

- Identify when plant can be shut down completely, e.g. during winter, overnight or at weekends.

- Consider potential for pre-cooling a building using an ice storage system using off-peak electricity.

- Investigate opportunities for heat recovery in the form of warm air or hot water. Suitable heat demands should be identified and matched to the quality and availability of recovered heat.

- Measure chiller plant water inlet and outlet temperatures and relate these to design data. Chilled water flow temperatures of between 5 °C and 9 °C are expected for most systems.

- Note compressor suction and discharge pressures where gauges are fitted and compare results with design specification. Refer to the manufacturer's data or refrigerant pressure–enthalpy diagrams to establish the expected suction and discharge pressure. Low suction pressures can indicate poor flow or lack of refrigerant. Faulty compressor valves can cause low discharge pressure. High discharge pressures may result from various faults including a fouled condenser or faulty cooling tower. Operation with pressure ratios or temperatures differing from the original design may result in significant loss of efficiency.

- Investigate the capacity/sequence controls for load matching. If several machines operate in parallel check that there are controls to avoid part-load operation and keep the minimum number of machines running on full load. Centrifugal and screw compressors in particular have poor part-load performance.

- Check maintenance procedures, including cleaning of heat transfer surfaces and water treatment. Common faults, notably fouling and faulty valve operation, can reduce performance progressively. This both restricts the available duty and increases running costs, perhaps by as much as 50% in some cases. A reported increase in oil consumption can usually be taken as a sure sign that fouling will be a growing problem.

- Check that water temperatures/refrigeration pressures/air temperatures across the condensers are correct and that performance is satisfactory. A water temperature rise of approximately 5 K is typical across a shell and tube condenser, with a leaving water temperature approaching 5 K below the condensing temperature. Air cooled condensers are usually designed to provide a condensing temperature in the range 10–20 K above entering air temperature.

- Check condenser maintenance procedures, including cleaning of heat transfer surfaces and screens/filters, water treatment and refrigerant leaks. A build-up of air and non-condensable gases can further increase condensing temperatures and reduce efficiency where maintenance is neglected.

- Check cooling tower performance by measuring inlet and outlet temperatures and ambient wet-bulb temperature. Relate these to specified requirements. The leaving water temperature should typically approach 5 K above the wet bulb temperature of the entering air.

- Check cooling tower maintenance procedures, including cleaning of screens and strainers, and water treatment, all vital to avoid bacterial growth. Poor sprays and damaged or missing baffles left unreplaced will reduce cooling efficiency and lead to longer plant running times.

- Investigate the balance of water flow through the condenser by-pass, if fitted. Too little flow through the condenser can

raise the condensing pressure. Restriction of flow through the bypass will increase the pumping head. It may be possible to check the bypass regulating valve setting against commissioning data as a first step.

Similar problems occur on cooling and heating distribution systems. Issues related to refrigeration distribution systems are therefore generally addressed within the heating section of this checklist.

Minimising cooling loads

☐ Reduce solar gains by using coated glasses, blinds and shading (see section 4). A cheaper alternative is to add reflective plastic coating to existing windows, although this may reduce daylight penetration and hence increase artificial lighting use.

☐ Reduce gains from lighting by using more efficient lighting and lighting controls. Air handling luminaires can reduce cooling loads by removing heat before it enters the occupied zone. This is particularly applicable in deep plan buildings where lighting is a major source of heat gain (see sections 7 and 9).

☐ Reduce gains from office equipment by using more energy efficient PCs, printers, photocopiers, etc. (see section 12).

Refrigeration plant

The use of refrigerants having zero ozone depletion potential may cause reductions in energy efficiency and refrigerant capacity. Information on strategies to respond to the need to phase out CFCs is given in CIBSE GN1[28] and BRE IP 14/95[29].

☐ Ensure that plant is not oversized; BSRIA GN13/97[30] covers the monitoring, assessment and remedial action that should be taken where plant is likely to be oversized.

☐ Replacement of inefficient compressors is unlikely to be cost effective unless there is very poor efficiency or excessive part load operation. However, a smaller machine to meet part load conditions could be cost effective. Very low loading of compressors should be avoided. As a rule of thumb, compressors should not operate at less than 50% of their full load.

☐ Check that the best form of heat rejection equipment has been chosen. A cooling tower will give a better coefficient of performance, but the extra costs of its maintenance, as well as the water and water treatment tend to mean that it is only economical for large systems.

☐ Consider the opportunity for recovering heat from refrigeration plant (see section 8.2.2).

☐ If waste heat is available, investigate the possibility of recovering or using it as the input for an absorption machine, see section 8.4.3.

☐ If an absorption machine is already being used, check to ensure all sources of waste heat are being employed.

☐ Check the condition and thickness of pipework insulation.

☐ Reduce condenser water temperature on water-cooled systems.

☐ Consider the possibility of using water direct from the cooling tower to give free cooling, thus avoiding the use of the chiller (see 8.1.3).

Refrigeration controls

☐ Ensure refrigeration plant is switched on only during periods when cooling will be required. Consider optimum start/stop or demand based controls where possible.

☐ Use efficient compressor capacity controls. Avoid hot gas by-pass and suction throttling where possible (see section 8.6.1). Consider use of variable speed drives for capacity control of compressors (see section 11.4).

☐ Ensure that the maximum acceptable chilled water flow temperature is maintained through automatic reset or direct compensation of the chiller. Significant savings can often be achieved during milder weather since the system can be operated at higher temperatures.

☐ Check sequence controls and sequence selection to ensure chillers are operating at maximum efficiency where possible, e.g. one compressor operating at full load will be more efficient than three operating at 33% load. In modular plants, the COP can sometimes increase at part load, since the reduced temperature lift can occasionally outweigh the compressor inefficiencies caused by unloading.

☐ Check that condenser fan and pump controls are operating correctly. Sequence control should also be applied for load matching. Some split system and packaged units are suitable for head pressure control to minimise condenser fan operation in winter.

☐ Check cooling tower for correct time, temperature and sequence control of fans and thermostatic control of frost protection.

☐ Variable-speed drives can be considered for reciprocating compressors; operation at half-speed can increase compression efficiency by 10%. This could replace stop/start or cylinder unloading control. Systems which control capacity by throttling gas flow to the compressor or allow gas to by-pass the condenser are extremely inefficient and should generally be avoided.

Lighting

In most buildings, lighting is the largest single end-use of electricity and, in offices, often the biggest single energy cost. The energy consumption of the lighting can be reduced by upgrading lamps, luminaires, ballasts and lighting controls. Where measures alter the overall lighting strategy or require a significant level of design, reference should be made to section 9. Energy issues related to lighting maintenance are covered in section 17. For further detail on lighting issues, refer to CIBSE *Code for lighting*[31].

A review of the lighting requirements and the methods of control should be undertaken. Investigations should then consider how to make the maximum use of natural light. Artificial lighting should be integrated with the available daylighting, using the most efficient appropriate source. The types of lighting system in use must be examined to identify where more efficient forms of lighting might be employed. The safety and comfort of occupants must be taken into account at all times. Lighting has a direct effect on productivity and so it is important to ensure that satisfactory conditions are maintained[31].

Requirements

Establish the specific or recommended requirements that determine the service to be provided, including any constraints on the types of fitting permitted:

- general illuminance or task lighting
- source: colour rendering, avoidance of flicker, avoidance of glare
- flameproof/weatherproof luminaires
- continuous or highly intermittent use
- aesthetic qualities of lighting or equipment

Requirements may have changed with the use of a building, e.g. greater use of personal computers and word processors requiring a lower level of background lighting. The standard service illuminances for various activities are given in Table 9.1.

Type and condition of the installation

- Note the types and ratings of the lamps, control gear and systems.
- Note the cleanliness of lamps, diffusers, reflectors, photocells and other surfaces which affect the light output. Mirror reflectors fitted in multiple-tube fluorescent fittings may allow one or more tubes to be removed while retaining a satisfactory level of illumination. Without cleaning, the illumination available in a dirty environment could easily fall by half over just two or three years.

- Assess the general level of maintenance, including planned lamp replacement. The light output of discharge lamps, e.g. fluorescent tubes and SON lamps, falls with use; at least 20% deterioration is likely over three years. After 2000 hours use the output from a fluorescent tube is likely to fall by about 2–4% per 1000 hours.

- Note any opportunities for greater use of daylight. Ensure that windows, rooflights and room surfaces are kept clean. Sources of daylight should not be obscured unless there are overriding reasons to prevent glare or control solar gain and heat loss.

Controls

- Lights should be switched off when not required; clearly labelled, accessible switches with reminder notices will encourage regular use. The addition of switches local to each user could also be considered as an aid to good housekeeping. Ideally, occupants should have to switch lights on manually but with some form of automatic control for switching off.

- Group switching should be avoided where possible or arranged so that as few luminaires as possible are left on unnecessarily, e.g. adjacent to windows or in unoccupied areas.

- Selective switching for security or cleaning purposes can provide an alternative level of background lighting.

Illuminance

Measure the illuminance at workplaces or other points of interest and compare with the specified requirements. The standard instrument used in lighting measurement is an illuminance meter. Measurements should be aimed at identifying opportunities for reducing the lighting load:

- Lamps and meters should be allowed to stabilise before readings are taken. Note that colour correction factors have to be applied to the readings from some meters.

- Specific point measurements are necessary for fixed workplaces.

- An average of as many points as are needed to give a representative value should be taken to assess general background lighting.

- Daylight should normally be excluded during measurements of the illuminance provided by artificial lighting.

- Measurements taken with daylight available can suggest where alternative switching arrangements could allow greater advantage to be taken of natural light, e.g. switching off perimeter lights.

Electric lighting

Identify where and when the contribution from electric lighting can satisfactorily be reduced:

- permanently, by removing or substituting alternative equipment
- occasionally, by selective switching to suit occupancy or available daylight
- by dimming
- by ensuring that lamps, luminaires, windows and building surfaces are kept clean and that discharge lamps are changed regularly.

Luminaire/lamp type

Explore the opportunities for changing the type of luminaire or lamp to reduce overall operating costs, particularly where systems are due for replacement or rewiring, or are used for extended periods. Allowance must be made for maintenance costs, including cleaning and lamp replacement. The reduced replacement frequency of long-life lamps is an important factor where access is difficult.

Typical schemes include:

- Replacement of tungsten filament lamps with fluorescent lamps; a 25 W rating compact fluorescent lamp gives a light output equal to that of a 100 W filament lamp and can sometimes be used directly in the same fitting.

• Replacement of older fluorescent tubes with 25 mm diameter energy saving tubes; restricted to switch-start circuits and those with certain electronic starters. A change of tube type is recommended to be carried out when existing lamps fail or are scheduled for replacement

• Installation of local task lighting allowing use of fewer luminaires for general background lighting.

• Introduction of high-frequency operation, normally 28–30 kHz, for fluorescent lighting circuits; high-frequency control gear is most economical in twin tube or four-tube circuits. High-frequency control gear also operates at a power factor near unity, unlike most conventional 50 Hz systems.

Luminaire refurbishment and replacement

Even installations that are only 5 to 10 years old, can benefit from refurbishment or replacement as the installation of modern equipment can often result in substantial energy savings and improved visual conditions[32]. Options are as follows:

☐ Ensure that the combination of light source, control gear and luminaire is the most efficient to meet the functional and aesthetic requirements of the system.

☐ Use modern luminaires with efficient reflectors; this allows fewer lamps or luminaires to be used to produce a given illuminance.

☐ Consider refurbishment before replacement. To assess viability, select a representative area. Clean and re-lamp the luminaires within the selected area, clean the wall and ceiling surfaces if possible and then measure the average illuminance over the working plane using a light meter (see CIBSE *Code for lighting*[31]). This will give a reliable indication of the initial illuminance that the existing equipment and installed load could achieve without further modification. Calculate the maintenance factor (see section 9.1.2) to arrive at the design maintained illuminance that would be achieved.

☐ Downrate lamps or remove lamps from multi-lamp fluorescent luminaires; this may be possible where illuminance is significantly higher than the design requirement. Where the illuminance is lower than design levels, appropriate measures should be taken to increase it to the design level, even though this may increase energy consumption.

☐ Replacement of luminaires may not always be cost-effective on the grounds of energy efficiency alone, although there are measures that can be taken to improve the overall performance of lighting systems. For example, the simple expedient of replacing old and yellowed prismatic or opal diffusers, linked with the measures listed below under *Lamp replacement*, can be very effective.

Task lighting

The use of local lighting (see section 9.1) at workstations with a lower background illuminance can provide an energy efficient alternative to a high general lighting level. Options are as follows:

☐ Lighting consumption can be reduced significantly due to the lower installed load and the close proximity of task lighting switches.

☐ Introducing localised lighting may be appropriate in some areas and allow a reduction in the general background lighting.

Specular reflectors

Specular reflectors are available to upgrade existing luminaires. Energy savings of 30–50% can be achieved, with payback periods of less than three years, due to the relatively low capital cost. However, not all luminaires are suitable for this modification, in particular because it can change the visual appearance of the space. The following simple checks should be carried out before proceeding with the complete installation:

☐ Measure the illuminance at several points over an area lit by an existing luminaire that has been cleaned and fitted with a new lamp.

☐ Repeat this procedure with the specular reflector fitted to the same or an identical luminaire.

☐ Calculate the average illuminance from each set of measurements. Check also that the distribution of illuminance has not changed to an extent that could adversely affect the uniformity of illuminance or the appearance of the space.

Lamp replacement

A change to a more efficient lamp type will reduce energy consumption. Some changes involve little or no capital expenditure, others may require the addition, or change, of control gear. Changing luminaire type and/or position will be less cost effective. A summary of lamp characteristics is shown in 9.3[33]. Options for lamp replacement are as follows.

Tungsten

☐ Replace tungsten lighting with compact fluorescent lamps (see section 9.3.4). A payback period of 3–5 years is possible, depending on use[34].

☐ Tungsten spotlights can also be replaced with low voltage (LV) tungsten–halogen systems. Although this requires some re-wiring and the installation of transformers, it can be cost effective in some circumstances, e.g. shops, museums etc. Tungsten–halogen lamps are susceptible to over voltage which can significantly shorten life. This is particularly important for LV tungsten–halogen lamps on a track system with a shared transformer which may have poor regulation when under loaded.

Fluorescent

Replace older 38 mm diameter fluorescent tubes with 26 mm diameter type with switch-start control gear. They cannot be used with starter-less circuits (see section 9.3.3)

Mercury and sodium

Replace high pressure mercury, MBF or MBTF lamps with high pressure sodium SON, or high pressure mercury MBI lamps. Energy savings are typically up to 20% with payback periods of less than three years (see section 9.3.5).

Control gear

☐ Replace standard glow-switch starters by electronic starters; 'soft' starting extends the economic life of the fluorescent tube, thus reducing maintenance costs. Energy savings can be 15–20%, with payback periods of 5–10 years (see section 9.4).

☐ Low-loss ballasts may be satisfactorily incorporated into new installations, or the installation of electronic high frequency control gear (with or without dimming) can achieve savings.

Lighting controls

The addition of lighting controls can be a highly cost effective retrofit measure, giving energy savings of 20–50% with payback periods of 2–5 years[35] (see section 9.5). Options for lighting controls are as follows:

☐ Self-contained luminaires, each with its own sensor and control, may be a more practical and economic solution than centralised control.

☐ Staff awareness campaigns may fail; control systems that are obtrusive are counter-productive and may even be sabotaged by the occupants. Minimise such problems by making staff aware of the purpose of the control system, how it works and how they can interact with it. Consult staff before introducing new controls.

☐ The following should be considered: presence detectors and/or delay timers for intermittently occupied areas; photocells where natural light is available and for outside lighting; timed controls to switch lighting off at the end of occupied periods; reset controls to allow individual lights to be switched back on locally, see section 9.5.

Heating

Heating is the single biggest component of the total delivered energy in most buildings and therefore provides significant potential for energy saving through upgrading primary plant, distribution systems and heating controls. Where measures alter the overall heating strategy or require a significant level of design, guidance is given in section 10. Energy issues related to heating maintenance are covered in section 17.

- Ensure that plant is not oversized; BSRIA GN12/97[36] covers the monitoring, assessment and remedial action that should be taken where plant is likely to be oversized.

Boiler plant

- Determine the type, rating and age of each boiler and burner and the types of fuel that can be used.

- Establish the annual fuel consumption of each boiler or group of boilers. This could be on a boilerhouse basis or, preferably, by service if heating and hot water boilers are separate. If not metered this might alternatively be determined from an assessment of the connected loads and the seasonal efficiency.

- Where possible, note the physical condition of each boiler and associated plant and examine the heat transfer surfaces for signs of fouling or corrosion.

- Examine the method and suitability of control of boiler operating time in relation to the type of load, e.g. optimum start control for variable preheating requirements. Examine the control of the boiler firing rate in response to demand; check that the water temperature or steam pressure match requirements within both high and low limits. High flow temperatures may increase system losses directly and low temperatures may lead to extended operating periods if user requirements are not satisfied.

- Check that on/off type burners are not cycling frequently and that high/low or fully modulating burners are set to match the range of demand experienced.

- For multiple boiler installations, examine the methods for controlling the number of boilers kept on-line in response to changes in load and consider automatic sequence control where not already fitted.

- Identify opportunities for restricting standing losses caused by flow through idle boilers, e.g. on the gas side automatic flue gas dampers or air dampers on burner inlets

- The thermal efficiency of any boiler should be determined both for the purpose of analysing energy use and with a view to improvement. Efficiency can often be improved by simple maintenance and adjustment of the burner to minimise excess combustion air. BSI-approved test procedures should be used. Efficiency is determined either by measuring the heat output in relation to the heat input (the direct method), or by inference from measurement of the losses (the indirect method). For short-term tests performed during a survey, when a boiler is on load, the indirect method is usually appropriate. The direct method, on the other hand, can be extended to provide information on long-term or seasonal efficiency over a range of load conditions but is normally only applied to major installations.

- Consider the advantages/disadvantages of decentralisation of boiler plant. Where plant is centralised the cyclic/seasonal pattern of heat use should be examined. The overall distribution loss as a proportion of the heat input may be equivalent to only 0.5% on a large peak winter load but could be as high as 50% in summer. A large site where the end users have widely diverse load patterns could present a good case for decentralisation. Consideration might also be given to possible future combined heat and power schemes where a centralised system could offer a useful base load.

- Check any electricity generating and combined generation (CHP) plant. Determine the type, rating and age of plant. Establish the fuel types, costs and quantities used and note where alternative, cheaper fuels might be suitable. Establish the operational times and load patterns on a daily/weekly/seasonal basis if possible. Calculate the cost of electricity, heat or steam produced and compare with other sources, e.g. boiler plant and imported electricity, see section 5.

- Feedwater and blowdown (steam boilers only): as water is evaporated so dissolved solids introduced with the feedwater concentrate in the boiler and settle to its base. The methods and requirements for removal of the total dissolved solids (TDS) that have accumulated should be reviewed. Consult the boiler manufacturer and/or water treatment specialist to establish the maximum recommended boiler water TDS value. The value will depend on the type of boiler and the operating pressure. Typical values are between 2000–3500 ppm for most shell-type boilers operating at below 10.0 bar pressure. Review the arrangements for using condensate return and mains make-up as feedwater. Condensate usually has a very low TDS and it is therefore essential to ensure maximum return and re-use as boiler feedwater in preference to mains water. Examine the procedures for blowdown and ensure that it is kept to the minimum necessary. Water may be blown down either intermittently by manual use of the main blowdown valve, or continuously via a valve set manually or adjusted automatically. The process can be extremely wasteful of energy and water if not controlled properly. Investigate the opportunity for heat recovery, if not already practised, using a continuous blowdown system discharging to a flash vessel.

- Flue gas heat recovery: investigate the opportunity for flue-gas heat recovery to improve the overall boiler thermal performance, particularly on large gas-fired plant operated for long periods. Consider the potential for application of gas-fired condensing boilers which are designed to condense water vapour and thereby recover its latent heat. Review the operation of existing economisers used to recover heat. With solid fuel fired boilers the flue gas is commonly cooled to between 150 and 160 °C but below about 145 °C the heat recovery equipment may be bypassed to avoid acid vapour condensation. With dual-fuel (gas and fuel oil) firing it is usual to bypass heat recovery equipment when oil firing to avoid corrosion and acid smut emission. Check that maintenance procedures are adequate to minimise the effect of fouling of heat exchangers when using solid or liquid fuels.

- Insulation: the outer surfaces of older boilers and associated steam and hot water vessels, pipework and fittings should be insulated to reduce heat loss. Examine the standard, condition and suitability of insulation. Note that insulating covers for valves and fittings should be easy to remove and replace for maintenance. Determine the economic thicknesses for the particular circumstances. A case can sometimes be made for upgrading or replacing insulation.

Low-temperature hot water systems

- Identify the system type and components; establish the methods of control and operation, noting the facilities for automatic control and any functions performed manually.

- Check control settings, compare with the requirements for occupancy and note whether the set values are achieved. Do not assume that settings indicate the actual conditions maintained. Poorly located or inaccurate temperature sensors may give unexpected results. Timeswitches may be running fast or slow by hours or even days, even though the set programs are otherwise correct.

- Check that the equipment responds satisfactorily to controls, taking care that any tests will not seriously inconvenience the occupants or adversely affect plant adversely. Change thermostat settings temporarily and check that equipment responds correctly. Similarly, operate overrides on timeswitches and other controls where it is safe to do so. Check that motorised valves are able to operate and that actuators have not become seized or disconnected.

- In systems where flow temperature is reduced during milder weather, the compensated flow temperature should be checked against the scheduled value for the prevailing outside air temperature. The case for complete system shutdown when the outside temperature reaches a pre-set level can be considered.

- Investigate zoning arrangements and local control facilities where areas on a common circuit have different needs, due for instance to building aspect, internal gains, or differences in occupancy. Discussion with occupants can help to identify poor balancing between different zones.

- Check the cleanliness of heat transfer surfaces and unit casings and note any obstruction of air movement or heat output from emitters. Identify problems of poor water circulation or inadequate air venting. Restricted heat output tends to result in excessive operating periods and the use of supplementary heating.

- Consider applying reflective foil to the inner surfaces of outside walls behind which emitters are installed. Heat losses through the building fabric can be reduced significantly where radiators are installed at windows.

- Review the effect of direct heat output from the distribution pipework. Unlagged pipework in a roof space or void may provide no useful heat input to the occupied space and could be susceptible to freezing when not in use. Large-diameter pipework may cause excessive heat input to an occupied space if flow temperature is not controlled, even if the individual emitters it serves are all switched off.

Warm air units

Units are either fired individually or fitted with steam, hot water or electric heater batteries.

- Check time and room temperature controls for correct location, setting and operation.

- Inspect the condition of fired units and check for correct burner and fan operation, cleanliness of heat transfer surfaces and filters, and integrity of casing and insulation. Test the thermal efficiency as described for boiler plant. Note that some directly fired units discharge the heat and products of combustion into the treated space.

- Identify any problem of stratification as this is common with convective heating systems in tall spaces. The temperature near a high roof or ceiling can be substantially higher than that at working level. Low-speed fans or simple ductwork systems to recirculate warm air to low level can often be justified, unless there is a requirement for fume extraction at high level.

- Check damper positions and outlet terminals where air is ducted from units. Ensure that air is directed only to where heat is required and that discharge is not obstructed.

- Consider replacement with a radiant heating system if the air change rate in the treated space is high.

Electric space heating

In addition to purpose-designed systems, it is common to find small individual units in local use.

- Check existing controls for correct operation and settings.

- Check cleanliness of heat transfer surfaces and unit casings, freedom of air movement and freedom from obstruction.

- Consider installation of automatic controls, e.g. timeswitches, room thermostats, presence detectors, for groups of heaters or individual units in regular use but switched manually at present.

- Pay particular attention to control of the charging of storage heaters. The charging should be reduced during mild weather and, if appropriate, at weekends. Automatic controls can often be applied to groups of heaters. Ensure that heaters are connected to a supply with an appropriate tariff.

- Consider alternative forms of heating that could offer lower operating costs than direct electric heaters. Storage heaters, gas-fired heaters and extension of an existing LPHW system are common alternatives. Note that local use of an electric heater may be cheaper than operation of a full LPHW system on some occasions, e.g. out of normal working hours.

- Ensure that effective manual control is maintained where this is most appropriate, e.g. for occasional, irregular use of individual heaters.

Domestic hot water

Local water heaters

Direct supply units are usually located next to sinks and are either of the instantaneous supply or of the storage type. The energy source may be electricity or natural gas. For small individual units the potential energy savings are limited.

- Check for satisfactory water temperatures and flow rates and correct operation of controls.

- Examine the insulation of storage cylinders.

- Consider providing timeswitch control for storage cylinders with immersion heaters. The timeswitch program should aim to make maximum use of off-peak electricity and to minimise maximum demand charges.

- Check that heaters without timeswitch control are isolated manually when appropriate, e.g. over holidays or weekends.

Central systems

Domestic hot water may be generated centrally or in distributed heat exchangers supplied from a central boilerhouse with primary hot water or steam. There may be gravity fed or, in larger installations, pumped secondary circulation of hot water, or direct draw-off through dead legs.

- Review the need to operate large centralised systems, particularly during periods with only small localised demand. The use of local gas fired water heaters or instantaneous units can sometimes produce major savings.

- Assess the distribution/standing losses. It may be possible to measure these by monitoring fuel consumption when the system temperatures are stable and the building is unoccupied, i.e. when there is no usage of hot water.

- Check the water temperature in storage and at the user end and ensure correct operation of controls. The hot water discharge temperature at the point of use should be 55–60 °C for normal use; this could mean temperatures above 60 °C the point of storage. The water must be hot enough to minimise the risk of infection by legionella pneumophila i.e. over 55 ± 2.5 °C, but not so hot as to result in excessive storage and distribution losses.

- Check the adequacy of storage cylinder and pipework insulation. Missing or damaged sections should be identified for early replacement or repair, but upgrading to increase thickness will probably not be justified. Recommended insulation thicknesses range from 25 mm for the smallest pipe size to 75 mm for flat surfaces.

- Check that flow rates at outlets do not result in wastage. Consider the application of flow restriction devices to taps or replacement with percussion taps on wash hand basins. Touch- or occupant-sensitive timed flow controls might be recommended in multi-use locations where taps or showers are left running.

- Relate actual consumption to occupancy where make-up water is metered. The provision of metering should be considered for heavy users without this facility. Average daily consumptions of hot water in commercial premises are given in CIBSE Guide G[37].

- Review storage capacities in relation to normal practice. CIBSE Guide G[37] suggests storage of approximately 1 litre per person for service and 2 litres per meal for catering in schools and offices with systems having a 1.5 hour recovery period.

- Consider replacing storage cylinders with plate heat exchangers to reduce standing losses.

- Identify dead legs with a view to eliminating them or reducing their length. Shortening runs reduces both draw-off and standing losses.

Distribution systems

- In large sites it may even be found that central plant is running purely to maintain the distribution losses. In these circumstances the distribution losses of central systems need to be distinguished from the end use.

- Inspect pipework systems visually for leaks or signs that they are occurring. Flooded ducts, plumes of steam and corrosion are some of the obvious indications.

- Determine and account for any imbalance between supply and end use as indicated by discrepancies in metered quantities or assessed consumptions. Unaccounted consumption may be due to leakage.

- Examine the type, condition and thickness of insulation on pipes and fittings. Identify the quantity, type and location of missing, wet or damaged sections of insulation that should be replaced. Note where additional weatherproofing or other protection is needed.

- Determine the economic thickness for the particular application, see FEB 16[19], and consider upgrading where necessary. Heat losses from insulated pipes are given in CIBSE Guide C[38]. The heat loss from an uninsulated valve is equivalent to that from 1 m of uninsulated pipe.

- District heating mains should be surveyed to confirm that all end users are correctly identified. The potential for rationalisation should be examined where mains are under-utilised. When a main is grossly oversized and in poor condition it may be possible to justify early replacement.

- Identify opportunities to reduce pumping rates in hot water systems, having due regard to system design and required temperature drops.

- Steam systems: consider using lower distribution pressures to reduce losses. The minimum permissible pressure will be determined by the pressure/temperature needs of the end users and the capacity of the pipework to handle increased steam volume.

- Check that steam traps are not allowing steam to pass. Portable meters can be used for test purposes, but the installation of permanent in-line devices should be considered for routine checks, particularly where access is difficult.

- Maximise condensate return for use as boiler feed to recover heat and to reduce the need for make-up water and treatment.

- Assess the amount of condensate returned to the boilerhouse on steam plants. This can usually be established by the difference between readings of the boiler feedwater meter(s) and the make-up water meter(s). Consider the quantity returned as a proportion of the mass of steam generated. Condensate should be available from virtually all steam users, except where steam is injected live or where condensate may be contaminated. Identify condensate losses due to leaks or overflow to waste from condensate collection vessels.

Minimising heating demand

☐ Keep distribution system losses as low as possible. Pipework and ductwork lengths should be kept to a minimum. In particular, long deadlegs in hot water systems should be avoided.

☐ Check the provision of thermal insulation. The Building Regulations[16–18] require that all pipework, ductwork and vessels for space heating and hot water supply should be insulated to the standards given in BS 5422[27].

☐ Add extra insulation, further reducing distribution losses, with typical payback periods of less than 3 years. Valves and storage vessels should always be insulated.

Heat generators

Boiler replacement can lead to a 5–25% improvement in energy consumption depending on the inefficiency of the existing plant.

Low temperature hot water boilers

Using high efficiency boilers can raise seasonal efficiency to over 80%; the use of condensing boilers can raise the efficiency further to 85–92% (see section 10.1.2). Options for low temperature hot water (LTHW) boilers are as follows:

☐ In the case of multiple boilers, control the plant to match the load more closely and hence maximise plant efficiency. A mixture of condensing and high efficiency boilers helps minimise capital costs although with little reduction in the seasonal efficiency of the overall plant, thus optimising the payback period (see section 10.1.5).

☐ Introduce effective measures to minimise standing losses with traditional heavyweight high water content boilers. Very old boilers can have standing losses of up to 7% and may benefit from the installation of an automatic shut-off damper on the burner or on the boiler flue off-take flue dampers to reduce losses. However, modern boiler losses are 0.1–1.5% and therefore boiler replacement may be preferable.

☐ Consider decentralising plant. In many cases the replacement of old centralised steam heating plant with local modern LTHW boilers and the elimination of extended steam distribution systems has provided considerable savings. This has often included the separation of heating and hot water plant to improve summer hot water efficiencies. Decentralisation is discussed in section 10.1.2.3.

☐ Provide common flow and return header system to ensure simple and reliable sequence control from return water temperature by providing a constant flow pumped primary circuit. Do not fit automatic isolation valves, or individual pumps on boilers, as these can cause the primary circuit flow to vary (see 10.3.2.5). Ensure that the boiler circuit flow is not affected by variable flow from other circuits (see 10.3.1).

Medium temperature hot water and steam boilers

☐ Introduce oxygen trim controls to maintain the correct air-to-fuel ratio and thus optimise combustion efficiency. Generally economic for large modulating boilers, these controls constantly measure the oxygen level in the flue gases and alter the air inlet damper to ensure the correct excess air level. Savings of 3–5% can be achieved and, although the capital cost is high, it is outweighed by the fuel saved in large boilers.

☐ Use variable speed control for the combustion air fan. For large modulating boilers, the average electrical demand of the combustion air fan motor can be reduced by up to 60% using a variable speed drive (VSD), see GPCS 35[39].

☐ Pre-heat combustion air using heat recovery equipment (see section 4.2.5.5). If the combustion air temperature is raised by 20 °C, the thermal efficiency of a boiler is increased by 1%.

☐ Consider economisers that recover waste heat from boiler flues using heat recovery equipment (see section 4.2.5.5). This is often cost-effective as a retrofit measure in very large plant. Install condensing economisers on gas fired boilers to raise efficiency even further.

☐ Around 3–5% of fuel consumption can be lost in blowdown from steam boilers. Blowdown can be automatically controlled to maintain the total dissolved solids at their optimum value, thus minimising losses.

☐ There are a number of cost-effective methods of recovering heat from blowdown which are covered in FEB 2[40]. Stagger or automatically time the blowdown cycle to spread the availability of waste heat recovery more evenly. Where more than one boiler is operated on an intermittent system, the cost effectiveness of waste heat recovery is improved because the equipment required will be smaller and will run for a higher proportion of the time.

Combined heat and power (CHP)

CHP should be considered where loads are suitable[41] (see section 5.3.1). Usually, there needs to be a simultaneous requirement for heat and power for at least 4500 hours per year to make CHP cost-effective[42,43].

☐   CHP plant requires careful sizing making a detailed feasibility study necessary.

☐   CHP can be installed in conjunction with boiler plant, but it should always take the lead role. In multiple building sites, the heat load may be significant enough to consider large scale CHP, e.g. gas turbines.

Warm air systems

A significant temperature differential (4–6 K) can often exist between the ceiling and the occupied space in large volume buildings, e.g. factories. Options for warm air systems are as follows:

☐   De-stratifying the air by forcing the warmer air down towards the occupied space reduces the heating requirements at working level. De-stratification fans are usually controlled thermostatically such that they operate once the temperature in the upper area reaches a pre-set level. Fan speeds are low to avoid perceptible down draughts and noise, thus fan energy requirements are also small.

☐   An air-jet circulation system is an alternative to de-stratification. This system draws warm air from the upper space and distributes it through a duct before blowing it vertically down at high speed to various locations. This stream entrains cooler air, preventing stratification and reducing energy requirements, although fan power is significant.

Radiant systems

☐   Radiant tube and plaque systems can be a cost-effective replacement for warm air systems in buildings with high air change rates, e.g. factories (see section 10.2.3).

☐   Ensure that radiant systems have good controls using black bulb sensors to ensure comfort levels and savings.

☐   Electric, quartz radiant heaters can be used for spot heating where requirements are highly intermittent. They have a very rapid response time and can be used in conjunction with occupancy sensors to control heat output but maintenance costs can be high.

Electric systems

☐   Existing systems should be replaced by fossil fuel heating where a life-cycle cost evaluation demonstrates that it would be cost effective. Compare with benchmarks in terms of CO_2 emissions rather than delivered energy.

☐   It may be cost effective to retain electric heating in parts of a building otherwise heated by a fossil fuel system where a limited area is heated at different times from the rest.

☐   Where electric heating is retained, install good time and temperature controls. Where heating needs vary, ensure that suitable heat emitters and controls have been chosen to allow the heat output to track variations in heat requirement.

☐   If electric storage heaters are retained, ensure that charge controllers are set correctly to minimise overheating on mild days.

Hot water services

☐   Minimising hot water consumption reduces energy consumption. Install spray taps, percussion taps, tap restrictors and showers instead of baths. Fix leaks and dripping taps as soon as they are detected.

☐   Consider whether the volume of hot water stored can be reduced, and whether pipe runs are longer than necessary.

☐   Turn off circulating pumps when the building is unoccupied.

☐   Calculate and install the economic thickness of insulation on storage tanks and pipework.

☐   Ensure that stored hot water is not over-heated.

☐   Ensure that thermostats are set correctly on electric immersion heaters and individual time controls are installed. Ensure immersion heaters for summer use are not left on through the winter.

Hot water controls

☐   Always employ time-control to ensure that hot water is only heated when required.

☐   Timeswitches should control the primary and secondary circulation pumps.

☐   Always use thermostatic controls to maintain hot water at the required temperature, e.g. a cylinder thermostat or a thermostat built into the storage water heater. Hot water should always be stored at (60 ± 2.5) °C to avoid legionella (see section 10.3.8).

Motors and building transportation systems

Significant energy savings can be realised by upgrading motors and motor controls[44]. When designing new systems with motors or replacing an existing motor, reference should be made to section 10. Maintenance and operation is discussed in section 17. Heat gains from electric motors are given in CIBSE Guide A[9]. The motor load should always be minimised by good system design prior to motor selection (see section 10.1). Effective system regulation and control are essential for efficient operation. Electric motors and drives can account for a significant part of the energy demand in buildings. A modest-sized 11 kW induction motor costing £300 can build up running costs of over £8000 in intermittently occupied buildings with seasonal system operation over ten years, and up to £30 000 with continuous operation over the same period.

The efficiency of typical three-phase induction motors operating at full load ranges from about 75% for a 1 kW motor to 90% for a 30 kW motor. Single-phase motors are some 5–10% less efficient.

Efficiency is reduced at part load and below one-third load the drop is very significant. Many motors are run for substantial periods at part load. Some oversizing is inevitable with variable or cyclic loads.

Check the motor load, from measurements of voltage, current and power factor, and compare with the rating. The load drawn by a three-phase motor operating on a 415 V, 50 Hz supply can be calculated as follows:

$$\text{Load (kV·A)} = \frac{\sqrt{3} \times 415}{1000} \times \text{running current (A)}$$

$$\text{Load (kW)} = \text{load (kVA)} \times \text{power factor (PF)}$$

The power input to a motor drawing a running current of 8 A and operating with a typical full load PF of 0.85 would be approximately 5 kW. Motors running at low load are likely to show power factors very much less than 0.85.

●   Examine the actual load requirements and identify where load reduction might be possible, e.g. reduced pumping rates. Also check for correct alignment, belt tension and satisfactory lubrication.

●   Consider the application of energy saving variable-speed controllers to motors operating predominantly at part load. Speed control is also an effective method of varying pump and fan duties.

●   Consider installing high-efficiency replacement motors. The small extra cost in original equipment is recovered typically in 1–2 years.

●   Identify where ancillary equipment is left running unnecessarily, including gland cooling circuits and DC generators for lift motors.

Assessing motor performance

The potential benefits of an investment in high efficiency motors or improved drives can be established by first checking the actual operating parameters for existing systems. The load determines the actual power drawn by the motor but the size of the motor does not necessarily relate to the power being drawn. For example, a 20 kW motor may be driving a 5 kW load very inefficiently. The rated motor power is the shaft power, i.e. the useful power it can provide to turn the load. However, due to the motor's internal losses, the power drawn by the motor at full load is greater than the rated shaft power. For example, a 30 kW motor which is 92.5% efficient at full load will, at full load, draw a power of (30/0.925) = 32.4 kW. Motor performance can be assessed using the following techniques:

- Estimate the actual running cost by multiplying the rated power of the motor by the number of hours running per year, and by the average cost of electricity in £/(kW·h). This ignores the motor efficiency and actual load conditions but provides a quick estimate of potential running costs and gives a useful guide as to where best to concentrate efforts on a site with many motor drives. For example, an 11 kW motor running for 5000 hours and costing 5 p/(kW·h) would have a potential annual running cost of £2750.

- Spot-check current measurement using a clip-on instrument. If the current drawn is close to the full load current as stated on the rating plate, it is likely that the motor is operating near to full load rated power. However, if the measured current is well below the full load value, all that can be said with certainty is that the power will be significantly less than the calculated kVA.

- Data logging is more accurate than spot-checks and reflects the variation of motor load with time.

- Fit kilowatt-hour meters or hours-run meters: these are particularly suitable for assessing savings on machines using large amounts of power.

Motors

- ☐ Higher efficiency motors should always be considered as they often have no additional capital cost and offer efficiency and economic benefit in virtually all situations (see section 11.2).

- ☐ Motors should be sized correctly to avoid the increased losses resulting from part-load operation.

- ☐ Improve efficiency of transmission systems, e.g. belt drives to reduce drive losses.

- ☐ Systems should be carefully designed to minimise pressure loss and hence reduce energy consumption.

- ☐ Efficient system regulation, achieved by matching fan and pump characteristics to the system (normally via speed change), can provide significant energy savings compared with increased system resistance. Energy savings are typically 20% for 10% flow regulation and 40% for 20% regulation.

- ☐ Variable flow control can provide significant opportunities for energy saving. Building services are sized for peak loads and, for most of their working life, operate well below their full output. Typically, only 20% of full volume energy is required to move air and water at 50% of maximum volume.

- ☐ The use of variable speed drives should always be considered for efficient system regulation and variable flow control (see section 11.4).

Minimising motor loads

There is little point in optimising the motor and its control if the driven equipment and the system it supplies are wasteful. The means of reducing the load are often inexpensive and provide an excellent starting point (see also section 11).

Transmission efficiency

- ☐ Use direct drives rather than belt drives, where practicable.

- ☐ Where belt drives are used, consider modern flat, synchronous, or ribbed-belt drives rather than traditional V-belts, to reduce drive losses.

- ☐ Replace all belts on a multiple belt drive, even if only one has failed.

- ☐ Check for correct pulley alignment.

- ☐ Ensure that the motor and load shafts are parallel.

- ☐ Check belt condition and re-tension on regular basis according to manufacturers' instructions, particularly with V- and wedge belts.

Pumping systems

- ☐ Select an efficient pump and operate it close to the point of most efficient operation.

- ☐ Consider variable flow systems that can provide significant energy savings.

- ☐ Ensure that the system is efficiently regulated by matching pump to system, rather than system to pump which is inherently inefficient.

- ☐ Maintain pumps properly; without maintenance, pump efficiency can fall to 10% of its value when new.

- ☐ Install a smaller impeller or trim the existing one if consistently under loaded.

- ☐ Minimise pressure drops: design for 2 m/s maximum flow in water.

- ☐ Minimise the number of sharp bends.

- ☐ Use low friction piping and consider coating the pump with friction reducers.

- ☐ Check that inlet pressures are satisfactory.

- ☐ Avoid unnecessary throttling.

- ☐ Establish a condition monitoring programme for large pumps in order to determine the optimum time for refurbishment.

Fan systems

- ☐ Select the most efficient fan for the application.

- ☐ Consider variable flow systems, which can provide significant energy savings.

- ☐ Ensure that the system is efficiently regulated by matching fan to system, rather than system to fan which is inherently inefficient.

- ☐ Clean blades regularly.

- ☐ Keep filters clean and avoid unnecessary pressure drops in ducting.

- ☐ Cut off the extract systems from unused machinery by fitting dampers.

- ☐ Where there is a bank of fans, switch units on and off to suit the demand.

Motor sizing, selection and repair

Consider replacing standard motors with high efficiency motors as part of a purchasing policy[45] (see section 15.3.5). Options for motor sizing, selection and repair are as follows:

- ☐ Ensure that motors are sized correctly for the application and consider replacement where over-sizing is identified (see section 11.2).

- ☐ It is seldom economic to repair standard induction motors much below 11 kW, and some companies draw the line at a much higher figure, e.g. 37 kW[46]. The effect on the environment of scrapping old motors and replacing them with new is outweighed by the reduction in carbon dioxide emissions through improved efficiency.

- ☐ Tests have shown that rewinding a motor can reduce its efficiency permanently by between 0.5% and 2%. Some motors are so badly damaged before they arrive at the repair shop that they should be scrapped rather than repaired.

Transportation

Detailed guidance on the management and operation of transportation systems in buildings is provided in CIBSE Guide D[47]. Where lifts, escalators and conveyors are to have a major refurbishment or are being replaced entirely then reference should be made to section 11. Transportation systems should be upgraded every 15–20 years to improve passenger service, increase reliability and performance, and reduce energy consumption.

Lifts

☐   Review the traffic patterns and consider the suitability of the lift controls to the application. Upgrading controls, particularly group controls, could reduce journeys and this may help reduce energy consumption.

☐   Consider the possibility of shutting-down some lifts at the end of the working day. This avoids two lifts being in service where one is adequate.

☐   In some multiple lift installations, it may be advantageous to omit the feature where unused lifts are directed to specific floors outside normal operating hours.

☐   Consider replacing older drives with energy efficient motors. In particular, old 'Ward-Leonard' DC systems are very inefficient and lead to high energy consumption.

Escalators and conveyors

Unlike lifts, escalators and conveyors operate continuously once they have been started.

☐   Delay starting escalators for as long as is practicable at the beginning of the working day.

☐   Stop single escalators when convenient after normal working hours

☐   Use start-up switches, or programme multiple escalators, to ensure they only operate when there is a demand. A balance needs to be struck between staff involvement and the energy saved.

General electrical power

Small power loads are an increasingly significant component of the total energy use in buildings. In particular, they have an important effect on the energy consumed in air conditioning and can influence the need to upgrade air conditioning due to increased internal heat gains (see section 12.4). There is significant potential to reduce the energy consumption of small power loads through sound purchasing policies and good housekeeping (see section 15.3.5).

Reducing cooling loads

All the energy consumed by appliances represents heat gain in the space where the appliance is located, acting to increase staff discomfort if no action is taken to dissipate the heat. Usually, this is achieved by increasing ventilation rates or cooling, which often leads to increased energy consumption (see section 7). Office equipment and appliances can therefore generate a double energy penalty.

Information technology

Surveys suggest that for most general purpose office buildings, the power demand of general IT equipment is likely to be in the range 10–15 $W \cdot m^{-2}$, or around 200 W/person. However, for intensive users, this load may increase to as much as 50 $W \cdot m^{-2}$. The introduction of large-scale IT can produce substantial increases in electricity consumption.

Reducing energy consumption of small power loads

☐   Limit the proliferation of non-essential equipment, e.g. kettles, electric heaters, desk fans. The provision of local hot water urns, adequate heating, and opening windows all help to discourage staff from using such appliances.

☐   Install time controls for vending and food dispensing equipment avoid machines being on overnight.

☐   Switch off photocopiers and other office equipment out of hours. In addition, the use of energy saving features, such as standby switches, can reduce energy consumption by up to 40%[48]. However, the use of standby mode out-of-hours is not energy efficient.

☐   Install automatic sensors for warm air hand dryers; dryers rated at 3 kW or greater are significant consumers of energy.

Reducing cooling loads

☐   Review the need for new office equipment in the light of its effect in increasing heat gains (see section 12)[49].

☐   Review the existing office equipment in the light of its effect on heat gains.

☐   Review the location of office equipment in relation to the air conditioning system to avoid 'hot-spots' where the air conditioning cannot cope.

☐   Position office equipment in groups, served by dedicated heat rejection plant. Providing a single room for fax machines, photocopying and printing machines, kettles, refrigerator etc. means that this room only may require air conditioning, rather than the entire office.

Information technology

Where equipment is replaced the following factors should be considered:

☐   Establish a purchasing policy to introduce 'energy star' computers wherever possible since this can have a significant effect on energy consumption (see section 15.3.5). Make sure the facility is enabled on equipment as it is commissioned.

☐   Make use of energy saving features, including automatic standby and switch-off modes.

☐   Introduce a 'switch-off' policy, even for some printers which take time to warm-up. Always switch off at night and weekends unless required. Research in Canada has indicated that computer operational time can be reduced by as much as 60%. Switching off monitors at lunch time, or when users are away from their desks, can save two thirds of the normal energy consumption.

19 Benchmarking, monitoring and targeting (M&T)

This section sets out some of the important issues in benchmarking, monitoring and targeting energy consumption in buildings, in line with the principles at the front of this Guide. Monitoring and targeting (M&T) is a continuous and disciplined approach to energy management that ensures that energy resources are used to the maximum economic advantage.

19.0   General

Monitoring and targeting (M&T) provides mechanisms for the long-term management of energy use and for highlighting potential improvements in the efficiency of energy use. However, M&T does not save energy; it is the action taken as a result of the M&T that provides real savings. Good M&T should aim to:

— establish current consumption

— compare current consumption with historical data and benchmarks

— set future targets

— compare current consumption with the targets

— identify trends in consumption

— produce exception reports when targets are exceeded.

Where consumption is identified as excessive or above norms, action should be taken quickly (see sections 17 and 18). Further details on M&T can be found in Good Practice Guides GPG 31[1] and GPG 231[2], *Energy — Containing the costs*[3], Fuel Efficiency Booklets FEB 21[4], FEB 7[5] and FEB 13[6].

Annual energy performance should be summarised in the building log book. This should show actual consumption compared to standard benchmarks and the designer team's estimates of future consumption, see section 14.

Procurement tendering and bill checking are valuable costs saving exercises that may be beneficially combined with the energy management procedures described here aimed at reducing consumption.

19.1   The M&T process

The M&T process first establishes a standard of energy performance for each energy accountable area (cost centre), which might be a department, a process or a cost accounting unit. For energy savings to be made, each accountable area needs to improve on the standard performance; this is the purpose of targeting. A target is selected to be an achievable improvement in performance. The process of monitoring and targeting is illustrated in Figure 19.1.

The process is broken down into the following four stages:

— *Data collection*: energy consumption data is usually obtained from meter readings and fuel bills. Also,

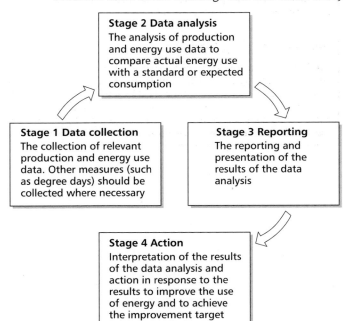

Stage 2 Data analysis
The analysis of production and energy use data to compare actual energy use with a standard or expected consumption

Stage 1 Data collection
The collection of relevant production and energy use data. Other measures (such as degree days) should be collected where necessary

Stage 3 Reporting
The reporting and presentation of the results of the data analysis

Stage 4 Action
Interpretation of the results of the data analysis and action in response to the results to improve the use of energy and to achieve the improvement target

Figure 19.1 Overview of the M&T process

half hourly data can be obtained electronically from the energy supplier.

— *Data analysis*: although it is possible to collect the data and analyse it manually, a modern system would use a computer to carry out the analysis and generate reports. The analysis would provide a comparison of consumption in each accountable area with the established standard as a means of controlling energy use. Also, by making comparisons with the target for an area (see section 19.5), it is possible to identify the potential for further savings and plan improvements in energy use. Checks should be made to confirm the accuracy and quality of the data during collection and input. Some form of reconciliation should be carried out to ensure a fit between the data and the results. A comparison of current consumption with historical data, benchmarks and targets can then be carried out.

— *Reporting*: to be effective, the M&T process must include management reports on energy use based on energy accountable areas. The management reports generated by the system provide the stimulus both to improve performance and to quantify the improvements made. Reports to management should provide a summary whereas reports to individual users should focus on their own consumption. Where possible, exception reports should be produced automatically when daily, weekly or monthly targets are exceeded.

— *Action*: it is essential that a management structure exists to make effective use of the reports generated by the M&T system. Those responsible for energy will need to plan future actions and obtain rapid feedback on the outcome.

This is a highly iterative process of successive measurement and comparison. M&T should be undertaken to a level of detail that relates to the size of the energy bill. The operation of an M&T scheme requires a clear energy policy supported by the organisational structures described in section 15.

19.2   Using energy data

An essential part of assessing building performance is to utilise readily available consumption data to its maximum potential. Some simple analysis techniques applied to suppliers information and sub-meter readings can help to identify areas of high consumption. Key sources of energy data are:

— energy invoice data (bills)

— half hourly energy data

— sub meter readings

19.2.1   Using energy invoice data (bills)

Typical data found on electricity bills can include:

— *Date of meter reading*: essential for determining the period of consumption.

— *Day time consumption*: cumulative energy consumption (kW·h), usually over a period 07:00 to midnight, depending on the particular electricity tariff.

— *Night time consumption*: cumulative energy consumption (kW·h), usually over a period midnight to 07:00, depending on the particular electricity tariff.

— *Total consumption*: cumulative total energy consumption (kW·h), the sum of day and night consumption.

— *Maximum demand* (MD): the peak power consumption (kW or kVA) reached over any 30 minute period during one month. This peak value needs to be kept to a minimum as MD charges in £/kW are high.

— *Power factor*: a rating of reactive power losses measured between zero and one. Above 0.9 is reasonable but below 0.9 should be investigated as the installation of power factor correction equipment could reduce costs.

— *Availability/capacity*: normally a fixed kW or kVA value limiting the capacity of the supply; severe financial penalties are incurred for exceeding the limit.

— *Price of electricity*: in p/kW·h, different for day and night usage.

— *Total cost*: over the consumption period, divide this by the total units (kW·h) to obtain the average price (p/kW·h).

Immediate analysis to be carried out should include:

— *Simple histograms*: plot consumption versus time for day, night and total data to look for trends; check that this matches actual occupancy and that seasonal trends look correct, e.g. rising in summer with air conditioning loads.

— *Averages*: calculate average kW values between each meter reading and compare against occupancy, seasons and expected values.

— *Day/night analysis*: look at day/night ratios throughout the period:

  — In buildings with 8- to 12-hour occupancy, night time consumption should be minimal or zero unless there is a significant UPS supply to server and telecommunications equipment. Significant night consumption should be investigated immediately.

  — In buildings with 24-hour occupancy, with significant night occupation, night consumption should be 10–40% of typical daytime consumption. Anything over 40% should be investigated immediately. A night survey can be profitable to ensure that this consumption is related to real occupancy/use at night, as this is often not the case.

  — MD analysis: plot MD data against actual occupancy and seasons to identify trends. If MD falls well below the availability limit then monetary savings can be achieved by lowering availability. Conversely, if the availability limit is being threatened then it may need to be increase to avoid penalties. Where the MD is much greater than the day time average, investigate large plant that may be causing short intermittent peaks.

Gas invoices usually provide just the total consumption over the period in kW·h, sometimes adjusted for pressure and temperature. Immediate analysis to be carried out should include:

— *Simple histograms*: plot consumption versus time to identify trends. Does this match actual occupancy?

— *Seasonal trends*: does space heating consumption correspond to changes in weather (see regression analysis in section 19.5.3)?

— *Averages*: calculate average kW values between each meter reading and compare with occupancy, seasons and expected values.

— *Base load*: does the non-space heating summer base load (usually HWS and catering) fit with expectations?:

    — In buildings with 8- to 12-hour occupancy with low HWS/catering requirements, base load consumption should be roughly 5–20% of the peak monthly total consumption including space heating. Greater than 20% should be investigated immediately.

    — In buildings with 24-hour occupancy with significant HWS/catering requirements, base load consumption should be roughly 10–40% of the peak monthly total consumption including space heating. Anything over 40% should be investigated immediately.

Oil is usually delivered by bulk tanker, making it difficult to monitor actual consumption with any degree of accuracy unless deliveries are frequent. Where possible, direct metering should be installed to address this. Immediate analysis to be carried out on oil consumption data should take the same approach as gas, above.

19.2.2   Using half-hourly energy data

Electronic data on electricity consumption measured every half hour are available from energy suppliers for most significant buildings/sites. Half-hourly data on gas consumption are also available for some larger buildings. This type of high accuracy data are also available on a real-time basis from a BMS connected to metering, or an automatic meter reading system, allowing real-time analysis with automatic exception reporting.

A spreadsheet is an ideal tool for analysing half-hourly suppliers data and can be programmed to produce 'weekly' plots as shown in Figures 19.2 and 19.3. These overlay profiles for seven days on one chart in order to identify changes, trends, differences and similarities. It is possible to set up the spreadsheet to allow the user to 'scroll through' the weeks to provide a visual impression of the profiles. This allows the shape, size and timing of the profiles to be assessed rapidly. Building operators are commonly surprised by the unexpected peaks troughs and

size of the profiles which usually gives rise to immediate action.

Immediate analysis of half-hourly data profiles should include:

— *Base loads*: look for high base loads at night and weekend indicating plant left on unnecessarily. Base loads should be viewed as absolute values (kW) and as a proportion of daytime consumption.

— *Night/weekend differences*: if there are significant differences between weekday nights and weekend day/night consumption then it could indicate plant being left on during weekday nights unnecessarily.

— *'Shoulder hours'*: excessive consumption during the hours leading up to full daytime consumption and falling away from it. e.g. 06:00–09:00 and 17:00–20:00

— *Profile shape*: unusual changes from day-to-day and week-to-week may indicate poor control. Changes with season and switching major plant on should be apparent.

— *Spikes, peaks and troughs*: unusual step changes and spikes in consumption may indicate erratic plant control

— *Occupancy*: above all, compare the profiles to actual occupancy patterns of the building.

The example in Figure 19.2 shows a very high base load of 900–1000 kW lasting throughout the weekday nights and right across the weekend. This represents roughly 65% of the 1400 kW peak load, which is excessive. Although this was said to be a 24-hour office with call centre facilities, a night survey revealed less than 20 people in the building at night. A programme of plant shut-down at night and weekend achieved major savings. Figure 19.2 also reveals other issues that need investigation. Why is Friday's consumption 100–200 kW less than other weekdays? Does the plant really need to operate from 05:00 to 21:00 and how does this relate to occupancy? Why are the weekend profiles not steady when there is minimal occupancy?

Figure 19.3 shows profiles from a second building and indicates only a 20% base load. This is mainly due to UPS systems supplying servers and telecoms (although UPS demand may be less than expected leaving scope for further savings). However, Monday night and early Tuesday morning show excessive consumption and both days indicate a lack of control during the day relative to the closely matched Wednesday to Friday. Weekend consumption is relatively constant, other than Saturday morning when the building is partially occupied, and is similar to weekday night consumption. These profiles indicate better control and less problems than those in Figure 19.2 but they still raise questions that could lead to energy savings.

19.2.3   Using sub-meter readings

Sub-meter readings can be used to provide a more detailed assessment of end uses within a building of where the energy is used. Sub-meters can help provide:

— *plant/area consumption data*: sub-meter readings can give a more accurate picture of the operation of

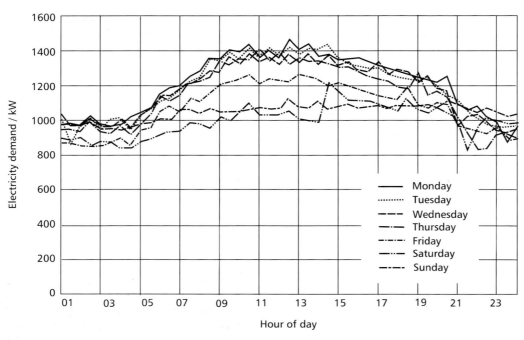

Figure 19.2 Example of daily electricity demand profiles over a week in office A

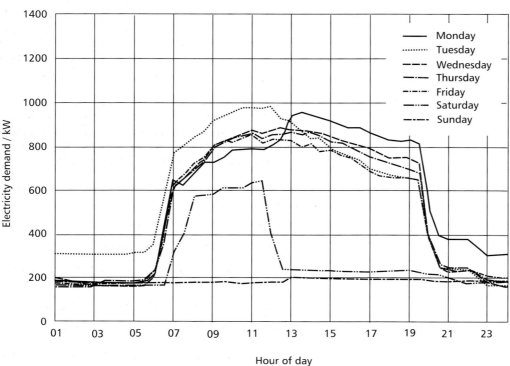

Figure 19.3 Example of daily electricity demand profiles over a week in office B

particular items of plant or particular circuits e.g. first floor lighting

— *plant/area profiles*: by taking sub-meter readings over a 24-hour period, manually or automatically, it is possible to build profiles similar to the half-hourly data (see above) which give rise to questions about the operation of plant/circuits in relation to occupancy

— *reconciliation*: in some instances it is possible to reconcile sub-meter readings with an end-use breakdown established using TM22[7] (see section 19.6). This confirmatory reconciliation can improve the reliability of the overall end-use breakdown. The TM22 software allows sub-meter data to be input and carries out a reconciliation with relevant end-uses.

19.3   Setting up an M&T system

It can be advantageous to set up energy accountable areas (cost centres). These may relate to a complete building or a distinct area or service within that building. Each cost centre should have a manager accountable for energy use who receives regular information on energy performance. Figure 19.4 shows the involvement in M&T at different levels in the management structure.

A manual M&T system may suit buildings having energy bills of less than £10 000 per year. Such a system may consist of checking invoices, plotting monthly energy consumption and comparing it with the same period in previous years. Annual totals could also be compared with benchmarks and a basic target.

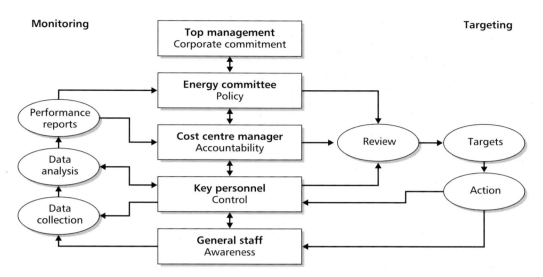

Figure 19.4 M&T operating at different levels of management

A simple spreadsheet may be appropriate when managing energy bills of up to, say, £100 000 p.a. Above this figure, an M&T software package may be more appropriate. The diversity of the estate also needs to be taken into account. For example, 10 buildings with a total bill of £100 000 will require more data and analysis than a single building costing the same amount. Since proprietary software is available, it is seldom cost-effective to develop bespoke in-house systems for circumstances where nothing more than a simple spreadsheet is required.

The advantages and disadvantages of specialist M&T software are discussed in GPG 31[1]. This also provides a checklist of features for consideration when selecting an M&T system. More detail on setting up M&T systems can be found in GPG 231[2].

Many M&T software systems cease to be used because they require excessive amounts of information when a few important indicators would suffice. Equally, over-detailed reporting can cause staff to ignore vital information. The number of buildings or cost centres, and the way information is to be collected needs to be established with care.

There is little to be gained from carrying out detailed analysis when only limited consumption data are available, e.g. quarterly invoices. Equally, detailed 'CUSUM' calculations and regression analyses are more appropriate if weekly energy consumption is available.

The ability to respond quickly is an important factor in the success of an M&T system. Data collection and input should be rapid. Exception reports indicating excessive consumption should be generated speedily to allow early action. Organisations should establish how they will respond to what the system highlights, and how this will integrate with the existing management information system.

Specialist training is essential and a minimum of two members of staff should be able to use the system. They should also be aware of their essential role in highlighting exceptional consumption and the potential for savings as quickly as possible.

Introducing an automatic means of reading meters and analysing the results such as a building energy management System (BMS) or a dedicated automatic meter reading system (AMR) can improve monitoring and targeting. BMS/AMR are ideal in larger buildings, for a large stock of buildings or on multi-building sites, and can promote the use of energy cost centres. Automatic systems should reduce manpower required for monitoring and may provide results more rapidly. An AMR provides automatic meter reading and automatic real-time analysis. The automatic presentation of consumption data as simple profiles and reports can be the most practical way to get users to recognise problems and take action. The whole process can be automated, providing the busy manager with reports only when something needs rectifying.

Automatic monitoring can be achieved using a BMS and standard M&T software but a dedicated AMR may provide a more tailored solution in some instances. Metering, communication technology and analysis software have become less expensive whilst becoming increasingly reliable.

M&T systems should undergo periodic review, auditing and development to:

— examine the system operation

— check the quality of data inputted

— ensure that reporting is adequate to support the decisions taken

— identify where improvements can be made

— determine the level of benefits achieved.

Targets should be set for the performance of the system, e.g. throughput times and reporting.

19.4   Data quality

Good quality data is the foundation of a successful M&T system. Careful validation during the data collection and inputting process is essential[2,8,9].

Time spent entering, analysing and reporting the data should not be underestimated. Savings may be made by using existing routes. For example, accounts departments that enter cost information could also enter energy data. Utility companies may be able to provide electronic data to users with many accounts.

It is common to find sophisticated analysis being carried out on suspect data, often without any data validation.

Simple checks to improve quality and accuracy include the following:

— How do the data compare with previous readings?

— Is the number of digits correct?

— Do the figures fall within acceptance bands?

— Are correct units used?

— Do meter readings reconcile with invoices?

— Are invoices estimated?

Training or guidance for meter readers can also help increase confidence in the results.

Since consumption needs to be compared over similar periods, the date of the meter readings is often crucial. Different definitions can also be the cause of errors. For example, if floor areas are used as a normalising factor to compare different buildings, it is important to ensure that the same definitions of floor area are used, e.g. net, gross or treated (see sections 13 and 20).

Coal and oil invoices often cause problems in M&T systems because they show bulk deliveries and therefore cannot provide a picture of the energy consumption patterns. It is more useful to meter the fuel that goes to the boilers etc.

19.5   M&T analysis techniques

The main aim of data analysis is to:

— highlight when/where corrective action is needed

— indicate when performance has been good and should be replicated

— evaluate the significance of changes in performance

— measure progress towards targets.

A range of analysis methods[2] are used for assessing building performance and the three main methods are shown below. With these methods, actual energy consumption is compared with the following:

— *League tables*: based on a range of factors e.g. highest CO_2/m^2, highest electricity $kW \cdot h/m^2$ etc. league tables can be used to identify the worst performing buildings in a large estate.

— *Benchmarks*: a comparison is made with a standard consumption benchmark (see section 20, Table 20.1) to establish how the building compares with typical and best practice buildings.

— *Performance lines*: these lines (e.g. variation of heating consumption with degree-days) make it possible to check whether the services continue to function in relation to key variables.

— *Historical data*: a comparison with a previous measurement to ascertain whether previously adopted energy efficiency measures have been effective, and to identify the need for further improvement

19.5.1   League tables

League tables are relatively easy to construct in spreadsheets to identify the worst performing buildings in a large estate. Simple consumption and floor area data can be prioritised on a range of factors e.g. highest CO_2/m^2, highest electricity $kW \cdot h/m^2$ etc. providing a useful first analysis to highlight buildings that require further investigation. League tables of the best performing buildings can also helpful to identify best practice that can be carried over into those performing poorly. Equally important is a league table based on floor area to provide a useful perspective on the estate size.

19.5.2   Performance indicators

The overall performance of a building can be crudely expressed as a performance indicator, usually in (kg CO_2/m^2) per year or separately for fossil fuel and electricity in ($kW \cdot h/m^2$) per year. The analysis is normally performed on annual data, allowing comparison with published benchmarks to give an indication of efficiency[10]. Some of these benchmarks are shown in section 20.

Although performance indicators for buildings are generally rated in terms of floor area, building volume and the amount of trade (e.g. number of meals) are sometimes used as normalising factors. Indicators, adjusted according to weather and/or occupancy are often called normalised performance indicators (NPIS). This 'normalisation' is intended to improve comparison between buildings in different climatic regions or with different occupancy patterns. However, this approach should be used with care as it can often distort the data and mask real patterns in consumption.

Where normalisation is essential and provided that consistent procedures are used, a valid comparison can be made of the NPI for a given building over successive years. However, care must be taken as errors in floor area, hours of occupancy etc. are common, particularly in large estates of buildings.

Section 20, Table 20.1, provides separate benchmarks for electricity and fossil fuels to allow for the widely different costs and CO_2 emissions per unit of energy delivered. Each unit of electricity results in two to three times more CO_2 being emitted as the direct use of fossil fuels in the building. In addition, a unit of electrical energy is more expensive than the equivalent amount of energy obtained through the consumption of fossil fuels in the building's heating system. It is recommended, therefore, that separate indicators be used for electricity and fossil fuel consumption. Where a single indicator is required, the electricity and fossil fuel consumption should each be converted to kg CO_2 and the two numbers added together (see section 13.3).

Performance indicators give only a broad indication of building efficiency and therefore must be treated with caution. It should not be assumed that a building with a 'good' performance indicator is in fact being operated as efficiently as is possible, or offers no scope for cost-effective savings. Overall performance indicators can mask underlying problems with individual end uses of energy. Techniques shown in CIBSE TM22[7] allow a more detailed analysis in terms of end-use consumption (e.g. lighting, fans

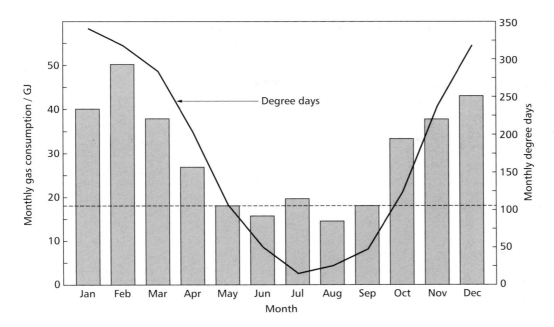

Figure 19.5 Histogram of monthly fuel consumption versus degree-days

etc.) in order to identify more closely where energy problems are occurring within the building. This is a staged approach, requiring more detailed input data at each stage and ultimately provides a comparison of actual end-use consumption with equivalent end-use benchmarks.

19.5.3   Regression analysis

It can be helpful to carry out an analysis to determine the relationship between energy use and the drivers that influence it. This involves developing a performance line equation (i.e. an equation of the form: $y = m x + c$). For example, heating consumption varies with degree-days, as shown in Figure 19.5.

Degree-day data provide a measure of the average outside temperature, which has a direct influence on heating or cooling loads. The data are normally used for analysis of monthly energy consumption. Monthly and annual figures are available from a number of sources. Tables usually show average figures for the year/month compared to an average over the last 20 years across seventeen regions in the UK. An average of the two nearest regions, or data recorded on site, may be preferred for locations remote from the central recording located in any one region. Heating degree-days are normally calculated to a base outside temperature of 15.5 °C, the base suitable for most commercial and industrial buildings[4].

Analysis of energy data often shows simple linear relationships, as shown in Figure 19.6. The correlation and base load data obtained from such plots can provide useful information on energy use, particularly relating to control and standing losses[1,2–5]. Once the performance line is established, consumption measurements can be easily compared with past results. The intersection of the sloping line and the y-axis indicates the base load consumption. This is a technique often used to identify hot water loads in buildings.

Initial attempts at producing a thermal performance line for a building sometimes reveal very poor performance or a wide scatter of points. This is invariably due either to poor adjustment, or to inadequacy or malfunction of the heating system controls. In any event, remedial action

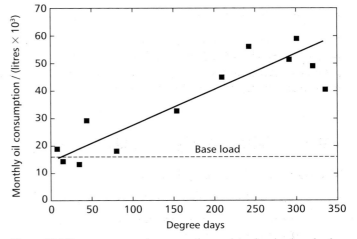

Figure 19.6 Energy consumption versus degree-days showing base load

should be taken. The correlation may also be poor if heating accounts for only a small proportion of the fuel requirement. GPG 125[11], GPG 112[12] and GIL 50[13] set out a number of forms that the weather dependency graph can take. Curved lines may indicate that constant temperature is not maintained throughout the year whereas broken/horizontal lines might indicate that consumption does not depend on weather over that period e.g. due to large distribution losses. This approach is heavily dependent on the accuracy of the degree day and consumption data. CIBSE are currently carrying out a review of degree days and their use. However, recent work[14] provides a method for determining the true base temperature leading to improved correlations between degree days and energy consumption, resulting in a better understanding of the building's problems.

A good thermal performance line can usually be produced if the controls are functioning and are reasonably adjusted. However, this does not mean that the building is operating efficiently, merely that its performance is consistent. Once established, the performance line can be used as a 'performance target' for the future operation of the building. Should any sudden significant deviation in fuel consumption occur, indicated by a change in the slope of the line, it should be investigated and corrective action taken. The best fit thermal performance line should be re-calculated annually[1,2–5].

19.5.4   Trend logging and CUSUM analysis

Figure 19.7 shows that simple histograms can help to identify trends and make comparisons against the previous year's consumption patterns. More complex ways of representing results, such as the CUSUM technique[5,6,15], can establish trends more clearly.

To construct a CUSUM graph, the baseline consumption is required. By calculating the cumulative sum of the differences of actual consumption from this base line, a trend line can be plotted to indicate performance and changes in performance as shown in Figure 19.8. A downward trend indicates savings beyond the base consumption and an upward slope indicates excessive consumption. The numerical value of CUSUM give the aggregate savings made to date, and the slope of the CUSUM line gives information on the performance trend.

19.6   Benchmarking end-uses

Once a building has been identified as an overall poor performer, a more detailed analysis of end-uses is the next

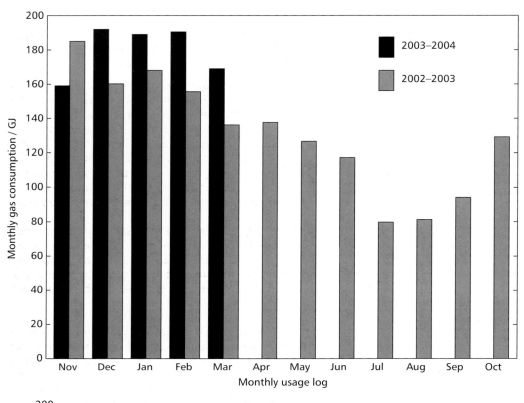

Figure 19.7 Monthly trend logging

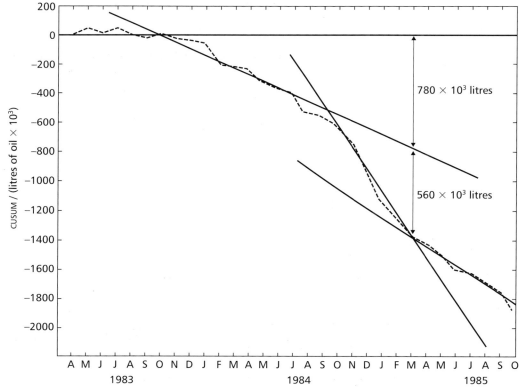

Figure 19.8 Example of a CUSUM plot showing cumulative energy savings (reproduced from Fuel Efficiency Booklet FEB 7[5]; Crown copyright)

step in identifying where, why and when inefficiency is occurring. M&T analysis may show that either electricity, fossil fuel or both are worse than standard benchmarks. A more focussed analysis is then required. For example, if electricity is the problem then a detailed analysis of electrical end-uses will reveal where this is happening and often how to solve it. This shows the value in keeping electricity and fossil fuel data separate in the M&T process.

The main tool for end-use analysis is the energy assessment and reporting method (EARM) provided by CIBSE TM22[7]. This approach, with its associated software package, was developed for offices, banks and agencies, hotels and mixed-use (industrial) buildings. The approach can also be modified for use in any other building. TM22 provides three five options for building assessment:

— *Option A — simple building assessment*: a one-page assessment of a simple building which has just one building type with at most two energy supplies including grid electricity, and does not have special energy or occupancy features which could be allowed for. The assessment is based on overall energy use although the electricity and non-electric supplies are assessed separately so that the different cost and environmental impacts of the fuels. Default carbon and building use factors are used.

— *Option B — general assessment*: an overall assessment of a more complex building which can include areas of different building types, with up to five energy supplies and special features or non-standard usage which are accounted for by exclusions or adjustment.

— *Option C — system assessment*: assessment of the energy performance of individual systems in a building against benchmarks for that building. The system energy use can be obtained either from metered energy data from the building log book required under Building Regulations, or from a detailed survey of plant and usage.

— *Option D — Design stage assessment and comparison*: assessment of design-stage energy performance against benchmarks and against actual performance. As an extension to the option C, design stage

Table 19.1 Normal and special end-uses

Normal energy end uses	Examples of special/atypical energy uses
Heating	Dedicated computer room or suite
Hot water	Catering kitchen and restaurant
Lighting	Dealing rooms
Ventilation	Sports and leisure facilities
Pumps	Covered car parks
Cooling	Exterior lighting
Humidification	
Office equipment	
Lifts and vertical transport	
Controls and telecoms	
Local kitchens and vending	

calculations such as the carbon performance rating (CPR) are compared with benchmarks and available system metered or surveyed data.

— *Option E — replacement AC/MV plant assessment*: a procedure for demonstrating compliance with the Building Regulations Approved Document L2[16] requirements for efficiency of fans in replaced air conditioning/mechanical ventilation (AC/MV) plant. This option is not dependent on options A to D, although the system benchmarks are common. The system efficiency requirements are given in a table that on completion demonstrates compliance.

Some options require more detailed data inputs but provide a more detailed assessment of the energy uses. Special/atypical end-uses like computer rooms, restaurant and car parks are separated out of the analysis in option B. Examples of normal and special end-uses are shown in Table 19.1.

Option C assesses the energy use of each system or end-use. The individual energy uses can be built-up into an overall picture in the form of a tree diagram, as shown in Figure 19.9, that provides a useful overview of the building. The value in each box is obtained by multiplying together the two values in the boxes below.

For example:

— Fan consumption (kW·h·m^{-2} per year) = (W·m^{-2} × hours run per year × control factor) / 1000

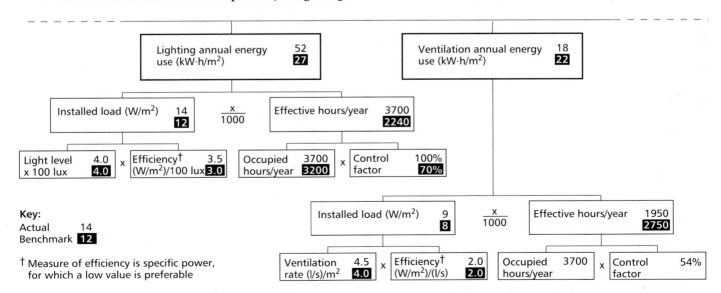

Figure 19.9 Tree diagram showing an example of actual versus benchmarks for lighting and ventilation (See CIBSE TM22)[7]

—   Lighting consumption (kW·h·m^{-2} per year) = (W·m^{-2} / 100 lux) × illuminance (100 lux) × operating hours per year × control factor / 1000

Each box shows actual consumption versus a benchmark, allowing detailed benchmarking of all end-uses across a number of different levels. For example:

—   each incoming energy consumption (kW·h·m^{-2} per year)

—   energy consumption of each system (kW·h·m^{-2} per year)

—   installed equipment loads (W·m^{-2})

—   efficiency indicators, e.g. fan efficiency (W·litre^{-1}·s^{-1}) or lighting efficiency (Watts·m^{-2} per 100 lux)★

—   service level, e.g. lighting (lux) or fan performance (litre·s^{-1}·m^{-2})

—   operating hours (hours per year)

—   control (management) factors.

Figure 19.10 shows a summary output in kW·h from stage 3. Representing this in terms of cost or CO_2 is often helpful in convincing management of the need for action and/or investment.

19.7   Setting targets

One of the objectives of an M&T system is to set targets that will stimulate management to make improvements. These targets must be realistic and achievable, taking into account the likely savings from improvements in 'house-keeping', maintenance and other efficiency measures. Management should use a consultation process to agree individual targets, rather than simply impose arbitrary figures. Targets should be set for each cost centre, to stimulate positive management action, and be reviewed annually.

19.7.1   'Top down' approach

Targets are often crudely set as part of an overall energy policy, for example, 'a 15% reduction in energy use to be achieved over five years'. Individual building targets can be set using the same 'top down' approach, e.g. 'an attempt will be made to save 10% in building 1 next year, but only 5% in building 2 as there is less scope for saving'. This broad-brush approach provides a means of starting the targeting process but, to be successful, requires agreement at all levels.

19.7.2   Standard benchmarks

Typical and best practice benchmarks exist for different kinds of building and these can be used as a target. Although they are fairly general, they give a more absolute measure of how certain types of buildings should perform, rather than a relative comparison with past performance. An extensive set

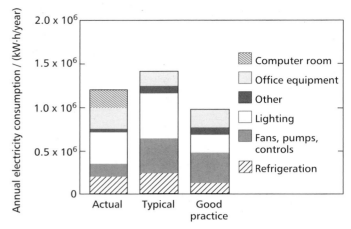

Figure 19.10 Comparison of actual consumption versus typical and good practice benchmarks

of benchmarks is presented in section 20, including a wide range of end-use/component benchmarks for various building types. Benchmarks are also available from Action Energy (www.actionenergy.org.uk) in the form of Energy Consumption Guides, most of which are summarised in section 20, Table 20.1.

Separate benchmarks are set for fossil fuels and electricity, since they have very different costs and CO_2 emissions. Most existing buildings should aim to have lower consumption figures than those in the 'best practice' column of Table 20.1. However, in inherently inefficient buildings, it may not be practicable or economic to bring the building up to this standard. In these circumstances, realistic targets should be set between the 'best practice' and 'typical' benchmarks, the larger figures providing a useful upper limit. The 'good practice' figures for existing buildings can be used as upper limits for new design, see section 13.2.2. New buildings should aim to achieve much lower consumptions than these figures.

These benchmarks will change as better quality data are gathered and as the energy efficiency of buildings improves. However, they provide useful targets for building operators. The shortfall between the actual consumed energy and the benchmark provides an indication of the potential for improvement. Analysis of the breakdown of energy use indicates where efforts should be directed to realise the improvement.

19.7.3   Targets based on historical records

Most targets are based on the historical consumption of each particular building. These targets may simply be the consumption for the previous year, an average over three years, or the consumption weather-corrected for the twenty-year average weather conditions. This method of targeting will not highlight any intrinsic problems in the building or its use but it does provide a target that is specific to the building being considered.

19.7.4   Targets based on key variables

As discussed in 19.4, energy consumption can be related to the most important variables, e.g. weather, number of

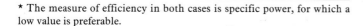

★ The measure of efficiency in both cases is specific power, for which a low value is preferable.

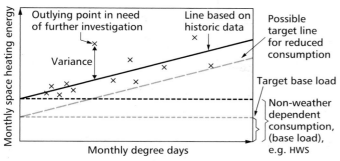

Figure 19.11 Typical linear relationship between degree days and space heating

meals, etc. Developing a performance line equation (i.e. an equation of the form: $y = mx + c$) can provide a target. For example, in Figure 19.11, the intercept theoretically represents the base load consumption, e.g. hot water. In practice, space heating is discontinued before the number of degree-days falls to zero and the true base load is higher than the intercept. The slope shows how the space heating demand relates to degree-days. The outlying point observed in winter, when the number of degree-days is highest, might be explained by a shutdown or plant breakdown. Targets could be set to reduce both the intercept and slope of the performance line, as shown.

The scatter of points often reflects the accuracy of control. A wider scatter suggests that control is poor, see section 19.4.2, but it can also be caused by a fluctuating base load. Good correlation could result from consistent control. However, that does not necessarily mean that the control settings are optimised, since they could have been maintained consistently at the wrong level.

19.7.5   The 'bottom up' approach (avoidable waste)

Targets can also be derived by using a 'bottom up' approach, i.e. estimating end-use energy consumption in order to develop a building target. This approach provides a building specific target, but requires a number of assumptions and estimates[6]. By subtracting estimates of what each service should use from the actual consumption, it is assumed that any remainder must represent avoidable waste or potential savings. However, the accuracy of the energy breakdown determines the accuracy of the likely savings. Unless a detailed analysis is carried out (e.g. CIBSE TM22[7] stage 3) then the resulting targets will give only a crude indication of potential savings.

19.7.6   Building modelling

Manual systems[17–20] and dynamic simulation software can be used to model buildings and hence derive targets. However, most of these systems are best used for comparing changes in a building design rather than predicting absolute energy consumption. CIBSE AM11[21] provides further details on building modelling.

19.7.7   Process energy

In many cases, particularly industrial buildings, the energy consumption for manufacturing and associated requirements may be substantially higher than, and may

overshadow or directly affect, that needed for environmental services. In general, process energy use should be analysed separately from that of the building services. Areas with processes or exceptional use should always be separated for the purposes of estimating consumption targets.

19.8   Maintaining the savings

Once energy saving measures have been introduced, immediate and ongoing checks should be made to ensure that energy efficiency measures have been installed and are operating correctly. These checks must confirm that the savings originally predicted are actually being achieved.

19.8.1   Post project evaluation

The PROBE studies[22] show the importance of overall post project evaluations and these are discussed in section 14.5. Following the implementation of particular energy saving measures, more focussed post project evaluation is desirable to establish that measures have been correctly installed and are achieving the predicted savings. Small measures may require only a cursory check but larger projects, e.g. those involving combined heat and power, require a thorough assessment. Evaluations should establish:

—   actual savings

—   final capital cost

—   impact on occupants

—   management implications

—   maintenance issues

—   other benefits achieved

—   practical pitfalls.

It may also be possible to compare actual savings with the savings achieved in published case study material. Problems identified well after implementation are often traced back to poor installation.

The energy manager should also provide a post project evaluation report to senior management on the effectiveness of the investment. For those managing a number of buildings, the evaluations can also help to indicate whether similar measures should be incorporated in other parts of the stock, while highlighting pitfalls to be avoided.

19.8.2   Continual monitoring

Again, where specific measures have been implemented, continual monitoring will help to maintain the level of savings achieved over successive years. This requires:

—   installing monitoring equipment where information is required to assess energy usage and savings

—   instituting a measuring and analysis scheme and allocate tasks to personnel

—   maintaining records of energy use and comparing them with targets

— checking records against utility bills to ensure cost savings are achieved

— reporting results to the building operator on a regular basis.

The following maintenance and management procedures also play a large part in ensuring continued savings:

— Review maintenance and operating procedures to ensure that efficiency of plant and system operation is sustained.

— Keep all personnel informed of progress and of results achieved.

— Keep a record of changes to the building and its use that may effect savings.

— Regularly review the monitoring programme and modify actions where necessary.

A formal monitoring system is invaluable when assessing performance and looking for further improvements, including environmental impact[23]. The whole programme for improving energy efficiency may fall into disrepute if savings cannot be proved. Confirming the results of investment helps to justify future investment.

References

1   *Computer aided monitoring and targeting for industry* Good Practice Guide GPG 31 (Action Energy) (www.action energy.org.uk) (1995)

2   *Introducing information systems for energy management* Good Practice Guide GPG 231 (Action Energy) (1998) (www.action energy.org.uk)

3   *Energy — containing the costs* (London: Chartered Institute of Management Accountants) (1992)

4   *Simple measurements for energy and water efficiency in buildings* Fuel Efficiency Booklet FEB 21 (Action Energy) (2001) (www.actionenergy.org.uk)

5   *Degree days* Fuel Efficiency Booklet FEB 7 (Action Energy) (1993) (www.actionenergy.org.uk)

6   *Waste avoidance measures* Fuel Efficiency Booklet FEB 13 (Action Energy) (1995) (www.actionenergy.org.uk)

7   *Energy Assessment and Reporting Methodology — Office assessment method* CIBSE TM22 (London: Chartered Institution of Building Services Engineers) (2004)

8   Field J, Soper J, Jones P G, Bordass W and Grigg P Energy performance of occupied non domestic buildings: Assessment by analysing end-use energy consumptions *Building Serv. Eng. Res. Technol.* **18** (1) (1997)

9   Field J W and Soper J H B Understanding energy performance of commercial and high street buildings *Proc. CIBSE Nat. Conf., London 5–7 October 1997* (London: Chartered Institution of Building Services Engineers) (1997)

10   *Introduction to energy efficiency in buildings* Energy Efficiency Booklets EEB 001–013 (Action Energy) (1994) (www.action energy.org.uk)

11   *Monitoring and targeting in small and medium sized companies* Good Practice Guide GPG 125 (Action Energy) (1998) (www.actionenergy.org.uk)

12   *Monitoring and targeting in large companies* Good Practice Guide GPG 112 (Action Energy) (1998) (www.actionenergy.org.uk)

13   *Energy saving in buildings — methods for quickly identifying opportunities* General Information Leaflet GIL 50 (Action Energy) (2001) (www.actionenergy.org.uk)

14   Day A R, Knight I and Dunn G Improved methods for evaluating base temperature for use in building energy performance lines *Building. Serv. Res. Technol.* **24** (4) (2004)

13   Harris P *Energy monitoring and target setting using CUSUM* (Cambridge: Cheriton Technology Publications) (1989)

16   *Conservation of fuel and power in buildings other than dwellings* The Building Regulations 2000 Approved Document L2 (London: The Stationery Office) (2001)

17   Baker N V and Steemers K *The LT Method 2.0. An energy design tool for non-domestic buildings* (Cambridge Architectural Research/Building Research Energy Conservation Support Unit) (1994)

18   *Energy demands and targets for heated and ventilated buildings* CIBSE Energy Code 1 (London: Chartered Institution of Building Services Engineers) (1999)

19   *Energy demands for air conditioned buildings* CIBSE Energy Code 2 (London: Chartered Institution of Building Services Engineers) (1999)

20   *Fundamentals* ASHRAE Handbook (Atlanta, GA: American Society of Heating, Refrigeration and Air Conditioning Engineers) (2001)

21   *Building energy and environmental modelling* CIBSE AM11 (London: Chartered Institution of Building Services Engineers) (1998)

22   Bordass W T, Bunn R et al. PROBE: Some lessons learned from the first eight buildings *Proc. CIBSE Nat. Conf., London 5–7 October 1997* (London: Chartered Institution of Building Services Engineers) (1997)

23   Bartlett P, Bishop T and Durrant H *The office toolkit. The guide for facilities and office managers for reducing costs and environmental impact* BRE Report BR 285 (London: Construction Research Communications) (1995)

Bibliography

Is your energy use under control? A practical guide to assessment and action Good Practice Guide GPG 136 (Action Energy) (1994) (www.action energy.org.uk)

Controlling energy use in buildings General Information Leaflet GIR 47 (Action Energy) (1997) (www.actionenergy.org.uk)

Practical energy saving guide for smaller businesses (Action Energy) (1992) (www.actionenergy.org.uk)

Energy managers handbook (London: NIFES/Graham Trotman) (1985)

Educated energy management (London: E and F N Spon) (1991)

Putting energy into total quality. A guide for energy managers Good Practice Guide GPG 169 (Action Energy) (1996) (www.actionenergy.org.uk)

Cheshire D N, Jones P G and Moss S Quality of data — an energy performance database *Proc. CIBSE Nat. Conf., London 5–7 October 1997* (London: Chartered Institution of Building Services Engineers) (1997)

Mortimer N D et al. *An energy based classification system for non domestic buildings* CIBSE *Proc. CIBSE Nat. Conf., London 5–7 October 1997* (London: Chartered Institution of Building Services Engineers) (1997)

Part C: Benchmarks

20   Energy benchmarks

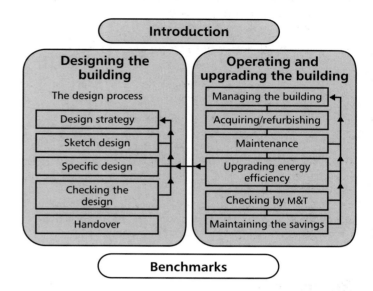

20   Energy benchmarks

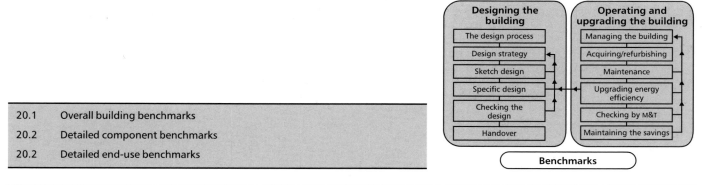

This section contains all the known UK energy and component benchmarks available at the time of publication (December 2003). 'Good practice' benchmarks are indicated by shading. In some cases, data from several sources are given; the reader must select a benchmark appropriate to the particular circumstances.

20.1   Overall building benchmarks

Table 20.1 Fossil and electric building benchmarks[1–22] (figures in shaded columns may be regarded as upper limits for new design)

Building type	Energy consumption benchmarks for existing buildings / $(kW \cdot h \cdot m^{-2})$ per year (unless stated otherwise)				Basis of benchmark
	Good practice		Typical practice		
	Fossil fuels	Electricity	Fossil fuels	Electricity	
Catering:[2]					
— fast food restaurants	480	820	670	890	Gross floor area
— public houses	1.5	0.8	3.5	1.8	(kW·h/m² per £1000 turnover)
— restaurants (with bar)	1100	650	1250	730	Gross floor area
— restaurants (in public houses)	2700	1300	3500	1500	(kW·h/cover[a])
Entertainment:					
— theatres	420	180	630	270	Gross floor area[b]
— cinemas	515	135	620	160	Gross floor area[b]
— social clubs	140	60	250	110	Gross floor area[b]
— bingo clubs	440	190	540	230	Gross floor area[b]
Education (further and higher)[17][c]					
— catering, bar/restaurant	182	137	257	149	Gross floor area
— catering, fast food	438	200	618	218	Gross floor area
— lecture room, arts	100	67	120	76	Gross floor area
— lecture room, science	110	113	132	129	Gross floor area
— library, air conditioned	173	292	245	404	Gross floor area
— library, naturally ventilated	115	46	161	64	Gross floor area
— residential, halls of residence	240	85	290	100	Gross floor area
— residential, self catering/flats	200	45	240	54	Gross floor area
— science laboratory	110	155	132	175	Gross floor area
Education (schools)[20]:					
— primary	113	22	164	32	Gross floor area
— secondary	108	25	144	33	Gross floor area
— secondary (with swimming pool)	142	29	187	36	Gross floor area
Hospitals:[19]					
— teaching and specialist	339	86	411	122	Heated floor area[d]
— acute and maternity	422	74	510	108	Heated floor area[d]
— cottage	443	55	492	78	Heated floor area[d]
— long stay	401	48	518	72	Heated floor area[d]
Hotels:[16][e]					
— holiday	260	80	400	140	Treated floor area
— luxury	300	90	460	150	Treated floor area
— small	240	80	360	120	Treated floor area

Table 20.1 Fossil and electric building benchmarks — *continued*

Building type	Energy consumption benchmarks for existing buildings / (kW·h·m⁻²) per year (unless stated otherwise)				Basis of benchmark
	Good practice		Typical practice		
	Fossil fuels	Electricity	Fossil fuels	Electricity	
Industrial buildings:[11][f][g]					
— post-1995; ≤5000 m²	96	—	—	—	Gross floor area
— post-1995; >5000 m²	92	—	—	—	Gross floor area
— pre-1995; ≤5000 m²	107	—	—	—	Gross floor area
— pre-1995; >5000m²	103	—	—	—	Gross floor area
Local authority buildings:[21]					
— car park (open)	—	—	—	1	Gross parking area
— car park (enclosed)	—	—	—	15	Gross parking area
— community centres	125	22	187	33	Agent's lettable area
— day centres	203	51	349	68	Agent's lettable area
— depots	283	37	311	39	Gross internal area
— sheltered housing	314	46	432	68	Gross internal area
— residential care homes	492	59	390	75	Gross internal area
— temporary homeless units	408	48	467	71	Gross internal area
— town hall (see also offices)	138	84	205	111	Gross internal area
Ministry of Defence (MoD) buildings:[15]					
— aircraft hangars (heated)	220	23	—	—	Treated floor area
— junior mess	2.5	1.4	—	—	(kW·h per meal)
— motor transport facilities	317	20	—	—	Treated floor area
— multi-occupancy accommodation	225	29	—	—	Treated floor area
— officers' mess	4.4	2.5	—	—	(kW·h per meal)
— stores/warehouses (occupied)	187	34	—	—	Treated floor area
— stores/warehouses (unoccupied)	54	3	—	—	Treated floor area
— workshops	175	29	—	—	Treated floor area
Offices:[10][f]					
— air conditioned, standard	97	128	178	226	Treated floor area
— air conditioned, prestige	114	234	210	358	Treated floor area
— naturally ventilated, cellular	79	33	151	54	Treated floor area
— naturally ventilated, open plan	79	54	151	85	Treated floor area
Primary health care (general practitioners' surgeries and dental practices)	174?	??	270?	??	Gross floor area
Public buildings:					
— ambulance stations[9]	350	50	460	70	Treated floor area
— churches[7]	80	10	150	20	Treated floor area
— courts (Magistrates)[22][h]	125	31	194	45	Treated floor area
— courts (County)[22][h]	125	52	190	60	Treated floor area
— courts (Crown)[22][h]	139	68	182	74	Treated floor area
— courts (combined County/Crown)[22][h]	111	57	159	71	Treated floor area
— fire stations[9]	385	55	540	80	Treated floor area
— libraries[21]	113	32	210	46	Agent's lettable area
— museums and art galleries[21]	96	57	142	70	Gross internal area
— police stations[9]	295	45	410	60	Treated floor area
— prisons[13]	18861	3736	22034	4460	kW·h per prisoner[i]
— prisons (high security)[13]	18861	7071	22034	7509	kW·h per prisoner[i]
Residential and nursing homes[18]	247	44	417	79	Gross floor area
Retail:[12]					
— banks and building societies	63	71	98	101	Gross floor area
— banks and building societies (all electric)	—	122	—	195	Gross floor area
— book stores (all electric)	—	210	—	255	Sales floor area
— catalogue stores	37	83	69	101	Sales floor area
— catalogue stores (all electric)	—	100	—	133	Sales floor area
— clothes shops	65	234	108	287	Sales floor area
— clothes shops (all electric)	—	270	—	324	Sales floor area
— department stores	194	237	248	294	Sales floor area
— department stores (all electric)	—	209	—	259	Sales floor area
— distribution warehouses	103	53	169	67	Sales floor area
— distribution warehouses (all electric)	—	55	—	101	Sales floor area
— DIY stores	149	127	192	160	Sales floor area
— electrical goods rental	—	281	—	368	Sales floor area
— electrical goods retail	—	172	—	230	Sales floor area
— frozen food centres	—	858	—	1029	Sales floor area

Table 20.1 Fossil and electric building benchmarks — *continued*

Building type	Energy consumption benchmarks for existing buildings / (kW·h·m⁻²) per year (unless stated otherwise)				Basis of benchmark
	Good practice		Typical practice		
	Fossil fuels	Electricity	Fossil fuels	Electricity	
Retail (continued):[12]					
— high street agencies	150	55	230	75	Sales floor area
— high street agencies (all electric)	—	90	—	160	Sales floor area
— meat butchers (all electric)	—	475	—	577	Sales floor area
— off licences (all electric)	—	475	—	562	Sales floor area
— supermarket (all electric)	—	1034	—	1155	Sales floor area
— post offices	140	45	210	70	Sales floor area
— post office (all electric)	—	80	—	140	Sales floor area
— shoe shops (all electric)	—	197	—	279	Sales floor area
— small food shops	80	400	100	500	Sales floor area
— small food shops (all electric)	—	440	—	550	Sales floor area
— supermarket	200	915	261	1026	Sales floor area
Sports and recreation:[14][f]					
— combined centre	264	96	598	152	Treated floor area
— dry sports centre (local)	158	64	343	105	Treated floor area
— fitness centre	201	127	449	194	Treated floor area
— ice rink	100	167	217	255	Treated floor area
— leisure pool centre	573	164	1321	258	Treated floor area
— sports ground changing facility	141	93	216	164	Treated floor area
— swimming pool (25 m) centre	573	152	1336	237	Treated floor area

Notes:

[a] 'Covers' are the number of place settings in the restaurant.

[b] Excluding balcony and circle areas

[c] Source quotes 'low' and 'high' instead of 'Good practice' and 'Typical'

[d] Derived from GJ/(100 m³ heated volume) assuming a floor-to-ceiling height of 2.9 m; divide by 8.06 to revert to GJ/(100 m³).

[e] For up-to-date information, see www.hospitableclimates.com

[f] Tailored benchmark is preferred; see www.actionenergy.org.uk/actionenergy/info+centre/tools for software tools.

[g] Building heating energy use only; based on building heated to 19 °C during occupied periods; 5-day, single 8-hour shift; 0.8 ACH for small buildings, 0.5 ACH for large buildings; decentralised, responsive heating system with optimised start and set-back when unoccupied; normal exposure; 2051 degree days. For any variation from these conditions, and to benchmark lighting energy, refer to www.actionenergy.org.uk for tailored benchmark.

[h] Magistrates and County courts will generally not be air conditioned and have only limited catering facilities (if any); Crown courts are more likely to be air conditioned, and to have extensive IT provision, high lighting levels, and catering facilities; combined courts are generally the largest and most modern courts and therefore relatively low specific heating use

[i] Denominator is number of prisoners averaged over the year

Table 20.1 provides energy benchmarks for existing buildings. The figures in the shaded columns may be regarded as upper limits for new design. Conversion factors for floor areas for offices are given in Table 20.2[10].

Data from earlier samples of retail buildings provide a rough indication of the average percentage of gross floor area given over to sales, see Table 20.3

Table 20.4 shows benchmarks based on buildings in the Northern Ireland public sector estate[24].

Although most of the benchmarks provide a strong indication of the likely consumption of typical public sector buildings, it should be recognised that some of the sample sizes are smaller than those required to provide good reliability. Care should therefore be taken when comparing a particular building with the benchmarks based on smaller samples. The sample size is a very important indicator of the reliability of the data. Using the results from small samples e.g. less than 50 buildings may be unrepresentative of the whole sector.

Table 20.5 shows benchmarks for retail buildings[12,25].

Table 20.6 shows benchmarks for various buildings based on data collected between 1992 and 1994[26].

Table 20.2 Floor area conversion factors for offices

Office type	Treated % of gross	Nett % of treated	Nett % of gross
Naturally ventilated:			
— cellular	95	80	76
— open plan	95	80	76
Air conditioned:			
— standard	90	80	72
— prestige	85	80	68

Table 20.3 Average percentage of gross floor area given over to sales

Type of retail outlet	% of gross floor area
Department/chain store	51
Other non-food	67
Superstore/hypermarket	61
Supermarket (no bakery)	43
Supermarket (with bakery)	52
Small food shop:	
— general	70
— fruit and vegetables	69

Table 20.4 Fossil and electric building benchmarks for some public sector buildings in Northern Ireland[24]

Building Type	Mixed fuel buildings					All-electric buildings			
	Electricity / kW·h·m⁻² p.a.		Fossil fuel / kW·h·m⁻² p.a.		Sample size	Electricity / kW·h·m⁻² p.a.		Sample size	Floor area type
	Good	Typical	Good	Typical		Good	Typical		
Community centres	29	39	140	183	18	72	94	12	Gross
Fire stations	64	74	223	275	19	171	197	47	Gross
Libraries	24	45	133	192	40	54	86	44	Gross
Nurseries	17	23	121	183	53	68	84	37	Gross
Offices:									
— naturally ventilated, cellular-	47	83	92	138	32	65	104	65	Net lettable
— naturally ventilated, open plan	65	81	143	166	38	118	149	12	Net lettable
Police:									
— headquarters	108	135	138	187	49	—	—	—	—
— stations	91	121	125	167	80	101	218	17	Net lettable
Public toilets	—	—	—	—	—	20	44	41	Gross
Schools:									
— dining centres	19	42	63	99	44	42	74	17	Gross
— kitchens	47	63	213	336	54				
— primary	12	18	91	119	822	56	66	69	Gross
— secondary	16	22	101	120	168				
University:									
— non-residential	29	39	103	142	39	79	115	22	Net lettable
— residential, mixed fuel: electricity	50	60	164	201	19	—	—	—	—
Youth centres	17	28	145	197	25	24	54	12	Gross

Note: the results from small samples, e.g. less than 50 buildings, may be unrepresentative of the whole sector

Table 20.5 Fossil and electric building benchmarks for some retail buildings[12,25]

Building Type	Mixed fuel buildings					All-electric buildings			
	Electricity / kW·h·m⁻² p.a.		Fossil fuel / kW·h·m⁻² p.a.		Sample size	Electricity / kW·h·m⁻² p.a.		Sample size	Floor area type
	Good	Typical	Good	Typical		Good	Typical		
Banks	71	101	63	98	1299	122	195	822	Treated
Bookstores	–	–	–	–	–	210	255	63	Sales
Butchers' shops	–	–	–	–	–	475	577	194	Sales
Catalogue stores	83	101	37	69	296	100	133	101	Sales
Clothes shops	234	287	65	108	38	270	324	1957	Sales
Department stores	237	294	194	248	221	209	259	182	Sales
Distribution warehouses	53	67	103	169	77	55	101	9	Treated
DIY stores	127	160	149	192	94	—	—	—	—
Electrical goods:									
— rental	—	—	—	—	—	281	368	577	Sales
— retail	—	—	—	—	—	172	230	298	Sales
Frozen food centres	—	—	—	—	—	858	1029	601	Sales
Off-licenses	—	—	—	—	—	475	562	131	Sales
Shoe shops	—	—	—	—	—	197	279	411	Sales
Supermarkets	915	1026	200	261	352	1034	1155	207	Sales

Note: the results from small samples, e.g. less than 50 buildings, may be unrepresentative of the whole sector

Table 20.6 Fossil and electric building benchmarks for various types of building[26]

Building type	Mixed fuel buildings					All-electric buildings			
	Electricity / kW·h·m⁻² p.a.		Fossil fuel / kW·h·m⁻² p.a.		Sample size	Electricity / kW·h·m⁻² p.a.		Sample size	Floor area type
	Good	Typical	Good	Typical		Good	Typical		
Banks	70	95	74	105	835	97	144	623	Gross
Bingo halls	117	128	203	261	29	–	–	–	Gross
Cinemas	64	81	203	261	56	–	–	–	Gross
Department stores:									
— general	238	294	199	248	221	237	371	29	Sales
— specialist	225	269	219	319	863	333	447	204	Sales
Dry cleaners	197	247	622	828	26	350	400	14	Gross
Fast food outlets	818	889	480	669	48	–	–	–	Sales
Frozen food centres	–	–	–	–	–	858	1031	602	Sales
Further education	35	49	146	216	49	–	–	–	Gross
Night clubs	106	292	50	89	13	247	297	11	Gross
Offices (multi-tenanted)	25	53	131	181	57	–	–	–	Gross
Post offices (main)	45	69	142	214	323	80	142	56	Gross
Shops/stores:									
— butchers' shops	–	–	–	–	–	475	578	195	Sales
— 'DIY' shops	128	160	151	192	94	–	–	–	Sales
— electrical goods (rental)	–	–	–	–	–	281	367	585	Sales
— electrical goods (retail)	–	–	–	–	–	172	231	299	Sales
— fashion shops	–	–	–	–	–	303	350	150	Sales
— non-food stores	224	258	82	127	59	238	307	1352	Sales
Warehouses:									
— distribution	53	67	114	175	71	–	–	–	Gross
— refrigerated	125	142	56	83	38	–	–	–	Gross

Note: the results from small samples, e.g. less than 50 buildings, may be unrepresentative of the whole sector

20.2 Detailed component benchmarks

20.2.1 General component benchmarks

The component benchmarks shown in Table 20.7 are based on offices[10] but provide useful indicators for other buildings.

20.2.2 Air conditioning equipment benchmarks

Table 20.8 shows performance indicators for a range of air conditioning products with cooling capacities up to 100 kW. Those with capacities up to 12 kW are characterised by the energy label system for air conditioners which came into force in January 2003. This uses the scale A (higher) to G (lower). For products with capacities over 12 kW, indicators are shown as numerical values for coefficient of performance (COP) or energy efficiency rating (EER). Close-control air conditioners are excluded. High performance targets are set to be challenging but achievable for the type of products that dominate the UK market at present. The high performance indicator is set at a level that separates the 10% most energy-efficient products in each class. Low performance targets are set to cut off the tail of market performance distribution. The

low performance indicator is set at a level that separates the 30% least energy-efficient products in each class.

This information forms part of an integrated, public domain database managed by the Department for Environment, Food and Rural Affairs (DEFRA) Market Transformation Programme (www.mtprog.com). The energy efficiency performance indicators have been set by analysis of the complete product database from Eurovent Certification (www.eurovent-certification.org). The database includes over 6000 products, nearly 5000 of which are under 12 kW. Product performance databases for air conditioners and other HVACR products are available at (www.ukepic.com).

Table 20.7 General component benchmarks

Component	Good practice	Typical practice	Units
Fan efficiency	1.0–2.0	1.5–3.0	W/(litre·s⁻¹)
Heating pump installed capacity	0.8–1.35	1.9–2.8	W/m² TFA
Cooling pump installed capacity	1.8–2.0	3.1–3.4	W/m² TFA
Humidification installed capacity	15–20	20–25	W/m² TFA
Lighting installed capacity	12	15–20	W/m² TFA
Lighting efficiency	3	3.75–5	(W/m²)/100 lux
Office equipment installed capacity	10–15	12–18	W/m² TFA

Note: TFA = treated floor area

Table 20.8 Performance indicators for air conditioners (based on data from Eurovent, July 2002)

Size ranges	Type	High performance indicators		Low performance indicators	
		Cooling	Heating	Cooling	Heating
1–12 kW	Air cooled:				
	— split and multisplit (cooling only)	B	—	F	—
	— split and multisplit, heat pump	B	B	F	F
	— packaged (cooling only)	B	—	F	—
	— packaged, heat pump	B	C	F	F
	Water cooled:				
	— packaged (cooling only)	C	—	G	—
	— packaged, heat pump	C	C	G	F
12–45 kW	Air cooled:				
	— split (cooling only)	2.77	—	2.35	—
	— split, heat pump	2.78	3.25	2.29	2.7
	— multisplit (cooling only)	2.67	—	2.4	—
	— multisplit, heat pump	2.9	3.11	2.3	2.78
	— packaged (cooling only)	2.85	—	2.22	—
	— packaged, heat pump	2.75	3.47	2.2	2.7
	Water cooled:				
	— packaged (cooling only)	★	★	★	★
	— packaged, heat pump	★	★	★	★
45–100 kW	Air cooled:				
	— split (cooling only)	2.73	—	2.29	—
	— split, heat pump	2.6	3.07	2.2	2.6
	— packaged (cooling only)	3.1	—	2.29	—
	— packaged, heat pump	2.57	3.2	2.19	2.7

★ Insufficient data to set reliable indicator

20.3 Detailed end-use benchmarks

20.3.1 Offices

The benchmarks in Tables 20.9 and 20.10 are taken from Energy Consumption Guide ECG 19[10], and relate to treated floor area.

Table 20.9 Offices: system and building energy benchmarks

System	Delivered energy for stated office types / (kW·h·m⁻²) per year							
	Type 1		Type 2		Type 3		Type 4	
	Good practice	Typical	Good practice	Typical	Good practice	Typical	Good practice	Typical
Gas/oil heating and hot water	79	151	79	151	97	178	107	201
Catering gas	0	0	0	0	0	0	7	9
Cooling	0	0	1	2	14	31	21	41
Fans, pumps and controls	2	6	4	8	30	60	36	67
Humidification	0	0	0	0	8	18	12	23
Lighting	14	23	22	38	27	54	29	60
Office equipment	12	18	20	27	23	31	23	32
Catering electricity	2	3	3	5	5	6	13	15
Other electricity	3	4	4	5	7	8	13	15
Computer room	0	0	0	0	14	18	87	105
Total gas or oil	79	151	79	151	97	178	114	210
Total electricity	33	54	54	85	128	226	234	358

Note: Type 1: cellular naturally ventilated; Type 2: open plan naturally ventilated; Type 3: 'standard' air conditioned; Type 4: 'prestige' air conditioned

Table 20.10 Offices: component benchmarks

System	Benchmark value for stated office type							
	Type 1		Type 2		Type 3		Type 4	
	Good practice	Typical	Good practice	Typical	Good practice	Typical	Good practice	Typical
Lighting:								
— installed loading (W·m⁻² floor area)	12	15	12	18	12	20	12	20
— full load hours/year (h)	1125	1500	1800	2100	2240	2720	2450	2975
— system hours/year (h)	2500	2500	3000	3000	3200	3200	3500	3500
— utilisation (%)	45	60	60	70	70	85	70	85
Fans (only):								
— consumption (kW·h per year)	0	0	0	0	22	42	24	44
— full load (W·m⁻² floor area)	0	0	0	0	8	12	8	12
— full load hours/year (h)	0	0	0	0	2750	3500	3000	3700
Desk equipment:								
— load (W·m⁻² floor area (local))	10	12	12	14	14	16	15	18
— percentage floor area (%)	60	60	65	65	60	60	50	50
— load (W/m² floor area (building))	6.0	7.2	7.8	9.1	8.4	9.6	7.5	9.0
— operating hours/year (h)	2000	2500	2500	3000	2750	3250	3000	3500

20.3.2 Banks and agencies

The benchmarks shown in Tables 20.11 and 20.12 are taken from CIBSE TM22[27]. The overall bank and agency benchmarks, with gas/oil heating or all-electric, are from *Introduction to energy efficiency in post offices, building societies, banks and agencies* and relate to gross floor area. These have been developed to allow for cooling, and end-use energy and system benchmarks. They have been developed based on information from surveys and comparison with office buildings[10].

Table 20.11 Banks and agencies: system and building energy benchmarks

System	Delivered energy for stated bank/agency type / (kW·h·m⁻²) per year							
	Type 1		Type 2		Type 3		Type 4	
	Good practice	Typical	Good practice	Typical	Good practice	Typical	Good practice	Typical
Fossil fuels:								
— gas/oil heating and hot water	70	100	0	0	150	230	0	0
Electricity:								
— heating	10	20	38	56	5	5	35	82
— hot water	5	7	5	7	5	7	5	7
— lighting	25	37	25	37	25	37	25	37
— fans, pumps and controls	3	4	5	8	3	4	4	7
— cooling	0	0	0	0	0	0	0	0
— office equipment	12	15	12	15	6	10	6	10
— server and communications rooms	3	3	3	3	0	0	0	0
— other electricity	12	14	12	14	11	12	15	17
Total gas or oil	70	100	0	0	150	230	0	0
Total electricity	70	100	100	140	55	75	90	160

System	Delivered energy for stated bank/agency type / (kW·h·m⁻²) per year							
	Type 5		Type 6		Type 7		Type 8	
	Good practice	Typical	Good practice	Typical	Good practice	Typical	Good practice	Typical
Fossil fuels:								
— gas/oil heating and hot water	70	100	0	0	150	230	0	0
Electricity:								
— heating	10	20	38	56	5	5	35	82
— hot water	5	7	5	7	5	7	5	7
— lighting	31	47	31	47	31	47	31	47
— fans, pumps and controls	9	14	11	18	9	14	10	17
— cooling	12	20	12	20	12	20	12	20
— office equipment	18	25	18	25	12	20	12	20
— server and communications rooms	3	3	3	3	0	0	0	0
— other electricity	12	14	12	14	11	12	15	17
Total gas or oil	70	100	0	0	150	230	0	0
Total electricity	100	150	130	190	85	125	120	210

Note: Type 1: bank, gas heating, no cooling; Type 2: bank, all electric, no cooling; Type 3: agency, gas heating, no cooling; Type 4: agency, all electric, no cooling; Type 5: bank, gas heating, with cooling; Type 6: bank, all electric, with cooling; Type 7: agency, gas heating, with cooling; Type 8: agency, all electric, with cooling.

Table 20.12 Banks and agencies: component benchmarks

System	Benchmark value for stated building type							
	Type 1		Type 2		Type 3		Type 4	
	Good practice	Typical	Good practice	Typical	Good practice	Typical	Good practice	Typical
Lighting:								
— installed loading (W·m⁻² floor area)	13	15	13	15	13	15	13	15
— full load hours per year (h)	1923	2467	1923	2467	1923	2467	1923	2467
— illuminance (lux)	450	500	450	500	450	500	450	500
— installed power density ((W·m⁻²)/100 lux)	2.9	3.0	2.9	3.0	2.9	3.0	2.9	3.0
— system hours per year (h)	2300	2800	2300	2800	2300	2800	2300	2800
— utilisation	84%	88%	84%	88%	84%	88%	84%	88%
Desk equipment:								
— load (W·m⁻² floor area (local))	8.0	9.0	8.0	9.0	4.0	6.0	4.0	6.0
— percentage of total floor area (%)	60%	62%	60%	62%	60%	62%	60%	62%
Equipment:								
— load (W·m⁻² floor area (building))	4.8	5.6	4.8	5.6	2.4	3.7	2.4	3.7
— hours per year (h)	2500	2700	2500	2700	2500	2700	2500	2700

System	Benchmark value for stated building type							
	Type 5		Type 6		Type 7		Type 8	
	Good practice	Typical	Good practice	Typical	Good practice	Typical	Good practice	Typical
Lighting:								
— installed loading (W·m⁻² floor area)	16	19	16	19	16	19	16	19
— full load hours per year (h)	1938	2474	1938	2474	1938	2474	1938	2474
— illuminance (lux)	500	550	500	550	500	550	500	550
— installed power density ((W·m⁻²)/100 lux)	3.2	3.5	3.2	3.5	3.2	3.5	3.2	3.5
— system hours per year (h)	2300	2800	2300	2800	2300	2800	2300	2800
— utilisation	84%	88%	84%	88%	84%	88%	84%	88%
Desk equipment:								
— load (W·m⁻² floor area (local))	12.0	16.0	12.0	16.0	8.0	12.0	8.0	12.0
— percentage of total floor area (%)	60%	58%	60%	58%	60%	62%	60%	62%
Equipment:								
— load (W·m⁻² floor area (building))	7.2	9.3	7.2	9.3	4.8	7.4	4.8	7.4
— hours per year (h)	2500	2700	2500	2700	2500	2700	2500	2700

Note: Type 1: bank, gas heating, no cooling; Type 2: bank, all electric, no cooling; Type 3: agency, gas heating, no cooling; Type 4: agency, all electric, no cooling; Type 5: bank, gas heating, with cooling; Type 6: bank, all electric, with cooling; Type 7: agency, gas heating, with cooling; Type 8: agency, all electric, with cooling.

20.3.3   Hotel benchmarks

The benchmarks shown in Tables 20.13 to 20.16 are taken from CIBSE TM22[27]. The main categories and the corresponding benchmark data are from Energy Consumption Guide ECG 36[16], which are compatible with Energy Efficiency Booklet EEB 9[8]. The ECG 36 benchmarks include a factor for air conditioning, applicable to all three types and a breakdown into end-uses for a typical luxury hotel. The remaining benchmarks have been derived to be compatible with this information.

The benchmarks relate to the number of bedrooms or the total hotel gross floor area. To avoid internal inconsistencies from other benchmark data, the 'kW·h per bedroom' benchmarks are based on the kW·h/m² benchmarks with a standard value of gross floor area per bedroom of 58 m².

Each category may have air conditioning and/or a swimming pool.

Table 20.13 Hotels: delivered energy benchmarks related to number of bedrooms

System	Delivered energy for stated hotel type / (kW·h per bedroom) per year					
	Type 1		Type 2		Type 3	
	Good practice	Typical	Good practice	Typical	Good practice	Typical
Electricity:						
— hotel with no pool or air conditioning	5220	8700	4640	8120	4640	6960
— additional for pool	580	1160	580	1160	580	1160
— additional for air conditioning	2320	4060	1740	3480	1160	2900
Fossil fuels (gas or oil):						
— hotel with no pool or air conditioning	17400	26680	15080	23200	13920	20880
— additional for pool	1740	2900	1740	2900	1740	2900
— additional for air conditioning	1740	2320	1740	2320	1160	1740

Note: Type 1: luxury hotel; Type 2: business or holiday hotel; Type 3: small hotel

Table 20.14 Hotels: electricity benchmarks related to floor area — basic data for hotel without pool or air conditioning

System	Delivered energy for stated hotel type / (kW·h·per m²) per year					
	Type 1		Type 2		Type 3	
	Good practice	Typical	Good practice	Typical	Good practice	Typical
Heating	0	0	0	0	0	0
Hot water	0	0	0	0	0	0
Lighting	40	70	35	65	35	55
Catering	23	32	23	32	23	32
Ventilation fans, pumps, controls	5	10	5	10	5	10
Cooling	2	3	2	3	2	3
Office equipment	5	10	5	10	5	5
Leisure pool	5	10	5	10	5	7
Other	10	15	5	10	5	8
Total electricity	90	150	80	140	80	120

Note: Type 1: luxury hotel; Type 2: business or holiday hotel; Type 3: small hotel

Table 20.15 Hotels: electricity benchmarks related to floor area — additional energy for pool and/or air conditioning

System	Delivered energy for stated hotel type / (kW·h·per m²) per year					
	Type 1		Type 2		Type 3	
	Good practice	Typical	Good practice	Typical	Good practice	Typical
Swimming pool only:						
— leisure pool	10	20	10	20	10	20
Air conditioning only:						
— ventilation fans, pumps, controls	25	40	20	35	13	30
— cooling	15	30	10	25	7	20

Note: Type 1: luxury hotel; Type 2: business or holiday hotel; Type 3: small hotel

Table 20.16 Hotels: fossil fuel benchmarks related to floor area — basic data for no pool or air conditioning

System	Delivered energy for stated hotel type / (kW·h·per m²) per year					
	Type 1		Type 2		Type 3	
	Good practice	Typical	Good practice	Typical	Good practice	Typical
Heating	180	260	160	230	160	230
Hot water	70	110	60	90	50	70
Catering	50	90	40	80	30	60
Pool	0	0	0	0	0	0
Other	0	0	0	0	0	0
Total gas or oil	300	460	260	400	240	360

Note: Type 1: luxury hotel; Type 2: business or holiday hotel; Type 3: small hotel

Table 20.17 Hotels: fossil fuel benchmarks related to floor area — additional energy for pool and/or air conditioning

System	Delivered energy for stated hotel type / (kW·h·per m²) per year					
	Type 1		Type 2		Type 3	
	Good practice	Typical	Good practice	Typical	Good practice	Typical
Swimming pool only:						
— leisure pool	30	50	30	50	30	50
Air conditioning only:						
— heating	30	40	30	40	20	30

Note: Type 1: luxury hotel; Type 2: business or holiday hotel; Type 3: small hotel

20.3.4 Mixed-use and industrial building benchmarks

The benchmarks shown in Tables 20.18 and 20.19 are taken from CIBSE TM22[27]. The categories for industrial buildings (Types 5–8), the corresponding benchmarks and Table 20.20 are taken from Energy Consumption Guide ECG 18[11], which are compatible with Energy Efficiency Booklet: *Introduction to energy efficiency in factories and warehouses.* Benchmarks relate to gross floor area. ECG 18 uses three levels of performance: 'typical', 'improved' and 'new building'; the 'new building' performance level from ECG 18 is used as the 'good practice' performance level in these tables.

The office categories and benchmarks are taken from ECG 19[10], although these have been modified by removing any computer room energy, and adjusting the benchmarks for use with gross internal floor area rather than treated floor area.

The benchmarks for industrial buildings shown in Table 20.20 are taken from ECG 18[11]. The number of shifts represents an average based on a typical 8-hour shift. Note that although ECG 81[28] has superseded some parts of ECG 18, the latter publication still contains valuable information.

Table 20.18 Mixed use buildings: system and building energy benchmarks

System	Delivered energy for stated building type / (kW·h·m⁻²) per year							
	Type 1		Type 2		Type 3		Type 4	
	Good practice	Typical	Good practice	Typical	Good practice	Typical	Good practice	Typical
Fossil fuels:								
— gas/oil heating and hot water	75	143	75	143	87	160	91	171
— catering gas	0	0	0	0	0	0	6	8
Electricity:								
— cooling	0	0	1	2	13	28	18	35
— fans, pumps and controls	2	6	4	8	27	54	31	57
— lighting	13	22	21	36	24	49	25	51
— office equipment	11	17	19	26	21	28	20	27
— catering	2	3	3	5	5	5	11	13
— other	3	4	4	5	14	25	24	36
— process/computer room	0	0	0	0	0	0	0	0
Total gas or oil	75	143	75	143	87	160	97	179
Total electricity	31	51	51	81	103	189	127	219

System	Delivered energy for stated building type / (kW·h·m⁻²) per year							
	Type 5		Type 6		Type 7		Type 8	
	Good practice	Typical	Good practice	Typical	Good practice	Typical	Good practice	Typical
Fossil fuels:								
— gas/oil heating and hot water	80	185	90	300	100	225	125	325
— catering gas	0	0	0	0	0	0	0	0
Electricity:								
— cooling	1	1	2	2	6	6	6	6
— fans, pumps and controls	5	8	6	10	10	15	10	20
— lighting	5	25	15	50	20	60	20	45
— office equipment	2	2	2	2	8	8	2	2
— catering	2	2	2	2	4	4	2	2
— other	5	5	4	4	7	7	10	10
— process/computer room	0	0	0	0	0	0	0	0
Total gas or oil	80	185	90	300	100	225	125	325
Total electricity	20	43	31	70	55	100	50	85

Note: Type 1: cellular naturally ventilated office; Type 2: open plan naturally ventilated office; Type 3: standard air conditioned office; Type 4: prestige air conditioned office; Type 5: distribution and storage; Type 6: light manufacturing; Type 7: factory office; Type 8: general manufacturing

Table 20.19 Mixed use buildings: component benchmarks

System	Benchmark value for stated building type							
	Type 1		Type 2		Type 3		Type 4	
	Good practice	Typical	Good practice	Typical	Good practice	Typical	Good practice	Typical
Lighting:								
— installed loading (W·m⁻² floor area)	11.4	14.3	11.4	17.1	10.8	18.0	10.2	17.0
— illuminance (lux)	380	428	380	428	360	450	340	425
— installed power density ((W·m⁻²)/100 lux)	3	3	3	4	3	4	3	4
— full load hours/year (h)	1125	1500	1800	2100	2240	2720	2450	2975
— system hours/year (h)	2500	2500	3000	3000	3200	3200	3500	3500
— utilisation	45%	60%	60%	70%	70%	85%	70%	85%
Fans (only):								
— consumption (kW·h per year)	0	0	0	0	20	38	20	37
— full load (W·m⁻² floor area)	0.0	0.0	0.0	0.0	7.2	10.8	6.8	10.2
— full load hours/year (h)	0	0	0	0	2750	3500	3000	3700
Desk equipment:								
— consumption (W·m⁻² floor area (local))	10	12	12	14	14	16	15	18
— percentage floor area (%)	57%	57%	62%	62%	54%	54%	43%	43%
Equipment:								
— load (W·m⁻² floor area (building))	5.7	6.8	7.4	8.6	7.6	8.6	6.4	7.7
— hours/year (h)	2000	2500	2500	3000	2750	3250	3000	3500

System	Benchmark value for stated building type							
	Type 5		Type 6		Type 7		Type 8	
	Good practice	Typical	Good practice	Typical	Good practice	Typical	Good practice	Typical
Lighting:								
— installed loading (W·m⁻² floor area)	3.0	6.0	4.0	9.0	12.0	18.0	5.0	9.0
— illuminance (lux)	150	200	200	300	400	450	200	300
— installed power density ((W·m⁻²)/100 lux)	2.0	3.0	2.0	3.0	3.0	4.0	2.5	3.0
— full load hours/year (h)	1667	4167	3750	5556	1667	3333	4000	5000
— system hours/year (h)	3000	4500	4500	5600	3000	4000	6000	6000
— utilisation	56%	93%	83%	99%	56%	83%	67%	83%
Fans (only):								
— consumption (kW·h per year)	2	4	4	6	6	10	6	12
— full load (W·m⁻² floor area)	1.0	1.0	1.0	1.0	2.0	2.5	1.0	2.0
— full load hours/year (h)	2000	4000	4000	6000	3000	4000	6000	6000
Desk equipment:								
— consumption (W·m⁻² floor area (local))	12	12	12	12	12	12	12	12
— percentage floor area (%)	6%	6%	4%	4%	22%	22%	3%	3%
Equipment:								
— load (W·m⁻² floor area (building))	0.7	0.7	0.5	0.5	2.6	2.6	0.4	0.4
— hours per year (h)	3000	3000	4500	4500	3000	3000	6000	6000

Note: Type 1: cellular naturally ventilated office; Type 2: open plan naturally ventilated office; Type 3: standard air conditioned office; Type 4: prestige

Table 20.20 Energy consumption for various types of industry

Industry	Shifts	Building related energy / (kW·h·m⁻²) per year			Process energy / (kW·h·m⁻²) per year
		Space heating	Other uses	Total	
Laboratories	1.5	669	538	1207	346
Chemical plant	3	543	85	628	3589
General manufacturing	2.3	328	81	409	495
Paper	3	298	88	386	2636
Electronics	2.5	298	65	363	341
Textiles	2.5	303	38	341	479
Plastics	2.3	288	52	340	532
Rubber	2.6	233	93	326	967
Light manufacturing	1.7	286	38	324	82
Engineering	1.7	257	45	302	85
Cooked food	1.8	170	121	291	795
Furnace/foundry	2.1	245	34	279	1012
Chemical factory	2.4	249	28	277	346
Distribution	1	164	44	208	0
Cold food	2.5	80	93	173	1247

20.3.5   Sports and recreation buildings

Tables 20.21 and 20.22 shows overall energy benchmarks for sports and recreation buildings. The component/zone benchmarks shown in Tables 20.23 and 20.24 are also taken from ECG 78[14], which provides a full methodology for developing specific benchmarks for individual sports and recreation buildings.

Table 20.21 Sports and recreation buildings: energy used by activity zone

Zone	Delivered energy* / (kW·h·m⁻²) per year			
	Electricity		Heating fuel	
	Good practice	Typical	Good practice	Typical
Leisure pool hall	208.1	318.4	999.6	2325.6
Conventional pool hall	208.1	318.4	824.9	1936.7
Sports hall	39.4	69.0	102.6	224.3
Bowls hall	31.8	51.9	67.6	130.5
Ice rink hall	204.8	307.7	73.8	158.8
Fitness/health suites	78.4	130.0	209.3	482.3
Internal courts	52.4	86.2	86.3	190.5
Wet changing and showers	93.4	167.1	529.7	1267.0
Dry changing and showers	92.4	149.6	299.4	676.0
Spectator	62.3	102.4	168.4	354.8
Common areas (mechanical ventilation)	74.1	117.7	168.4	354.8
Common areas (natural ventilation)	52.7	80.9	109.5	185.3
Plant rooms	74.1	117.7	168.4	354.8
Stores	52.7	80.9	109.5	185.3
Car park	4.6	6.6	0.0	0.0
Floodlit court/pitch	3.3	5.8	0.0	0.0

* related to zone area, not total building area

Table 20.22 Sports and recreation buildings: energy used by facilities

Facility and unit for energy assessment	Delivered energy / (kW·h / unit) per year			
	Electricity		Heating fuel	
	Good practice	Typical	Good practice	Typical
Snack bar (hot meals/day)	109.5	182.5	0.0	0.0
Sauna/steam room (number of persons)	1168.0	1752.0	0.0	0.0
Solarium (number of sunbeds)	2628.0	3942.0	0.0	0.0
Exercise machines	788.4	1051.2	0.0	0.0
Wave machine	13140.0	17520.0	0.0	0.0
Flume	3504.0	6570.0	0.0	0.0
Spa pool/jacuzzi (number of persons)	876.0	1752.0	0.0	0.0

Table 20.23 Sports and recreation buildings: energy used by building services systems — 'typical' benchmark level

Zone	Local electricity use by stated system* / kW·h·m⁻²					Local heating fuel used by stated system* / kW·h·m⁻²			
	Lighting	Ventilation	Pumps	Other	Total	Fabric	Ventilation	Pool/other	Total
Leisure pool hall	49.9	104.6	148.9	15.0	318.4	361.1	866.9	1097.6	2325.6
Conventional pool hall	49.9	104.6	148.9	15.0	318.4	294.6	707.2	934.9	1936.7
Sports hall	42.9	9.1	7.0	10.0	69.0	107.1	83.4	33.9	224.3
Bowls hall	42.9	1.8	4.7	2.5	51.9	107.1	16.7	6.8	130.5
Ice rink hall	49.9	49.3	8.5	200.0	307.7	0	83.4	75.4	158.8
Fitness/health suites	61.3	49.0	9.7	10.0	130.0	170.6	294.8	16.9	482.3
Internal courts	60.0	9.1	7.0	10.0	86.2	107.1	83.4	0	190.5
Wet changing and showers	46.0	97.9	13.1	10.0	167.1	284.3	982.7	0	1267.0
Dry changing and showers	46.0	84.0	9.7	10.0	149.6	170.6	505.4	0	676.0
Spectator areas	46.0	36.7	9.7	10.0	102.4	170.6	184.3	0	354.8
Common areas:									
— mechanical ventilation	61.3	36.7	9.7	10.0	117.7	170.6	184.3	0	354.8
— natural ventilation	61.3	2.9	9.7	7.0	80.9	170.6	14.7	0	185.3
Plant rooms	61.3	36.7	9.7	10.0	117.7	170.6	184.3	0	354.8
Stores	61.3	2.9	9.7	7.0	80.9	170.6	14.7	0	185.3

* related to zone area, not total building area

Table 20.24 Sports and recreation buildings: energy used by building services systems — 'good practice' benchmark

Zone	Local electricity use by stated system* / kW·h·m⁻²					Local heating fuel used by stated system* / kW·h·m⁻²			
	Lighting	Ventilation	Pumps	Other	Total	Fabric	Ventilation	Pool/other	Total
Leisure pool hall	26.3	65.0	106.8	10.0	208.1	273.5	248.5	477.6	999.6
Conventional pool hall	26.3	65.0	106.8	10.0	208.1	221.7	201.5	401.7	824.9
Sports hall	26.0	4.3	4.1	5.0	39.4	61.0	25.3	16.3	102.6
Bowls hall	26.0	0.6	3.3	2.0	31.8	61.0	3.4	3.3	67.6
Ice rink hall	26.3	23.3	5.3	150.0	204.8	0	28.2	45.6	73.8
Fitness/health suites	41.4	25.9	6.1	5.0	78.4	102.9	98.2	8.1	209.3
Internal courts	39.0	4.3	4.1	5.0	52.4	61.0	25.3	0	86.3
Wet changing and showers	29.6	51.7	7.1	5.0	93.4	182.1	347.6	0	529.7
Dry changing and showers	29.6	51.7	6.1	5.0	92.4	102.9	196.4	0	299.4
Spectator	29.6	21.6	6.1	5.0	62.3	102.9	65.5	0	168.4
Common areas (mech. vent.)	41.4	21.6	6.1	5.0	74.1	102.9	65.5	0	168.4
Common areas (nat. vent.)	41.4	2.2	6.1	3.0	52.7	102.9	6.5	0	109.5
Plant rooms	41.4	21.6	6.1	5.0	74.1	102.9	65.5	0	168.4
Stores	41.4	2.2	6.1	3.0	52.7	102.9	6.5	0	109.5

* related to zone area, not total building area

20.3.6 Hospital buildings

Table 20.25, page 20-14, shows overall energy benchmarks for hospital buildings derived from ECG 72[19]. Energy benchmarks in hospitals are often quoted in GJ/(100 m³) of heated volume to take account of different ceiling heights. A ceiling height of 2.9 m has been assumed in Table 20.25. To convert kW·h·m⁻² to GJ/(100 m³), divide by the factor given in Table 20.26.

Table 20.26 Correction factor for ceiling height

Ceiling height (m)	Factor
3.6	10
3.3	9.17
3.0	8.34
2.9	8.06
2.7	7.50

Table 20.25 Hospitals: energy used by services

System	Delivered energy for stated hospital type* / (kW·h·m⁻²) per year							
	Teaching		Acute		Cottage		Long stay	
	Good practice	Typical	Good practice	Typical	Good practice	Typical	Good practice	Typical
Fossil fuels:								
— space heating	215.3	249.4	296.3	308.2	322.1	345.1	251.8	332.4
— base load	123.4	161.6	126.1	202.1	121.2	146.7	148.9	186.0
Electricity:								
— lighting	20.0	40.0	20.0	40.0	11.8	23.5	11.0	22.0
— HVAC	17.3	25.6	15.8	23.2	10.2	12.5	7.0	10.0
— other building services	11.9	13.4	11.8	13.1	10.1	13.1	9.9	13.1
— IT equipment	6.0	6.7	5.9	6.5	1.2	1.6	1.2	1.6
— supplementary heating	2.8	3.1	2.7	3.0	4.7	6.0	4.5	6.1
— personal small power	11.0	14.0	11.0	14.0	11.0	14.0	11.0	14.0
— medical equipment	15.3	17.0	3.9	4.4	1.5	1.9	0.7	0.9
— catering	1.9	2.1	3.3	3.7	4.3	5.5	3.0	4.0
Total fossil	338.7	411.0	422.3	510.4	443.3	491.8	400.7	518.4
Total electricity	86.2	121.9	74.4	108.0	54.8	78.2	48.4	71.8

* based on a ceiling height of 2.9 m

References

1   *Building energy efficiency in schools. A guide to a whole school approach* Energy Efficiency Booklet EEB 001 (Action Energy) (1999) (www.actionenergy.org.uk)

2   *Introduction to energy efficiency in catering establishments* Energy Efficiency Booklet EEB 002 (Action Energy) (1994) (www.actionenergy.org.uk)

3   *Introduction to energy efficiency in shops and stores* Energy Efficiency Booklet EEB 003 (Action Energy) (1999) (www.actionenergy.org.uk)

4   *Introduction to energy efficiency in further and higher education* Energy Efficiency Booklet EEB 005 (Action Energy) (1994) (www.actionenergy.org.uk)

5   *Introduction to energy efficiency in offices* Energy Efficiency Booklet EEB 006 (Action Energy) (1999) (www.actionenergy.org.uk)

6   *Introduction to energy efficiency in sports and recreation centres* Energy Efficiency Booklet EEB 007 (Action Energy) (1999) (www.actionenergy.org.uk)

7   *Introduction to energy efficiency in museums; galleries; libraries and churches* Energy Efficiency Booklet EEB 008 (Action Energy) (1999) (www.actionenergy.org.uk)

8   *Introduction to energy efficiency in hotels* Energy Efficiency Booklet EEB 009 (Action Energy) (1994) (www.actionenergy.org.uk)

9   *Introduction to energy efficiency in prisons; emergency buildings and courts* Energy Efficiency Booklet EEB 012 (Action Energy) (2002) (www.actionenergy.org.uk)

10   *Energy efficiency in offices* Energy Consumption Guide ECG 19 (Action Energy) (2000) (www.actionenergy.org.uk)

11   *Energy use in industrial buildings and sites* Energy Consumption Guide ECG 18 (Action Energy) (www.actionenergy.org.uk)

12   *Energy benchmarking in the retail sector* BMI special report (Building Maintenance Information: London) (1999)

13   *Energy use in prisons* Energy Consumption Guide ECG 84 (Action Energy) (2001) (www.actionenergy.org.uk)

14   *Sports and recreation buildings* Energy Consumption Guide ECG 78 (Action Energy) (2000) (www.actionenergy.org.uk)

15   *Energy use in Ministry of Defence establishments* Energy Consumption Guide ECG 75 (Action Energy) (1999) (www.actionenergy.org.uk)

16   *Energy efficiency in hotels — a guide for owners and managers* Energy Consumption Guide ECG 36 (Action Energy) (1999) (www.actionenergy.org.uk)

17   *Energy management study in the higher education sector* Management Review Guide (Bristol: Higher Education Funding Council) (1996)

18   *Energy consumption guide for nursing and residential homes* Energy Consumption Guide ECG 57 (Action Energy) (1996) (www.actionenergy.org.uk)

19   *Energy consumption in hospitals* Energy Consumption Guide ECG 72 (Action Energy) (1996) (www.actionenergy.org.uk)

20   *Saving energy — a whole school approach* Good Practice Guide GPG 343 (Action Energy) (2003) (www.actionenergy.org.uk)

21   *Energy benchmarks for local authority buildings* Energy Consumption Guide ECG 87 (Action Energy) (2002) (www.actionenergy.org.uk)

22   *Energy use in court buildings* Energy Consumption Guide ECG 82 (Action Energy) (2002) (www.actionenergy.org.uk)

23   *Energy use in government laboratories* Energy Consumption Guide ECG 83 (Action Energy) (2002) (www.actionenergy.org.uk)

24   Jones P G, Turner R N, Browne D W J and Illingworth P J Energy benchmarks for public sector buildings in Northern Ireland *Proc. CIBSE Nat. Conf., Dublin, 2000* (London: Chartered Institution of Building Services Engineers) (2000)

25   Jones P G, Bond M and Grigg P F Energy benchmarks for retail buildings *Proc. CIBSE Nat. Conf., Harrogate, 4–5 October 1999* (London: Chartered Institution of Building Services Engineers) (1999)

26   Jones P G and Cheshire D Bulk data for benchmarking non-domestic building energy consumption *Proc. CIBSE Nat. Conf. Harrogate, 1996* (London: Chartered Institution of Building Services Engineers) (1996)

27   *Energy assessment and reporting methodology: Office assessment method* CIBSE TM22 (London: Chartered Institution of Building Services Engineers) (1999)

28   *Benchmarking tool for industrial buildings — heating and internal lighting* Energy Consumption Guide ECG 81 (Action Energy) (2002) (www.actionenergy.org.uk)

Appendix A1: CIBSE policy statements

A1.1 Energy

A1.1.1 Objective

It is the Institution's policy to encourage the installation of those building services systems which minimise pollution or the consumption of energy.

The main objectives of this policy are:

— to mitigate the demands placed on the world's reserves of fossil fuels

— to reduce the consumption of fossil fuels, in order to reduce pollution

— to promote the use of renewable and sustainable energy sources and passive design solutions.

A1.1.2 Policy

Whilst actively pursuing this policy it is accepted that any energy efficiency measures must demonstrate that they are cost effective and can maintain appropriate standards.

To meet these aims the Institution commits to:

— support the Government's energy policy in promoting energy efficiency measures and the achievement of the UK's carbon emissions reduction targets

— encourage the design and refurbishment of buildings which minimise energy consumption

— encourage a holistic view of building design, operation and specification which enables effective collaboration between the professions to be achieved

— advise owners/occupiers of new and existing buildings on methods for reducing energy consumption

— support research into the development of energy efficient systems.

A1.2 Combined heat and power

A1.2.1 Objective

Combined heat and power (CHP) is a well-proven technology, which generates both electricity and heat at the point of use.

CHP is appropriate for both new build and refurbishment and, when used in the correct applications, can contribute to or provide:

— space heating requirements

— domestic hot water requirements

— cooling requirements (when used in conjunction with absorption chillers)

— improved security of electrical supply

— significantly reduced carbon emissions

— an environmentally friendly image

— substantial energy cost savings

— substantial returns on investment.

CHP is expected to provide a sizeable proportion of the UK's commitment to reducing its CO_2 emissions, and the government is supporting the use of CHP accordingly, most noticeably through its exemption from the Climate Change Levy.

A1.2.2 Policy

CIBSE recognises that CHP is a very effective means of reducing the energy costs and the environmental impact of buildings. It is therefore CIBSE's policy to encourage Institution members to consider CHP for use in all suitable applications.

A1.3 Air conditioning

A1.3.1 Objective

The Institution's objective is to encourage the adoption of energy efficient design solutions which achieve environmental, functional requirements and air quality standards.

A1.3.2 Policy

— To encourage building services engineers to adopt a rational approach to the use of air conditioning in new and refurbished buildings.

— To encourage building services engineers to adopt a holistic approach to design solutions which utilise available opportunities for passive energy use.

— To encourage the use of refrigerants or alternatives that minimise environmental damage in accordance with the policy defined in the CIBSE

Guidance Note GN1: *CFCs, HCFCs, HFCs and halons*[1].

— To support the Government's initiative of reviewing building regulations to include demonstrating compliance with performance requirements for air conditioning and mechanical ventilation by the use of the energy performance index method.

— To support the 1997 Kyoto Protocol on Climate Change which sets targets for reducing the emissions of greenhouse gases for 2008 to 2012.

— To support the Government's May 1999 initiative *A better quality of life: a strategy for sustainable development for the UK*[2] on sustainable development.

A1.4   Global warming

A1.4.1   Objective

To recognise that global warming is a major threat to the stability of the Earth's ecosystems. To promote an approach to design, operation and maintenance that minimises the contribution of buildings to global warming. The objectives are wholly consistent with the policy on sustainability.

A1.4.2   Policy

To encourage building services engineers to adopt a co-ordinated approach to environmental issues at all stages of the life cycle of buildings, including conception, briefing, design, procurement, construction, maintenance and ultimate disposal by:

— Liaising closely with designers, design teams, clients, operators and owners at all stages of the design and construction process.

— Developing and improving techniques for quantifying the global warming potential of materials, components, equipment and processes.

— Encouraging the development of designs, materials, components, systems and processes with reduced or zero effects on global warming.

— Adopting techniques and products which minimise the use of designs, materials, components, systems and processes which contribute to global warming in their construction, transportation, installation and use.

— Encouraging the use of designs, materials, components, systems and processes which do not contribute to global warming on final disposal.

— Ensuring building operators are advised of the importance of properly maintaining systems to minimise global warming.

— Encouraging programmes for replacement and substitution of designs, materials, components, systems and processes with those having a reduced or no contribution to global warming.

A1.5   Passive measures for energy efficiency in buildings

A1.5.1   Objective

To recognise and promote the benefits and advantages of passive measures in achieving improved energy efficiency in buildings.

A1.5.2   Policy

To encourage building services engineers to apply their understanding of thermal environmental technology and expertise in design and construction techniques to the benefit of clients and other construction profession disciplines by highlighting and promoting the cost effective application of passive energy efficiency measures including:

— appropriate thermal insulation standards for building envelopes

— controlling unwanted building solar heat gains

— the exposure of internal surfaces of building mass to allow thermal inertia to minimise the effect of peak heat gains

— improved standards of building envelope airtightness to minimise spurious air infiltration

— the use of vegetation to reduce unwanted solar heat gains

— determining and demonstrating the effect of diversities in periodic heat gains and losses

— the provision of arrangements to permit natural ventilation of buildings or appropriate parts of buildings during mid-season or other suitable weather conditions

— the use of night time ventilation by natural or mechanical means to pre-cool the building by the introduction of cool, outside air to mitigate the need for daytime cooling

— the use of appropriate 'free-cooling' techniques.

A1.6   Renewable energy sources

A1.6.1   Objective

It is the Institution's policy to limit the energy requirements of buildings, and therefore to encourage the effective integration of renewable energy sources into buildings and building engineering services.

The main objectives of this policy are:

— to mitigate the demands placed on the world's reserves of fossil fuels

— to reduce the consumption of fossil fuels, in order to reduce pollution

— to promote the use of renewable and sustainable energy sources and passive design solutions.

A1.6.2 Policy

Whilst actively pursuing this policy it is accepted that any renewable energy system must demonstrate that it is cost effective or that its significant environmental or social benefits outweigh any financial overcosts compared to the traditional alternatives.

To meet these aims the Institution commits to:

— EU Council Resolutions on renewable energy

— support the UK Government's energy policy in promoting the adoption of 10% increase of renewable energy systems by 2010

— encourage the incorporation of renewable energy sources in new and refurbished buildings so as to minimise fossil fuel derived energy production

— encourage a holistic view of building design, operation and specification which enables effective collaboration between the professions to be achieved

— advise owners/occupiers of new and existing buildings regarding methods and options for integrating renewable energy systems

— support research into the development of new renewable energy sources and their successful integration into buildings.

A1.7 Sustainable development

A1.7.1 Objective

The Institution's objective is to promote awareness and encourage greater consideration among designers, installers and operators of the longer term direct and indirect effects of design solutions on the environment as a whole, and how they can contribute to providing a better quality of life for everyone.

A1.7.2 Policy

A commonly used definition of sustainable development is: 'development which meets the needs of the present without compromising the ability of future generations to meet their own needs'[3]. CIBSE advocates a co-ordinated approach to sustainability issues at all stages of the life cycle of buildings and their components including conception, briefing, design, procurement, construction, maintenance and ultimate disposal by:

— Liaising closely with other professionals, technical and commercial, within the industry at all stages of the construction process.

— Developing and improving techniques for predicting building performance to provide an increasingly reliable basis for energy labelling.

— Consider within the design of systems and products how, through design, to reduce energy use, waste and pollution in construction, transportation, installation and use.

— Encouraging the use of components which have a high recyclable element on final disposal.

— Ensuring building operators are educated in the importance of properly maintaining systems from the point of view of energy efficiency and reduced waste.

— Encouraging programmes for replacement and substitution of materials and components with less environmentally damaging alternatives.

References

1   *CFCS, HCFCs, HFCs and halons* CIBSE Guidance Note GN1 (London: Chartered Institution of Building Services Engineers) (2000)

2   *A better quality of life: a strategy for sustainable development for the UK* Cm 4345 (London: The Stationery Office) (1999) (ISBN 0-10-143452-9) (www.sustainable-development.gov.uk)

3   *Sustainable Development — the Government's approach* (www.sustainable-development.gov.uk)

Appendix A2: Conversion factors, properties of fuels and correction of meter readings

A2.1   Conversion factors and fuel data

Table A2.1 Conversion factors for energy units

Original units	Multiply quantity in original units by factor to give quantity in units below			
	Joule	Kilowatt-hour	Therm	Btu
Joule (J)	1	0.2778×10^{-6}	0.948×10^{-9}	0.948×10^{-3}
Kilowatt-hour (kW·h)	3.6×10^{6}	1	34.12×10^{-3}	3.412×10^{3}
Therm	105.5×10^{6}	29.31	1	1×10^{5}
Btu	1.055×10^{3}	0.2931×10^{-3}	1×10^{-5}	1

Table A2.2 Conversion factors for miscellaneous quantities

Quantity	Imperial units	Multiply by stated factor to give quantity in SI units	
		Factor	SI units
Calorific value (volume basis)	Btu/ft^3	3.726×10^{-2}	MJ/m^3
Calorific value (mass basis)	Btu/lb	2.326	kJ/kg
Density	lb/ft^3	1.602×10^{1}	kg/m^3
Force	lbf	4.448	N
Heat flow rate	Btu/h	2.931×10^{-1}	W
Heat flow rate intensity	Btu/(h ft^2)	3.155	W/m^2
Heat flow rate per unit length	Btu/(h ft)	9.615×10^{-1}	W/m
Heat flow rate (refrigeration)	ton	3.517×10^{3}	W
Mass	ton	1.016	tonne
	pound	0.454	kg
Power	hp	7.457×10^{2}	W
Pressure	lbf/in^2	6.895	kPa
	bar	1×10^{2}	kPa
Specific heat capacity	Btu/(lb °F)	4.187	kJ/kg
Specific volume	ft^3/lb	6.243×10^{-2}	m^3/kg
Thermal conductivity (λ-value)	Btu/(h ft^2 °F)	1.442×10^{-1}	W/(m K)
Thermal transmittance (U-value)	Btu in/(h ft^2 °F)	5.678	W/(m^2 K)
Volume	ft^3	2.832×10^{-2}	m^3
	gallon	4.546	litre
Volumetric flowrate	ft^3/min	4.719×10^{-1}	litre/s

Table A2.3 Prefixes and multiplying factors for SI units

Symbol	Prefix	Multiplying factor
T	tera	10^{12}
G	giga	10^{9}
M	mega	10^{6}
k	kilo	10^{3}

Table A2.4 Calorific values of typical fuels

Fuel	Calorific value (MJ/kg)	
	Gross	Net
Class D fuel oil†	45.0	42.2
Natural gas‡	38.6	34.7
LPG:		
— butane	49.5	46.0
— propane	50.0	46.5
Solid fuels (washed smalls):		
— anthracite	29.65	28.95
— dry steam coal	30.60	29.65
— coking coals (medium volatile)	30.80	29.75

† to BS 2869
‡ at 15 °C, 101.3 kPa

Table A2.5 Calorific value of renewable energy sources

Renewable source	GJ per tonne	Notes
Domestic wood	10.0	50% moisture content
Industrial wood	11.9	Average
Straw	15.0	
Poultry Litter	8.8	
Meat and bone	17.3	
General industrial waste	16.0	
Hospital waste	14.0	
Municipal solid waste	9.5	Average
Refuse derived waste	18.6	Average
Short rotation coppice	10.6	As received
	18.6	Dry
Tyres	32.0	

Source: *Digest of UK Energy Statistics* (DUKES) (London: HMSO) (2001)

Table A2.6 Conversion factors to obtain energy contents of fuels in kilowatt-hours

Fuel	Measured units	Factor*
Electricity	kW·h	1
Natural gas	m³	10.7
	hundred cu. ft.	30.3
	kW·h	1
	therm	29.31
Class D oil (35s)	litre	10.6
Class E oil (290s)	litre	11.2
Class F oil (950s)	litre	11.3
Class G oil (3500s)	litre	11.4
Propane	tonne	13780
	kg	13.78
Coal (typically)	tonne	9000
	kg	9

* Multiply by stated factor to obtain energy content in kW·h

Table A2.7 Carbon dioxide equivalents (1998 data)

Energy source	$(kg\ CO_2)\ /\ kW{\cdot}h^{(1)}$
Grid electricity:	
— 1990	0.74[2]
— 1991	0.76
— 1992	0.72
— 1993	0.70
— 1994	0.65
— 1995	0.58
— 1996	0.57
— 1997	0.53
— 1998	0.43[3]
Coal (typical)	0.29
Coke	0.42
Coke oven gas	0.24
Smokeless fuel	0.39
Natural gas	0.19
Petroleum (average)	0.27
Heavy fuel oil	0.26
Diesel	2.98 kg/litre
Petrol	2.54 kg/litre
Propane	1.75 kg/litre

Notes:
(1) Divide by 3.67 to obtain carbon equivalent
(2) Electricity figures are per kW·h delivered
(3) The figure of 0.43 has been adopted as the official standard for carbon dioxide reporting until further notice

Table A2.8 Example building CO_2 calculation

Fuel	kW·h	CO_2 ratio	kg CO_2
Oil (27000 litres)	286200	0.27	77274
Gas	140000	0.19	26600
Electricity	35000	0.43	15050
		Total:	118924

A2.2   Correction of meter readings

A2.2.1   Fuel oils

Fuel oils are sold by volume and not on an energy basis. The calorific value of oils may usually be obtained from the supplier. The heat value may be in kJ/litre or kJ/kg. In the latter case, conversion to heat per unit volume requires a knowledge of the oil density in kg/litre, and this value may also be obtained from the supplier. Again, the density is quoted at the standard temperature, 15.5 °C.

The oil temperature at the metering points may be as high as 120 °C for the heaviest grade. The volume changes by approximately 1% when the temperature changes by 15 °C. This effect is slightly more significant for lighter grades of oil, but these are not heated to the same extent.

For residual fuel oils, the approximate temperature correction factor by which meter readings should be multiplied to give standard volume is:

$$1 / (1 + 0.0007\, t)$$

where t is the actual oil temperature (°C) minus 15.5 °C.

For example, the volume of a heavy fuel oil metered at 110 °C should be corrected by the factor:

$$1 / (1 + 0.0007\, (110 - 15.5)) = 0.938$$

Furthermore, if the above oil had a density of 0.98 kg/litre and a quoted calorific value of 41 130 kJ/kg the calorific value per standard litre would be:

$$41\,130 \times 0.98 = 40\,307 \text{ kJ/litre}$$

Where the consumption of the heavier fuel oils is determined by the delivery and tank stock method, minor errors will occur if a float-type contents gauge is used, due to volume changes with temperature. However, tank gauges which measure the weight head of oil are calibrated for each grade of oil density and are therefore self-compensating.

A2.2.2   Natural gas

Care should be taken to ensure that data are related to standard, purchased conditions. Volume varies by approximately 1% for a gas temperature change of 3 K and by approximately 1% for a pressure change of 10 mbar (4 inches water gauge). Minor variations from the standard conditions of 15.5 °C and 1013.25 mbar can usually be ignored, but where gas is metered at high pressure/temperature the temperature correction factor f_t and pressure correction factor f_p are given as follows:

$$f_t = \frac{273 + 15.5}{273 + t_a} \tag{A2.1}$$

where t_a is the actual temperature (°C).

$$f_p = \frac{p_a + 1013.25}{1013.25} \tag{A2.2}$$

where p_a is the actual pressure gauge reading (mbar).

As an example, consider a meter supplied with gas at 16 °C and a gauge pressure of 600 mbar.

To correct the meter data to standard conditions the overall correction factor will be:

$$\frac{273 + 15.5}{273 + 16} + \frac{600 + 1013.25}{1013.25} = 1.59$$

Appendix A3: Consultants and model briefs

A3.1 Using consultants

A3.1.1 Selecting a consultant

A clear idea is needed of the tasks to be performed so that the services available from a consultant can be matched to the project requirements. The particular combination of services required and the scale of a project determine the type of consultancy likely to be found of best value.

Small energy consultancy practices often provide only an energy audit and survey service. The client then seeks separate services from suppliers and contractors to design and implement the schemes recommended in the survey report. Other consultancies may concentrate on design services, or might offer a specialist survey and design service for a particular type of plant or building. Larger consultancies can be expected to offer the broadest range of services and to be able to maintain support throughout all stages of a project from initial planning to final implementation.

The greatest benefits are obtained when a consultant is chosen and briefed carefully. When choosing a suitable consultant, consideration of the following points will enable a commission to be placed with confidence:

— background of consultancy; it is best to use a well established business that has tackled similar projects and can demonstrate long-term commitment

— references from recent clients or direct previous experience of the services offered

— details of the experience, qualifications and supervision of individuals who actually carry out the commission

— resources; ability to meet the programme; ability to meet temporary instrumentation requirements

— independence from interests in supply of equipment or fuel that could compromise impartiality of advice

— fee bases; fixed sum, time charge, scale fee, percentage or performance related charges may be preferred.

Advice on where energy consultancies can be contacted may be obtained from professional institutions, Action Energy (www.actionenergy.org.uk) and Regional Energy Efficiency Officers. Further information is available from the Energy Systems Trade Association (ESTA) (www.esta.org.uk) which includes the Independent Energy Consultants Group.

A3.1.2 Use of model brief

If the intended scope of a commission has to be determined then preliminary discussions should be held and, perhaps, outline proposals invited from prospective consultants. Clients should satisfy themselves that their requirements are covered and that no unnecessary items are included.

Formal proposals should detail the fees involved, the objectives, procedures and reporting format, and indicate the anticipated benefits. To ensure that the terms of reference are clearly defined, and to assist with the comparison of proposals from alternative consultants, the use of a standard form of brief is recommended.

The models for comprehensive and concise audit and survey briefs given below are intended for this purpose. Deletions or additions of specific items should be made to match the precise needs of a particular site.

A3.1.3 Making best use of consultants

To make the most effective use of a consultant's time it is necessary to identify the information and assistance that the consultant can expect to receive, and to ensure that maximum co-operation is available. If the consultant knows with confidence what support is being provided then work can be priced accordingly and effort directed properly.

The findings and recommendations of a consultant are rightly challenged so as to ensure confidence in the results of an audit and survey and establish a firm case for implementation. Finding are most likely to be implemented successfully where the parties have worked together and maintained a constructive dialogue.

A3.2 Model brief for a concise energy audit and survey

This section outlines the objectives of a concise energy audit and survey, and the report format to be used to detail the findings and recommendations of the audit and survey.

A3.2.1 Objectives

The objectives of a concise energy audit and survey are:

— to identify opportunities for reducing energy costs

— to estimate the potential savings, and where applicable, implementation costs

— to provide an audit for the site on the basis of the previous 12 months' invoiced accounts.

Methods of achieving these objectives are:

— by observations and, where applicable, analysis of how efficiently energy-consuming equipment is being used.

— by considering possible improvements to energy management control.

A3.2.2   Report format

A short report shall be written to outline the findings and recommendations arising from the survey. The report shall be preceded by a summary outlining the potential energy savings available at the site. These will primarily be of the good housekeeping and low-cost type but will also indicate where further opportunities may exist. The body of the report shall contain the following sections:

— site information

— energy audit

— energy use

— energy management.

A3.2.3   Scope of survey and report

The following shall be covered.

A3.2.3.1   Site information

The site, its functions and services, shall be described.

A3.2.3.2   Energy audit

Based on data obtained from the previous 12 months' fuel invoices, a table showing annual fuel consumptions and costs shall be compiled for the site. Performance indicators shall be determined and commented upon.

A3.2.3.3   Energy use

Boiler plant

Combustion efficiency, based on waste gas analyses, shall be assessed for the main boiler plant under operating conditions as found. The general condition of the boiler plant and associated pipework insulation shall be checked. Recommendations for improved energy efficiencies within the boiler house shall be based on the above analysis and observations.

Space heating and domestic hot water

The heating and hot water systems shall be assessed and recommendations made on:

— the heating period compared with occupancy periods

— the condition, settings and siting of existing controllers and sensors

— instantaneous temperature measurement taken during occupancy periods

— the condition of insulation on pipework, valves and flanges

— the condition and siting of heat emitters and any obstruction

— HWS temperature.

Electrical power and lighting

Observations of power and lighting systems shall be carried out to determine the following:

— the condition of lighting equipment

— any unnecessary use of lighting

— the type of existing luminaires and possible replacement by higher-efficiency lighting

— use of electric heating and its control

— the operation and loading of refrigerators and air compressors

— efficient use of large electric motors.

Recommendations to reduce energy costs shall be made on the basis of the above observations.

Air conditioning plant

The settings of existing time and capacity controls shall be obtained and included in the report, together with comments on control, operation and potential energy savings.

Building fabric

Observations shall be made of:

— insulation standards

— excessive uncontrolled ventilation into buildings due to badly fitting doors and windows.

Recommendations shall be based on the above observations.

A3.2.3.4   Energy management

Existing energy management procedures shall be assessed, and outline recommendations shall be made on any improvement which can be made to the existing system. An assessment of any potential for fuel and/or tariff changes shall be outlined.

This Appendix outlines the objectives of a comprehensive energy audit and survey, and the report format to be used to detail the findings and recommendations of the audit and surveys.

A3.3 Model brief for a comprehensive energy audit and survey

A3.3.1 Objectives

The objectives of a comprehensive energy audit and survey are to:

— provide an audit of site energy

— identify areas of potential energy cost savings

— provide an estimate of potential annual energy savings with implementation costs and payback periods

— identify how methods of energy management should be developed to achieve, maintain and recognise further potential savings.

Methods of achieving these objectives are by:

— analysis of invoiced and metered fuel consumptions

— observations and measurements on energy-consuming equipment during the survey period to determine energy efficiency and wastage

— establishment of a basis for continued monitoring of energy consumptions and setting achievable targets

— on completion of the survey, preparation of a report in the format outlined below containing recommendations supported by data, which, if implemented, would result in energy costs savings

— presentation of the report to senior management.

A3.3.2 Report format

A report is written to detail the findings and recommendations arising from the survey. It consists of the following.

A3.3.2.1 Management summary

This outlines the potential energy savings identified by the survey. The summary shall also show tables of individual recommendations based on good housekeeping and low-cost measures and capital expenditure schemes.

A3.3.2.2 Report

The report details findings and recommendations in the following sections (delete any sections to be excluded):

— Site information

— Energy audit

— Energy use:

    (a) Boiler plant

    (b) Space heating

    (c) Domestic hot water

    (d) Air conditioning and ventilation

    (e) Electrical power and lighting

    (f) Catering

    (g) Other energy uses

    (h) Building fabric

— Energy management.

A3.3.2.3 Appendix

The Appendix includes graphs, calculations and miscellaneous data which are relevant to the report.

A3.3.3 Scope of survey

The following items should be covered and reported on (Delete any items to be excluded).

A3.3.3.1 Site information

The site, its functions and services, shall be described in this section. A building or site plan shall be included.

A3.3.3.2 Energy audit

Based on information obtained from fuel invoices, metered consumptions, observations and calculations, the following shall be produced:

— a table showing the consumptions, unit costs, and total costs for all purchased fuels for the previous 12 months

— a table showing the percentage changes in energy costs over the previous 3 years

— a summary of energy intakes e.g. supply meters and tariffs

— table(s) and pie chart(s) showing a breakdown of fuel types and costs for each major fuel user, for the previous 12 months.

Energy performance indicators for the building(s) shall be calculated and commented on.

A3.3.3.3 Energy use

Boiler plant

— Combustion efficiency tests shall be carried out on all boilers at high, medium and low fire rates (where applicable). Recommendations for the improvement of combustion efficiency shall be made where necessary.

— Seasonal efficiency of boilers shall be estimated, based on observed operating conditions and past records. The effect of producing hot water only, during summer periods, on seasonal efficiency shall be assessed if applicable.

— Where low seasonal efficiencies are found, recommendations shall be made on savings achievable by replacement boilers, separate hot water heaters, or other facilities for seasonal operation.

— The general condition of the boilers shall be

assessed with particular reference to insulation and air infiltration and recommendations made for improvements where necessary.

— The condition and thickness of insulation on pipework, valves and flanges shall be assessed and recommendations made for improvement where necessary.

— Suitability and settings of time and temperature or pressure controls shall be assessed and recommendations for improvement made where necessary.

— The use of waste heat recovery from boiler blow-down on steam boilers and the use of economisers on gas-fired boilers shall be evaluated and recommendations made on the viability and practicality of such schemes.

— Use of cheaper/alternative fuels shall be considered.

— Consideration shall be given, in certain circumstances, to the viability of the use of waste incinerators.

Space heating

The heating systems shall be examined and recommendations made on:

— the heating periods compared with occupancy

— the type of heating system installed

— the condition, settings, positioning and operation of existing controllers and sensors

— the need for additional controls

— the condition and thickness of insulation on pipework, valves and flanges

— the condition, positioning, and any obstruction of heat emitters.

A temperature record, over a period of 7 days, shall be carried out to obtain a heating profile in representative area(s).

Domestic hot water

The hot water system shall be examined and recommendations made on:

— calorifier storage and delivery temperatures and control systems

— calorifier insulation, condition and thickness

— calorifier storage capacity in relation to draw-off requirements

— hot water outlet temperatures and flow control from taps and showers

Electrical power and lighting

Observations and measurements shall be carried out to determine:

— the 'maximum demand' profile over a period of 7 days

— the most economical supply tariff, based on the 'maximum demand' profile and past invoices

— the need for power factor correction, if low power factors are penalised by the supply authorities

— excessive transformer losses due to low loading of transformers

— an assessment of connected power and lighting loads

— the type, condition, siting and switching arrangement of existing luminaires, and possible replacement by high-efficiency lamps.

— any unnecessary use of lighting and power equipment, with particular attention to electric heating equipment.

— the control of electric heating, and possible replacement by other types of heating.

— the performance and loading of air compressors, and the potential for waste heat recovery.

— the effectiveness of the distribution and utilisation of compressed air.

— the type, size and loading of motors to suit the application.

— the potential for combined heat and electricity generation (CHP).

Recommendations shall be made on the basis of the findings from the above observations and measurements.

Air conditioning and ventilation

— Air flows shall be measured and the heating/cooling loads assessed.

— Controls shall be examined for switching, settings and operation of existing time and capacity controls.

— Ductwork shall be examined for leakage and for correct operation of dampers.

— The performance and loading of refrigeration compressors and the potential for waste heat recovery shall be studied.

— The distribution and insulation standards of the refrigeration system shall be examined.

— The power consumption of major fans, chillers and pumps shall be assessed for audit purposes.

Catering and other energy use

— The use of cheaper alternative fuels and heat recovery shall be considered.

— Any unnecessary use of equipment shall be identified.

Building fabric

The following shall be examined and appropriate recommendations made:

— insulation standards of roofs, walls and floors

— glazing standards of windows

— excessive air infiltration due to badly fitting doors and windows

— excessive air infiltration due to doors and windows being left open.

A3.3.3.4   Energy management

An assessment shall be made of the existing energy management procedures, information available, and metering at the site. Recommendations shall be made on any improvement which can be made to the existing system. These recommendations shall take account of manpower availability and the cost requirements setting up an improved system of energy management.

Systems of energy management shall be based upon quantitative measures of performance using:

(*a*)   performance indicators calculated for the particular situation, or

(*b*)   monitoring and target setting, relating energy consumption to known variables.

The merits of suitable methods shall be outlined on the basis of the availability of information, cost of implementation, metering availability and the suitability of variables against which to compare energy consumption.

Management structures for collecting and processing data and taking action in response to the findings shall be reviewed.

Further reading

Choosing an energy efficiency consultant, what is energy consultancy and how can it benefit you FL89 (Action Energy) (2002) (www.actionenergy. org.uk)

Appendix A4: Useful websites

Name	Website address*
Action Energy	www.actionenergy.org.uk
American Society of Heating, Refrigeration and Air-Conditioning Engineers (ASHRAE)	www.ashrae.org
Association of Environment Conscious Building (AECB)	www.aecb.net
British Council for Offices (BCO)	www.bco.org.uk
British Institute of Facilities Management (BIFM)	www.bifm.org.uk
British Photovoltaic Association	www.pv-uk.org.uk
British Standards Institution (BSI)	www.bsi-global.com
Building Regulations (England and Wales)	www.safety.odpm.gov.uk/bregs/index
Building Research Establishment (BRE)	www.bre.co.uk
Building Services Research and Information Association (BSRIA)	www.bsria.co.uk
CADDET (EU energy information site)	www.caddet-ee.org
(The) Carbon Trust	www.thecarbontrust.co.uk
Chartered Institute of Building (CIoB)	www.ciob.org.uk
Chartered Institution of Building Services Engineers (CIBSE)	www.cibse.org
(The) CHP Club	www.chpclub.com
Combined Heat and Power Association (CHPA)	www.chpa.co.uk
Commissioning Specialists Association	www.csa.org.uk
Construction Industry Research and Information Association	www.ciria.org.uk
Department for Environment, Food and Rural Affairs (DEFRA) Market Transformation Programme	www.mtprog.com
Department of Trade and Industry (DTI) Renewable Energy Programme	www.dti.gov.uk/renewables
Energy Institute	www.energyinst.org.uk
Energy Saving Trade Association (ESTA)	www.esta.org.uk
Energy Saving Trust	www.est.org.uk
Enhanced capital allowances	www.eca.gov.uk
Federation of Environmental Trade Associations (FETA)	www.feta.co.uk
Heating and Ventilating Contractors Association (HVCA)	www.hvca.org.uk
Hotel and Catering International Management Association (HCIMA)	www.hospitableclimates.com
Institute of Domestic Heating and Environmental Engineers (IDHE)	www.idhe.org.uk
Institute of Plumbing	www.plumbers.org.uk
Institute of Refrigeration (IoR)	www.ior.org.uk
Oil Firing Technical Association for the Petroleum Industry (OFTEC)	www.oftec.org
Royal Institute of British Architects (RIBA)	www.architecture.com
Sustainable development	www.sustainable-development.gov.uk
UK Electricity Association	www.electricity.org.uk
UK Environmental Products Information Consortium	www.ukepic.com
Usable buildings	www.usablebuildings.co.uk

Note: correct at the time of publication (January 2004)

Index